TAMING MEGALOPOLIS

VOLUME I

What Is and What Could Be

H. WENTWORTH ELDREDGE received the A.B. degree from Dartmouth College and the Ph.D. degree from Yale University. He is currently Professor of Sociology and Chairman of the Department at Dartmouth College. Previously he served as Chairman of the City Planning and Urban Studies Program at Dartmouth, and has been Visiting Professor of City Planning at the University of California at Berkeley, and Visiting Lecturer in City Planning at Harvard.

Professor Eldredge has published numerous articles and reviews in professional journals, periodicals, and an encyclopedia. He is the author of *The Second American Revolution: The Near Collapse of Traditional Democracy*. In addition he has lectured on planning at many universities in the United States and abroad.

Professor and Mrs. Eldredge live with their two sons in Norwich, Vermont.

TAMING MEGALOPOLIS

Volume I

What Is and What Could Be

EDITED, WITH A PREFACE AND HEADNOTES,

BY H. WENTWORTH ELDREDGE

Anchor Books
Doubleday & Company, Inc.
Garden City, New York

The Anchor Books edition is the first publication of
Taming Megalopolis: Volume I, What Is and What Could Be

Anchor Books edition: 1967

Library of Congress Catalog Card Number 67–12878

To Diana, Jamie, and Alan,
who survived

PREFACE

The city, "man's noblest creation," hardly merits such an accolade in its late twentieth-century form. In order to tame that sprawling beast, the metropolis fast becoming megalopolis, it is first necessary to understand his characteristics and have some idea of the sort of useful and handsome creature one would like. Having achieved an idea of the qualities and goals desired, one must elaborate ingenious administrative structures and physical forms to be used in molding urban society into something of "style and quality," however defined. Clearly this is a mountainous task and very close to the fringe of our present skills—and the number of skills to be enlisted in such an effort are legion. Traditional city planners—flanked by lawyers, housing experts, civil engineers, public health specialists, students of air pollution, conservationists, social psychologists, real estate agents, sociologists, anthropologists, urban designers and architects, public administration scholars, computer programmers, political scientists, regionalists, economic geographers, economists, traffic engineers, recreation planners, purveyors of the higher culture, etc.—may be able to at least get on with the job. There apparently is an urban dimension to every sophisticated occupation. But the mere complexity of the matter demands that new higher levels of human thought and skills must be involved. These may take the form of an overarching synthesizing profession of *planner of the total environment* and of total systems analysis employing all professional specialities to serve the political decision-makers counseled in detail by the entire planning skill consortium. It is difficult enough to keep up in one's own field, much less absorb the key thinking of neighboring and distant ones, with the flood of new knowledge pouring in daily, but to make a quantum jump to a valid synthesis of all fields through systems analysis and computer-based mathematical models, preliminary to managing the total environment is a stupendous intellectual *and* operational task. It takes more than thought; it takes successful doing. Furthermore, all serious students of the urban scene by now agree that there are not going to be any new and shining cities without new and shining people in some as yet not entirely clear reciprocal relationship. And the people must eat and have shelter which spells out the truism that space, social and economic planning are parts of a trinity—and cannot be worshiped separately with any anticipation of reward.

The logical plan of this book is simplicity itself: Part One, *What Is;* Part Two, *What Could Be;* and Part Three, *How to Manage an Urbanized World,* or how to get there. In reality, the material and my valued contributors could not be contained in any such tidy mold. Robert Wood in telling us *what is* about urban political things, can't help making some suggestions for *what could be* and even *how to manage an urbanized world;* Economist Thompson does exactly the same. While Planner Abrams in a concluding chapter in *how to get there* on regional planning in developing areas gives a wise *tour d'horizon* of planning and housing problems that might well be in *what is.* But the material does fall reasonably well into the three divisions, which seem to fit total logicality. The slipping back and forth may serve to tie diverse material together, as I endeavor to do in my brief chapter introductions with the end of making this collection a coherent entity. Quite frankly there is much too much in "urban planning and urbanism" to capture the whole story in one work. Feeling somewhat the way Diderot must have in the eighteenth century, as he faced bringing all of extant human knowledge together in one encyclopedia, I finished my stimulating task acutely aware of my own limitations and of the lacunae in the result. Specialists in various fields will feel their pet interest slighted; *aficionados* of the single solution will be hurt. But if they all will forgive me, I have made one valid point: the process of building an urban society of style and quality must rest eventually on a unified, but many-pronged, attack with results feeding back into goals and operations in a rising spiral to cope with rising complexity. Finally, societal scale is far beyond the city today: regional, national and international plans are in order. In *functions, space* and *time,* we must go beyond present practice.

One can dream of a fat loose leaf book with the latest knowledge in each of hundreds of urban skills, with all variables cross-referenced in a quantified fashion, ready at hand for the decision-maker. Only it won't be a book; it will be a computer storage and retrieval system changing every day. For such will be the task of coping with so many people in

such ascending complexity in the city of mankind: the earth.
If that day has not already arrived.

H.W.E.

Tarn House
Norwich, Vermont
5 June 1967

CONTENTS

VOLUME I

VOLUME II

PART THREE. HOW TO MANAGE AN URBANIZED WORLD

PART ONE. WHAT IS

Chapter 1

URBANIZATION AND MODERNIZATION

It is becoming increasingly more difficult to talk and write about "the city." Max Weber and Louis Wirth could catalog the city's qualities as opposed to rurality and describe the people and life to be found there. But in the latter half of the twentieth century it is nearly impossible to analyze the city as place; the indeterminacy of this urban area befuddles all careful qualification and quantification, of its form, style, and inhabitants. People and their institutions overflow the central city bowl, course through suburbia and the hinterland to coalesce once again into a next urban place. Psychically the presumed urban qualities, spread by the ever more efficient transportation and communication of ideas, people and goods, blanket all but isolated marginal ponds of rurality. Life styles tend to become increasingly similar with shared technics, things and ideas. Although differentially shared by social sub-groups, there is little evidence of significant rural-urban dichotomy any longer in industrialized and modernized nations.

The non-Western world—once too glibly characterized as composed mainly of folk and peasant cultures—is now striving to adapt Western industrial society, the skeleton of modern urbanization. This process of modernization has best been described as technological and organizational resulting in focused power and not simply by co-ordinates of place/physical form. Modernization and urbanization may be roughly equivalent terms although dispersion could conceivably accompany urbanism. The high density of rural Ceylon and Indonesia do not *a city make* nor the low densities of Westchester non-urbanism. In fact, what is *urban* (as differentiated from the physical fact of city) can be defined as a socio-cultural structure rather than mere space. The urbanists are frankly still in the process of redefining their target area and tend more and more to think in terms of high technology and high organization—as Scott Greer has phrased it in the "increase in societal scale," which has spelled the doom of the relatively closed defunct system of *the* city. The relevant system for the study of urbanism has increased to regional or national scale or in some cases, as in the German-Belgian-Dutch complex, to an international scale. In the non-West urbanism linked to modernization is a societal quality beyond mere higher population density, once the universal fixed criterion of urbanism.

To explore all the qualities of urbanization would be an endless task resulting in a quasi-delineation of modern society. Here three important aspects relevant to planning problems have been singled out: First, Christopher Tunnard, planner, has sketched out the gargantuan spatial dimensions of the eastern seaboard regional city—now more generally named *megalopolis*—which has "just growed" for a thousand clustered miles from southern Maine to northern Virginia as the leading exemplar of what is happening to urban scale in North America, Western Europe and elsewhere—in the Tokyo area for example. Second, Alan K. Campbell, political scientist, substantiates with hard data that the most dynamic sector of the entire American economy—both public and private—is local government expenditures. Unquestionably this is where the high costs and heavy investments are in modern society: the *public sector* of urban places, needed badly to make them function as human habitations. Finally, Melvin M. and Carolyn C. Webber explore the professional's *nonterritorial community* of time/distance rather than space alone, electronically possible for the growing intellectual-managerial elite of advanced societies. In contradistinction, they check this tendency against the folk culture-like behavior in the communities of urban workers, whose life styles are generally space oriented.

The implications of the three aspects of modern urbanism explored here are clear; increasingly large areas must be managed as meaningful systems; these urban areas will require a large and ever-increasing shrewd allocation of resources and must be managed with mounting bureaucratic complexity. And finally, altered space/time relations can conceivably foster new types of human society and settlements in the future with shapes and social structure as yet unglimpsed. This then is *modern* society. How to devote scarce resources with a long lifetime of use in an open-ended planning process for such a misty large-scale future is a matter of mounting interest and concern both to students of urbanism and to the urban planners, both physical and socio-economic-political, who must rely on their findings.

America's Super-Cities

CHRISTOPHER TUNNARD*

There is a new eastern American city, a product of the mid-twentieth century. In 1965, close to forty million people lived in it, and an increase of about thirty percent is expected in the next two decades. A great proportion of the economic

* Professor of City Planning, and Department Chairman, Yale University. Trained in Canada and England, he became a Visiting Lecturer in Harvard's Graduate School of Design in 1939 and after holding a Wheelright Travelling Fellowship in Architecture, came to Yale in 1945. He has been a visiting lecturer or critic at M.I.T., North Carolina State College, University of Minnesota, University of Winnipeg, and

power of the entire world is now concentrated in it, and the possibilities of what its ultimate shape and character may become are staggering.

Start driving down the coast from Bangor, Maine, along the Old Post Road, and keep going until you swing out at the end of the journey at Norfolk, Virginia. You will have traveled through the heart of Anglo-America, the land-before-the-frontier, the financial center of the world, the heart of the communications industry, the part of the United States called by Westerners "older." The region has something of all 350 years of our history in it—historic houses and ranch houses, water-powered mills and steel rolling mills, farms and suburban estates, company towns and seaside resorts, the nation's capital and the world's largest city,[1] drive-in movies, regional shopping centers, summer theaters. It has no mountains to speak of, but it has some picturesque scenery, especially east of New York, where upland meets the drowned Atlantic plain, creating little bays and rocky harbors.

This is the spine of the great city, which is being reinforced by new superhighways, tunnels and bridges, bringing its parts ever closer together in time-distance. City, you say? From its appearance, a great deal of the landscape through which you drive on this route is still countryside, but if you were to think of it as rural, in the strict sense of the term, you would be fooling yourself. By any realistic standard of calculation you have traveled six hundred miles through a giant city. Look at

Clemson College. He was awarded a Guggenheim Fellowship, a Fulbright Fellowship at the *Institut d'Urbanisme* at the University of Paris, and a Fulbright Grant to serve as Lecturer on City Planning at the Academy of Fine Arts in Istanbul, Turkey. In 1966, he was the chairman of the American Faculty at the Salzburg Seminar on Urban Studies dealing with the planning and development of the urban community. He is the author of *The City of Man* (Scribner, 1953), *American Skyline* (with Henry Hope Reed, Houghton Mifflin, 1955), and co-author with Boris Pushkarev of *Man-Made America: Chaos or Control* (Yale University Press, 1963) which was picked as one of the fifty notable books of 1963 by the American Library Association and won the highly coveted National Book Award in 1964.

This article is adapted from "America's Super-Cities," *Harper's Magazine*, Vol. 217, Issue 1299, August 1958, © and reproduced with permission.

[1] *What size region should we plan for?* The present (1965) population of the Tri-State New York Region is about 17 million. We anticipate a growth to 25 to 30 million around the year 2000, according to present trends in natural increase and economic growth." Stanley Tankel "Planning for the New York Region," p. 63 in *Planning, 1965*, ASPO, Chicago, 1965.

a map, the kind that deals with people and their activities—sales, densities, traffic volumes. Or look at the Standard Metropolitan Statistical Areas: they are contiguous from Lawrence-Haverhill, Massachusetts, on the New Hampshire border in the north to Fairfax County, Virginia, in the south. It is perhaps even more meaningful to point out that *municipalities with a density of more than 100 people per square mile* (that is, those that show definite signs of urbanization) stretch in a *continuous five-hundred mile* belt from Kittery, Maine, to Quantico, Virginia . . . a belt which is still growing.

This sprawling city is the Atlantic Urban Region, as we have called it at Yale. H. G. Wells gave it part of its name. In his *Anticipations,* which was published in 1902, he accurately foresaw—as no one else seems to have foreseen—what cities were going to turn into. "Enough has been said," he wrote, "to demonstrate that 'town' and 'city' will be, in truth, terms as obsolete as 'mail coach'. For these new areas that will grow out of them we want a term, and . . . we may for our present purposes call these coming town provinces 'urban regions.' "

Although it is the world's largest, the Atlantic Urban Region is by no means the only one of its kind in existence.

Starting in 1950 with an examination of the "urban core" of Connecticut (the fast urbanizing belt that stretches from the New York state line along the coast, turning up at New Haven toward Springfield in Massachusetts) Yale developed the early theory of the Atlantic Urban Region and pointed out the existence of others. There is the steel belt—Pittsburgh–Youngstown–Canton–Akron–Cleveland—and the cities that are growing together around Detroit. The Chicago-Milwaukee area is another, and a new strip seems to be joining Chicago and Detroit. In the Far West there is the Los Angeles-San Diego strip: and Charlton Chute, of the Institute of Public Administration, has pointed out that the Seattle-Tacoma area is still another urban region. One is developing in Florida as a linear city grows up between Palm Beach and Miami: the region is in the process of changing from just a playground to a southern industrial center.

Not so very long ago an outlying community was drawn to the nearest city, however small, as its cultural and financial and commercial lodestone. But the automobile has changed that; and as mobility increases and distances shrink, a small town today can easily have access to several regional centers, only one of which is the old city to which it was formerly tied.

This is something now being realized by the federal government, which is making its first tentative efforts to deal with transportation problems along the "Northeast Corridor," as the region is being termed in Washingtonese.

An urban region six hundred miles long cannot, of course, be called one big city for any but the most specialized purposes. Nobody in his right mind would say it should be under one government. (Even in New York's borough system, some political scientists think, the units are too large to permit effective administration.) Nobody would agree that the long Atlantic linear strip is one community with common interests, activities and experiences. Maine's Down Easterners don't think or vote like Virginians.

But they usually share some of the same problems. Down Easterners and Virginians have to worry about highways, recreation, and water supply, for example, and they travel surprisingly long distances back and forth along parts of the strip for work and pleasure. From Maine to Virginia there is a constant overlapping of interests and activities, and for the purposes of physical and economic planning, as well as for sociological reasons, it has become essential to know what this overlapping is, how it happens, and how communities which may be many miles apart are tied to one another.

If you will look again at the map you will see that within the big Atlantic Urban Region one city, New York, dominates the whole area. But Boston, Philadelphia and Washington dominate considerable areas of their own. Boston, for instance, although no longer "The Hub of the Universe," nevertheless holds sway over an area which meets New York's region somewhere between Hartford and Springfield, especially in such matters as banking and newspaper circulation. Within these big orbits of influence are smaller ones. Hartford and New Haven have their own zones of influence and, while these two cities are about the same size, their influence is markedly different. Hartford dominates or services a much larger region than the university city.

The size of each of the great new urban regions, of course, has its limitations. Albany-Troy-Schenectady, for geographical reasons, are still outside the Atlantic Region and so are Harrisburg-Pittsburgh and the steel towns. The southernmost boundary of the Atlantic Region is likely to remain at Norfolk-Portsmouth-Hampton Roads because of the absence of good harbors and the long stretch of Cape Hatteras below this point. This has hindered the growth of modern industry, just as it plagued the early settlers on that part of the coast. But there are no exact boundaries that one can be sure will limit an urban region; its extent depends on the orbit of influence of its regional centers. Don Bogue, the demographer, has suggested, for example, that the influence of Boston, if you measure it by its trade, reaches northwest almost to Montreal.

"CITY PLANNING" IS OBSOLETE

Any careful consideration of the urban regions and how they grow should make it quite plain that old concepts of regional planning just don't apply to them. As life in America becomes more and more urbanized, the sectional and historical boundaries which we have long taken for granted have less and less meaning.

Take New England as an example. Southern New England has a great deal more in common with the New York-New Jersey area than with any part of New Hampshire, Vermont or Maine. In a part of the country whose resources consist largely of the skills of urban workers, it doesn't make much sense to apply the old concept of "regional resources" to planning. You can't foster the idea of an agrarian culture in Connecticut, for example, when the base of the culture has become urban. You are wasting your time when you hold onto the ideal of the small town (as television soap opera does and as politicians and popular novelists do) as the place where rural virtue persists, when the typical small town is merely part of a fringe area that sends its inhabitants as commuters to many different business and industrial centers. These are not people who live on the land: they live on the highway.

But old concepts of planning die hard. Though there have been some champions of the city-regions, the promoters of the garden-city idea—most notably Lewis Mumford—have held the floor. The garden cities, according to their doctrine, were to be built outside large centers to take the overspill of the population. They were to have their own industries, and thus achieve a built-in financial balance. They would cut down on commuting and be protected from the encroachment of developers by greenbelts. The ideal garden city should never exceed 50,000 residents, for only communities from 25,000 to 50,000 represent the "biological norm" that can reproduce itself. They were the answer to the dying "megalopolis"—a favorite word of the Scot, Patrick Geddes, coined by Oswald Spengler in *The Decline of the West*, and recently revived by the geographer Jean Gottmann, who has applied it to the Atlantic Urban Region.

But the trouble with the garden city theory was that it ignored what was actually happening to the modern city. Frank Lloyd Wright used to say that our cities have become "just hopeless" and that they are centers of "sin and banking." It is not as simple as that. Leaving aside sin, which is universal, Wright should have added that cities are centers of wholesale and retail trade, newspapers, central telephone offices, population density, cultural activities, and a host of other factors that affect the lives of people who live far outside the city limits. The automobile, the Federal Housing Administration, the forty-hour week and the do-it-yourself craze have exploded cities like baskets of popcorn. Their circles of influence spread wider and wider and communities within their orbits have become more and more interdependent.

While it would be altogether too optimistic to say that regional planning which makes sense has already taken hold in this country, there is plenty of evidence that it is being considered, and the new Department of Housing and Urban Development, in spite of its name, is through sheer force of circumstances, bound to be regionally oriented. While bills continue to be presented in the Congress calling for carving up the nation into "natural" or "resource" regions, a good deal of practical planning which doesn't ignore the existence of cities is going on. The new federal requirements for evidence of regional planning before money is allocated for highways, hospitals and airports is an indication of impatience with urban sprawl and a mandate for local communities to join forces instead of continuing their municipal particularism.

Some years ago, when Abraham Ribicoff was governor of Connecticut, he complained to the Stamford Good Government Association that "few voices are raised on a regional basis in this state. Most of the voices come from organized pressure groups that have special interests." He asked for study, appraisal and suggestions for ways which could better contribute to "regional planning". Since then his state has set up many Regional Planning Agencies, which are beginning to be regarded as the logical vehicles for broad-scale planning formerly done on a hit-or-miss basis by forward-looking communities or ignored completely.

Race and other forms of prejudice, which cannot be solved by regional planning, nevertheless are involved in making planning decisions. There is still an iron ring around northern cities, held there by the suburbs which refuse housing to Negroes. The "new towns" in process of replacing the "garden city" concept in the United States, will reinforce this barrier if they build only for an income group which can afford the current prices of the free housing market.

Typical of the jealousies and special interests which work against the common good is the case a few years ago of the Bronx, which found itself embroiled with Westchester County over the use of the suburban county's recreation facilities.

Westchester closed its golf courses and beaches to nonresidents, and in retaliation the Borough President of the Bronx threatened to prevent Westchester dwellers who work in the city from parking their cars in his borough. It becomes ridiculously apparent that community interests overlap at more and more points, that the idea of solving the city's problems with outlying garden cities is, if it ever made any sense, now obsolete, and that the Urban Region must be the center of focus.

Let me give you an example of the sort of life we at Yale found when we arbitrarily chose for study a section of Connecticut which included seventy-nine towns, an area comprising several urban cores surrounded by rural-urban fringe.

We discovered, first of all, that 24 percent of the population lived on 86 percent of the residential land. On this land some people have built their homes with their own hands, others have ordered expensive country estates, and still others have bought houses in subdivisions. We paid particular attention to the land beyond the suburbs, known as the rural-urban fringe, making case studies which were later published in a book called *Man-Made America*.[2]

This is the kind of district where a housewife's remark that she is just going to step out to take the children over to the neighbor's house means that she is going to drive them five miles down a country road. Or if she says she's just running down to the store, she may drive fifteen miles to a shopping center, or a supermarket, or an upholsterer. She lives in an infinitely more complicated world, both socially and financially, than the one Spectorsky describes in *The Exurbanites*. The economist Richardson Wood, who was one of our advisers and persuaded the business world to take its first good look at the new phenomenon through the aegis of its insurance companies, has called it "interurbia."

[2] Yale University Press, 1963.

The family that lives in the rural-urban fringe is not beholden to any one central business district either for shopping or for employment. Travel time is the chief factor here, not distance, and it is quite possible that husband and wife may go in opposite directions to get to their jobs. In all of Connecticut only 3 percent of the population lives on farms—which means that almost everybody commutes to work. They do not necessarily commute to cities but to factories and offices located in small towns about the state or they may even cross the state border into Massachusetts and New York. These people are urbanized folk, and for all practical purposes the entire state of Connecticut might properly be considered part of an urban region.

LIVING ON THE FRINGE

As we can see, the growth of interurbia is by no means an eastern seaboard phenomenon. During a recent five-year period, 43 percent of the total population increase happened on the rural fringe of metropolitan areas. The rural fringe has grown faster than the suburbs, and the fringe is a busy place. Family life is geared not to a town but to a region. The children may go to a regional school, and health is looked after by regional public-health districts, and those who are hard up can look to regional welfare schemes. If father loses his job in a textile mill, and can no longer go back to work on a farm, he may, by turning around and driving off in another direction, get a job in an electronics plant or a light metals factory that is taking up the slack.

But this is only a start. A whole new set of regional institutions will have to be set up to deal with the needs and aspirations of interurbia. With the community taking on the dimensions of the region, the planner's and the social scientist's approach will have to change. The idea of community "self-sufficiency" which has been used for so long to justify the self-contained garden city approach falls apart in the face of interdependent regions. The "balanced town" with its own industries, stores, businesses, and homes is giving way to specialized communities in which industry or shopping or residences dominate. Some parts of a region may have no industry, no agriculture, no houses; while other parts may have nothing else. The balance between urban and rural landscape, for example, between built-up and open land will not be the problem for a single township but for a whole region. Agricultural land and recreation areas will serve the region, not just the individual community—and unless the region is served, interurbia is going to waste its land, despoil the very qualities that attract so many families to it, and turn into a slum, miscellaneously peppered with houses, hot-dog stands, and factories.

Picture if you can, what the laissez-faire attitude to the urban region means; it is pretty terrifying. Power lines, clearings for gas pipelines, oil storage tanks cut across the landscape in a haphazard fashion; strings of houses cut themselves off from the very landscape their owners moved out to enjoy; new roads are built without regard for topography or the existing order—merely to solve mounting traffic snarls or to take advantage of the least costly right of way. Private developers of gravel pits or subdividers are not always to blame—after all, they are controlled in those states and communities which have set up strong zoning and planning regulations. Government agencies, from highway traffic departments to the Atomic Energy Commission, are equally culpable and often "above" the usual restrictions. Recent efforts by citizen groups to curb the powers of state highway departments reflect a growing concern with the activities of single-purpose or autonomous authorities. We are well on the way to creating, often with official sanction, a man-made American mess.

But if interurbia, rife with special-interest exploitation, becomes a slum, what about the centers of big cities, so many of them blighted already? The older cities are developing more and more as office and communication centers, as centers for specialty shopping, for head offices of national firms, for television and advertising companies. But there are attempts in many of them to turn their slums into attractive residential areas. Just how attractive is another matter. The bloodless redevelopment projects with their towering brick boxes, set about on lawns where children are not allowed to play, offer poor competition to interurbia with its room for children to romp and for father to build a boat in the back yard. In the long run the public will accept or reject the urban redevelopment projects, not for their efficiency or for their nicely calculated arithmetic of man-per square-foot, but because of the way they look and the pleasures and amenities they provide. As William H. Whyte, Jr. wrote recently of urban development: "The institutional approach is dominant, and unless the assumptions embalmed in it are re-examined the city is going to turn into a gigantic bore." American redevelopment architects could learn a great deal from some of the European postwar reconstruction schemes in which architects have tried hard and often successfully to fit the designs into the fabric and character of the older city.

The intolerable congestion that now plagues cities may not be their permanent fate. One of their problems is created by the fact that highway networks, instead of being built according to the needs of a region, now are built merely to join big cities, with the result that masses of traffic are dumped from one city to another. The federal highway program can help to relieve this congestion if the highway engineers and construction co-ordinators see the wisdom of introducing connector streets to take traffic through or around densely populated areas and central business districts, rather than relying on local roads to do the job. If this is true of major cities it is equally true of smaller centers. The many new pedestrian walks in shopping districts of European cities were born of the impossibility of parking there; they will remain because people have found them attractive. In the United States, urban freeways which slash through neighborhoods or cut off waterfronts from public use should be considered as crude mistakes of the forties and fifties, to be replaced by a more sophisticated and sensitive urban highway policy. Unfortunately, these mistakes are continuing into the sixties in far too large a number.

The mounting problems of the central cities are providing the spur for broad changes in administration and in the manner of financing local government activities. More and more one hears responsible city officials in New York and Cleveland calling for "a new type of federalism across state lines" or "a joint interstate metropolitan government development commission." Municipal pride and self-interest die hard, but serious and mounting problems of competition for water supply, interstate transportation and pollution control are beginning to alert the public to the foolishness of trying to deal with common problems on an individual basis. The recently formed New York Metropolitan Council bears testimony to this.

No one has worked out the machinery for handling problems of this sort in any detail, but it looks as though—without destroying the structures of local governments—the regional council is the answer. Under such a council towns might have a status similar to that of city boroughs, each with its elected officials. Tax burdens would be shifted and revenues redistributed on a regional rather than a town basis. There are some authorities who believe that this is a problem that should be handed to the states to administer and that the responsibility should be shifted to them, but it seems to me that we will have to know a good deal more about the nature of urban regions than we do now before it would be wise to suggest governmental and fiscal changes. As the Renaissance humanist Alberti wisely observed five hundred years ago, "It is useless to bend the bow if you don't know where to aim the arrow."

SUPER-PROBLEMS FOR SUPER-REGIONS

Actually the target grows bigger and bigger. The urban region already shows signs of entering a new stage, even before most people are aware that urban regions exist at all. The land that is back from the urban strips, the "interland," is filling in and is creating a merger of the present regions. A super-region is beginning to appear that will create super-problems, and super-opportunities. We can already trace its course through the East and Midwest, where the Atlantic Urban Region is linking up through New York State to Cleveland, Detroit and Chicago and bulging out through Pennsylvania to Pittsburgh and the Ohio Valley, then stretching down toward St. Louis. If you will trace the truck highways you will find the path of the super-region. It is now the economic center of the world, and someday it may be its cultural center as well.

The super-problems that face urban regional planning are many. Probably the most urgent of these are:

(1) To increase the choice in price, type and location of housing throughout the region, especially for low-income and deprived families;

(2) to determine a rational use of land on a broad scale;

(3) to design a highway network that makes industry, decentralized offices, and regional commercial centers accessible to more people;

(4) and to provide a vastly increased recreational system of parks and reservations as well as hold agricultural open space.

These are a few of the things that city, town or county planning in the classical sense cannot conceivably accomplish.

The Bureau of the Census wisely makes a practice of hedging its bets, and you can't even choose a mid-point among its several projections; however, an increase of sixty or sixty-five million people for the U.S. between 1965 and 1985 is not too far from an official estimate. One thing we do know, that these additional millions won't be living "down on the farm." Only by planning entire urban regions instead of towns and cities in isolation, by introducing regional councils with adequate local representation and by an equitable redistribution of the taxpayer's money, can a desirable living pattern for the future be achieved. There is absolutely no reason why the new urban regions, with their hierarchies of places large and small, should not provide an expanding context for American economic and cultural life—more opportunities for employment, more communication between more people, more institutions and new and interesting kinds of recreation.

Here are a few of the directions we should be moving in:

(1) *Conservation of space*. In spite of the efforts of conservationists, we have no real policy for buying up open land in the urban region and saving it for public use. We need a forward-looking policy that includes state and county committees working on land as it is about to become available. Breathing spaces that once were thought inviolate are now coming on the market—small water company reservations, golf courses, even army bases. Many of these spaces, including about-to-be-abandoned army reservations around Chesapeake Bay and Washington, D.C., have formed natural buffer zones between industrial and residential areas. If the communities don't get them, the subdividers will. The various federal programs which are now helping communities and counties to acquire recreation space and the private money being used to acquire nature reserves are steps in the right direction; however, regional thinking should lie behind an acquisition policy. The shoreline reservation, the Allegheny National Park stretching from Canada to Georgia, the national plan for recreation . . . all these and more are indicated in the light of expected population increase and new habits of employing leisure time.

(2) *Federal action*. As already indicated, concern with urban affairs will demand regional planning in order to avoid sending good money after bad. A model is to be found in the Soil Conservation Districts, originally set up by the states, but staffed and funded from Washington. New regional councils could be responsible for creating the national plan, in which the future use of urban and rural land is projected. But we

must make sure whose plan it will be. The current preoccupation with the problems of the cities themselves must not blind us to the necessity of conserving and developing resources or protecting wildlife. Biologists must be included among the planners; the curators of non-human life must help to create the new regional environment as a viable ecosystem for all life.

(3) *New towns.* Government aid in the construction of large housing-cum-shopping-cum-industrial developments should carry the proviso that a wide range of income groups should be provided for. Otherwise, that which is promoted as a brave new world can become just another means of escape for those who can afford the country club.

(4) *New regional centers.* The village green, the local shopping street and town square have been replaced in our generation by at best the regional shopping plaza and at worst by a strip along a highway junked up with stores, motels, automotive service facilities, hot-dog stands and billboards. The enticing feature is usually lots of parking space. The central business district is trying to compete by providing parking space too, and usually ends up by looking as ugly as the other, with gaps, holes and the inevitable billboards as well. Do we realize the number of good or plain decent buildings that are being swept away in this unplanned nightmare activity? In some communities we have good land-use controls, but in all too few do we have regulations which would preserve the best of the past and encourage adequate new design.

(5) *Preservation.* Until recently, very little attention has been paid to preserving the past, in architecture, in city districts or in the monuments of our industrial society. We are waking up to the fact that there soon will be nothing of the past left, and the historic preservation movement, spearheaded by the National Trust for Historic Preservation, is the result. Our thinking should be regionalized here, too, in the form of historic waterfront districts, scenic river valleys and the preservation of chains of villages and towns in states like Vermont and California. Visible history is an essential part of the creation of new regions: it enriches the experience of life, just as does the preservation of nature.

(6) *Design.* "Project" mentality, which is creating the "colossal bore" of the rebuilt city centers, must be replaced by a critical and informed public mentality, focused in design committees who will choose civic designers with as much care as they elect the new conductor of their symphony orchestra.

Further, the entrepreneur at present has a stranglehold on design in redevelopment areas and should be forced to submit to criticism by the public; in many cases the entrepreneur can be eliminated entirely by municipalities doing their own developing (and incidentally making money in the process) as a common practice in the countries of northwestern Europe. Design on the regional level is just as important, and environmental designers should be trained in our universities to deal with urban regions, their transportation problems, the location of public facilities and the enhancement of their beauty.

(7) *Urban regional planning.* Let us focus our attention on cities, not only as the currently fashionable "problem," but as man's supreme creation. Back in 1935 the National Resources Committee turned away from urban regional planning and announced: "To construct regions which would adhere to cities rather than to the broader aspects of resources, economic patterns, and regional interests is to place the emphasis upon one factor rather than the total region. Upon such a basis, regional planning tends to become an expanded form of city planning." Of course, this was just what was needed. We are now faced with large urban areas as well as parts of cities which face disaster economically and for which huge "poverty" programs have to be devised.

The National Resources Planning Board, as it came to be called, did a great deal to stimulate local planning, but its weight wasn't thrown behind the idea of urban regional planning. Thus the first important metropolitan planning body today in North America is to be found in Canada, at Toronto. It is already discovering that the logical planning area today is the Toronto-Hamilton urban region, much of which is outside the jurisdiction of Metropolitan Toronto. If we can care for the individual "trees" as well as husbanding the "forest," if we can create a beautiful environment as well as a healthy one, if we can guarantee plurality of choice in housing for everybody and not just the majority we shall have created a regional environment.

THE URBAN REGIONS OF THE FUTURE

What will the new planned urban regions look like? Let me refer you again to the author of *Anticipations* and his sixty-five-year-old vision. You must make allowances for trans-atlantic differences and imagine a broader distribution of national income than his picture allows for. But it suggests, I think, that "interurbia" need not necessarily be a new kind of hell:

It will certainly be a curious and varied region, [Wells wrote] far less monotonous than our present English world, still in its thinner regions, at any rate, wooded, perhaps rather more abundantly wooded, breaking continually into park and garden, and with everywhere a scattering of houses. These will not as a rule, I should fancy, follow the fashion of the vulgar ready-built villas of the existing suburb, because the freedom people will be able to exercise in the choice of a site will rob the "building estate" promoter of the local advantage . . . each district, I am inclined to think, will develop its own differences of type and style. As one travels through the urban region, one will traverse open, breezy, "horsy" suburbs, smart white gates and palings everywhere, good turf, a grandstand shining pleasantly: gardening districts all set with gables and roses, holly hedges, and emerald lawns: pleasant homes among heathery moor lands and golf links, and river districts with gaily painted boat-houses peeping from the osiers. Then presently a gathering of houses closer together, and a promenade and whiff of band and dresses, and then, perhaps, a little island of agriculture, hops, or strawberry gardens, fields of gray-plumed artichokes, white-painted orchard, or brightly neat poultry farm. Through the varied country the new wide roads will run, here cutting through a crest and there running like some colossal aqueduct across a valley, swarming always with a multitudinous traffic of bright, swift (and not necessarily ugly) mechanisms; and everywhere amid the fields and trees linking wires will stretch from pole to pole . . . All that is pleasant and fair of our present countryside may conceivably still be there among the other things. There is no reason why the essential charm of the country should disappear: the new roads will not supersede the present high roads, which will still be necessary for horses and subsidiary traffic: and the lands and hedges, the field paths and wild flowers, will still have their ample justification. A certain lack of solitude there may be perhaps, and . . .

Will conspicuous advertisements play any part in the landscape?

But I find my pen is running ahead, an imagination prone to realistic constructions is struggling to paint a picture altogether prematurely . . .

And now the prophecy has become the reality, with "conspicuous advertisements" everywhere, and public taste showing its power and nature in the split-level or the ranch house. I don't think Wells would have been too discouraged; he would have found our hedge-hopping fringe dwellers quite fascinating. Looking across at our "nameless city set in a distant sea" he would have at once made suggestions to improve its well-being, its science, and its culture.

Without the help of this man who foresaw the new environment, Americans will now have to create Utopia in the midst of the biggest population dispersal of all time.

Most Dynamic Sector

ALAN K. CAMPBELL*

The most dynamic part of the American economy today is the state-local government sector of that economy. Although public discussion and debate about the appropriate role of

* Professor of Political Science and Director of Metropolitan Studies, Maxwell Graduate School, Syracuse University. Formerly: Faculty of Salzburg Seminar in American Studies, Spring 1965; Deputy Controller for Administration, State of New York 1960–61; Chairman of the Political Science Department of Hofstra College, and on the faculty at Harvard University. He served as research consultant in 1959 to the New York State Commission on the Governmental Operations of the City of New York and as a member of the staff of the New York Metropolitan Region Study. He was a contributor to the *Anatomy of a Metropolis* (Harvard University Press, 1959) and co-editor of *Case Studies in American Government* (Prentice Hall, 1962), as well as author of numerous articles in professional journals and monographs. He has played an active role in New York State Democratic politics as well as serving professionally on the Committee on Urban Economics of Resources for the Future 1965–, the Advisory Committee to the Committee for Improvement of Management in Government of the Committee for Economic Development 1965–, and the Temporary New York State Commission on the Revision and Simplification of the Constitution 1965–. This article is an adapted version of "Most Dynamic Sector," *National Civic Review*, Vol. LIII, No. 2, February 1964, and published with permission.

government concentrates most of its attention and fire on national government, that level is relatively stagnant compared to state and local levels. In fact, the rate of growth in expenditures, revenues and employment by state and local governments outstrip the growth rate of all other parts of the economy, public or private.

This growth has been accompanied by rather severe political growing pains. Recent state and local elections demonstrate that mayors, governors and suburban government officials find political survival extremely difficult as the demands for new and improved services invariably require greater revenues. The nature of the financing of public services causes the public to simultaneously favor improved services and lower taxes. The stronger forces, however, are on the side of increased expenditures and it is these increases which necessitate rising revenues. The dynamics of growth therefore has its origin in expenditures and these must be examined as a prelude to an analysis of the nature of the revenue response.

One indication of the comparative growth of the state and local sectors is to relate it to the growth of the federal sector. Federal general expenditures increased 24 per cent in the past decade while state and local expenditures increased 126 per cent.[1]

This greater growth has caused its proportion of all general expenditures (federal, state and local) to approach the pre-World War II relationship of federal to state and local expenditures. State and local expenditures in 1964 constituted 41.7 per cent of total general expenditures, the highest proportion it has reached since 1940.

If defense and foreign policy expenditures are excluded and only domestic expenditures compared, the relative growth of the state and local sector is even more pronounced. Measured in this way, they constituted 63 per cent of all general expenditures in 1962; the similar figure for 1946 was 44 per cent. The 1962 proportion is comparable to the pattern of the 1920s.

All of these comparisons demonstrate the growing role of state and local government in the total governmental system

[1] Unless otherwise stated, comparisons are of general expenditures as that term is defined by the Census Bureau, comprising "all expenditures other than (a) benefit and refund payments of public-employee retirement and other social-insurance systems, and (b) spending for state and local liquor stores and for local water, electric, transit and gas utilities."

but perhaps of even greater interest is the role of the state and local sector in the total economy. Total government purchases of goods and services constituted 19.16 per cent of gross national product in 1964, a figure which shows a small decline from 1954 when it was 21.84 per cent. In other words, the total public sector as measured by purchases of goods and services has not increased its proportion of the total economy during the past decade.

This overall stability hides important internal shifts. For this same ten-year period the federal government purchases, as a proportion of gross national product, declined from 13.96 per cent to 10.01 per cent while the state and local sector grew from 7.89 per cent to 9.14 per cent. In relative terms, therefore, the proportion of gross national product represented by state and local expenditures for goods and services increased 16 per cent while similar federal expenditures declined 28 per cent.

TABLE 1

PROPORTION OF GENERAL DOMESTIC EXPENDITURES*
BY LEVEL OF GOVERNMENT

Year	Per Cent Federal	Per Cent State	Per Cent Local	Per Cent State and Local
1922	34.6	12.9	52.5	65.4
1936	48.7	14.9	36.4	51.3
1946	56.1	12.6	31.3	43.9
1952	39.5	20.1	40.5	60.6
1954	39.8	19.8	40.3	60.1
1962	37.2	21.2	41.5	62.7
1963/64	36.3	22.3	41.4	63.7

(Totals do not add to 100 per cent because of rounding)

* Excludes Defense and Foreign Policy Expenditures.

SOURCE: U.S. Bureau of the Census. Census of Governments: 1962. Vol. VI, No. 4, *Historical Statistics on Governmental Finances and Employment.*

U.S. Bureau of the Census. *Governmental Finances in 1963–64.* Series G-GF64-No. 1.

SHIFTS IN FUNCTIONAL ALLOCATION

This increase in expenditure levels has been accompanied by different rates of growth for the various functions performed by state and local governments. While total state and local general expenditures have increased by 126 per cent during the past decade, education has increased by 151 per cent. The large growth in expenditures for education, added to the large proportion of the total expenditures represented by this function, results in most other functions increasing less than the increase for all functions. The exceptions are local parks and recreation which have grown 141 per cent since 1954 but the absolute amount in this category is so small that the proportion of total expenditures had increased by 1962 to only 1.5 per cent. Interest on debt has also increased more than the overall increase—224 per cent.

TABLE 2
GOVERNMENT PURCHASES OF GOODS AND SERVICES
AS A PER CENT OF GNP (IN CONSTANT 1958 DOLLARS)

Year	GNP Billion	All Governments Billion	Per Cent	Federal Government Billion	Per Cent	State and Local Billion	Per Cent
1929	$203.6	$ 22.0	10.81	$ 3.5	1.72	$18.5	9.09
1940	227.2	36.4	16.02	15.0	6.60	21.4	9.42
1946	312.6	48.4	15.48	30.1	9.63	18.4	5.89
1950	355.3	52.8	14.86	25.3	7.12	27.5	7.74
1952	395.1	92.1	23.31	63.8	16.15	28.4	7.19
1954	407.0	88.9	21.84	56.8	13.96	32.1	7.89
1962	530.0	107.5	20.28	60.0	12.00	47.5	8.62
1964	577.6	110.7	19.16	57.8	10.01	52.8	9.14

SOURCE: U.S. Department of Commerce, Office of Business Economics: *Survey of Current Business*, XLV, 8, August 1965; Table 2.

The education expenditure increase reveals an interesting contrast when it is divided between local schools and higher education. Local school expenditures have increased at just about the average national increase—a growth of 127.9 per cent. The higher growth rate for education is accounted for by the increase of 289.6 per cent for institutions of higher education, the greatest increase for any function.

Because of the domination of the total figures by educational expenditures, it is revealing to analyze separately non-education expenditures which had an over-all increase of 112 per cent. Looked at this way, the greatest growth for a large function was highways which increased its expenditures by 111.0 per cent while welfare, with an increase of 88.4 per cent, is growing less rapidly than the average of all non-education functions.

Despite the different rates of growth for individual functions, the proportionate allocation of the total resources used in the state and local sector has not changed drastically over

TABLE 3

STATE AND LOCAL GENERAL EXPENDITURES WITH AND WITHOUT EDUCATION: GROWTH AND PROPORTION, BY FUNCTION, 1954–1963/64

	Growth 1954–63/64 per cent	with education 1954 per cent	with education 1963/64 per cent	without education 1954 per cent	without education 1963/64 per cent
Total	125.7	100.0	100.0	100.0	100.0
Education	151.3	34.4	38.3		
Local Schools	127.9	29.1	29.4		
Insts. of Higher Ed.	289.6	4.6	7.9		
Non-Education	112.3	65.6	61.7	100.0	100.0
Highways	111.0	18.0	16.8	27.4	27.3
Public Welfare	88.4	10.0	8.3	15.2	13.5
Hospitals & Health	103.8	7.8	7.1	12.0	11.5
Police	109.4	3.7	3.6	5.6	5.5
Local Fire Protection	87.1	2.1	1.8	3.2	2.9
Sanitation	114.3	3.5	3.3	5.2	5.3
Natural Resources	140.8	2.4	2.6	3.8	4.3
Parks & Recreation	141.0	1.4	1.5	2.1	2.4
Hous. & Comm. Redev.	86.9	2.0	1.6	3.0	2.7
General Control	86.7	4.5	3.7	6.8	6.0
Interest on Debt	223.6	2.3	3.4	3.6	5.5
Non-Hwy. Transportation	110.3	1.0	0.9	1.5	1.5
Others and Unallocable	137.2	6.9	7.2	10.5	11.7

Proportion of Total Expenditures 1954, 1963/64

SOURCE: The U.S. Census of Governments, 1962: *Historical Statistics on Governmental Finances and Employment.* The Bureau of the Census: *Governmental Finances in 1963–64.*

the last ten years. The biggest gainer has been education, which has climbed from 34 per cent of the total to 38 per cent. Welfare has declined, while highways has just held its own.

What will happen in the future? Will the present pattern continue, will there be a leveling off, or will rates of change increase or decline? The easy and correct answer is that nobody knows. Nevertheless, informed guesses are possible and several have been made in recent years which are based on an analysis of need and resource availability as measured by such factors as potential increase in school population and economic growth.[2]

Contrasting three of these projections with predictions based on a mcehanical straight-line projection indicates that, in the opinion of the soothsayers, future growth will proceed at a somewhat slower pace than that of the past decade. For one of the projections it is possible to check its current accuracy since it was made in 1958 with estimates of annual increases over the next decade.[3] When current expenditures are translated into the definitions used in this prediction, the actual growth to date is somewhat greater than the prediction. Such direct comparison is not possible for the other projections since they were not made on an annual basis. Nevertheless, when these projections are compared to straight-line projections based on the actual experience of 1952–62, the general indications of both the substantive and mechanical projections is for substantial growth.

On a functional basis, the differences in the various substantive projections are caused primarily by differences in the estimates made for education and urban renewal. The Colm-Helzner projections assume much greater growth in these areas than do Netzer and Eckstein. In part, this difference is based on different assumptions about economic growth and, in part, on political factors. Eckstein, with a comparatively low projection in the urban development field, specifically argues that "A rising construction program, especially for

[2] Otto Eckstein, *Trends in Public Expenditures in the Next Decade,* Committee for Economic Development, 1959. Gerhard Colm and Manuel Helzner, "Financial Needs and Resources Over the Next Decade: At All Levels of Government" and Dick Netzer "Financial Needs and Resources Over the Next Decade: State and Local Governments" in *National Bureau Committee for Economic Research,* a report of the National Bureau of Economic Research, 1961.

[3] Eckstein, *op. cit.*

TABLE 4

A COMPARISON OF ANALYTICAL PROJECTIONS OF STATE AND LOCAL
EXPENDITURES TO STRAIGHT-LINE PROJECTIONS[1]
(BILLIONS OF DOLLARS IN 1958 CONSTANT DOLLARS)

Projections: Eckstein Definitions

Year	Substantive	Straight Line
1962	$43.3	$44.8 (actual)
1963	45.2	49.2
1964	47.4	53.4
1968	53.7	68.8
1970		75.7
1972		82.1

Projections: Netzer Definitions

Year	Substantive	Straight Line
1962		60.2 (actual)
1963		66.4
1964		72.4
1968		93.9
1970	65.8–78.4	103.6
1972		112.6

Projections: Colm-Helzner Definitions

Year	Substantive	Straight Line[2]
1962		61.9 (actual)
1963		70.2
1964	64.6	78.2
1968		107.3
1970	90.0	120.3
1972		132.4

SOURCE: Otto Eckstein, *Trends in Public Expenditures in the Next Decade*, Committee for Economic Development, 1959. Gerhard Colm and Manuel Helzner, "Financial Needs and Resources Over the Next Decade: At All Levels of Government" and Dick Netzer, *Ibid*, in *National Bureau Committee for Economic Research*, a report of the National Bureau of Economic Research, 1961.

[1] A straight-line projection is provided for each of the other projections. In each case the straight-line projection follows the definitions and constant dollar assumptions used by the authors of the other projections.

[2] The 1962 figures of the straight-line projections are actual figures adjusted for appropriate definitions and constant dollars. The straight-line projections are based on the experience of the 1952–62 period.

urban renewal, is projected, but the magnitude is moderate due to local obstacles to projects."[4]

[4] *Op. cit.*, p. 4.

Overall, the actual experience of the past decade and the projections based on an analysis of individual functional areas indicate that the growing rate of increase in state and local expenditures will slacken, at most, very little. It seems fair to assume that a larger and larger portion of the total national product will be allocated to this sector of the economy. Obviously much depends on the state of the economy and on the willingness of government to maintain the present level of responsibilities.

Within these indications of an overall increase there is some evidence that the pattern of need may be shifting. Until recently, for example, the primary pressure for increased expenditures in the suburbs has been for education, while in central cities the big increase has been in the municipal sector —an increase necessitated by the neglect of capital plant during the depression and war and by new needs created by population shifts. Now, however, there are suburban areas where the growth in educational expenditure seems to be slowing slightly but this slowdown is more than offset by the increase in non-school municipal expenditures.

The older suburban areas, those which experienced their great increases in population in the late '40s and early '50s, are beginning to feel the need for the traditional municipal services—sanitation, police and fire protection, and highways. The central city picture, in contrast, is one of educational costs rising more rapidly than municipal costs. This shift is caused by the need for new school plant in central cities and

TABLE 5

TAX REVENUES AS A PER CENT OF NATIONAL INCOME, 1940-1963/64

Year	All Govts.	Federal	State	Local	State & Local	National Income Billion dollars
1940	15.64%	6.01%	4.09%	5.55%	9.63%	$ 81.1
1946	25.51	19.96	2.72	2.84	5.55	181.8
1950	21.19	14.60	3.29	3.31	6.60	241.1
1952	27.14	20.49	3.40	3.26	6.62	291.4
1954	27.86	20.59	3.66	3.62	7.28	303.1
1962	27.05	17.98	4.50	4.59	9.09	457.7
1963	27.25	18.04	4.60	4.60	9.20	481.1

SOURCE: The U.S. Census of Governments, 1962: *Historical Statistics on Governmental Finances and Employment.*

U.S. Bureau of the Census, *Governmental Finances in 1963-64.*

The U.S. Department of Commerce, Office of Business Economics: *Survey of Current Business XLV,* 8 (August 1965) Table 4.

by the special educational problems associated with the increasing number of culturally disadvantaged pupils. Simultaneously, at the fringe of the older suburban areas, the suburban population boom continues and the pattern of rapidly rising educational costs experienced earlier in the nearer-in suburbs is being repeated.

The total impact of these shifts is likely to increase pressures for increased expenditures. The metropolitanization of the country is continuing and will accentuate these shifts while simultaneously creating a demand for a generally higher level of public services.

REVENUE RESPONSE

"Where's the money coming from?" This question takes on a rather special urgency in the light of state and local expenditure growth during the past decade and the projections of future growth.

The overall general revenue increase has had to keep pace with these expenditure increases but the significant questions revolve around changes in sources of revenue and shifts in the pattern of sources used. As with general expenditures, federal tax revenues have increased less rapidly than similar state and local revenues. As a proportion of national income, state and local taxes have increased from 7.3 per cent in 1954 to 9.2 per cent in 1962. Federal tax revenue in 1954 equalled 20.6 per cent of national income; it declined by 1963 to about 18 per cent and has remained at that figure since.

Despite a large increase in the total, the sources of state and local tax revenue have not shifted markedly. Perhaps most remarkable, particularly in view of many dire predictions about its future, has been the performance of the property tax. In 1954 the property tax contributed 45.2 per cent of state and local tax revenues; in 1963–64, 44.6 per cent. At the local level its proportion was 87.2 per cent in 1954, and 87.5 per cent in 1963–64.

Over a longer time span, the significant change in the property tax has been its abandonment by most states, causing it to become almost exclusively a source of local revenue. For example, in 1922, 37 per cent of state tax revenues was provided by the property tax. This had declined by 1940 to 8 per cent, declining to 4 per cent in 1952, and to 3 per cent in 1962. This change has not, however, reduced its total contribution since its abandonment by the state has simply resulted in its being used more extensively by local governments.[5]

Although the overall pattern of state general revenue sources had been established by 1952, the contribution made by the various sources of revenue has shifted somewhat in the past decade. Gains have been made in the proportion of general revenue contributed by the individual income tax, fees and charges, and federal aid. The individual income tax had increased its proportion of total state general revenues from 6.6 to 9.1 per cent, while fees and charges increased from 8.7 to 10.5 per cent and, most significantly, federal aid had grown from 17.4 to 24.0 per cent.

The pattern of local general revenue sources has not shifted as much during this same period as has the state pattern. Over a longer period, about the last four decades, the significant change has been the increasing proportion of local general revenues provided by state aid. During the last ten years, however, the various sources have remained relatively constant. Fees and charges increased from 13.6 to 15.2 per cent. It is only in this source that a major increase in the proportion contributed has been accomplished. While property taxes have fallen slightly from 49.0 per cent to 46.5 per cent, the other sources have remained fairly constant with individual income tax increasing from a .6 per cent to .9 per cent; sales from 3.6 to 4.1 per cent; while federal aid has increased from 1.5 to 2.2 per cent.

The most remarkable aspect of state and local revenue sources has been their stability over the past decade. There have not been any dramatic developments in traditional revenue sources nor has there been any major new source of revenue found. Nevertheless, there have been some shifts and these should be carefully examined to determine their possible implications for the future.

It appears clear that state and local governments are turning more and more to direct charges for public services where the service lends itself to that kind of treatment. Another sig-

[5] The abandonment by the state governments of the property tax as a major source of revenue has resulted during the last quarter of a century in their adopting non-property taxes and non-tax sources of revenue. By 1952 a new pattern of revenue sources had been established. All states, with the exception of one, Nebraska, have adopted one or two broad-based taxes—the individual income tax and/or the sales tax. New Hampshire's income tax is a limited one, and the state has responded to its fiscal pressure with a state-sponsored lottery. The revenue results to date have been disappointing.

TABLE 6

PERCENT OF STATE GOVERNMENT GENERAL REVENUES CONTRIBUTED BY REVENUE SOURCE: 1940–1963/64

	1940	1946	1950	1952	1954	1962	1963/64
Total Gen. Rev.*	100.0%	100.0%	100.0%	100.0%	100.0%	100.0%	100.0%
Taxes	75.5	78.6	70.4	73.5	72.5	66.1	64.4
Indiv. Inc.	4.7	6.2	6.4	6.8	6.6	8.8	9.1
Corp. Inc.	3.5	7.0	5.2	6.2	5.0	4.2	4.5
Sales	42.3	44.6	41.5	42.7	43.0	38.6	37.1
Property	5.9	4.0	2.7	2.8	2.6	2.1	1.9
Licenses	8.8	7.0	6.7	6.9	7.2	5.4	5.1
Other	10.3	9.8	7.9	8.1	8.2	7.0	6.7
Charges	7.9	7.7	8.1	8.1	8.7	10.0	10.5
Intergov'tal Rev.	16.5	13.8	21.5	18.5	18.8	24.0	25.1
From Federal	15.2	12.8	20.2	17.3	17.4	22.8	24.0
From Local	1.3	1.0	1.3	1.2	1.4	1.2	1.1

SOURCE: The U.S. Census of Governments, 1962: *Historical Statistics on Governmental Finances and Employment*. The U.S. Bureau of the Census, *Governmental Finances in 1963–64*.
* Due to rounding, the totals do not add to exactly 100 per cent.

TABLE 7

Percent of Local Government General Revenues Contributed by Revenue Source: 1940–1963/64

	1940	1946	1950	1952	1954	1962	1963/64
Total Gen. Rev.	100.0%	100.0%	100.0%	100.0%	100.0%	100.0%	100.0%
Taxes	64.9	62.6	57.0	55.8	56.1	54.7	53.4
Indiv. Inc.	0.3	0.4	0.5	0.5	0.6	0.8	0.9
Sales	1.9	2.2	3.5	3.7	3.6	3.8	4.1
Property	60.1	57.6	50.2	48.9	49.0	48.0	46.5
Others	2.6	2.4	2.8	2.7	2.9	2.1	1.9
Charges	7.3	11.2	11.4	13.0	13.6	14.9	15.2
Intergov'tal Rev.	27.8	26.0	31.6	31.2	30.3	30.4	31.4
From Federal	4.0	0.6	1.5	1.4	1.5	1.5	2.2
From State	23.8	25.4	30.1	29.8	28.8	28.4	29.2

source: The U.S. Census of Governments, 1962: *Historical Statistics on Governmental Finances and Employment.* The U.S. Bureau of the Census, *Governmental Finances in 1963–64.*

nificant development has been the increased contribution of federal aid to the states. This increase is primarily the result of the introduction of the new aid program for the National Defense Highway system and the increase through formula adjustment in the amount of aid provided for welfare.

This demonstrates an important characteristic of the federal aid system relative to state and local revenue. Increases in this source are primarily a result of the federal government deciding to provide federal aid for the first time to a traditional state and local responsibility or to revise its formulas for already aided activities. Increases, therefore, in the proportionate role of federal aid as a source of revenue are dependent on specific action by the national government rather than the result of evolutionary increases growing out of automatic adjustments or economic growth.

Of interest, too, is the relatively small proportion of local general revenues provided by direct federal aid. In the postwar period there has been a great deal of discussion about federal-city relations, with many predicting that the national government would provide more and more assistance directly to city governments. Major new programs providing such aid have been adopted, most notably in the housing and urban renewal and anti-poverty field, but as yet this aid has not had a substantial impact on local revenues. Many of the projections of future state and local expenditures put considerable stress on this field and, if the local obstacles to urban renewal can be successfully overcome, it is possible that federal aid for renewal and other metropolitan development programs may play a more and more important role in providing additional revenue to local governments.

On the whole, however, it seems likely that the additional revenue needed to finance the increasing expenditures of both state and local governments will be simply more of the same. The property tax has been found to be remarkably responsive to new needs and recent studies indicate that, at least in suburban areas, it is a fairly adequate surrogate for a local income tax, since a high relationship has been found between property values and income levels.[6] It is possible that the one state which has not adopted a broad-based tax, will do so, and

[6] Robert Fairbanks, *Property Tax Behavior in New York State, 1949–1961*, DSS Dissertation, Syracuse University, 1963; and Jesse Burkhead, *State and Local Taxes for Public Education*, Syracuse University Press, 1963.

some of those states which have adopted only one of the two such taxes, will adopt the other.

It can be anticipated, too, that the pattern of debt increase of the past ten years will be continued. Total state and local debt increased from 34 to 67 billion dollars, a 97 per cent increase, while federal debt increased 39 billion, or 15 per cent.

REVENUES AND EXPENDITURES

Although these national figures provide a good general picture of what is happening in state and local finance, they do not provide any explanation of variations in fiscal behavior among the states or within individual states. There are substantial differences in many aspects of fiscal behavior, including differences in per capita expenditures, in rates of growth and in the proportion of expenditures employed for different functions, and in the patterns of revenue sources.

The art and science of state and local public finance is unable to explain all these differences but significant progress has been made in explaining some of them. Most effort has been expended in understanding differences in per capita expenditures and significant results have been obtained. One of the earlier studies,[7] done in 1942, attempted to explain variation in state and local expenditures by relating the different state levels to three variables: population density, degree of urbanization and personal income. Using multiple regression analysis, the study succeeded in "explaining" 72 per cent of the variations in per capita total operating expenditures in 1942; that is, 72 per cent of the variation of per capita total general operating expenditures was associated with or related to variances in per capita income, population density and per cent urban. In a later study,[8] the same variables were used in analyzing 1957 data and the results were not substantially different from the 1942 results except that the proportion "explained" declined to 53 per cent.

Further light was shed by a study done of 1960 data[9] when

[7] Solomon Fabricant, *Trend of Governmental Activity in the United States Since 1900*, National Bureau of Economic Research, 1952.

[8] Glen Fisher, "Determinants of State and Local Government Expenditures: A Preliminary Analysis," *National Tax Journal*, December 1961, pp. 349–55.

[9] Seymour Sacks, Robert Harris, and John J. Carroll, *The State and Local Government . . . The Role of State Aid*, Comptroller's Study in

TABLE 8
STATE AND LOCAL GENERAL REVENUES AND EXPENDITURES:
PROPORTIONS BY REVENUE SOURCES AND BY FUNCTIONS FOR
EXPENDITURES, PERCENTAGE INCREASE AND PER CAPITA AMOUNTS

General Revenues	New Jersey %	New York %	Ohio %	Texas %	Washington %
Total General Rev.	100.0	100.0	100.0	100.0	100.0
Proportion Contributed by:					
Federal Aid	7.3	7.4	11.3	14.5	12.6
Taxes	79.3	79.0	72.3	67.0	69.1
property	53.3	35.3	37.5	32.6	21.8
others	26.0	43.7	34.7	34.4	47.3
Charges and Misc.	13.4	13.6	16.4	18.5	18.3
% Increase of Gen. Rev. 1957–61	54.8	38.0	43.5	30.8	39.1
Per Capita, Gen. Rev. 1961	$300.6	$370.8	$268.5	$244.8	$346.9
General Expenditures	%	%	%	%	%
Total General Exp.	100.0	100.0	100.0	100.0	100.0
Proportion Expended for:					
Education	36.7	30.4	37.2	38.6	40.0
Highways	12.2	13.4	19.1	22.6	15.4
Public Welfare	5.4	7.4	9.0	7.4	10.4
Health & Hospitals	7.1	9.6	6.6	5.7	5.5
Public Safety	10.0	6.6	5.6	5.2	4.3
Sewage and Sanitation	5.1	3.5	4.6	3.2	3.4
General Control	2.8	2.4	2.3	1.9	1.6
All others	20.6	26.8	15.6	15.3	19.4
% Increase of Gen. Exp., 1957–61	37.5	38.1	34.2	32.1	34.6
Per Capita, Gen. Exp. 1961	$293.1	$388.4	$278.0	$253.7	$369.9

SOURCES: The U.S. Bureau of the Census, *Compendium of Governmental Finances*, 1957 Census of Government, Vol. III, No. 5.
The U.S. Bureau of the Census, *Governmental Finances in 1961*.

two new variables were added—per capita federal and state aid. The result of these additional variables increased the amount of variance "explained" to 87 per cent. This new finding would seem to indicate that state and federal aid does not reduce state and local revenues but is additive to these revenue levels which are determined by other factors independent of the amount of aid received.

There are, of course, other factors which may help explain different levels of expenditures in various jurisdictions. For example, the nature of the governmental system within the state may have an impact. What fiscal difference does it make whether a function is performed at the local level, the state level, or at the local level but financed in part by the state? The answer is not clear, but the hypothesis most attractive to the writer is that the performance of a function at the local level, whether state aided or not, tends to increase expenditures. The belief is based on the assumption that the wealthier communities will spend sufficiently to produce a higher average of expenditures than will be achieved by state performance of the function at a minimum level throughout the state.

It is also possible that state and local expenditures are influenced by the character of the local system of government. What, for example, is the effect of many overlapping governments within an area, compared to a system of more general governments?

Another set of issues revolves around the role of central cities in metropolitan areas. What significance does their size relative to their entire metropolitan area have?

SUMMARY AND CONCLUSIONS

The state and local sector of the economy is the fastest growing. This growth is likely to continue and will put extraordinary pressure on the governmental system to find the revenues necessary to finance it.

The expenditure growth areas, both functionally and by area, are likely to be the same as those of the past decade but with some internal shifting. Education will continue to be the biggest user of public resources but the greatest growth of this function may shift from suburbia to central city and suburban fringe areas. Within education, higher education costs may grow more rapidly than elementary or secondary education. Urban renewal and associated metropolitan programs may, if political obstacles can be overcome, constitute a larger and larger share of state and local expenditures.

Revenue sources will remain much the same but some of the sources will increase their contribution more than others. In general, fees and charges are bound to grow and the political pressure for more state and federal aid is likely to increase the role of aid in overall state and local finances. States and local governments which have not taken full advantage of the already cultivated tax sources will move into those areas which remain to be tapped.

State and local governmental systems will continue to produce various levels of expenditures, these levels being determined in part by the state's economic characteristics and, in part, by its governmental system. The revenue system will also reflect these characteristics. Exact or even approximate relationships between these characteristics and fiscal behavior need extensive investigation.

The upward pressure, however, on expenditures and revenues will not subside while such investigations are made. These pressures and their contradictory directions—better services and lower taxes—will retire many mayors, suburban government officials and governors from public office unless they are able to move fast enough to reach the relative political safety of the White House or Congress.

Culture, Territoriality, and the Elastic Mile

MELVIN M. WEBBER AND CAROLYN C. WEBBER*

Conventional analysis of spatial relations in cities are built upon a commonly held conception of the nature and meanings of space. The underlying idea, borrowed from Euclid, supplies the foundation for much of the new-found interest among economists and sociologists, no less than among engineers and city planners. But it is now becoming apparent that this com-

* Melvin M. Webber, M.C.P. from the University of California, Berkeley, is presently Professor of City Planning and Acting Chairman of the Center for Planning and Development at that institution. He served as editor of the *Journal of the American Institute of Planners* (1958–62), as Visiting Research Associate at Resources for the Future, Inc., and as Senior Metropolitan Planner for the San Francisco Bay Area Rapid Transit Study. He has been a consultant for the Metropolitan Transit Study for Santiago (Chile), to the State of Hawaii on its general plan as well as to New York University on its urban studies program and to various federal agencies. He contributed "The Urban Place and the Nonplace Urban Realm," in *Explorations into Urban Structure* (Philadelphia: University of Pennsylvania Press, 1964) which he edited and "Order in Diversity Without Propinquity," in Lowdon Wingo, Jr., editor, *Cities and Space* (Baltimore: The Johns Hopkins Press, 1963). Carolyn Webber, his wife, an M.A. in Econom-

mon intellectual property is really a very heterogeneous commodity. In only a limited sense is space measurable as mileage distances on the surface of the earth, or even as the various costs of traversing those mileage distances.

Space is turning out to be a very complex phenomenon, having far more than the simple three dimensions that are revealed through our senses of sight and touch. Current work in mathematics is describing several of its complex geometries. The group dynamicists have been seeking to measure its many social dimensions. The economists are of course exposing a diversity of cost dimensions. The experimental psychologists are exploring individuals' perceptions of conventional three-dimensional space and the ways in which they cope with spatial distortions. Various anthropologists have commented on the meanings of territorial space in primitive communities, and others have been exploring the cross-cultural variations in perceptions of personal space and time.

Now, most recently, several sociologists and social psychologists are examining some of the social-cultural variants in perceptions of space and in social meanings, as these are affected by space. In turn, they are inquiring into the culturally specific behavior with respect to space in several of the subcultures of complex urban-industrial communities. The findings of these latter studies, and especially the investigations into the culture of working-class ethnic groups, are revealing some striking variations in responses to space among population subgroups. They suggest that culturally specific spaces must be measured against a wide variety of transformations of the linear-distance scale and of the time scale, and against a varied collection of value scales. In an effort to identify some of these scale differences, we should like first to speculate about the space-related behavior of the intellectual elites and then to summarize some of the more relevant findings of the recent inquiries into working-class behavior.

ics and Sociology, from the University of Texas, has had recent research association with the Institute of Industrial Relations and the Institute of International Studies at the University of California, Berkeley.

This is a modification of an earlier article appearing in the *Papers of the Regional Science Association*, Vol. XIII, 1964, pp. 59–70, and is reproduced with permission. The authors are indebted to Marc Fried and Herbert J. Gans for many of the generalizations about the working class presented here. They have also profited from the critical comments of Michael Teitz and the late Catherine Bauer Wurster in the presentation of their ideas.

In turn, then, these suggest some policy guidelines for city-building programs.

THE INTELLECTUAL ELITES

At one extreme, along the continua that differentiate the population into status and occupational subgroups, we find the intellecual elite. This class includes university professors, high-level administrators in business and government, working scientists in private research establishments, and creative contributors to the arts. The members of the intellectual elite are marked by a primary orientation toward achieving excellence in their work, as a self-sufficient end, and toward defining intellectual, scientific, and/or policy problems and then discovering solutions to them. As a group, they are largely responsible for the tremendous recent additions to the stock of knowledge; and they have made marked contributions to governmental policies and the expansion of industry. Their personal and professional standards are forged from a searching self-criticism and from the evaluations of their professional peers around the world.

Their contacts with friends and colleagues at distant places are maintained through a large number of channels—the academic journals, books, the mails, the long-distance telephone, the telegraph, and of course the long-haul transportation lines. Although most of their colleagues and associates are physically distant in space, the quality of interaction engendered by shared interests is very intimate even when face-to-face conversations are infrequent. Together these specialized intellectuals comprise closely knit communities to which each member *belongs* and to which his professional loyalties are assigned. It is these spatially dispersed peers who will understand his work and, in evaluation, convey the rewards that matter most to him.

As with all other professional elites, the primary group is not based on kinship, ethnicity, nationality, *or* place. Rather, it is a voluntary association of men joined by shared interests and shared values. And today, when gratuitous expense accounts fix the dollar costs of long-distance travel at zero, the intellectual elites exhibit a much higher-average propensity to travel than do others having comparable taxable incomes. As men who trade in information and ideas, they must necessarily maintain intensive communication with other members of their spatially dispersed, *nonplace* communities.[1] These folk approximate the true cosmopolites, for whom territorial distance is a minor barrier to interaction and whose professional social communities are the least shaped by territorialism. For these, social propinquity is least dependent upon spatial propinquity.[2]

Of course, these world-wide or nation-wide communities of specialist elites make only partial claims upon their participants. It is only in his segmental roles as specialist that a man is even a member of these cosmopolitan communities. In others of his role—as teacher, laboratory worker, grocery shopper, PTA member, parent, husband, and many more—his communities are likely to be more nearly *place*-based. Each of the many communities to which he belongs has its own set of peers, each set distributed within spatial realms somewhat different from each of the others. As parent and husband his world typically fixes on the suburban lot. As grocery shopper or participant in the local PTA, perhaps a few statute miles. As "neighbor" he may have virtually no contact with those who live on his block, for he probably selects his social friends largely, if not solely, on the basis of common interests; and he may therefore travel dozens of miles for an evening visit.

The life spaces of these highly specialized professional types are multi-dimensional and supraterritorial, being scaled against measures of social rank, generation, age, stage in the life cycle, educational attainment, and, almost incidentally, geographic distance. The cosmopolite *himself* is also pluralistic: each individual represents a variegated bundle of role-persons, each at least somewhat different from the others. Each *role* also carries its own special demands, opportunities, and sources of potential gratification.[3]

But the striking thing about these men, when playing out their specialist roles, is the ease with which they are able to operate within *ex*tensive space. In their professional roles they are likely to be at home in Washington, Denver, Los Angeles, London, Warsaw, or Tokyo. Even in their more localized

[1] Melvin M. Webber, "The Urban Place and the Nonplace Urban Realm," in M. M. Webber *et al.*, *Explorations into Urban Structure* (Philadelphia: University of Pennsylvania Press, 1964).

[2] Melvin M. Webber, "Order in Diversity: Community Without Propinquity," in Lowdon Wingo, Jr., editor, *Cities and Space* (Baltimore: The Johns Hopkins Press, 1963).

[3] Erving Goffman, "Role Distance," in *Encounters*, two studies in the sociology of interaction (Indianapolis: Bobbs-Merrill, 1961).

roles as parents or grocery shoppers, they accommodate to *alternate* locational settings with seeming ease, moving their households from one end of the country or world to another with remarkable frequency. The high rates of residential mobility among these groups seem to be sustained by the large adaptive capacities of their families; seldom does a long-distance move represent an adjustment crisis of serious proportions. To be sure, in part this reflects the decline of cultural differences among the regions of the nation, such that a move from Long Island to Santa Monica is nearly equivalent to a move of a few blocks within either of those places.[4] In part it reflects the association of a move with an expanded role-opportunity that is positively sought and with the enhanced economic opportunity that may accompany the move. But in part, too, it reflects their internal, psychic resources for coping with change.[5]

Middle-class Americans, and especially those whose education has exposed them to conditions in the world at different times and at different places are thereby better equipped to anticipate conditions they will confront at different places and at later stages in time. In the normal course of acculturation to middle-class ways, one assimilates a concept of futurity, the notion that the future is in some degree controllable, and a capacity to forego present gratifications for potentially greater future gratifications. The cosmopolite's life space is not only geographically extensive; it also extends forward (as well as backward) in time.

THE WORKING CLASS

Now consider another group, at the opposite end of the continua that extend from the professional cosmopolites to the working-class locals.[6] These people might be located in

[4] Herbert J. Gans, "Effects of the Move from City to Suburb," in Leonard Duhl, ed., *The Urban Condition* (New York: Basic Books, 1963), pp. 184–200; also his "The Balanced Community: Homogeneity or Heterogeneity in Residential Areas," *Journal of the American Institute of Planners,* XXVII: 2 (August 1961) pp. 176–84; and his "Planning and Social Life: Friendship and Neighbor Relations in Suburban Communities," *Journal of the American Institute of Planners,* XXVII: 2 (May 1961) pp. 134–40.

[5] Marc Fried, "Transitional Functions of the Working Class Communities: Implications for Forced Relocation," in Mildred Kantor, ed., *Mobility and Mental Health* (New York: D. Van Nostrand, 1964).

[6] The terms "cosmopolites" and "locals" may have been first used in this sense by Robert K. Merton in *Social Theory and Social Structure*

pre-industrial peasant villages in almost any part of the world
or in the high-density slum of any large European or American metropolitan area.[7]

The accumulating studies are revealing some remarkably
similar patterns among all these groups, suggesting that locational setting and physical surroundings are not the crucial
determinants of social structure and behavior, as the early
civic and housing reformers assumed. The consistent findings
indicate that the so-called working class, whether residents of
central city slums or suburban housing tracts, have retained
the "intense localism" and the limited "close-knit-networks"
of social relations that are also found in many peasant societies.[8]

(New York: Free Press of Glencoe, Inc., 1957, 2nd edition), Chap. X,
"Patterns of Influence: Local and Cosmopolitan Influentials," pp. 387 ff.
    [7] Oscar Lewis, *Five Families* (New York: Basic Books, 1959) and
"The Culture of Poverty," in John J. Fisher and Sidney N. TePaske,
eds., *Explosive Forces in Latin America Today* (Columbus: Ohio State
University Press, 1964, pp. 149–56).
    [8] Bennett Berger, *Working Class Suburb: A Study of Auto Workers
in Suburbia* (Berkeley, University of California Press, 1963), pp. 34–36,
Ch. V. Elizabeth Bott, *Family and Social Network* (London: Tavistock
Publications, 1957) Ch. III, esp. pp. 92–96; Ch. IV. Marc Fried, "Griev-
ing for a Lost Home," in Leonard Duhl, ed., *The Urban Condition*
(New York: Basic Books, 1963), pp. 151–71; and Fried, "Transitional
Functions of the Working Class Communities," *op. cit.* Herbert J. Gans,
The Levittowners, Ways of Life and Politics in a Suburban Community
(New York: Institute of Urban Studies, Teacher's College, Columbia
University, 1965, mimeo); and Gans, *The Urban Villagers* (New York:
The Free Press of Glencoe, 1962). Nathan Glazer and Daniel Patrick
Moynihan, *Beyond the Melting Pot* (Cambridge, M.I.T. and Harvard
University Press, 1963). Gerard Handel and Lee Rainwater, "Persistence
and Change in Working Class Life Style," in A. Shostak and W. Gom-
berg, eds., Blue Collar World, *Studies of the American Worker* (Engle-
wood Cliffs: Prentice-Hall, 1964). Hoggart, Richard, *The Uses of
Literacy* (London: Oxford University Press, 1961). Clyde Kluckhohn,
"Culture and Behavior," in Gardner Lindzey, *Handbook of Social Psychology*, Vol. I (Cambridge, Mass.: Addison Wesley, 1959, pp. 931–33).
Mirra Komarovsky, *Blue Collar Marriage* (New York: Random House,
1962). Hylan Lewis, *Blackways of Kent* (Chapel Hill: University of
North Carolina Press, 1955), pp. 27–36. Oscar Lewis, *Five Families,
op. cit.*, and "The Culture of Poverty," *op. cit.* Lee Rainwater, R. Cole-
man, and Gerard Handel, *Workingman's Wife: Her Personality, World
and Life Style* (New York: Oceana, 1959). Robert Redfield, *The Little
Community: Peasant Society and Culture* (Chicago: Phoenix Books,
1960). Geirardo and Alicia Reichel-Dolmatoff, *The People of Aritama:
The Cultural Personality of a Colombian Mestizo Village* (Chicago:
University of Chicago Press, 1961). W. I. Thomas and Florian Znani-
ecki, *The Polish Peasant in Europe and America* (New York: Dover
Publications, 1958), originally published in 1918. W. Lloyd Warner, *So-*

Life in the working-class subculture is highly structured to accord with the formalized networks of social relations among immediately proximate kin and neighbors, and to accord with the unambiguously prescribed obligations, prerogatives, and behavioral norms. The primary social unit is the extended family—that tight network that ties mother and father, married children and their children, cousins, aunts, uncles and grandparents into a close community of interaction and mutual dependence. Especially in early childhood and then after marriage, one's intensive interpersonal relations are primarily with nearby members of the extended family and nearby neighbors. Older children and unmarried youth maintain close ties with members of their own localized peer groups. Working men maintain close associations with co-workers during the day and with proximate neighbors who may frequent the same tavern at night. Housewives maintain a running conversation with the women who live nearby. These overlapping close-knit networks of association, *based upon the residence,* are manifested in the intensive interaction and in the rapid exchange of information on day-to-day happenings that reinforce a cohesive and mutually interdependent social organization.[9]

A great many of the residents of some American and British working-class neighborhoods have lived within the same block, or within a radius of a few blocks, for at least a generation. Willmott and Young reported that many families had lived in London's Bethnal Green for well over a century. There, when the community was studied in the early fifties, the researchers found that the ties within a family (especially the ties between a married daughter and her mother) were so strong that few were willing to live farther than a few minutes' *walking* distance away. As a result, it was common to find parents and married children living within the same apartment building or in adjacent buildings. Aunts, uncles, and cousins were clustered nearby, and this high degree of accessibility facilitated the daily visiting among kinfolk and neighbors, through which mutual supports and aid in emergencies were personally provided.[10]

---

cial Class in America (New York, Harper & Bros., 1960). William F. Whyte, *Street Corner Society* (Chicago: University of Chicago Press, 2nd edition, 1955). Michael Young and Peter Willmott, *Family and Kinship in East London* (Glencoe: The Free Press, 1959).

[9] Fried, "Transitional Functions of the Working-Class Communities," *op. cit.*

[10] Young and Willmott, *op. cit.*

Although visiting among the members of a working-class family may be largely localized within the house or apartment (one's home is frequently a private place, exclusively reserved for "blood relatives"), the continuous babble among non-kin neighbors reverberates at such places as corridors, front stoops, streets, taverns, stores, and, among women, from window-to-window and window-to-street.[11] The street thus becomes an extension of the house, itself a place where people *live,* and where much of the social interaction takes place. Where the house is the habitat of kin, the street is the habitat of neighbors. And, in striking contrast to middle-class groups, *social organization* (encompassing both family and friends) *is territorially coterminous with neighborhood place.*[12]

The members of these societies rarely leave their spatial environs. Of course, the job holder may have to leave the neighborhood daily, but he follows a fixed transit course to his destination, and returns with little intercourse en route. The family may make a trip to visit an upwardly mobile member of the family who has moved some distance away; but such journeys are rare, even if the distance is only a few miles.

In this way the insular life in the working-class culture resembles life in a Colombian peasant village where:

> Most people move only between their houses and their fields. Year after year they use only a certain trail and when asked about trails in another direction they are often ignorant or uncertain of them. They may know a few neighboring trails, those used by villagers who have their fields in the same general direction, but a man who owns a field on the slopes west of the village does not necessarily know how the slopes to the east of it can be reached. And there is little interest in knowing. The trail a man uses and knows is "his trail" . . . because it leads from his home to his field, and other people's trails are not his concern.[13]

This pattern of generational localism has never been as in-

---

[11] Gans, *The Urban Villagers, op. cit.*
[12] Bernard J. Frieden, "The Legal Role in Urban Development," *UCLA Law Review,* Special issue, *Land Planning and the Law, Emerging Policies and Techniques,* Vol. 12, No. 3 (March 1965), pp. 856–79. See also Fried, "Transitional Functions in Working-Class Communities, *op. cit.*; Richard Hoggart, *op. cit.*; and Young and Willmott, *op. cit.*
[13] Alicia and Geirardo Reichel-Dolmatoff, *op. cit.,* pp. 26–27.

tense in the United States as in European cities. Here, within a generation or two, many of the children of working-class immigrants moved into the middle class and away from the old neighborhoods. But it has persisted among the older non-mobile working-class residents of large cities on the Eastern Seaboard.

Even when some working-class families have moved out of the old neighborhoods—whether because redevelopment projects have taken their homes, because their factories have moved to the suburbs, or because they chose to leave the central city for better housing in the gray areas or in the outskirts —these behavior patterns have been transferred, unchanged, to the new environment.[14] Although these physically mobile members of the working class have often achieved an improvement in the quality of their housing, their primary socialization is still limited to the house and, within it, mainly to the close family. As a substitute for the company of their female relatives, housewives with young children may participate in neighborly visits over the fence or even in occasional coffee-klatches in the homes of neighbors nearby. But their husbands rarely socialize with other men in the neighborhood. The prosperity of recent years has permitted a markedly higher standard of living, but their basic life style remains relatively unchanged.

Just outside the few blocks that surround the working-class resident's home lies foreign territory. Even though it too may be inhabited by families having apparently identical demographic and cultural characteristics, there is typically no way into its close-knit network of family ties and neighbor associations; and its residents may therefore be seen as strangers and regarded with suspicion and hostility. This sort of parochialism is seen in its extreme form in the localism of male, teen-age gangs who fight to defend the turf of their street corner or candy shop against the threat of invasion by gangs from the immediately adjacent but foreign blocks.[15] Here, in

---

[14] Berger, *Working-Class Suburb, op. cit.*; his "Suburbia and the American Dream," *The Public Interest* No. 2 (Winter 1966), pp. 80–91; and his "Suburbs, Subcultures, and Styles of Life: Problems of Cultural Pluralism in Urban America," *The Public Interest*, forthcoming. See also Gans, *The Levittowners, op. cit.*, and Willmott and Young, *op. cit.*

[15] William F. Whyte, *op. cit.* The California motorcycle gangs may be perceived as a variant on this pattern of territorially linked personalization of social space. Although the members are deployed extensively in space throughout the state, the congregating points for the motorcycle gangs appear to comprise a known network of bars, race-tracks,

the only genuine social neighborhoods of our cities, one's physical life space acquires a highly personalized meaning.[16]

The physical place becomes an extension of one's ego. The outer worlds of neighborhood-based peer groups, neighborhood-based family, and the *physical* neighborhood-place itself, seem to become internalized as inseparable aspects of one's inner perceptions of self. In the highly personalized life of the working-class neighborhood, where one's experiences are largely limited to social contacts with others who are but minutes away, the physical space and the physical buildings become reified as aspects of the social group. One's conception of himself and of his place in society is thus subtly merged with his conceptions of the spatially limited territory of limited social interaction.[17]

Fried has insightfully suggested that the highly structured spatial arrangements of the typical working-class slum area (composed, as they typically are, of the densely compacted and physically delineated alleys, streets, basement cubicles, and the like) seem to conform to the highly structured organization that marks the residents' society. Proprietary rights to public spaces are staked out by different groups of tenants; and, in accord with the traditionalist and rigid allocation of rights and obligations, others in the community then respect those space allocations. But more important than that, and in marked contrast with contemporary intellectual elites, the underlying conceptions of order and the protocols of social propriety among working-class groups seem to demand clean boundaries and clearly articulated structure. The literature on the working class has been emphatic about its highly formalized social structure; and recent research is now suggesting that these patterns of social organization may be mirrored in preferred organization of physical environments and in spatial patterns of social interaction.

The hypothesis is reinforced by our understanding of several related traits of working-class persons. However rich in subtleties of interpersonal associations, life in the working class

---

and drag strips that have become invested with the same proprietary exclusiveness as the drugstores and street corners of the big-city slum gangs.

[16] Alvin L. Schorr, *Slums and Social Insecurity*, Research Report No. 1, Division of Research and Statistics, U.S. Social Security Administration (Washington: U.S. Government Printing Office, 1963). See also Bennett Berger, "Suburbs, Subcultures, and Styles of Life," *op. cit.*

[17] Fried, "Transitional Functions of the Working-Class Communities," *op. cit.*

tends to be concrete and particularistic. One typically knows where he stands, whether in the social hierarchy of his family and friends or in the territorial domain of his physical world. He lives with well-defined rules of behavior. His prerogatives and his limits are clearly understood. The objects of attention are tangible. And they exist in the present.[18]

Life for the women is a never-ending burden of "making-do" on limited funds and of household chores and child care lightened by a never-ending round of gossip about the interpersonal relations among kin and neighbor. For the men, whose education may not have gone beyond the grade school, work, when available, is, at its routine best, only a means for earning a livelihood. Its performance may be physically arduous and its tenure uncertain. There is virtually no interest in the work as such, either as an outlet for self-expression or as a means of social advancement.[19] Whatever his level of skill, he scarcely expects that he'll ever do much better. Among the working-class residents of a California subdivision, ownership of a $12,000 house seemed to be the ultimate goal in life.[20] In all other respects they were scarcely concerned with the future.

At least within the stable working-class white communities that have been studied (there is little published evidence of the space-related behavior of either lower-class whites or of Negroes), the people have had a characteristically limited education and follow a parochial and present-oriented life style. For them, only the spatially concrete and the temporally immediate are understandable and real. When faced with threatening situations or with uncertainties about the future, the prototype working-class person is poorly equipped to cope, and so he relies heavily on family and social networks to provide a cushion against disaster. Perhaps as an adaptive response, he resignedly accepts the outcomes as the inexorable workings of fate. ("What is to be, will be." "When your number comes up, that's it." "You've got to take life as it

[18] Edward T. Hall, *The Silent Language* (New York: Doubleday, 1959). See also Gans, *The Urban Villagers, op. cit.*, and Richard Hoggart, *op. cit.*

[19] When Elaine Cumming asked a sample of working-class males which of their many jobs they liked best, the respondents seemed not to even understand the question!

[20] Berger, *Working-Class Suburb, op. cit.* See also Carl Werthman, Jerry Mandel and Ted Dienstfrey, *Planning and the Purchase Decision* (Berkeley: Center for Planning and Development Research, University of California, 1965).

comes." "The bitter with the sweet.") Just as in some primitive societies, the idea of movement forward in time is tied to concrete sequential episodes in the culture.[21] A birth, a wedding, perhaps a weekend's holiday, a religious festival, and death comprise the determinate events to which the passage of time may be related. Just as distant places are unfamiliar and hence unreal, so too is the future unreal. In part this is because the future really is unmanageable within the psychic, cognitive and economic resources at his command. But possibly it is also because his basic thoughtways and his style of life are oriented to that which is *here*, and that which is here *now*.

SOME IMPLICATIONS FOR PUBLIC POLICY

It should be apparent that we discuss these two special groups as a way of marking the extremes of a continuum, and not because either of them represents any sort of cultural mean. But we do so also because so much of contemporary analysis and the resulting public policy treats space-related behavior as though populations were homogeneous and as though space and time were homogeneous. We therefore mean to direct attention to the wide spectrum of interaction propensities extending from extreme cosmopolitanism to extreme localism. If, in the determination of public policies, it were possible to take account of these differences, the burden of costs and the enjoyment of benefits might be distributed more sensitively and more equitably among the subgroups in the population.

The public policies that affect life in cities are often voiced in the language of broad welfare goals, and the action programs that follow are directed to serve a generalized public interest that accords with a single-dimensional national image of the good life. And yet, as public intentions get crystallized in the political arena and written into law, and as programs become operational through the workings of the administrative governmental agencies, declarations of intent and consequences may not match. The effect may be inevitable, for the heterogeneous composition of the population is such as to permit few public programs to serve all segments of the population equally. Indeed, diversities of values and life styles are so wide as to make for conflicting wants among sub-

[21] Kluckhohn, *op. cit.*

groups, such that programs that serve some groups may thereby also disserve others. If public services are to be supplied to all groups in the society, they may have to be specifically designed for each of them. In few instances will a single public policy or a single services package serve all.

This principle has not escaped governmental officials, of course. A large number of governmental programs have been installed to serve special groups in the society—examples include special tax regulations allowing for oil depletion, utilities regulations that stabilize non-competitive industries, public housing for the poor, Medicare for the elderly, civil rights legislation for the Negroes and the Economic Opportunity Program for the groups living in poverty.

Other federal programs, such as those providing the interstate highway system, mortgage insurance and urban renewal were intended to serve a broad segment of the urban population by reshaping the larger environmental conditions—in these examples, the conditions affecting travel accessibility, access to housing, and the economic vitality and physical structure of the central cities. But even here, the benefits have not been distributed to all who live in the benefited cities.

As these programs and others like them are executed by operating agencies, administrative criteria often intervene between the broad welfare goals expressed in the legislation and their actual implementation. Given a complex program with a varied clientele, many administrators have lacked the technical skill for evaluating the multiple effects of any action on the publics they serve. Their personal understandings of social value systems and their personal perceptions of space and time probably come closer to those of the intellectual elite than to those of the working classes. Lacking an explicit understanding of the probable responses of various groups within the city to any specific proposal, these administrators and their staffs have often designed programs either on one-dimensional premises that would be acceptable to a middle-class population, or else on narrow cost-efficiency criteria that are unrelated to the preferences of some publics the programs are devised to serve. In either case, because the preferences of the lower and working classes were not understood, they were not likely to be satisfied.

By now the initial murmur of protest about the effects of urban renewal on working-class populations has grown loud enough to make the point clear to all. Half a dozen or more books and numerous journal articles have appeared criticizing the program.[22] Conceived originally as a major national effort to reverse the processes of central city decay, the program sought to replace the dilapidated buildings in which poor households lived, to attract the middle-class suburbanites back to the metropolitan centers, to re-establish the traditional central business district's economic functions, and thereby to re-create the fiscal stability of the older municipalities. The legislation and the administrative regulations formalized a procedure for assembling sites in "blighted" or "gray" areas, demolishing the buildings, and then selling the cleared and redesigned sites to private developers who would build to accord with a publicly prepared plan.

Only after some of the initial sites had been assembled and the land cleared, was it pointed out that many areas that had been classed as "slums" were in fact the neighborhoods of stable working-class social communities. The housing was poor but habitable. The neighborhoods provided a comfortable physical framework for familiar activities, for interaction with relatives and long-time friends. Rents were low. Many families had lived in these areas for a generation or more, and few had any desire to leave. Their forced evacuation induced costs far greater than the immediate pecuniary cost of the move, and the typically higher rents they had to pay in the relocation housing was crowding the families' budgets for food, clothing and other commodities that they valued higher than housing.[23]

When tenement housing in the working-class neighborhoods was emptied and cleared, the complex networks of social interconnections that existed within them were disrupted. Friends and relatives were dispersed. The familiar habitat of corner drugstore, tavern, church and social hall went down with the houses. The small neighborhood shopkeepers, who provided informal caretaker services or small loans in emer-

---

[22] Chester Hartman, "The Housing of Relocated Families," *Journal of the American Institute of Planners*, Vol. 30, No. 4 (November 1964), pp. 266–86. Scott Greer, *Urban Renewal in American Cities* (New York: Bobbs-Merrill, 1965). Bernard J. Frieden, *The Future of Old Neighborhoods* (Cambridge: M.I.T. Press, 1964), and his "The Legal Role in Urban Development," *op. cit.* Marc Fried and Peggy Gleicher, "Some Sources of Residential Satisfaction in an Urban Slum," *Journal of the American Institute of Planners*, Vol. 27, No. 4 (November 1961), pp. 305–15. Fried, "Grieving for a Lost Home," *op. cit.*, and "Transitional Functions of Working-Class Communities," *op. cit.* Gans, "The Balanced Community," *op. cit.*, "Planning and Social Life," *op. cit.*, and *The Urban Villagers, op. cit.*, especially the final chapter.

[23] Hartman, *op. cit.*; Gans, *The Urban Villagers, op. cit.*

gencies, lost their sites and patronage. Some, often the older ones, were unable to find other suitable locations. Many residents found the locale of their new housing strange, although it may have been only a few blocks distant from the old. Lacking the support of familiar surroundings and associations, the evictees perceived the new neighborhoods as hostile; their recollections of the old ones were sometimes tinged with a "grief" reaction akin to the stresses of mourning for a loved friend or relative.[24]

Although for the potentially mobile members of these working-class areas redevelopment may have accelerated mobility into middle-class society, the costs of readjustment for most relocatees were far in excess of their limited capacity to accommodate to change. Had the legislators and professionals who conceived the urban renewal program seen these neighborhoods as functioning social systems, rather than as blighted buildings on valuable central-city land, the program might have taken a different turn. In fact, the abundant criticism that has followed on observation of the social dislocations wrought by urban renewal, has by now resulted in some significant changes in the program and in the stimulation of new types of programs.

In mid-1966 the program emphasis is turning from housing clearance to housing rehabilitation. It now appears likely that a massive new effort will be launched during the next few years to renovate decaying buildings and then to replace those old houses with new ones, in such a fashion that present tenants will be permitted to remain in their old houses or neighborhoods. With the possibility of governmental rent supplements and other subsidies, they may even be able to do so with no additional out-of-pocket rental outlays. As a further reflection of the growing understanding of cultural differences in values, preferences, and behavior patterns, the War on Poverty, initiated by the Economic Opportunity Act of 1964, has sought to equip better the culturally deprived groups for participation in the complex industrial society—primarily by installing training programs designed to implant the cognitive, occupational, and social skills that are common among the middle-class groups.

The message has not yet gotten through to all government agencies, however. In many cities the no-man's-land of empty housing and partially or totally cleared sites that resulted

[24] Fried, "Grieving for a Lost Home," *op. cit.*

from the early urban renewal program is mirrored in large if not equivalent sites taken for freeway and rapid-transit rights-of-way. Transportation engineers have been guided by a rather delimited concept of efficiency that has made them notably insensitive to the redistributive effects of transportation facilities. With considerable sophistication in analytic method, they have succeeded in measuring volumes of traffic flow through cities, in forecasting probable future volumes and patterns of flow, and they have then designed new transport systems that would move traffic efficiently, by minimizing aggregate costs to travelers.

Of course, the differences in travel habits among middle-class and lower- and working-class groups are very large. Those who travel long distances within the metropolitan areas are likely also to own automobiles and to hold an interest in improved highway facilities. Localites who stay close to home and who are too poor to own cars, are likely to be disinterested in highways. Except, of course, when the highways are built through their neighborhoods and affect the social life of the residents.

Freeways or transit lines passing through a working-class neighborhood of localites may bisect the social community, dividing friends and kin from each other, children from their schools, and induce a reshuffling of patterns of movement and social interaction. Often freeways function as barriers, real or symbolic, between low-income areas and higher status neighborhoods where low-income residents, particularly low-income Negroes, are not welcome. Where housing for low-income residents is in short supply, demolition of residences to make way for transportation routes only accentuates the shortage and results in further overcrowding.[25]

Proposals to construct transportation lines through middle-class areas on the outskirts of cities or in the suburbs are frequently greeted by organized public protests that sometimes result in less offensive reroutings. But the working-class residents of central cities are poorly equipped, conceptually and educationally, to influence the highway bureaucracy. Just as they view all life fatalistically, so too do they view the public interventions that will cause them inconvenience. Efforts to identify the real administrative source of the inconvenience, to draft a petition specifying a particular or general complaint, to circulate the petition for public support, and to

[25] Frieden, "The Legal Role in Urban Development," *op. cit.*

appear at an adjudicatory hearing all require a generality of
world view and a cluster of social skills that the prototype
working-class person rarely possesses. His response is likely
to be the defensive reiteration, "You can't fight City Hall,"
and then resignedly to accept the personal costs that the highway will engender.

Both in England and in the United States, public-housing
policy has been similarly handicapped by the failures of inter-
cultural understanding. Even though the housing has been
specifically intended for lower- and working-class households,
its design has typically reflected the space preferences of the
middle-class reformers, designers, and administrators who installed it. In an attempt to increase privacy, high in the hierarchy of middle-class values, and to provide the garden that
would symbolize affinity with the gentry, the design of British
working-class suburbs was partly modeled on the early British
garden-cities. Some of the initial studies of working-class
populations centered on residents' behavior in the British
housing-estates of the interwar period and the post-World War
II British new towns.[26] In the new towns, after the initial
occupants had moved into the twelve-to-the-acre houses with
gardens front and back, it quickly became apparent that the
isolation imposed by removal from the familiar old neighborhoods, and from their supportive network of friends and relatives, placed a great strain on the young emigrant working-
class couples. Accustomed to frequent daily contact with
female relatives, the wives found the modest cushion of space
around their houses a barrier to interaction with their neighbors. Their husbands found the frequently long commutes to
work costly in time and money. At night and on weekends
they missed the neighborhood pubs and other city recreation.
Observers of the new towns found that their occupants made
many trips back to the old neighborhoods, and in some instances, in spite of the improved housing that all valued
highly, the isolation exacted too great a cost and the emigrants
moved back.

The understanding of the space-related behavior of
working-class persons that has resulted from these studies of
the early British new towns, has contributed to reshaping the
design proposals for the recently constructed new towns of
Cumbernauld and Glenrothes. There the individual gardens
have been replaced by larger open spaces for community use,

---

[26] Willmott and Young, *op. cit.*

while the entire pattern of siting and land use was conceived at higher, more "urban" densities.

In the United States, too, a few public-housing projects have been located on the outskirts of cities, in neighborhoods where some Negro project residents have been subjected to an alienation and abuse from the surrounding middle-class white community that they have found difficult to tolerate. In cases where the projects have been located in inaccessible areas poorly served by public transportation, their residents have had difficulty seeking and traveling to work. Frequently, to save land costs, large public-housing projects in large cities are designed as high-rise apartment buildings separated by large, undifferentiated spaces between them. With no specific function, the spaces between buildings have sometimes become a hazard to children and adults alike, a hunting ground for malevolent elements, and a jungle of empty bottles and broken glass.[27] Where projects are designed in smaller units, often to maintain a middle-class image, the lawns, front and back, may then be fenced between dwellings, leaving little usable play spaces for young children, and no central commons where neighbors may visit each other.

Within the buildings the designs frequently reflect a limited understanding of the preferences of working-class occupants and an incompatibility of objectives. On the one hand walls may be built of materials that permit ubiquitous noises to penetrate throughout the buildings; while at the same time there may be an attempt to create the effect of privacy by providing access to the apartments through small hallways accessible and visible to only four or five families. In lower-class and working-class communities where public scrutiny often insures safety, sheltered entryways may furnish a real or potential safety hazard; and, in any case, may inhibit the interaction between neighbors that is the basis of mutual aid in the frequent emergencies that beset them.

In the provision of public facilities, a sensitivity to the space preferences of working-class users would result in different designs than have been formulated for the middle-class. Where a middle-class housewife may easily travel from several blocks to several miles to a shopping center, the prototype working-class homemaker, often tied to the house by young children, is less mobile and typically unwilling to travel

[27] Roger Montgomery, "Comment on Fear and House-as-Haven in the Lower Class," *Journal of the American Institute of Planners,* Vol. 32, No. 1 (January 1966), pp. 31–37.

more than a block or two to shop. She may make some of her major purchases from door-to-door peddlers.[28] Instead of large community shopping centers, small shops carrying a variety of grocery and household items, yet located within the block, would be more acceptable to her. Similarly, if the hospitals, clinics, schools, and recreation facilities are to be effectively used by working-class and lower-class persons, they should be located at a number of sites and at small scale, rather than in a single large facility at a central location. Where distance in space presents an obstacle to the working-class person, he is less likely to use the community facilities that might help him.

The long-term historical changes in industrial society have been toward an ever-increasing scale of the society, reflecting increasingly complex networks of interdependence, rising social mobility, lower real transportation and communication costs, and, with it all, ever-increasing mileage distances of social interaction. Although in the United States public education and the mass media have exerted an important leveling effect, these changes have by no means touched all segments of the heterogeneous population. We find it sobering to be reminded that very large numbers of central-city and some suburban residents follow styles of life and adhere to systems of values that are in many respects unchanged from those that were brought over from the European peasant villages several generations ago. At the same time that social organization of cosmopolite groups is being largely freed from the restraints of territorial place, the "urban villagers"[29] live out their lives in territorially bounded and territorially perceived societies.

These facts, and the interpolations for the spectrum of other groups that lie between, suggest that these findings need to be incorporated into the studies that form the bases for public-policy and for public-service programs. Were we alert to the cultural differences among the various sectors of the population, and prepared to look for the cultural determinants behind the economist's demand functions, our public policies could be more sensitively tuned to the underlying wants of the many different publics we seek to serve.

[28] David Caplovitz, *The Poor Pay More: Consumer Practices of Low-Income Families* (New York: The Free Press of Glencoe, 1963).
[29] Gans, *The Urban Villagers, op. cit.*

Chapter 2

AIR, WATER, LAND AND PEOPLE

The environment of man is nature, but man interferes with nature, as Ian McHarg has brilliantly expounded in Chapter 12. The more people, the more concentrated and the higher the level of industrialization, the more interference; all of which can be reliably quantified. The state of the natural environment is increasingly the concern of civilized men and responsible officials.

Clean air is no longer "free" as the fossil fuels now in vogue poison the atmosphere. New chemical processes produce compounds unknown in nature with results often unpredictable. Amenities, as well as physical health, are imperiled by the scale of activities far beyond city boundaries; New York's Department of Air Pollution is less successful because of New Jersey's carelessness; Belgium, Holland, and the German Ruhr make difficult each other's breathing; a Russian atomic test in Siberia rains fallout on a New England village.

Man can live for surprising periods without food; without water he will die within days. The industrial plant gulps water faster than its human masters and throws it away befouled as do cities. Presumably, there is enough H_2O on the face of the globe; although much of it is salt (not immediately usable), and the rest often badly distributed. The way it is needed and treated by man is the planning problem.

Land, as space, is at a heavy premium in desired locations both within and without urban places. Unfortunately for us, the American heritage of land exploitation does not operate in our favor; something like the Dutch attitudes and devices covered in Chapter 23 by Dr. de Cler are needed. The relation between people and land—the man-land ratio—is crucial merely considered arithmetically. Physical cities and social structures are ancillary to, but strongly influenced by, pure human numbers—neglecting the quality of those numbers socially defined. Planning for people includes planning people whether democratic mores understand this yet or not.

Abel Wolman, natural scientist and practical engineer, has explored the metabolism of the city as a quasi-organism with large inputs of water and of air, later excreted. These problems are worldwide, enormous and increasingly difficult to solve. Edward L. Ullman, geographer, reconsiders the city as a service-producing center. He questions present forms of urban life and inquires into city siting and metropolitan internal structure. Urban sprawl, as a non-pejorative statement, may be the ideal physical form for modern society. Spread-city is our future, it would seem. I have summarized purely demographic urban data for developed and developing nations. *Urbanization*, as a process, and *city growth* are both examined in the high density, current clustering of mankind in urban places or metropolitan areas. In turn the centrifugal forces within the metropolitan area and just beyond are touched on, as well as the age structure and especially the "racial" composition of urban places today. Both of these demographic qualities are clearly vital desiderata for urban planning and basic to the sociological analysis of comparative urbanism that follows in Chapter 3 by Gideon Sjoberg.

The Metabolism of Cities: Water and Air

ABEL WOLMAN*

The metabolic requirements of a city can be defined as all the materials and commodities needed to sustain the city's inhabitants at home, at work and at play. Over a period of time these requirements include even the construction materials needed to build and rebuild the city itself. The metabolic cycle is not completed until the wastes and residues of daily life have been removed and disposed of with a minimum of nuisance and hazard. As man has come to appreciate that the earth is a closed ecological system, casual methods that once appeared satisfactory for the disposal of wastes no longer seem acceptable. He has the daily evidence of his eyes and nose to tell him that his planet cannot assimilate without limit the untreated wastes of his civilization.

No one article could describe the complete metabolism of the modern city. Moreover, many of the metabolic inputs such as food, fuel, clothing, durable goods, construction materials and electric energy present no special problem. Their supply is handled routinely, in part through local initiative and in

* Emeritus Professor of Sanitary Engineering at Johns Hopkins University and consultant to various municipal, state, federal, and foreign governments including the TVA, U. S. Public Health Service, the World Health Organization, and the Israeli Jordan River Project. Currently he is chairman of a panel on water resources of the U. S. Agency for International Development. He was a member of the Princeton, University of California (Berkeley), and University of Chicago faculties prior to joining Johns Hopkins in 1937, and has been editor or associate editor of a number of professional journals among them the *American Journal of Public Health*, the *Journal of the American Water Works Association*, and *Municipal Sanitation*. This article is reprinted with permission. Copyright © 1965, by *Scientific American Inc.* All rights reserved. It appeared as "The Metabolism of Cities," in the September 1965 issue.

part through large organizations (public or private) that operate about as effectively in one city as another. I shall be concerned therefore with three metabolic problems that have become more acute as cities have grown larger and whose solution rests almost entirely in the hands of the local administrator. Although he can call on many outside sources for advice, he must ultimately provide solutions fashioned to the unique needs of his own community. These three problems are the provision of an adequate water supply, the effective disposal of sewage and the control of air pollution.

That these three problems vary widely from city to city and that they are being managed with widely varying degrees of success is obvious to anyone who reads a daily newspaper. It is ironic, for example, that New York City, which houses the nation's (if not the world's) greatest concentration of managerial talent, should be running short of water while billions of gallons of fresh water flow past it to the sea. It is not easy for people living in arid countries, or even for those living in the southwestern part of the U.S., to have much sympathy with New York's plight.

This summer, while New Yorkers were watching their emptying reservoirs and hoping for rain, Californians were busy building an aqueduct that would carry water some 440 miles from the Sacramento River, near Sacramento, to Los Angeles and other cities in the southern part of the state. And thanks to earlier examples of foresight, people in southern California were watering their lawns and filling their swimming pools without restriction, while in New York and New Jersey lawns were dying and pools stood empty. In the water-rich Middle Atlantic states water shortages are largely the result of delayed action and failures of management—sometimes exacerbated by political jockeying.

If American cities have had such unequal success in supplying their citizens with water, it is hardly surprising that some should have an even less satisfactory record in controlling water and air pollution, areas in which the incentives for providing remedies are much weaker than those that motivate the supplying of water. To make matters worse, pollutants of water and air often do not respect state boundaries. For example, the wastes of five states—Michigan, Indiana, Ohio, Pennsylvania and New York—have contributed to the accelerated pollution of Lake Erie. "The lake," according to the U.S. Public Health Service, "has deteriorated in quality at a rate many times greater than its normal aging process." The fourth-largest and shallowest of the five Great Lakes, Lake Erie is the main water supply for 10 million U.S. citizens as well as for the huge industrial complex that extends for 300 miles along the lake's southern shore from Detroit to Buffalo. The combination of treated and partially treated municipal sewage and industrial wastes that enters Lake Erie directly, and also reaches it indirectly through a network of rivers, has disrupted the normal cycle of aquatic life, has led to the closing of a number of beaches and has materially changed the commercial fishing industry. Last month the five states, in consultation with the Public Health Service, reached agreement on a major program of pollution abatement.

Although engineers concerned with water supply, sewage disposal and air pollution are accustomed to thinking in terms of large volumes, few laymen quite appreciate the quantities of water, sewage and air pollutants involved in the metabolism of a modern city. Figure 1 expresses these quantities in the form of an input-output chart for a hypothetical American city of one million population. The input side of the chart shows the requirements in tons per day of water, food and fuels of various kinds. The output side shows the metabolic products of that input in terms of sewage, solid refuse and air pollutants. The quantities shown are a millionfold multiplication of the daily requirements of the average city dweller. Directly or indirectly he uses about 150 gallons (1,250 pounds) of water, four pounds of food and 19 pounds of fossil fuels. This is converted into roughly 120 gallons of sewage (which assumes 80 percent recovery of the water input), four pounds of refuse (which includes food containers and miscellaneous rubbish) and 1.9 pounds of air pollutants, of which automobiles, buses and trucks account for more than half.

As of 1963 about 150 million out of 189 million Americans, or 80 percent, lived in some 22,000 communities served by 19,200 waterworks. These 150 million people used about 23 billion gallons per day (b.g.d.), a volume that can be placed in perspective in several ways. In 1960 the amount of water required for all purposes in the U.S. was about 320 b.g.d., or roughly 15 times the municipal demand. The biggest user of water is irrigation, which in 1960 took about 140 b.g.d. Steam electric utilities used about 98 b.g.d. and industry about 60 b.g.d. Since 1960 the total U.S. water demand has risen from about 320 b.g.d. to an estimated 370 b.g.d., of which municipalities take about 25 b.g.d. (See Figure 2)

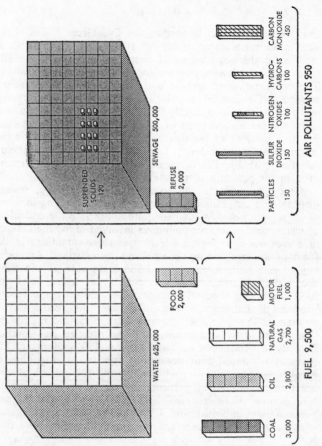

FIGURE 1. METABOLISM OF A CITY involves countless input-output transactions. This chart concentrates on three inputs common to all cities, namely water, food and fuel, and three outputs, sewage, solid refuse and air pollutants. Each item is shown in tons per day for a hypothetical U.S. city with a population of one million. Water, which enters the city silently and unseen, overshadows all other inputs in volume. More than .6 ton (150 gallons) must be supplied to each inhabitant every day. After about 20 percent of the water has been diverted to lawns and other unrecoverable uses, it returns, contaminated, to the city's sewers. The city's most pervasive nuisance, air pollution, is accounted for chiefly by the combustion of fuels. (If refuse is burned in incinerators, it can also contribute heavily, but that contribution is not included here.) The various air

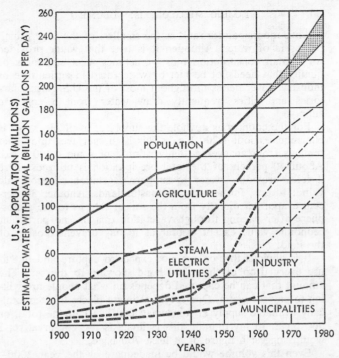

FIGURE 2. U.S. WATER REQUIREMENTS will be 53 percent greater in 1980 than in 1960, according to the most recent estimates of the Department of Commerce. Virtually all water used by agriculture is for irrigation; nearly 60 percent of all irrigated land in the U.S. is in five Western states (California, Texas, Colorado, Idaho and Arizona) where water tends to be scarcest. Steam power plants need water in huge amounts simply to condense steam. In 1960 municipalities used about twenty-two billion gallons per day (b.g.d.), which represented only about 7 percent of the total water withdrawal of about 320 b.g.d.

pollutants are keyed by shading to the fuel responsible. Most of the particle emission (soot and fly ash) is produced by coal burned in electric power plants, and in well-designed plants more than 90 percent of the particles can be removed from the stack gases. For this hypothetical city one may assume that 135 of the 150 tons of particles produced by all fuel consumers are removed before they reach the atmosphere. All other emissions, however, pollute the atmosphere in the volumes shown. Sulfur dioxide is based on use of domestic fuels of average sulfur content.

Thus municipalities rank as the smallest of the four principal users of water. Although it is true that water provided for human consumption must sometimes meet standards of quality that need not be met by water used in agriculture or industry, nevertheless throughout most of the U.S. farms, factories and cities frequently draw water from a common supply.

For the country as a whole the supply of available water is enormous: about 1,200 b.g.d. This is the surface runoff that remains from an average daily rainfall of some 4,200 b.g.d. About 40 percent of the total precipitation is utilized where it falls, providing water to support vegetation of economic value: forests, farm crops and pasturelands. Another 30 percent evaporates directly from the soil or returns to the atmosphere after passing through vegetation that has no particular economic value except insofar as it may prevent erosion of the land.

It is obvious that one cannot expect to capture and put to use every drop of the 1,200 b.g.d. flowing to the sea. The amount that can be captured depends on what people are willing to pay for water. One recent estimate places the economically available supply at somewhat less than half the total, or 560 b.g.d. In my opinion this estimate is too conservative; I would suggest a figure of at least 700 b.g.d.

Even this volume would be inadequate by the year 2000—if all the water withdrawn for use were actually consumed. This, however, is not the case now and will not be then; only a small fraction of the water withdrawn is consumed. In 1960 "consumptive use," as it is called, amounted to about 90 b.g.d. of the 320 b.g.d. withdrawn. Most of the remaining 230 b.g.d. was returned after use to the source from which it was taken, or to some other body of water (in some instances the ocean). A small fraction of the used water was piped into the ground to help maintain local water tables.

Estimates by a Senate Select Committee a few years ago projected a consumptive use of about 120 b.g.d. in 1980 and of nearly 160 b.g.d. in the year 2000, when total demand may reach 900 b.g.d. Agriculture accounts for the biggest consumptive use of water. It is conservatively estimated that 60 percent of the water employed for irrigation is lost to the atmosphere as the result of evaporation directly from the soil or indirectly by transpiration through the leaves of growing plants. (The amount of water incorporated into plant tissue is insignificant;

roughly 1,000 gallons of water is needed to produce about 10 cents' worth of crop.) In contrast, from 80 to 98 percent of the water withdrawn by municipalities, industry and electric utilities is available for reuse. It is for this reason that the projected withdrawal rate of 900 b.g.d. in the year 2000 should not prove difficult to meet, whether the economically available supply is 560 b.g.d. or 700 b.g.d. Of the 900 b.g.d. that may be required in A.D. 2000 to meet human, industrial and agricultural needs, approximately 740 b.g.d. should be available for reuse.

These estimates, moreover, are pessimistic in that they make only minor allowances for reductions in industrial or agricultural demands as a result of technological changes and in that they provide for no significant increase in the cost of water to hasten such changes. Thus we must reasonably conclude that for many years beyond A.D. 2000 total water shortages for the U.S. as a whole are highly improbable.

If water is going to remain so plentiful into the 21st century, why should New York and other cities find themselves running short in 1965? The immediate answer, of course, is that there has been a five-year drought in the northeastern U.S. With the completion in 1955 of two new reservoirs in the upper reaches of the Delaware River, and with the extension of the Delaware aqueduct to a total distance of more than 120 miles, New York City believed it could satisfy its water needs until the year 2000. This confident forecast reckoned without the unprecedented drought.

There is no point in criticizing New York's decision to depend so heavily on the Delaware watershed for its future needs. The question is what New York should do now. As long ago as 1950, in an earlier water shortage, New York was advised to build a pumping station on the Hudson River 65 miles north of the city to provide an emergency supply of 100 million gallons per day, or more as needed. (New York City's normal water demand is about 1.2 b.g.d. The average flow of the Hudson is around 11 b.g.d.) The State of New York gave the city permission to build the pumping station but stipulated that the station be dismantled when the emergency was over. By the time the station was built (at a point somewhat farther south than the one recommended) the drought had ended; the station was torn down without ever having been used. This July the city asked the state for permission to rebuild the station, a job that will take several months, but as of mid-August permission had not been granted.

Meanwhile there has been much talk of building atomic-energy desalination plants as the long-term solution to New York's water needs. The economic justification for such proposals has never been explained. New York now obtains its water, delivered by gravity flow to the city, for only about 15 cents per 1,000 gallons (and many consumers are charged only 12 cents). The lowest predicted cost for desalination, assuming a plant with a capacity of 250 million or more gallons per day, is a highly optimistic 30 to 50 cents per 1,000 gallons. Since a desalination plant would be at sea level, its entire output would have to be pumped; storage and conveyance together would add about 20 cents per 1,000 gallons to the basic production cost. Recent studies in our department at Johns Hopkins University have shown that if desalinated water could be produced and delivered for as little as 50 cents per 1,000 gallons, it would still be cheaper to obtain fresh water from a supply 600 miles away. (The calculations assume a water demand of 100 million gallons per day.) In other words, it would be much cheaper for New York City to pipe water 270 miles from the St. Lawrence River, assuming that Canada gave its consent, than to build a desalination plant at the edge of town. New York City does not have to go even as far as the St. Lawrence. It has large untapped reserves in the Hudson River and in the upper watershed of the Susquehanna, no more than 150 miles away, that could meet the city's needs well beyond the year 2000.

Few cities in the U.S. have the range of alternatives open to New York. The great majority of inland cities draw their water supplies from the nearest lake or river. Of the more than 150 million Americans now served by public water supplies, nearly 100 million, or 60 percent, are reusing water from sources that have already been used at least once for domestic sewage and industrial waste disposal. This "used" water has of course been purified, either naturally or artificially, before it reaches the consumer. Only about 25 percent of the 25 b.g.d. now used by municipalities is obtained from aquifers, or underground sources. Such aquifers supply about 65 b.g.d. of the nation's estimated 1965 requirement of 370 b.g.d. Most of the 65 b.g.d. is merely a subterranean portion of the 1,200 b.g.d. of the precipitation flowing steadily to the sea. It is estimated, however, that from five to 10 b.g.d. is water "mined" from aquifers that have been filled over the centuries. Most of this mining is done in West Texas, New Mexico, Arizona and California.

The fact that more than 150 million Americans can be provided with safe drinking water by municipal waterworks, regardless of their source of supply, attests the effectiveness of modern water-treatment methods. Basically the treatment consists of filtration and chlorination. The use of chlorine to kill bacteria in municipal water supplies was introduced in 1908. It is fortunate that such a cheap and readily available substance is so effective. A typical requirement is about one part of chlorine to a million parts of water (one p.p.m.). The amount of chlorine needed to kill bacteria and also to "kill" the taste of dissolved organic substances—many of which are introduced naturally when rainwater comes in contact with decaying vegetation—is adjusted by monitoring the amount of free chlorine present in the water five to 10 minutes after treatment. This residual chlorine is usually held to about .2 p.p.m. In cases where unusually large amounts of organic compounds are present in the water, causing the public to complain of a bad taste, experience has shown that the palatability of the water can often be improved simply by adding more chlorine. Contrary to a widely held impression, free chlorine itself has little taste; the "bad" taste usually attributed to chlorine is due chiefly to organic compounds that have been too lightly chlorinated. When they are more heavily chlorinated, the bad taste usually disappears.

Throughout history impure water has been a leading cause of fatal disease in man; such waterborne diseases as typhoid fever and dysentery were still common in the U.S. less than a century ago. In 1900 the U.S. death rate from typhoid fever was 35.8 per 100,000 people. If such a rate persisted today, the deaths from typhoid would far exceed those from automobile accidents. By 1936 the rate had been reduced to 2.5 per 100,000, and today the disease is almost unknown in the U.S.

In underdeveloped nations, where many cities are still without adequate water supplies, waterborne diseases are among the leading causes of death and debility. In Central and South America more than a third of 75 million people living in towns or cities with a population of more than 2,000 are without water service. Similarly, in India about a third of the urban population of 80 million are without an adequate water supply. Calcutta is regarded as the endemic center of cholera for all of southeast Asia.

No general prescription can be offered for bringing clean water to the vast urban populations that still lack it. I have found in my own experience, however, that the inhabitants of communities both large and small can do much more to help themselves than is customarily recognized. If the small towns and villages of India and elsewhere wait for their central governments to install public water supplies, most of them will wait indefinitely. It is surprising how much can be accomplished with local labor and local materials, and the benefits in health are incalculable.

In the larger cities, where self-help is not feasible, municipal water systems can be built and made to pay their way if an appropriate charge is made for water and if the systems can be financed with long-term loans, as they have been financed traditionally in the U.S. Such loans, however, have only recently been made available to underdeveloped countries. A few years ago, when loans for waterworks had to be paid off in six to 12 years, the total value of external bank loans made to South American countries for water supply and sewerage projects was less than $100,000 in a six-year period. Under the leadership of the Pan-American Health Organization and the U.S. Agency for International Development bankers were encouraged to extend the repayment period to 28 or 30 years. Today the total value of bank loans made to South American countries for waterworks and sewerage systems has surpassed $660 million.

Outside the U.S., as within it, adequate water resources are generally available. The problem is to treat water as a commodity whose cost to the user must bear a fair relation to the cost of its production and delivery. The total U.S. investment in municipal waterworks is about $17.5 billion (replacement cost would approach $50 billion), or about half the nation's investment in telephone service. More significant than investment is the cost of service to the consumer. The average American family pays about $3 a month for water, which it cannot live without, compared with about $7.30 for telephone service. One might also note that the average household expenditure for alcoholic beverages is more than $15 a month. It should be clear that Americans can afford to pay for all the water they need.

The question of fair payment and allocation of costs is even more central to the problem of controlling water pollution than to the problem of providing water. Whereas 150 million Americans were served by waterworks in 1963, only about 120 million were served by sewers. Thus the wastes of nearly 70 million Americans, who live chiefly in the smaller towns and suburbs, were still being piped into backyard cesspools and septic tanks. When these devices are properly designed and the receiving soils are not overloaded, they create no particular sanitation hazard. Unfortunately in too many suburban areas neither of these criteria is met.

The principal pollution hazard arises where sewage collected by a sewerage system is discharged into a lake or river without adequate treatment or without any treatment at all. As of 1962 the wastes of nearly 15 million Americans were discharged untreated and the wastes of 2.4 million received only minor treatment. The wastes of 32.7 million were given primary treatment: passage through a settling basin, which removes a considerable portion of the suspended solid matter. Intermediate treatment, which consists of a more nearly complete removal of solids, was applied to the wastes of 7.4 million people. Secondary treatment, the most adequate form of sewage treatment, was applied to the wastes of 61.2 million people. The term "secondary treatment" covers a variety of techniques, often used in combination: extended aeration, activated sludge (an accelerated form of bacterial degradation), filtration through beds of various materials, stabilization ponds.

Although there was a significant improvement in sewage treatment in the U.S. between 1942 and 1962, a big job remains to be done. Only in the past five years of this period did the rate of sewer installation begin to overtake population growth. The present U.S. investment in sewers and sewage-treatment works is about $12 billion (again the replacement value would be much higher). The Public Health Service estimates that replacing obsolete facilities, improving the standard of treatment and providing for population growth will require an annual investment of more than $800 million a year in treatment works for the rest of the decade. This does not include the cost of extending the sewage-collection systems into new urban and suburban developments. This may add another $800 million to the annual requirements, making an approximate total of more than $1.6 billion a year.

Unfortunately some municipalities have not found a satisfactory or painless method for charging their residents for this vital service. Many simply float bonds to meet capital costs and add the cost to the individual's bill for property taxes.

In Baltimore (where the tax bill is completely itemized) it was decided some years ago that sewerage costs should not be included in the citizen's *ad valorem* taxes but should be made part of his water bill. In the Baltimore system the charge for sewerage service is half the water service charge. A good many other cities charge for sewerage service on a similar basis.

Cities, of course, account for only a part, and probably not the major part, of the pollution that affects the nation's waterways. Industrial pollution is a ubiquitous problem. Industrial pollutants are far more varied than those in ordinary sewage, and their removal often calls for specialized measures. Even in states where adequate pollution-control laws are on the books, there are technological, economic and practical obstacles to seeing that the laws are observed. The Federal Water Pollution Control acts of 1954 and 1962, which enlarged the role of the Public Health Service in determining the pollution of interstate waterways, have sometimes been helpful in strengthening the hand of local law-enforcement agencies.

My final topic—air pollution—is much harder to discuss in quantitative terms than water pollution, which it otherwise resembles in many ways. It is never going to be possible to provide a collection system for air pollution emissions, almost all of which result from combustion processes. Every house, every apartment, every automobile, truck, bus, factory and power plant is vented directly into the open air and presumably will have to remain so.

There are perhaps only three general approaches to controlling the amount of pollutants entering the atmosphere. One is to switch from a fuel that produces undesirable combustion products to one that produces fewer such products. Thus fuel oil produces less soot and fly ash than bituminous coal, and natural gas produces less than either. The second expedient is to employ a new technology. For example, atomic power plants produce none of the particulate and gaseous emissions that result from the burning of fossil fuels. One must then decide, however, whether the radioactive by-products that are released into the environment—either in the short run or the long—by an atomic power station are more or less hazardous than the fossil-fuel by-products they replaced. The third recourse is to remove the undesired components from the vented gases. Fly ash, for example, can be largely removed by suitable devices where coal or oil is used in large volume, as in a power plant, but cannot readily be removed from the flue gases of thousands of residences. The problem of dealing with many small offending units also arises in trying to reduce the unburned hydrocarbons and carbon monoxide emitted by millions of automobiles.

At this point it is worth asking: Why should air pollution be considered objectionable? Many people enjoy the smell of the pollutants released by a steak sizzling on a charcoal grill or by dry leaves burning in the fall. The cigarette smoker obviously enjoys the smoke he draws into his lungs. In other words, a pollutant per se need not necessarily be regarded as a nuisance. If by accident or design the exhaust gases emitted by a diesel bus had a fragrant aroma (or worse yet, led to physiological addiction), not many people would complain about traffic fumes.

The criteria of what constitutes an objectionable air pollutant must therefore be subjectively defined, unless, of course, one can demonstrate that a particular pollutant is a hazard to health. In the absence of a demonstrated health hazard the city dweller would probably list his complaints somewhat as follows: he objects to soot and dirt, he does not want his eyes to burn and water, he dislikes traffic fumes and he wishes he could see the clear blue sky more often.

Many conferences have been held and many papers written on the possible association of air pollution with disease. As might be expected, firm evidence of harmfulness is difficult to obtain. The extensive epidemiological data collected in the U.S. on smoking and human health suggest that in general place of residence has a minor influence on the incidence of lung cancer compared with the smoking habit itself. British statistics, however, can be interpreted to show that at times there is something harmful in the British air. In any event, it will be difficult to demonstrate conclusively—no matter how much one may believe it to be so—that air pollution is associated with long-term deterioration of the human organism. Eric J. Cassell of the Cornell University Medical College recently summarized the situation as follows: "I do not think that it is wrong to say that we do not even know what disease or diseases are caused by everyday pollution of our urban air. . . . We have a cause, but no disease to go with it."

Two diseases frequently mentioned as possibly associated with air pollution are chronic bronchitis and pulmonary emphysema. In Britain some investigators have found strong associations between chronic bronchitis and the level of air pollution, as measured by such indexes as fuel use, sulfur dioxide in the air and sootfall. In California the death rate from emphysema increased fourfold in the seven-year period from 1950 to 1957. This increase may indicate nothing more than the fact that older people go to California to retire, but there is objective evidence that emphysematous patients in Los Angeles showed improved lung function when allowed to breathe carefully filtered air for 48 hours.

In response to mounting public concern, and the urging of President Johnson, Congress two years ago passed the Clean Air Act, which states in its preamble that "Federal financial assistance and leadership is essential for the development of cooperative Federal, state, regional and local programs designed to prevent and control air pollution." The regulatory abatement procedures authorized in the act are similar to those found in the most recent Water Pollution Control Act. When an interstate pollution problem is identified, the Public Health Service is empowered, as a first step, to call a conference of state and local agencies. The second step is to call a public hearing, and the third step, if needed, is to bring a court action against the offenders.

The Clean Air Act takes special cognizance of air pollution caused by motor vehicles; it requires the Secretary of Health, Education, and Welfare to report periodically to Congress on progress made on control devices. He is also invited to recommend any new legislation he feels is warranted. Eventually the secretary may help to decide if all new U.S. motor vehicles should be equipped with exhaust-control systems, such as "afterburners," to reduce the large amounts of unburned hydrocarbons and carbon monoxide that are now released.

California studies in the 1950's showed that exhaust gases accounted for 65 percent of all the unburned hydrocarbons then produced by motor vehicles. Another 15 percent represented evaporation from the fuel tank and carburetor, and 20 percent escaped from the vent of the crankcase. As a first step in reducing these emissions California began in 1961 to require the use of crankcase blowby devices, which became standard on all U.S. cars beginning with the 1963 models.

A new California law will require exhaust-control systems on all 1966 automobiles and light trucks sold in the state. The law is intended to reduce by 70 or 80 percent the amount of hydrocarbons now present in exhaust gases and to reduce the carbon monoxide by 60 percent. All the carbon monoxide is generated by combustion and is now released in the exhaust.

The steady rise in carbon monoxide vented into the atmosphere of Los Angeles County is plotted in Figure 3.

No one questions that an affluent society can afford to spend its money without a strict accounting of benefits received. Any reasonable expenditure that promises to improve the quality of life in the modern city should be welcomed. It is not obvious, however, that any American city except Los Angeles will be significantly benefited by the installation of exhaust-

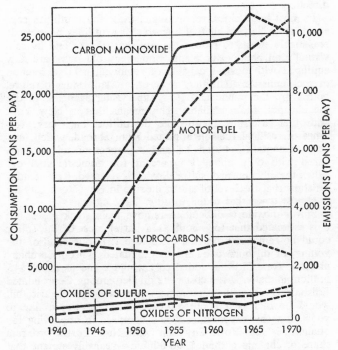

FIGURE 3. LOS ANGELES AIR POLLUTION is tied closely to the steep rise in automobile use in Los Angeles County. This chart compares gasoline consumption with the computed output from all sources of carbon monoxide, hydrocarbons, oxides of nitrogen and oxides of sulfur. Motor vehicles produce only small amounts of the last two substances, and their output has been controlled chiefly by curbs on the emission of pollutants by industry. Carbon monoxide and hydrocarbon emissions should decline when cars start carrying exhaust-control systems.

control systems in motor vehicles. The cost of these systems will not be trivial. At an estimated $40 to $50 per car, such systems would add more than $300 million to the sales price of new cars in an eight-million-car year—and this does not include the annual cost of their inspection and maintenance. If one objective of reducing the air pollution caused by automobiles is to increase the life expectancy of the city dweller, or simply to make his life more pleasant, it can be argued that $300 million a year could be spent more usefully in other directions.

In most large cities, for example, the electric utilities consume up to half of all fuel burned. Most utilities have made reasonable efforts to reduce the emission of soot and fly ash; virtually all new power plants, and many old ones, are now equipped with devices capable of removing a large fraction of such emissions. Utilities, however, are still under pressure, both from the public and from supervising agencies, to use the cheapest fuels available. This means that in New York and other eastern-seaboard cities the utilities burn large volumes of residual fuel oil imported from abroad, which happens to contain between 2.5 and 3 percent of sulfur, compared with only about 1.7 percent for domestic fuel oil. When the oil is burned, sulfur dioxide is released. Recent studies show that the level of sulfur dioxide in New York City air is almost twice that found in other large cities.

Sulfur dioxide is difficult to remove from stack gases, but it is estimated that for about $1 a barrel most of the sulfur could be removed from the oil before it is burned. For the volume of oil burned by the Consolidated Edison Company in New York City the added cost would come to about $15 million annually. If the cost were divided among Consolidated Edison's three million customers, the average electric bill would be increased about $5 per year. One would like to know how this expenditure would compare in improving the quality of New York City's air with New York's pro rata share of the more than $300-million-a-year investment that would be required by the installation of exhaust-control systems in motor vehicles. That share would be on the order of $8 million a year. Perhaps New Yorkers should insist on both investments. But these are only two of many options, all of them expensive. It is the responsibility of the city administrator and the public health officer to make choices and assign priorities, even while admitting that air pollution is never beneficial.

One must also recall that when large-scale changes are contemplated, the whole spectrum of society is involved. Rarely do all forces march forward in step, particularly where public policy and scientific verity are not crystal clear. Competitive forces delay correctives until public opinion rises in wrath and pushes for action on an *ad hoc* and intuitive basis.

Let me sum up by observing that in the case of water supply the accomplishments of the U.S. have been extraordinarily good, not only in the prevention of waterborne and water-associated diseases but also in providing water generously for comfortable living in most places at most times. The prospect for the future is likewise good. The realities are that we are not running out of water and that we are capable of managing our water resources intelligently.

In the area of water and air pollution our successes are only partial. Rapid urbanization and industrialization have intensified the problems of controlling both. At the same time one must concede that there is much stronger scientific justification for mounting vigorous programs to abate water pollution than to abate air pollution. Nevertheless, public pressure on behalf of the latter is increasing, and as has happened so often in the past, we may find action running ahead of knowledge. This is not necessarily to be deplored.

My own view coincides with that recently expressed by P. B. Medawar of University College, London, at a symposium on the interaction of man and his environment. "We are not yet qualified," he said, "to prescribe for the medical welfare of our grandchildren. . . . I should say that present skills are sufficient for present ills."

The Nature of Cities Reconsidered

EDWARD L. ULLMAN*

Are cities really necessary? . . . or even farms, for that matter? Recent trends prompt one almost to raise this question or at the least to ask what kind. This does not necessarily

* President, Washington Center for Metropolitan Studies, Washington, D.C., on leave as Professor of Geography, and formerly Associate Dean of the Graduate School, University of Washington, Seattle. He was Associate Professor of Regional Planning, Harvard University, 1949–51, and has published widely in professional journals. With Ronald Boyce

mean that most people will live nowhere and do nothing (but it might help!). Cities have been growing in size, expanding even more in area, and declining in overall density. Analysis of these developments will bring up to date some of "The Nature of Cities" written in 1944[1], which emphasized, among other facets, that "The support of a city depends on the services it performs not for itself but for a tributary area. Many activities merely serve the population of the city itself." In this presentation the degree to which a city actually is "supported" by performing services for itself will be measured and related to the size and growth of cities. The second and larger part of this study will analyze the expansion of urban areas and bring up to date the increasing importance of the "Multiple Nuclei" concept of urban structure first suggested in the earlier study.

THE GROWTH OF CITIES

Not only is rural and much small town population declining absolutely, but the very largest cities appear to be increasing more rapidly than any others. Actual figures for relative growth of metropolitan areas in the U.S. between 1950 and 1960, however, indicate that small and large have all grown about the same in terms of percentage increase. Rates are: over 3,000,000, 23% increase; 1,000,000 to 3,000,000, 25%; 500,000 to 1,000,000, 36% increase (the largest); 100,000 to 500,000, 26%. Still other groupings indicate about the same.

However, if the absolute amount of growth is allocated by groups still another interpretation can be made. For example, the five cities over 3,000,000 had an absolute increase of about 5,000,000. The second group also had an increase of about 5,000,000, but this was spread out over 16 cities. The next smaller groups had about 5,000,000 increase but the in-

and Donald J. Volk, he is author of the much discussed *The Meramec Basin: Water and Economic Development* (Washington University Press and Meramec Basin Corporation, 1962), and with Michael F. Dacey, "The Minimum Requirements Approach to the Urban Economic Base," in *Papers and Proceedings of the Regional Science Association*, Vol. 6 (1960), pp. 175–94. The article that follows was delivered as the Presidential Address to and published in *Papers and Proceedings of the Regional Science Association*, Vol. 9 (1962), pp. 7–23; it is reprinted in its entirety with permission of the Association.

[1] Chauncy D. Harris and Edward L. Ullman, "The Nature of Cities," *Annals of the American Academy of Political and Social Sciences*, Nov. 1945, pp. 7–17.

crease was distributed over still more cities. Thus an increasing quantity of U.S. population was concentrated on the average in each of the largest cities. This, then, is presumably the justification for emphasizing metropolitan growth.

If, in general, each of the largest cities on the average have been growing somewhat more, what is the explanation? No pat answer is possible but the following three factors may be involved: (1) Mere size attracts size—a mass, gravity effect; the larger the center the more innovators, the more persons who have relatives and friends who are attracted as in-migrants, etc. (2) The external economies of larger centers provide a greater range of interdependent specialities and facilities. (3) A relative improvement in internal, urban transit has occurred, primarily because of the short haul advantages of the auto and truck; this latter factor has been particularly significant in the expansion of urban area. Leon Moses suggests that the truck allows suburban factories to develop and thus enables the metropolitan area now to compete with outlying regions by providing not only relatively cheap land, but also urban nearness and access to the scale economies just noted.

All three of these forces presumably are given greater scope to influence growth because of the well known shift from primary, to secondary, and particularly to tertiary activities—toward more processing and consequent lesser orientation of production to resource locations.

SCALE ECONOMIES

What is the evidence for the scale economy factor, which has been mentioned so much recently by Vernon, Hoover, and others? In this connection some new findings will be advanced, indicating the degree to which a city is self-contained —takes in its own washing, if you please—which varies according to size and other particulars.

According to studies which Michael Dacey and I, and others, have made using what we call the "Minimum Requirements" method, there is, on the average, a definite relationship between size of a city and its degree of self-containment.[2] (Figure 1) Thus, towns of 10,000 have about one-third of their employment serving internal needs and two-thirds exter-

[2] Edward L. Ullman and Michael F. Dacey, "The Minimum Requirements Approach to the Urban Economic Base," *Papers and Proceedings of the Regional Science Association*, Vol. 6, 1960, pp. 175–94.

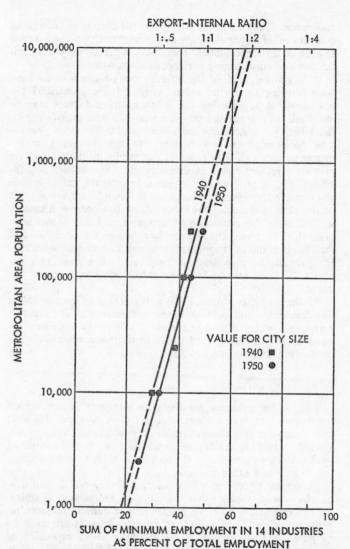

FIGURE 1. Association of Internal (Service or Non-Basic) Employment with City Size, Based on Minimum Requirements Method

nal, for an Export-Internal or Basic-Service ratio of about 1:.5; cities of 500,000 are about evenly divided, one-half internal, one-half external, etc.

This exponential relationship also fits approximately other logical relationships. When extended downward it crosses 0% at about four persons, where it should according to logic, since a family unit can sell nothing to itself; when extrapolated upward, a more dubious procedure, it crosses within about 10% of the expected for the United States population, as a whole, if one assumes the United States to be about 90% self-contained.

If this relationship holds, then the only deduction one can make about the optimum size of cities is that the larger cities are, the more self-contained they are. By extension, on the basis of this measure *alone,* we tentatively conclude that the larger the city, the more efficient it is, since it can trade more with itself and save transport costs to and from other places. We cannot say there is an optimum size, other than that the larger the better, by this measure.

The following table indicates some other measures of the gain. Thus the amount of "external" employment "captured" increases, but is the increase really proportionate in effective terms to increase in size of city? For example, is there more

	Approximate % Total Employment		Approximate % of "Remaining" External Employment "Captured" by Increasing City Size Ten-Fold
City Size	Internal	External	
1,000	21	79	—
10,000	32	68	14
100,000	43	57	16
1,000,000	54	46	19
10,000,000	65	35	24

"scale economy" gained in increasing from 10,000 to 100,000 than from 1,000,000 to 10,000,000? We do not know and will not know until we know a great deal more about the workings of urban economies.

In any event it does not mean that many metropolises will become multimillion population centers in the next 50 years, first for the obvious reason that the total population of the U.S. will not be large enough to accommodate many, and secondly because many activities are top hierarchical, one-of-a-kind functions—national headquarters, United Nations, etc. They cannot pyramid in numerous cities. Does the latter consideration mean that one city, New York, (or two or three) will become the super giants, as Haig speculated some years ago?[3]

In considering this possibility we encounter other factors—persistence of some resource orientation, whether it be the old ones of minerals and agriculture or the newer role of resort climate, and possible *diseconomies* of scale, or simple lack of scale economies in a significant number of activities, as in government. Foremost among the diseconomies today *may* be environmental limitations—increasing cost of controlling air, and secondly water pollution from large concentrations, although future technology may alter this in unknown ways.[4]

Still other forces are at work in individual cities, as the rapid growth of aviation and electronics centered in the attractive climate of Los Angeles which in turn grows as a second center of the U.S. in its own, somewhat protected, western territory. With the small number of giant cities over 5,000,000 (3 in the U.S.) it is impossible to single out one common force more important than the individual influences at work on each of the cities. To a lesser degree this is true also of the 19 cities from 1,000,000 to 5,000,000, which range from Dallas to Seattle to Philadelphia. The individual differences outweigh the similarities, but the scale economy factor would appear to be an underlying force of varying magnitude. Just how this operates and the magnitude of the effect of increasing size, now and in the future, is an explicit question needing further research.

THE INTERNAL EXPANSION OF URBAN AREAS

As our cities grow in size paradoxically their overall densities appear to decline. Suburbs and satellites boom, some

[3] R. M. Haig, Toward an Understanding of the Metropolis: "Some Speculations Regarding the Economic Basis of Urban Concentration," *Quarterly Journal of Economics*, XL (1926), pp. 179–208.

[4] A highly urbanized region may also have scale economies. *Cf.* Chauncy D. Harris, "The Market as a Factor in the Localization of Industry in the U. S.," *Annals of the Association of American Geographers*, Vol. 44, 1954, pp. 315–48, and Edward L. Ullman, "Regional Development and the Geography of Concentration," *Papers and Proceedings of the Regional Science Association*, Vol. 4, 1958, pp. 179–98. See also references to Gottmann and others in footnote six.

fringe areas are by-passed, blight produces a gray area around most of the closer-in parts of central cities, and downtowns decline. This unsettles land values and existing tax bases and alarms powerful groups. The central cities are particularly hit because most of them are unable to expand their city limits. Some conclude that cities are therefore suffering from some unknown disease. There is, however, a logical explanation, already alluded to, related to improved circulation and communication, and particularly to the nature and wide-spread use of the automobile. Improvements in transportation and communication have benefited short hauls and especially self-loading and unloading commodities like passengers or telephone messages dialed by the individual. These are improvements at metropolitan scale distances.

Before analyzing the forces promoting change, let us attempt to establish what actually has been happening in our cities, a somewhat difficult task both for statistical reasons and because of the recency of the change.

For the country as a whole the census bureau indicates that SMSA's (all central cities and their counties over 50,000) have increased 26 per cent in population, but the central cities alone, based on holding city limits constant to 1950, increased only 1.5 per cent as compared to 62 per cent in the remainder of the metropolitan areas. This is natural; as cities grow, they might be expected to expand in all directions. However, even within the 1950 city limits there is vacant land, especially on the edges, so that actually the innermost portions of cities have declined. In some areas increase in other activities has pushed out residences, but, as will be seen, on an overall basis, probably not even this has compensated for the loss. A net, although unevenly distributed, decline is evident.

For other measures beyond population, it is difficult to obtain data from the census, except for retail trade, and for the office function on a consistent basis it is impossible. To obtain as much consistency as possible a representative group of cities, of all size classes has been chosen and changes in the central city have been compared to the whole metropolitan area. (Tables I and II) The measures were limited to eighteen cities which from 1947 to 1958 had virtually no change in boundaries. Percentage calculations for the average of these cities are given on Table I.

These eighteen metropolitan areas and their central cities grew slightly faster than all U.S. metropolitan areas, with the

TABLE I. CHANGES IN PROPORTION OF SELECTED ACTIVITIES FOR 18 U.S. CENTRAL CITIES AND METROPOLITAN AREAS, VARIOUS DATES 1929–1960[a]

#		Unweighted Mean Percent
1	*Population:* proportion of SMSA located in central city, 1948	64
2	" " " " " " " " " " 1960	52
3	change in SMSA/central city concentration, 1960/1948	81
4	(1948/1958:84)	
	change, SMSA 1960/1948	133
5	change, central city 1960/48	106
6	*Manufacturing:* production workers in central city, 1929	74
7	" " " " " " 1939	71
8	" " " " " " 1947	70
9	" " " " " " 1954	64
10	" " " " " " 1958	60
11	establishments in central city, 1947	75
12	" " " " " 1954	69
13	" " " " " 1958	67
14	*Wholesale trade:* paid employees in central city, 1948	89
15	" " " " " " 1954	88
16	" " " " " " 1958	82

17	establishments in central city, 1948	86
18	" " " " 1954	83
19	" " " " 1958	80
20	*Selected services:* paid employees in central city, 1948	86
21	" " " " 1954	82
22	" " " " 1958	80
23	establishments in central city, 1954	72
24	" " " " 1958	69
25	*Retail trade:* paid employees in central city, 1948	79
26	" " " " 1954	77
27	" " " " 1958	72
28	*Manufacturing:* change in concentration of prod. workers, 1958/1947	88
29	*Wholesale trade:* " " " " paid employees, 1958/1948	91
30	*Selected services:* " " " " 1958/1948	93
31	*Retail trade:* " " " " 1958/1948	91

ᵃ Central cities chosen were those with virtually no boundary change 1947–58: metropolitan area (SMSA) figures adjusted to 1958 area.

Numbers refer to numbers of columns in following table for individual cities.

SOURCES: U.S. Census of Manufactures 1947, 1954, 1958; Census of Business 1948, 1954, 1958; Census of Population 1960.

D. J. Bogue, "A Technique for Making Extensive Population Estimates," *Journal of the American Statistical Association,* 45 (June, 1950), pp. 149–63.

Table II. Ratios of Activities of Selected Central Cities to SMSA's

#	1	2	3	4	5	6	7	8	9	10	11	12	13	14	15	16	17	18	19	20	21	22	23	24	25	26	27	28	29	30	31
Buffalo	56	41	73	124	93	60	50	48	43	42	69	62	61	87	85	80	84	80	75	81	72	70	60	55	70	65	59	88	92	86	84
Chicago	66	57	86	115	99	74	72	70	65	59	83	75	71	88	87	79	88	83	77	85	81	76	71	63	70	70	64	84	90	89	91
Cleveland	65	49	75	123	93	89	86	83	70	68	87	80	76	93	93	87	92	87	81	88	84	83	70	69	78	74	69	82	94	94	88
Detroit	61	44	72	129	94	75	58	60	53	49	69	56	52	86	77	74	87	77	73	86	78	75	66	59	71	65	56	82	86	87	79
Philadelphia	57	46	81	122	98	66	61	71	56	55	71	65	62	89	82	77	85	75	70	75	75	72	62	57	69	63	58	90	87	96	84
St. Louis	52	36	69	126	88	61	61	71	63	55	78	71	68	—	86	80	80	73	70	77	76	73	58	55	70	59	59	79	80	95	84
Akron	68	57	84	125	103	89	82	82	81	67	71	64	59	94	92	85	88	86	82	91	88	78	74	69	81	78	74	82	77	90	91
Miami	53	31	58	209	103	79	77	74	70	50	64	66	57	94	79	72	93	82	70	73	46	45	60	54	66	63	55	98	62	62	83
New Orleans	85	72	85	131	111	78	77	77	68	61	89	83	79	95	91	88	93	90	87	96	90	90	86	82	93	90	86	68	93	94	92
Portland	54	45	83	126	107	68	63	63	60	58	68	56	59	81	91	89	78	85	84	89	84	85	73	68	79	79	77	79	110	96	97
Rochester	69	54	78	123	97	92	94	95	94	92	90	87	84	95	95	92	93	92	91	97	93	87	88	84	85	90	82	92	97	90	96
Syracuse	64	51	80	131	105	76	71	47	43	40	55	49	49	84	79	71	76	74	71	82	78	69	54	51	67	65	60	97	85	84	90
Baton Rouge	79	66	84	145	121	18	17	28	23	37	57	77	83	87	94	92	88	95	93	89	98	95	97	89	91	96	94	132	106	107	103
Des Moines	79	78	99	122	121	91	95	86	77	69	93	84	85	—	96	94	91	93	92	98	96	95	92	90	92	95	92	80	94	97	100
Erie	62	55	89	121	107	67	69	54	56	57	70	67	64	90	90	87	83	82	79	89	85	83	72	67	82	81	77	106	97	93	94
Flint	62	53	85	147	125	96	99	98	80	68	62	56	65	—	89	54	82	83	79	89	90	89	69	71	85	83	79	69	54	100	93
Salt Lake City	67	49	73	150	111	70	61	70	71	72	84	80	77	92	95	93	91	90	90	90	90	91	78	81	85	87	85	103	101	102	100
South Bend	59	56	95	122	115	82	81	80	81	73	74	66	66	83	77	81	81	79	78	77	81	83	73	71	81	79	75	91	98	108	93
Average	64	52	81*	133	106	74	71	70	64	60	75	69	67	89	88	82	86	83	80	86	82	80	72	69	79	77	72	88	91	93	91

* Adjusted to 84 for 1958
# Numbers at top of columns are identified on Table I.

central cities showing a six per cent increase compared to one and one-half per cent nationally. This probably means, therefore, that the other measures of decline of central city proportion of all metropolitan activity are slightly understated in Table I. Also, as noted for population, the measures used probably actually understate the degree of inner decline since the city limits themselves are drawn fairly far out. Finally, the figures are for 1958; later data would show still more relative decline.

Even with these qualifications, relative decline of the central city is apparent. The decrease from 1948 to 1958 in the degree of central city concentration as a percentage of the metropolitan area is shown in the last four figures (28, 29, 30, 31) where Manufacturing in 1958 is eighty-eight per cent of 1947, Wholesale Trade ninety-one per cent of 1948, Selected Services ninety-three per cent, and Retail Trade ninety-one per cent, as compared to eighty-four per cent for Population.

The actual per cents of population or employment in the central city in 1958 were as follows: Population about fifty-four per cent, Manufacturing sixty per cent, Wholesale Trade eighty-two per cent, Selected Services eighty per cent, Retail Trade seventy-two per cent.

It is clear that population leads the way to the suburbs, but jobs are not far behind, especially in manufacturing. Factories appreciate the roominess of the suburb just as much as ranch houses. One-story structures with ample parking are the rule. Walk-up or elevator factories in town are abandoned as soon as conditions permit by most industries, save some with high labor requirements and production processes not sensitive to poor layout or with light weight raw materials and end products. Wholesaling, especially warehousing, should increasingly join manufacturing in low density structures, although its traditional nature, and especially greater market within the city, in contrast to manufacturing, probably explains the greater urban concentration up to now.

The number of individual establishments in manufacturing are more concentrated in the city than is employment, indicating that the larger, more self-contained industries, requiring more space, have led the way to the suburbs. In wholesale trade the reverse appears, indicating probably relatively more warehouse, low labor activity in suburbs.

These general trends in themselves are not conclusive evidence of expansion and lower density, but several studies of individual cities, among them New York, Chicago, Boston[5] indicate the dispersal as well as the classic example of Los Angeles, a city which has grown up in the recent period.

REASONS FOR THE PRESENT AND FUTURE REARRANGEMENT OF CITIES

Before citing other evidence of the expansion and rearrangement of cities, let us examine the fundamental changes in background which have made this possible. As is well known, improvement in transportation and circulation has changed the nature of urban space, allowing greater distances to be covered[6] and particularly the development of *favored*

[5] Perhaps the most significant finding along these lines of the New York Regional Study is buried in a footnote added after the study was completed and using last minute, 1960 census returns: ". . . . the tendency to fill up the previously by-passed land of the inlying counties does not appear to be quite as strong as our projection assumes. . . . In general the dispersive population forces in the region seem even stronger than those built into our model." Raymond Vernon, *Metropolis 1985*, Harvard University Press, Cambridge, 1960, footnote, p. 222.

Examples of two earlier but recent quantitative studies proving the shift in urban structures are: John R. Hamburg and Robert Sharkey, "Chicago's Changing Land Use and Population Structures," *Journal American Institute of Planners*, Vol. XXVI, Nov. 1960, pp. 317–23, and, *A Report on Downtown Boston*, Greater Boston Economic Study Committee, 1959.

[6] *Cf.* the prophetic statement of H. G. Wells in "The Probable Diffusion of Great Cities" in *Anticipations* (London, 1901) where, in discussing urban growth promoted by improved methods of transport he says, "It is not too much to say that before [2000]—the vast stretch of country from Washington to Albany will be all of it available to the active citizen of New York and Philadelphia—This does not for the moment imply that cities of the density of our existing great cities will spread to these limits" (quoted by K. C. Edwards, "Trends in Urban Expansion," *Advancement of Science*, No. 62, Sept. 1959, p. 60.)

Jean Gottmann (*Megalopolis*, New York, Twentieth Century Fund, 1960) eloquently describes the human geography of the whole area from Boston to Washington as one unit. Norton S. Ginsburg, "The Dispersed Metropolis: The Case of Okayama," *Toshi Mondai*, (Municipal Problems, in Japanese), June 1961, pp. 67–76, equally eloquently proposes a new type of city based on several centers and improved transportation.

Some less careful enthusiasts have overplayed the urban explosion, however, partly sparked by a change in definition of metropolitan areas in 1950 by the U.S. Bureau of the Census from a minor civil division basis to a county basis. When mapped it appeared as though urbanization had taken a gigantic leap into the countryside. Actually open country still surrounds all major metropolises even on the eastern seaboard of the U.S., even though the built-up area and ribbon development, much of it low density, has spread greatly. *Cf.* Lester E. Klimm, "The

sites—parts of the city more on the basis of their intrinsic natural and cultural characteristics, and less because of their location or situation. For example, before the automobile, some poor water recreation areas reached by streetcar or train on the edges of cities were very popular. Since the automobile has taken over, these nearby areas, if of poor quality, have declined drastically and visitors travel up to 100 or 200 miles to new impoundments or natural water bodies with better water and scenery, or build swimming pools. In this case, both the opportunity to travel and the ability to pay for something better in our increasingly affluent society have created a change.

Thus the stage is set for urban areas. First, as is well known, provision of streetcars and mass transit enabled cities to expand especially out along radial corridors; the volume required for this type of transport tended to focus on one large center—downtown. With the widespread use of the automobile, not dependent on large volume, the interstices could also be served which provided access to enormous additional amounts of land on the expanding circumference. The area of a circle increases by πr^2, which means, for example, that doubling the distance from the center increases the area four times.

Most of the inventions in communication also seem to favor a more open pattern. The telephone with its postage stamp rate over wide areas freed dependence on messengers, the movie made it possible to bring entertainment into the communities and neighborhoods from downtown, and the TV now brings it into the individual house and makes the home even more independent of other localities in the city.

What is happening in cities can be compared to what happened to world land use in the 19th and 20th centuries when improved transport enabled distant fertile lands to produce for the world market and in the process compete with less fertile lands nearer the market. Thus, the steamship and railway brought agricultural products to Europe from fertile prairies in America, Argentina, or Australia and either forced

Empty Areas of the Northeastern U. S.," *Geographical Review*, Vol. XLIV, 1954, pp. 25–45. What has happened is more to be measured by invisible indicators in the landscape: commuting, shopping and other trips, telephone calls, TV, etc., spreading out and beyond suburbia and exurbia. For an example of quantitative indicators of this see: Edward L. Ullman, Ronald R. Boyce and Donald J. Volk, *The Meramec Basin*, Washington University Press, St. Louis, Mo., 1962, Chapter 1.

abandonment or drastic alteration of agriculture in many less fertile lands in the European market. Thus the present subsidy to European agriculture might be compared to the subsidy to cities through redevelopment programs, although no value judgment is implied.

Cities might thus initially be compared to the Von Thünen model of land use around a city, with intensity generally decreasing as distance increased from the central market. Urban transportation, especially the automobile, removes much of the handicap of distance just as the steamship and railway did for the world's regions.[7]

One might thus paraphrase and add to some well known economic principles by coining a new law of *urban expansion* and *specialization* as follows:

As urban transport improves cities not only can expand in area, but the range of location choice is widened; the more desirable sites within a city can be reached and developed according to their intrinsic advantages.

The second part of the generalization, relating to *site* qualities rather than *situation* qualities, as geographers would define them, is just as important as the first, or expansion part of the law. The monopoly quality of close-in urban locations is weakened.

Even in parts of Europe the same phenomenon is occurring as witness a statement in 1960 by Dr. Aage Aagesen of the Geography Department of the University of Copenhagen:[8]

The Intensive urbanization which has developed in proximity to the railway stations seems to have been transformed into a more general, less pronounced urbanization of more extensive areas; this is a natural result of the fact that the importance exercised by motor-cars and other motor-vehicles on the daily transport is constantly increasing. Another consequence is that there are almost no limits to the choice of residence; this allows preference to be given to *esthetic* considerations by choosing the site in coastal regions, in undulating land, at the edge of a wood or of a lake. A combination of these factors has

[7] Homer Hoyt anticipates me somewhat in this interpretation (as he constantly does) in "Changing Patterns of Land Values," *Land Economics,* Vol. XXXVI, 1960, p. 114.

[8] Aage Aagesen, "The Copenhagen District and its Population," (paper presented to 1960 Symposium on Urban Geography, Lund, Sweden, August, 1960), published in *Geografisk Tidsskrift,* Vol. 59, 1960, pp. 204–13, (citation on p. 210).

caused the expansion of the Copenhagen district toward the north, in the sub-glacial stream-trenches of North Zealand filled with lakes and woods. To the west and to the southwest of Copenhagen, in a flat and fertile moraine-land, the relief of the landscape is far from being as attractive and, therefore, has not invited an expansion of the same dimensions.

The same occurs in American cities where waterfront property, as on Lake Michigan in Chicago or Lake Washington in Seattle, is sought, or attractive wooded hill lands in part draw high class residence as in western St. Louis or north-western Washington, D. C. Likewise, close-in hilly sites are by-passed by factories in favor of out-lying, level lands.

Thus specialization on the basis of natural site qualities occurs, whereas 100 years ago, before the streetcar or auto, close-in Back Bay in Boston was filled in for high class residential use, or centrally located Nob Hill in San Francisco was built up in mansions and Leland Stanford reportedly got cable car service, an invention of the time uniquely fitted to serve hills. Today many, if not most, of these residents have moved to more spacious sites in the suburbs. Thus different natural factors may apply to urban sites than to rural areas, such as scenically attractive land for high grade housing or level land for factories rather than fertile land for crops.

Urban sites, however, for various reasons, probably cannot be rated so much on their natural characteristics as rural lands, but rather more because of certain man-made or *cultural* attributes. The result is a *push-pull* relationship.

First, close-in locations generally are relatively unattractive because of smoke, noise, traffic, crime, and other well known attributes of crowding.

Secondly, closer-in lands may be by-passed by new building for two principal reasons: 1) the generally smaller size of parcels close-in compared to large outlying tracts suitable for large subdivisions and the lower cost mass building techniques of today, and 2) the greater cost of acquiring old structures and paying high land prices near the center as opposed to using raw land farther out.

The cost of acquiring close-in sites may run from $100,000 to $200,000 and more per acre[9] as compared to $10,000 to

[9] Raymond Vernon, "The Economics of the Large Metropolis," in "The Future Metropolis," *Daedalus*, Winter, 1961, Vol. 90, *Proceedings of the American Academy of Arts and Sciences,* p. 44.

$25,000 per acre for outlying land. As a result, few one story or even two story structures can afford costs of close-in sites, whether for house or factory; at the same time the demand for multi-story apartments or other intensive uses is simply not great enough to cover all the gray areas. As a further result the government must subsidize redevelopment, contributing two-thirds or more and the local government the remainder to get site costs down to competitive levels. Even so, the temptation is to build to high densities, which in the past has produced high rise, low income housing, in many cases of dubious attractiveness.

Furthermore, anywhere in the city it appears that low density—that is two story group houses—are the cheapest way to house people because of lower construction costs, lack of elevators, etc. Even in England this is claimed.[10] As Hans Blumenfeld notes the cheapest cost building in a country is apt to be the type which is built most.[11] The higher standard buildings may last somewhat longer, but even the average annual payments do not appear to be significantly less.

It is argued that cost of utilities—sewers, water, electricity, is higher if dispersed building is allowed on the fringes. As Lovelace remarks, "The underground system of sewers and water mains is about all that is holding [the city] together.[12] Even this is questionable, as Lovelace also notes.

Cheaper methods of lagoon sewage treatment or small package plants have been developed for small subdivisions, septic tanks at low densities are suitable on many soils, and even farmhouses have electricity and telephone at not excessive rates. It is true that new schools and other community facilities may have to be built, but these may replace similar facilities close-in which have outlived their usefulness. One story schools, requiring more land, are preferred to the old urban two, or three story structures with inadequate playgrounds.

As a concrete example, Lovelace points out that much of southwestern Michigan outside the cities is developed for low density, non-farm uses in an area of sandy soils with high

---

[10] Cf. "The two story house on new land is still the cheapest form of development in Britain," Myles Wright, "Further Progress" in Land Use in an Urban Environment, Liverpool, 1961, p. 251.

[11] Hans Blumenfeld, Urban Land, Vol. 21, No. 7, Aug. 1962.

[12] Eldridge Lovelace, "Urban Sprawl Need not be a Tragedy," Landscape Architecture, Vol. 51, 1961, pp. 230–1.

water table so that sewers and water mains are not required.[13] This illustrates graphically a natural site advantage which can now play a role with cheap transportation. Areas unsuitable for septic tanks can be skipped over.

Furthermore, low density sprawl on the fringes of a city is not unattractive simply because it is low-density, but rather because of the way it is done with ribbon development, removal of trees, growth of junk yards and the like. It is not the low density itself that is to blame. Restraining cities to dense, contiguous settlement is not the only answer, nor even the best answer to unsightly sprawl. Sprawl does however produce some obvious inefficiencies.

THE CENTRAL BUSINESS DISTRICT

The core of the city is generally declining relatively and in many cases absolutely. The best data indicating these trends are for retail sales. The top part of Table III shows change in CBD sales and SMSA sales in terms of constant value dollars from 1948 to 1958. The decreases for CBD's range from sixteen per cent for cities over 1,000,000 down to about 10 per cent for those from 100,000 to 250,000. At the same time the remainder of the SMSA's outside the CBD's were increasing from thirty-three to sixty-four per cent. The lower portion of Table III shows what percentage CBD sales are of total SMSA's. Note the decline from sixteen per cent to ten per cent for those over 3,000,000, from twenty-six to fifteen per cent for 1,000,000 to 3,000,000 etc. Note also the lower percentage of total SMSA sales in the CBD in the larger cities, as would be expected, ranging from 9.6 per cent in the largest group to 32 per cent in the smallest. Pre-war, the only firm figure we had, was the special census under Proudfoot for Philadelphia which reported 37.5 per cent in 1937.

These figures show the effect of the construction of large branch department stores and shopping centers and the general movement of shopping to customers. If much of the retail trade leaves downtowns what will replace it?

Before attempting to answer this question, two fundamental points about downtowns should be noted:

1) Most large cities have developed on water and have grown more in one direction than another so that the central business district is not now centrally located in many cities.

[13] Lovelace, *op. cit.*

As a result it loses sales and economic activities as cities grow away from it.[14] Street grids and mass transport focussing on the CBD mitigated this handicap in the past and the construction of radial superhighways to downtown will probably help overcome it to some extent in the future, especially if the parking problem can be solved.

2) Even more serious than the off-center location, in many cases, is the surrounding of the CBD by the low income, blighted, "gray area" of cities. Redevelopment, therefore, in many cases is pushed in part as a means of providing customers. In addition, a market for high and medium income apartments can be developed around downtowns, especially as older people with grown children come onto the market, as well as a new wave of post-high school and young college graduates. This market in most cities, however, does not appear large enough to effect a significant change. Probably a larger natural apartment market for retired persons exists in suburbs and other centers.

The remaining large activity for CBD's is the office function. This is growing, and growing particularly in New York which has witnessed a boom in central office and other activities locating there for national control, in part made possible by the airplane. To a degree the same is happening in Washington. For most cities this does not appear so likely. Even Chicago's recent expansion and planned new construction will only result in the same per capita office space as in 1930, although it will help the Loop.[15] Most other cities are worse off.

The unknown question is how much is face-to-face contact —linkages of various kinds—necessary for various functions, especially outside New York City. Many activities apparently do not require it, particularly in insurance and in single-function office buildings.

In some cities, even beside Los Angeles, notably St. Louis, outlying office centers are now starting to develop. Clayton, seven miles west of the CBD and more centrally located in reference to the high income area, has many modern, city-wide or nation-wide office buildings, with rents as much as

[14] Cf. Ronald R. Boyce's forthcoming study suggested this point of the relation of CBD retail sales to CBD centrality. Also note William Weismantel, "A Multicenter Transportation Plan," *Washington University Law Quarterly*, June, 1962, pp. 310–37, for an excellent discussion of St. Louis' growth patterns in relation to transportation.

[15] *Urban Land*, April, 1961, p. 8.

three times higher than downtown, but with land values only about 1/3; Clayton illustrates a location nearer the geographic center of a city as well as closer to executives' homes. Ancillary businesses and social services, including luncheon clubs, have sprung up, although the center is not as large as downtown St. Louis. Executives, however, can still go downtown for luncheon club conferences. They drive to their offices in Clayton, then drive downtown for lunch and return in the afternoon, avoiding all rush hour traffic.

Many activities are downtown just because they are there, or in response to linkages which disappeared years ago. Many could be served better elsewhere. In any case, the average downtown should be greatly improved in order to compete with the greater number of sites now accessible by modern transportation. This will be increasingly difficult in view of the outward movement of housing, retail trade, manufacturing, and other activities which now begin to reinforce each other elsewhere in the city.

It looks as though the CBD may become one of the many centers in a city, in many cases the most important, but a center of much less relative importance than in the past. A logical development would make it the shopping center for the large, low income area around it and an office center on a reduced scale for older activities or smaller concerns needing poor, vacant space or using large amounts of cheap labor. The high grade activities characteristic of the top hierarchical position of the CBD will abandon it for centers better located to serve the high income areas.[16]

Other centers elsewhere will develop on a regional or specialized basis, strengthening the multiple nuclei generalization suggested in the earlier "Nature of Cities." Conventions and out of town visitors will find it increasingly more convenient to locate near the airport which, because of its own space needs locates on the periphery; outlying shopping centers will handle retail trade; large factories and employment centers will be on the outskirts on large tracts of land; special entertainment, educational, cultural, and recreational centers will be scattered all over the city to serve the whole population.

Many have said that a city cannot exist without a heart, the CBD. The metropolis of today and increasingly in the future is not only one city, but a federation of general and

---

[16] This will eliminate some of the cross hauling now occurring as executives travel from the residential suburbs into the center and workers travel from the center outward to suburban industrial sites.

TABLE III. CENTRAL BUSINESS DISTRICT SALES DATA

I. *Changes in Retail Sales CBD and Metropolitan Areas, 1948-58 Adjusted to 1948 Dollars and for 1960 SMSA's.*

SMSA Population (1960)	All Retail Sales						Women's Specialty Stores (Clothing)					
	Changes in CBD Sales			Changes in SMSA Sales (Less CBD Sales)			Changes in CBD Sales			Changes in SMSA Sales (Less CBD Sales)		
	1948-54	1954-58	1948-58	1948-54	1954-58	1948-58	1948-54	1954-58	1948-58	1948-54	1954-58	1948-58
3,000,000 or more (5 cities)	−11.6%	− 5%	−16%	+21%	+11%	+33%	− 2.1%	+11.5%	+ 9.3%	+13%	+ 4%	+17%
1,000,000 to 3,000,000 (14 cities)	− 7.8%	− 7.8%	−16.3%	+31%	+17%	+50%	−16.8%	− 5%	−21%	+12%	+32%	+48%
500,000 to 1,000,000 (25 cities)	− 7%	− 8%	−14.4%	+38%	+23%	+64%	−11.7%	− 6.7%	−17.5%	+16%	+29%	+49%
250,000 to 500,000 (32 cities)	− 4.3%	− 6.7%	−10.6%	+35%	+18%	+55%	−10.3%	−13.7%	−23%	+60%	− 3%	+55%
100,000 to 250,000 (14 cities)	− 2.3%	− 7.1%	− 9.7%	+30%	+18%	+50%	−10%	−10%	−20%	+101%	+13%	+118%
U.S. Average	− 6.6%	− 7%	−13.4%	+30.4%	+16.8%	+51%	−10%	− 4.8%	−14.4%	+40.2%	+15%	+57%

SOURCE: Calculated from U.S. Census of Business, 1958, 1954, *Central Business District Statistics.*

II. CBD Retail Sales as Percentage of SMSA Sales, 1948-58.

SMSA Population (1960)	All Retail Sales			Women's Specialty Stores (Clothing)		
	% of SMSA Sales in CBD			% of SMSA Sales in CBD		
	1948	1954	1958	1948	1954	1958
3,000,000 or more (5 cities)	15.6%	11.4%	9.6%	33.8%	27.4%	26.8%
1,000,000 to 3,000,000 (14 cities)	26%	18.8%	15.4%	58.8%	47.5%	41.1%
500,000 to 1,000,000 (25 cities)	34.3%	24.3%	19.7%	78.3%	65%	55.3%
250,000 to 500,000 (32 cities)	38.7%	28.5%	24.4%	84.8%	75.6%	70.8%
100,000 to 250,000 (14 cities)	44.5%	37.2%	32.1%	91.7%	81.8%	77.8%
U.S. Average	31.8%	24%	20%	69.5%	59.5%	54.4%

SOURCE: Calculated from U.S. Census of Business, 1958, 1954, Central Business District Statistics.

special centers. As such it is likely to have several hearts better located than one, and basically will be better off because of reduction in travel time, congestion, and utilization of better sites.

CONCLUSION

The generalizations about urban growth and re-arrangement will vary with individual cities because individual natural environments, economic bases, and civic actions vary. Many of the location changes in cities hinge on small margins with inertia and tradition holding many activities in uneconomical, old areas. Identical offices and industries can thrive in CBD's, suburbs, and small towns. They adjust accordingly.

If we were to start over, however, we would not build our cities as they are today. If we were to apply private enterprise depreciation principles to the inner portions of cities we would write them off—just as machinery is scrapped, and throw them away, but where would we throw them?

As a citizen I recognize that the major problem of cities—slums and the gray area—cannot be tolerated. We may well have to eliminate them before we eliminate all the causes, including poverty, ignorance, and racial discrimination against the new arrivals, or the other manifold ills of our society both old and new.

Some might say that the new pattern of our cities is the result of a plot hatched by Detroit, the sub-dividers, and land speculators. Inflated land values are a part of the "pernicious" process of urban sprawl.[17] The auto does not pay its fair share for use of the city and hidden costs are passed on to the public in urban expansion. This may be true, but three points seem germane: 1) the magnitude of the underpayment is probably not enough to result in anything more than a slowing down in the process, even if corrected. 2) Countervailing forces are already deployed on the other side, sparked in part by the threatened decline in land values in the center. Urban redevelopment is subsidized, and priority is given a radial pattern for the interstate highway system focussing on downtown, reflecting old flow patterns, with generally only one circumferential, when some inner or intermediate belts are also required. 3) Even if the whole process is a plot, it is our

---

[17] Cf. the thoughtful article by Mason Gaffney "Urban Expansion-Will it ever Stop?," *1958 Yearbook of Agriculture* (Washington, Govt. Printing Office, 1959), pp. 503–22.

foreseeable institutional arrangement and as a geographer I see it producing the future expansion—specialization—federation patterns sketched above.

A key question then will be the interrelations between the centers and parts. How much will they benefit from being adjacent, or would separate cities of 100,000 to 500,000 be as good or better? The latter seems unlikely since there are still some specialized services, such as jet aircraft flights, that are better performed for millions than thousands. The problem remains to design cities to take advantage of scale economies and the other advantages of concentration, and at the same time to provide optimum livability.

People: Urbanization and City Growth
H. WENTWORTH ELDREDGE

People grouped together make cities. The spatial distribution of the population and its composition by age, sex and "race" are the demographic bases for urbanization and urbanism. Cities may profitably be perceived as social, economic, political or ecological (by institution) systems, but there is no escaping the fundamental reality that "the city is the people." Attention here will be devoted to the arithmetic and general location, urban demographic facts in a dynamic context.

The *urbanization* process is not very old in human history; only within the last few centuries has more than a minority of the world's population lived in cities. The modern pattern of industrial city living is something new, although prefigured first over five thousand years ago by the pre-industrial cities of the Fertile Crescent in the eastern Mediterranean and later by the cities of classical Greece and Rome, and by medieval Europe. The city folkways dominate not only the urban inhabitants, but with increasing communication and transportation they also tend to dominate the rurality. This process has not ended as developing countries urbanize more rapidly than developed areas, and all cities grow at least at a speed equal to general population growth within each nation. Before the year 2000, when the earth's human population will probably have reached close to seven billion, if concentration continues at 1950–60 rates, over half will live in cities of over 100,000 in an "urbanized world".[1]

Urbanization appears now to be a finite process with four stages: (1) an initial stage of centripetal rural migration to the city; (2) a smaller centrifugal movement to the city fringes (streetcar suburbs); (3) a larger centrifugal movement to suburbia extending urbanism to metropolitan dimensions (electric commuter railroads, high-speed buses and especially private motor cars); this movement appears to reach an apogee in the neighborhood of a 65% to 70% "urban" population; (4) a slowdown of urban concentration either in reality, or by statistical quirk, or by the beginnings of the end of the urban-rural dichotomy into a loose-grained grid of world urbanism. Megalopolis quite possibly begins this stage. Barring unforeseen catastrophe or an international population policy, plan and program, something like the pattern sketched as Stage 4 will be the world's demographic future. Under such circumstances, urban society and urban physical form will take on quite different characteristics than today. Urbanization is technically the percentage of persons in areas defined as cities by national or United Nations criteria for a given national state. Its extent rests basically on agricultural productivity (and transport) which enables the rural population to create sufficient food surplus to feed non-food-producing city dwellers. Food producers with increasingly advanced technology at command need not be just up the road but can be on the next continent. If, however, rural populations, kept alive by modern medical knowledge, are displaced by industrial farming methods and increase at such numbers as they are in today's developing areas, the phenomenon of "over-urbanization" will take place with city, as well as rural, starvation becoming a fearful reality barely controlled by forced feeding from the granaries of Western suppliers. If rural populations expand as rapidly as they are now in developing areas, *urbanization* (presently at a far higher rate than in developed areas) will decline even though *city growth* will continue keeping up with general population growth. In 1900 only one society, Great Britain, could be regarded as urbanized; today the definition fits all industrialized nations; in fact by 1960 it has been estimated that 33% of the entire world's population were already in that state.

[1] Kingsley Davis, "The Urbanization of the Human Population," *Scientific American*, Vol. 213; No. 3, September 1965, pp. 41 and 52. Many of the ideas for this section were drawn from the Davis article.

THE TREND IN WORLD URBANIZATION,
1800 to 1960

The last 150 years, more or less concomitant with the industrial revolution, have seen a more rapid urbanization than during the whole of recorded history. The entire world has become, as indicated above, the agricultural hinterland for the city; the rural-urban ratio, still high in some areas, has dropped to one actual food producer for fifteen or higher in the West. Great Britain led the world in urbanization; from 10% of the population in cities of 100,000 or more in 1801 reaching 35% in 1901 and 38% in 1951; from 58% in 1901 in cities of 20,000 or more to 69% by 1951. The total world population did not attain the British level of 1801 until the second or third decade of the twentieth century. Table 1 shows the percentage of world urbanization in cities of 100,000 and over from 1800 to 1960.[2]

TABLE 1
PERCENT OF THE WORLD'S POPULATION IN CITIES OF 100,000
AND OVER, 1800–1960

1800	1.7
1850	2.3
1900	5.5
1950	13.1
1960	19.9

While the world's population has increased rapidly since 1800 (2.9 billion by 1960), the urban population has grown more rapidly. The 15.6 million living in cities of 100,000 or more in the world of 1800 had increased almost forty times by 1960 to 590 million more or less. The fifty cities of 100,-000 in 1800 had grown to almost 1400 by 1960. But this urbanization was not distributed equally throughout the globe. Table 2 indicates the urban population in cities of 100,000 and over by world regions in percentage terms.[3]

[2] Kingsley Davis, "The Origin and Growth of Urbanization in the World," *The American Journal of Sociology*, Vol. IX, No. 5, March, 1955, p. 433 and Homer Hoyt, *World Urbanization: Expanding Population in a Shrinking World* (Washington, D.C.: Urban Land Institute, 1962), p. 31 for 1960 figure.

[3] Gerald Breese, *Urbanization in Newly Developing Countries* (Prentice-Hall, Inc.: Englewood Cliffs, N. J., 1966), Table 4, p. 22.

TABLE 2

PERCENT OF REGIONS' POPULATION IN CITIES OF 100,000
AND OVER, 1960

World	19.9
Asia	12.3
Europe	29.6
Africa	8.1
America	42.0
Oceania	43.3

The highest levels of urbanization are found in those areas
that are highly industrialized with Oceania (New Zealand and
Australia), the United States and Western Europe leading.
The correlation at this stage in history of urbanization with
industrialization is high, but there is evidence that urbanization (percentage of total population) tends to level off. While
today developing nations are far from this saturation point of
urbanization, it would seem that they too with a present
faster rate of growth will level off in due course.

There is a reminiscent quality about the initial surge to the
city of rural people in developing areas; moreover there are
already signs of suburbanization evident as bicycle, bus, motor
bike and automobile affluence slowly seep in. The city pulls
and the rural pushes are at work with local variations and
with new elaborations the result of twentieth century variables
fed in from a more closely knit world system of trade and
communication. Models of Western urbanization that affect
both official and private decisions in developing areas are so
much more visible in farm, jungle and plain today than one
hundred years ago. In advanced countries the city model glit-
ters somewhat less than it once did. Central city woes are
widespread and the excitement of central city is exported in
any case by electronic means and cheap wheels to the hinterland. Thus ecologically minded demographers have predicted
a loose grained settlement pattern which the U.S. East Coast
megalopolis may prefigure. Mathematically, it is obvious that
as the reservoir of youth declines, as the total percentage of
population in rural areas declines, urbanization as a process
is bound to slow down. This centralizing process or centripetal
phase was followed in the Western world by explosion to the
city fringe.

METROPOLITANIZATION

An awkward word, metropolitanization, defines this large-scale movement spreading from central city. As the rural and/or foreign millions poured in with successive waves, they pushed or better enabled the older migrants in central city to move out to the suburban greener pastures in two related movements: the first impelled by the late nineteenth- and early twentieth-century technology of the streetcar and steam train and the second more dramatic and further reaching sprawl by the private automobile subsidized by the national road system. These metropolitan areas are now touching each other in the United Kingdom, Holland, West Germany, Belgium and the United States, for example, in megalopolitan blobs. "The real super-city is a gargantuan metropolitan collection of central cities, suburbs and satellite cities. Looking into the future, at least eleven in the U.S.A. should pass the population mark of five million within the next three or four decennial censuses; some sooner, some later, some already have."[4]

The six largest of these metropolitan areas in the United States with the 1960 census figures in parentheses are:

1. New York (14.8 million)
2. Chicago (6.8 million)
3. Los Angeles (6.7 million)
4. Philadelphia (4.3 million)
5. Detroit (3.8 million)
6. Baltimore-Washington (3.7 million)

The political city of New York today holds 8,000,000 people; the functional metropolitan area of New York is estimated to grow to 20,000 by 1980 presumably linking with fourth-ranking Philadelphia and through Wilmington with sixth-ranking Baltimore-Washington to the south. To the north Bridgeport, New Haven, Springfield and New London will be locked in orbit as Providence, Worcester and Boston in turn connect. More alarmingly, Indian cities, if the present accelerating rate of growth should continue, are predicted to reach the magnitude of 36,000,000 to 40,000,000 inhabitants by A.D. 2000 without necessarily linking in a series of megalopolitan regions. How planners can cope adequately with prob-

[4] Ben J. Wattenberg, *This U.S.A.* (Garden City: Doubleday, 1965), p. 75.

lems of such grandiose dimensions remains to be discovered.

The second aspect of metropolitanization and beyond is the distribution within the metropolitan area (which has as yet been unable to find a government in the United States). A succinct statement of the internal distribution trends is given in Table 3:[5]

TABLE 3

PERCENTAGE INCREASE IN U. S. POPULATION WITHIN AND OUTSIDE METROPOLITAN AREAS IN THE PRECEDING DECADE, 1910–1960

	1960	1950	1940	1930	1920	1910
Total U. S. Population	18.5	14.5	7.2	16.1	14.9	21.0
All metropolitan areas reported	26.4	22.0	8.1	28.3	26.9	34.6
Central cities	1.5	13.9	5.1	22.3	25.2	33.6
Suburban areas	61.7	35.6	15.1	44.0	32.0	38.2
Area outside metropolitan areas	7.1	6.1	6.5	7.9	9.6	16.4

The 1960 census was the first to show population declines in a number of large cities. More than one quarter of all cities around which the Standard Metropolitan Statistical Areas of the Census Bureau are formed lost population during the decade preceding, even as reporting metropolitan areas grew at a rate above that of the entire population. That, of course, is spelled out by the 1.5% total central city increase shown in Table 3 as compared to suburban areas which increased at an astounding 61.7%. Our giant metropolitan central city areas fared badly from 1950 to 1960, if losing population quantity is to be considered bad; social quality is at least as important from a local point of view. From 1950 to 1960, intra-metropolitan movements are shown for the five largest metropolitan areas in the United States in Table 4.[6]

Sprawling Los Angeles merely filled in as well as exploded; the pattern within the others is clear. In that recent decade the population "wanted out" of central city; with the enormous expenditures in central city renewal during the sixties it will be interesting to learn in 1970 whether this powerful demographic trend continued. It is more than likely that more

[5] Adapted from Noel Gist and Sylvia Fava, *Urban Society*, 5th edition (New York: Crowell, 1964), p. 73, Table 5. The statistics were carefully assembled and adjusted.

[6] *Ibid*, p. 74, Table 6, as adapted.

TABLE 4
PERCENTAGE OF CHANGE BY AREA IN THE FIVE LARGEST SMSA's
IN THE U.S.A., 1950–1960

	Central City	Outside
New York	− 1.4	+75.0
Chicago	− 1.9	+71.5
Los Angeles	+27.1	+82.6
Philadelphia	− 3.3	+46.3
Detroit	− 9.7	+79.3

SMSA population will live in the suburbs than in central city or elsewhere.

THE COMPOSITION OF THE URBAN POPULATION

In addition to intra-metropolitan distribution of population, two other important demographic indices, relevant to the planning process, are generally at hand from the decennial census (a) age and (b) racial composition. Factors such as class, religion and ethnicity of relevance are hard to get at and are of a more sociological than narrowly demographic nature—the object of attention here.

According to the 1960 census, within the entire SMSA population there were 29.1% children under fourteen; within the central city population 26.7% and in the suburban population 31.4%, which is hardly surprising. At the other end of life, sixty-five years and over, there were in the SMSA population 9%; in the central city population 9.8%; in the suburban population 7.2%. In short, central city is weighted slightly on the old person side as compared to suburbia, and children are slightly under-represented. Planners had better cope *with* senior citizens in central city and cope *for* youngsters, if more with their parents are wanted in central city.

Non-white population, specifically Negroes, are the latest migrants to American cities on a large scale. Both World Wars played a large role in the movement. In 1900, 40% of the total population lived in urban places; with 22.7% of them Negroes. By 1960, with 69.8% of the total population living in urban places, 73.4% of the Negroes had moved in. In the 1950–1960 decade with a total increase of 38.4% in urbanized areas the non-white population increased 64.9%:[7]

[7] *Ibid,* Table 7, p. 130, as adapted.

TABLE 5

NEGRO PERCENTAGE OF POPULATION IN THE FIVE LARGEST SMSA'S:
PLUS WASHINGTON, D.C., 1950 AND 1960

| | SMSA | | Central City or Cities | |
	1950	1960	1950	1960
New York	8.9	11.5	9.5	14.0
Chicago	10.5	14.3	14.6	22.9
Los Angeles	5.0	6.9	7.9	12.2
Philadelphia	13.1	15.5	18.2	26.4
Detroit	11.9	14.9	16.3	28.9
Washington, D.C.	23.1	24.3	35.0	53.9

This, of course, is the growing reality of the ghetto central city and the "lily-white" suburbs. Moreover, Negroes are not spread equally throughout the urban tissue of central city, but are in impacted areas. Suburbia shuts out Negroes pretty solidly for practical purposes; they are trapped in central city with social and pecuniary diseconomies—not to mention increasing political diseconomies. Some advocates of "Black Power" see these ghettos as a useful base for political action of a new and rambunctious level; they are against Negro suburbanization. Washington, D.C., already 53% Negro, has 80% of its school population colored. This concentration seems almost certain to increase in central city, as the ghetto bonds can only be loosened slowly even with the evident purposeful action on the part of the federal and many state governments. The easy release of movement to suburbia duplicating the social and spatial mobility of past white migrant waves seems barely opened. The results for the United States urban scene are beyond present comprehension. Without unnecessary hyperbole, this is the most serious unsolved urban problem. To the complex enough woes of central city everywhere, this country has an admixture of explosive racialism as recent events attest.

It has been said that the city is increasingly the haunt of the colored, the old, the poor and the odd. The decennial census confirms the first two; income and crime statistics suggest the second two characteristics might be true also. All of which calls for some considerable ingenuity, if we would make livable cities.

Finally, such planning may seem a futile exercise, since the struggle to renew cities boils down merely to negative coping with a too rapidly expanding and concentrating population in both the developed and developing portions of the urbanizing globe. From a macroplanning position, it would seem far wiser to plan and program the over-rate of population growth, rather than attempt to remedy chaos after the event through highly unreliable and extremely costly physical forms and social-political-economic structures.

Chapter 3

CITIES IN DEVELOPING AND INDUSTRIAL SOCIETIES: A COMPARATIVE SOCIOLOGICAL APPROACH

Urban sociology, at least the urban sociology of the American industrial city, has been an enthusiastic concern of sociologists here since the first decade of the twentieth century, when the Chicago school first commenced dissecting that "wicked" city. As sociological methodology has become increasingly sophisticated, and prodded by the anthropologists poaching on preindustrial urban places, the sociologists have moved toward richer and more embracing theories about urbanism and urbanization—even reaching out through history to the prehistorical findings of archaeology. As modern urban society (read modern industrial society) has become increasingly better understood through quantifying technologies, the exponentially more difficult task of comparative urbanism has been tentatively explored. In this task, Gideon Sjoberg has been a pioneering leader in the search for the golden independent variable or variables in the barrel of worms comprising the complex of variables in the bewildering bundle of urbanization—and its connections with modernization. Indeed the sociologists, after a quiescent period in which they recuperated from early reformist inclinations, have once again joined the operationally oriented as the Great Society linkage of physical and social planning is aborning and underdeveloped area urbanism has turned out to be an obvious disaster. Into the knowledge and skill vacuum now clear to all in "city planning," the sociologist is slowly working his way, building carefully and reasonably solidly the eminently practical "good theories" of the middle range which planners in future decades may well find operationally powerful. The quantifying methodology of sociology, with an assist from the mathematical precision of economic research, is fast becoming the social science underpinning for building "the good city" in Western and non-Western societies.

Cities in Developing and Industrial Societies: A Comparative Sociological Approach
GIDEON SJOBERG*

Our primary aim is not to summarize existing research but rather to focus on certain crucial theoretical issues and to delineate problem areas that merit intensive study.[1] In addition to our effort to isolate the structural correlates of industrial cities, we devote special attention to the matter of social integration and the division of labor and the role of mediators in modern industrial-urban systems. This general problem—central to much of sociological analysis—is too frequently ignored.

THEORETICAL BACKGROUND

If we are to understand the city in both its historical and its current social settings, our scope must be broad. A wide perspective is essential, for social systems do not arrange themselves into neat compartments that conform with arbitrary disciplinary boundaries or the divisions sociologists establish for teaching purposes. We believe that the search for structural correlates of industrial cities is of sufficient theoretical and practical import to warrant acceptance of the risks that inhere in any macroscopic cross-cultural investigation.

Although the obstacles to cross-cultural research and analysis loom discouragingly large, there is cause for optimism, for

* Associate Professor of Sociology at the University of Texas. He is the author of *The Preindustrial City: Past and Present* (The Free Press, 1960), and has published numerous articles on urban sociology. He served from 1958 to 1964 as a member of the Social Science Research Council's Committee on Urbanization. This article, with slight textual changes by the author, is reprinted with permission from Hauser and Schnore, *The Study of Urbanization,* copyright © 1965, by John Wiley and Sons, Inc., where it appeared as Chapter 7.

The author acknowledges with thanks the assistance of his wife, Andrée F. Sjoberg, in examining various materials in foreign languages.

[1] At this stage of cross-cultural research, we believe that the emphasis must be upon "discovery" or "asking questions" rather than upon the formal testing of well-defined hypotheses. We are oriented to the procedure set forth in Norwood Hanson, *Patterns of Discovery* (Cambridge: Cambridge University Press, 1958).

by limiting ourselves to isolating the *shared* characteristics of industrial cities our task is simplified. We are spared concern with a host of niggling traits peculiar to one or a few systems at most.

The macroscopic orientation, in contradistinction to the microscopic one, maximizes synthesis and minimizes analysis.[2] Sociologists who adhere to a macroscopic perspective, as we do, are often accused of removing themselves from social reality. However, generalizing across cultures usually demands a relatively high level of abstraction. Patterns that appear to diverge perceptibly on a concrete, empirical plane frequently seem quite similar on a more abstract level. Moreover, the macroscopic orientation brings to the fore relationships that scholars who concentrate upon particular organizations are apt to ignore.

With respect to our theoretical perspective, we take technology as the key variable for explaining the nature of the industrial city. Technology involves the tools, the sources of energy, and the know-how connected with the use of both tools and energy that a social system employs. Industrialization is that kind of technology that relies on inanimate energy sources, highly complex tools and the specialized know-how required to tap those power sources and utilize these advanced tools.

Sociologists tend to use the concept "technology" uncritically. Our conceptualization diverges from most in that it incorporates the notion of "know-how"—thereby making science, or the scientific method, an essential ingredient of modern industrial technology. Such a viewpoint sidesteps the pitfalls of a stark materialism and articulates with the current conceptual drift in social science. Unlike researchers of a few decades ago who spoke mainly of the impact of the factory system on modern society, scholars nowadays are much more concerned with the effects of the "scientific revolution."[3] Viewed in these terms, a city with a highly specialized labor force—say, a university community harboring a large number of scientists—is highly industrialized along at least one of its dimensions.[4]

---

[2] Roger Nett, "System Building in Sociology—a Methodological Analysis," *Social Forces*, 31 (1952), pp. 25–30.

[3] Robert A. Brady, *Organization, Automation, and Society* (Berkeley: University of California Press, 1961).

[4] As employed in this essay, "technology" has several dimensions. We could perhaps simplify our analysis by using only "energy" as a

Although technology is our primary variable, we do not reject out of hand other orientations but rather use these to supplement our analysis. Certainly we cannot ignore the role of cultural values. For one thing, industrial cities, even in divergent cultural settings, share certain values.[5] But each may also display certain "unique" values that in turn are associated with differing structures. These structural differences, however, are meaningful from a scientific viewpoint only if we contrast them with the structural similarities. We must isolate, therefore, the structural similarities before we can hope to establish the cultural or stylistic differences among industrial cities.

Nor do we disregard the impact of the city on social organization, for some rural-urban differences persist even in industrial orders. So, too, if we are to explain the rise and proliferation of industrial centers, we must pay heed to the impact of social power. Because of the interplay between a society's power structure (on both the national and the international planes) and its value system, different nations follow somewhat different paths to industrial urbanization—a point stressed by Kerr and others as well as by Moore and Feldman.[6]

Yet, the impact of technology on urban social structure is our main point of departure. For purposes of analysis we distinguish among three "constructed types" of cities: the preindustrial, the transitional, and the industrial. Actually these are subsystems within broader social orders: the preindustrial civilized (or feudal), the modernizing (or developing), and the industrial, respectively. And one of our primary assumptions is that the city cannot be understood except in its relationships to the broader society of which it is a part.

Still another facet of our theoretical orientation requires clarification: in our examination of the key structural arrangements of industrial cities we adhere to a structural-functional

variable. For such an approach, see Fred Cottrell, *Energy and Society* (New York: McGraw-Hill, 1955). Even so, we could not ignore the dimension of "know-how."

[5] See Alex Inkeles, "Industrial Man: The Relation of Status to Experience, Perception, and Value," *American Journal of Sociology,* 66 (1960), pp. 1–31.

[6] Clark Kerr, John T. Dunlop, Frederick Harbison, and Charles Myers, *Industrialism and Industrial Man* (Cambridge: Harvard University Press, 1960); Wilbert E. Moore and Arnold S. Feldman (Eds.), *Labor Commitment and Social Change in Developing Areas* (New York: Social Science Research Council, 1960).

frame of reference—with significant modifications.[7] We recognize that alternative structures may serve given "imperatives."[8] However, the number of such alternatives is far from infinite; there are some limits to the kinds of structural arrangements that can obtain. At times we can more easily assess these limits than determine the particular structure a system requires for its operation. The negative case approach is especially useful for establishing these structural limits. Nor can we ignore the dilemma posed by structural-functional theorizing. For though a given structure may be "imperative" for the functioning of an industrial city, this same structure may depend on industrialization for its existence. This is true of advanced or specialized education, for example.[9]

Above all, we incorporate into our theoretical framework the concepts of "contradictory structures" and "contradictory functional requirements."[10] By and large, structural-functionalists have stressed the matter of internal integration in social orders; some see it as essential for a society's maintenance or "survival." But to us, recognition of the coexistence of antagonistic structures, and even their essentiality for the maintenance of the system, is empirically more realistic.

THE PREINDUSTRIAL CITY[11]

Until barely two centuries ago all cities were of the preindustrial type. From the time they arose approximately five and a half millennia ago in the Mesopotamian riverine area, they spread outward until they spanned much of the globe, forming the nuclei of preindustrial civilized societies.

[7] Structural-functional analysis has been subjected to sharp attack in recent years for its "teleological bias." See Carl G. Hempel, "The Logic of Functional Analysis," in Llewellyn Gross (Ed.), *Symposium on Sociological Theory* (Evanston: Row, Peterson, 1959), pp. 271–310. But Hempel takes a reductionist position, denying that the "collectivity" is more than the sum of its parts. But such actors as key decision-makers in modern societies think and act *as if* a social system were teleologically oriented.

[8] Although some writers draw the fine distinctions among the terms "imperatives," "requisites," and "prerequisites," these concepts are employed synonymously herein.

[9] For a critical analysis of the idea of "prerequisites of modern industrialization," see Alexander Gerschenkron, *Economic Backwardness in Historical Perspective* (Cambridge: Belknap Press, 1962), Chap. 2.

[10] Gideon Sjoberg, "Contradictory Functional Requirements and Social Systems," *Journal of Conflict Resolution*, 4 (1960), pp. 198–208.

[11] For a detailed analysis, see Gideon Sjoberg, *The Preindustrial City: Past and Present* (New York: Free Press of Glencoe, 1960).

Of the cities that flourished before the spread of industrialization, few attained populations of over 100,000, and many sheltered fewer than 10,000 persons. Moreover, subjected as they have been to the vagaries of nature and the instabilities of the political systems supporting them, preindustrial cities have fluctuated considerably in size over time. Yet, over broad regions and in diverse social orders their *structural* characteristics have remained more or less the same, whereas their specific cultural content has varied widely.

Preindustrial cities have always functioned primarily as governmental and religious centers, and only secondarily as commercial establishments. As to the internal spatial structure, the elite typically has resided in or near the center, with the lower class and outcaste groups fanning out toward the periphery. Added to this ecological differentiation in terms of class are land-use patterns reflecting occupational and ethnic distinctions. Typically, each occupational group lives and works in a particular street or quarter, one that frequently bears the name of the trade in question. And ethnic groups form relatively self-contained subsystems that frequently are spatially isolated from one another. Yet despite the high degree of socioeconomic differentiation, a minimum of specialization in land use is the rule: a single site frequently serves multiple functions.

With respect to the preindustrial city's social structure, the effects of social class tend to be all-pervasive. The small upper class, readily identifiable by its distinctive garb, speech, and personal mannerisms, controls the key organizational units of government, religion, and education. This privileged group—whose locus is mainly urban rather than rural—dominates not just the cityscape but the entire preindustrial civilized society. In striking contrast to the elite is the vast bulk of the populace. Though these two broad groups evince internal gradations of status, the wide gap between the elite and the lower class is the most obvious feature of the stratification system. The lower class includes both the urban commoners and the rural peasantry. Standing apart from and below this lower class are the outcastes, whose locus is primarily urban, and whose chief function is carrying out activities that are essential to the continuance of the system yet clearly outside the pale of respectability. Some mobility occurs among the several strata, including some movement between the lower class and the elite, as a result of shifting political fortunes, contradictory structural arrangements, and the like, but from the purview of the individual actor this mobility seems slight indeed.

The revered societal forms in feudal orders reach their fullest flowering within the urban upper class. This group sets the standards for the entire society. For example, the preindustrial urbanite functions within a family system to which he must subordinate his own interests. Consequently marriages are familial rather than individual arrangements. The large, extended family, with numerous relatives residing within a single "household" and functioning more or less as a social and economic unit, is the urban ideal. But preserving close ties among family members and keeping the entire unit under a single "roof" is generally possible only for the elite. Economic circumstances prevent the urban poor and the peasantry alike from maintaining such households; for them the *famille souche* is the more usual form. Families in the lower strata, existing within a "culture of poverty" and having higher morbidity and mortality rates, are more unstable and fragile than upper-class families.

Within the urban elite family the men lord it over their womenfolk. "Respectable" women are isolated from many facets of community life, whereas women of the urban lower class play a far more salient role in the family and the community. But almost everywhere in feudal societies it is the rural woman who enjoys the most freedom.

The family is the primary socializing agency in the community and serves for women and children, and to a lesser degree for men, as the focus of leisure-time activity. More significantly, given the relatively limited social mobility, one's family becomes the chief determinant of one's occupational position. The society's leaders, bureaucratic personnel, and most craftsmen are recruited primarily on the basis of kinship and other particularistic ties.

By industrial standards the technology and the economic organization of the preindustrial city are simple. Commercial activities, manual labor, or "practical pursuits" in general are depreciated and shunned by the elite. Except for a few large-scale merchants, persons engaged in commerce or the crafts belong to the lower class or the outcaste group.

Within the economic realm the main unit is the guild, typically a community-bound organization. Through the guilds, handicraftsmen, merchants, and members of various service occupations seek to minimize competition, determine standards and prices, and control the recruitment and training of personnel in their particular economic activity.

From the viewpoint of the industrial-urban order, the production of goods and services depends on a division of labor that involves little specialization of knowledge. The craftsman performs all or most of the steps in the fashioning of an article and often also markets it himself. Thus we find relatively little standardization of process in manufacturing; rather, specialization is according to product.

So too in commerce a modicum of standardization exists in prices, currency, weights and measures, and in the grading of commodities. In the main the price of an item is fixed through haggling between individual buyers and sellers. Different systems of currency may be in use at a given moment, even in a single community or region; similarly, weights and measures frequently vary among crafts and markets within a city. On top of this, the widespread adulteration of goods impedes standardization in production and marketing.

Economic development is inhibited by the educated stratum's negation of business activity and work with the hands, the paucity of standardization, and the meager facilities for credit and capital formation. All of these tend to slow technological innovation and, conversely, the inadequacies of the technology hinder advance in the broader economic realm.

As for the political system, we find the upper class in command of the key governmental posts. The political apparatus tends to be strongly centralized, with the chief provincial and local administrators (some of whom share kinship ties with the societal ruler) being personally accountable to the leaders in the capital. Although the sovereign exercises autocratic powers, countervailing forces mean that the "absolute despotism" posited by Wittfogel is never really attained.[12]

The authority of the ruling group and the bureaucracies it commands rests upon appeals to tradition and to absolutes. As in the educational and religious spheres, the political bureaucracy is characterized by rigid hierarchical arrangements. However, the lines of authority tend to be imprecise. As a result, decisions are arrived at more in terms of the incumbent's personal prestige than in accordance with any set of impersonal rules. The office, in other words, is largely a function of the "person." This pattern is reinforced because bureaucracies usually select their key personnel and serve their

[12] Karl A. Wittfogel, *Oriental Despotism* (New Haven: Yale University Press, 1957).

clientele according to particularistic criteria. These norms, combined with the lack of a fixed salary system, provide a favorable climate for "graft" and similar activities whereby bureaucrats supplement their earnings by extracting gratuities for the services they perform. This pattern is an accepted and legitimate part of the normative order.

Like the political structure, the bureaucracy supporting religious values is a potent integrative and stabilizing mechanism. The highly prescriptive norms control numerous facets of the urbanite's everyday existence. The religious personnel and their functions and beliefs exhibit the same tripartite (elite, lower class, outcaste) division that is so apparent in other realms of activity in the preindustrial-urban order. Members of the upper class command the key posts in the religious hierarchy and are the most faithful adherents to the ideal religious norms. Consequently, the preindustrial city, though it is in one sense a focus of change, is also the chief bastion of orthodoxy.

Magic also plays a vital role in the preindustrial city, for in this setting man seeks not to remake the natural and social order but rather to adjust to it, and to do so he resorts to a variety of magical practices. Protective magic serves to maintain the world on an even keel; restorative magic attempts to right it when it goes awry; and through predictive magic one seeks to determine how to avoid disturbing the natural equilibrium in the future.

The formal educational structure, serving primarily the elite and usually only males, does much to perpetuate this magicoreligious heritage. The traditional learning is overwhelmingly of the religious-philosophical variety and tends to be standardized over time and space. It is because the upper class acquires this common body of ideas and knowledge that it is far more homogeneous than the lower class. This pattern reinforces and sustains the elite's privileged position in the social order.

Experimental science, wherein abstract thought is coherent with practical knowledge, and through which man endeavors to manipulate the natural order (both physical and social), is almost absent in the traditional society. The existent technology is perpetuated primarily by the lower class and is only slowly enhanced. The educated minds that could fertilize these seeds of knowledge have been narrowly attuned to the traditional learning, which must not be questioned and revised. The elite's avoidance of practical pursuits and work with the hands has further sundered the theoretical aspects of knowl-

edge from the practical. It was only in the centuries just prior
to the Industrial Revolution in Europe that the two coexisting
traditions merged, giving birth to modern science and the
industrial-urban order.

The foregoing typology is offered not as an end in itself but
rather as a basis for deriving hypotheses about existing cities
that are still largely preindustrial. And our constructed type
provides a reference point for analyzing modernizing and industrial cities. Obviously its utility can be tested only within
the crucible of research experience.

THE INDUSTRIALIZING CITY

Cities in traditional civilized orders do not undergo any sudden and complete transformation into the industrial form. As
transitional cities, they are partly industrial, partly preindustrial in character. (We could obviously distinguish among
types of transitional cities—for example, those that are largely
the products of Western colonial rule, such as Calcutta or
Shanghai, and those that are indigenous to the preindustrial
civilized order. Although such types are worthy of detailed
consideration, we cannot examine them here.)

In our analysis of the industrializing city, we are obliged to
stress social *processes* rather than form or structure, which is
the focus of our attention in sections devoted to preindustrial
and industrial cities.

Reasons for, and Patterning of, Industrial Urbanization

Sociologists who study transitional cities in such areas as
Africa and Asia soon encounter two major questions: (1)
Why is the society to which these cities belong so anxious to
industrialize? (2) How does it seek to attain this goal?

Nowadays most nations, large and small, are striving to
achieve a higher degree of industrial urbanization. Indeed,
some countries are taxing all their resources to achieve this
goal. A prime motivation is the desire to attain "the good life,"
with freedom and plenty for all, but apparently more compelling is the struggle among nations for power and status. The
societies that enjoy high prestige, and are emulated by others,
are usually those that wield political and military advantage,
and this depends on an advanced industrial-urban base in today's world. Social orders farther down the scale that have
recently thrown off the colonial yoke have set their sights on
imitating the powerful nations. Most significant of all is the

fact that societal rulers are implementing such policies even at the expense of the traditional authority structure that supports their own power position. They recognize that unless the society industrializes and urbanizes, it may revert to its former colonial status, a possibility that is so repugnant that industrial urbanization becomes the lesser of the evils.

Social scientists' knowledge of the power structure in the traditional society and its effects upon industrial-urban development is all too meager. We must learn more about the relationships among a country's resource base, its political organization, and industrial urbanization.[13] A common research focus for students of the city—sociologists, anthropologists, economists, historians, and political scientists—is the differential impact upon industrial urbanization of various power structures and ideologies.[14] The rate of industrial-urban growth and the social structure of transitional cities appear to differ in "totalitarian" and in "democratic" societies. Those modernizing nations that adopt the Communist model are more prone, or so it seems, to stress heavy industry than are nations that seek inspiration from the democratic model. The latter are likely to emphasize light industry—attempting even to salvage or sustain the earlier handicraft orientation—and are much less intent upon revising the traditional social structure.[15]

Nations committed to some variant on the democratic model also tend to differ markedly from totalitarian ones in their ideology concerning which groups are to bear the "human cost" of industrial urbanization. The Communists, certainly in the U. S. S. R., have called upon the traditional elite and the peasantry to assume a disproportionately heavy share of the burden.[16] They have also sought, via political con-

[13] One proposition in particular needs to be tested: If a nation cannot draw upon a varied and complex resource base, it must resort to some kind of "colonialism" to further its industrial urbanization. For suggestive leads on this problem, see George W. Barclay, *Colonial Development and Population in Taiwan* (Princeton: Princeton University Press, 1954), and K. Berrill, "International Trade and the Rate of Economic Growth," *Economic History Review*, 12 (1960), pp. 351–359.

[14] See Francis Seton, "Planning and Economic Growth," *Soviet Survey*, No. 31 (1960), pp. 38–44; John Kenneth Galbraith, "The Poverty of Nations," *Atlantic Monthly*, 210 (1962), pp. 47–53; Gerschenkron, *op. cit.*; Morton A. Kaplan (Ed.), *The Revolution in World Politics* (New York: Wiley, 1962).

[15] Galbraith, *op. cit.*

[16] Barrington Moore, Jr., *Terror and Progress: USSR* (Cambridge: Harvard University Press, 1954).

trols, to suppress the wants of urban consumers, whose expectations would otherwise rise very rapidly.[17] The leaders believe that capital should be channeled toward large-scale industrial enterprises and used to advance scientific knowhow. In contrast, the democratic model ideally seeks to equalize the cost of industrial urbanization among the various classes, and it gives greater attention to rising consumer demands, but this in turn fosters a "revolution of rising expectations"; and when these expectations cannot be met political turmoil is likely to result.

The contrast we describe between the totalitarian and the democratic models is admittedly somewhat overdrawn. Some totalitarian regimes (for example, that of Peron in Argentina) have sought to further industrial urbanization while catering to the rising expectations of the urban working class. Even granting this limitation, however, the democratic and totalitarian models are a convenient basis from which to initiate research.

Urban sociologists should not overlook the forces that impede the industrial city's development. In most preindustrial civilized orders now in the throes of industrialization, considerable hostility, latent and manifest, toward the introduction of the newer urban forms is apparent on both the community and the national levels. The incipient industrial forms in the cities become targets of resentment for those who would preserve the traditional, "sacred" order. Knowledge of the sources of this anti-industrial urbanism is an urgent need, because present evidence indicates that under certain conditions they effectively slow the industrial-urban process. This is especially likely, we hypothesize, where traditional values are reinforced by a long-standing and deeply entrenched bureaucratic apparatus. The historical role of the Catholic Church in southern Europe is a case in point. The manner in which the Church has resisted, adapted to, and disseminated industrial-urban lifeways deserves intensive study. In some countries it has effectively opposed industrial urbanization; in others it has sought to mold the social structure of emergent industrial cities in conformance with its own ideology.[18] Of

---

[17] Naum Jasny, *Soviet Industrialization, 1928–1952* (Chicago: University of Chicago Press, 1961), especially Chap. 5.

[18] Although the Catholic Church has generally aligned itself with anti-industrial forces, it has also made certain adjustments to this trend. Some have been successful, some unsuccessful. See William Bosworth, *Catholicism and Crisis in Modern France* (Princeton: Princeton University Press, 1962); Emile Poulat, "La découverte de la ville par le

course, any such research would have to take into account the sharp disagreements within the Church itself over policy vis-à-vis the industrial-urban order.

More generally, a comparison of the Nazi movement in Germany, the Poujade movement in France, and the conservative reaction in Turkey after the Second World War supports the proposition that the inhabitants of small towns and villages (those most closely linked to the feudal past) have been the backbone of movements with strong anti-industrial-urban sentiments.[19] Usually these are the groups who have profited least from the industrial-urbanizing efforts of the new order; in effect, they are reacting against the new order from which they are "alienated."

Unfortunately, the attempts at analysis of industrial urbanization in modernizing societies have been riddled with unstated ideological premises. Whether consciously or not, American social scientists tend to reject industrial urbanization as an ideal for these transitional societies; instead they favor the development of moderate-size towns with handicraft industries and the preservation of many rural traditions. The fact that social scientists who hold to "democratic" ideals should implicitly oppose extensive industrial urbanization is somewhat ironical,[20] for recent research supports the hypothesis that democracy flourishes most vigorously within advanced industrial-urban societies.[21] Some constructive self-criticism by social scientists regarding their own implicit or explicit assumptions is in order.

This ideological stance, moreover, involves a question: are people better off in large metropolises or should they stay in the smaller centers, or even in the villages, making a living following the ox and the plow? The answer depends partly upon one's conception of "the good life." But of more immediate significance for us is the concept of "overurbaniza-

catholicisme français contemporain," *Annales,* 15 (1960), pp. 1168–1179; Alfred Diamont, *Austrian Catholics and the First Republic* (Princeton: Princeton University Press, 1960).

[19] See Dankwart A. Rustow, "Politics and Islam in Turkey 1920–1955," in Richard N. Frye (Ed.), *Islam and the West* (The Hague: Mouton, 1956), p. 92; S. M. Lipset, *Political Man* (Garden City: Doubleday, 1960), pp. 145–146; Jacques Fauvet and Henri Mendras, *Les Paysans et la Politique,* Cahiers de la Fondation Nationale des Sciences Politiques, No. 94 (Paris: Armand Colin, 1958).

[20] There are exceptions to this pattern. See W. W. Rostow, *The Stages of Economic Growth: A Non-Communist Manifesto* (New York: Cambridge University Press, 1960).

[21] Lipset, *op. cit.,* Chap. 2.

tion" used generally by social scientists who view the burgeoning of large cities as an impediment to optimum economic development. Some of these writers feel that large metropolises are not only inefficient but that they also inevitably breed slums, disease, and poverty. That these conditions do exist in cities in many modernizing countries can hardly be denied.[22]

However, these fundamentally anti-urban views are deserving of searching criticism, for city dwellers in most modernizing countries enjoy many economic, educational, and other social advantages over ruralites. Consider the economic dimension. Urbanites are the greatest beneficiaries of the few welfare programs that exist in these societies. The fact that ruralites continue to flock to the large cities—in India, Egypt, Greece, Mexico, and elsewhere—suggests that the urban communities are providing these people with certain advantages not found in the villages.[23]

American social scientists are perhaps misled by the greater concentration and higher visibility of poverty in the city; the misery of the countryside, though often greater, is inevitably more diffuse and less transparent. Actually, the high visibility of urban problems encourages the formulation of programs to cope with the "ills" that beset transitional societies, thereby intensifying the industrial-urbanization process. And from a long-run perspective, the inhabitants of large cities are more likely to acquire the skills and values of the emerging industrial system than are people who live in small towns or villages.

Barring nuclear warfare, industrial-urban forms are likely to proliferate at an increasing rate. If sociologists persist in their anti-urban tendencies they will be ill-equipped to generalize concerning the vast urban agglomerations of the future that Davis predicts will encompass tens of millions of people.[24] They must admit the possibility of the emergence in these metropolises of novel social and ecological patterns.

[22] A convenient summary of some of the data on Indian cities can be found in Bert F. Hoselitz, "Indian Cities: The Surveys of Calcutta, Kanpur and Jamshedpur," *Economic Weekly*, 13 (1961), pp. 1071–1078.
[23] See Vasant P. Pethe, "Congestion and Over-Crowding in Cities and Towns: A Scrutiny of Some Popular Beliefs," *Asian Economic Review*, 3 (1960), pp. 1–11; Doris G. Phillips, "Rural-to-Urban Migration in Iraq," *Economic Development and Cultural Change*, 7 (1959), pp. 405–421; Dimas Maulit, "Income Ratio Between Rural and Urban Workers in the Philippines," *Economic Research Journal*, 6 (1959), pp. 83–95.
[24] Kingsley Davis, "Urbanization in India: Past and Future," in Roy Turner (Ed.), *India's Urban Future* (Berkeley: University of California Press, 1962), pp. 3–26.

Urban Patterns and Differential Change

Whether industrial urbanization has resulted in a broadening rather than a narrowing of the gap between rural and urban subsystems is a question open to research. Rural-urban contrasts seem to differ in Communist and in non-Communist societies, and the divergency between rural and urban communities may be greater today in some countries of Asia than it was in Western Europe in the nineteenth century. Yet, while the transitional city is importing from abroad much advanced industrial-urban know-how that is intensifying its differentiation from the village, the latter is more than ever before being influenced by mass media, thereby reducing to a degree the gap between city and country. In any event, marked differences between villages and cities persist in developing societies. Consequently, one urgent research need is to examine the means by which ruralites, and preindustrial urbanites, adjust to the modernizing city. To appreciate this process we must understand the changing structure of this kind of city.

We might begin with the general proposition that different elements of the transitional city's social structure change at different rates: those traditional arrangements most closely associated with the economic-technological order seem to buckle first under the impact of industrial urbanization. More specifically, we observe the following processes occurring more or less simultaneously: (1) the persistence of traditional forms, (2) revision or modification of traditional forms, (3) disappearance of traditional forms, and (4) emergence of new structures.

Although much has been written of the tenacity of traditional patterns in modernizing cities, surprisingly few cross-cultural generalizations have been formulated. We are unable to state with confidence which traditional structures are most likely to persist in cities in divergent cultural settings; we sorely need this information.

The most obvious pattern is the reshaping of preindustrial forms—familial, economic, political, and so on—to accord with the needs of the emerging industrial-urban system.[25] Many

[25] See Bertram Hutchinson et al., *Mobilidade e Trabalho: Um Estudo na Cidade de São Paulo* (Rio de Janeiro: Centro Brasileiro do Pesquisas Educacionais, 1960); Donald Willmott, *The Chinese of Semarang: A Changing Minority Community in Indonesia* (Ithaca: Cornell University Press, 1960); Aileen D. Ross, *The Hindu Family in its Urban Setting* (Toronto: University of Toronto Press, 1961). Although much re-

of these structures are tending toward the industrial model discussed later. Even special types of organizations evince patterns of this sort. In India some facets of the traditional caste system are dying out, whereas others are being remolded along extracommunity lines and are acquiring new and novel functions. The castes, for example, serve as special interest groups in the political arena on both the regional and the national levels.[26] Vogel contends that the marriage broker in Japan plays a more critical role in the transitional order than he did in the preindustrial setting, for his is a key accommodative mechanism between the older patterns and the new.[27]

Some of these changes may generate "ruptures" in segments of the urban social structure and, from the actor's perspective, his social environment may lack integration. It is not uncommon for hiatuses to develop between the newer urban ideals and the institutionalized means available for their achievement. This occurs in marriage patterns in many transitional societies. On the basis of his research in a Tokyo ward, Dore contends that young people consider romantic love as an ideal in courtship and marriage; yet no satisfactory structural means has developed to make this goal attainable.[28] Similar patterns appear in the economic realm. People in industrializing cities are being socialized into certain ideals, especially a high standard of living, that are still unattainable. The result is political and social unrest.

Another dimension of social change in transitional cities is the matter of class. Though it exhibits considerable fluidity and ambiguity, the class structure is typified by a yawning gap between the upper and lower socioeconomic levels.[29] The

search on transitional cities is still to be carried out, we have reached the point where a systematic evaluation of current data is mandatory.

[26] See Selig Harrison, *India: The Most Dangerous Decades* (Princeton: Princeton University Press, 1960); M. N. Srinivas, *Caste in Modern India* (London: Asia Publishing House, 1962), Chaps. 1 and 6; and various articles in the special issue of the *Sociological Bulletin*, 11 (1961), on the "Nature and Extent of Social Change in India."

[27] Ezra Vogel, "The Go-Between in a Developing Society: The Case of the Japanese Marriage Arranger," *Human Organization*, 20 (1961), pp. 112–120.

[28] Ronald P. Dore, *City Life in Japan* (Berkeley: University of California Press, 1958), p. 170.

[29] For data that bear upon this argument, see Hutchinson, *op. cit.*, and J. C. Olivé Negrete and B. Barba de Piña Chán, "Estudio de las clases sociales en la Ciudad de México," *Anales del Instituto Nacional de Antropología e Historia*, 14 (1962), pp. 219–262.

elite's close involvement with the formal educational structure, which disseminates the knowledge emanating from science and the new technology, means that this class is usually the first to assimilate the new industrial-urban forms. Some of its members have been educated abroad, in advanced industrial-urban settings. Nevertheless, many of them cling to traditional ways that are not easily obliterated. A vexing dilemma for many modernizing countries is how to socialize educated persons into accepting "work with the hands" as a dignified rather than degrading activity. The leaders in China have made intensive efforts to induce "intellectuals" to share in tasks demanding physical labor; one method is insistence upon physical exercise sessions for scientists, students, and the like to rid them of so-called "archaic" values.[30] Government planners in India, too, are distressed by the educated man's aversion to practical pursuits, work with the hands, and entrepreneurship, all of which are essential for industrial urbanization.[31] Indeed, in many societies certain elements of the traditional elite have been the most fervent opponents of industrial urbanization. The bases for the upper socioeconomic group's acceptance or rejection of industrial-urban forms merit detailed investigation.

The adaptation of the lower strata to the emerging industrial-urban milieu is an even more complex matter. Some studies suggest that lower-class persons in the cities and in the villages are striving to attain traditional ideals at the very time that the higher groups are rejecting them and are moving toward the industrial-urban forms. Thanks to the indirect subsidy of industrialization, the common man is now able to realize certain traditional ideals that he could not achieve in the past. From this perspective, industrial urbanization may well breed conservatism. While many Indians in the upper strata are discarding features of the traditional Sanskritized culture, various disadvantaged groups, their lot improved somewhat by industrial progress, are bent on acquiring at long last some of the traditional ideals; this is especially true of certain older family and religious values, and even those relating to caste.[32]

[30] Tuzo Wilson, *One Chinese Moon* (New York: Hill and Wang, 1959), p. 80.

[31] See K. M. Munshi, *The Gospel of the Dirty Hand* (Delhi: Government of India, 1952).

[32] See Bernard S. Cohn, "Changing Traditions of a Low Caste," *Journal of American Folklore,* 71 (1958), pp. 413–421; A. P. Barnabas, "Sanskritisation," *Economic Weekly,* 13 (1961), pp. 613–618.

As Friedl has observed, contemporary Greek villagers still take the preindustrial city model as their reference point; in the meantime the cities of Greece are modernizing and industrializing.[33]

Yet certain forces contravene this pattern. Modern mass media can directly and rapidly socialize the common man into the industrial-urban way of life. Communist regimes purposively utilize movies, the theater, newspapers, and so on to this end.[34] In nations having close contacts with highly industrial-urban orders such as Mexico vis-à-vis the United States, some lower-class urbanites are bypassing the traditional forms, moving directly toward the industrial-urban ideals.[35]

Minority groups in many transitional cities present a special problem; the traditional outcaste groups are the most notable example. On the other hand, the emerging values generally call for greater equality of opportunity, thus setting in motion forces that undermine the long-perpetuated segregation of minority or outcaste elements. On the other hand, it is often easier for members of minorities to climb within the broader society by identifying with their respective groups than by functioning as lone individuals. In some modernizing societies minorities are given preferential treatment in the political and educational spheres as a means of advancing the ideals of democracy. Thus, the Harijans, or Outcastes, in India are nowadays accorded special advantages to assist them in overcoming their lowly status.[36]

Ultimately we are led back to an examination of the formal and informal organizations through which persons are enabled to adapt to the industrializing urban milieu. Sociologists and anthropologists have come to recognize that newcomers to the city do not function as isolated individuals; rather, they identify with earlier in-migrants from their own village or region and/or persons of the same class, ethnic, or occupational grouping.[37] The enclaves that arise as a result of these similar

[33] Ernestine Friedl, "Lagging Emulation in Post-Peasant Society: A Greek Case," *American Anthropologist,* 66 (1964), pp. 569–586.

[34] See Frederick T. C. Yu, "Communications and Politics in Communist China," in Lucian W. Pye (Ed.), *Communications and Political Development* (Princeton: Princeton University Press, 1963), Chap. 16.

[35] Oscar Lewis, *The Children of Sánchez* (New York: Random House, 1961). Some data on the impact of the mass media on lower socioeconomic groups can be found in Daniel Lerner, *The Passing of Traditional Society* (New York: Free Press of Glencoe, 1958).

[36] Harrison, *op. cit.*

[37] See Janet Abu-Lughod, "Migrant Adjustment to City Life: The Egyptian Case," *American Journal of Sociology,* 67 (1961), pp. 22–32;

interests or cultural backgrounds are analogous to the immigrant communities that were typical of American cities some decades ago.[38]

These subsystems in transitional cities perform at least three major functions: (1) Through them the migrant from the village or from another city is oriented to the new and complex urban milieu. Often composed of relatives or acquaintances of the newcomer, the members of these subsystems indoctrinate him into the unfamiliar lifeways and provide him with at least a modicum of knowledge concerning such essentials as how to secure employment and how to avoid arrest. Moreover, it is through these informal subsystems that the newcomer gains access to formal organizations such as schools and unions, which assist him in adapting to the demands of the industrializing city. (2) These informal subsystems are the prime means by which the urbanite sustains ties with the rural traditions. Frequently these groupings sponsor ceremonies whereby the past is re-created and thus perpetuated. (3) It is through these urban groupings that elements of industrial-urban lifeways are carried back to the villages. Some of this knowledge is diffused via the visiting patterns that arise between the rural villagers and out-migrants who have moved to the city.

The Role of Tradition

Analysis of the aforementioned patterns leads us to a strategic question: are these internally integrated subcommunities functional or dysfunctional to the industrial-urban process? Generalizing from his findings in Turkey, Suzuki argues that these kinds of subsystems perform a positive function in furthering industrialization.[39] He argues that the social stability that derives from membership in them makes for a more efficient and effective labor force. On the other hand, some

---

Peter Suzuki, "Village Solidarity Among Turkish Peasants Undergoing Urbanization," *Science*, 132 (1960), pp. 891–892; Donald Petesch, "Mexican Urban Ecology," unpublished M.A. thesis, University of Texas, 1960, pp. 200ff.; Edward M. Bruner, "Medan: The Role of Kinship in an Indonesian City," to be published in Alexander Spoehr (Ed.), *Pacific Port Towns and Cities;* Robert B. Textor, *From Peasant to Pedicab Driver,* Cultural Report Series No. 9 (New Haven: Yale University, Southeast Asia Studies, 1961). Textor, in particular, points up the fragile nature of the organization among some of the urban in-migrants.

[38] See John MacDonald and Beatrice D. MacDonald, "Urbanization, Ethnic Groups, and Social Relationships," *Social Research*, 29 (1962), pp. 433–448.

[39] Suzuki, *op. cit.*

scholars contend that integrated subcommunities which sustain ties with the rural past are an impediment to industrial urbanization.[40] Thus, in many cases the in-migrant's prime loyalty is to his village; so too, the lifelong urbanite may be firmly attached to traditional groupings whose structural links are with the preindustrial way of life. In either case, the members of these subgroups are oriented more to the past than to the future; as such, they tend to resist the goals and values of the emergent industrial-urban order.

The aforementioned controversy results in part from the divergent frames of reference employed by social researchers. Some sociologists study industrial urbanization from the standpoint of the individual and his subgroup, whereas others view this process from the perspective of the total society. Suzuki belongs in the first category, for he neglected to place his subcommunity in the context of the broader Turkish society. He also failed to state explicitly that the community in which he did his research was semi-industrial in nature.

The kinds of subcommunities about which Suzuki wrote have a role to play, but they cannot possibly train and socialize the labor force required to build and sustain a complex industrial city. For this purpose complex, large-scale organizations—for example, formal education media supported by the state—become imperative. Moreover, a society bent on constructing an advanced industrial-urban order must sever most of its ties with the feudal past, although some links with tradition may be essential.

We cannot possibly understand or predict the future course of transitional cities if we do not examine them in their broader societal context. Organizations are being created in many of today's societies for the purpose of rupturing the urbanite's past allegiances and hastening the adoption of industrial-urban forms. In Russia, the Communist Party and the labor unions have been prime vehicles for instilling in workers the norms of discipline, punctuality, and efficiency. In China, the Party as well as the urban communes have been employed to socialize native urbanites *and* newcomers to the city into the desired norms, including those of health and sani-

---

[40] Galbraith, *op. cit.;* Bert Hoselitz, "Urbanization in India," *Kyklos,* 13 (1960), p. 369; Scarlett Epstein, "Industrial Employment for Landless Labourers Only," *Economic Weekly,* 11 (1959), pp. 967–974; Srinivas, *op. cit.;* Arthur Niehoff, *Factory Workers in India,* Publications in Anthropology, No. 5 (Milwaukee: Milwaukee Public Museum, 1959).

tation.[41] One can picture the Party leaders regularly haranguing the workers with speeches and slogans calling for greater and greater effort. Even in India the labor unions are an important channel through which the urban factory worker is indoctrinated into his role.[42] In all modernizing societies, of course, the formal educational structure is the prime medium for socializing urbanites into the new industrial way of life.

Just as some societal structures foster change, so others help the urbanite sustain some ties with the past. We have already indicated how certain local community organizations may serve this end. The role of the national government in maintaining continuity is easier to overlook. Here charismatic leaders are especially vital. If sociologists are to interpret correctly the transformation of preindustrial cities, they cannot ignore the function of nationalism.[43] For this ideology calls for a glorification of the society's heritage, its history and traditions.[44] Such idealization of the past provides people with a sense of belonging and a feeling of continuity, making it easier for them to shed much of the preindustrial organization and to adopt new structural forms. The Russian leaders, in particular, have purposively encouraged resuscitation of the art, literature, and music of the Turkic peoples of Soviet Central Asia at the very time they have been striving to destroy these groups' traditional economic, political, familial, and religious organizations. In Communist China, too, the leaders are encouraging the revival of the folk arts. Even in India, folk art, music, and literature are gaining in prestige and favor as the preindustrial structure undergoes fundamental change. One consequence of this pattern is the resurgence of traditional ceremonies that have lost their former functions and "content" and thus can readily be adapted to new ideologies.

[41] Shih Ch'eng-chih, *Urban Commune Experiments in Communist China* (Hong Kong: Union Research Institute, 1962).

[42] Morris David Morris, "Labor Discipline, Trade-Unions, and the State in India," *Journal of Political Economy*, 63 (1955), pp. 293–308; Karl de Schweinitz, Jr., "Industrialization, Labor Controls, and Democracy," *Economic Development and Cultural Change*, 7 (1959), pp. 385–404.

[43] See Gideon Sjoberg, "Political Structure, Ideology, and Economic Development," The Carnegie Faculty Seminar on Political and Administrative Development (Bloomington: Department of Government, Indiana University, 1963), for an argument to the effect that the charismatic leader and his ideology are necessary conditions for *rapid* industrial urbanization.

[44] See "Folk Dances," *The Hindu*, January 31, 1957, p. 10; Felix Greene, *China* (New York: Ballantine Books, 1962), pp. 231ff.

This search for stability and continuity—the fact that during rapid industrialization urbanites require some link with the past—points up certain contradictory functional imperatives whose theoretical and empirical ramifications have not been explored by sociologists, urban or otherwise. To further revolutionary change, a social order must sustain or revive certain traditions. But just where the balance lies between rapid change and continuity is exceedingly difficult to determine, except in extreme instances.

THE INDUSTRIAL CITY

In our treatment of the transitional city, we have discussed the main problems relating to research on the processes of change from the preindustrial to the industrial type. We can now delineate the key issues concerning investigation of the social structure of the industrial city, the form toward which the transitional city is moving.

Ecology

Systematic efforts to examine cross-culturally the spatial organization of industrial cities are virtually nonexistent. This holds for the relationship of cities to their hinterland (including other cities) and for their internal arrangements as well. Without a doubt, the efforts to rectify this situation in urban sociology deserve high priority, for an impressive body of research materials on the subject has accumulated. Although the data on cities in Germany, England, France, Japan, the United States, and so on, are not strictly comparable since the levels of industrialization differ, they can provide the basis for some major advances in urban sociology.

The existing propositions concerning urban dominance must be examined cross-culturally.[45] Those who study the industrial city and its relationships to its hinterland must come to grips with the proposition that advanced industrial-urban systems require some all-encompassing political superstructure if they are to achieve economic and social stability and attain the goals implicit in industrial urbanization. The Common Market is one such superstructure.

On the matter of spatial arrangements *within* industrial cit-

---

[45] Some of these can be found in Otis Dudley Duncan et al., *Metropolis and Region* (Baltimore: Johns Hopkins Press, 1960).

ies, we can offer certain generalizations that can serve as a guide for research.[46] Industrial cities, in contrast to preindustrial ones, are more likely to revolve about a commercial and/ or industrial focus than around a religious-governmental complex. (The larger political capitals in industrial orders tend to be exceptions to this pattern.) Symbolically as well as physically, the typical industrial city's commercial and industrial edifices tower over those of government and religion.

Industrial cities exhibit a high degree of specialization in land use. Unlike the situation in preindustrial centers, residential and occupational sites in the industrial milieu tend to be separated. The continual outward expansion of suburbs in the modern metropolis is one expression of this trend. In marked contrast to the privileged class in preindustrial and modernizing societies, the upper and middle socioeconomic groups in the industrial city tend to reside beyond the city's core, leaving the central area to various low-status groups, and elements of the elite as well.

In many European cities, including those in the U. S. S. R., the persistence of the feudal tradition has inhibited suburbanization because high status has attached to residence in the central city. Contrast this with the pattern in American cities, which lack a feudal heritage. Still, suburbanization in Europe is proceeding relentlessly, hand-in-hand with the diffusion of the "automobile culture." As new residential suburbs arise, a variety of shops and services springs up in the area. Specific types of businesses no longer concentrate in a narrowly defined sector of the city.

The residence patterns of the industrial city's status groups are not so clearly distinguishable as those in the preindustrial context. Just as the lines between classes, ethnic minorities, and occupations are less clearly drawn in the industrial-urban milieu, so too they are much less obvious spatially. But what about the many studies pointing to "islands of segregation" in

---

[46] André Cornette, "Arras et sa banlieue," *Revue du Nord,* 42 (1960), pp. 9–137; Jean Daric, "La localisation de quelques professions liberales dans Paris et le Departement de la Seine," *Population,* 8 (1953), pp. 555–578; P. H. Chombart de Lauwe et al., *Paris et l'Agglomération Parisienne* (Paris: Presses Universitaires de France, 1952); P. Gourou, "L'agglomération bruxelloise," *Bulletin de la Société Royale Belge de Géographie,* 82 (1958), pp. 3–83; René Lebeau, "Zurich, métropole de la Suisse," *Revue de Géographie de Lyon,* 35 (1960), pp. 7–47; Rainer Mackensen et al., *Daseinsformen der Grosstadt* (Tubingen: Mohr, 1959), and other sources cited in the original article.

highly industrialized cities?[47] These cases dramatize the fact that complete residential equality for all urbanites has not been attained; nor is there unlimited social and spatial mobility. With some exceptions, such as the Negroes in America, these enclaves are fewer and less isolated today than in the past, for advancing industrialization has drawn various "minority groups" increasingly into the mainstream of community activity. Looking to the future, we can expect some forces for neighborliness and exclusiveness to persist in the industrial city. While some kinds of spatial segregation are declining others are likely to emerge. Beyond this we cannot safely make any predictions about these new strains toward exclusiveness.

The spatial distribution of the industrial city's people and institutions is also tied to a distinctive set of values. In contrast to preindustrialites, industrial urbanites adhere far more to secular than to sacred or traditional values. Where people do hold sacred conceptions of space (for example, with respect to some historical sites), and the power structure reinforces these views, land-use change and even industrialization itself may be inhibited. Conversely, the values associated with industrialization—punctuality, efficiency, and so on—find expression in particular kinds of spatial arrangements such as newer, more effective transportation routes.

When we move beyond these limited generalizations, we encounter serious difficulties. Recent studies of industrial cities in Europe suggest that a number of common features are discernible despite certain differences among these cities. By way of illustration, consider the city's central core. As people abandon it for the suburbs, the central area is taken over by such units as specialty shops and the managerial and administrative offices of large-scale organizations.[48] By locating in the downtown area, the managers of key enterprises maximize the possibility of personal contacts with one another; such contacts are essential if they are to carry out their functions effectively. Meanwhile, industries are fanning out toward the periphery. This is true of the United States, but whether simi-

---

[47] See John Barron Mays, "Cultural Conformity in Urban Areas: An Introduction to the Crown Street Study in Liverpool," *Sociological Review*, 6 (1958), pp. 95–108; Ruth Glass, *Newcomers* (London: George Allen and Unwin, 1960); Otis Dudley Duncan and Stanley Lieberson, "Ethnic Segregation and Assimilation," *American Journal of Sociology*, 64 (1959), pp. 364–374; Albert J. Mayer and Thomas F. Hoult, *Race and Residence in Detroit* (Detroit: Institute for Urban Studies, Wayne State University, 1962).

[48] See *The Paper Metropolis, op. cit.*; Hoover and Vernon, *op. cit.*

lar kinds of industrial enterprise exhibit similar spatial patterns in cities in different societies is a question that needs to be answered.

Delineation of urban land-use patterns in modern cities is complicated by various current trends: automation, the rapid rise in the proportion of white-collar workers, the increasing amount of leisure time, and the burgeoning of urban agglomerations.[49] While some pressures push the city's boundaries ever outward, contrary forces are at work. For example, we might hypothesize that the automobile will in time "choke itself off" and thus greatly slow, or perhaps even reverse, the trend toward suburbanization.

An industrial technology both demands and makes possible new urban land-use forms. However, at the present state of our knowledge it is exceedingly difficult to determine how particular land-use patterns sustain the industrial complex. Which land-use arrangements provide "optimum" gains for the industrial city as a whole? More specifically, how much separation of work and residence is required for an industrial city to function effectively, and what are the limits of this separation?[50]

Social Differentiation and Stratification

Two facets of the stratification system in industrial cities require detailed cross-cultural study: (1) differences in the nature of the organization of various status groupings within the city, and (2) basic trends in the overall class structure.

On the first point, the evidence suggests that members of the upper socioeconomic strata are the leaders and main participants in the activities of formal organizations on both the community and the societal levels. Although persons in the upper strata also engage in informal activities, the lower status groups fall back upon them almost to the exclusion of formal associational ties. Of course, we can expect this differential to decrease with the advance of automation and education.

As for the permanency and stability of the bonds among persons in the different status groupings, the early Chicago sociologists made much of the disorganization of the lower

[49] Some of the effects of the proliferation of tertiary industries have been suggested by Jean Gottmann in *Megalopolis* (New York: Twentieth Century Fund, 1961).

[50] The extreme segregation in South African cities is a "test case" for a number of ecological propositions about industrial cities; see Leo Kuper et al., *Durban: A Study in Racial Ecology* (New York: Columbia University Press, 1958).

class and immigrant groups in the city; this was the pattern dramatized by Zorbaugh in his study of *The Gold Coast and the Slum*.[51] But Whyte and others have shown that the slum is organized in its own way.[52] Still, some sectors of the urban community are more loosely organized than others, displaying less cohesion and stability. The lower strata, in particular, enjoy much more fragile personal relationships than do persons who belong to the middle and upper classes. Poverty in itself generates uncertainty and instability. Consider the "beats" in Greenwich Village, described in a sensitive essay by Ned Polsky.[53] As a result of their withdrawal from the formal structures of industrial-urban life, they evince relatively little social integration and stability. Mention of the "beats" brings to mind the role of the rebel in industrial cities in diverse cultures. Are there standardized patterns in this realm? Although the *stilyagi* in Russian cities differ in significant respects from the "beats" in America,[54] the similar actions of youth in various industrial societies suggest the presence of some standardized patterns in the realm of deviant behavior.

Of special significance to the student of differential organization in industrial cities are numerous "mediators"—social workers, teachers, social scientists, among others. These functionaries stand between the lower-class and deviant groups on the one hand and the middle- and upper-class groups on the other. These go-betweens diffuse information to the disadvantaged elements and also seek to socialize the latter into the views of the dominant groups within the city and the broader society.

As to the overall patterning of the class structure, many social scientists posit a close association between industrial urbanization and class fluidity, whereas others detect an opposite trend—a firming up of class barriers in such highly industrialized societies as the United States and the Soviet Union.[55]

---

[51] Harvey W. Zorbaugh, *The Gold Coast and the Slum* (Chicago: University of Chicago Press, 1929).

[52] William F. Whyte, *Street Corner Society* (Chicago: University of Chicago Press, 1943); Herbert Gans, *The Urban Villagers* (New York: Free Press of Glencoe, 1962); Michael Young and Peter Willmott, *Family and Kinship in East London* (New York: Free Press of Glencoe, 1957).

[53] Ned Polsky, "The Village Beat Scene: Summer 1960," *Dissent*, 8 (1961), pp. 339–359.

[54] See Allen Kassof, "Now the Angry Young Ivans," *New York Times Magazine*, November 19, 1961, pp. 22 et passim.

[55] See Claude S. Phillips, Jr., "Class Stratification in Soviet Russia: A Bibliography Survey of Recent Literature," *Michigan Academy of Sci-*

One reason for this divergency in current theorizing is that social scientists are examining the empirical data through different conceptual lenses. Those who claim to observe trends toward greater rigidity in industrial cities often contrast observed reality with the model of a classless society, with the result that these cities appear to be class-ridden. On the other hand, social scientists who compare the class system of industrial cities with that in preindustrial centers arrive at quite different conclusions: from this perspective the industrial-urban community seems quite fluid. Further confusion arises when sociologists who are seeking to assess the changes in a society's class structure take different time periods as their reference points.[56] Add to this the fact that contradictory forces are at work within the industrial city, some encouraging greater rigidity and some discouraging it.

Yet it is clear that the industrial city's poor are neither so stiflingly poor, nor the elite so far removed from the common man, as their counterparts in preindustrial or transitional cities.[57] Nor are ethnic minorities so clearly distinguishable in the industrial-urban milieu. Although pressures to preserve ethnic ties persist, as members of minorities search for identity or use their minority group connections to ascend the social ladder, the overall structural change, as well as the value system that calls for status by achievement rather than ascription, serves to override many of the traditional patterns.

There are several dimensions to the industrial city's class system that require special attention. One significant pattern concerns the standardization of personal attributes—speech, personal mannerisms, and dress. In contrast to the preindustrial setting, these attributes are vague and amorphous. Yet urban sociologists have given little attention to the implications

ence, Arts, and Letters, 42 (1956), pp. 195–216. The divergent views concerning social class in American cities can be perceived by comparing the writings of W. Lloyd Warner, Leonard Reissman, David Riesman, C. Wright Mills, Harold E. Lasswell, Talcott Parsons, Bernard Barber, and Robert J. Lampman, among others.

[56] Cf. Alex Inkeles, "Social Stratification and Mobility in the Soviet Union: 1940–1950," *American Sociological Review*, 15 (1950), pp. 465–479; and Alex Inkeles and Raymond A. Bauer, *The Soviet Citizen* (Cambridge: Harvard University Press, 1959). It appears that Inkeles' views regarding the Soviet class system changed during the 1950's, largely because of a shift in reference points.

[57] Irving B. Kravis, "International Differences in the Distribution of Income," *Review of Economics and Statistics*, 42 (1960), pp. 408–416; and Jean Fourastié, *The Causes of Wealth*, trans. and ed. by Theodore Caplow (New York: Free Press of Glencoe, 1960).

arising from the loss of personal attributes within the secondary-group setting of large metropolitan areas. The ambiguity of these personal markers facilitates a person's escape from his class or other status identities, with multiple consequences for the social control patterns within modern cities.

Occupation is another dimension of class, or stratification more generally, that is of special interest to sociologists. Clearly, there is much more upward mobility within industrial than preindustrial cities. Moreover, the mobility patterns in the urban sector of industrial societies—at least as measured by the movement of urbanites from manual to nonmanual occupations—appear to be rather similar across national boundaries.[58] Without this individual mobility the many new occupational positions being created by the advancing technology could not be staffed. In addition, entire occupational groups continue to experience major shifts in their relative power, prestige, and monetary rewards. And automation will likely heighten this type of mobility in ways that urban sociologists must explore.[59] For example: Will the cybernetics revolution, which is eliminating many blue-collar and white-collar workers, lead, as some writers suggest, to a few intellectuals, scientists, and managers working long hours in contrast to the mass urban population, who will live in relative leisure? Or will service occupations proliferate so as to absorb those occupational groups now being eliminated from the labor force by automation, with a consequent restructuring of the class system?

But one must analyze not only the movement of individuals and groups but the supposed cross-cultural similarities of social rankings in industrial cities and societies. Some unexplained anomalies exist. The work of Inkeles and Rossi,[60] among others, indicates that in diverse industrial cities and societies leading governmental officials, professional persons (notably doctors, lawyers, and teachers), and industrial managers all

[58] Seymour M. Lipset and Reinhard Bendix, *Social Mobility in Industrial Society* (Berkeley: University of California Press, 1959).

[59] These issues are being raised largely by writers outside the mainstream of academia—for example, Peter Irons, "The Cybernation Revolution," *Progressive*, 29 (1965), pp. 18–21.

[60] Alex Inkeles and Peter H. Rossi, "National Comparisons of Occupational Prestige," *American Journal of Sociology*, 61 (1956), pp. 329–339; Melvin M. Tumin (with Arnold S. Feldman), *Social Class and Social Change in Puerto Rico* (Princeton: Princeton University Press, 1961), pp. 425ff. See also J. Clyde Mitchell and A. L. Epstein, "Occupational Prestige and Social Status Among Urban Africans in Northern Rhodesia," *Africa*, 29 (1959), pp. 22–40.

enjoy elevated social standing. The industrial-urban structure supports, and is apparently sustained by, a common core of values with respect to the ranking of occupational groups. Still, the imperatives of the industrial-urban order do not account for all the similarities, for certain high-status pursuits in industrial cities have traditionally carried high prestige in preindustrial orders as well. Apparently all large-scale social systems require that certain occupations, such as key governmental roles, enjoy elevated status. However, a number of occupational groups having low prestige in the preindustrial city—physicians, managers of manufacturing or commercial enterprises, and entertainers—have risen considerably in status under the aegis of industrialism. At the same time, some traditionally high-status occupations like the clergy and certain categories of intellectuals seem to have declined.

The patterning of the power dimension of social class is of utmost significance. The intensive specialization of occupational roles that characterizes the industrial city tends to delimit the effective dominance of ruling elites on both the local and the societal levels. The complexity of the industrial-urban order makes it impossible for those in positions of power to keep before them all pertinent facts concerning the system's manifold activities. Although he is not a manager or administrator, the highly trained specialist can exercise a degree of authority because of his monopoly of strategic information. Indeed, the acknowledged leaders in political or other spheres may become "captives" of the experts below them. Concentration of vital technical information in the hands of these specialists is furthered also by the nature of authority in a democracy; here the leaders derive their authority from "the consent of the governed."

Along with the greatly increased fluidity in the class system, certain requirements of the industrial-urban order call for some kind of stratification.[61] Sociologists in the Durkheimian tradition reason that stratification is intensified by the industrial society's complex division of labor, a feature which many sociologists believe minimizes class distinctions and reduces the ruling group's authority. Thus managers, or persons of superior prestige and power, are needed to coordinate or synchronize the activities of specialists who operate, with only

[61] For a first-rate essay on contradictory tendencies in the Soviet Union's class structure, see George Z. F. Bereday, "Class Tensions in Soviet Education," in George Z. F. Bereday and Jaan Penmar (Eds.), *The Politics of Soviet Education* (New York: Praeger, 1960), pp. 57–88.

a minimal understanding of one another's roles, on both the community and the societal levels. Extrapolating from this fact, some social scientists doubt that democracy can survive the onslaught of advanced industrialization with its demands for a managerial elite.[62]

Significantly, however, most students of ruling elites overlook the distinctive nature of leadership in industrial-urban systems. Whereas the preindustrial-urban elite rationalizes its dominance by appeal to absolutes and to tradition, the elite in industrial-urban orders depends for its self-justification upon the popular largesse. This is true of the political realm as well as the economic and cultural spheres. Since popular opinion is more capricious than are tradition and absolutes, the new elite's power and authority in various spheres of activity is far more tenuous than that enjoyed by the preindustrial system's leaders. The emergence of an elite based upon mass support, on either the community or the national levels, is deserving of more attention than it has received. Overall, sociologists have made only meager efforts to examine the contradictory structural arrangements that obtain in the class and power structure in the industrial city.

Family

Most sociologists assume that the ideal and the usual family form in mature industrial cities is the conjugal unit, as opposed to the large, extended type with members of three or more generations living under a single "roof." However, some dissenting voices have recently been heard. As noted earlier, the urban lower class and the peasantry in feudal orders have typically been unable to sustain the society's ideal of a large extended family residing within a single "household." It is this esteemed form, achievable mainly by the upper class in the cities, that is dysfunctional in the industrial-urban context.

The conjugal unit, as the ideal family type, has perhaps reached its most striking development in American cities, though it is becoming increasingly dominant in industrial cities in Great Britain, Germany, the U. S. S. R., and apparently even Japan. The industrial city's conjugal family is closely associated with heightened status and freedom for women and adolescents within the family and the community at large.

---

[62] C. Wright Mills seems to have feared industrial-urban development in the United States while apparently favoring its expansion in other societies. See his *The Power Elite* (New York: Oxford University Press, 1956).

In turn these patterns are functionally linked to other trends. One is the formation of a "youth culture" and the accompanying "social problem" of juvenile delinquency. The Russian leaders are distressed by the young "hooligans" in the cities who clearly lack dedication to Soviet ideals; Japan worries over its youthful beatniks and revolutionaries; and so on.[63] The high standard of living in industrial cities frees young people from the need to seek employment in order to eke out a livelihood and contribute to the family's earnings. Then, too, few positions can be filled by adolescents; the industrial-urban order demands of its workers more and more formal education or specialized training. Consequently, adolescents with considerable time on their hands are thrown together and left to their own devices. The mass media further sever them from the adult world and help to loosen family ties by emphasizing certain lifeways to which young people aspire.

This unfolding of a "youth culture" sets the stage for "romantic love" as a legitimized basis for marriage. Contrary to the allegations of some social scientists, romantic love as a foundation for marriage and family life is a relatively recent and unique phenomenon. Where parents no longer select mates for their offspring according to strictly social considerations, romantic love serves as the chief medium in the development of mutual understanding, particularly where the couple have quite different social backgrounds.

One of the most striking features of the industrial city concerns the role and status of women.[64] As industrialization has advanced, "respectable" women have sallied forth from

[63] See the special issue of *Daedalus* (Winter 1962) and *The Annals* (November 1961), both of which deal with youth in the United States and in other societies. See also William R. Vizzard, "Taiyozoku: A Youth Problem in Japan," *Sociologus*, 9 (1959), pp. 162–178; and Mark G. Field, "Alcoholism, Crime, and Delinquency in Soviet Society," *Social Problems*, 3 (1955), pp. 100–109.

[64] See Rene König, "Family and Authority: The German Father in 1955," *Sociological Review*, 5 (1957), pp. 107–127; Paul Chombart de Lauwe et al., *Famille et Habitation*, II (Paris: Centre Nationale de la Recherche Scientifique, 1960); Kent Geiger, "The Family and Social Change," in Cyril E. Black (Ed.), *The Transformation of Russian Society* (Cambridge: Harvard University Press, 1960), pp. 447–458. Italy also has been moving toward the "industrial model." See Franco Archibugi, "Recent Trends in Women's Work in Italy," *International Labour Review*, 81 (1960), pp. 285–318. But Italy and Japan have witnessed considerable resistance to the "emancipation" of women. See Yoshiharu Scott Matsumoto, *Contemporary Japan*, Transactions of the American Philosophical Society, Vol. 50, Part 1 (Philadelphia, 1960), pp. 17–33.

the home to carve a niche for themselves in the world outside. One index of their heightened status is the extensive formal education they have been acquiring, and their role as wage-earners, decision-makers, and so on outside the home has sharply elevated their status within the family. Both in the labor market and in the home, the formerly clear-cut division of labor has largely disappeared. As a result, industrial cities evince a wide range of possible adaptations in husband-wife roles, about which we have only a modicum of information.[65]

Although women have invaded almost every occupational field, sex discrimination survives in industrial cities. Full equality in the labor market has not been achieved, and perhaps it never will be. One factor is the periodic withdrawal of many women from the labor force for the bearing and rearing of children. Another is the stress given to femininity, or to woman as a "sex symbol."[66] These emphases contravene some of the egalitarian tendencies. Sociologists have paid surprisingly little attention to the contradictions that inhere in the roles played by women in modern cities.

We can now return to the conjugal family and pose two questions. (1) Why is this the prevailing form in industrial-urban centers? (2) What are some of the countertendencies? One reason for the prominence of the relatively small, flexible family system is that it seems to accord best with a highly trained mobile labor force. Mass education and the opening up of countless new occupations demand loose family ties; without this freedom, urbanites could not take advantage of the new opportunities and adjust to the ever-changing scientific technology. Simultaneously the conjugal family has come to serve as a prime source of emotional security for the individual. Yet this tendency also acts to loosen family bonds, for the notion of "emotional well-being" is a highly individualistic matter and, as such, is difficult to institutionalize as part of a normative order. One result has been the proliferation of counselors, lawyers, psychiatrists, and other mediators who can arbitrate differences among family members.

Some groups in the industrial city profit economically and

[65] See Elizabeth Bott, *Family and Social Network* (London: Tavistock Publications, 1957).

[66] See Max and Tobia Frankel, "New Soviet Plan—Feminine Females," *New York Times Magazine*, December 6, 1959, pp. 30 et passim; Vera Bacal, "The Latest Fashion News—from Moscow," *New York Times Magazine*, November 20, 1960, pp. 16 et passim. These and similar data indicate the nature of this trend in Soviet cities.

politically from maintaining extensive kinship ties. The recent studies by Townsend[67] and others on London's lower class have created quite a stir; some sociologists assume these findings refute the proposition that the conjugal family is a necessary adjunct of the industrial city. But this is hardly the case. The data do seem to refute the notion that the conjugal family unit lacks extensive kinship ties. But they do not point to a resuscitation of the preindustrial-urban ideal, namely a large, extended family gathered under a single "roof." Rather, Townsend found that even where old people reside with the family of a son or daughter many would prefer to live alone, albeit near at hand.[68]

In practice, family forms in industrial-urban centers differ according to social class. On the basis of an extensive survey of the literature, Goode contends that

> . . . the contacts of upper-strata families with their kin form a smaller proportion of their total social interactions, since the higher strata belong to more voluntary organizations, clubs, and formal groups than the lower strata. On the other hand, they have more resources with which to maintain their ties with kin, and because of these means, mutual exchanges are also more frequent than in the lower strata.[69]

As cities industrialize, especially in the context of a feudal past, the lower strata may well adopt the preindustrial-urban family model, for as their income rises they come closer than ever to achieving the ideal that has long been held before them. This may account for some of Townsend's findings.

Looking ahead, we discern still other changes under way in familial organization. We know little about how lengthening

[67] Peter Townsend, *The Family Life of Old People* (New York: Free Press of Glencoe, 1957); Young and Willmott, *op. cit.*

[68] See J. B. Cullingworth, "Some Implications of Overspill: The Worsley Social Survey," *Sociological Review*, 8 (1960), pp. 77–96; Cullingworth indicates that the patterns delineated by Townsend and Young and Willmott change as people move to the suburbs. Moreover, Cullingworth believes that there is an untenable hidden assumption in the work of Young and Willmott, i.e., that the poor are basically happy. We believe that he is correct.

[69] William J. Goode, *World Revolution and Family Patterns* (New York: Free Press of Glencoe, 1963), p. 76. This is a very important volume for students of industrial urbanization. Unfortunately, Goode's analysis is compromised by his failure to clearly delineate the familial structure of preindustrial societies.

life expectancy or the expanding leisure time will modify family patterns, but we can expect the relationships among generations to become more complex. We should also explore the interconnections between the broader kinship system and the actions of individuals and bureaucratic structures in the industrial-urban setting.[70]

Economic Structure

Industrial cities diverge dramatically from preindustrial cities in their economic organization. Within the industrial city, extended leisure, a product of new production methods and a shorter work week, is increasingly the prerogative of the common man.[71] Today many high-status persons work longer hours than do those in low-status occupations, a situation quite the reverse of that in the preindustrial-urban setting.

Within affluent industrial cities the ordinary man lives far above the survival threshold. The economic rewards for his labor, as well as his overall health standards, have improved markedly. Industrialization has also made possible and imperative the development of a host of services, many of them totally unknown to the preindustrial urbanite. These range from special welfare benefits to provisions in the cultural arts and include facilities that cater to industrial man's self-perpetuating appetite for consumption goods of various kinds.

In the process the composition of the labor force (as suggested earlier) is undergoing marked change. Industrial technology demands more and more professional persons, scientific specialists, and skilled technicians who are committed to the ideals of efficiency and rationality as well as to "the good life" in the material realm. Actually, automation has progressed to the point where the question of how to integrate the little-educated person into the city's economic system has become a major social problem in some industrial orders.

The proliferation of specialists has been associated with the evolution of a highly complex educational apparatus. Formal

[70] See Daniel R. Miller and Guy E. Swanson, *The Changing American Parent* (New York: Wiley, 1958); Dennison Nash and Peter Berger, "The Child, the Family, and the Religious Revival in Suburbia," *Journal for the Scientific Study of Religion*, 2 (1962), pp. 85–93; Erwin K. Scheuch, "Family Cohesion in Leisure Time," *Sociological Review*, 8 (1960), pp. 37–61; Marvin B. Sussman and Lee Burchinal, "Kin Family Network: Unheralded Structure in Current Conceptualizations of Family Functioning," *Marriage and Family Living*, 24 (1962), pp. 231–240.

[71] Fourastié, *op. cit.*

educational systems are found side by side with a bevy of special institutes, seminars, and on-the-job training programs whose task is to socialize workers into the demands of the industrial order. And this educational system shares with the mass media the responsibility for keeping the populace informed about technological innovations and their social implications.

Sociologists are in general agreement concerning the patterning of these features of the economy, but the theoretical implications are another matter. Considerable argumentation revolves about one question in particular: Does the heightened division of labor in the urban community foster integration or disunity? The followers of Durkheim have long contended that it leads to greater interdependency among segments of the social order and, therefore, to integration. In general the data support this view of the industrial city as compared to the preindustrial, but certain qualifications must be interjected.

First, an intensive division of labor can breed disunity. In industrial-urban systems it fosters the vested interest groups that crystallize about specialized occupations and vie for the social rewards that derive from industrialization. Second, a vast extension of education and mass communication has accompanied further division of labor; this has fostered greater homogeneity along ethnic, class, and regional dimensions.[72] Perhaps it is the broader commonality of values, added to the complex division of labor, that lends cohesion to the industrial-urban order.

While recognizing these qualifications, we believe that the industrial city's division of labor plays a strategic role in social integration, though an empirical test is difficult. The division of labor in the contemporary city involves a set of *social norms* that demand interdependency among workers having special technical knowledge. Such a pattern is quite different from that in the preindustrial city, where the division of labor involves specialization according to product rather than process, and where the technical information possessed by any one person is quite limited. Here only a modicum of cooperation among workers is required for the system to function. Udy and other sociologists fail to differentiate between the kind of division of labor in industrial cities and that found in

[72] See Sanford Irwen Labovitz, "Regional Analysis of the United States," unpublished M.A. thesis, University of Texas, 1962.

preindustrial centers; as a result, they cannot adequately interpret modern urban social and economic patterns.[73]

A corollary of this intensive specialization is the demand on both the local and the national levels for large-scale bureaucracies to direct and integrate the operations of manifold segments of the labor force. The industrial order's bureaucratic structure, unlike that in the feudal system, tends to gigantism. Essentially interurban in character, it encourages linkages of an extracommunity sort. Moreover, the industrial-urban bureaucracy requires an echelon of managers to prod the system toward achievement of its objectives. As a result of their training, these functionaries stress innovation and entrepreneurship. Certainly, there appear to be a number of common features in the industrial manager's role across sociocultural boundaries.[74] In addition to the managers, another highly significant group of functionaries has emerged in industrial-urban orders. It includes such mediators as labor negotiators and members of grievance committees. Almost no attention has been given to the function these mediators play in harmonizing the many complex, and often contradictory, roles that exist within various sectors of the occupational structure, and in integrating them with those in the broader social order.[75]

Overall, industrial-urban bureaucracies display many of the characteristics Weber assigned to rational, capitalistic structures. Weber's theory, of course, has been seriously questioned in recent years. If we take the preindustrial-urban order as our point of comparison, however, modern bureaucracies appear highly rational and efficient. The industrial city's economic structure is characterized by intensive planning and by numerous reports, audits, and investigations by experts, all of

[73] Stanley Udy, Jr., *Organization of Work: A Comparative Analysis of Production among Non-Industrial Peoples* (New Haven: HRAF Press, 1959).

[74] Mason Haire, Edwin E. Ghiselli, and Lyman W. Porter, "Cultural Patterns in the Role of the Manager," *Industrial Relations*, 2 (1963), pp. 95–117; David Granick, *The Red Executive* (Garden City: Doubleday, 1960); Frederick Harbison and Charles A. Myers, *Management in the Industrial World* (New York: McGraw-Hill, 1959); J. E. Humblet, "A Comparative Study of Management in Three European Countries: Preliminary Findings," *Sociological Review*, 9 (1961), pp. 351–360.

[75] For the emergence of some of these mediator roles in the Soviet Union, see Emily Clark Brown, "Interests and Rights of Soviet Industrial Workers and the Resolution of Conflicts," *Industrial and Labor Relations Review*, 16 (1963), pp. 254–278.

which are lacking or rudimentary in the preindustrial city, where they are unnecessary for the functioning of the economic system. The present-day budgeting and auditing procedures, the maintenance of personnel files, the recruitment of workers according to universalistic criteria so as to obtain the most highly qualified persons—all these presuppose social and technological innovations that are unquestionably more industrial than preindustrial in form.

The advance of social science itself is inextricably associated with the striving for rationality. We may consider only one example. Although social science activity in the Soviet Union is sharply restricted, the demands for empirical data are incessant, and the barriers surrounding social research must be lowered for reasons of political expediency.

The achievement of greater rationality and efficiency in the industrial city presumes a fairly high level of technical knowledge, and it also requires considerable standardization in the production and distribution processes. This is possible only if the economic and political organizations formalize their rules and procedures. Regularization of coinage, weights and measures, prices, and the quality of goods and services far exceeds that in the preindustrial city.

Counterpressures obviously act to reduce standardization. Even in the Soviet Union different styles in radios, clothing, and so on are produced for different consumer levels. Furthermore, even a small degree of competition among producers helps to sustain the quality of consumer goods; theoretically, the consumer will buy the "best" and thus will weed out the producers of inferior goods.[76] Thus advertising, though decried as sheer capitalistic wastage, plays a role in the Soviet Union. It stimulates a degree of competition among producers, and it is a means of educating consumers to accept the new products that result from technological innovation.

Another question arises: "How much centralization of decision-making in the economic and/or political orbits is feasible in industrial-urban societies?" There do seem to be functional limits to both centralization and decentralization.[77]

[76] Marshall I. Goldman, "Product Differentiation and Advertising: Some Lessons from Soviet Experience," *Journal of Political Economy,* 68 (1960), pp. 346–357.

[77] This issue has been raised in a somewhat different manner by Michael Polanyi, "Towards a Theory of Conspicuous Production," *Soviet Survey* (October–December 1960), pp. 90–99. The comments on Polanyi's article by Devons, Grossman, Jasny, Nove, Seton, and Wiles

According to some observers, the Soviets are retreating from their commitment to extreme centralization, whereas in the United States the heightened demands for national planning have been nibbling away at the local community's autonomy.

A critical issue in industrial-urban orders concerns the amount of autonomy the local community can wield in an industrial-urban society. We hypothesize that the range within which urban communities can function effectively is rather wide, although it may be narrower than in the preindustrial, civilized society. It is difficult to specify with precision what is the optimum "balance," or point of equilibrium, between the opposing structural requirements. Given our present state of knowledge, we may have to be satisfied with delineating, through the use of "negative cases," the boundaries to feasible centralization and decentralization.

Political Structure

A comparison of the political organization of the preindustrial or the modernizing city and society with that found in advanced industrial-urban orders suggests some significant hypotheses. For example, there seems to be a close association between democracy and an industrial-urban way of life, though it is by no means a perfect one. But just what is meant by "democracy"? A "democratic" political system is characterized by (1) an institutionalized opposition vis-à-vis the group in command, and (2) the consent of the governed as the ultimate basis of authority. The two criteria are obviously interrelated. Only as the existence of an opposition becomes institutionalized can one governing element effectively transfer authority to another without detriment to the system's stability.

Lipset contends that certain traits we associate with highly industrialized orders—an open class system, mass literacy, and so on—are factors that favor the rise and effective functioning of a democratic political system.[78] Restating this hypothesis we advance the proposition that democracy is a necessary, though perhaps not a sufficient, condition for the maintenance of a relatively stable industrial-urban system on both the local *and* the national levels.

The rise of democracy is also related to the division of labor

---

raise issues that have been ignored by urban sociologists concerned with such problems as "the hierarchy of cities."

[78] Lipset, *op. cit.*; J. J. Spengler, "Economic Development: Political Preconditions and Political Consequences," *Journal of Politics,* 22 (1960), pp. 387–416.

within the industrial-urban order. The vast proliferation of experts has diffused both knowledge and authority over a broad spectrum of the social system. It is through the democratic process that the industrial-urban system harmonizes and integrates the conflicting views of experts and of the various interest groups that form about them.

Earlier we mentioned that specialists in the economic, political, and educational bureaucracies tend to carve out niches for themselves—little islands of localized power and authority. Whether in the white-collar or the blue-collar category, many individuals are organized into special interest groups, including professional associations, unions, and the like. These associations not only cut across bureaucratic structures but tend to be extracommunity oriented. Kerr and his co-authors believe that the cleavages among various special interest groups will eventually supplant the schisms along class lines that have so long prevailed in civilized societies.[79] This is an hypothesis that requires intensive investigation.

Moreover, political and other leaders in industrial cities seek vital information from experts—the "trustees of scientific knowledge." Indeed, recourse to these specialists is deemed the only rational mode of decision-making. Thus politicians in various societies argue for military or economic progress in terms of the knowledge provided them by military or economic experts.[80] At the same time, experts often fail to perceive the broader community or societal implications of their own actions, and as a group they are frequently incapable of reaching consensus on many vital issues. Indeed, social scientists cluster at opposite poles on questions of how to cope with economic recessions, while physical scientists are at odds over the long-run effects of radiation. More often than not it is the politician who must mediate the opposing viewpoints and keep the system on a relatively even keel. At times the politician must balance the opinions of the experts against the views of the mass populace upon whose votes he depends for his continuance in office. Ultimately, the politician serves as a strategic mediator among various interest groups, who reflect the internal contradictions within the industrial-urban system.[81]

[79] Kerr et al., *op. cit.*

[80] The impact of the expert even on the local community should not be underestimated. The pattern of local government seems to change once scientifically oriented experts are introduced into the formal structure.

[81] Some of the inherent contradictions that plague a democratic order have been outlined in Bernard Berelson, Paul F. Lazarsfeld, and

Questions may arise concerning our argument to the effect that democracy is a product of and is functionally essential to the maintenance of an industrial-urban order. What about the industrial-urban societies that have deviated from this pattern? Germany under Hitler comes to mind. One could argue, however, that in large degree the basis of Hitler's power lay in the support he received from proponents of the older feudal structure and its values.[82] The Soviet Union is another case in point. It is especially strategic for either disproving or confirming the hypothesis regarding the relationship of democracy and industrial urbanization. Some fragmentation in the power and authority structure of the Soviet system is quite apparent nowadays, and there is a concomitant enhancement of the status of the scientific expert. In addition, leaders are more and more concerned with "feedback" from below, with the public's reactions to various programs the government initiates. The emergence of public opinion polls, though they are limited in scope, is a development of significance. For some years the Russian leadership has permitted and even encouraged the public to use the letters-to-the-editor columns in newspapers to upbraid lesser officials who deviate from the system's ideals. These partial ruptures with the authoritarian past demand attention from students of urban life.[83]

More generally, the dictatorships we associate with

William N. McPhee, *Voting* (Chicago: University of Chicago Press, 1954), pp. 313–323.

[82] The support for Hitler came from those who were marginal or outside the mainstream of the industrial-urban process. See Rudolf Heberle, *Social Movements* (New York: Appleton-Century-Crofts, 1951), pp. 222–236. On the other hand, the structure of the industrial-urban order, and the nonideological character of the middle class, leaves this system vulnerable to extremist movements. This may account for the passivity of the middle class in Germany and their rationalizations for the actions of the Nazis. See Raul Hilberg, *The Destruction of the European Jews* (Chicago: Quadrangle Books, 1961).

[83] Among the writers who believe that some "democratization" is under way in the Soviet Union are Ullman, Djilas, Deutscher, and Bell. See Isaac Deutscher, *Russia in Transition*, rev. ed. (New York: Grove Press, 1960); Daniel Bell, "Russia's Eroding Ideology," *New Leader*, 46 (1963), pp. 18–23. Various data bear out this growing flexibility in the system: "Youth Paper Opens a 'Public Opinion Institute,'" *Current Digest of the Soviet Press*, 12 (1960), pp. 24–29; Patricia Blake, "Russia: The Scientific Elite," *Reporter*, 20 (November 14, 1957), pp. 17–22; Paul Jacobs, "The Boys on Gorki Street," *Reporter*, 23 (July 7, 1960), pp. 35–38. For an opposing view see Z. K. Brzezinski, *Ideology and Power in Soviet Politics* (New York: Praeger, 1962). It is significant that Brzezinski ignores science and the scientific method, as well as the technological revolution.

industrial-urban systems are of a different kind than those in the preindustrial context, at least in their mode of rationalizing their power. The modern dictator gives at least lip service to the notion of "the consent of the governed"; he does not appeal to absolutes such as "divine right" to justify his rule.

Still, industrial urbanization will not lead to any utopia. Many urbanites are said to experience a sense of alienation as a result of the complexity of modern life. Even in a democracy the individual may feel powerless to influence the political course of events. Then, too, an industrial-urban order is beset by instabilities that emerge from contradictions within the system as well as strains between external and internal imperatives. The external requirements, in particular, lead to deviations from the democratic ideal. Thus secrecy in many areas of international relations is the accepted mode of action. Leaders strive to seal themselves off from the conflicting and sometimes uninformed opinions of the populace in order to cope with certain external problems.

Another dilemma confronting the democratic industrial-urban order can be phrased as a question: How much "pluralism" and how much "homogeneity" are required for the system's effective functioning? Many American social scientists assume that pluralism of some sort is essential to offset the mass society's inherent instability, as well as to curb the authoritarian tendencies of any ruling elements.[84] In this context, "pluralism" refers to heterogeneity in terms of power and authority. But it appears to be highly fragile and little understood. It is not the political pluralism, as in France, that tends to stultify the democratic process. Nor is it the pluralism of language and caste characteristic of cities in India.[85] Democratic pluralism signifies the erasing of ethnic and religious barriers and an end to the kind of fragmentation that characterizes the feudal society and its cities. It implies commonality in the overall goals of the society; any divergencies of opinion are confined to the selection of the proper means to these ends. It implies a spirit of trust and compromise and

[84] Among others, Galbraith, Riesman, Parsons, and Kornhauser think in these terms. See William Kornhauser, *Politics of Mass Society* (New York: Free Press of Glencoe, 1959); Talcott Parsons, *Structure and Process in Modern Societies* (New York: Free Press of Glencoe, 1960), especially Chap. 6.

[85] Henry C. Hart, "Urban Politics in Bombay," *Economic Weekly*, 12 (1960), pp. 983–988.

tolerance of rather divergent values. But such tolerance may make this system vulnerable to extremist movements.[86]

This reasoning leads us back to our earlier discussion concerning the heightened specialization of the labor force in industrial cities. The close integration of diverse elements of the social order, which some sociologists attribute to the complex division of labor, may be partially a result of the cultural homogeneity that obtains in industrial centers. In the end, the question of how much homogeneity and how much heterogeneity are feasible in an industrial-urban order can best be determined by specifying the limits within which democracy can function rather than by seeking to establish some optimum balance point.

In our consideration of the political structure and the integration of modern industrial cities, we cannot ignore the legal system. Like politicians, those who occupy roles in the legal structure are often called upon to compromise the differences among vested interest groups or among occupational specialists. They must also deal with the fundamental conflict between the rights of the individual and those of the collectivity. The individual versus collectivity dilemma has attracted little attention in urban sociology.[87]

Unlike the politician, who typically seeks accommodation through negotiation, mainly by probing for areas of common interest, the legal functionary employs highly formalized procedures. Moreover, the administration of these legal norms differs markedly from one system to another. The modes of ascertaining guilt or innocence are quite distinct in industrial and preindustrial cities. In the latter, one is assumed to be guilty until proved innocent, and magico-religious rites are common means of determining the result. The law offers little protection for the accused. In the industrial city, however, the trend is toward universalism and a deepening rationalization of the legal structure, a pattern that seems to be developing even in the U. S. S. R., albeit slowly and painfully.[88]

[86] Hilberg, op. cit.

[87] Some American sociologists have dealt with limited aspects of this issue. See Sidney M. Willhelm, Urban Zoning and Land-Use Theory (New York: Free Press of Glencoe, 1962), and Robert Dubin (Ed.), Human Relations in Administration, 2nd ed. (Englewood Cliffs, N. J.: Prentice-Hall, 1961). Although the Marxists have historically denied the existence of an individual-group dilemma, some, like the Pole Adam Schaff, have recently reconsidered the matter; see " 'Socialist Ethics' Studied by Poles," New York Times, April 30, 1961, p. 19.

[88] See George Ginsburgs, "Objective Truth and the Judicial Process in Post-Stalinist Soviet Jurisprudence," American Journal of Compara-

These changes result in part from the greater authority of the common man today, and in part from the need for some standardized rules so that differences among scientific experts can be more satisfactorily adjudicated.

Mass Communication and Education

Industrialization fosters the rapid proliferation of communication media—including magazines, newspapers, radio, television, and movies. In turn, the industrial-urban order depends for its very existence upon the functioning of these media; the complex body of knowledge that must continually be disseminated cannot be diffused simply by word of mouth.

In addition to transmitting technical information vital for the city's operation, the mass media keep the populace informed about the many technological innovations that lead to revisions in the economic, political, and educational realms. Education is an ongoing, day-by-day process. Moreover, it is through the mass media that much purposive control is exerted, whether by leaders bent on influencing popular thinking or by elements of the citizenry who seek to prod the leaders into initiating particular reforms.[89]

We have also witnessed the rise of "popular culture" in the industrial-urban system as a byproduct of the mass media. The proliferation of this culture reflects not only the common man's growing importance but also the expanding leisure time he enjoys. Today urbanites of divergent social backgrounds and residing in widely separate communities can share in many popular leisure-time pursuits. This pattern also seems to integrate elements of the urban community in ways that sociologists have not examined. Actually some elements of popular culture such as jazz thrive so well in the individualized urban milieu that they have diffused even to societies whose leaders actively oppose such influences.

Intellectuals in Europe and America have commented on the so-called deleterious effects of the mass media on urban

---

tive Law, 10 (1961), pp. 53–75; Harold J. Berman, "The Struggle of Soviet Jurists Against a Return of Stalinist Terror," *Slavic Review,* 22 (1963), pp. 314–320. For a discussion of the impact of scientific thought upon American legal norms, see William M. Evan, "Value Conflicts in the Law of Evidence," *American Behavioral Scientist,* 6 (1960), pp. 23–26, and James R. Richardson, *Modern Scientific Evidence* (Cincinnati: Anderson, 1961).

[89] Letters to the editor in Soviet newspapers serve as one device for pressuring lower-level bureaucrats into adhering to the norms of universalism and efficiency.

man.[90] But the results are actually rather contradictory. Although the mass media may foster certain kinds of disintegration, they also exert a standardizing influence on the thinking, beliefs, and tastes of the ordinary urbanite, and this fosters social integration. The mass media also open up to societal leaders possibilities of manipulating the average urbanite to a degree unimagined in the preindustrial city. Yet these same channels provide the ordinary man with the sophistication he needs to protect himself against the machinations of leaders who would exploit the mass media for questionable ends.

Still more significant for diffusing information in the industrial-urban order is the formal educational system. Advanced industrialization, having freed man from the incessant struggle for bread, provides him with the leisure necessary for formal study. But just as imperative, the industrial city (and the broader society) demands assiduously trained experts for its advancement and very continuance. As automation hurries its pace, the demands upon the educational structure increase accordingly. Thus, many industrial-urban orders in Europe are in the throes of an educational revolution that bids fair to revise fundamentally the social structure of their cities.[91] Not only are more persons gaining advanced education, but most of the newly educated are specialists steeped in scientific know-how rather than in the humanities, which so long dominated European education. The resultant proliferation of scientific specialists generates even more rapid change. And scientific research becomes a major economic enterprise into which vast funds are channeled.

The impact upon the city of an educational system committed to the scientific method has been largely ignored. But if one views science as part of technology, as we do, analysis of this problem area is central to an understanding of the social and cultural patterns within industrial communities.

While on the matter of the relationship of education and scientific learning, it seems appropriate to raise a critical ques-

[90] One reason for the traditional intellectual's opposition to industrial urbanization is his loss of the ability to "predict" and "control" the future. This was the basis of his authority and power in the preindustrial city.

[91] Frederic Dewhurst et al., *Europe's Needs and Resources* (New York: Twentieth Century Fund, 1961), Chap. 10; George Louis Payne, *Britain's Scientific and Technological Manpower* (Stanford: Stanford University Press, 1960). Cf. Nicholas DeWitt, *Education and Professional Employment in the U. S. S. R.* (Washington: National Science Foundation, 1961).

tion: What are the essential ingredients and consequences of this new kind of knowledge for the industrial-urban order? Given our own theoretical commitment—one that views science as part of technology—the answer to this question is central to our analysis. Our thesis is that many of the values and beliefs of the industrial-urban system have their origin in the scientific method. In science, positive values attach to "negation" and to the notion of "institutionalized opposition." Quite unlike the knowledge that typifies the preindustrial city, modern science thrives on a degree of scepticism; it advances by negating existing interpretations of the physical and social systems and by substituting more adequate ones. The industrial technology is constantly undergoing revision; indeed it involves a "permanent revolution."[92] Not surprisingly, a degree of secularization results from application of the scientific method.

Furthermore, science fosters institutionalized opposition in other realms of human activity. The period since the Industrial Revolution gives evidence of a causal connection between the advancement of science and the rise of political democracy. Yet the association is by no means perfect. Industrial urbanites—and scientists are no exception—display a remarkable capacity for playing multiple roles, for compartmentalizing their thought and action patterns. Thus Nazi scientists found themselves faithfully pursuing their labors amid the horrors of concentration camps, all the while gaining security and satisfaction from performance of their technical duties. All the same, we hypothesize that such an extreme divergency in one's roles cannot be sustained over a long period of time.

Another facet of the scientific method, and one that shapes the industrial urbanite's "world view," consists in explaining physical and social phenomena (including disasters such as earthquakes, disease, and economic depressions) in natural rather than divine terms. One who is committed to the scientific method sees the physical and social worlds as manipulable and controllable. In contrast, the preindustrial urbanite attributes disasters, physical and social, to divine will or the caprices of hostile supernatural forces; he does not ordinarily attempt to revise the existing order. Rather he assumes that it is not to be tampered with by mere human beings. This fundamental divergency in the interpretation of reality lies at the heart of

[92] Dewhurst, *op. cit.*, Chap. 25.

many of the structural and ideological disparities between preindustrial-urban and industrial-urban societies.

Furthermore, science must stress universalism over particularism if it is to be successful. One cannot hope to falsify or confirm hypotheses on particularistic grounds. So, too, scientific personnel must be recruited primarily on the basis of achievement rather than in terms of ascription. This gives rise to the following proposition: the more closely social organizations depend for their operation upon modern science, the more likely they are to emphasize norms like universalism and achievement when dealing with their employees and their clientele. We would expect a religious order to deviate from these ideal norms to a greater degree than would a scientific institute. Even in the latter, however, the existence of contradictory requirements prevents the full realization of these norms.

Still another effect of the scientific method upon the industrial-urban system derives from the fact that science flourishes when scientists can identify with a loosely organized professional group and effectively exchange data and thus cross-fertilize budding ideas. From this perspective, scientists are committed to maintaining an "open society." As a result, they seek to sustain contacts with colleagues in other communities and beyond national boundaries. The local community is clearly unable to hold these persons in its grip, and even the nation must compete with these transcultural, multinational professional ties for the scientist's allegiance.

Finally, the idea of "ethical neutrality," intrinsic in the scientific method, serves the cause of science in that it challenges the efforts of politicians who would confine the scientist to some narrow ideology. The very notion of neutral, objective knowledge facilitates compromise among competing individuals or interest groups in modern society. Mediators, including politicians, may appeal to the "facts" as the basis for achieving consensus among conflicting parties.

Yet the principle of ethical neutrality generates problems of its own. Consider the educational realm. An industrial-urban system, which must educate its members into accepting the principle of ethical neutrality, has to train certain persons to make sound "extrascientific" judgments. Scientists seem to have grasped the issues here more clearly than sociologists, as witness the writings of C. P. Snow.[93] Nor is this dilemma

[93] C. P. Snow, *Science and Government* (New York: New American Library, 1962); see also *Science, An Interview by Donald McDonald*

confined to industrial-urban systems in the democratic West; the Soviet Union also is groping for a more effective means of balancing the demands for technicians with those for persons educated in the humanities. Training party functionaries to be the primary "moralizers" in the society leaves much to be desired.[94] It allows little room for such intellectuals as social philosophers and novelists to probe for meaning in the industrial-urban setting apart from the immediate concerns of practical politics.

Once more we encounter the question that troubled Durkheim and has plagued other sociologists since his time: Is a complex division of labor sufficient to sustain an industrial-urban order? The demand for persons who moralize, who make extrascientific judgments, indicates that an industrial-urban system requires more than just skilled technicians.

Religious Structure and the Value System

Although much is still to be learned by sociologists about certain facets of industrial-urban life, our ignorance of the religious structure and its related value system is particularly glaring. One proposition, however, seems well documented in the literature: a heightened secularization of religion occurs in the industrial city, particularly as opposed to the preindustrial city type. Religious values no longer permeate the entire social fabric. Indeed, large sectors of activity have become exempt from religious injunctions in the industrial city. The existing religious norms tend to be permissive rather than prescriptive. Inasmuch as industrial urbanites often are called upon to play multiple and even contradictory roles, any rigid moralization would subject people to incessant conflict and indecision.

True, some industrial-urban orders are less secular than others, and considerable variation with respect to religious ties persists within and among societies.[95] Even the Soviet

---

with Hans Bethe (Santa Barbara: Center for the Study of Democratic Institutions, 1962). Another facet of this problem is discussed by Wallace S. Sayre, "Scientists and American Science Policy," in Bernard Barber and Walter Hirsch (Eds.), The Sociology of Science (New York: Free Press of Glencoe, 1962). The book edited by Barber and Hirsch also provides us with data on the ideology of scientific enterprise.

[94] See the special issue of Daedalus (Summer 1960) on "The Russian Intelligentsia," especially the essay by Burg.

[95] For data on variations among societies, see "Les attitudes réligieuses de la jeunesse," Sondages, 21 (1959), p. 21. On variations within societies, see David Moberg, The Church as a Social Institution

Union, which has pursued a vigorous antireligious policy and envisages no place for religion in the social system, is experiencing efforts to revive religion.[96] Some observers claim that the United States has undergone a religious revival in urban centers during recent decades. Other sociologists doubt the validity of the statistics cited. Actually it is highly unlikely that religion is having a greater impact upon the daily life of urbanites now than a few generations ago.[97]

Overall, the following working hypothesis seems in order: religion continues to shape the lives of many urbanites, but less so than in past decades, and certainly to a far lesser degree than in preindustrial cities.[98] In the process religion has become more a private than a public matter.[99] Even many devoutly religious persons are applying their religious ideals to only limited spheres of daily life.

Concerning the organization of the church itself, we can offer only the most tentative of hypotheses. Close on the heels of industrial urbanization have sprung up numerous sectarian groupings that seem in many ways to meet the needs of certain lower-class urbanites.[100] Yet given the generalized weakness of the religious commitment, these fragmented ecclesiastical bodies tend to be unstable; they eventually disappear or merge with others of their kind.

Still unanswered is the following question: Can urbanites

(Englewood Cliffs, N. J.: Prentice-Hall, 1962), Chap. 15, and Antonio Donini, "Practica y Actitudes Religiosas (Parte II)," *Sociologia Religiosa*, 8 (1962), pp. 9–172.

[96] Seymour Topping, "Rise in Religion Worrying Soviets," *New York Times*, February 12, 1961, p. 14; Seymour Topping, "Soviet Whittling at the Roots of 20 Churches in Leningrad," *New York Times*, April 2, 1961, p. 18.

[97] For a discussion of the contradictory evidence, see William Petersen, "Religious Statistics in the United States," *Journal for the Scientific Study of Religion*, 1 (1962), pp. 164–178. One of the main reasons for our assumption that there has been a decline of religious commitment is the growing "tolerance" of different religious faiths for one another.

[98] For an analysis of the influence of religion in a highly industrialized city, see Gerhard Lenski, *The Religious Factor*, rev. ed. (Garden City: Doubleday, 1963).

[99] Thomas Luckmann, "On Religion in Modern Society: Individual Consciousness, World View, Institution," *Journal for the Scientific Study of Religion*, 2 (1963), pp. 147–162.

[100] Some of these sectarian groups serve as socializing agencies for members of the lower socioeconomic strata, helping them adapt to and become assimilated into the urban environment. It is significant that in the U. S. S. R. the most active sects in the urban centers have been those catering to the lower class. See Walter Kolarz, *Religion in the Soviet Union* (New York: St. Martin's Press, 1961), Chap. 9.

function effectively over a long period without the stabilizing influence of some traditional religious ideology, particularly one that seeks to provide a meaning for life after death?[101] Most sociologists would probably respond in the affirmative. Nevertheless, the problem of meaning for the individual continues to trouble social philosophers and social scientists in industrial-urban orders. By and large, this problem has been the province of religion throughout history.

Some industrial urbanites seek meaning in life by embracing such secular religions as nationalism and scientism. We know little about the function of either of these ideologies. Although nationalism in industrial cities is not as potent a force as it is in transitional ones, it still provides a rationale for living and for dying and, like religion, it demands sacrifices. And it is highly significant that in the U. S. S. R. the intellectuals have taken the "scientific socialism" of the nineteenth century as the basis for their utopian model for industrial-urban living.[102]

Other industrial urbanites have found meaning in a kind of secular ceremonialism or "ritualism." In a city oriented to consumption and leisure-time pursuits, parties, sports, and vacations—associated with a "fun morality" that is highly stylized and ritualized—become a way of life for many people. Those who engage in these activities feel they are "in the swing of things" and thereby gain a sense of personal direction. Such a pattern of existence—dramatized effectively in the movie *La Dolce Vita*—stresses only the present and minimizes any concept of the past or of the future. A major research problem is to understand how large segments of the urban populace are able to maintain a sense of direction when work or traditional religion are no longer dominant forces in their lives.

THE END PRODUCT: A REASSESSMENT OF SOME BASIC ISSUES

That industrial cities over the world are becoming alike in many aspects of their social structure is our main thesis. Im-

---

[101] We need also to investigate the persistence of magic even in supposedly "rational" spheres of urban life. See Neil Ulman, "Some Investors Turn to Stars for Answer to Market's Riddles," *Wall Street Journal*, April 16, 1963, p. 1 et passim.

[102] Walter Laqueur and Leopold Labedz (Eds.), *The Future of Communist Society* (New York: Praeger, 1962), especially the "Introduction."

plicit in our analysis is another hypothesis: as technology becomes increasingly complex, a significant number of structural imperatives become more narrowly defined. Thus preliterate societies with their simple technology display greater diversity in their economic and familial organization than do preindustrial civilized societies, and the latter in turn display greater diversity in these realms than do industrial ones.

Yet we cannot ignore the potential objections to our primary thesis. A Marxist, for one, would insist upon the fundamental dissimilarities between cities in communist and in capitalist societies, for he is committed to the thesis that these divergent types of economic systems lead to basically different kinds of social organization within a community or a society as a whole. It is of some ideological consequence that West European and American social scientists have generally abandoned the capitalist-socialist dichotomy for the industrial-nonindustrial one; by so doing, they recognize many more similarities among industrial systems than do the Soviet theorists. This is true even of writers like Parsons, who were nurtured in the Weberian heritage.

Another constellation of scholars who challenge the notion of an increasing similarity among industrial-urban orders are those who insist upon the preeminence of cultural values.[103] We also believe that cultural values induce stylistic differences among industrial cities that cannot be ignored. However, a value system cannot modify structural arrangements in an infinite variety of ways. Industrial cities share certain values because of their dependence on the scientific method and modern technology. Overemphasis of cultural values as an independent variable leads to historicism and a denial of the possibility of making cross-cultural generalizations.

A third source of opposition to our theoretical perspective finds its reference in the French Revolution. Writers steeped in this tradition emphasize the impact of different political values and institutions upon industrial-urban systems. They stress the differences between the social structures of democratic and of totalitarian systems. It cannot be denied that some divergencies exist in urban forms as a result of differing political structures, but this should not allow one to disregard the similarities.

Sociologists like ourselves, who champion the notion of

---

[103] This view seems implicit in Herbert Blumer, "Early Industrialization and the Laboring Class," *The Sociological Quarterly*, 1 (1960), pp. 5–14.

the "convergence" of industrial societies and their cities, clearly focus on the similarities. Our antagonists have recourse to variables other than technology and on this basis they stress the differences among industrial-urban systems. Add to this the emphasis given to selected features of industrial cities and the dissensus becomes even more pronounced.

These disagreements affect the social scientist's analysis of industrial-urban systems in specific societies. It has been argued that Japan's industrial organization, and many other features of its urban life, diverges sharply from those in the West because of the unique cultural milieu within which it has been shaped. Abegglen stresses those patterns in Japanese factories that diverge from the factory organization in Western cities.[104] But his reasoning is not persuasive. As Drucker indicates, some recently emergent sectors of the Japanese industrial complex are quite unlike the traditional forms of which Abegglen speaks; they resemble their Western counterparts far more closely.[105] Odaka supports Drucker's thesis and goes on to criticize Abegglen for overemphasis on the positive contribution of tradition to industrial-urban development in Japan.[106] Approaching the problem from another perspective, Dore also concludes that Japanese urban life is moving toward some approximation of the Western model.[107] Significantly, Dore has been concerned with comparing the present with the past within a Tokyo ward. From this vantage point, the present structure is closer to Western urban-industrial forms than to Tokyo's preindustrial past.

So it is with scholars who contrast the United States and the Soviet Union. Those who stress the structural similarities see much in common between the two, especially in contrast to modernizing or preindustrial civilized societies.[108] The more

[104] James Abegglen, *The Japanese Factory System* (New York: Free Press of Glencoe, 1958). Odaka includes William A. Lockwood, Solomon B. Levine, Frederick Harbison, and Charles A. Myers in this school of thought as well; see K. Odaka, "Traditionalism and Democracy in Japanese Industry," a paper delivered at the Fifth World Congress of Sociology, Washington, D. C., September 1962.

[105] Peter F. Drucker, "The Baffled Young Men of Japan," *Harper's*, 222 (1961), pp. 65–74.

[106] Odaka, *op. cit.* Odaka argues that American social scientists who have imputed "positive functions" to the traditional social structure have served to bolster the conservative cause in Japan.

[107] Dore, *op. cit.*

[108] Marshall E. Dimock, "Management in the USSR—Comparisons to the United States," *Public Administration Review*, 20 (1960), pp. 139–147.

intrepid thinkers assume some kind of convergence in the development of these industrial giants. Even those who underline the differences recognize that in matters of education and literacy, the structure of the labor force, and so on, cities in the United States and in the Soviet Union resemble one another more closely than they do the cities of, say, India or Iran.[109] Of course, not even the most committed of the writers who perceive marked similarities would claim that the Soviet Union and the United States are alike in all major respects. Obviously, important differences exist. Yet for the scientist these differences acquire significance only in terms of the similarities.[110]

We should recognize, of course, that many structural imperatives are not absolute. The industrial-urban society is often free—within certain limits—to work out alternative solutions. It is because of the presence of these alternatives that sociologists need to pay special heed to the negative cases that demarcate the limits within which the economic, political, and educational structures must function.

Furthermore, industrial technology is ever changing or evolving. On several occasions we have indicated that automation and the cybernetics revolution are remaking many facets of the industrial city's social structure. Although this structure obviously will not revert to the preindustrial form, merely projecting from current industrial-urban patterns seems inadequate as a method for predicting the future.

CONCLUSIONS

The preindustrial city's social structure has served as the basis for our interpretation of both industrializing and advanced industrial cities. When we considered the transitional city we focused on those processes that accompany the shift from a preindustrial to an industrial-urban form. Especially significant are the differential changes in the social structure

---

[109] For example, William Petersen, "The Soviet Subject Viewed as Citizen," *Antioch Review* (Spring 1960), pp. 101–111.

[110] Some of the methodological and theoretical issues that inhere in comparisons of industrial-urban societies, especially the economies of the Soviet Union and the United States, are set forth by various writers in "Comparisons of the United States and Soviet Economies," Joint Economic Committee, Congress of the United States (Washington, D. C.: Government Printing Office, 1960). Also see the essay by Alex Inkeles, and Sorokin's rebuttal, in P. J. Allen (Ed.), *Pitirim A. Sorokin in Review* (Durham: Duke University Press, 1963).

and in the role of tradition in the industrializing or transitional city, matters that have been little studied.

Our main emphasis has been upon the industrial city. Here are the primary conclusions we draw from our analysis of this kind of urban center:

1. Although sociologists generally agree on the broad outlines of the structural correlates of industrial cities, there are significant areas of disagreement. Some of the confusion stems from differing frames of reference, some from apparently contradictory data. But one reason for the supposedly contradictory findings is the existence of contradictory functional requirements, and consequently contradictory structures, within industrial cities and societies. For example, some writers see the class system as becoming more rigid, whereas others view it as becoming more flexible. We contend that the empirical data run counter to the assumption of Parsons, Weber, and many other sociologists that structures or social systems are rather neatly and consistently arranged. Because of structural contradictions, sociologists must make explicit their bases of comparison if we are ever to achieve a modicum of consensus as to the nature of industrial-urban systems. The preindustrial city is our basic reference point.

2. We believe that the structural arrangements of the industrial city are functionally related to the nature of modern technology—a technology that encompasses scientific know-how. In turn, the scientific method seems to support and is itself sustained by an ideology that gives rise to and promotes the democratic process, and such norms as universalism and emphasis on achievement in modern bureaucracies.

3. Cutting across our analysis of the common structural correlates of the industrial city is the problem of the division of labor, a major concern to students of industrialization and urbanization since Durkheim. We have noted some of the neglected theoretical aspects of the division of labor for the industrial-urban system. For example, a clear distinction must be drawn between the division of labor that characterizes the preindustrial city and that which typifies the industrial center if we are to answer such questions as the following: What is the function of the division of labor as an integrative mechanism, and as a divisive force, in the industrial-urban setting? And how is the division of labor related to the emergence of a "society of mediators"? Family counselors, welfare workers, labor arbitrators, politicians, and legal functionaries, including lawyers, come to mediate differences (1) among indi-

viduals, (2) between individuals and the broader society, and (3) among special interest and occupational groups that may support contradictory structures within the society. Some mediators, such as family counselors, function quite informally as they search out areas of value consensus among disputants; others, such as legal functionaries, employ rather formalized procedures when they seek to resolve disagreements.

Admittedly, the existing knowledge on the nature of integration and consensus in the industrial city is limited. We need to know much more about the interrelationships of the value system, the division of labor, and the role of mediators. This is an area of research to which urban sociologists could make a particularly significant contribution.

Chapter 4

URBAN ECONOMICS

The last social science to rally around to the study of urbanism is economics; classical economists have not been spatially oriented and only within recent times has a new breed of economist come to the fore, able and willing to attempt the delicate task of breaking economic data apart into urban packages. Pure economic considerations, without social, political and administrative overtones usually not within the skill spectrum of traditionalistic economists, are incapable of shedding much light on, much less managing urban economies. The economic factor is tangled with non-economic factors, and operational considerations beyond mere research obtrude themselves into all questions. There is heavy pressure for action. Wilbur R. Thompson has in the pages that follow exemplified the approach of a multi-skilled urbanist with the primary emphasis on his forte, the economics of urbanization. Having dichotomized the city into "small urban areas" and "large urban areas," he has characterized the essential problems of each type: the "small urban area" must cope with either growing or dying as an open system in a large scale economic world throwing variables at it from the heights of a national economy far beyond any local possibility of control. The "large urban area" tending more and more to be similar economically in industry-business mix, must concentrate energies on the prickly problem of how to take care of itself. If the small place must be as nimble as a bright chipmunk to stay ahead of chance disaster, the large area or metropolis tied to national growth rates, sometimes seems like an awkward herbiverous dinosaur unable to think and to coordinate quickly enough to survive well. Strategies of growth for small places, including capital investment in non-economic factors (education and amenities), might well merit federal subsidy beyond that accorded larger areas who enjoy externalities of scale already. This suggests that fascinating will-of-the-wisp idea of optimum city size for maximum service at minimum cost; no one has yet spotted this delicate point which obviously changes with technological-managerial increasing capabilities. Large urban areas are plagued on one hand by too-low incomes needing extra services badly and on the other by too-high incomes demanding amenities. Affluence creates its own political-economic problems. Population pressures, too, are expressed in central city costs and suburban sprawl. Finally Thompson plays political scientist or public administration expert from an economic standpoint and introduces a novel discussion of "pricing" municipal services and skillfully lays bare the dearth of a public entrepreneurship equal to private. Just as Alan K. Campbell, political scientist, in tabulating service costs in the "Most Dynamic Sector," Chapter 1, entered into economic analysis; so Thompson slips over into political science. It is patent, further, that he is not satisfied to study merely *what is*, but is highly motivated to picture *what could be* and explore *how to get there*. Urbanists tend to be multidisciplinary in approach and operationally minded.

Urban Economics

WILBUR R. THOMPSON*

PART I: GROWTH AND DEVELOPMENT OF SMALL URBAN AREAS

"Urban economics" has barely been born whole, but this paper will argue that it was predestined to split amoebalike into two viable entities. The natural division of the subject matter is along the lines of urban size. The small urban area, heavily export-and-import oriented, faces outward on a capricious, even hostile, national economy which can turn toward or away from its precious few life-giving local exports without notice or qualms. A rising per capita income, with almost all the increase adding to discretionary income, and a rapidly advancing technology, which continually offers new choices in products and processes, steadily increase the vulnerability of the narrowly based, small urban economy. Confronted by an inexorable natural increase in its labor force, the smaller urban area is dominated by a deep concern for its competitive position in the system of cities and for the rate of local job formation. In sum, for the smaller urban area the "gut issue" is how to grow.

The larger urban area, in sharp contrast, faces inward on what is often dramatized as the "awful mess." The felt need of the large urban area is not how to grow, for growth from its broad industrial base and deep infra-structure is unusually stable and seems assured, but rather how to manage the prod-

* Professor of Economics, Wayne State University, Detroit, and formerly Director of the Committee on Urban Economics of Resources for the Future, Inc. Holder of a Ph.D. in Economics from the University of Michigan, he is the author of *A Preface to Urban Economics* (Baltimore: Johns Hopkins Press, 1965) and with J. Mattila *An Econometric Model of Postwar State Industrial Development* (Detroit: Wayne State University Press, 1959).

uct of inexorable growth—great city size. Thus the economics of the large urban area rests more on *intra*-urban analysis, quite distinct from the *inter*-urban economics of the smaller place.

The plan here is to begin with the small urban area, work through the growth process, especially as it affects income patterns, and conclude with the internal managerial problems of the metropolis.

The Goals of an Urban Economy

Since the beginning, economists have analyzed economic life by function and in time, but seldom in space, except, of course, "economic geographers." The economy was implicitly the national economy, disaggregated by industry and traced through time, as in Alfred Marshall's "short run" and "long run" planning periods of the firm and industry. Economists are turning slowly to spatial disaggregation and to the study of the urban place. It is wholly understandable that the economist, in venturing into sub-national economics should bypass both broad regions (e.g. the "South") and the states and proceed directly to "metropolitan areas." For if today the nation is the primary unit of employment and income generation in the long run, the commuting radius about a cluster of work places is quickly appreciated as the primary short-run economic welfare unit. Short and long run are, moreover, used here in a context striking analogous to their traditional use in firm theory. In the short run, prospective employment and income depend largely on the balance of demand and supply in the local labor market, locked in as the worker is to a reasonable daily journey to work from his current residence (the fixed factor). In the long run, however, intra-urban commuting gives way to inter-urban migration and the worker's economic welfare rests more with the state of the national economy.

Urban economics, then, is essentially complementary to national economics and more explicitly treats the economics of the *spatial short run*. It is quite appropriate, therefore, to begin by accepting the income goals traditionally identified at the national level:

1. Affluence: A high and rising level of income, as expressed in both money and real terms;
2. Equity: A "fair" distribution of income, as a product of natural market forces and as altered by government in-

tervention in the market or through public services and transfer payments;

3. Stability: Stability of employment and income, expressed both over the business cycle and secularly in the local growth trend.

None of these seemingly simple objectives are as operational at the local level as at the national level. To measure the level of money income is not enough; we should be able to convert money income into real income. To do this requires an *inter-urban* cost-of-living index that measures more than the cost of potatoes in each of the many cities, or even land prices; we need to quantify the value of varying ranges of choice, for that is what "urban-ness" is all about. And we have virtually none of this information. Again, equity is not equality, but sooner or later we must come to grips with the desirable degree of income inequality, given the degree of national income inequality.

The nation has had through the past a sizable business cycle, but its growth has been remarkably stable; therefore, it is understandable that economics has stressed cyclical instability. But at the local level we are at least equally interested in the frequency and sharpness of the breaks in trend—"growth instability." Budget officers are most interested in prospective tax receipts next year and the public welfare commissioner is concerned with the likely case load next quarter, and so the local business cycle is highly relevant. But the city planners and public works officials are looking ahead ten, twenty or even fifty years, for their actions must stand the test of very long amortization periods. To these latter planners, the real unknown is whether the current growth trend will accelerate and create congestion in the lagging physical facilities or decelerate and leave the locality burdened with excess capacity. How stable—predictable—is the local growth rate?

From Industry Mix to Income

If the economist first establishes rapport with the subnational, urban economy as a local labor market, he will next most often see the urban-region as a more or less distinctive industry mix. Different industries exhibit very different income and employment characteristics, so that much (most?) of the variation in the level, distribution and stability of income among areas may be traceable to their industrial specializations. Since, moreover, the distinctive part of the local industry mix is the local export sector (just as the "shoe-maker" exports shoes), we have an "export (economic) base" theory of local economic welfare. In effect, the economist might say to a community: tell me your leading industries and I will tell your fortune.

Certainly, it is not enough to say that high-wage industries create high-income urban areas or that unstable industries create cyclically sensitive areas. (On the one hand such a statement is trite; on the other hand it is not quite true!) Still, if one could have only one piece of information from which to forecast an urban economy, its export base would probably be the most relevant dimension to know—at least for short and perhaps intermediate periods of up to, perhaps, a decade.

More substantively, one would expect high incomes in ur-ban areas that specialize in industrial activities that (1) use relatively high proportions of the more skilled occupations, (2) have high capital-to-labor ratios and (3) sell in oligopo-listic markets, and all three enriching factors may be highly inter-related and cumulatively reinforcing. High capital-to-labor ratios imply not only high labor productivity but also heavy fixed costs, decreasing unit costs over a considerable range of output, and few firms. "Oligopoly" ordinarily turns "non-price competition," and "administered prices" into high profits, yielding thereby the means with which to invest even more heavily in capital equipment, again raising the produc-tivity of labor. Further, the advent of only a few big buyers of labor in a given industry tends to evoke the "countervailing power" of a trade union, virtually ensuring that the gains of higher product prices will be shared by labor in higher wages. Further, higher wage rates reinforce the corporate orientation toward mechanization by providing an incentive to substitute their cheap, abundant (redundant?) supply of capital for in-creasing expensive labor.

Perhaps even more important heavy retained earnings—a joint product of high profits and management control of the corporation with widely distributed (weak) ownership—lead to the institutionalization of research and development, with the growing technological sophistication embodied in larger capi-tal investments. Thus if the few firms in the given industry do not become fewer, the heavy and rapidly growing capital re-quirements and the high and rapidly advancing technology impede new entry and virtually ensure that they will not in-crease in number and their price power will persist even in the long run. Finally, a capital-intensive, technologically progressive industry is clearly one in which the occupation mix will stress education and reward it well. In sum, a good occupational mix, a high capital-to-labor ratio and monopoly power are more a tight nexus of income-determining forces than three independent forces. The whole may be greater than the sum of the parts when the parts interact.

Again, manufacturing towns show a very marked tendency to have more equal distributions of income than non-manufacturing places. The differences in inequality among the two hundred-odd metropolitan areas are moreover, not trivial, with the most unequal income distributions exhibiting twice the inequality of the least unequal ones.[1] Easy inferences come to mind to explain the greater income equality in manufacturing places. The factory as a workplace probably calls for a relative narrow range of skills and imposes similar personal demands, especially in the more routine assembly plant operations, where jobs must mesh with each other. In addition, the egalitarianism of the trade union further compresses wage rate variation, as is well testified to by the periodic unrest of the skilled workers.

But the forces underlying the local distribution of income are very subtle and complex. Cross-section, statistical analysis of the many metropolitan areas reveals that the female labor force participation rate is significantly correlated with income equality: the larger the proportion of females in the labor force, the lower the inequality of *family* income. Many have noted the higher propensity for lower-income families to employ the wife as a second earner; therefore, the availability of jobs for females tends more to raise low incomes and reduce inequality. Since commercial, financial and tourist areas tend to generate more such work, the second-earner characteristic tends to offset the manufacturing-unionization effect (but only partly).

Nothing could seem more certain deductively than a close relationship between industry mix and cyclical stability. An integral and not inconsiderable part of the lore of economics is that durable goods are much more cyclically unstable than non-durable goods and that non-durables fluctuate much more than services. For example, durables exhibited average peak-

---

[1] Using as an index, the inter-quartile deviation of family income divided by the arithmetic mean. This degree of inter-urban variation in income inequality approximates the variation in income level, which also registers a high of roughly twice the lowest value.

to-trough declines of 3.6 and 10.8 percent in the 1953–54 and 1957–58 recessions respectively; non-durables remained nearly constant in both; consumer expenditures on services exhibited average *increases* of 5.3 and 3.2 percent respectively, despite the recessions. We would be quite surprised if those areas specializing in durable goods were not substantially more unstable over the cycle than those emphasizing non-durables. And surprising it is to find, for example, no significant correlation between the percent of total local manufacturing employment engaged in durable goods production and the percent peak-to-trough decline in total employment, 1957–58, for the larger 135 of the two-hundred-odd standard metropolitan areas. Certainly it would be most premature to reject on the basis of such casual empiricism the powerful deductive hypothesis that since durables are more unstable than non-durables, durable good areas would tend to exhibit a greater local business cycle than non-durable areas. Still, urban areas are, it would seem, something more than simple bundles of industries in space, and urban economics something more than industry location theory. The local cycle seems more related to the local rate of growth, a subject to which we now turn.

From Industry Mix to Growth to Income

The local industry mix influences more than the three income goals of the community, it also affects the second of our income determinants: the rate of aggregative growth of the locality. A number of sources of growth originating in the local industry mix may be cited. A relatively large proportion of new industries in the accelerating, exploitation-of-the-market stage of growth would act to create a rapidly expanding local economy, while specialization in the more mature industries, adjusting to the dampened replacement-market stage, would tend to slow the locality to a less-than-average rate of increase in total population and total income. Second, an income elastic demand for local exports would almost ensure at least moderate growth. Consumers with rising per capita income increase expenditure on automobiles more than proportionately, boosting automobile towns to rapid growth, while food-processing and tobacco-manufacturing towns find their exports responding little if at all to higher incomes (income inelastic demands). Third, a locality may grow even with old industries subject to income inelastic demands, if they can gain a larger share of the stagnant national industry total output and employment. Southern textile towns have followed this path; Atlanta has been rising rapidly as a regional service center by assuming wholesaling, corporate administration, financial and other "old" functions formerly performed up North.

There is a significant element of substitution at work among these growth forces. Larger urban areas tend to exhibit fast growing mixes coupled to declining shares of these industries, while the smaller urban areas tend more to grow by acquiring greater shares of the slow-growing industries. New York, for example, has lost nearly every industry it has ever had—flour mills, foundries, meat-packing plants, textile mills, tanneries and, more recently, this most dynamic economy has spun-off apparel and printing while retaining its share of the higher functions of designing and selling garments and publishing. Such a pattern befits a high-wage, high-rent area that can continue to earn these high returns to labor and land only by ceaselessly exploiting the newest industries during their early (pre-competitive) high-price, high-profit-margin stages. Conversely, as operations become more routine with industrial experience they seek lower cost sites to be competitive, filtering down to the lower-skill, lower-wage areas. This filtering down of maturing industries may have as a socially valuable counterpart the "filtering up"—upgrading—of the less industrially advanced urban areas, assuming that the new industries tend to be more technically sophisticated not only at their inception but also throughout their lives.

For whatever reason rapid local growth in output and job formation may occur, it acts to tighten the local labor market and to raise the average income by pushing up wage rates and by generating fuller work weeks and work years. A tight local labor market usually acts to increase the lower incomes more than proportionately, as employers under pressure of manpower shortages accept the inconvenience and expense of hiring and upgrading the more marginal members of the local labor force. Thus, a rapid rate of local job formation tends to reduce unemployment and wage rate differentials, and reduces family income differentials even more, as the wives from low income households find employment. But rising wage rates and incomes serve, in the long run, as beacons attracting workers from other areas, especially the more disadvantaged ones. In the last analysis, therefore, the degree of local income inequality may revert to its original, high level and the principal *long-run* effect of a greater-than-average rate of growth in local employment opportunities may be a larger local population, spanning as before the full range of education, productivity and income. An open economy grows by adding individuals at both ends of the income spectrum, a fact-of-life with a policy moral to be explored below.

The rate of local aggregative growth is also significantly associated with the local business cycle. The percent increase in total population (or employment), 1950–60, exhibits a correlation coefficient of .49 with the percent decline in total employment from 1957 peak to the 1958 trough, in a sample of 135 of the larger metropolitan areas. With, then, roughly 25 percent of the differentials in cyclical severity among urban areas associated with their respective rates of growth, in sharp contrast to the lack of any significant correlation between local specialization in durable goods and the local cycle, some rationalization of this relationship is in order.

A rapidly growing urban area would almost certainly have a relatively high proportion of total employment in the construction industry. Buildings, streets and utilities are not only durable goods, easily postponed in a recession, but are investment goods, subject to speculative actions. To the extent that a rapidly growing area alters its rate of growth frequently and substantially—is subject to "growth instability"—long-run projections are made more difficult, speculative influences are greater, and over- and under-investment is common. Again, to the extent that rapid growth is based on income elastic exports, growth and cyclical instability will be linked. As the secular rise in per capita income which is supporting the strong trend gives way to a short-lived reversal in the recession, the booming local economy finds its exports sales declining more than proportionately, temporarily. Income elastic demands, then, may be at the source of both the rapid rate of local growth and the sharp recessions experienced on the way up.

From Growth Rate to Size to Growth Stability

Just as the first income-determining force, the industry mix, not only acts directly on each of the three income goals, but also generates a side effect on the second income-determining force, the rate of aggregate growth, so too, the growth rate acts not only directly on the income goals but generates a second side effect on the third income-determining force, urban size. The mathematics of change and ensuing size are certain and relatively simple. Still, much can be learned by keeping the various mathematical identities in mind. So often the residents seem to want their community to grow (to generate the new jobs that will keep their children at home) but seem not to want it to get bigger (and lose cherished amenities). Or some seem to want to be bigger (especially, the more urbane consumers and the local merchants) but seem not to want to bear the pains of growth (e.g. housing shortages, traffic congestion, inflated prices and long delays in construction and repair services). It seems appropriate, therefore, to remind ourselves that our growth rate and city-size decisions must be consistent.

The effect of urban size on the various income goals is probably the simplest and perhaps the most powerful of all. Empirical materials drawn from the 1940, 1950 and 1960 Censuses of Population show a very significant tendency for urban economies to become more alike with larger size. Simply said, the smaller urban areas may specialize in very high-wage industries (e.g. automobiles in Flint, Michigan) or somewhat more often in very low-wage industries (e.g. textiles in Greensboro, North Carolina). The larger urban areas tend instead to concoct a blend of industries with diverse wage rates, biased a little toward the higher-wage ones, producing a (slightly above) average per capita income. Again, the smaller urban area is likely to have either durable or nondurable goods industries, inclining it toward substantially greater-than- or less-than-average cyclical instability, while the larger urban area is likely to mix durables and non-durables and services in near-national proportions, producing an average cycle. Again, the smaller urban area may be dominated by manufacturing or virtually free of it; and, therefore, reflect either the great egalitarianism of the unionized assembly line or the great inequality of a profit-based, service-industry town, while the larger urban area again would presumably fashion an average degree of income inequality by sampling the broad range of possibilities. Size normalizes urban income patterns.

The most critical and subtle set of interactions of all may be the feedback of urban size on the local industry mix and the ensuing local growth pattern, serving thereby to reinforce and amplify all the causal connections sketched above. Ever greater urban size serves to stabilize the rate of aggregate growth in a number of ways. First, and most obvious the larger the local economy, the larger the number of products (or services) in its export base, to the end that an average rate of growth is likely to result from this offsetting of growth patterns of young, mature and declining industries and from the mixing of income elastic and inelastic exports as well. Since the industrial structure of a sub-national economy does not ordinarily undergo drastic changes within so short a time period as, say, five years, the current industry mix is probably *the* key to the *near* future.

But a reading of American urban economic history teaches us that in the long run a competitive, open economy can ensure its economic future only by continually reaching for new industries. And certainly the rapid (accelerating?) rate of technological change characteristic of the day is not likely to change this pattern. While we are a long way from achieving a satisfactory theory of change in local industry mix, we hazard here a simplistic hypothesis. The largest urban areas are probably more than proportionally places of invention and, especially, innovation. Hosting, then, the newest industries and assuming that the rate of growth is fastest in the early stages of exploiting a new market and slows later when the market is saturated and replacement production is the rule, the largest areas probably grow principally by planting and harvesting "growth industries." And the larger urban areas do have a more than proportionate share of the graduate schools, laboratories, libraries, museums and other rich sources of invention, plus the investment banking, management consultants, advertising firms and other rich sources of innovation.

Third, the larger urban areas are also better based to adapt to innovations originating elsewhere. With a wider assortment of educational institutions and more professional counseling, local workers may be more quickly retrained from declining to expanding occupations. Re-employment can often (usually?) be achieved within the same local labor market, eliminating the very difficult residential relocation characteristic of smaller places. Finally, in the most general way, urban scale extends the range of consumer and occupational choice, consistent with high and rising levels on income and education, luring and holding the more creative and urbane individuals.

Toward an Income Policy

As thin as the literature is on the determinants and processes of urban economic growth and development, even less has been written on the general objectives on which local development policy should rest—"goals." This becomes most understandable when one tries to specify precisely an opera-

tional set of local income objectives. A nation may rationally
seek to maximize the per capita income of its given set of
inhabitants, but such a prescription degenerates at the local
level, for an "open" urban economy would maximize per
capital income by evacuating everyone except the richest man
in town. The constraint could, of course, be added that a
rational local objective would be to maximize the income of
the current residents, but even this creates the unrealistic
image of a fortress city, with walls that both lock in and lock
out.

In an open, sub-national economy, there is merit in framing
a broad social account in which the local welfare function is
seen as spanning three groups: (1) those who are now residents and will likely remain so, (2) those current residents
who will (or should) migrate out of the area, and (3) those
outsiders who will (should) migrate into the area. The need
for such an extended view and the nature of the income problems posed by migration can be most quickly and clearly
appreciated by recourse to a simple numerical illustration.
Consider three individuals: (1) a current resident earning
$10,000 a year who can realize a maximum increase in earn-
ings of $2,000 by remaining at home; (2) a current resident
earning $12,000 who would increase his income most
($2,000) by moving to another (larger?) urban area; (3) a
resident of the (rural?) hinterland earning $6,000 who would
increase his income most ($2,000) by moving into this urban
area.

We face the paradox where, with unrestricted migration,
each individual would be better off by $2,000, the nation
would be richer, but the local economy would be poorer,
slipping from an average income of $11,000 (10 + 12) to
$10,000 (8 + 12). A community into which the unskilled
(rural) poor come and from which the more educated and
productive members leave is performing the very commenda-
ble service of upgrading the labor force, but in a self-
sacrificing way. We should not be surprised to find such a
community resisting the nation-serving role of human resource
development center, especially if the social costs are borne
locally and the social benefits "spill-out" to the nation. We
might easily argue for substantial federal financial support for
any such area, for example, federal aid to education. The
smaller urban areas in agricultural regions come quickly to
mind in this context, but the central cities of the very largest
metropolitan areas perform a similar function, as the poor

in-migrants flood into the old, cheap housing of the core and push persons with rising expectations into the suburbs.

Certainly, we cannot hold up the maximization of the per capita income of any given piece of real estate—city, county or state—as either an ennobling or operational goal. Our end is people, not land area. It would be naïve perhaps to expect localities to show such national altruism, but, fortunately for the nation at large, localities are powerless to prevent that in-migration and out-migration which aids the migrants but beggars them. Still, it is unfortunate from both a national and local standpoint that we have not seen fit to recognize the net contribution of the locality to the nation and reward this service with a compensating payment, not just for the sake of equity but also to provide an incentive to the community to undertake this critical educating and acculturating function less reluctantly. In the absence of outside (federal) financial assistance, fewer resources will be devoted to education and retraining than would be optimal from a national point of view. (Formally, a region will perform below optimal level any activity for which it bears the full marginal cost and receives only part of the marginal benefits.)

A realistic local policy on the distribution of income is, again, much more difficult to formulate than its national counterpart. The locality operates within the constraint of the national distribution of income; a sub-national economy open to inflows and outflows of capital, both physical and human capital, must look toward assembling the full spectrum of human capital. To lack the most able and ambitious persons is to run the risk of not creating the new industries that generate the new growth indispensable to absorb an inexorably increasing local labor force. The more talented and energetic entrepreneurial and professional groups not only earn a high income for themselves but also raise the productivity and the income of the less talented and educated members of the local labor force. Thus having the most productive and highest-paid persons does not necessarily increase local income inequality, and by lifting the lower end of the income spectrum, almost surely raises the average income of the community, the first of our goals.

Again, an urban area, unlike an exclusive suburb with fixed boundaries does not have and cannot erect a protective wall around itself. It is, therefore, unlikely to lack a nearly pro-rata share of the poor; stagnant urban economies generate the poor and prospering ones attract them, through both better job opportunities and higher public assistance payments. Open economies and migration provide an equilibrating mechanism that acts to distribute the have-nots so as to equalize the burden of and responsibility for the poor. A national average distribution of income becomes, then, both a local norm and a local projection (especially so with larger size). Major changes in the distribution of income can be best accomplished through national policy.

Toward a Growth Policy

Students of urban economic development have been very hesitant to suggest an optimum rate of local growth, or even a desirable one. Given the state of our knowledge about the nature of small-area economic development, some reasonable degree of humility is well taken, but surely some rough benchmarks are defensible. To form jobs locally at less than the natural rate of increase of the local labor force is to invite heavy chronic unemployment and to force net out-migration. Certainly, it is hard to argue against out-migration—the natural market force corrective—when retaining a redundant local labor force piles up heavy public welfare loads, engenders despondency and creates a culture of poverty and dependency. But, while out-migration may solve the problem of the out-migrants, the lot of the remaining residents may improve or deteriorate, depending on whether the local contraction turns out to be an equilibrating adjustment in the supply of labor or leads to cumulative disequilibrium.

Out-migrants tend to be the more mobile members of the local labor force: the young adults, almost certainly, and often the more skilled persons, or at least potentially so in the case of the young. Each wave of out-migration could easily weaken the *long-run* productivity of the local economy, requiring further out-migration, even as it is adjusting the *short-run* supply of labor to the inadequate current demand. And if the rate of out-migration reaches the point at which absolute decline in local population and employment results, idle capacity in public plant will appear, reflected in a rising per capita cost of government, further burdening a population that is laboring under a static or even falling per capita income. Absolute decline also narrows the range of consumer and occupation choice, weakening the attraction of the place to the more affluent and educated.

A community that *grows* at less than the natural rate of

increase in its labor force runs the risk, therefore, of not *developing,* and so slow growth requires local management of the highest order. Especially critical is the design of a local manpower policy that will hold the net out-migration neutral with reference to the quality of the population. Some of the brightest young men might be kept at home with premium pay and with travel and education allowances that permit these ambitious people to maintain intellectual contact with the rapidly advancing technology of their chosen professions (e.g. attendance at professional meetings and post-graduate seminars at leading universities).

Conversely, an urban area which creates jobs at a rate much greater than the natural rate of increase in the labor force runs the risk of outrunning local physical capacity, raising local costs in money (e.g. overtime prices and wage rates) and time (e.g. congestion and waiting). Overburdened facilities deteriorate more rapidly, moreover, and much blight is due to overloading streets, housing and other lagging physical facilities. Who would argue that the social costs of housing shortages and crowded schools on half-day sessions do not, in the long run, create social costs that rival those of too-slow local growth? To be sure, there will be strong voices in the community that would risk erring on the side of too-fast growth as the lesser evil; rapidly rising local sales and property values are healing salve to local merchants, landlords and landowners. But the local economy pays as well as receives high rents and land prices in a set of pure fiscal transfers that do not create new wealth or income; growthsmanship need not be blindly served.

Local job formation at a rate roughly equal to the rate of natural increase in the local labor force may be, therefore, a good first approximation of an "optimum" or at least desirable rate of local aggregative growth. Strengthening this first impression is the hard fact that an above-average rate of growth in one place must be matched by a below-average rate of growth in some other place of equal size. One of the two deviations from average is almost certain to lead to lower economic welfare, and both deviations will create serious social costs in most cases. Still, none of this argues for artificial (federal?) support of an average rate of increase for urban areas that lack the long run economic potential to justify, ultimately, the continuing existence of the locality, much less the larger size which results from growth.

Toward a Size Policy

An operational concept of the optimum size of an urban area is equally elusive, but again rough formulation may be manageable. Quite likely there is some fairly wide range of city sizes which are not markedly superior or inferior to each other as production or residential sites, and where choice would be a matter of taste. Those who indulge in movies and fishing and who have more general occupations (accountants) would probably find a given money income yields a higher real income in urban areas of, say, 200,000 population, while the museum and theatre-going financial analyst would seek an urban area of a million or over to maximize consumer satisfaction and occupational expression. But this conjectured city-size-welfare plateau may or may not extend over the full range of cities; there may be urban pathology of the extremes. Urban areas of less than, say, 50,000 population may often be too small to provide the range of consumer choice that permits increasingly affluent households to enjoy their rising incomes, too narrow a range of occupations to educate and employ a population in which college graduates may come to predominate, and too small to build the local infra-structure that would make science and technology the servant of a better life rather than an exogenous taskmaster that forces radical and painful adaptation on the local community.

Less demonstrable, urban areas may become too big and press too hard on their natural resource bases, creating water shortages, water and air pollution, shortages of accessible land space and the like. In the last analysis, the viability of ever larger urban areas, not unlike larger automobile firms and universities, rests largely on advances in management science, especially in communication and organization theory and practice, and we have been remarkably resourceful in this direction. A number of critics of very large cities have allowed their personal values to intrude in their judgment about the desirability of multi-million population metropolis and have even prematurely written the obituary of the metropolis. Still, we cannot blithely assume that natural market forces will ensure greater size only if the added benefits outweigh the added costs. Most locational decisions are in private hands, and private costs and benefits may not fully reflect the full social costs and benefits; if the added costs of pollution, congestion or *anomie* are blurred and borne at large in concealed ways, urban expansion may run on too long.

Industrial Development Policy for Small Areas

No urban policy would seem harder to formulate than an industrial development strategy for the isolated, smaller urban area (less than 50,000 population). Industry diversification sufficient to ensure stable growth is virtually out of reach. These smaller places often depend on a single industry and often a single firm, exposing them to the uncertainty of shifting brand loyalties and/or incompetent management even if the product-industry outlook is bright. With long-run forecasting virtually impossible, forward planning requires a new tack. Forewarned may be forearmed, but it is not necessary to know the future to prepare for it. A small community, rather than trying to guess what it will be doing a decade hence, might instead devote its efforts to preparing for whatever task the national economy may call on it to perform.

A strategy of industrial flexibility is much easier to sketch broadly than to detail operationally. The local labor force will surely be called on to shift from one type of semi-skilled work to another frequently, as the local shirt factory fails or moves on and the paper box factory moves in, tentatively. A local labor force that has a reasonably good basic general education, rather than some vocational training in depth, would seem to be appropriate. Rudimentary quantitative skills, sold in the school curriculum as "business arithmetic" or "shop practice," and communication skills sugar-coated as manual reading and report writing, if necessary, strike the image in mind. Labor-management relations that go well beyond industrial peace to the point of identification of common interests would seem to be a prerequisite to achieving the job occupational flexibility at stake. Occupational counseling in depth would contribute to managing the unending labor reassignment puzzles.

Wage-rate policy needs also to be well handled. If local wage rates outstrip local productivity, local unit costs will not be competitive, discouraging new entry and weakening existing local firms. But the lower, the better, does not follow. If a large share of profit, interest and rent income flows out of the local economy to absentee property owners, wages become almost the sole source of local value added and local income. Too low a wage rate impoverishes the community and thereby reduces its attractiveness to local-market-oriented firms. Even more critical, depressed wage rates starve the local public economy, practically ensuring inferior schools and other public services essential to area development. An area does not rise far if it can attract only those industries and personnel who will tolerate a low-quality environment. The ratio of local wage rates to wage rates elsewhere should keep up with the ratio of local productivity to the productivity of labor elsewhere.

The availability of local equity capital for small, struggling business known only locally has been widely recognized and occasionally institutionalized in community industrial development funds. The critical importance of borrowed working capital to the new firm is less well recognized and points to the need for a mildly venturesome local banking group. Recent studies, however, have emphasized the ready availability of *real capital,* especially vacant plant space, ready for immediate occupancy. Rising per capita incomes, leading to more than proportionate increases in discretionary spending, ensures a growing importance of impulse buying. The ability to get into production quickly to exploit a transitory market (hoola hoops) often overshadows all other cost considerations. A community with a vacant multi-purpose (shell) plant may easily out-compete rivals with lower tax rates, lower wage rates, or better transportation facilities.

Clearly, a strategy of "industrial flexibility" is a euphemism: a call for the smaller urban area to live by its wits in a world of great uncertainty. But, the small urban place is not unlike a small businessman, opportunistically filling market interstices temporarily missed or ignored by multi-product corporate giants. Some new institutionalization of social entrepreneurship seems to be indicated; the more successful forms of the increasingly common non-profit, local development corporation will probably be widely adopted.

Another possible industrial development strategy for the vulnerable, small urban area—preferably complementary to rather than substitutive for the flexibility strategy outline above—is to simulate greater scale. If the local economy is within, say, fifty miles of a substantially larger city and is connected with good highways, long-distance commuting may be used as supportive tactic. Commuting this far may not be tolerable as a permanent measure, but as a stopgap between local employments, it may dull the sharpest edges of the recurring layoffs that accompany the continuing radical reformation of the local economic base. With a little luck, moreover, the current suburbanization of manufacturing in the not-too-distant metropolis will spin off plants appreciably closer in miles and much closer in time, as movement through the heavily built-up areas to the core could then be avoided.

Greater city size might be simulated by informal inter-urban confederations. Two or three urban areas, perhaps a dozen or two dozen miles apart or even more, might create an integrated local labor market by the appropriate co-ordination of employment and manpower policies. Expansions and contractions in various local industries might then be offset, stabilizing regional employment and rationalizing both in- and out-migrations. Moreover, co-ordination in the planning and use of urban public capital (e.g. hospitals, auditoriums, sports arenas, and colleges) would permit a much richer array of public goods than otherwise, helping to hold the young people at home. While co-operation among separate political entities is never easy, it is not obvious *a priori* why the rationalization of a set of too-small, separate economies in a sparsely populated region would be more difficult to arrange than inter-governmental co-operation in the politically fragmented larger metropolitan areas.

An economic crisis brought on by the lack of sufficient scale could provide the incentive to co-operate with other small urban places nearby—a latter-day version of hanging together or hanging separately. Perhaps one of the places is bigger and/or more aggressive and a natural leadership situation could develop. Or rivalry between near-equals might be resolved by a form of the price mechanism. Suppose each community opts for the regional auditorium and offers the other the new improved jail. An economist's solution would be to let each community bid for the auditorium by offering to assume a higher share of the cost: "No, we will take the auditorium and pay 60 percent of the cost—65 percent—." In the most sanguine terms, "Where there is a will, there is a way," and where there is a crisis, there is a will.

PART II. FORM AND FUNCTIONING OF LARGE URBAN AREAS

The economics of the small urban area is essentially growth and income analysis, the study of the income and employment implications of industrial specialization in a small "open economy"—an economy which is heavily engaged in exporting and importing, into and from which capital flows and labor migrates easily. In the larger urban area of perhaps a half-million population and over and certainly those of over one million population, "urban economics" becomes less the study of inter-urban competition and differentiation and more the study of intra-urban form and function; less the concern with atypical income characteristics, uncertain job formation and how to ensure growth, and more the problem of how to accommodate and manage inexorable growth and great size.

In the popular literature, the large metropolitan area is most often described in terms of its internal problems: Chapter 1. Blight, Chapter 2. Crime in the Streets, Chapter 3. Traffic Jams, Chapter 4. Pollution, Chapter 5. The Empty Public Purse, and so forth into a full recounting of the "urban crisis." It is intriguing to try to factor out of the unending list of "problems" a few root causes. This exercise leads to a certain clarity and incisiveness, at the cost of some oversimplification —the trademark of the economist.

The intra-urban economics of the large metropolitan area will be drawn out in a simple framework. Urban spatial patterns, especially those relating to land-use and the organization of local government, and urban economic processes, especially those relating to the supply of local public services, will be rationalized with reference to:

1. The level and distribution of income;
2. The population size of the area;
3. The adequacy of various mechanisms of control, especially the role of the price system and urban public management.

The Income Paradox

The pattern of income distribution has a powerful effect on the form and functioning of the city; it is commonplace to recognize that many urban problems are in large part surface reflections of poverty. Slums are where the poor live. Desperate or alienated people commit crimes, and it is unlikely that they will steal paint to help fight blight. A good case might be made, therefore, that the great complex of programs designed to raise incomes constitutes our most basic urban improvement policy. Federal fiscal and monetary policies that increase the aggregate demand for labor and reduce unemployment would qualify. Federal-state and local manpower programs which project changing occupational demands, retrain workers in new and expanding lines of work (whether before or after the fact), relocate workers from depressed areas to growing areas, counsel in depth and open up new occupational horizons or otherwise tailor the supply of labor to fit the pattern of new demands are also powerful, if indirect, slum-clearance programs.

Further, income-maintenance policies that act outside of the labor market touch at least as many persons in the poverty category as do full-employment policies. Social insurance in all its forms—old-age retirement, workman's compensation, categorical aids to the handicapped, aid to dependent children —supports a major share of the life of the core area. A major piece of "urban legislation" passed last year was Medicare: elderly people, a major constituent group of our urban core dwellers, impoverished by heavy medical and hospitalization bills cannot afford to repair or repaint their houses. The ties among age, illness and physical blight, moreover, should not be expected to weaken as medical science learns how to keep us alive longer and longer, but at a higher and higher price. National socio-economic planning is, in short, a clear corequisite and perhaps even a prerequisite to effective urban planning.

The paradox of the day seems to be that we are able to produce full employment, that is, reduce unemployment to around 4 percent of the labor force, only by generating mild inflation. Tight labor markets produce skilled-labor bottlenecks and a favorable climate for wage demands that outrun productivity increases. Given the unfortunate fact that our social insurance programs lack cost-of-living "escalator clauses," we have seen secular inflation slowly but inexorably erode the purchasing power of these fixed payments: workman's compensation programs have slipped from a support level of about two thirds the wage earned prior to incapacitation when the program was enacted to a current support level of about one half. A point is reached where the expansion of aggregate demand through fiscal and monetary policy creates through inflation as much poverty among those on fixed income outside of the labor force as it eliminates among the marginal members of the labor force through increased employment.

Poverty has, in fact, become so dominant an issue that the urban policy conference of the day often becomes in effect a poverty conference. It is, therefore, most timely and productive to ask the utopian question: if poverty were eliminated, what if any urban problems would remain? From this vantage point, it is but a short step to see that an almost equally important source of urban "problems" is growing affluence. Rising incomes, widely shared, increases the number of automobiles and adds to traffic congestion, as Europe is now discovering. Growing mass affluence has elevated the priority of water pollution problems, as rising output increases the supply of wastes to be disposed of in our river sewers precisely at the time when rising incomes increase the demand for outdoor recreational facilities. Frustrated drivers become frustrated boaters and fishermen.

Again, widespread affluence and automobile ownership have led to the power to command greater land space. A large lot in a distant suburban location which demands long journeys to work and shop and play—"sprawl"—is a natural product of affluence and the automobile. (An implicit price structure that may be quite irrational is also at issue, to be considered below.) Sprawl has, moreover, interwoven the problems of affluence and poverty.

In hindsight, we now see how the affluence of the great majority of Los Angeles residents led to the development of low-density residential areas and to an elaborate automobile freeway network, the combined effect of which eroded mass transportation service to the point where important parts of the metropolitan area become inaccessible to those who could not afford to own an automobile or could not drive. The riots in the Negro suburb, Watts, were in large measure a manifestation of the growing inaccessibility of decentralizing job opportunities and the growing cultural isolation of the inhabitants of the Watts "compound." The city must (be planned to) accommodate all income groups and some very critical linkages between land-use, transportation and employment were missed. The rich and poor, with very different consumption patterns, may be mixed in proportions that create public service demands that are hard to process, especially since "public goods" are highly indivisible and subject to the rather insensitive process of majority rule. Even a pluralistic big-city transportation system can never be designed to fully satisfy any one class of users; the units of consumption —expressways, transit lines—are much too lumpy.

"Problems" can also be seen as unmet demands growing out of rising expectations, reasonable or not. Rising incomes, education and leisure increase the demand for public goods and services at least apace with private goods. There is mounting evidence that local government services increase more than in proportion to rising income, that is, they exhibit income-elastic demands. Further, public goods and services are more complicated to supply and finance; the public economy exists largely to process goods and services which the market place cannot handle efficiently or equitably. Again, public entrepreneurship may be less responsive or dynamic, as a result, perhaps, of irrational constraints or multiple-purpose objectives that complicate response. In any event, new gaps are opened between citizen expectations and government performance: the "revolution of rising expectations" applies also to the local public economy—the game is never won. Affluence leads, then, to "problems," in the same sense that curing a disease that kills at sixty years of age brings to notice a new disease that kills at seventy years.

Exaggerating to make a point, one sometimes feels in reading the urban problems literature (at least the "crisis" variety) that most urban problems would be greatly softened if not dissolved by a distribution of income in which most families lived a little above the poverty line ("genteel poverty") and a substantial number were very rich. The former would live densely and inconspicuously in decent, if dull, houses (terraces?) and ride mass transit, while the latter, as patrons of the arts including architecture, would sponsor the parks and plazas which grace a city. It is the numerically small, lowest-income group and the very large middle- and low-upper income classes which cause trouble. The latter class "congests" the city during the day with their automobiles and then journeys home in the evening to "sprawl" in suburbia, and then makes exorbitant demands on park space and water sports facilities on the weekends, always reluctant to pay taxes from their new-found wealth. The poor, of course, blight the city.

The Pressure of Population

Sheer population size is a major source of many, even most, urban problems. A growing population is accommodated in part by horizontal expansion sweeping over the surrounding rural areas. Greater distances must then be traversed if any semblance of economic and social unity are to be preserved, if, that is, the urban area is to be more than a collection of villages in accidental proximity (as Tokyo was once said to be). Population growth leads, then, to a more than proportionate expansion in transportation demands (as *per capita* movements increase). To the extent, therefore, that government plays a significant role in supplying transportation facilities and services, the public sector tends also to expand more than proportionately.

It is almost inevitable, moreover, that local government

will be forced to assume a greater responsibility for internal transportation as the volume of movement mounts. Transportation arteries need to be widened and bordering private property must be taken. Larger operations often dictate transportation forms that employ much larger initial investments, resulting in heavy fixed cost, unit costs which decrease over long ranges of output, and very long amortization periods. Decreasing unit cost leads to monopoly which must be either publicly owned or regulated, and long payoff periods may discourage private enterprise.

The horizontal extension of the city also operates to increase the distance and lessen communication between the various socio-economic population clusters that seem always to form in cities. Perhaps in a relative sense, residential segregation by income, and to a lesser extent by occupation, was just as true of urban places a century ago as it is the iron law of urban living today. The poor have nearly always lived "on the other side of the tracks" but the distances were short and contacts frequent, as in the schoolrooms and town halls. But the all-slum block becomes first the all-slum school, next the all-slum community—the ghetto—and threatens now to become the all-slum city. What was once, if not benign, at least digestible *apartheid* at small scale, portends a large-scale unemployability, anti-social behavior and, ultimately, recourse to ever more centralization of authority. Slum schools "graduating" unemployables and political enclaves of the poor lacking the tax base to support minimum public standards of health and safety (vice havens, perhaps) invite either state or federal intervention.

The horizontal extension of the city has, therefore, laid on the public sector new responsibilities in effecting greater inter-group communication, reflected in the burgeoning poverty programs. We are learning the lesson that a structure, such as residential segregation by income, which is viable at small scale is not necessarily viable at very large scale. A synthesis of the Burgess Concentric Zone Theory and the natural history of the dinosaur seems indicated.

A growing population is also accommodated in part by vertical expansion and by sheer crowding. Higher land rents in the ever denser core area are a substitute for the higher cost of traveling ever farther to the receding edge of town. Those activities which inter-act frequently with others in the core, or those which need to command the full sweep of the urban area from a single base, often find the rising cost of constructing higher floors or economizing on space below, the most economical course. (Achieving larger size rapidly—a rapid rate of growth—also serves to increase densities temporarily as the supply of new space lags behind the booming demand; crowding occurs throughout the urban area.)

Greater urban densities generate greater inter-personal inter-actions, both planned increased contact and unplanned increased friction. Greater density and inter-action is perhaps the principal objective of city-building. Still, densely packed populations get in each other's way (e.g. traffic delay—"congestion") or annoy each other (e.g. noise, noxious odors—"pollution") or otherwise impose "neighborhood effects," as in driving automobiles or burning garbage. Spillover costs and benefits require the mediation of some impartial third force, such as government.

In the extreme, high-population densities convert previously free goods into scarce (economic) goods (e.g. fresh air) and in many cases into "public goods"—goods which are highly indivisible and are "collectively consumed," such that individual benefits cannot be identified or separated out. With the voluntary mechanism of the private market inoperative, resort must be had to compulsory payment—taxes. Adam Smith's unseen hand is replaced by the clearly seen and keenly felt hand of government.

The Spatial Pattern of the Local Public Economy

One of the principal advantages of the large urban area is, or at least should be, lower unit costs of various utilities and public services. Many of the activities basic to the support of urban life—dense habitation—involve large initial investment and heavy fixed costs, for example, the provision of water, sewage disposal and transportation, and are thereby subject to significant decreases in unit costs of production with larger outputs. Thus with greater urban size comes potential "internal economies of scale," which may not be fully realized if this growing market is subdivided by political boundaries and many small, high-cost installations are substituted for an efficient area-wide public monopoly. Of interest is the fact that it is the privately owned and operated public utilities that most often command area-wide jurisdictions and capture the full economies of scale (e.g. electricity and gas).

The most sanguine view of political fragmentation is one which carefully distinguishes between two quite distinct functions: (1) *decision-making* on the quantity and quality of the various public services which should be provided and (2) the actual physical production of those services. The argument is advanced that internal economies of scale in the production of, say, water supply, sewage disposal, garbage incineration and police road patrolling can be captured by small local governments, either through joint action or through a quasi-market system. A number of the smaller municipalities of a politically fragmented metropolitan area might jointly finance and operate an optimum-size plant or they might contract out this work and stimulate the formation of efficient-size independent suppliers. These suppliers may be either larger public authorities, such as the central city or the county water departments, or large private enterprises, common in refuse disposal.

Not content to rest their defense on merely matching the *potential* output and *potential* internal economies of scale of big government, those who would rationalize political fragmentation rather than beat the drums for "METRO," press farther and argue that the potential economies would probably be more nearly achieved in a system where two or more public and/or private suppliers of a service were competing for the garbage business of the small municipality. Competition would provide a healthy pressure toward both technical efficiency in production and responsiveness to the needs of the principal buyers, two objectives often lost in the bureaucracy of big government. Political scientists have rediscovered that competition is "a thing of beauty"; economists have long found it to be "a joy forever."

Still, most often the number of suppliers will be very small, and oligopolies, by one route or another, generally arrive at or near monopoly price and output patterns. The gains through "competition" would probably be modest at best. Shifting from a static to a more dynamic context, however, oligopoly promises more in quality competition and product improvement through research and development, some of which surely gets to the consumer even through the resistance of an administered price structure.

The political subdivisions of the large and growing metropolitan area might either achieve population sizes which permitted most of the internal economies of scale in water, sewer, transportation and police systems to be realized internally or they might achieve production efficiencies externally by contracting. Or the point might be reached where the "diseconomies" of larger local government more than offset further economies; the imputed subjective value of greater political participation in the political process and greater responsiveness of public officials to the electorate might tip the balance.

But internal economies of scale may not be the principal point at issue in rationalizing the spatial pattern of local government. To the extent that the cost or quality of a public service is a function of the degree of spatial coverage (relative size) rather than the level of output of a service (absolute size), then efficiency increases with growth to the full extent of the market (urban area). If, for example, transportation facilities are adjusted to accommodate peak movements and the journey to work generates that peak, and if the metropolitan area is a single indivisible labor market or nearly so, then the web of movement is spun in an economic space that transcends political boundaries and cannot be rationalized within a politically subdivided space no matter how large, in absolute measure, the constituent municipalities are or become. (Recent evidence of a new peak, the Sunday evening return from *regional* outdoor recreational facilities, does not alter this conclusion as a projection, for that too is a supra-municipal pattern of movement.)

That the rationalization of metropolitan area-wide transportation flows are complicated by political subdivision of the area is readily apparent—intuitively. Still, it is useful to express the problem more formally in terms of "spillover costs." If the residents of political subdivision A who benefit from moving through subdivision B pay only part of the traffic costs they impose on B, then the citizen-taxpayers of B will probably allocate fewer resources to (spend less on) those sections of the transportation system which lie in their domain than the commuters from A would prefer and be willing to help finance. The allocation of resources will be carried only to the point where the marginal benefit of another unit of transportation services to B is equal to the marginal cost of that service, borne wholly by B. The socially optimum position is at a higher output at which the rising marginal cost becomes equal to marginal benefit of A plus B. This will only occur if A shares in financing the service. What usually happens is that A avoids paying and beggars B who, in turn, underinvests in facilities that also service A and inconveniences his exploiter. Both inequity and allocative efficiency result, as our metropolitan areas produce both traffic jams and inequitable redistributions of income.

In sum, growing population increases population density and inter-personal spillovers, as my storm water floods your basement. At the same time, a growing population expands horizontally across fixed political boundaries, hardened by cumbersome political annexation procedures (e.g. veto by any existing political entity rather than the more common rule of majority). Thus, inter-personal spillovers become intergovernmental spillovers too, further defying economic rationalization in the usual absence of any immediate, competent jurisdiction encompassing both my storm water run-off and your basement, except the courts.

The Discipline of Price

Low residential density at the edge of the urban area and heavy, slow movements through the area—"sprawl" and traffic jams—reflect the growing size of the local population, the rising level of income and, perhaps to a lesser degree, a public sector which responds only sluggishly and weakly. These shortcomings of the local public sector reflect, in turn, both political fragmentation, itself a partial function of size and sprawl, and other binding constraints on the exercise of imaginative urban public management, discussed below. To all this, the role of price is now added.

While rising incomes and mass automobile ownership have been the principal determinants of falling residential densities, postwar lots have grown bigger and the extent of the leapfrogging over contiguous vacant land much greater than if full cost prices had been charged for extending water, sewers, roads and police and fire protection out into these new, low-density areas. Again, rapidly rising automobile ownership and use are largely attributable to affluence, but here too an important element of subsidy is present in the costs of traffic control, noise, dirt, air pollution and delay, even though the gasoline tax provides much of the road surface. More significant, off-peak drivers overpay and subsidize on-peak drivers, as when four lanes of expressway or bridge capacity are needed in the morning and evening rush hours where two lanes would have done if movements had been random in time and direction, that is, near constant in average volume.

If the cost of the additional facilities needed to accommodate the rush-hour traffic were charged to the peak-hour users, by means of tolls or special licenses to travel at those hours, rather than spread over all users through the gasoline tax, both greater efficiency in the allocation of resources and greater equity in the distribution of income would be achieved. To the degree that the rush-hour user paid the toll and continued his use at that time, the funds would be provided to expand the crowded system; to the degree that rush-hour automobile drivers shifted their time of use or became riders in buses or other cars, price would be serving to ration the existing road and bridge space efficiently. In either case, an inequitable redistribution of income from off-peak to on-peak users would have been eliminated.

Thus, while the level of income may largely explain the ownership of automobiles, it is price which largely explains the traffic jam. The problem of congestion stems from the absence of some mechanism, such as price, to: (a) ration the current scarce supply of street space, (b) signal the need to allocate more resources into automobile transportation facilities—better, signal the *demand* for additional capacity as evidenced by rationing prices that exceed the cost of the additional facilities—and (c) arrange the actual financing of the additional facilities.

Our failure to use prices to rationalize allocation of resources among the various functions of the local public economy has turned back on us and complicated the spatial rationalization of local government. Public subsidization of large lots, leapfrogging land use, and the use of the automobile has accelerated the horizontal expansion of the urban area and thereby reinforced the trend toward political fragmentation (principally attributable to population growth, however). Automobile movement back and forth across communities and political boundaries has, moreover, generated mounting inter-personal and inter-governmental spillovers, elaborated above.

Below-cost pricing of automobile movement also acts against economic efficiency in resource allocation by reducing the incentive to live near one's work. We see much more criss-crossing in home-to-work trips than would occur if the extra costs of accommodating the peak-hour user were assessed fully and directly on the journey-to-work trip. In all fairness, user charges designed to encourage people to live near their work would be feasible only if supporting changes were made in our housing and residential land-use patterns. A substantial increase in the number of high-income houses and neighborhoods would need to be added to the core of the metropolitan area, near the central business district, for professionals who work downtown, and low-income houses and neighborhoods added in the suburbs for the unskilled laborers and domestic service workers who must commute to suburban plants and homes. Thus the conditions necessary to effect an efficient and equitable land-use and transportation pattern—in simulation of the workings of the private market place—includes the supply of a wide range of housing throughout the metropolitan area (local labor market) and automobile user charges that capture most of the high on-peak movement costs of this most expensive mode of travel.

User charges are, however, difficult to introduce into the public economy both because their applicability is limited and their advocacy most impolitic. The public economy is charged especially with the production of goods and services which are either: (a) highly indivisible and must, therefore, be "collectively consumed," to the end that individual benefits cannot be separated out and the service rendered only to those who will voluntarily pay (e.g. justice, defense, public safety); or (b) "merit goods" judged to be more beneficial to society or the individual himself than many persons recognize, to the end that the majority chooses to subsidize them and increase their consumption or (c) designed to benefit those who cannot afford to pay for them, to the end that a desired redistribution of income is achieved (e.g. public assistance payments and poverty programs in general).

The continuing transfer of functions to the public sector has brought a virtually automatic extension of the tradition of "free" public services, despite the clear trend in local government toward the assumption of more and more functions that do not fit this neat schema ("proprietary activities" in the earlier literature of public administration and political science). The provision of free public facilities for automobile movement in the crowded cores of our urban areas can hardly be defended on the grounds that: (a) motorists could not be excluded from the expressways if they refused to contribute their fair share of the costs, or (b) the privately operated motor vehicle is an especially meritorious way to move through densely populated areas, or (c) the motorists cannot afford to pay their own way and that the general (property) taxpayers should subsidize them. And all this applies with a vengeance to municipal marinas and golf courses.

Finally, we might argue that to subsidize motorists, boaters and golfers is to redistribute income toward greater inequality, assuming that the proportion of these services used by the upper-income groups is greater than their share of the local (property) taxes that finance the subsidy. Even if the redistributive effects were neutral, these proprietor-type activities draw on a scarce supply of tax money which must be depended on to support the classic-type public functions. Given continuing resistance to higher local (property) taxes, the "opportunity cost" of adding more marina space is to give up additional judges, teachers or social case workers. Marina user charges would, on the other hand, allow us to have both. In sum, failure to apply user charges wherever possible and appropriate leads to: (a) overallocation of resources in that sector, (b) underallocation of resources in some classic-type public function, and (c) a possible and even probable unintended and adverse redistribution of income.

An Entrepreneurship Gap?

Let us bring together the arguments from above. A rising standard of living increases the absolute and *relative* size of the public sector, assuming an income elasticity of demand for public services of greater than one. The persistence of an impoverished group left behind in the climb to general affluence reinforces the expansion of the public role. The growing population size of the urban area extends its horizontal dimension, forcing the public sector to take on the added tasks of holding it together with new programs in transportation and inter-group communication. Size also leads to greater density, turning previous free goods into "public goods" (e.g. fresh air and "community development") and causes inter-personal spillovers that require the impartial mediation of government. This growing role of the public sector is thrust on local government at just the time when its financial, decision-making and production functions have been heavily constrained by political fragmentation. Finally the limited applicability of price to the public sector and the failure of public managers to use price explicitly as a system of control when it is applicable has created significant misallocations of resources (shortages and congestion), misplaced rewards and penalties (windfall gains and hardship exactions) and generally aimless development.

All of this suggests the heroic role reserved for a beleaguered urban public management. This closing section of the chapter is addressed to the question of whether the urban public sector is capable of responding to so great a challenge. Does a large part of what we loosely label the urban crisis arise from an "entrepreneurship and management gap" between the public and private sectors?

Civil service salaries have always lagged behind the rates

for comparable work in business. The highest posts carry the glamour of high visibility or the lure of power, such that recruiting at this level may not suffer. But at second-echelon levels and below—in the shadow of the leader—there is neither the lure of money nor any good substitute; consequently these critical technical slots are the hardest to fill. How many cities could hire a first-rate professional economist within their present salary structure? A most revealing question that might be put to the heads of local government departments would be: which would you prefer, a bigger total budget for staff, or the power to pay higher salaries out of your present budget? Perhaps the federal government should apply pressure by specifying professional appointments which carry competitive salaries on supported projects (e.g. one professional economist, Ph.D., at $20,000). The great outcry recently raised against paying salaries of $15,000 to $20,000 for top professional jobs in the poverty program—jobs which call for great skill on the frontiers of social science, or beyond—suggests such a strategy may be politically premature.

Raising the rewards for local public service to levels competitive with private business will not be an easy task. The average stockholder of a large corporation is probably more sophisticated, at least about economics, than the average citizen, especially with reference to the opportunity cost of top talent. The stockholder typically has a higher income and is less reluctant to pay competitive salaries. Probably more relevant, the large business corporation is almost invariably management rather than stockholder controlled, while the municipal corporation exhibits much tighter citizen control. Space is critical here: the stockholder must travel across the country at considerable cost in time and money to the annual stockholders' meeting, while the citizen can vote down the block from his house. What may result, then, is a competition for managerial talent between a centralized, sophisticated business sector and very democratic, naïve public sector.

Perhaps this comparison of private and public enterprise misses the mark in that the public economy was not designed with efficiency foremost. The public sector is where the business world's heavy emphasis on efficiency is redressed; equity and humanitarianism are important goals and those who have failed or fared poorly in the competitive arena are here attended. A less sanguine interpretation is that government jobs are political spoils to be divided. Robert Wood has wondered whether the student of urban affairs may not wait in vain for an aroused citizenry to reform local government; the citizen has never really expected local government to be efficient.

Certainly, the popular image (caricature?) of the corrupt politician and the lazy civil servant reinforces this low expectation. A form of "underdevelopment trap" quickly follows where a low expectation justifies low pay which attracts low talent which merits only low pay. The most obvious, if not especially popular, remedy is to break the circle by overpaying the current clique, ultimately attracting personnel which merit the pay. The hope would be that mediocre legislative bodies who opportunistically raise their own salaries might succeed in legislating themselves back into private practice.

Not only is the municipal corporation subject to relatively tight citizen control, but its present "management" is subjected to an organized, institutional opposition dedicated to destroying the credibility of its performance. There may be some limited analogy here with competition in the business world, but market competition would seem to lead more often to linked private and public gain through product improvement, while the political process stresses more the destructive competition of disparagement.

The two arenas differ further in that the private economy makes full use of advertising in its merchandising strategy, while the public economy is prohibited from advertising its "products." Perhaps it would give an unfair political advantage to the incumbents to allow public funds to be used to herald their reputed triumphs. Still, can the public economy expect to sell civic beauty and amenity over the din of Madison Avenue? This is a battle for discretionary income—impulse spending on weakly felt wants—and it is not a fair game.

Denied the weapon of advertising, the public enterprise is further disadvantaged with a line of merchandise that is hard to sell. Most products of private enterprise are relatively simple and small, can be built in advance of sale, can be exhibited to stimulate demand and carry a certain price. Conversely, the public economy must try to sell the public on very complicated, abstract goods and services which entail uncertain costs. The automobile may not seem so simple, but compare it to a new mass transit system; contrast a model home with the blueprints for a "new town."

Embattled by a tough, alert, patient opposition on one flank, the municipal leaders are constrained on the other flank by an electorate which tends to reward timid, safe political behavior. A most hallowed political axiom is that citizens vote against, not for, candidates. Quite understandably politicians tend to become caretakers rather than entrepreneurs. The communications media might help inculcate a popular demand for experimentation and innovation and help rationalize occasional errors and losses as the cost of progress. But newspapers seem convinced that their readers have a taste for blood and are more inclined to feed them a petty grafter than recount quiet successes of great significance. Too often they inflame controversy and highlight minor errors of commission; they should more often blast timidity and major errors of omission. Public acclaim is the most distinctive reward of public office and is bestowed largely by the mass communication media—neither especially fairly nor constructively to date.

Perhaps most of all and more directly in line with main themes drawn out above, public enterprise also suffers from the limited horizons of the job both in space and time. Political fragmentation of our larger metropolitan areas limits the absolute size of local government and thereby the total budget available to support the high specialization and professionalism needed for a first rate staff. Perhaps even more important, municipal employment may be frustrating to the most able people because the spatial extent of their power falls short of that necessary to effect bold and fruitful policies.

Consider, for example, urban renewal and housing authorities limited to the central city, where little or no vacant land is available on which to build low-income housing in advance of the demolition of dilapidated units. Not only are the housing and renewal programs forced to put added pressure on the low-income housing supply before they can improve the situation, but the central city authorities are limited to maintaining large clusters of poor in the core area, regardless of any evidence that other spatial arrangements would be preferable, with reference to education, the financing of public services, transportation requirements and other closely related public policy objectives. It would be most surprising if a central city housing authority could come near rivaling a metropolitan area-wide housing authority in attractiveness to professional economists or sociologists.

Not only do local government posts often lack powerful challenges, but they also suffer from limited tenure—the time horizon necessary to respond to whatever creative opportunities do exist. The top jobs that carry decision-making power are political, and re-election is uncertain, and the civil service personnel who carry over from one administration to the next are often conservative in outlook and owe little allegiance to the changing political leaders. The paradox is that political entrepreneurs and managers have short personal horizons (even to the point of being ineligible for re-election) and must deal with very long life capital (e.g. street patterns) while business corporate decision-makers deal more with capital that has relative short amortization period (e.g. tools and machines) from the secure position of near certain tenure far ahead to retirement.

Chapter 5

THE CONTRIBUTIONS OF POLITICAL
SCIENCE TO THE STUDY OF URBANISM

There patently can be no urban planning in Western society without wary and assiduous attention to governmental structure, administrative behavior, practical politics, pressure blocs and the consent (at least to a certain extent) of the governed. This situation is exacerbated in labyrinthian complexity under three-tiered American federalism. Until very recent years, urban America poured money into the national till only to have a rurally stacked Congress parsimoniously short-change the cities and pour funds out to the 30 percent agricultural minority. With Baker versus Carr (1962) the glacially slow redistricting for state and national legislatures is at least underway to reduce the rural bias in voting power. This may end up shifting power to suburban voters—still slighting the central city, which has been labeled "the haunt of the old, the poor, the colored, and the odd."

With the final establishment under President Johnson of the Department of Housing and Urban Development (1965), more sophisticated federal forms are slowly falling into shape to administer at a level at least equal to the Department of Agriculture, the affairs of our 70 percent urban nation. It is estimated that 90 percent of all future population growth will occur in metropolitan urban areas. As the world starves in pieces with mounting food shortages, the huge U.S. domestic agricultural supports pushed by a frenetically active and successful lobby will become recognizably less needed and less voted.

Robert C. Wood, as one of the best-known students of American urban political affairs, has the strategic position of Under Secretary of the Department of Housing and Urban Development in a crucial and constructive period during which the federal government is moving massively in a many-pronged attack planning the political, economic, and social life of urban America—which is after all modern America. What Wood, as a scholar, thinks is of crucial importance as he plays a key operational role "in the armpit of the tortoise" as the federal government experiments with a whole new battery of instruments ranging from Demonstration or Model Cities and the Poverty Program to upgrading commuter and megalopolitan rail transport.

The Contributions of Political Science
to the Study of Urbanism
ROBERT C. WOOD*

In the United States historically, neither public policy nor research in public affairs have had a major positive impact on the course of urban development. Although the tempo of popular concern and governmental activity in city-building has increased in recent years, and political decisions of great moment to the pattern of urbanization are made daily, a comprehensive consistent philosophy is only slowly beginning to emerge.

Why this is so—and how it could be changed—is the subject of this paper. Essentially, the explanation of our present situation comes in three parts. In summary these seem to be the reasons.

Substantively, the American urban political process is best understood as chronically beset with such tensions, conflicts, and diversity of participants as to be always in danger of disintegration and collapse. Since pre-Revolutionary days and thereafter throughout our national life, the problem of amassing sufficient power to enable the development and execution of reasonable public policy has never been adequately solved. Hence, the conscious impact of political decisions on the development of urban form has been slight in comparison to other influences.

Secondly, a solid base in scholarly analysis on which sound policy could be built—given power—has been slow in coming. The deficiencies and gaps in professional study have been such that students of urban politics constantly walk on eggshells,

* On leave as Chairman of the Department of Political Science at M.I.T., currently the Under Secretary of the Department of Housing and Urban Development. Best known of his recent publications are *Suburbia: Its People and Their Politics* (Boston: Houghton Mifflin Co., 1959) and *1400 Governments: The Political Economy of the New York Metropolitan Region* (Boston: Harvard University Press, 1961). He served on the presidential task forces of 1964–65 and 1965–66 which led up to H.U.D. The following is an adaptation of his article in *Urban Life and Form*, edited by Werner Z. Hirsch, copyright © 1963 by Holt, Rinehart and Winston, Inc. and including portions of a lecture, "A Generation of City Builders" delivered at the University of Ohio, February 25, 1965.

confront each other with apparently self-contradictory conclusions and submit conflicting policy recommendations.

Finally, the central thrust of the academic community supporting urban study seems basically misdirected. Before progress in policy-making is possible, and contrary to present proclivities, the student of urban politics needs a role closer to the engineer in his profession than to the pure scientist embarked on "basic research."

This fragility in our formulations of analysis and prescription seems the root cause of our inability accurately to understand indigenous processes and to generate meaningful public policy. As a subsection of political science, inquiry into urban politics has been caught up in a more general debate over purposes and methods which has continued for at least a generation and which only now appears to be in part, on point of resolution. Within the realm of political science as well, the study of urban politics has shown an unusual proclivity in the twentieth century to select the wrong properties of urban political behavior as relevant for investigation, and has thus provided descriptions of manifest, rather than real forces at work. Moreover, urban scholarship has faced special complications and special subtleties. In the broadest sense of the word a comparative study, urban politics, in its original definition as "state and local," involves the comprehension of 212 metropolitan areas, 3,047 counties, 34,381 cities and towns, and 54,459 special districts, or one government for each 2,000 people and each 40 square miles in the United States. Thus a discipline unsure of its objectives has applied overly simple assumptions to an enormously complex field of investigation in the hope of producing, in some quick and dirty way, satisfactory generalizations for action.[1]

POLITICAL SCIENCE: DESCENT FROM THE PEAKS

The general liabilities of political science as a discipline are perhaps the most disabling. In an age of analysis, the rich historical and philosophical legacy of political science has often seemed to operate as much as a handicap as a resource. To the last two generations of political scientists, at any rate, the question of what to do with their heritage has been a

[1] Walter A. Rosenblith, "On Some Social Consequences of Scientific and Technological Change," *Daedalus* 90:3 (Summer 1961), pp. 510–17.

perplexing, recurrent question. Andrew Hacker has summed up the nature of the dilemma in this way:

> For better or for worse, the term "political theory" has two quite distinct meanings for contemporary students of politics. It stands, first of all, for the history of political ideas. . . . studies with due regard for historical circumstances which produced them, and their influence on political practice . . . This understanding of political theory is the more traditional of the two, and an honorable tradition of scholarship supports it. The other conception of the theory is newer and, in consequence, less sure of its methods and purposes. Nevertheless, it can be said that this approach calls for systematic study of political behavior in the modern world. . . . sees as its subject the actual behavior of men and institutions in our own time. Systematic theory, then, is concerned to create generalizations which describe and explain contemporary political phenomena. By and large it places great importance on the methods of collecting data, for systematic knowledge must be founded on evidence rather than intuition. On the whole, this approach to theory tries to avoid making value judgments or entering into ethical controversies.[2]

It is not clear at all that these approaches are contradictory or mutually exclusive. Indeed, Hacker emphasizes both the empirical basis on which the great political thinkers from Plato to Mill have rested their arguments and the norms implicit in the newer approach as it undertakes to speak to the relevant issues of the day. And certainly methodologically elegant inquiries make little or no contribution if the knowledge they produce can simultaneously be acquired by casual observation, common sense, or cruder methods of inquiry.

But the fact remains, as Daniel Lerner has pointed out, that there is a basic difference between a perspective which emphasizes the dialectic and that which stresses the systematic interjection of new information into the consideration of relevant propositions.[3] Recurrent themes in political life there certainly are, each to be set in the circumstances of its own time. But what the circumstances are, how they modify the themes,

[2] Andrew Hacker, *Political Theory: Philosophy, Ideology, Science* (New York: The Macmillan Company, 1961), p. vii.
[3] Daniel Lerner, *The Human Meaning of the Social Sciences* (New York: Meridian Books, Inc., 1959), Preface.

what light they throw on the latter's viability are increasingly significant considerations and, in the complex world of urban political behavior, vital ones.

Moreover, a sizable number of political scientists today are persuaded that the potential for identifying relevant circumstances of the environment, for specifying the relevant properties of political behavior, and for modifying that behavior deliberately is vastly greater than ever before. In particular, the increasing sophistication of the attitudinal study and the rapid development of the high-speed computer offer the prospect of testing empirically propositions on a scale and in depth that no other generation of scholars has possessed.

This emerging view of the character of political science suggests a narrowing of the range of concerns, a forswearing of undiluted normative speculation, and a descent from the peaks of political inquiry as the queen of philosophy to the substratum approximating that much maligned and misunderstood calling of "social engineering." There are sacrifices in this reordering, of course. Great names may appear less and less frequently within our ranks; fewer political scientists will sit immediately at the feet of policy makers. But the net result of cumulative knowledge may be something novel in urban politics: the capacity of political action actually to contribute decisively to urban form and to touch more fundamental aspects of urban life. In place of cities built by the Invisible Hand and the occasional aesthetic whim of strategically located individuals, there may emerge purposeful public policy which has aspects of rationality and clearer satisfactions of public needs attached to it.

WHAT WE THINK WE KNOW ABOUT URBAN POLITICS: KEY COMPONENTS IN THE PRESENT SYSTEM

With this introduction as to the atmosphere of ferment and revisionism in which the urban political scientist works today, what generalizations can we make about the urban political process? What operating assumptions underlie the research now going on?

An answer to these questions turns, of course, on the definition chosen for "the urban political process." Perhaps the most popular conception of this process today focuses on decision-making and decision-makers, the choices exercised by political activists to settle, postpone, or bypass public issues in urban life. Here, the characterization is one of actors responding to a diverse set of social, economic and political pressures, defining objectives, obtaining political influence of various types, striving to increase that influence through its strategic employment in coalition with or in opposition to other political actors in an assortment of arenas. In analyzing behavior in this process, the substance of the issue, and its effect outside the immediate arena, is less important than what happens to the objectives, resources, and relative positions of the participants and how they devise and utilize their strategies.

But we shall have to employ a larger conception of the urban political process if we are to discharge our assignment of linking politics to urban form and political science to its companion disciplines in the social sciences. We need a model that encompasses the decision-makers and their activities but goes further to identify the generators of public matters and the consequences of public actions. There must be inputs and outputs related to the urban political process, transformers to channel "pressures" into "decisions," power exchanges coupling choices to programs so that one can fix the boundaries of urban politics in relation to the general process of urbanization and specify the particular variables with which it is concerned.

One way to approach this task is to conceive of the urban political process as a system of some seven identifiable and interlinked components, and then to fashion out of our present knowledge the best propositions we can about their properties. Ideally, any specific impulse ought to be capable of being traced from entrance to exit within the system and its mutations and modifications duly noted.

We undertake such a characterization of the system and the propositions about its operations in the next few pages. Thereafter, we may be in the position to inquire what we still need to know and how to go about acquiring the new information.

1. *Urban Social Mobilization.* The designation of this first component is borrowed from our colleagues working with the politics of newly developing areas that are faced with comparative problems resembling our own. In these studies, the concept speaks to the transformation of rural, traditional societies into modern urban ones. So, the investigation focuses on the relationship between the more or less impersonal forces of urbanization and industrialization and resulting social and political attitudes toward change, including the willingness for

the newly developing countries to engage in radically new processes of political recruitment and socialization.[4]

The concept has obvious relevance to our own domestic experience: the pressures that urban growth generates on government in terms of resources utilization, and the expectations and attitudes of urban populations toward government. As a starting point for understanding the urban political process at work, one identifies "real needs" that result simply from the interaction of people in a spatial area—the relevance of size, density and income to the expansion of public services—and also those of a more elusive character where the cultural attributes of the population, their ideology and class structure come into play, and where expectations and values are superimposed on the simpler notion of need.

The distinction among the different categorizations of needs is a critical one, for it performs the functions of comparing characteristics of urban populations with the character of their politics. "Real needs" correspond to the language of economists when they inquire as to indivisible social capital required to support an industrial complex and as they distinguish these requirements from "private wants": streets per houses, water and sanitary facilities per families, hospital beds per 1,000 persons. They are the public activities provided in various communities and correlated to various indices of urbanization, regardless of variations in local political patterns, and regardless of whether the activities are actually undertaken by government or not. However calculated, whether or not measurable, these tests are theoretically the prerequisites for organized urban existence. But "real needs" rapidly transform themselves as they enter the urban political process. They are capable of many interpretations and reinterpretations before they reemerge in the new wrappings of a "solution" to a public problem.

One proposition about urban social mobilization, close now to tautology, we borrow largely from the economists: *Real needs almost uniformly occasion an expansion in the resources devoted to the public sector, and their magnitude and rate of expansion is related to the environmental characteristics and stage of particular localities involved.* The first part of this proposition has been the acknowledged property of public fi-

[4] James S. Coleman, Gabriel A. Almond, Lucian Pye, and Carl Deutsch are among those who have pioneered in this field. See, for example, Almond and Coleman, eds., *The Politics of Developing Areas* (Princeton, N.J.: Princeton University Press, 1960).

nance for a century. The second has become clearer and more
precise chiefly in the last decade, when the studies in St. Louis,
Cleveland and New York began to disentangle the snarl of
correlated variables subsumed under the notion of urbanization. The a priori studies of Walter Isard and Richard Meier
further clarify the proposition of "minimal needs" by calculat-
ing costs of developing a new urban settlement or maintaining
a city above the starvation level.[5]

From the political scientists' point of view, however, a more
relevant aspect of the mobilization process is the filter interjected by the perception of needs by political activists and
influentials in the body politic. What generates the demand for
"quality" in public services and the intercity differentials
among apparently like communities, what accounts for the
"unexplained" portions of the New York factor analysis, what
role do personal or group pressures play when the production
of goods and services is removed from the market place? An
extreme position here is that of Edward Banfield who argues
that the capacity of urban politics to ignore service and policy
pressures approaches the infinite:

> The rapid growth of the metropolitan population will
> not necessarily have much political effect. To be sure,
> many new facilities, especially schools, highways and wa-
> ter supply and sewage disposal systems, will have to be
> built and much private activity will have to be regulated.
> But such things do not necessarily have anything to do
> with politics . . . Difficulties that are "political" arise
> (and they may arise in "private" as well as in "public"
> undertakings) only insofar as there is conflict . . . The
> general political situation is affected, therefore, not by
> changes in population density or in the number and com-
> plexity of the needs that government serves ("persons,"

[5] Of the many sources in the literature of local public finance, the
most relevant summarizing pieces can be found in Werner Hirsch's contribution in John Bollens, ed., *Exploring the Metropolitan Community*
(Berkeley: University of California Press, 1961); Seymour Sacks and
William F. Hellmuth, Jr., *Financing Government in a Metropolitan
Area* (New York: The Free Press of Glencoe, 1961); Walter Isard,
Methods of Regional Analysis (New York: John Wiley & Sons, Inc.,
jointly with Technology Press, M.I.T., 1960); Jesse Burkhead, "Metropolitan Area Budget Structures and Their Significance for Expenditures," *Proceedings of the National Tax Association*, 1959, pp. 279–95;
and Nick Netzer's "Financial Needs and Resources Over the Next Decade: State and Local Governments," *Public Finance: Needs, Sources
and Utilization* (Princeton, N.J.: Princeton University Press, 1961).

the human organisms whose noses are counted by census takers, are not necessarily "political actors") but rather by actions which increase conflicts in matters of public importance or make the management of it more difficult.[6]

One does not have to adopt Banfield's position (indeed one may suspect that the number of people and their density of interaction are importantly and directly associated with the character, number and frequencies of conflicts) to recognize the capacity of politics to distort and shift the ordering of priorities of apparently objective needs or to invent new ones of psychic and class character. The stern face which the town fathers of the early American cities turned against the provision of relief, in an industrial age clearly caught up in the business cycle, maintained the ideology of the English poor laws for almost two centuries. Alternatively, the capacity of the latter-day nineteenth- and early twentieth-century boss to focus almost exclusively on welfare activities, although in a highly personalized and selective way, led to gross negligence of a wide array of services. For example, Frank Hague's hospital center in Jersey City flourished while other public facilities fell into abandon; but for a time at least, this strategy enhanced Hague's role. Hence, a second proposition: *The urban political process is not directly concerned with the provision of goods and services, except when these "problem solving" activities can be translated into useful resources for the resolution of political conflict or its avoidance, or when, at infrequent intervals, in times of breakdown and emergency, an outright failure of law and order seems imminent* (for example, the Galveston flood and the invention of the commission form of municipal government). The latter is a critical qualification. Regimes that escape from "objectivity" in the satisfaction of the desires of the actors ultimately collapse in the face of nature.

2. *The Expression of Needs.* An understanding of the subjective dimension in public need leads directly to an exploration of how the needs become articulated or reformulated in terms of goals or objectives. Civic textbooks make the connection almost in terms of a one-to-one correlation of felt needs and instant expression. Our third proposition runs to the contrary: *The great bulk of the urban population neither is conscious of its public needs nor anticipates that urban gov-*

[6] Edward C. Banfield, "The Political Implications of Metropolitan Growth," *Daedalus* 90:1 (Winter 1961), p. 67.

ernments will fulfill them. Vast is the violence that has been done to the grass-roots mythology by such studies as Scott Greer's discovery of suburban isolates in St. Louis and Murray Levin's clinical examination of the alienated voter of Boston.[7] True, the axiom may not surprise the close student of local election turnouts, or lack of turnouts. But it substitutes measurable indices of withdrawal for impressionistic descriptions of the average citizen's view of the politician, Nast cartoons, and editorials against apathy.

The Levin formulation of a citizenry that feels powerless, normless, and estranged from the political process makes "need expression" a largely negative affair. Wanting nothing from the government except, perhaps, personal favors, believing themselves incapable of effecting political decisions or the kind of public service offered, the voters withdraw—or never participate in the first place. Popular action, therefore, becomes less and less meaningful to urban politics, and campaign activities less and less reasonable. And these studies are buttressed by the extraordinarily intriguing studies of political socialization in the American public school, which seek to establish at what age and into what groups the air of cynicism seems to set in and the relevant relationship to personality and to family situations.

To posit that a great number of people in an urban population expect nothing of their government, that a few expect everything in terms of personal livelihood, and that the majority become conscious of their expectations only in times of emergency or breakdown may be disillusioning. But it makes more understandable the popular failure to turn out for elections and school referenda, the critical role of communication strategy in the dissemination of information and the difficulty of devising campaign strategy when voters believe nothing a candidate promises.

Parenthetically, the proposition also secures urban political science's links with psychology and sociology in much the same way as the first two propositions identify our relationship with economics. What it suggests is that the wide gap in the identification of the characteristics of an urban complex and the observable responses of governments as identified by financial indices of "output" is only occasionally explicable in

[7] See Greer's paper on the Metropolitan Community prepared for the 1961 Syracuse Seminar on Metropolitan Research, and Murray B. Levin, *The Alienated Voter: Politics in Boston* (New York: Holt, Rinehart and Winston, 1960).

terms of the behavior of the public at large. We need to turn elsewhere to understand the actual workings of urban politics, and to modify the notion of need from one of individual to group interest.

3. *The Effectuation of Responses to Need.* The vacuum of electoral response leads the urban political scientist to that will-o'-the-wisp of urban studies, the composition and characteristics of the urban elite. Here again, present doctrine conflicts with the stereotyped image of urban politics as boss-led or special interest dominated, for the fourth proposition runs: *Perceptions and decisions about public needs are made by highly diverse and segregated power centers, each operating with little relation to, or knowledge of, the other.* This characterization is put forth with considerable diffidence. We have only begun to assemble persuasive evidence on elite structures, and the most probable pattern is hardly a settled matter. Yet, the evidence we have points in this direction. Norton Long has the distinction of first formalizing the theorem in his *Ecology of Games.*[8] But Wallace Sayre, Herbert Kaufman, Robert Dahl, Edward C. Banfield and Frank Mungar have arrived at similar conclusions of many actors, in many arenas, pursuing separate goals in such a way that the total output of one urban political system is a laundry list of diverse items, coming to a total which is never added by a single hand.[9] At least in our larger metropolises, the urban ship of state breaks up into flotsam and jetsam, a highly fragmented series of conflicts, with groups forever assembling, disbanding, and reorganizing.

Quite different judgments as to the desirability of such a scattering of influentials are made by each observer, ranging from applause that from such diversity an open society is nourished at the local level to the conclusion that only nonsense results, since there is little correlation between elite goals

[8] Norton E. Long, "The Local Community as an Ecology of Games," *American Journal of Sociology,* LXIV (November 1958), pp. 251–61.

[9] Wallace S. Sayre and Herbert Kaufman, *Governing New York City: Politics in the Metropolis* (New York: Russell Sage Foundation, 1960); Robert Dahl, *Who Governs?* (New Haven: Yale University Press, 1961); Edward C. Banfield, *Political Influence* (New York: The Free Press of Glencoe, 1961). For an extensive bibliography of periodical literature, see Wallace Sayre and Nelson Polsby memorandum on research in urban politics, undertaken for the Social Science Research Council (Summer 1961), footnotes 21 and 22. See also, David B. Truman, "Theory and Research on Metropolitan Political Leadership: Report on a Conference," S.S.C.C., Items, 15 (March 1961).

and constituency needs, let alone "real needs." But, at present, the general consensus emerges that Lincoln Steffens' one man who "runs things" for better or for worse is replaced by cliques, coteries, and casual coalitions, operating with imperfect information, a high degree of uncertainty, and no fixed channels of either influence or power.

4. *Issue Resolution. The Ordering of "Needs."* If the requirements for maintaining law and order above the minimum for a great number of people engaged in highly specialized personal pursuits and living in relatively densely settled circumstances are obscure, the political outlook of the populace, passive, and their representation, haphazard and often invisible, how do things happen in urban politics? Who decides what issues become debatable in urban politics, which ones receive priority, and how competing definitions of needs are resolved? Budget processes and formal grants of authority notwithstanding, a fifth proposition stands: *Conflicts are resolved and activities authorized usually on the basis of the lowest common denominator of voluntary assent of the active participants.* In one sense, this rule re-establishes the legal possessor of authority as the actual decision-maker, since his is the strategic role of finally legitimizing an acceptable decision. But it makes him a most reluctant dragon. The convergent forces that play upon the official or officials who cannot avoid making decisions, dictate postures of vacillation and postponement as long as possible. Even after the action is taken, there is considerable doubt as to whether the decision will stick. One cluster of evidence here, of course, is the biographies of contemporary strong mayors and supposed shadow bosses, who ten years ago were heralded by the popular press as new urban "leaders." Now Lindsay in New York, Daley in Chicago, Tate in Philadelphia, find the crown of mayors tarnished and the manageability of their large enterprises more dubious. They have vast difficulty in fashioning a political strategy sufficient to maintain public acceptability. And bosses disappear overthrown by motley assemblies of rank amateurs. So, too, the exhaustive comparative studies of George Duggar in the more restricted field of urban renewal revealed a mare's nest over which cautious administrators agonizingly preside.[10]

[10] George A. Duggar, "A Framework for the Analysis of Urban Redevelopment Policies: Some Financial Factors in Local Programs and Some Implications," *Papers and Proceedings of the Regional Science Association,* 2 (1952).

There are exceptions to the rule, though we are uncertain about their absolute magnitude. A sixth corollary proposition states: *A determined minority in command of its subfield may push its item of public business quickly to the top of the agenda.* So, the new sensitivity to the aspirations of the Negro community in central cities, to suburban organizations sponsoring mental health; or to opponents of what once appeared a routinized technical decision on fluoridation of public water supplies. Here perceived needs, usually in terms of seeking changes in governmental attitudes or ideology, can frequently, in Sayre's words, "energize" officialdom to action. These sudden thrusts may be widespread and it is difficult to predict the circumstances under which they appear. But when they occur, they produce, not generally balanced responses, but makeshift palliative intended to meet immediate demands rather than provide long-run solutions. They tend to deflect conflict and to obscure problems—not to resolve them.

5. *Issue Validations. The Role of Institutions and Authority.* A "treading water" characterization of minimal response to conflict, arising from urbanization and the rapid ballooning of programs where consensus among the prime actors can most easily be achieved, raises the question of the relevance of structures and organization in urban government. A few years ago, many political scientists were on the verge of dismissing institutional analysis as irrelevant. Now, questions of institutional organization are dealt with increasingly in terms of the resources, strategy and tactics they make available to the elite groups and the decision-makers. Who is advantaged or disadvantaged by the strong-mayor form of government? What minorities have an opportunity to express their needs in a fragmented pattern of urban government and what minorities in a centralized one? What is the function of various kinds of elections in recruiting various kinds of people, and what do particular offices offer for the advancement of individual political careers? Charles Adrian's exploration of city manager governments suggests, for example, the interjection of strong institutional biases in favor of business, and middle-class definitions of needs and requirements; a contrary influence is often attributed to the mayoralty office in large cities.[11] Hence,

---

[11] Charles Adrian, "A Typology of Non-Partisan Elections," *Western Political Quarterly* (June 1959), pp. 449–58, as well as an unpublished paper by Duane Lockard, "On Non-Partisan Elections," (1960); C. A. Harrell and D. G. Weidford, "The City Manager and the Policy Process," *Public Administration Review* (Spring 1959), pp. 101–7; and

the seventh proposition: *Governmental form is less related to the execution of tasks or provision of services than it is to the distribution of resources and means of access to decision making by elite groups.*

But organizational arrangements of a purely local nature do not exhaust the field, and political scientists have been increasingly dissatisfied with descriptions of the relevant institutions which operate in an urban area as those constitutionally defined as municipal in nature. The participation of state highway departments, the Federal Bureau of Public Roads, the Department of Housing and Urban Development, the Department of Defense in many urban fields—and the ever present "authority"—now parallels the customary local units of government. Their modes of behavior have to be described in terms largely unrelated to local constituency and local elites. So, an eighth proposition: *The urban political process is further interrupted and focused on separate substantive concerns by the interjection of higher levels of government chiefly through interbureaucratic negotiations.*

6. *Externalized Relations. The Metropolitan Dimension of Urban Politics.* The diffusion of jobs and households beyond the boundaries of the core city and the development of suburban political consciousness further complicate the process of the articulation, formulation, and expression of "need" in policy terms—and the task of analysis for the political scientist. Though our information about suburban political behavior remains impressionistic and at times contradictory, the following propositions are now current in the field:[12] Nine: *By reason of size and homogeneity, the suburban political process submits much more readily to the rule of an elite or a few elites.* Ten: *Participation or nonparticipation by the suburban public is more the result of satisfaction and civic consciousness than it is of alienation or frustration.* The act of participation, however, may bear little relation to "needs," real or perceived. Eleven: *The needs felt by suburbanites or recognized by their elite are for the most part capable of being resolved within their own political boundaries.* Therefore, proposition twelve:

Adrian *et al.*, "Leadership and Decision-Making in Manager Cities: A Study of Three Communities," *Public Administration Review* 3 (Summer 1958), pp. 208–13.

[12] Fred I. Greenstein and Raymond E. Wolfinger, "Suburbs and Shifting Party Loyalties," *Public Opinion Quarterly*, XXII (Winter 1958), pp. 473–82 vs. Jerome C. Manis and Leo C. Stine, "Suburban Residence and Political Behavior," *Public Opinion Quarterly*, XXII (Winter 1958), pp. 483–89.

The resolution of area-wide conflicts rarely takes place because the issues have no arenas in which to be raised. Minimum "real need" requirements are met in ways (for example, authorities) which are structured to preclude conflict.[13] Attempts to articulate "metropolitan needs" are taken by self-appointed elites rarely possessing power resources of votes, money or strategic positions.[14]

These characterizations of suburban behavior as essentially self-conscious isolation were probed in some depth by Bradbury Seasholes in the Boston area. His findings, based on leadership interviews in sixteen of that city's sixty-five suburbs, revealed the absence of a metropolitan outlook not so much as a matter of conscious, parochial separatism—ignorance of or unwillingness to deal with more general affairs—as it was a result of absence of opportunity and motivation for involvement and the high cost in time and effort of such a concern. The chief links with affairs of other communities appeared to be by joint use of scarce professional talents (planners) and an occasional seeking of abundant outside advice (professors). Those suburbs most disposed to consider the larger region had the highest incomes and were located in the farthest distance from the central city—presumably attributes permitting some objectivity.[15]

7. *Consequences and Output.* Given the diffuse character of urban politics and the potential for irrational behavior, it has been fashionable in recent years for political scientists to deprecate attempts to build links between the urban political process and the social and economic repercussions which it occasions. Perhaps as an ultrasensitive reaction against a treatment of urban politics as the black box that receives problems and produces solutions and in an effort to emphasize the equilibrium function of political systems—the capacity to preserve a modicum of social stability and build consensus rather than to solve the problems—many political scientists prefer not to link political decisions to changes of economic and social systems. Nonetheless, the magnitude of the resources urban governments now command and the range of their clientele suggest some interconnection as inevitable. A thirteenth proposition, to end our list on an ominous note: *Pro-*

[13] Robert C. Wood, *1400 Governments,* (Cambridge: Harvard University Press, 1961), Chapter 5.

[14] Greer, *op. cit.*

[15] Bradbury Seasholes, *Boston Political Atlas,* Falk research memorandum, mimeo., M.I.T., 1961.

gram expansion of urban governments is initiated from without the system (that is, federal or state sources) or by highly mobilized elite groups successful in separating their activities from the process (for example, schools). Other outputs of regulatory or policy nature (Miami Metro or New Haven renewal) are random.

The burden of the argument here is that federal and state assistance programs augment the resources of local participants active in these particular endeavors and relieve the budgetary and administrative ordeals of the presiding officials. Similarly, school programs and the activities of the authorities feature self-contained systems capable of defining needs and supplying their own resources. But dramatic breakthroughs, like a major reorganization or a renewal program, are more likely to be the result of accident, not design. They are not the creature of a conscious effort by a powerful coalition; they are uncalculated occurrences of an improbable but possible convergence of forces in temporary agreement.

Taken together, these thirteen propositions about the properties of the main components of the urban political system suggest that the total system is characterized by

(1) A substantial divorce from the process of social mobilization as it produces "real needs" occasioned by interaction of people in space—that is, it functions only minimally to "solve problems" except the most routine ones;

(2) On the part of the public, indifference to, at best, or frustration by, at worst, the operations of the system;

(3) Incapacity on the part of active participants to coalesce in meaningful power centers;

(4) A disposition on the part of authority-wielders to seek automatic or voluntary resolution of conflict rather than actively to secure settlement;

(5) The use of institutions to raise issues rather than to settle them;

(6) The creation of new power centers across the metropolitan terrain faster than the merger or regularizing of relations among old ones;

(7) An increasing disposition of the system's output to be a function of stimuli from outside its own boundaries. In short, compared to criteria which suggest that government normally possesses qualities of purposefulness, rationality, regularized processes, and the power for the deliberate resolution of issues and conflicts, urban politics is devoid of most of the properties of a manageable enterprise.

Note that these observations carry no implications about what the urban political process ought to produce, or how it should go about transforming the inputs of social mobilization. Their criteria are the much simpler ones of a well-constructed system, whatever it turns out: What is its efficiency ratio, the results achieved for energy expended? How much power is effectively applied and how much wasted? How well engineered are the parts for the functions they perform? It is the question of system design and operation which concerns us here, not disputations on ultimate purpose.

Yet, even with these limitations, the characterization remains only what we think we know about urban politics, a rash summary of the concepts and hypotheses a good number of political scientists might be ready to accept. What do we actually know about the system in the sense that if we undertook to apply the model to a given area there would be a high probability that we would find data conforming to our specifications? Here we are on shaky ground. Only two foundations seem secure: that older models are demonstrably unsatisfactory and that some versions of the new model, properly applied, make no impossible demands on methodology and data collection.

What We Know Now:

1. *The Collapse of the Classic Model.* When we say that old ways of looking at urban politics no longer work, we are suggesting, again in an engineering analogy, that students selected the wrong "signals" for analysis out of the many discordant "noises" the system produces. Either they filtered out signals of obvious political power manifestations to the exclusion of those constraining or disrupting power, or they chose spurious signals that provided an apparent explanation of behavior but did not touch more fundamental variables—and therefore proved incapable of manipulation. Two research memoranda —that of Wallace Sayre and Nelson Polsby, undertaken for the Social Science Research Council, and that prepared by Delos D. Hughes, for the Urban Studies Program at Chapel Hill—summarize brilliantly the deficiencies of studies of Bryce, Steffens, and the successive waves of municipal reformers.[16] Their bibliographical and critical reviews will not be repeated here, though they are required reading for anyone wishing to trace the history of research in urban politics to its present

[16] Sayre and Polsby, *op. cit.,* and Delos D. Hughes, "Research in Urban Politics" (Chapel Hill: May 1961).

state of development. But it is important to describe the two critical errors—the attribution of real power to the total system, and the essential superficiality of the properties examined on many occasions.

The Muckrakers were primarily guilty of the first error. Though they provide some of the most realistic literature in urban history, essentially their focus was narrow and their approach episodic.[17] Their attention was almost exclusively on the nomination, election, and re-election process and the circumstances necessary for effective boss rule. But the facts about the exercise of political power once amassed, the sharp limits to the kinds of activity local governments undertook and their generally weak response to the pressures of the day were scarcely touched on at all. Carl Bridenbaugh, Arthur Schlesinger, Sr., and Oscar Handlin put the role of urban politics in vivid perspective in their contrast of the mounting tide of immigration and the growing conditions of social and physical disorder with the puny responses of the political system.

But power, in the eyes of the Muckrakers, seems finally to have been defined as the capacity of the politicians of the day to depart in their personal behavior from middle-class norms, not in their capacity to resolve conflicts, make substantive decisions, or use governing powers in any systematic way. And, in careless interpretations, this definition of power as the management of the political organization was transformed into an all-inclusive image of a tightly controlled, closely directed, self-sustaining enterprise across the entire range of urban politics. So, our backward glances at urban political history now often posit a stable equilibrium of town fathers succeeded by immigrant bosses in league with shady business interests, which, in fact, was continually being undone by the pressures of growth and the intrusion of new participants and new interests. James Curley now appears in fiction as a boss, though his bases of support were shifting and unreliable, his relations within the Boston Democratic organization competitive and insecure, and his concerns with the conduct of his offices negligible.

The error of reformist analysis was not that it failed to be broad, but that its methods of procedure in data assembly and its assumptions were heavily ideological in bias. The reformers were intent on making a case, and their approach

[17] Sayre and Polsby, *ibid.*, pp. 1–12; Hughes, *loc. cit.*, pp. 1–4.

resembled that of lawyers. Thus, they rarely paused to test a priori beliefs by the noises the system was emitting. Their descriptions of each of our prime components bear testimony to their limitations.

So far as the definitions of needs or values are concerned, the reformers, from Bryce through the major metropolitan studies of the fifties, never conceived that there was any real question of the needs that a municipality existed to fulfill or of the values it chose to guard. In the classic phrase of Charles Taft, there were "no Republican or Democratic ways to pave the street"; many a political scientist accepted this proposition of an urban government as a bundle of services derived from impersonal indices of urban mobilization as proposed by functional specialists.

With needs treated as a priori items incapable of being tampered with (at least in any legitimate fashion), no allowance was made for the filter process of either the constituency or the elites. From objective standards of service, one moved to a definition of the constituency as composed of active, interested citizens capable of rational behavior concerned about the affairs of the city, and willing to accept some generalized definition of the public interest.

Nor was the concept of an elite either formulated or looked for. The influentials in the classic model were uniformly the publicly elected officials or the "best citizens." All others— bosses, immigrants, bookies—once discovered, were rejected as exogenous factors, introduced from some obscure source and required to be removed to prevent the malfunctioning of the system.

In such a framework, issues were related to simple honesty or dishonesty—indicators of the deviations from appropriate behavior. Institutions were accorded a majestic, almost magical role. Properly structured and properly developed, they were presumed to have a strange feedback effect of cleansing the system of the distorted influences of boss-led minorities and restoring the "real needs" as the generators of political activities. The emergence of the suburban and exurban clusters in the urban region with their characteristics of escape, of status, and psychological identity were summarily dealt with as so many units of government, so many duplicatory services and facilities, so many overlapping bureaucracies, so many separate tax levies and budgets which again prevented "efficient" functioning. The outputs of the system were simple: not the residue of bargains drawn up among groups with different values and different needs but the social capital required to allow the American economic system to perform its production and distribution functions.[18]

In the end, then, the observations which earlier urban political scientists chose to make were formalistic, categorical, and norm-laden. The point is not that these noises did not exist, nor that in one way or another they have to be comprehended. The point is that they were essentially the ideological banners of one group of participants in the urban political process of the time, mistakenly paraded as systematic analysis.

One should not write off this analysis in terms of simple derogation. Faced with awesome choices and an abundance of material, few resources, and little time, the early students took what observations they could and fashioned them into an explanation of behavior of urban politics. That their observations are not now substantiated is largely a function of time, of more resources, of improved research aids. At a minimum, the history of the study of local politics provides us all now with a clearer understanding of where not to look and with the obligation to fit early observations into a more generalized and more accurate scheme. The performance raises, too, the question as to the relevance of the observer-actor role, a dual assignment treated with suspicion today, and to which we return later.

2. *New Methodological Approaches.* What reasons do we have to suppose that the signals that students of urban politics now select from noises are more reliable than those of their predecessors? Why accept our new formulations or suppose that political science is not still engaged in the process of endlessly raking coals of old fires?

The quick answer is that there is little basis for accepting the propositions as valid in their present form; much, for utilizing them as a basis now for calculated exploration. If the past ten years have seen the elaboration of new hypotheses, concepts, and perspectives, they have seen painfully little testing of the new approach on a basis that permits valid inferences. Somewhat maliciously, we have trod on the ruins of past scholarship, but our positive production remains scanty and turned out at enormous expense. Thus, the reliability of our present knowledge turns on our capacity to solve some

[18] J. R. Herson, "The Lost World of Municipal Government," *American Political Science Review*, 51 (June 1957), pp. 330–45.

stubborn methodological problems and to expand considerably the scope of our empirical testing.

As to the methodological problems quickly glided over in earlier sections, they run as follows:

a. Urban Mobilization. We have made substantial progress in the perfection of mathematical and statistical techniques suitable for display as the association among the dimensions of the community environment and governmental financial series, although problems in time-series and classification remain. But, existing procedures still pay too little attention to the roles that human perception and political manipulation play to distort and alter relationships. How to come to grips with the phenomenon of "rising expectations," how to deal with needs the census statistical series do not report, and how to anticipate new needs and new programs are most immediate problems.

Here, the work of William B. Storm and Wallace H. Best in Los Angeles dealing with measurement of public awareness of urban problems through carefully designed survey techniques, particularly in the development of an "apathy index," has opened up new lines of exploration.[19] The inverse relation between low visibility of services like fire and police and high satisfaction with them on the part of the public provides a provocative clue as to how to distinguish between settled needs and emerging ones that partake of conflict, and alternative means of resolution by different cities. This more systematic advance over the adventurous work of Thorndike and Simons in the thirties gives promise that we can interpret mathematical results with new perception and that we can broaden the array of indices that are measurable.

b. Expression of Needs. To know that the public has attitudes on some services is comforting, but to probe its willingness to express them actively and with some optimism requires survey work of a different nature. Greer, Levin, and others have, after all, made only isolated forays, and one is entitled to wonder if the picture is so black, say, in Milwaukee, San Francisco or Baltimore. In this area, the possibility of combining attitudinal studies with computer simulation, inquiring what the public would do and how different groups of voters might respond, shines brightest. Conditional formu-

[19] William B. Storm and Wallace H. Best, "Public Awareness of Metropolitan Problems: Some Survey Research Estimates," *Metropolitan California: Papers Prepared for the Governor's Commission on Metropolitan Area Problems,* (Sacramento: 1961).

lation of questions and then computer calculations of the resulting attitudes of different alternatives offer, perhaps, the first major occasion for urban political scientists to use the machines to their fullest capacity. But we have scarcely begun research in this direction.

c. Effectuation of Responses. Studies of the elite bubble now with alarms and excursions, mostly between the sociologist and the new community specialist in urban politics. Sayre and Polsby have brilliantly traced the running controversy of the last decade whether a "general" elite rules in its own interests or a more fragmented pattern is more typical; there is little call to review their findings here. Suffice it to say, after five years of probing in widely separated areas, we have developed a refined theory of actors, resources, roles, strategies, and rules. Now the need is to relate the studies to some typology of communities so that our generalizations have a broader base of support than the cities in which the leading researchers happen to reside. Robert Salisbury, in an earlier critique of this paper, has suggested how the task might be tackled with more precision and more utility than we have managed up to now. He proposes that we compare variations in the power of governmental officials to reallocate resources with variations in (1) the formal centralized authority of the officials, (2) their electoral security, (3) their technical skills, and (4) the configuration of group support of and opposition to the officials and the proposed resource reallocation. And Salisbury argues persuasively that the payoff will come with a more adequate understanding of the last category. Not until we can relate the kind and magnitude of group support necessary to effect a given amount of reallocation on a comparative basis, he believes, can we have meaningful answers to the implications of different patterns of power structures.

d. Issue-resolution and Issue-validation Research. Studies of elites, by extending observations through the process of examining actual decisions, have subsumed, for the most part, research on resolution and validation of issues. Theoretically, we encounter little difficulty in viewing officials and institutions as participants in the game, and some of our most important propositions are found in this area. But our method remains the episodic, expensive, and debatable case study, which continually raises issues of coverage and implementation. In competent literary hands, the case study can always refute an overly enthusiastic generalization. But, its capacity to advance positive knowledge and to build new generalizations on the present opportunistic basis by which cases are selected remains sharply limited.

We need here to begin to categorize types of decisions and develop a shorthand for identifying relevant participants and outcomes so that we can begin to catalogue the growing store of cases. "Differentiation of pluralistic decision-making" is the most common way of phrasing this objective.[20]

e. Externalized Relations. Methodological opportunities in suburban studies are perhaps as great as in many subfields in political science. The possibility of skillful manipulation of public opinion polls and electoral behavior and financial statistics improve as our more precise classification of a typology of suburbs progresses. What the suburban mosaic offers to the political scientist is a chance to abandon the case study (almost inevitable in central city research), and to deal with suburban political behavior on a more probabilistic basis. By describing suburban units according to a few indices of both environmental and attitudinal dimensions and then going on to rank, categorize, sort, and re-sort their behavior, we should be able to make proper samples of the largest universe afforded to the political scientist.[21]

f. Outputs and Consequences. Finally, we move now to join forces with our colleagues in planning. If more political scientists can be persuaded to abandon the view that their findings should have few consequences for social and economic systems, they acquire the opportunity to participate in pragmatic and policy-making concerns, to investigate the conflicts inherent in managing development, in guiding industrial location, in subdivision control, and in renewal of the core city. This is, in effect, the "politics of change," and here our understanding of the nature of urban renewal or the process by which the mass developer overruns the rural community is the least satisfactory of all. Why, for example, do the politics of highways produce "solutions," or at least action, while the politics of urban renewal tend to lag considerably behind; why are planners so far removed, usually, from sources of influence; what is the political implication of the new immigrants, Negro and southern white, to the central city and their pressures outward? These are questions which we have scarcely begun to tackle.

[20] Sayre and Polsby, *op. cit.*, pp. 26–27.
[21] Cf., Charles S. Liebman, "Functional Differentiation and Political Characteristics of Suburbs," *American Journal of Sociology,* 67 (March 1961), or Wood, *op. cit.*

FILLING THE GAPS

1. *A Moratorium on Theory*

A review of research needs and problems promises excitement and progress in the years ahead, but it underscores the slender bases on which our present understanding of urban politics rests. What we do not want to study is fairly clear at the present time. How we proceed in the immediate future is also a subject of some consensus. But the gaps in our knowledge are awesome, and the catalogue of research needs grows every day. If the ten years which have just passed have seen the reformation of doctrine, they have also opened up a vast horizon of facts that we should, but do not, possess.

In these circumstances, where the elbow room for speculative thinking is still substantial and appealing and the methodology and data-gathering problems sticky and grubby, the temptation is strong to continue the research strategy of reconnaissance and selective inquiry. Our most recent literature displays a strong preference to search for refinements in theory that make propositions self-evident or capable of easy generalization. The emerging spectacle of multiple power centers, the continuing disintegration of governmental capacity to move towards solutions in important public policy areas, the day-to-day, busy-day atmosphere in which urban politicians wallow, striving desperately to build some kind of popular reputation but avoiding the effort to solve problems, make it open season for impressionistic, intuitive, and derisive commentary. Such an appraisal of the urban political scene establishes the role of the observer as superior and comforting. So much variety, so many actors, so large a stage, so many touches of irony and comedy delight the clever and aggressive academic. They are grist for his mill; they provide selective analogies for new game theories; they offer a richness of comparisons of extremes never before available.

But the temptation of more theory should be resisted, at least until we work through the round of present hypotheses. The need now is to steel ourselves to more disciplined scholarship. Actors, resources, motivations, goals, arenas, strategies are perfectly acceptable points of departure for examining the internal workings of a city's politics. Suburban behavior viewed as a process of jostlings and maneuvers among domestic principalities provides an adequate framework for the assembly of available data. The whole can fit reasonably well in some ecology of games. But, if we continue to dabble at the edges, we will find ourselves with enough knowledge to know that old answers are not adequate, but with not enough information either to end a dialectic or to provide reasonable policy suggestions that might significantly change the current state of affairs. And that, it should be recalled, is precisely the basis for distinguishing between high-status and low-status sciences.

2. *Urban Observatories*

How do we test, in a way that allows us to move forward in resolving current methodological problems and provides a rapid, reliable feedback for the refinement and modification of theory? Obviously, not on a particularistic, individualistic basis that delights in the use of the old logical proposition that a single contrary fact destroys a carefully advanced theorem. Some notion of a collective enterprise has to be introduced into the ranks of urban political scientists.

One way to approach the problem is to reconsider the role of university centers of research in urban affairs, and the current practice of foundation grants to particular cities and for individual proposals of individual scholars in the hopes of immediate, "demonstration" payoffs. In this reconsideration, a useful analogy may be with the field stations, data centers, and observatories that natural scientists employ. With an agreed upon set of tools, an accepted field of observation, a common understanding of the phenomena to be observed, these institutions work together to build a cumulative record. It does not seem too far-fetched to suggest this procedure in our present research.

How would these observatories operate? Principally by making a common series of investigations under a single research plan which for the first time would provide us with professionally reliable findings simultaneously in a number of areas. Consider the possible benefits that might have been achieved if the same format for the study of New York City had been applied to Chicago, or that of St. Louis, undertaken in San Francisco. Think what might have happened if the same set of questionnaires (for all their limitations) administered to some 300 leaders in the Boston suburbs over the last two years had had their counterpart in the Cleveland, Kansas City, and Tulsa areas. Conceive of a set of reports periodically bringing together decisions in urban renewal on the same basis that integration conflicts are now analyzed throughout the South. Suppose the new Minnesota study of urbanization had been carried forth in the same framework as that of the New York Metropolitan Region. Suppose the Houston and Syracuse investigations had utilized a single research frame; or that a sample of different sized urban regions with different economic mixes now generated, not a single, but a continuing report over time.

THE POTENTIAL OF A NEW APPROACH: TOWARDS A STRATEGY OF ACTION

What would we gain by reorganizing our research efforts along the lines just suggested and by less reliance on piece-meal and sporadic data assembly? For one thing, there should be an increasing disposition to report negative results. One principal distinction between the social and natural sciences to-day is the latter's capacity to indicate what explorations have proven fruitless and what experiments should not be under-taken again. Steps like these contribute a focus and a com-mitment of energies to a single research objective, such as the massive coordinate effort which the International Geo-physical Year represented. With the vastly expanded terrain that urban political scientists have to investigate, the more we can avoid dissipation and duplication of effort, the better off we are.

Second, a common agenda and a common system of re-porting would allow us to tap resources not now available. The young instructor at the small college would provide ob-servations, analyses, and findings which would add importantly to the extension of our knowledge. They would also allow him a constructive opportunity in scholarship not now avail-able, and permit other research than the exercise of literary ingenuity. The few efforts political science in general has un-dertaken in this direction—the study of presidential nominat-ing politics and the compilation of national election statistics —have paid dividends in the finding of talent as well as the ordering of data.

Third, more coordinate efforts might bring the resources necessary to pay for the tools we need to use now. A simu-lation of urban traffic flow that demonstrates the effect of dif-ferent strategies for moving traffic on the transportation sys-tem capacity, and which also indicates the attitudes of elites and voters alike respecting each strategy—before any one is executed—seems now a feasible undertaking. Its potential for demonstrating to cautious elites how they may be leaders without political danger appears sizable. The funds required to develop and perfect such a simulation, however, are available only in the largest of foundations or in government agencies. Yet, given a place as an item on a national research agenda, this simulation could be completed in one year.

Fourth, and perhaps most important, the research regrouping of urban political science might help to end the disturbing controversy about the appropriate behavior of the professions in their research and policy roles. Sayre, Polsby, and Hughes are not alone in their severe criticism of the earlier generation of municipal reformers for posing as "social engineers." The recent Syracuse seminars on metropolitan research reported a continuing debate on whether scholars can advise as well as observe policy-makers and still maintain their integrity.

The question was posed as if there were a choice. Again, the contrast with the "hard side" of scientific endeavor is instructive. Natural scientists defend strenuously their right to engage in basic research, unfettered by the issue of relevance. But few seem to doubt for the moment that there will be a practical effect; that what Robert Oppenheimer has called the "ennobling" and the "utilitarian" purposes of scientific inquiry are ultimately joined; and that calculated manipulation of the natural universe will result. When we have enough to say in urban politics about actual behavior, then the possibilities of manipulation and development will become clearer. It is only when advice proceeds from ignorance, half truths, ill-understood diagnoses that the charge of charlatanism arises. One does not avoid involvement in the real affairs of the world by honest inquiry. One becomes inevitably caught up in the enterprises men care about.

To reinstate the role of policy advice and cool the controversy over professional integrity does not mean that the urban political scientist emerges as the bearer of panaceas and all-purpose plans for reforms. If the last decade has made any contribution in this respect it has not been to indicate the clear policy alternatives which lie before us but to emphasize the difficulty in finding any realistic alternatives at all. The post-research experiences in St. Louis and Cleveland reflect the fate of major proposals for reordering urban government and politics. The ways we proceed will more likely be by discovering the possibilities for incremental advances in assembling political power at the urban level and for bringing together greater—but not great—coalescences of authority, and improvements in communication. It is the exploration of these far more limited choices which promises real comfort to ourselves and the policy-makers.

But the end purpose remains the production of knowledge and then reflection as to how it may bear on the issues of the day. If we are right in our present supposition that the foundations of urban politics have always been weak and are in the process of further dissolution, that most Americans are likely to live out their everyday lives under circumstances of disorder, confusion, temporizing and indecision, then the need to know enough to act increases in direct proportion. With the present urban political process requiring management, we should not view our prospects for gaining more information in monistic terms nor confuse conscious policy making with manipulation and manufactured consent. The world of learning and reason has always been the source of providing notions about "a better way out) since the process of building urban civilization began. It ought to continue to serve the same function, all the more so as our capacity to know, to establish, to demonstrate, and to prove increases rapidly over time.

THE CASE FOR ACTION

Fundamentally, of course, the call for a drastically revised research approach to urban politics should not rest on narrow professional self-interest. It is the real problems of urban America—not a plea for "the good of the order"—that should motivate our efforts. American cities may be capable of survival under present circumstances. Yet clearly they are capable of improvement. It is that task that justifies reform.

It is abundantly clear for example that good homes and good communities are not everywhere about us; that the new migrants flooding into our cities from the rural South and West often failed in their hopes for adjustment; that public facilities and services necessary for the good of community life are not everywhere about us. Our cities do not provide an environment of beauty, with ample opportunity for recreation and leisure pursuits. They offer few genuine choices for the individual. These are the important tasks that spur improved analysis and recommendation.

If there are benefits not presently included in our urban

milieu; if our cities can and should be better planned and organized; then a few cautions are in order as we begin the job of policy making from a new research stance. They are drawn from the mistakes of the generation that tried to direct the development of complicated metropolitan areas after World War II. The perils to watch for are these:

—First, *we should not be preoccupied exclusively with physical development*. The great mistakes in the last fifteen years of urban renewal was the belief that a new downtown, with new office buildings and new city halls, constituted a strong new city. One great need in urban building today is to make *residential* neighborhoods in the central city more attractive, manageable, appealing, and human. Another must is to consider the human beings who live there. We have reduced the number of the poor from ⅓ to ⅕ since 1933, while the rest of us have grown more affluent. But that is actually slow progress and we need to redouble our efforts to bring the marginal man into the mainstream of American society. We need also to be sure that all of us have more choices for our own self-development: city centers and parks and playgrounds and marinas. The simple refurbishing of commercial real estate is not sufficient to these demands.

—Second, *let us not fall into the trap of believing that the public sector of the local economy is unproductive*. When we spend money for schools, for parks, for renewal, we improve the functioning of the private sector of the economy. We add to our total real resources. It is no longer correct to say that any private purchase is more valuable than any public purchase. One cannot defend the third car in the garage or the new outboard motor every two years—if it makes impossible the addition of another school desk in an elementary school.

—Third, *we should work with the political system as it is constituted recognizing its slow tractability*. Let us not believe that the formal reform of governmental institutions and new blueprints of metropolitan governments are prerequisites for guiding urban growth. If our propositions about urban politics are even half-way correct, the political, social, and economic systems that abound in urban areas are complex, interdependent, and, for the loads they bear, they are weak. But they are extraordinarily tough and persistent and one will not see neat and tidy metropolitan governments presiding over new and tidy metropolitan areas. So we must learn to deal with *systems* of decision making, just as engineers deal with systems of weaponry and space vehicles. The task of reform is not that of inventing new structures. It is the infinitely complicated task of mobilizing public interest, bringing together coalitions of support, negotiating, bargaining, and teasing the present institutions into collaboration. Local and state and federal governments will all be involved, so will private groups. City builders who would be effective will be engaging in parapolitical operations just as most of our military action today involve paramilitary operations. Sophistication, elegance, and style are the key political characteristics for the urban reformers—not slogans, demonstrations, and debates.

So compulsions to build cities are powerful. Alternatives exist that seem better than just muddling through. Mistakes made in the past need not be made again. But what of the promise? Why make the effort? The answer does not just lie only in aesthetics—better architecture, better use of space, a city form that the average citizen can comprehend and enjoy—though this value should not be discounted. Nor is it just a matter of justice, a concern in an affluent society, that American standards of social service for the young, the old, the poor and the minorities become at least equal to those of every other nation in the western world. Nor is it only self-interest that demands better health, less pollution of air and water, more safety in our streets.

The great challenge is to see that if in building great cities of massive size, the United States can create a community dialogue and a set of common activity that we fondly believe existed in the grass roots now left so far behind in our history. Can we, in short, build an urban society that can allow encounters before they become confrontations?

PART TWO. WHAT COULD BE

Chapter 6

GOALS FOR DEMOCRATIC PLANNING

City planning, stemming originally from architecture, has long suffered from a decided lack of intellectual sophistication in goal setting and in the creation of valid yardsticks to measure the product. Inspiration, rather than a coldly cumulative scientific approach, has generally been the rationale behind the allocation of billions of dollars of scarce resources both here and abroad. Somewhat mistakenly in recent years, physical planners have increasingly turned to social scientists for definitions of the "good society"—as well as some leads on how to get there. The latter breed can undoubtedly map effectively what a given society or subsector believes to be "good" or "bad." But social science is neither geared nor qualified to provide eternal or even immediate verities—neither optimum societies nor emergent "high goals" are its meat. Whether in the long run "scientifically ascertained values" can be plotted—ever changing in the planning process—remains to be seen. Without such values, no firm goals—much less quantitative goals—can be easily set. Thus goals for planning a better urban civilization still rest in the hands of inspirational or operational types: philosophers (no matter how logical), theologians (no matter how sacrosanct), and politicos (no matter how elevated)—as well as mind-stretching utopians and the planning profession *per se*.

Various schemes have been advanced to nail down a precise formulation of valid, reachable goals in order to make explicit largely implicit notions in the planning operation. The list has varied, from this editor's itemized, but not quantified, catalogue of biological, social and cultural (largely derived) goals—long used in an introduction to planning course—to the New Zealander, Gerhard Rosenberg's, careful inventory[1] centered around the "needs" of children, the old and adults, and for a good environment and mental health. Lewis Mumford has long given us pause to think and David Riesman's "autonomous personality" lurks in every planner's mind as he moves restlessly toward his often fuzzy private dream world. But no one yet has given us a scientific ten commandments in positive form—connecting both physical form and social structure in an evolving system.

The Declaration of Delos expresses an urgency and purpose acceptable to varied ideologies, nations, and professions, for remaking the urban human environment. As Marshall McLuhan concentrating

[1] "City Planning Theory and the Quality of Life," *The American Behavioral Scientist*, Vol. IX, No. 425, December 1965–January 1966.

on mass media has indicated, the environment created by man is an extension of man's ability to perceive and in turn is and makes man; Kevin Lynch has said somewhat the same thing in analyzing the reciprocal relationship between man and the aesthetic qualities of his created environment. President Johnson, magnificent politician that he is, backs into the city through the rural back door of "natural beauty" from the wide-open spaces of "America the Once Beautiful" and has undoubtedly through this device been able to marshal great skill and very considerable resources to upgrade the style and quality of urban life under the Great Society's banner of physical form and social context. Thomas A. Reiner, economically oriented regionalist, suggests in his article (a) that new communities are splendid experimental systems in which to test values and results and (b) that regional resource allocation can clarify what value criteria may be used and what each will cost in increasing the productivity of goods and services for the "good life." John Dyckman, a most philosophical and behaviorally oriented planner, mordantly lays bare the functional lag between physical planning and "social planning" (defined by him to mean approximately total societal or national planning). He believes that planners can produce some social therapy, do adequate caretaking (when alerted after the act) and possibly move toward radical reform with more clarified national goals breaking the conservative ideology of the U.S. present.

Finally, we "Anglo-Saxons" must "love that city"; Morton and Lucia White have shown that American intellectuals don't, and a similar survey of British intellectuals makes clear that this antipathetic stream had a source higher in the hills. Contrariwise, the French, as evidenced in the towering Balzac, Stendahl and Proust, revel in urbanism, which it would seem is a more rewarding emotional and intellectual set to assume in an increasingly urbanized world.

The Declaration of Delos*

Meeting in Delos on this, the twelfth day of July, 1963, we the undersigned, drawn from a wide range of different disciplines, nations, political allegiances and cultural groups, affirm and declare that:

The city throughout history, has been the cradle of human

---

* On the occasion of the symposium *Delos One* held in Greece during the Summer of 1963 and sponsored by the Athens Technological Institute, headed by Constantinos Doxiadis, the following manifesto for total planning to remake the urban environment was endorsed by an impressive and varied list of signers. It is here reprinted with permission from *Ekistics,* the journal devoted to the conception of wholistic community design based on "the science" of human settlements, Vol. 18, No. 107, October 1964, pp. 268–69.

civilisation and progress. To-day, like every other human institution, it is profoundly involved in the deepest and widest revolution ever to overtake mankind.

This revolution proceeds under the sign of dynamic change. In the next forty years, the world's population will rise to seven thousand million. Science and technology determine more and more of the processes of human living. As they advance, man's social behaviour is profoundly modified. These changes present themselves in every field as a danger matched by an even greater opportunity. Man can use atomic power to reduce every human settlement to the shambles of Hiroshima. It may give them enough energy to fulfill all human needs. The world's population may far outstrip its food supply. Even to keep pace, to-day's food production must rise threefold by the year 2000. Yet for the first time, we also have the means of securing enough food for everyone.

These paradoxes are widely felt. What is not realised is that the failure to adapt human settlements to dynamic change may soon outstrip even disease and starvation as the gravest risk, short of war, facing the human species.

A universal feature of the worldwide revolution is the movement of people into urban settlements at an ever faster rate. World population increases by 2 per cent a year, urban population by over 4 per cent. In the next forty years, more urban construction will take place than hitherto in the whole history of man. It is already evident that wrong projections of urban development produce inexcusable waste. The absence of any forecasts leads to chaos, in the cities, to the undermining of civic order and the destruction of precious and diverse historical traditions. Thus, the need for the rational and dynamic planning of human settlements both now and in the foreseeable future is inherent in the urban situation to-day.

Man can act to meet this new crisis. There are sufficient resources for the task. Modern technology permits the mobilisation of material means on a wholly new scale. Developed nations spend 150,000 million dollars a year on armaments and still their national incomes go up. Billions are spent each year on social services, some of which are made necessary by the inadequacies of urban life. Once a problem is recognised, the resources for meeting it can be found. These resources are not, it is true, uniformly available. Some societies still lack the means for action. But this is not an absolute shortage and while they achieve modernisation, their lack can be made good by sustained assistance from more technologically advanced areas.

Guide lines for policy are also clearer than ever before, thanks in part to the great extension of systematic studies in human behaviour. The aim must be to produce settlements which satisfy man not only as parent and worker, but as learner and artist and citizen. His active participation is essential in framing his own environment. He must be able to use creatively the still unforeseen possibilities of advancing technology. Planning itself must ensure that such possibilities are not excluded by a static view of human settlements. Above all, the citizen should feel at ease in his own culture and open to the cultures of others.

When we turn to the application of these principles to the problems of urbanisation, we feel the need for the most far-reaching reform and reinforcement of existing institutions and procedures. At present, educational systems at every level have not yet taken sufficient action to meet the new problems of human settlement or to explore the possibilities of meeting them through rational planning. In the universities, the application of the basic sciences to human welfare has been fragmented. They have dealt with parts of man—his health, his nutrition, his education—not with the whole man, not with man in community. Thus, we underline with all possible urgency our belief that in every action of ours, in the agencies dealing with these problems at a national or international level, in the institutions of higher learning, whether public or private, our society requires:

   a. to establish in its own right a new discipline of human settlements;

   b. to initiate basic research of the most far-reaching kind;

   c. to bring together specialists from other relevant disciplines to work together on projects in this field;

   d. to work out new methods of training the men who can assume leadership and responsibility in the sphere of action;

   e. to attract some of the best young minds into this new area of research, development and practice.

We come from different nations, from different cultural backgrounds. Our politics differ, our professions are various. But we believe that the problem of human settlements is a general and fundamental problem in our new dynamic world and that it must be viewed and studied in such a way that it will, in common with all great scientific disciplines, transcend our local differences. We agree that the practical implementation of policy—in such vital fields as land use, the location of investment or the planning of cities over time—will be determined by domestic politics and needs, and as citizens we pledge ourselves to attempt to bring these issues into the active political dialogue of our local societies. But we are not divided in what we wish most strongly to affirm—that we are citizens of a worldwide city, threatened by its own torrential expansion and that at this level our concern and commitment is for man himself.

CHARLES ABRAMS (U.S.A.).
Housing expert and Visiting Professor, Massachusetts Institute of Technology.

EDMUND N. BACON (U.S.A.).
Executive Director, Philadelphia City Planning Commission.

STEWART BATES (Canada).
President, Central Mortgage and Housing Corporation.

PEDRO BIDAGOR LASARTE (Spain).
Director General of Planning, Ministry of Housing.

A. K. BROHI (Pakistan).
Senior Advocate of the Supreme Court.

C. S. CHANDRASEKHARA (India).
Sec. Gen., East Asia Regional Organization for Planning and Housing.

WALTER CHRISTALLER (Germany).
Professor Emeritus of Regional Geography; Vice President, Regional Science Association, U.S.A.

JACOB L. CRANE (U.S.A.).
City Planning Consultant.

RICHARD LLEWELYN DAVIES (Britain).
Chairman, Department of Architecture, London University.

C. A. DOXIADIS (Greece).
President, Athens Technological Institute.

LEONARD DUHL (U.S.A.).
Psychiatrist, National Institute of Mental Health.

O. E. FISCHNICH (U.N.).
Assistant Director-General, Technical Department, F.A.O.

LYLE C. FITCH (U.S.A.).
President, Institute of Public Administration, New York.

R. BUCKMINSTER FULLER (U.S.A.).
Director, Generalized Science Exploration, Southern Illinois University.

CLIFFORD FURNAS (U.S.A.).
President, State University of New York, Buffalo.

S. GIEDION (Switzerland).
Professor of Art History, Zürich and Harvard University.

J. GORYNSKI (Poland).
Undersecretary, Ministry of Communal Administration and Housing.

EIICHI ISOMURA (Japan).
Professor of Sociology, Tokyo University.

BARBARA WARD JACKSON (Britain).
Economist and author.

STURE LINNER (U.N.).
Director of United Nations Special Fund Programmes in Greece, Representative of the United Nations Technical Assistance Board.

M. S. MAKIYA (Iraq).
Principal, Department of Architecture, University of Baghdad.

EDWARD S. MASON (U.S.A.).
Lamont University Professor, Harvard University.

SIR ROBERT MATTHEW (Britain).
President, Royal Institute of British Architects.

MARGARET MEAD (U.S.A.).
President, American Anthropological Association; Associate Curator of Ethnology, American Museum of Natural History, New York.

MARSHALL McLUHAN (Canada).
Director, Centre for the Study of the Extensions of Man, University of Toronto.

WACLAW OSTROWSKI (Poland).
Professor of Town Planning, Technical University, Warsaw.

ALFRED R. OTOO (Ghana).
Chief Development Officer, Accra-Tema Metropolitan Area.

DAVID OWEN (U.N.).
Executive Chairman, Technical Assistance Board of the United Nations.

CHARLES H. PAGE (U.S.A.).
Professor of Sociology, Princeton University.

E. PAPANOUTSOS (Greece).
Vice-President, Athens Technological Institute.

SHAFIK H. EL-SADR (U.A.R.).
Undersecretary of State for the Ministry of Housing and Public Utilities.

Carl Schweyer (Germany).
  President, International Federation of Housing and Planning.
C. H. Waddington (Britain).
  Professor, Animal Genetics, University of Edinburgh.
Sir Robert Watson-Watt (Britain).
  Center for the Study of Democratic Institutions, Santa Barbara, California.

Beauty for America

LYNDON B. JOHNSON*

For centuries Americans have drawn strength and inspiration from the beauty of our country. It would be a neglectful generation indeed, indifferent alike to the judgment of history and the command of principle, which failed to preserve and extend such a heritage for its descendants.

Yet the storm of modern change is threatening to blight and diminish in a few decades what has been cherished and protected for generations.

A growing population is swallowing up areas of natural beauty with its demands for living space, and is placing increased demand on our overburdened areas of recreation and pleasure.

The increasing tempo of urbanization and growth is already depriving many Americans of the right to live in decent surroundings. More of our people are crowding into cities and being cut off from nature. Cities themselves reach out into the countryside, destroying streams and trees and meadows as they go. A modern highway may wipe out the equivalent of a 50-acre park with every mile. And people move out from the city to get closer to nature only to find that nature has moved farther from them.

The modern technology which has added much to our lives can also have a darker side. Its uncontrolled waste products are menacing the world we live in, our enjoyment and our health. The air we breathe, our water, our soil and wildlife, are being blighted by the poisons and chemicals which are the byproducts of technology and industry. The skeletons of dis-

---

* A message to the Congress of the United States, February 8, 1965. 89th Congress, 1st Session, House of Representatives, Document No. 78.

carded cars litter the countryside. The same society which receives the rewards of technology, must, as a cooperating whole, take responsibility for control.

To deal with these new problems will require a new conservation. We must not only protect the countryside and save it from destruction, we must restore what has been destroyed and salvage the beauty and charm of our cities. Our conservation must be not just the classic conservation of protection and development, but a creative conservation of restoration and innovation. Its concern is not with nature alone, but with the total relation between man and the world around him. Its object is not just man's welfare, but the dignity of man's spirit.

In this conservation the protection and enhancement of man's opportunity to be in contact with beauty must play a major role.

* * *

Certainly no one would hazard a national definition of beauty. But we do know that nature is nearly always beautiful. We do, for the most part, know what is ugly. And we can introduce, into all our planning, our programs, our building, and our growth, a conscious and active concern for the values of beauty. If we do this then we can be successful in preserving a beautiful America.

There is much the Federal Government can do, through a range of specific programs, and as a force for public education. But a beautiful America will require the effort of government at every level, of business, and of private groups. Above all it will require the concern and action of individual citizens, alert to danger, determined to improve the quality of their surroundings, resisting blight, demanding and building beauty for themselves and their children.

* * *

Federal assistance can be a valuable stimulus and help to such local efforts.

I have recommended a community extension program which will bring the resources of the university to focus on problems of the community just as they have long been concerned with our rural areas. Among other things, this program will help provide training and technical assistance to aid in making our communities more attractive and vital. In addition, under the Housing Act of 1964, grants will be made to States for training of local governmental employees needed for community development. I am recommending a 1965 supplemental appropriation to implement this program.

We now have two programs which can be of special help in creating areas of recreation and beauty for our metropolitan area population: the open space land program and the land and water conservation fund.

I have already proposed full funding of the land and water conservation fund, and directed the Secretary of the Interior to give priority attention to serving the needs of our growing urban population.

The primary purpose of the open space program has been to help acquire and assure open spaces in urban areas. I propose a series of new matching grants for improving the natural beauty of urban open space.

The open space program should be adequately financed, and broadened by permitting grants to be made to help city governments acquire and clear areas to create small parks, squares, pedestrian malls, and playgrounds.

In addition I will request authority in this program for a matching program to cities for landscaping, installation of outdoor lights and benches, creating attractive cityscapes along roads and in business areas, and for other beautification purposes.

Our city parks have not, in many cases, realized their full potential as sources of pleasure and play. I recommend on a matching basis a series of Federal demonstration projects in city parks to use the best thought and action to show how the appearance of these parks can better serve the people of our towns and metropolitan areas.

* * *

In almost every part of the country citizens are rallying to save landmarks of beauty and history. The Government must also do its share to assist these local efforts which have an important national purpose. We will encourage and support the National Trust for Historic Preservation in the United States, chartered by Congress in 1949. I shall propose legislation to authorize supplementary grants to help local authorities acquire, develop, and manage private properties for such purposes.

* * *

In my 33 years of public life I have seen the American system move to conserve the natural and human resources of our land.

TVA transformed an entire region that was "depressed." The rural electrification cooperatives brought electricity to lighten the burdens of rural America. We have seen the forests replanted by the CCC's, and watched Gifford Pinchot's sustained-yield concept take hold on forest lands.

It is true that we have often been careless with our natural bounty. At times we have paid a heavy price for this neglect. But once our people were aroused to the danger, we have acted to preserve our resources for the enrichment of our country and the enjoyment of future generations.

The beauty of our land is a natural resource. Its preservation is linked to the inner prosperity of the human spirit.

The tradition of our past is equal to today's threat to that beauty. Our land will be attractive tomorrow only if we organize for action and rebuild and reclaim the beauty we inherited. Our stewardship will be judged by the foresight with which we carry out these programs. We must rescue our cities and countryside from blight with the same purpose and vigor with which, in other areas, we moved to save the forests and the soil.

The Planner as Value Technician: Two Classes of Utopian Constructs and Their Impacts on Planning

THOMAS A. REINER*

An appealing and plausible idea attracts planners the world over: we are scientists, or at least capable of becoming such. As scientists, or technicians, we work with facts to arrive at truth, using methods and language appropriate to our tasks, and our way of handling problems are not subject to outsiders' criticism.[1] This stand should be challenged because in fact it

* Associate Professor of Regional Science, University of Pennsylvania, and Research Associate, Regional Science Research Institute, Philadelphia; formerly URA Field Representative in Puerto Rico, consultant to the Puerto Rico Planning Board and associated with Adams, Howard and Greely in Cambridge, Massachusetts. Among professional publications, relevant to the following article is his *The Place of the Ideal Community in Urban Planning* (University of Pennsylvania Press, 1963).

[1] See, e.g., F. S. Chapin, "Foundations of Urban Planning," in Werner Z. Hirsch, ed., *Urban Life and Form*, New York, Holt, 1963; and citations in P. Davidoff and T. A. Reiner, "A Choice Theory of

does not represent much of what the planner does or can do, and because the underlying picture of the scientist is a caricature.

A central feature of the technocratic view of planning is that, as a scientist, the planner's work removes him from the realm of values: there is an imperative to action in the facts on which he bases his decisions. But if there is one truth in the world of the planner, it is that he is indeed deeply immersed in values at every turn. Some examples: the technician's plan must be based on adequate data. Yet which data to collect is essentially a matter for choice, based on notions of what is right and what is relevant.[2] Standards on which to base land-use allocations, for example, are but value statements, though ones which can be buttressed by some reason. Measurement itself, central to all scientific tasks, is a prime example of a value-laden activity.[3] The purpose of an investigation and hence the direction of the investigator's efforts likewise are not absolutes but rather have strong volitional and value components.[4] These problems, of course, are not peculiar to the planning profession. They are embedded in the entire scientific effort and professional milieu.

The total planning process—as applied to city development and like problems—involves the planner in a series of choices. If we define planning as a method for determining appropriate future action, we can see that such choices are made at three levels: *first,* the selection of objectives and criteria; *second,* the identification of a set of alternatives consistent with these general prescriptives, together with the selection of one of these as a preferred alternative; *third,* guidance of action toward determined ends. Since choice permeates the whole planning sequence, a clear notion of the ways in which choices are made and of the ends pursued must lie at the heart of the planner's task.[5]

Planning," *Journal of the American Institute of Planners,* Vol. 28, No. 2, May 1962, pp. 103–15.

[2] For an extensive treatment of this argument see, for example: C. West Churchman, *Prediction and Optimal Decision,* Englewood Cliffs, N.J., Prentice-Hall, 1961, esp. Chap. 4.

[3] See: Churchman, *op. cit.,* Chap. 5, and references therein.

[4] See, for example, the discussion of applied research in Russel L. Ackoff *et al., Scientific Method: Optimizing Applied Research Decisions,* New York, Wiley, 1962.

[5] Such a framework for planning is elaborated in Davidoff and Reiner, *op. cit.* A similar argument (without reference, though, to urban planning) is given in Robert Boguslaw, *The New Utopians,* Englewood Cliffs, N.J., Prentice-Hall, 1965.

Values and judgments by definition have no absolute base. But in making such choices, the planner can undertake several vital tasks and perform them rationally. He can identify a set of plausible objectives for the system to pursue. Indeed, one formulation of the planner's job, the one area where it is appropriate for him to say: "This is a uniquely defined area of expertise," is precisely in this area.[6] The planner should, further, identify the points where, in a policy question with technical components, values or judgments can arise; and prescribe proper analysis for these.[7] Finally, he can perform a signal service where he identifies the consequences of the pursuit of certain objectives, and contrasts these. To do this, of course, again involves choices: in the selection of alternatives whose impact is studied, and in the selection of criteria by which to compare impacts and select one or another as preferred.[8]

Of the many questions with which planners deal, two suggest themselves as meriting close attention from the point of view of value analysis. Though these questions differ in substance, they nevertheless illustrate nicely the interaction of values in the "science of planning," and they allow one to remark on the role of the planner in confronting judgment-loaded issues. Both are illustrations of the difficulties encountered in determining goals for democratic planning. The first problem is the design of ideal towns or communities: of fairly practical and precisely designed Utopias. The second arises in regional planning: the allocation of funds by a central planning authority to a set of regions undergoing development. Both problems arise in many parts of the world, though local conditions (economic as well as political) govern the specific form of the analysis.[9]

[6] The planner as goal technician is discussed in Davidoff and Reiner, *op. cit.*, and references therein. Also see J. W. Dyckman, "Social Planning, Social Planners, and Planned Societies," *Journal of the American Institute of Planners*, Vol. 32, No. 2, March 1966, pp. 66–76.

[7] For a case in point see, for example, the analysis of the work of the Philadelphia Planning Commission in William H. Brown and Charles E. Gilbert, *Planning Municipal Investment*, Philadelphia, University of Pennsylvania Press, 1961, Chap. IV and Part 2.

[8] Further discussion of such "impact" analyses (and the way in which these differ from optimizing studies) is found in Davidoff and Reiner, *op. cit.*

[9] See, e.g., the citations given in R. J. Osborn and T. A. Reiner, "Soviet City Planning," *Journal of the American Institute of Planners*, Vol. 28, No. 4, November 1962, pp. 239–50; and T. A. Reiner, "Sub-

There exists a rich collection of proposals for new communities developed over the last century or so. These prescribe, to varying degrees of specificity, the physical environment which its creator feels is best associated with a desirable life style. The ideal community proposals generally have the following format: 1) presentation of social objectives; 2) explanation of the way in which such objectives are translated into physical form; 3) design of the environment. Ideal communities vary, of course, in the sophistication with which each of these steps is developed and in the extent to which they successfully establish the relationship.[10]

What then is the purpose of a design for an ideal community? First and foremost, the ideal community model serves as a device for exploring alternative objectives for urban development. As suggested above, among the skills most needed in urban government are those of the "goal technician"; one of the goal technician's functions being the formulation of plausible, compatible and feasible values and criteria for consideration by the policy-maker.

This formulation of goals can be the creative work of an individual designer, or, at the other extreme, can result from fine investigation of the preferences and attitudes of the eventual clients. Since such goals do not exist in a vacuum, the ideal community construct can serve as a vehicle for their expression and development.[11]

Specifically, the ideal community should serve as a device for anticipating the consequences of a wholehearted commitment to the pursuit of one or a closely linked set of objectives related to the structure and function of the environment. With such a design, the political body then would be able to judge whether the objective or group of goals merit support—provided, of course, that there have been (implicitly if not explicitly) developed criteria for making such evaluative judgments and provided that feasibility studies give favorable answers. In this way, planners can function as goal-technicians:

National and National Planning: Decision Criteria," *Papers, Regional Science Association,* Vol. 14, 1965, pp. 107–36.

[10] The use of ideal communities is discussed more extensively in Thomas A. Reiner, *The Place of the Ideal Community in Urban Planning,* Philadelphia, University of Pennsylvania Press, 1963, esp. Chaps. 1 and 5.

[11] A number of ideal communities which explore alternate goals are summarized in Reiner, *The Place . . . , op. cit.,* Chap. 3.

this is an exciting example of the potential linkage between design and political skills.[12]

Ideal communities demonstrate, using whatever tools are available (from intuition to the computer), the richly interwoven nature of economic, social, physical and other facets of urban life. The ideal community typically is a vehicle for the study of a host of relationships which most experts, with their specific technical skills, generally study from one or only a few viewpoints. With due allowance for a possibly inappropriate analogy, the ideal community corresponds to the economist's search for a workable general equilibrium (in contrast to the greater detail of a partial or sectoral one). Study of the impacts of one facet of urban life on another gives the analyst a chance to measure, even if in most general terms restricted by available analytic techniques, the relative worths of the projects proposed as seen from various perspectives. Again this evaluation is essentially a question of values.

Perhaps the most successful example of an ideal community model is to be found in *Communitas*, written some twenty years ago by the collaborating brothers Goodman.[13] This is an excellent example of experimental goal construction for the study is, in reality, a trio of ideal communities, exploring the physical layout generated by, and supposedly in harmony with, alternate sets of socio-economic objectives. These goals are related to the economic fundamentals which underlie the social structure of the respective cities. Thus, the first "paradigm" is a design for a business core surrounded by a radiocentric system of easily accessible residential areas consistent with a high consumption ideal of what today is labeled an "affluent society." The second model is based on a more modest production-use sequence, with greater emphasis on the direct benefits from participation in work. The result is a polynu-

[12] Frank Lloyd Wright's Broadacre City is a good case in point. This proposal is a fairly complete specification of what would be entailed—given the U.S. technology and resources—by wholehearted commitment to one particular type of rural life. See, e.g., Frank Lloyd Wright, *The Living City*, New York, Horizon Press, 1958; and Reiner, *The Place . . .*, *op. cit.*, pp. 71–75.

[13] See Paul Goodman and Percival Goodman, *Communitas*, Chicago, University of Chicago Press, 1947. Also see the critiques in Reiner, *The Place . . .*, *op. cit.*; and a review by D. Riesman, "Some Observations on Community Plans and Utopia," *Yale Law Journal*, Vol. 57, No. 2, December 1947, pp. 175–200 (also reprinted in David Riesman, *Individualism Reconsidered*, Glencoe, Ill., Free Press, 1954; reissued New York, Doubleday Anchor Books, 1955).

cleated city mirroring its anarcho-syndicalist premises. The
third version is a city keyed to maximum production and military security. Separation of home and work, minimal and
compact living space, and rudimentary community facilities
are some of its features.

Clearly, physical form is made to reflect the initial premises
and, indeed, in *Communitas,* the forms are as distinct as the
underlying objectives. The Goodmans' work emphasizes the
linkages between physical and social elements.[14] Yet the critic
of the Goodmans' model and indeed of the ideal communities
literature in general will wish to question much in this approach. For a one-to-one correspondence between life-style
sought (the objective) and the resulting physical pattern is
difficult to establish. This is a reflection of a rather fundamental discovery—one which has only recently received the recognition it deserves—that we have but the most fragmentary
evidence to support what can be labeled "ecological determinism."[15] By this term we mean the existence of a rigid
causal chain from the physical environment to the behavior
and attitudes of individuals and groups living in the habitat.
Yet, for reasons not at all clear, different people react in quite
distinct ways to uniformly structured environments; and, what
may seem paradoxical, equivalent social forms are created in
quite distinct places. It is, therefore, no surprise to find that,
as the creators of ideal communities try to fit together pieces
of the evidence (which all too often is anecdotal) models are
created which show distinct physical features in response
to similar socio-economic conditions, and ideal communities
which are physically similar in shape and size nevertheless are
ones which harbor most diverse living conditions. Thus, the
style of life which is to be preferred in, say, Le Corbusier's
well-known city plans is quite similar to that which the Anglo-
American planner, Thomas Adams had in mind, yet the former is a city core of skyscrapers set in a rigid pattern, while
the latter is envisaged as a relatively low-density semi-
suburban setting for the pursuit of the middle-class virtues.
To take another example: the new-town model has been proposed as a cure for urban ills in societies which differ as much
as do the USA and the USSR; and these two nations among

---

[14] The social and economic elements are the source of objectives
and, as empirical evidence, constitute the major independent variables
of the models.

[15] See the critical bibliography, M. Heyman, "Space and Behavior,"
Landscape, Vol. 13, No. 3, Spring 1964, pp. 4–10.

many others, have seen development of parallel examples of neighborhood, or *mikroraion* plans with contrasting social goals underlying the schemes.[16]

Yet, even with the limitations just noted, the ideal community model and its modification for a particular city has a vital place in planning. The model explicitly forces attention on significant aggregate objectives for city development and so can be a vital force in political decision-making. Second, planning for the ideal community is a vehicle for the translation of general objectives into specific goals which have far greater reality, and potential for conflict, for the ultimate clients. Finally, the ideal community approach can be a framework for the amassing of evidence linking space, structure, attitudes and behavior.

Let us now consider the second problem. Again, we focus on the value components and on the methods of analysis.

How do public bodies make major investment decisions? Assume that planners have at their disposal a certain sum which must be allocated to projects to be built or to run over a given period. The question should be approached from at least two directions. First, what is an optimal allocation decision when choices must be made between broad types of programs; for example, to satisfy demand for highways as compared with demand for education, or housing needs pitted against requirements for industrial development. It would seem that this problem is related to issues which gave rise to the economists' literature on sectoral investment criteria. Second, the decision-maker faces the task of intelligent determination of allocations made spatially. Should investments be made in locality A or in locality B? As in the sector case, the answer is "it depends on what one is trying to do." By now the sector issue is rather well understood.[17] However, the decision-maker, in the spatial phase of the investigation, has few analytic formulations on which to build. Yet in this case, too, the objectives for planning are of paramount importance. Not that there are no decision-making rules which have been devised to identify the preferred spatial distribution of allocations and development—and any worker in the field is keenly

[16] For further discussion of this point, see Reiner, *The Place . . .*, *op. cit.*, Chap. 5; and Osborn and Reiner, *op. cit.*

[17] See, for example, the several excerpted articles in Gerald M. Meier, *Leading Issues in Development Economics*, New York, Oxford University Press, 1964, Part 5, Chap. 1.

aware of the pressures originating from political circles. What appears to be lacking is understanding of the consequences of pursuit of spatial or regional allocation criteria, an appreciation of their properties, and knowledge of what happens when they are integrated into a framework that in addition takes account of sector criteria.[18]

But in reality, long- and short-term objectives are jointly sought, different programs establish rival claims pursuant to conflicting interpretations of societal means and ends, and regions vie with each other and with the nation in identifying proper benchmarks for successful action. We are faced with a common problem in the public as well as the private domain: the pursuit of plural objectives each with *prima facie* validity. New techniques are needed to chart a proper course in such a world—techniques which are typically more complex and yet more fruitful than is the relatively simple maximization of one class of entities (as output measured by Gross National Product) subject to a given set of constraints (such as resource limitations). Comparison of alternate and multiple regional objectives and their relation to one simple national end should give insight to the more general development of multi-objective models.[19]

In the analysis of economic development, nation and region frequently receive distinct treatment in conceptualization as well as in administration. Economists and economic planners have worked almost exclusively on the national level; urban planners at most at the regional. Two types of studies to some extent do link region and nation in development. The first seeks to measure and analyze regional differentiation in well-being; the second focuses on the extent of urbanization. Study at the geographic levels of nation and of region of the objectives underlying the policies and the more specific targets (as these are elements along an end-means continuum) should be most helpful in our attempt to get a deeper understanding of the interplay of values in conflict.

The numerous criteria proposed in the economic development literature for allocation of investments are repeatedly expressed in terms of national indices: Gross National Product (G.N.P.), growth in G.N.P., maximum social marginal productivity, and the like. The evaluation procedure differs, of

[18] Time is another factor. Ideally, the analyst will identify the proper sequence of allocation to sectors or programs in a spatial setting.

[19] Plural objectives are discussed in Reiner, "National and Sub-National Planning . . . ," *op. cit.*

course, with each of the specific criteria. However, there is one common methodological thread: an allocation is tested, through impacts on sectors of the economy, for effect on the national economic indices. These sectors may be expressed in very general terms (referring to productive as contrasted to overhead uses) or in terms of specific sectoral disaggregations (such as the steel vs. the chemical industry). Such models can be adapted to incorporate the results of location analysis. When such comparative cost-locational equilibrium considerations are introduced, a spatial dimension is, of course, present. However, when such locational factors are introduced, the criterion of optimal allocation is still expressed in terms of some national (or system) index of economic welfare.

These models and analytic methods at best allow for a differential in regional productivity (long or short term) on which to capitalize in the quest for greater national output. Regional considerations also enter, of course, as knowledge of unequal endowment in the resource base. But the effect on national economic indicators again remains as the hallmark of a successful investment decision.

Yet, just as national plans have spatial or regional impacts, regional planning activities are conducted at the national level as well. This conclusion follows from a definition of regional planning as those efforts which lead to allocations made consciously (if not necessarily scientifically) on a spatial basis. As such, regional planning differs from the national planning approach with returns analyzed in terms of sectoral decisions and with reference to national welfare indices. Two related regional planning formulations appear. On the one hand, regional development is sought to bring about some notion of optimal self-fulfillment or utilization of the total resource base. On the other hand, regional development is sought to enable the area to achieve a better balance among the major components in the regional socio-economic sphere: for example between human resources and capital, supply and demand of locally consumed goods, etc.[20]

Regional planning decisions might also be directed toward

[20] The self-fulfillment notion (with certain inevitable vagueness) is expressed, e.g., in India; Planning Commission, *Third Five Year Plan*, Delhi, Planning Commission, 1961, pp. 142–44; and J. G. Saushkin, "Large Areal Complexes of Productive Forces of the Soviet Union," *Papers, Regional Science Association*, Vol. 8, 1962, pp. 93–104. The balance of objectives are cited, for example, in "National and Regional Economic Planning in Italy," in Walter Isard and John H. Cumberland, eds., *Regional Economic Planning*, Paris, OEEC-EPA, 1961.

spatial and size distribution of urban concentrations, and in specification of the service, welfare, and amenity levels therein through decisions on infrastructure investments.[21] Or, regional planning activity might lead to a pattern of distribution of public projects related to a concept of equity in development.[22] Under some circumstances, improved ability to withstand cyclical shocks is sought. In other cases, adaptation to technological change or to shifts in the nation's military posture would be the goals. And under some crisis circumstances, an appropriate set of objectives would focus on regional autarky.[23] Finally, regional planning may be a vehicle for the intelligent adaptation to major exogenous impacts on a given region.[24]

One further choice remains: allocation procedure itself. As noted above, the decision-makers may approach the space question directly: asking first where to place the investment, and only then making industrial sector determinations. Or the decision-makers, with some national objective in mind, first make a choice as to sector of allocation, and then, given the sectoral determination, so locate the investment to this sector as to achieve a spatially oriented objective. The actual solu-

[21] See, for example: Lloyd Rodwin, "Metropolitan Policy for Developing Areas," in Isard and Cumberland, eds., *op. cit.* The distribution of urban places can be evaluated as an objective in itself, or as an instrumentality to optimum growth of the system of regions which constitute the nation. Here we are largely beyond the realm of analytic models, though the scale, external economy, and agglomeration considerations (which underlie, among others, the "development poles" approach) are susceptible to mathematic formulation.

[22] See, for example, the papers of several of the Delegations reporting to the European Productivity Agency Conference on Problems of Economic Development (1960) in Isard and Cumberland, eds., *op. cit.* One of the rare but significant attempts to apply intensively economic techniques in such a regional planning context is discussed in Hollis B. Chenery and Paul G. Clark, *Interindustry Economics*, New York, Wiley, 1959, Chap. 12.

[23] See, for further discussion of some of these regional objectives: J. L. Fisher, "Concepts in Regional Development," *Papers and Proceedings, Regional Science Association*, Vol. 1, 1955, pp. W1–W20; C. L. Leven, "Establishing Goals for Regional Economic Development," *Journal of the American Institute of Planners*, Vol. 30, No. 2, May 1964, pp. 100–10; and D. F. Bramhall, "Projecting Regional Accounts and Industrial Location: Reflections on Policy Applications," *Papers, Regional Science Association*, Vol. 7, 1961, pp. 89–118.

[24] Perhaps the bulk of regional planning analyses fall in this category. See, for example: A. Ganz, "Regional Planning as a Key to the Present Stage of Economic Development of Latin America," *Cuadernos de la Sociedad Venezolana de Planificación*, special issue, September 1963, pp. 117–28.

tion or final choice may depend on the strategy. When two constraints or objectives of this sort are placed on an activity, the order is significant. Thus, steel may be preferred to chemicals as yielding the highest G.N.P. increment (the criterion associated with sectoral determination); and the second choice might be that, spatially, southern investment—because, say, of some equity policy—is to be preferred to investment in the North. The final directive is to allocate to steel in the South. But what if the other sequence is followed? The South is selected as the location for investment, and if decision-makers only then ask "To which industrial sector do we allocate?"— where they still seek to maximize G.N.P., but where their determinations are made after the regional determination—the answer then may well be: "Allocate to chemicals." For, given the constraint that allocation be limited to the South, it could be that a greater G.N.P. may be generated if investment is made in the chemical sector. This would be the case if steel, the most efficient industrial sector nationally, is, by virtue of location factors, a highly efficient industry when located in the North, but is less efficient when located in the South. Only where both decision sequences lead to the *optimum optimorum* (or other extreme cases) is the result known to be independent of the decision order taken.[25]

Within the context of national planning there are four circumstances under which such criteria, strictly *regional* allocation criteria (as distinct from those related to sector activity), may profitably be used:

1. The most obvious task is the study of regional impacts of exogenously determined investments (ones set by forces outside the region) as these are made pursuant to national plans with their sectoral determinations. This may lead to adaptation to the impact by decision-makers in the regions and to positive steps to take advantage of these. Comparison of impacts at the regional level should provide additional information to help in the relative assessment of such investments at the level of the national plan.[26]

2. A second field for regional planning endeavors with

[25] It should be emphasized that problems similar to those noted here arise in urban planning. For example, decisions to invest public funds in various parts of a city are parallel to the national decisions discussed in this paper.

[26] See, e.g.: Ganz, *op. cit.;* and A. Mayne, "Designing and Administering a Regional Economic Development Plan," in Isard and Cumberland, eds., *op. cit.;* regarding such studies for Venezuela and Puerto Rico, respectively.

allocation criteria is the exploration and effectuation of regional policies under conditions where national constraints and objectives are not fully binding. For example, given relative abundance or pressing political considerations, regional criteria can be considered a "luxury" which the national planning agents calculate (or concede) can be afforded.[27]

3. Where *sector* allocation decisions have been made with a certain objective in mind, *regional* allocation levels might subsequently be made pursuant to a different objective appropriate to regional considerations. This seems to be a particularly worthwhile attack on the problems of regional planning. So as to make the analysis manageable, it may prove fruitful to assume that, as the result of a first stage of analysis, a decision as to sector or program of allocation has been made. Confronting such a decision, the analyst proceeds to a spatial determination of the allocation.[28]

4. Finally, national aggregative criteria (of the type "Allocate so as to maximize G.N.P., and allocate accordingly to a given sector at a particular location") are not particularly informative or determinate—given the state of the economist's art and the scope of economic analysis—in matters of social overhead and such allocations which are virtually welfare transfers. Certain regional investment criteria can serve as handy tools for determining spatial assignments of these types.

Regional allocation criteria, as is clear if the above planning framework is accepted, are value statements; they stand or fall by reference to other elements of a value hierarchy. But this is not to say that each regional criterion is without costs or benefits in terms of other regional criteria, or in terms of national considerations. Thus one of the main forms which analysis of regional criteria can take is the measure of opportunity cost implicit in each.

Further, if we accept the notion that values exist in a hierarchy, then the general propositions that regions and their inhabitants should be treated equitably—widely voiced in development circles—must be rendered more specific. Equity is a slippery concept and several popular notions compete for attention.

[27] Thus, it is evident that East and West Pakistan are entitled, in many sectors, to virtually equal allocations under the national plan. See Pakistan Planning Commission, *The Second Five Year Plan,* Karachi, the Commission, 1960, Chap. 19.

[28] This procedure reduces the complexity of the problem; it also seems to correspond to the reality of certain tasks facing operating agencies.

Is equity a matter of equal growth rates, or one of an equal share in benefits of growth? Is equity achieved with no further aggravation of present inequalities, or is it tantamount to the eradication of such differences in well-being? What part of a person's income is proper subject of concern: total income, including imputed income, or income which originates as inter-regional transfer? Or is the proper subject of concern only the income which can be ascribed to social services, welfare payments, and other government activities? Is equity to be measured (as seems to be the usual implication) by indices of central tendency—the mean or median income levels—or is a more meaningful index of well-being to be found in the analysis of the spread of values? Is the intention of the equity-directed program to raise the level of well-being of those whose income today is the lowest, or is it to raise the median regional income.[29] Furthermore, what is the proper relation between "equity" and "balance"? When growth rates are viewed regionally, is sectoral imbalance to be tolerated? Are there class inequities generated with regional equity programs? And, to what extent, à la Hirschman, are "imbalance" and "inequity" useful growth-inducing instruments?[30]

Does equity refer to that population now living in the region, or to those remaining or brought in as a result of development programs? Plans affect location of productive activity, and location decisions therefore have migration implications. Precisely, as a result of those equalizing measures embodied in an allocation scheme, population shifts are sure to arise. Such population flows can, of course, negate or accelerate achievement far in excess of any equalizing programs. The equalization criterion chosen would, ideally, recognize the implications of this dynamic factor.[31] Another temporal

[29] Some of the alternate equity notions regarding regional development have been presented in L. Rodwin, "National Urban Planning and Regional Capital Budgets," *Papers and Proceedings of the Regional Science Association*, Vol. 3, 1957, pp. 223–32; and S. H. Robock, "Regional and National Economic Development in India," *Papers and Proceedings of the Regional Science Association*, Vol. 6, 1960, pp. 65–82.

[30] See Albert O. Hirschman, *The Strategy of Economic Development*, New Haven, Yale University Press, 1958, esp. Chap. 10.

[31] Clashing attitudes toward migration reflect the world-wide conflict between the many vested interests favoring immobility and the very evident volitional population shifts to urban areas. Where migration is restrained—in the face of evidence that it is associated with beneficent shifts in productivity, education, birth rates, etc.—equalization of per capita incomes on a regional basis becomes a more difficult undertaking. This conflict is a facet of the following question, one which has been

factor is choice of a date by which to achieve equality.[32] Clearly the nature of a given program hinges quite directly on the answer to questions such as these. Again, we say that the most significant contribution the planner-analyst may have to make is to bring such (and other) alternative considerations to the attention of responsible decision-makers and encourage an explicit commitment to a particular path in the direction of development.

Finally, limits to the acceptable range of homogeneity or heterogeneity within a given region must be set. This, it might be argued, interregional equality is relatively meaningless where, within regions, there remains (or possibly there is built up) greater disparity. Such internal inequality may be expressed spatially, in which case a finer regionalization might resolve the problem.[33] It may be nonspatial disparity, as where minorities, or disfavored age groups, are scattered throughout a region. In the latter case, the "grain" of regionalization is irrelevant.

Let us now consider analytically some rather simple regional allocation criteria. Though examples can be drawn from other nations, the development programs of the U.S. Government, particularly as these stimulate the flow of resources to urban areas, are all built on such allocative devices. The criteria are presented with sufficient generality so that elementary analysis is possible.

---

insufficiently probed in planning circles: "What condition represents 'stability': can stability be consistent with lack of change in the rate of change? In more homely terms, is a region or community 'stable' when a given population remains resident there, though with changing economic features, changing family size, new travel and consumption patterns and other behavior shifts as the cohort ages or becomes wealthier? Or should one speak of stability in terms of groups exhibiting similar patterns of behavior even though individuals composing the region have changed; new faces having come to assume old roles?"

[32] A dynamic income-equalization model (with an objective of maximizing G.N.P.) is given in M. A. Rahman, "Regional Allocation of Investment," *Quarterly Journal of Economics,* Vol. 77, No. 1, February 1963, pp. 26–39.

[33] A simple representation of the effects of different regionalization patterns on intraregional measures of welfare is given in T. A. Reiner, "Organizing Regional Investment Criteria," *Papers, Regional Science Association,* Vol. 11, 1964, pp. 63–72.

CRITERION 1: EQUALIZE REGIONAL PER CAPITA INCOMES

India is among the several nations where the national plan declares that achievement of interregional equality in per capita income (or consumption) is one of the aims, albeit a subsidiary one.[34] Such plans implicitly provide that equalization should not take place below a certain level of system welfare, or at the cost of direct interregional transfers, and subject to other such constraints. Inequalities must persist pro tem, where national levels are low. In other words, equalization is to be achieved by raising incomes in the poorer areas and not be reducing the wealth of the richer. Deferred equalization purchases, so it is maintained, a higher level for all. One crucial variable, then, is the target date for achievement of equalization.

A more modest version of this equity criterion, and one which is perhaps more palatable politically, is that the disparity be gradually lessened period by period. Thus, if one region exceeds the other in per capita income by 50 percent, the criterion for allocation might be an investment pattern such that at the end of one period, the maximum national product be attained provided the disparity did not exceed 25 percent. A limiting version of such a modified criterion would call for allocations such that existing disparities not be further aggravated by the investment pattern. In a situation where one or more regions are of declining importance economically, this might be the most that a reasonable politician could demand.

CRITERION 2: ALLOCATIONS IN PROPORTION TO WEALTH

An equitable allocation can be interpreted as one which counterbalances current inequity in well-being. Thus an equitable allocation would be one where investments to regions are made in some fashion inverse to their current wel-

---

[34] See, e.g., India, Planning Commission, *Second Five Year Plan: A Draft Outline*, New Delhi, the Commission, 1956, p. 20. Such a framework, where minimum regional consumption levels appear as constraints, can be stated as a linear program.

fare.[35] Since regional population does vary, this requires that a system of weights be used to reflect variation in size. An alternate formulation of essentially the same criterion is based on the assumption that regions with higher income are in greater need of certain classes of investments than are the poor, or that the wealth is in itself an index of the logic and sensibility of investment (say because of the higher returns secured in regions with high agglomeration economies). Criteria may therefore be established to allocate in direct proportion to existing income levels. Furthermore, a region's willingness to avail itself of certain types of funds hinges on the ability to contribute its local share. It may therefore be said that (at least on the aggregate, for a whole set of programs) funds would be distributed roughly in proportion to existing income.[36]

CRITERION 3: ALLOCATION IN PROPORTION TO POPULATION

Perhaps the simplest scheme for allocating equitably is by reference to population size. The "population," depending on the particular program, may be identified as the total regional population, or as some relevant subset of this universe: the unemployed, school-age children, residents of urban areas, etc., as these identify clients related to the intent of the allocation. A criterion of this type is usually an important element in the formulae employed to determine regional eligibility for welfare, health, and education programs.

CRITERION 4: ALLOCATIONS IN PROPORTION TO SPACE

The allocation pattern sought may be expressed strictly in terms of space. There is some evidence that, in certain nations, investments for railway track and irrigation are being made pursuant to an area criterion. During one period in the fifties, certain Puerto Rican programs (urban renewal and industrial development, among others) were conducted to pro-

[35] Obviously, there are other forms which could be given to such a compensation criteria: for example, allocate in proportion to deviation from some standard per capita income level. Grants made by the U.S. Government in several fields of social welfare follow this pattern.

[36] Thus, there are certain grants-in-aid allocated by the U.S. Government which seem to be distributed in proportion to wealth.

vide one project for each civil subdivision.[37] Since most nations have large interregional differences in density of settlement and intensity of development, such area-equal criteria are likely to be coupled with high opportunity costs.

In another paper, there has been developed a simplified, comparative static model which is designed to study the effects of adherence to one or another such criterion.[38] The main point to be stressed is that each criterion can lead to distinct and possibly to conflicting policy directives. Each criterion, when explicitly stated, provides the basis for rational action. Such criteria underpinnings are indispensable elements of rationality, yet in themselves are value statements, and nothing more. Finally, each criterion can result in distinct allocation of resources, and so in distinct pattern of urban places.

Where does analysis of such values lead? If nothing else, it allows the measurement of opportunity costs, or the mutual costs, in terms of the set of goals or criteria. Careful study of criteria therefore allows the planner to establish the impacts of the pursuit of values. And if he does this task well and nothing else, he has more than earned his keep.

[37] See, e.g., Puerto Rico Industrial Development Corporation, *Master Plan for Industrialization*, San Juan, the Corporation, 1956.
[38] Reiner, "Sub-National and National Planning . . . ," *op. cit.*

Societal Goals and Planned Societies

JOHN W. DYCKMAN*

Social planning is a belated and tentative response of American planners to functional lag. Physical planning, particularly of cities, has been accepted as a legitimate activity at the gov-

* Professor of City and Regional Planning and Chairman of the Center for Planning and Development, University of California, Berkeley. With a master's degree in economics and a Ph.D. in planning from the University of Chicago, he served on the faculty of the University of Pennsylvania for eight years and with Arthur D. Little, Inc. in San Francisco as Chief of the Regional Development and Urban Economics Section prior to the University of California. Visiting Professor at several institutions, Dyckman has consulted for the National Park Service, the New York City Planning Department, the Planning Board of Puerto Rico, ACTION, The Philadelphia Redevelopment Authority, as well as serving on a number of important advisory committees both public and private. He is presently associated with Vladimir Music at the Urbanistici Institut in Ljubljana, Yugoslavia. The author of a consid-

ernmental level for more than half a century. Economic planning, though partial and inconstant, has been an established part of the governmental scene since the 1930's. Social planning, on the other hand, has been openly recognized only more recently, and then it has proceeded under a cover of confusion which has prevented public debate on its scope and its intentions.

For the most part, social planning in the USA is defensive, and arises from the crises which are spun off as by-products of action programs of government. Public intervention in urban development and renewal, for example, has cast up problems of relocation which are so intertwined in the fabric of social life of the affected communities that "social" planners are called upon for relief.

At the same time, the residual issues of the affluent society are so clearly social issues that earlier concerns of physical and economic planning have in some cases given way to priorities for direct planning of social outcomes. The Poverty Program, for example, recognizes that the problem of poverty is not merely a problem of economics, but is also a problem of the culture of poverty which can be addressed only by direct social action. Juvenile delinquency, mental health, and a range of other social ills are, in the view of the behavioral scientists who examine them, more than economic problems. Indeed, there are many who argue that a planned economy cannot eliminate these problems. The presence of social pathology alongside planning then becomes an argument against an excessively "materialistic" view of society. Paradoxically, opponents of the excessive economic determinism often attributed to Marxism are cast in the role of advocates of increasing planning in the social sphere.

Other types of social planning have been made necessary by rejection of the "planned society" of socialist economists. The whole complex of welfare services which have grown up in the United States were traditionally, and still remain, devices to compensate for the wastage and breakage in a competitive,

erable number of valuable articles in professional journals, he contributed the summary chapter to Melvin Webber, Ed., *Explorations Into Urban Structure* (Philadelphia: University of Pennsylvania Press, 1964), and with Reginald Isaacs, published *Capital Requirements for Urban Development and Renewal* (New York: McGraw-Hill, 1961). This article is partially based on a 1963 "Memorandum on Social Issues in Planning Puerto Rico," and reprinted here with permission from the *Journal of the American Institute of Planners,* Vol. XXXII, No. 2, March 1966.

individual-serving, industrial society. They have existed to cushion the blow of this competitive struggle for those so disadvantaged as to be unable to compete effectively. The traditional social services, both privately and publicly provided, are ad hoc solutions for specific problems. They have not, until recently, drawn upon a common context or comprehensive planning outlook.

The notion of coordinated social services, of planned cooperation between agencies, is relatively recent in the field of social welfare and social work. But even where such coordinating councils exist in cities or metropolitan areas, their planning is roughly advisory (except for determinations which enter into the division of the Community Chest) and lacks measures of progress which would guide the allocative decisions. Even more important, the social goals which planning would presumably help to advance are vague and are often stated so as to obscure rather than to adjudicate differences between the goals of the independent agencies.

As a result, there is a great deal of remedial social action, and some social planning in the United States, but this goes on in the absence of even a schematic societal plan which will guide the individual plans of the operating agencies. Societal planning in the United States is principally hortatory, as in the National Goals Reports issued during the Eisenhower Administration.

Some of the most thoughtful work on the meaning of social planning in the American context was instituted several years ago under the direction of Everett Reimer for the Puerto Rican Planning Board. Reimer, assisted by Janet Reiner, commissioned thoughtful papers by Herbert Gans, Abraham Kaplan, and other consultants, and produced many useful internal memoranda. In one of these papers Gans clearly distinguished "societal planning" from "social programs." The former is much more difficult to treat, since it entails some specification of the goals of the society, while the latter are farther along in the "means" end of the means-ends continuum. Gans developed a paradigm for locating programs and actions in this framework which is an excellent statement for orientation to the problem of social planning in the context of the remedial actions of social agencies traditional in the United States.[1]

Let us extend this line of reasoning, and take *social planning*

[1] Herbert Gans, "Memorandum," an unpublished paper of the Puerto Rican Planning Board.

to mean the effort to plan for the fate of a whole society. This view emphasizes the interdependence of activities and the shared consequences of program actions. It recognizes that there may be unplanned consequences of planned actions, and that these may deserve attention equal to that given the programs themselves. Much of the concern with social planning among city planners in the United States stems from the unplanned social dislocations and stresses that follow upon public programs such as redevelopment. In a comparable vein, the interest in social planning in developing economies arises from similar stresses that follow upon planned economic development. Indeed, the former draws heavily on the literature developed in the latter, and both have made liberal use of studies developed in crisis situations such as bombings, floods, and deportations. The problems of disrupted working class urban neighborhoods described by Gans and others are in one perspective a pale copy of the disruptions and strains on social goals of political realization, social justice, and cultural self-expression which have accompanied pursuit of the goal of economic development in preindustrial societies.

When societal goals are advanced by unilateral programs of service agencies, unexpected or perverse results may emerge. Thus the goals of economic justice may dictate an emphasis on low-cost meritorious consumer goods such as housing, and the goals of social justice may indicate that the housing should be placed in neighborhoods as favored as those claimed by higher income groups, but the actual programs for achieving these goals may make for outcomes that disturb the harmonious relations between groups, aggravate class tension, and encourage some forms of antisocial actions. Programs of economic development have almost inevitably favored certain classes whose cooperation was vital to the program, to the relative disadvantage of others. More specifically, these programs have been concerned with incentives necessary to realization of the goals, such as high rewards to entrepreneurs, which may have been paid for by relatively disadvantaged groups. One can proliferate examples of this kind, both in economic development and in urban renewal. These examples dramatize the need for a true social planning framework in which to evaluate the social consequences of individual programs.

To clarify these relations, we might distinguish three operational meanings of *social planning,* and three levels of action.

　　1. At the societal planning level, social planning means

the selection of the social goals of the nation or state, and the setting of targets for their achievement. It requires a ranking of these goals, and assessment of the cost (in terms of other objectives) of achieving them, and judgments of the feasibility of such programs.

2. Social planning, in a closely related meaning, involves the application of social values and action criteria to the assessment of programs undertaken in the pursuit of economic or political goals. Thus, it can mean the testing of the consequences—in terms of intergroup or interpersonal relations—of everything from broad economic development programs to specific redevelopment projects.

3. Social planning can mean specifically "social" programming arising from the broad social goals of the community. The traditional welfare activities of public and private agencies have been the principal focus of such planning in the United States. The coordination of programming for and by the multitude of caretaker agencies that have grown up in our free enterprise economy is a popular task for this type of social planning.

Much of the discussion of social planning, and the identification of activities under this label, belongs in the third category. It is my contention that this category has developed in a variety of directions without an adequately specified set of objectives at the first and second levels. This view is independent of considerations of the planned society, though subsequent discussion will make clear that the latter are not irrelevant to it.

Social planning has long been treacherous ground for the city planner because of the ever present danger that the expert determination of need might degenerate into the imposition of class or professional prejudices upon a resistant clientele. Social planning, in the sense of determination of the social needs of a community or a group within the community is torn between the desire to require certain levels of consumption of merit goods on the one hand, and the recognition of the legitimacy of individual choice on the other. Many social planners assert that their interest is in the maximization of opportunity, or freedom of choice. But as a practical matter, no society has found a feasible way of maximizing choice for all groups or individuals at all times. For the exercise of one man's choice is a limitation on the freedom of choice of another.

It is not surprising that social planning has often turned

away from goals, in the direction of means. For one thing, it is firmly in the tradition of modern clinical psychology, and the positivism of sociology, to accept individual determined ends as legitimate, and to emphasize means of realizing these ends. But it is a matter of some subtlety, worthy to challenge the professional social actionist, or clinical caretaker, to emphasize the manipulation of behavior, rather than the alteration of goals of behavior. Let us consider some of the problems encountered in these tasks.

FINDING APPROPRIATE REMEDIES: DIAGNOSIS OF THE CLIENT

Remedial social planning is necessary in our society because the major forces shaping our lives are unplanned. Social planning has come to the fore because we have been unable to predict, control, or shape the repercussions of technological change or of our planned programs. Because we do not plan our technology, but allow it to follow opportunistic lines, we do not control the repercussions of its development. These repercussions cast up many of the persistent social problems of our times, such as the sharp segregation of the poor, the aged, and the minorities in the cities; the left-behind regions of economic depression; the unemployable cadres of displaced workers; and the great gaps in educational attainment. In many respects, the advanced technological societies need therapeutic social planning as badly as the countries experiencing the stresses of early technological change. For example, urban renewal, which was embraced avidly by liberals and city planners in 1949 at passage of the Housing Act, has proven a specific source of embarrassment and friction to liberal politicians for fifteen years. It is the realization of this fact that has created the call for a Domestic Peace Corps in the United States.

These problems have traditionally been easier to identify in the newly developing economies. One might swiftly recognize the particular problems raised for Puerto Rican planning by a host of world and hemispheric developments: the emergence of a new stage in world industrialization; the extension of the urban life style and the obliteration of differences between city and country in the most industrially developed nations; the sharpening of differences between the "educated" and "uneducated"; the development of new technological advances in transportation and communication. Until a Michael

Harrington, or some other prophet, calls attention to the lags in our perception, we are likely to miss the similar phenomena which take place in societies starting from a more favored base. It is the merit of urban renewal that it called attention to problems of the city, to implications of public intervention in the city, and to undeveloped perspectives in city planning.

Further, the issue of relocation in urban redevelopment emphasizes the interdependence of the social fabric of communities. It has underlined the reality that one cannot intervene in any important portion of this web without disrupting the structure and entangling himself in the consequences.

But the urban renewal issue is complicated by the complexity of modern government and its ingrown bureaucracy in response to technological pressures operating through the inexorable drive of organizational efficiency. In the course of this transformation of government, many of the more purely "social" concerns, which were adequately handled in the days when political community and social community were identical, have disappeared in the larger governmental apparatus. As a result, the need for social planning is one symptomatic side effect of the organizational conquest of government. This bureaucratization is present at all levels—the distance between the local communities and city government is evident at a public hearing in a major city on the subject of a freeway location or a redevelopment proposal—though it is most intense at the federal level, where the bureaucracies are relatively rationalized and professionalized. Because we have not been conscious of the organizational and technological revolutions in our modern life, we approach the discovery of disparities between local community feeling and bureaucratic objectives with indignation. Truly effective social planning, even in a limited therapeutic sense, would need to deal more self-consciously with the relation between local social objectives and larger organizational requirements.

It is largely this sense of bureaucratic distance, which exists between city planners and citizens, almost equally with practitioners of welfare services and their clients, that has led to the social planning emphasis on *client analysis*. Presumably, by detailed sociological analysis of the client population, akin to the market analysis conducted by firms seeking outlets for their products, social planning can be equipped to overcome this bureaucratic disability. Client analysis has drawn upon, and has developed, substantial insights into the aspirations and motives of the target populations. Presumably, client analysis will also help uncover and recognize the interest of groups who are disenfranchised of power, and whose real aspirations would rarely be reflected in public programs. This more dynamic, or even revolutionary, aspect of client analysis has been widely stressed by social planners operating in minority group areas. It may be likened to a caretaker variant of the civil rights position that the society must do some things to help disadvantaged groups which have not yet been discovered by the disadvantaged groups themselves. In the advertising analogy, client analysis thus leads to taste-making, as well as taste-serving.

In this latter formulation, the client analysis position strikes a responsive note in the ideology of city planners, who have commonly felt that the citizens of the megapolitan world must be saved from themselves. In the social planning context, the inarticulate disadvantaged are saved from a temporary ignorance of their own best interests in order that they can more effectively express those interests over time.

The client analysis position, however, has one great advantage over that of traditional city planning. It explicitly identifies these interests, and neither subsumes them in vague categories of public interest, nor freely ascribes the prejudices of the bureaucracy to the long run best interest of the poor. Client analysis, moreover, begins from the presupposition that many of the bureaucratic standards will be ill-suited to serve the real client population. Nevertheless, one cannot escape the reality that social planning with client analysis merely substitutes market research for the operations of the market. That is, client analysis notwithstanding, social planning is the antithesis of laissez-faire.

Social planning, in fact, cannot escape the ire of the conservatives by adopting some of the instruments of the market. Indeed, the violence of objections to the rent supplements included in last year's Housing Bill is evidence that indirectness and subtlety in social programs, which place a greater premium on planning than on direct action, may be more deeply resented by opponents of the programs' purposes. One is reminded that the late Senator Bricker belaboured his compatriot Senator from Ohio, Robert Taft, for introducing the "Trojan Horse" of private redevelopment into the publicly subsidized 1949 Housing Act. There is no particular ground for believing that social planning and market mechanisms make public spending any more palatable to enemies of the programs. The very informational requirements of social planning may make the priests of that planning more suspect of hoarding secrets.

CARETAKERS AND LONG-RUN CLIENT INTERESTS

Most social planners have at least a modified "caretaker" orientation. In his statement on "Meeting Human Needs" in *Goals for Americans,* the report of the President's Commission in 1960, James P. Dixon, Jr. wrote, "[society] can develop ways by which people can meet their own needs more readily and fruitfully, and it can develop ways by which society as a whole can meet needs that would otherwise be unmet. There are individuals who will not meet their own needs, and others who cannot."[2] The caretaker responsibility presumably extends to those who will not as well as those who cannot. Few societies take a wholly permissive view towards freedom of choice. In addition to the collective goods which we make available for the use of all citizens, from national defense to national parks, there are public programs encouraging the consumption of certain goods and services, and discouraging others. Economists recognize that societies encourage the consumption of the "merit" goods and discourage the consumption of demerit goods. Thus we exempt certain foods from sales taxes and place punitive taxes on alcohol, tobacco, and other products, and severely restrict the use of narcotics.

Americans have been understandably wary of social planning, since these responsibilities place the planners in the role of caretakers of "safety," "health," and "morals." The technological competence of highly organized government is today so great that there is widespread suspicion and apprehension about government power. We are afraid of the information handling capabilities which modern technology has placed at the disposal of government, for the "disutopians" have warned us of the threat to liberty which may lurk in such power. We all tend to be slightly apprehensive about the governmental capacity for storing information about the individual and recalling it by means of his social security number, zip code, or other identification. These fears may be legitimate even when it is recognized that the information technology is itself morally indifferent, and can be used with equal effect for widely approved and undesirable social purposes. The is-

---

[2] James P. Dixon, Jr., "Meeting Human Needs," *Goals for Americans,* The Report of the President's Commission on National Goals (Prentice-Hall, 1960), p. 249.

sue of what is "desirable" is an openly divisive one. Humanists have never been reluctant to prescribe remedies for fellow humans, but a central problem of democratic planning, as Davidoff and Reiner have emphasized, is that of preserving an adequate area of individual choice in the face of expert judgments of the "good."[3]

This issue is a persistent stumbling block in all social planning programs aimed at overcoming some of the undesirable consequences of our great technical efficiency. The Poverty Program is split, from the very start, on disagreement over the meaning of poverty. The traditional libertarian nineteenth century economists argue that the problem of poverty is one of inadequate income, and the provision of that income will eliminate the poverty. Some of the contemporary liberals argue the contrary, maintaining that there is a culture of poverty independent of income which cannot be redressed by simple money payments. The choice of a measurement of poverty engages this issue. A "market basket" approach as contrasted with an income level approach commits one to a definition of poverty in terms of merit goods, and required consumption, rather than income payment. In short, it takes some of the choice away from the poor, and refers the determination to an objective standard.

In social planning, the caretaker issue directly confronts choice. The case of planning for mental health, for example, is fraught with instances of value conflict. Even at the margin, where relatively clear-cut issues of community interest can be adduced, there are few clear-cut policy directions. Take the control of dischargees from mental hygiene programs. It serves the cause of effective treatment to continue the contact with the patient over a period of time. To maintain this contact normally requires a legal hold on the patient. But it is a matter of great administrative delicacy to decide when the imposition of that hold, usually by court order, is genuinely "protective," and when it is a violation of the patient's civil liberties.

In such cases, the welfare economics rule, crudely paraphrased, would be to restrain the patient only when the marginal social benefit from the continuing contact exceeds the marginal social cost of diminishing individual liberty. In practice, the probability of relapse once removed from contact is the decisive "factual" input. When the social cost of relapse, weighted by the probability of relapse once the patient is removed from contact, exceeds the social cost of deprivation of liberty multiplied by the probability of such deprivation in enforced contact, the restraint is justified. Clearly, administrators may be divided on their relative valuation of the social damage of the behavior of the mentally ill and of freedom to come and go at will. But it is sometimes overlooked that the social sciences, on which such calculus is dependent for its "factual" inputs, are often equally at variance over the behavioral probabilities. As Hans Morgenthau once observed, social sciences are not only uncertain about the nature of causes, given effects, but are also uncertain about the evaluation of the effects, given the causes.

The problem of choice is therefore shifted uncomfortably to the social planner. He finds that he must have a theory of long-run client interests. If he is to engage in this perilous activity, he cannot afford the luxury of positivist detachment. He will not be handed a ready-made packet of goals in the form of a set of well-ordered preference functions, and the task of discerning "latent" goals will take great patience and much free interpretation. The enterprise of social planning has always been facilitated by strong ideology. At the least, it requires determined leadership.

SOCIAL PLANNING AND SOCIAL LEADERSHIP

If the democratic ideals of decentralized decision and individual choice are to be pursued concurrently with the officially defined community goals of health and welfare, including increased consumption of meritorious goods and services, extraordinary efforts must be made to bulwark the choosing processes of the disadvantaged with vast amounts of technical information, political leverage, and economic means. In particular, it may be necessary for the poor and disadvantaged to have their own planners. This realization is quickly forced upon those who hold uncompromisingly democratic goals, and who become engaged in the action processes. For example, Paul Davidoff has on various occasions urged that planners take up the role of advocates for the disadvantaged.[4]

[4] Good statements of the Davidoff position may be found in Paul Davidoff, "The Role of the City Planner in Social Planning," *Proceedings of the American Institute of Planners, 1964 Annual Conference*, pp. 125–131, and, "Advocacy and Pluralism in Planning," *Journal*

The problem is closely analogous to that of foreign aid. In making grants or loans to undeveloped nations, the donors are always faced with the difficult task of insuring efficient use of the funds, without imposing imperialistic controls. The difficulties in such action may account for the predilection in Soviet aid programs for concrete development projects, rather than outright grants. If the projects chosen are popular, some of this difficulty can be avoided. Presumably, if federal programs followed indigenous market choice rather than bureaucratic determination of merit, they would provide freedom schools, key club memberships, and cut-rate Cadillacs rather than public housing, Job Corps camps, and school lunches. It would then be up to local planners, working in the community as advocates, to both extend the impact of the actual choices of the community, and to reshape the choice, by dramatizing the relations between means and ends.

Taken seriously programs like the rent subsidy provisions of the present Housing Act, which are aimed at encouraging the consumption of merit goods, entail a basic reeducation of consumers. Indeed, real incomes measured by consumer satisfaction, may not go up in the short run under such programs even if the objective level of consumption is raised. (In the case of relocation of slum dwellers in housing estates in England, Ireland, and elsewhere, there is even some evidence that the objective level of living has at times declined slightly with the increased consumption of a particular merit good, housing.)

The closer one gets to the community level, and the closer to the client, the more acute are these problems of individual liberty and choice. The main problem of social planning at the national level is to establish social goals which are attainable, or at least approachable, which can be given some hierarchical ordering, and which can be programmed. National planners should use program guides, standards, and other bureaucratic controls sparingly, lest they make demands on localities which are unreasonable in this sense.

At the local level, where these goals are to be implemented, the democratic ideal would hold out the opportunity for citizens to participate in defining the operational form of their goals. In practice, however, there is a tendency toward organizational efficiency which requires each local agency action to be measured against the operating rules of output which are established by the national bureaucracies. While planning as an activity is independent of the issue of centralization, the same organizational forces that make for planning push for the efficiencies realizable by central control. What is more, the planners are often impatient with the delays, losses, and frictional costs imposed by decentralized administration. The conduct of the Antipoverty Program is an example of such costs, and the uneasiness which these arouse in the planners.

SOCIAL PLANNING AND ADMINISTRATIVE EFFICIENCY

The Great Society is determined to be The Efficient Society, not content to provide butter with its guns, but bent on having the most Bang for the Buck and the smoothest spreading, high-score product in Dairyland. The success of economic thinking in the Defense Department's planning and the great growth of efficiency analysis techniques supported by government contract effort have encouraged governmental planners to apply performance tests to social welfare programs as well as to military procurement. The city planning profession, which has long vacillated between social utopianism and managerial efficiency aims, now must increasingly accommodate to the imposition of the latter by the administering federal bureaucracies. Local social planning has barely begun to digest the implications of this trend.

The drive for evaluation of the effectiveness of social service programs is eminently reasonable. In the absence of well articulated national social goals, individual program progress is difficult to measure; in a society only recently concerned with defining more subtle measures of social progress than income and employment some confusion of direction is to be expected. The presence of established bureaucracies poised to soak up the new program funds does not reassure the operations analyst. After all, what percentage of applicants to the U.S. Employment Service are placed in jobs by that service? What percentage of referrals to Mental Health clinics are successfully treated? Existing welfare agencies tend to be audited in terms of operations performed, not results achieved. Senator Ribicoff's recent observation that federal agencies may lack the competence to administer the new social programs enacted by Congress is only half the picture; Congress has failed to give clearly the direction of results expected from these programs. Administrative audits may be premature until these purposes are clarified. There is even a danger that too-hasty efficiency measures will impede the development of these goals, for the latter must be defined by the interactions between the clients and the supply agencies.

Since a prime goal of administration is efficiency, and since individuals may be legitimately indifferent to the efficiency of the system or organization, individual behavior is a friction to be overcome in administration. Resistance to the imposition of preference rankings from above is a fundamental democratic tenet, but it is almost inevitably in conflict with programs planned by experts, whether social planners or physical planners. Efficiency-minded physical planners become impatient at the economic and engineering inefficiencies produced by obdurate human behavior, and the social planners, since the origins of the settlement house movement, have marvelled at the capacities of the poor for resisting "self-betterment."

Robert Moses, one of the more impatient of planners, recently gave vent to this common annoyance, commenting on an engineering feasibility report for a proposed Long Island Sound Crossing which he favors. Since the feasibility depends, to some extent, on the ability of the planners to persuade people to use the crossing at times other than summer months and week-ends, Mr. Moses complained that "the usual short season, dependent on the opening and closing of schools, and occasional mid-summer peak loads due to silly, gregarious travel hours, are the despair and curse of those who operate our seashore." The stickiness of this behavior puzzled Mr. Moses, for he continued, "as to hourly schedules, why should motorized lemmings instinctively crawl in huge armies to cast themselves into the sea just at high noon, instead of staggering their arrivals? Why can't they listen to radio and other mechanical instruction? Why must a driver behave like an ant, and if he must, why isn't he an obedient ant?"[5]

The administrative, or management, sciences differ in their approach to planning, depending on the scope and degree of control exercised by the management. More centralized management leans to a "hard" style, with decentralized or democratic management styles featuring a "soft" approach. The mnemonic public administration acronym POSDCORB (plan, organize, staff, direct, coordinate, report, budget) is appropriate to the hard style, while its counterpart DECOCOMO (de-

---

[5] Remarks by Robert Moses on the proposed Long Island Sound Crossing, Triborough Bridge Authority, 1965.

cide, communicate, coordinate, motivate) is more representative of the soft. The soft style in administrative planning
does not ask why man is not an obedient ant, it assumes that
strict obedience is not feasible, and that manipulation of the
actor's motives will be necessary to achieve the desired performance. But both POSDCORB and DECOCOMO are "top-
down" procedures, as the words "direct" and "decide" reveal.
The ends, in either case, are given.

The Community Action Committees set up by the Office of
Economic Opportunity in its "Poverty Program" wish to have
a hand in setting these ends. They wish to exploit the "maximum feasible participation" phrase in the enabling legislation
to take a major part in the direction of the program. The
Bureau of the Budget, guardian of administrative efficiency
and witting or unwitting ally of the established big-city political machinery, has moved to curb the power of the clients
in policy-making. Administrative efficiency and mass democracy have often been in conflict; Veblen's Engineers could not
leave the conduct of the economy to so anarchic a mechanism
as the Price System. Elites and the electorate are constantly
in tension, both about the proper ends of the society and the
appropriate forms of participation in decision-making.

SOCIAL PLANNING AND RADICAL REFORM

Proponents of social planning in the United States are impeded from developing a coherent plan of action by the ideological strictures of the society in which they operate. Our
pragmatic, conservative, democratic ideology holds that *one,*
the structure of power cannot be changed from below, and
two, behavior and taste cannot be changed from above. Under
the first, not only are revolutionary *means* excluded, but radical ends are ruled out as well. By the canons of presupposition
two, democracies must resist the imposition of preferences
upon the weak by the strong. Despite welfare economists' demonstration that aggregation of individual values into a community value function is greatly facilitated by acceptance of
the preference of authority as the preference of the group
(the dictatorship case) this convenience is denied social
planners.

Given these limitations, social planning is split, with its left
wing rejecting presupposition *one* and accepting *two;* an administrative right accepting *one* but altering *two;* and a political right accepting both *one* and *two* and insisting on confining

operations within the alternatives of the status quo. Only the last mentioned has no crisis of legitimation. Radical social planners bent on changing the distribution of power and available actions to maximize individual choice and administrative social planners accepting the power distribution and attempting to secure behavior of the wards to conform to the tastes of their guardians are both pushing for social change. The left wishes substantial redistribution so that its clients will be allowed to transform themselves (along lines of their choosing) while the administrative right wants the clients to transform themselves so that the whole game will work more smoothly, even if the chief beneficiaries of smoother functioning prove to be the more powerful. Examples of these ideal types are not hard to find in city planning.

The task of the radical social planners is difficult. Society is less tolerant of those who would tamper with the goals than of those who would alter the means, and its organized apparatus is especially uneasy at efforts to incorporate machinery for regularly changing the goals, through radical indulgence of free choice, even when the rhetoric of the social planners uses venerated slogans. The experience of Mobilization For Youth in New York is evidence that revolutionary programs guided by social planners are not likely to be treated by the custodians of civil order with the degree of indulgence sometimes accorded illegal sit-ins. Mobilization For Youth, moreover, was challenging the local governmental administration more directly than it was threatening some vague "power structure." This was true even when it supported tenant movements, for the slum landlords "power" is vested in their relations with local political figures rather than in connections with financial and economic powers.

In comments at the workshop on "Centrally Planned Change" two years ago, John R. Seeley expressed the fear that the federal involvement in traditional local social planning would create a more formidable bureaucratic administrative barrier to the "grass roots" choice school of social planning. Observing that "a number of the executive departments of the federal government have moved into a species of planning and plan-forcing on a scale so massive as to constitute almost a new force in American life, and, incidentally, to render peripheral and probably powerless the previous incumbents of "the social planning activity," he went on to cite Karl Mannheim as labelling "correctly the major danger on which would turn the fate of planning as between the dictatorial and democratic varieties. The former fate would be sealed if planning fell into the hands of the bureaucracies."[6] But the dilemma for social planning leadership is clearly not "bureaucracy or grass roots," but "what bureaucracy?" In a society in which the "establishment" has vast bureaucratic, rationalizing, technically competent apparatus at its disposal, can a more tolerant, permissive, choice-maximizing movement succeed in redistributing power? And if the radical social planners are allowed to keep presupposition *two* on condition that they give up their opposition to *one,* that is, that they retain democratic choice at the price of foregoing revolutionary redistribution, will they not become the leaders of the lost, the counselors of despair?

This tension in the leadership condition of the radical social planners in the American ghetto slums has been bared by the anarchic outbreaks of Harlem last summer and Los Angeles this year. The democratic social planner resists being made a recruitment officer for the Establishment. He wants the client to be taken on his own terms, to be taken seriously as an arbiter of his own values. He may even attempt to protect indigenous forms and life styles when they are illegal. But he has no revolutionary role or power. In a direct confrontation of authority and the frustrated aspirations of his clients, he has no function, for he cannot relinquish or curb his doctrine of self-determination—that would mean rejection of position *two* —and he cannot speedup the transfer of power.

SOCIAL PLANNING, SOCIAL SCIENCE, AND SOCIETAL GOALS

At best, our contemporary social planning can achieve some coordination of welfare agency efforts, some limited participation by community groups in welfare planning, and a readiness to be measured against such goals as the discerning savants of our society can muster. Positive social science, which is steadfastly descriptive, and determined to be value-free, can play an important diagnostic role, but without the informing graces of ideology it is remarkably mute on prescription. Social scientists tell us of the plight of the bottom fifth of our society, of the obstacles to social mobility, of the frustrating flight of meaningful work, of intergenerational

[6] John R. Seeley, "Central Planning: Prologue to a Critique," *Centrally Planned Change: Prospects and Concepts,* ed. Robert Morris (New York: National Association of Social Workers, 1964), p. 58.

transmission of dependency, and even of the private grasp of public decision, but they leave program to the reformers and ideologues. Ideologically sustained societal planning, as the socialist experiments show, virtually dispenses with social science.[7]

The ideological socialists are steadfast in their commitment to equity principles, though in practice efficiency considerations of economic development may be allowed to supersede these as "temporary" expedients. The utilitarian postulates of the economic-efficiency administrative analysts are regarded by social critics as convenient oversimplifications. As a nation we have slipped into a program of broad social reform which involves the organization of our economy, of the space organization of our cities, and even of interpersonal relations, without benefit of societal planning. At the same time our social scientists have compiled some of the best social statistics in the world, and have supported these with unexcelled social analysis and a great deal of partial social theory. At the local community level we are on the verge of comprehensive social accounts.[8]

We are now in an increasingly good position to measure the impact of public programs on their various clients, to establish the benefits and costs of programs, and to measure, in limited terms, the efficiency of public actions, thanks to a host of social studies, social measurements, and social accounts. Our social intelligence system is potentially powerful. Some, like Seeley, fear that this power will be manipulated by the planner-bureaucrats. Others feel, somewhat wryly, that the bureaucrats will keep this knowledge from being mobilized for social action. The "broad citizen involvement and participation" sought in community social planning is frustrated by the lack of basic social democracy. Without this involvement, the political legitimacy of social planning is open to challenge, for we have no consensus on a national social program to guide the community effort.

In any event, the social democracy which is a precondition to collective social planning in a political democracy depends on social gains which will be engineered, for the most part,

[7] A well-documented case for this conclusion appears in a yet-unpublished paper on Soviet Social Science prepared by Peter R. Senn for the Annual Meeting of the American Association for the Advancement of Science at Berkeley, December, 1965.

[8] See Harvey Perloff, "New Directions in Social Planning," *Journal of the American Institute of Planners*, XXXI (November, 1965), 297–303.

from Washington. The achievement of economic democracy, the securing of equality in civil rights, the abolition of gross regional differences in education, and other major social gains will be forged by federal power, or not at all. But the societal plan which will set the targets against which all the ad hoc programs will be measured does not exist.

If such national social planning were to be instituted in the USA, substantial reorganization and improvement of our social data might be required. It is obvious, for example, that the relation of economic planning to social planning requires a national manpower policy, and that the latter, in turn, requires a national manpower budget with great regional and local detail. The material for such a budget is abundantly available, but the policy—which would require the setting of targets on full employment, local and regional labor force mobility, and similar matters—is not available to organize the data.

Social science can inform policy directly, as well as contribute to social accounting. The findings of social scientists have influenced the highest councils in the land, as the wholesale citation of Myrdal's *American Dilemma* by the Supreme Court in its civil rights decisions showed, and the revival of brain-trusting style in the executive branch is now graced by richer social science material than was available to the New Deal. At times it seems we have fallen back on "objective" social science findings because our political ideology offers so few positive guides to social reconstruction. Thus a program which might be openly embraced in other countries out of commitment to an ideology might be introduced in the USA under the seemingly nonarbitrary cloak of social "science." There is a danger in this process, for it could lead to the tyrannical "scientism" predicted by intellectual opponents of planning.

More likely, however, it would lead to much ad hoc social planning. For the social scientists cannot supplant the goal-making role of ideology, or relieve the political decision makers of their responsibility for setting the public preference scale and the targets to be embodied in a societal plan. The protection of the citizen against administrative abuses, the biases of planners, the condescension of caretakers, and all arbitrariness in social planning depends upon the open articulation of coherent national social goals, and the public acceptance of social planning targets. The Poverty Program, Appalachia Bill, aid to education, and other "Great Society"

Acts need a national social accounting against which to be measured. Even more, they need a national social plan which articulates policy, and target dates, for achieving minimum levels of income and consumption, direction and amount of redistribution of population, reduction of intergenerational dependency, equalization of education, and a host of other social goals.

Chapter 7

AESTHETICS

During the past few years there has been a determined drive to define in a precise fashion aesthetic values at a city-wide level and to develop a calculus for measuring them. The exact notation of musical sounds is an ancient skill and its relation to mathematics clearly recognized. Somewhat allied to this, psychologists are now at work on perception quantifiers for aesthetic visual experience and are building note-taking devices so that both (a) movement into and within a city as well as (b) the total aesthetic impact involved in living there may be fixed for evaluation and replication. The leader in this has been Kevin Lynch of the Massachusetts Institute of Technology—backed by Gyorgy Kepes, who in basic research into the *Education of Vision* (New York: George Braziller, 1965) has carried the study of total aesthetic perception still further. Lynch with his concentration on the urban scene has illumined the city and its aesthetic impact with legibility, identity and imageability as key components. His five anchor points for the urban pattern of paths, edges, districts, nodes and landmarks, as well as their interrelations and shifts, have been widely studied and applied. He now sees the movement system, array of centers and subcenters, and the pattern of open spaces as leverage points to manipulate whole metropolitan areas for increasingly rewarding sensual returns as well as dollar-measured cost/benefit analysis in narrow economic *cum* efficiency terms. Backed by the President, Karel Yasko, a Yale-trained architect, in the U. S. General Services Administration is dedicated to the use of federal buildings as an important factor in sophisticating the dullish American cityscape; while Ada Louise Huxtable, heavily design-oriented, is a much-quoted New York *Times* special correspondent and critic of urban planning and architecture. President Johnson himself hammers the beauty theme constantly, enthusiastically and shrewdly, seconded by Mrs. Johnson. Urban design is clearly in.

Despite all this excitement about the precise quality of the urban scene growing out of a belated, if widespread, recognition of its miserable aesthetic character, it must be recorded (a) that there are no clear scientifically established criteria for *eternal beauty*, and (b) no studies of any significance on the relationship of aesthetics to individual well-being or the good life. We are here still in the realm of intuitive art; sadly and quite possibly, moreover, the democratic process of low-level consensus cannot produce a city-building art. On the other hand neither Stalin's skyscrapers nor Hitler's blockhouse constructs argue for dictatorial aesthetic fiat. Perhaps, democracy can eventually free its practitioners of the humane art of microscale design and allow them to connive with nature on the large scale. Boris Pushkarev's article on the design of the road in Christopher Tunnard's *Man Made America* (New Haven: Yale University Press, 1964) indicates the possibility. All this (if it does not cost too much) including the retention of the graceful—even interesting—old, may well spell a "rewarding" (whatever that may mean) townscape to nurture the dulled citizens of the urban jungle and desert. The British and French have officially tried long and hard in the artistic tradition to define "good design" for the urban scene; perhaps to their humanism can be added some measure of reliable quantification that can define excellence or decadence and also serve as the firm basis for a positive forming of the human-made environment—valid at least for one culture and possibly for all cultures. It may be that one man's rewarding cityscape may very well be another's aesthetic junk heap—especially if the move is from Occident to Orient.

The American Institute of Architects are striving to lift their sights (and sites) beyond the one building to a macrolevel using tried and true *design* criteria and even rushing up into the macrolevel vacuum of the metro-area.[1] Harvard's program in urban design defines its task as follows: "Urban design is that part of city planning concerned with perceiving and contributing order, with the developing of a master form and a master program. It is the most creative phase in which inspiration and artistic capacity play an essential role. This process must be based on rationality as a system of procedure, which does not exclude inspiration which acts as an acceleration on the path to the desired goal. Inspiration is a special moment in a rational process. The two are inseparable."

In the first selection in this chapter, one of America's fine practitioners of the graceful city, Edmund Bacon from Philadelphia, sums up the Townscape Panel Report for President Johnson's Natural Beauty Conference of May 1965—with Bacon's experienced hand showing through the common effort. Wilhelm von Moltke has had a splendid opportunity in molding Ciudad Guayana, the new town building in Venezuela for a future population of 700,000. Thus we have the good old city thoughts and a new city plan for human townscape juxtaposed. But there is obviously still much to be learned before man can build large scale beauty and the public by perception enhance as well as recognize the product. The object aesthetically is felt to be related to the level of education of the beholder which poses a nice philosophical problem not to be explored here. As the third article, S. B. Zisman shrewdly points out that a big factor in design is "not so much as what is, as what ain't"—namely space—increasingly a most scarce, expensive and precious public and private commodity within the urbanized area.

[1] See Paul D. Spreiregen, *Urban Design: The Architecture of Towns and Cities,* New York: McGraw-Hill Book Company.

The Townscape: A Report to the President
EDMUND N. BACON*

While stressing positive steps that should be taken to implement the objectives of a national policy for natural beauty, as outlined by President Johnson in his special message, the Townscape Panel most strongly emphasizes these facts:

Efforts made to date to beautify the American city have been totally inadequate. Government, municipal, State, and Federal, is responsible for much of the disorder and clutter of our cities, and must assume the leading role in a concerted attack on these problems.

Likewise, private industry has been a major offender in fouling the American environment. Private industry must, therefore, play a much larger and more positive role in the development of beauty in cities. This should be done not only through more careful attention to industry's own environs and waste disposal, but also through private encouragement of a higher order of beauty, sponsored and financed by private business.

As a vital first step, the panel recommends immediate passage of the Housing and Community Development Act of 1965, containing provisions for urban beautification and expansion of the existing open space land program. This badly needed legislation should carry with it full funding as recommended by the administration. Such amounts are adequate only to gain a foothold on the massive problems of developing more and better city parks and beautifying urban areas. A

* Executive Director of the City Planning Commission of Philadelphia, since 1949. Holder of a Cornell Bachelor of Architecture degree, he came to Philadelphia in 1940 after planning and architectural experience in Shanghai, and Flint, Michigan. He has been prominent in various projects of national importance: Franklin Delano Roosevelt Memorial Competition; Task Force on the Potomac River Basin Plan for Secretary Udall, as well as President Johnson's Citizens' Advisory Committee on Recreation and Natural Beauty. He is a Visiting Lecturer at the University of Pennsylvania, a Trustee of the American Academy in Rome; on the Advisory Council of the School of Architecture, Princeton; and Executive Director of *Urban America*. Holder of a number of awards, he has published under a Rockefeller Foundation grant the *Design of Cities*.

much broader federal effort should be made as soon as possible.

The panel also wishes to put special stress upon the new provisions of the proposed 1965 legislation pertaining both to urban beautification and the development of neighborhood centers, as these provisions can be applied to impoverished areas of cities. These programs, limited as they are in funds and scope, should be particularly directed to the poorest areas of cities, to insure that all American families share in the effort to beautify our townscapes.

There must be a much greater, more intensive push toward better education for beauty in the cities on at least two levels:

(1) We must develop in the youth of the nation a greater awareness of and sensitivity to all aspects of the environment. They must be made aware of what comprises a stimulating environment and what every citizen can do to insure its development and maintenance. Perhaps most important, we must involve young people in the actual development of a stimulating environment. Programs to accomplish these objectives should be established and administered locally, but with aid from both private industry and the federal government.

(2) There must also be a nationwide program of education for our urban leadership, public and private. Many of the conditions which are blighting our cities today are the result of ignorance, apathy and neglect. These are forces which can be dispelled, and education can be our major weapon in this task. Such a program should be initiated immediately, with the help of federal, state, and local funds as well as contributions from foundations and private industries. It should be aimed not only at mayors, city councilmen, county supervisors, boards of education, zoning and building commissions and planning boards, but also at heads of private industry such as insurance companies and other large industries which bring to bear powerful influences on the urban environment. All must be made to see most clearly their responsibilities, as leaders, in the development of a more stimulating environment.

The technological capacity of American industry must be harnessed with our design knowledge if we are ever to create a higher order of urban environmental design. To achieve this objective, the panel recommends that the professional societies concerned create, with federal aid, a National Urban Design Center. Such a center would co-ordinate the work of architects, planners, landscape architects, industrial and interior designers, manufacturers and research corporations—with all who contribute to total townscape design. The center would also co-ordinate the needs of all agencies of federal, state, and local government who post signs, specify materials and fixtures, determine spaces and relationships and uses. The federal government should assist, through grants and other types of aid in the establishment of a National Design Center and support its activities and educational program in the same manner as it assists the Highway Research Board.

Every city should develop a comprehensive design plan embracing elements of the environment, as part of its comprehensive planning program. The federal government should require that such design planning be developed in comprehensive planning before federal development funds are released to a city or urban county. Every American community must have an organizational framework for performing the functions of sound environmental design. Where such a framework does not now exist, it should be created as soon as possible. In some cases, it might be feasible to establish a special agency to oversee all elements of design in city development. In every case, the function of urban design must be performed in an effective and comprehensive fashion.

Moreover, comprehensive design planning must be an integral part of the decision making function of local or regional government. Design should not be allowed to become a meaningless exercise, existing only in paper form to clutter up the municipal library shelves. It must be a living, continuing, dynamic function of city government, made meaningful in the everyday lives of all the city's people.

There must be a much broader effort made throughout the nation to preserve historical structures and areas. A higher degree of public awareness of what is worth keeping, particularly in terms of local values, must be instilled and developed if preservation is to become a source of local pride. The current inadequate program of education for more effective historic preservation must be broadened and intensified.

Specific action proposals for historic preservation include:

1. An inventory, throughout the nation, of major landmarks, taking into account a wide range of historic, architectural, and unique community values. The National Park Service program for classifying and identifying historic buildings is inadequate to do this broader task.

2. A program of certification of historic and landmark structures or areas, with accompanying legal protection.

3. The creation of historic districts, wherever appropriate, including the whole of some historic towns.

4. A special program of compensation to private owners for losses suffered or for damages accruing from delay or deprivation in legal protection cases.

5. Special FHA mortgage insurance for improving landmark structures.

6. Expanded public programs of ownership of historic structures and areas.

7. Machinery should be developed for a co-ordinated private-public program of preservation. The federal government should take the lead in this endeavor.

8. The panel underscores the President's call for more funds for the work of the federally chartered National Trust for Historic Preservation.

The panel recommends a thoroughgoing overhaul of federal, state, and local tax policies to encourage the implementation of natural beauty policies. Specific areas for further study would include possible revision of tax policies to encourage greater private investment in the preservation of approved historic and landmark structures and areas, through revision of income, inheritance, property, and admission taxes. Local taxing bodies should also review policies which penalize property owners who maintain their properties in a decent fashion.

Any survey of taxation policies should consider a broad range of possible tax actions which would encourage business and private citizens to maintain properties in orderly and aesthetic fashion.

The planting of shade trees must become a paramount objective of all those who would improve the appearance of cities. A prompt start should be made to improve and coordinate the technical process of large-scale mass moving of big trees and the reduction of the costs of such operation.

American cities should profit from the British example and make better use of forest lands or large estates in or near cities as a source of trees for replanting in small neighborhood parks as well as along streets and boulevards.

Tree planting programs should proceed within the broad context of the previously recommended urban design plan, as part of the comprehensive planning process.

The urban highway is often cited as the worst defiler of townscape, and the principal reason why it seems so difficult to develop and maintain any semblance of order and beauty in cities.

Yet the panel believes the highway can contribute measurably to a higher order of beauty in metropolitan areas, if it is carefully planned, designed, and controlled.

Most important, highways must be planned within the total urban design context of the metropolitan area, rather than as something apart, designed strictly for moving numbers of people, in cars, from here to there. In this context, highways can be an important element for unifying the diverse components of vast metropolises, and can serve the city's people in beauty as well as efficiency.

The Visual Development of Ciudad Guayana
WILHELM VON MOLTKE*

INTRODUCTION

The Guayana region is one of the richest natural resources areas in the world not yet fully developed. It has:

—One of the world's finest concentrations of high grade iron ores.

—The greatest potential supply of hydroelectric power of any single river system in the Western Hemisphere.

—Direct deep water access to the Atlantic Ocean.

—Direct connection by oil pipeline to the oil and gas fields of Eastern Venezuela.

—An operating steel mill with an output-capacity of 750,000 ingot tons, already selling its products to eight foreign countries.

* Professor of Urban Design and Director of the Urban Design Program, Graduate School of Design, Harvard University. He received his architectural degree from the Technische Hochschule, Berlin, and an M.A. in architecture from Harvard. He has been associated with architectural offices in England and Stockholm, Sweden; as well as with Alvar Aalto; Hugh Stubbins; Howe, Stonorov and Kahn; Marcel Breuer; Skidmore, Owings and Merrill; and Eero Saarinen and Associates. Among the projects on which he has worked are the campus plans for Brandeis University and the University of Michigan. He took First Prize at the Museum of Modern Art, N. Y. in 1941 and Second Prize in the Carson-Pirie and Scott Centennial International Competition for Design of Center City, Chicago, in 1954. This article originally appeared in *Connection*, June 1965 issue, and is reprinted with permission.

—Deposits of other minerals, including manganese, nickel, chrome, industrial diamonds, gold—the full extent of which is still under investigation.

—Forestry and fishing potentials still in their initial phase of development.

—A young and vigorous population.

—A dramatic setting for a new city.

At the confluence of the Orinoco and Caroni rivers a new city—Santo Tome de Guayana—is rising to exploit these resources. It is already one of the most rapidly growing urban zones in the country, having increased from 4,000 in 1950 to over 50,000 inhabitants in 1962. Its development offers a unique opportunity to integrate regional planning and industrial development with an urban form appropriate to contemporary needs and incorporating the best principles of civic design. Its population has been projected to 400,000 by 1975, increasing to over 600,000 in the 1980's.

The rationale for this development lies in Venezuela's need to sustain a booming growth. Due largely to the exploration, production, and export of petroleum, the Venezuelan economy has grown at the phenomenal rate of 7% per year over a twenty-five year period—a virtually unequalled long-sustained high growth rate. At the same time, Venezuela's population growth has risen to 3.1%—one of the world's highest. Venezuela's present population of some 8,000,000 will roughly double in the next twenty years. To continue its past rate of economic increase Venezuela must quadruple its output of goods and services in the next two decades.

The key to achieving this goal is Venezuela's industrial production, which must expand at the rate of at least 12% per year. Such growth can only be achieved by substantial diversification of Venezuelan manufacturing industry. Although the country's industrial base is one of the largest and most dynamic in Latin America, it is now characterized by final assembly based on substantial imports of basic and intermediate products. Such industries have increased employment and raised the standard of living, but have also accentuated the import demand for components and intermediate products without contributing to export earning of foreign exchange.

For Venezuela to move forward there must be an increase in industrial production of metals, petro- and electrochemicals, and heavy and light machinery to supply the burgeoning Venezuelan industrial economy with basic and intermediate products. It is this urgency for industrial diversification and substantial new imports that has led to a priority role for the Guayana Region Economic Development in the National Plan recently promulgated by CORDIPLAN, the central planning and coordinating agency of the Venezuelan government.[1]

THE SETTING

In order to meet national and regional goals for industrial production, Ciudad Guayana, the heavy-industrial focus of the Guayana Region, will need more than half a million people within the next ten to fifteen years.

The industrial activities and the population it needs will best be served by a well-designed city, for economic and for social reasons. A city offers the opportunity to share services and facilities, achieving economies of scale. A well-designed city offers the social benefits of scale; the stimulation of the highly-skilled technicians, administrators, and professional people needed to achieve the economic goals. And a well-designed city may go a long way in overcoming the sense of isolation, a major deterrent for the many skills needed for this enterprise.

The city is located where the Caroni, with its tremendous hydroelectric potential, joins the Orinoco, whose deepwater channel gives access to world markets. Here too are the spectacular rapids and falls of the Caroni—symbols of power and source of pleasure—making this a unique place for Ciudad Guayana.

The climate is hot, but almost constant breezes from the east-northeast bring refreshment. These breezes, which blow from this direction seventy per cent of the time, are strongest around 4 p.m.—the hottest time of the day—and the relative humidity is also lowest at this hour. These factors make the climate quite agreeable. The vegetation is sparse except in the many valleys and along the shores of the rivers. The levels of the rivers fluctuate considerably between the dry and the rainy seasons. The level of the Orinoco varies by as much as 14

[1] The Corporacion Venezolana de Guayana is a special public authority ("Instituto Autonomo") established by the Venezuelan Government in December, 1960, with broad powers and responsibilities to develop the Guayana region and all its resources. To assist in specialized aspects of its work, the Joint Center for Urban Studies of the Massachusetts Institute of Technology and Harvard University has been acting as consultant to the Corporacion since 1961, employing Professor von Moltke as Director of Urban Design.

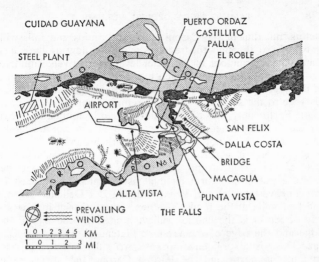

CUIDAD GUAYANA

PUERTO ORDAZ
CASTILLITO
PALUA
EL ROBLE

STEEL PLANT

AIRPORT

SAN FELIX
DALLA COSTA
BRIDGE
MACAGUA
PUNTA VISTA

ALTA VISTA
THE FALLS

PREVAILING WINDS

1 0 1 2 3 4 5 KM
1 0 1 2 3 MI

THE LINKAGE OF OLD AND NEW NODES

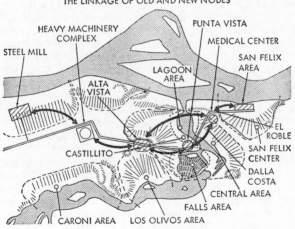

HEAVY MACHINERY COMPLEX

STEEL MILL

PUNTA VISTA

MEDICAL CENTER

SAN FELIX AREA

ALTA VISTA

LAGOON AREA

EL ROBLE

SAN FELIX CENTER

CASTILLITO

DALLA COSTA

CENTRAL AREA

FALLS AREA

CARONI AREA   LOS OLIVOS AREA

CIVIC CENTER
PUNTA VISTA   MEDICAL CENTER

HEAVY   COMMERCIAL   SAN
MACHINERY   CENTER   FELIX
STEEL MILL   CARONI   CENTER

FIGURE 1

meters, but that of the Caroni above the rapids and falls will be stabilized through the regulation of the flow at the Guri Dam. The fluctuations of the water level alternatively inundate and lay bare large areas, which can only be used during part of the year. Therefore, only in areas with steep banks will the distance to the shores of the river remain approximately constant. Fortunately, most of the intermittently inundated areas are sandy or wooded, and therefore they are not unsightly when bare and do not represent a health hazard.

The terrain is generally flat, about 140 meters above the level of the Orinoco, and slopes gently to the shores of the rivers. These slopes form distinct visual units. In the east is the concave bowl of San Felix, with the Las Delicias Lagoon and San Felix at the focus. The next visual district in a westerly direction is the central valley, limited by the San Felix ridge and the edge of the Western Plateau above Puerto Ordaz. This visual unit encompasses two subareas, the lagoon area to the north and the Parque Caroni, the area of the rapids and falls, to the south. The two are linked by the Punta Vista peninsula, which lies at the focus of the central valley and from which springs the first bridge across the Caroni.

To the west is a large plateau, bordered by the districts of the Orinoco to the north and those of the upper Caroni to the south. It includes the promontory, called Alta Vista, which projects east into the central valley beyond the crescent-shaped cliff west of Puerto Ordazm at the apex of a convex mass. Alta Vista, Punta Vista, and the Lagoon of Las Delicias are very important points in our development strategy.

Man-made restraints are also influencing the urban design of the new city. The vast new steel plant of the Venezuelan government, located 17 kilometers from the nearest settlement, the ore-loading facilities at Puerto Ordaz and Palua, the Macagua hydroelectric dam, the San Felix port, the bridge across the Caroni, the 100-year-old commercial and political center of San Felix, 29 kilometers to the east of the steel mill, the rapid influx of immigrants from all parts of the country—all of these magnify the complexity of the planning task.

OVERALL DEVELOPMENT STRATEGY

In our search for an overall form for the city a number of alternatives were examined. The plan for three separate communities—San Felix, Puerto Ordaz, and a new town south of the steel mill on the upper Caroni—was discarded because it would result in one town and two camps (Puerto Ordaz and the new settlement) with the social problems and the continued administrative burden resulting from this type of development. This alternative would also increase the need for initial investment since all services and community facilities would have to be started afresh for the new settlement before the existing ones in the area had been used to capacity. Moreover, such a strategy would have retarded the creation of an urban mass sufficient to assist in attracting the special skills needed to achieve the economic goals of the city.

Another alternative was a design based on the concept of development along the shores of the rivers, with the major focus on Punta Vista, on which would be located the city center. This would have left large areas between developed sections unused, resulting in a very dispersed city, difficult if not impossible to develop and control.

These and other alternatives, which are more fully discussed elsewhere, were rejected in favor of a linear city, extending from the steel mill to San Felix, and which will be developed from these extremities towards the center. This overall strategy is based on the following two premises:

1) The *raison d'être* of this city is the heavy industrial complex, therefore its location is a basic determinant of the overall form. Its many linkages with the steel mill make it mandatory that this complex be developed adjacent to the mill. This location has other advantages for industry. Here eight kilometers of shoreline close to the deepwater channel of the Orinoco offer the opportunity to construct special-purpose ports for industry. Here also the heavy freight traffic generated by this industry can reach domestic markets to the west and north without passing through the city. Furthermore, the prevailing winds will carry noxious air away from the city. Finally, in this location there is an adequate supply of flat terrain for future expansion.

2) Contiguous growth from east to west will have substantial political, social, economic, and visual benefits for residential development. An abandonment of the traditional political center of San Felix would be likely to result in political opposition. Contiguous development can overcome a sense of isolation in the different parts of the city by creating early a larger single urban mass, and it

will facilitate the use of the existing services and community facilities, rather than building complete new systems, reducing their costs—especially in the early stages when demands for public capital are very great.

A linear city is the only form that will tie together the existing elements, which are scattered over a distance of 30 kilometers. Almost all of the important existing centers of activity can be connected by a central spine which extends from the steel mill to the new San Felix port. This will help in overcoming one of the site's major physical problems, the extreme dispersion of existing facilities. Even so, it will be some time before the scale of development will be in proportion to this oversize frame. This can occur when the population reaches 250,000 people, provided the overall development strategy is implemented.

The existing elements connected to the central spine include the steel mill, the Matanzas Industrial Park, the Puerto Ordaz Airport, Parque Caroni and the Caroni Falls, Dalla Costa, El Roble, San Felix, and the San Felix port. The only important node not included is the commercial center of Puerto Ordaz, which, at a distance of two kilometers from the spine, will remain an important center for the community of Puerto Ordaz. For geographic reasons it was impossible to attach this center to the spine. This circumstance will strengthen the development of Alta Vista, the site selected for the city center, since all major traffic will pass through Alta Vista, bypassing the Puerto Ordaz center, presently the most vital commercial node west of the Caroni.

The price we have to pay for this strategy is a sizeable burden in cost for transportation facilities and in time for the journey to work, especially in the early stages of development. Moreover, these facilities will not be efficiently used since the traffic flow is tidal as a result of the fact that the dominant center of employment is at one and the residential areas at the other end of the system. It has been estimated that, when the city reaches a population of 250,000, approximately eighteen per cent of the disposable income of its residents will be spent on transportation, as compared with twelve to fifteen per cent in the United States. However, this factor will become more favorable as residential development grows westward and industry grows eastward, reducing commuting distances and proportionately, the cost of transportation.

OVERALL DESIGN STRUCTURE

The design structure of the city must have clarity, establish order, and organize activities. It must be congruent with the terrain, the natural conditions, the forces acting upon it, and the functional organization of activities. It must facilitate orderly development and accommodate change over time. It must offer interesting visual experiences. Above all, it must create order, a sense of unity, and a memorable image, and it must have a sense of beauty which will foster pride in and loyalty to the city.

The scattered character of the existing settlements results in a lack of visual continuity. But one of our goals is to create order, a sense of unity, and a memorable image, and for this visual continuity is a prerequisite.

As mentioned earlier, the area falls into three major visual units, those of San Felix, the central valley, and the western plateau. There are two major visual barriers: the San Felix Ridge and a slight elevation in the western plateau, west of the airport. And there are three major natural foci:

1) the lagoon of Las Delicias and the core of San Felix, at the focus of the concave San Felix bowl,

2) the peninsula of Punta Vista, between the Caroni lagoon and the Caroni falls at the focus of the central valley, and

3) Alta Vista, a promontory of the western plateau projecting into the central valley at the apex of a convex mass, which dominates the valley and is the natural site for a visual link between the western plateau and the central valley.

In order to create a sense of unity, it is proposed to develop along "Avenida Guayana" the central spine, which connects almost all major existing elements, a series of nodes which will be intervisible and will thus further continuity of activities along it.

On the western visual barrier is to be developed the *heavy machinery complex*, which will be visible from both the steel mill and the Alta Vista Center. The *Alta Vista Center*, in turn, will establish intervisibility between the western plateau and the central valley. Alta Vista is the midway point between the steel mill and San Felix. This location was tested in a potential model, which indicated a location close to Alta Vista as the most accessible in the future city, and thus the most appropriate site for the Centro. This site has ample land for easy development, it has adjacent areas highly suited for residential development to strengthen it, and it dominates the central valley; it is a symbolic focus of the urban area.

Furthermore, this site benefits even in the present disorganized condition of the city structure from the fact that all traffic from existing residential areas to central Venezuela and to the western industrial areas passes through it. Moreover, it is proposed to strengthen it through the early development of residential areas in its vicinity and to provide adjacent areas with a street system which converges on the Centro.

The next node to the east is at *Punta Vista*. This important focus, between the confluence of the two rivers and the Caroni falls and site of the first bridge across the Caroni, is appropriate for the development of the cultural center, the seat for research and higher education, a center for city-wide recreation and higher education, and for residences of high quality. This is the appropriate place for activities which symbolize the highest aspirations of the city. It is proposed to develop here for the various functions clusters of buildings in a park-like setting, creating a unique environment at this unique site.

Going eastward, we come to the future location of the Medical Center on the *San Felix Ridge,* which will include a 280-bed general hospital, now being developed. This node will establish visual continuity between the central valley and the San Felix bowl.

Finally, we reach the *lagoon of Las Delicias,* adjacent to San Felix, around which will be grouped clusters of apartment buildings, sports areas, a club, and a shopping center, and which will lead to the San Felix waterfront with its Paseo, marina, and mercado libre.

This series of nodes along the urban spine will establish visual continuity from the steel mill in the west to San Felix in the east; it will also provide continuity of experiences and activities. This development strategy has as its goal to use the Avenida Guayana as a catalyst for public and private investments through the creation of a strong image and through cross-fertilization of activities along the main transportation route in the early stages of the city's development. This will promote the sense of unity which is so essential in creating the image of the city, and which will help to overcome the sense of isolation.

It is quite apparent that in the long run the central spine

will be unable to accommodate all east-west traffic. It is there-fore proposed to construct bypasses to the north and south, once concentration of traffic becomes congested. These by-passes, which will have the character of expressways, will telescope the time-distance for the journey to work. The Avenida Guayana will then only serve the activities which are developed along it.

VISUAL DEVELOPMENT STRATEGY

The visual development strategy must strengthen the design structure, activities, and constructive forces. It is based on a number of visual goals. It would be idle to try to establish a priority amongst these goals, since the policies, which grow out of the strategy, will incorporate most of them.

The following are the most important goals of the visual development strategy:

1) To develop a visual structure which will accommodate change and yet maintain visual consistency and a sense of order in the long run.

2) To develop as rapidly as possible the elements which will strengthen the image of the city.

3) To protect and enhance the natural assets of the site.

4) To create the physical conditions which will promote the participation of private enterprise in the building of the city, particularly in the fields of industry, housing, recreation, commerce, and communication.

5) To develop housing for the rapidly increasing popu-lation in a manner that will strengthen the city's image and accommodate future change.

In developing a strategy for achieving these goals we must carefully allocate our limited resources in funds and man-power for the greatest benefit and we must strive to use pri-vate initiative to the greatest extent possible.

The most important element which will strengthen the image of the city is Avenida Guayana. This central spine will create a sense of unity by connecting nearly all of the city's major activity centers. It will open up sites for private and public development and will establish the order which is presently lacking in dispersed developments. Therefore, this spine should be developed as rapidly as possible. All of its elements must be used to strengthen it: the road-bed, the landscaping—particularly the planting of trees, the water-plays, and the street-lighting must be developed as soon as possible. At the same time, earth-moving, advertising, and the use of special devices for promotion must be used to strengthen it. These devices, which should be illuminated at night, might include the development of temporary sheds for exhibition purposes—on Alta Vista to show the industrial products of the areas, and on Punta Vista to house a constantly-changing city-planning exhibition, signs indicating the different important locations and their purposes, and a coordinated and imaginative use of advertising.

The site's most important asset is the rapids and falls of the Caroni. Therefore, the Parque Caroni must also be developed as rapidly as possible for the enjoyment of the people and to strengthen the image of the city, with particular emphasis on Punta Vista, which is the most accessible part. The lagoon on Punta Vista must be cleaned and a shuttle service between Punta Vista and the island of Pica Pica must be initiated to give easy access to the spectacular Llovisna Falls.

In addition, land for the entire park system must be reserved and steps must be taken to stem soil erosion and to commence reforestation in designated areas. Facilities for water sports must be constructed soon, and the upper Caroni should be reserved for sailing, sculling, and canoeing, except that power boats can be used on transportation routes giving access to the Campamento Caroni, Macagua, and the Mission Church from Los Olivos and Pica Pica. Another area of importance which needs early attention is the area around the lagoon of Las Delicias, which should also be cleaned. The adjacent waterfront of the Orinoco in San Felix should be developed as soon as possible.

In the area of residential development it must be our aim to further the overall development strategy by strengthening the Centro at Alta Vista through the early development of the Los Olivos community with highest densities in the vicinity of Alta Vista, and by furthering continuity through the development of Dalla Costa. However, the building up of the San Felix and Puerto Ordaz areas will continue, to meet the immediate housing needs in areas which already have some of the public services, the community facilities, and the road system needed. In the area of residential development the principle of change-over-time must also be recognized. Certain areas which should contain higher densities may have to be developed initially at lower densities since a large sector of the housing construction in the initial stages will be self-help or low-cost housing, which is most appropriately developed at relatively low densities. In this case care should be taken to make this change possible within the frame of roads and public utilities. Tree planting in residential areas should be commenced as soon as possible.

In the area of transportation, Avenida Guayana will provide in the first stage the most important—in places the only—transportation route for city-wide east-west movement. However, once the activities along it have developed and once the traffic has become congested, bypasses will be constructed which will provide alternative routes, relieve the congestion, and shorten the time-distance for the journey to work. Then Avenida Guayana will serve primarily the activities along it. Avenida Guayana will be used throughout the city's development to order and promote city-wide activities, to create unity and continuity between the different parts of the city, thus strengthening the image of the city. The development strategy for other transportation arteries is similar. Develop first the avenues that connect the community facilities, reserve the right of way for the expressway routes, and develop them once traffic becomes congested on the avenues. An exception should be Northern Artery which will cross the mouth of the Caroni. This expressway should be constructed ahead of the time needed, to relieve traffic congestion on Avenida Guayana, and to provide a truck route without steep grades between the heavy industrial complex and the San Felix port and the region east of the Caroni. The noise of the truck traffic, which will have to use the Avenida Guayana in the early stages and which will have to overcome grades of over six per cent between Punta Vista and Alta Vista, will be a blighting influence on the adjacent residential areas.

Certain elements must be developed ahead of the time needed in order to attract private initiative and to channel its activities for the greatest benefit of the total community. These might include streets, streetlighting, water and sewers, landscaping, in some instances the construction of buildings, and the visual promotion through signs, symbols, and an up-to-date model of the planned development. Needless to say, this type of program must be supplemented by literature containing data and projections, illustrating the investment opportunities, and by the efforts of an adequate promotion staff.

This development strategy will go a long way in creating

order and unity, and to overcome the sense of isolation. This is essential for the achievement of the goals of the city.

Open Spaces in Urban Growth

S. B. ZISMAN*

The great issue in planning is not where to build but where not to build. In the decades ahead there will be a vast amount of building, greater than in the decades just past. Cities will grow, expand, and rebuild. New towns will rise. Wider, longer, and more highways will ribbon the country, pushing remorselessly through neighborhood and nature. The metropolis will continue to explode over the countryside.

In the past, building reflected the feeling of the old frontier, that to escape crowding in one place you simply could move out to build farther out. By and large the concern always has been where to build for space almost always was unlimited—the wide open space of a "continent so huge in its resources of land and forests, so unbounded that though men chopped away at them with only their own interests in mind, the great bulk of things remained unspoiled."[1] We built everywhere, sometimes wisely but more often indiscriminately.

In planning the great emphasis was on land use, reflected in planning maps by colored patches to show where residential, commercial, or industrial development had taken place, or could—with some bits of color for a school or park. Open spaces were left most often as vacant white patches, presumably unused space to be colored in at a later date when

* Planning Consultant, San Antonio, Texas, and Visiting Professor, University of Utah. He has been on the faculties of both M.I.T. and Texas A. & M. University; and was associated with the National Resources Planning Board, the U. S. Departments of Defense and of the Interior, and the H.H.F.A. He wrote *Action for Cities: Guide for Community Planning* (Chicago: Public Administration Service, 1943), was co-author with Charles F. Hoban and Charles F. Hoban, Jr., of *Visualizing the Curriculum* (New York: The Cordon Co., 1937) and *New Campuses for Old: A Case Study of Four Colleges that Moved* (New York Educational Facilities Laboratories, Inc., 1962) as well as various professional articles and reports. This article is reprinted with permission, as adapted, from "Open Spaces in Urban Growth" which appeared in the *Proceedings of The 1964 Institute on Planning and Zoning*, The Southwestern Legal Foundation, Dallas, Texas, copyrighted © 1965 by Matthew Bender & Co., Inc., Albany, New York.
[1] *The Public Happiness* 232 (New York: Athenian Press, 1962).

the urbanized area would exceed sober predictions of early dreams and the maps had to be redone.

The urban scene was viewed as a fairly comprehensible city-scape of a finite shape and size, in which buildings, pavements, and other man-made forms so predominated that the matter of open spaces as an urban concern hardly reached the stage of consciousness.

NEW VIEWS OF THE URBAN SCENE

The urban problem is so dominant in our time and the changes in the urban scene are so pervasive that a world of attention is being given to the issues of urban growth and the views of urban space and form.

The view of extreme dispersion is, "The spatial patterns of American urban settlements are going to be considerably more dispersed, varied and space consuming. . . ."[2] Another view holds:

"The future use of urban space will tend toward a more dense, more nucleated, more clustered pattern than we are now building in our urban areas. Accompanying the tighter development and stronger centers, there will be less private open space (that is, we will have smaller lots) and at every scale of development, substantial continuous open space, commonly enjoyed and publicly or commonly owned."[3]

Or, it is suggested, the future urban scene may need to consider a series of alternative patterns: present trends projected, general dispersion, a concentrated super city, or a constellation of relatively diversified and integrated cities.[4] The future view has been projected further by Greek Planner Doxiadis to "Ecumenopolis—the Universal City," involving huge regional, and even continental, areas in size and urban settlements on the order of hundreds of millions of people.

The question arising throughout these projections is not merely the *quantity* of open space but the *location, deploy-*

[2] Webber, "Order in Diversity," in *Cities and Space* (Baltimore: Johns Hopkins Press for Resources for the Future, Inc., 1963).

[3] Tankel, "The Importance of Open Space in the Urban Pattern," *id.* p. 70.

[4] Catherine Bauer Wurster, "The Form and Structure of the Future Urban Complex," *id.* pp. 78, 79.

ment, and *use* of open space as an essential factor of urban spatial organization.

OPEN SPACE IN URBAN DEVELOPMENT

In *Cities and Space,* a series of essays on the future use of urban land, Editor Lowden Wingo, Jr.,[5] notes, "The open land problem . . . presents us with a major issue." Law Professor Charles M. Haar[6] says, "Today, the most disputed subject is open space, whether park, playground, recreational or simply undeveloped land." And Planner Stanley B. Tankel observes,

> "Open space has become the subject of a remarkable new interest. The words are echoing even in the halls of Congress and the state legislatures. . . . This is no faddist movement: it is a direct expression of concern about the present and future use of urban space."[7]

The Functions of Open Space

The nature and function of open space in urban terms are now being stated, defined, and classified. Mr. Tankel refers to Charles Eliot's distinction between open space for *service* and open space for *structure* and to Tunnard-Pushkarev's four functions served by open space—*productive, protective, ornamental,* and *recreational.* He offers this interpretation as to the kind of open space of which people personally are aware:

> ". . . it is *used*—for the wide range of active and passive recreation activities, for circulation; it is *viewed*—from the home, the road or other vantage points and it is *felt*—it gives privacy, insulation, or sense of spaciousness and scale. . . ."

And the open space of which people may be unaware but which, nevertheless, affects their daily lives:

> "Open space which *does urban work*—protects water supply and prevents floods by soaking up run-off, acts as a safety zone in the path of aircraft take-off and landings; and open space which *helps shape the development*

[5] "Urban Space in a Policy Perspective," *id.* p. 17.
[6] "The Social Control of Urban Space," in *id.* p. 16.
[7] *Supra* N. 2, p. 57.

pattern—as space between buildings or communities, as space which channels development, as a land reserve for the future. . . ."

Marion Clawson[8] catalogs major open space uses as:

1. Open space surrounding public buildings,
2. Open space for recreation,
3. Open space for ecological protection or for the preservation of certain desirable natural characteristics,
4. Open space for urban structural and esthetic purposes, and
5. Space provisions for future urban growth.

These statements underscore the significance of open space as an urban element, with a positive urban function to perform. It is becoming a major competitor for the use of urban land. It may be a key determinant of urban growth and development.

Types of Open Space

In the urban context, all open space has utility. It is not the rural leftover land nor the sentimental remnant of the countryside. In this context open space may be seen as three major functional types:

1. *Open utility spaces:* These are the surface spaces needed for water supply, for drainage and flood control, the air spaces for aircraft movement, and the space for production.
2. *Open green spaces:* Lands and areas used for parks and recreation, greenbelts and greenways, building entourage, and natural and scenic protection.
3. *Corridor spaces:* Rights-of-ways for movement, transportation, and passage.

Within these broad categories are a multitude of open space forms and uses ranging from large land reserves through regional parks, water reservoirs, natural life preserves, wetlands, river and creek ways, local parks, playgrounds, plazas, and expressway routes to the street itself. In the broader planning aspects, even such areas as campuses, cemeteries, zoos, or airfields take on some characteristics and uses of open space in such systems.

[8] "A Positive Approach to Open Space Preservation," in 28 *A.I.P.J.* (May, 1962).

The catalog of open spaces and the analysis of types and uses can help toward a fuller understanding of the role each can play in urban spatial planning and clarify planning issues, such as those raised in the classic case of the *North Expressway* in San Antonio, Texas.

The Case of the North Expressway

For more than five years a bitter controversy has continued over the location of an expressway route through San Antonio's famed Brackenridge Park and related open spaces. This park is part of a system of open spaces reaching from the northern parts of the city to its center by way of the San Antonio River which has its source in this area. It includes not only undeveloped land and a major flood control facility and parkland but recreation and sports areas, picnic grounds, zoo, college campuses, a renowned landscaped Sunken Garden and outdoor theatre, a city school stadium, a municipal golf course, and stretches of the natural water course.

The proposed expressway curves and winds through this open space system, crossing an Audubon bird sanctuary and Olmos Creek, a tributary waterway in its natural state. It moves along a picnic ground and recreation area obliterating a Girl Scout camp and nature trail. It plunges across the Olmos Flood Basin and rises to enormous heights to go over the Olmos Dam. It severs the campus of the College of the Incarnate Word and stretches across the lands of the San Antonio Zoo. It blocks off the half-built public school gymnasium, slides along the rim of the Sunken Garden, hovers over the edge of the outdoor theatre—squeezing between that and the public school stadium—blocking a major entrance. It slashes through residential areas and slices along the golf course and a wooded portion of the natural watercourse of the San Antonio River.

How many irreplaceable trees of magnificent size and age, how much spoil of adjacent area, how much auxiliary space for interchanges, drainage, and other highway structures will be needed have not, as yet, been calculated fully.

It has been observed that, in many similar cases of expressway controversies, the fight has been centered on the despoliation of a park *or* the disruption of a neighborhood *or* the severing of a campus *or* the loss of trees and landmarks *or* the crossing of a zoo *or* other single problems. But, in the case of the *North Expressway*, practically all of these would be disrupted, severed, or destroyed in one wholesale invasion.

Two bond issues, the second powerhoused after the defeat of the first; a divided community in which deep scars and enmities still remain: legislative challenges and legal action not yet over—all these have resulted from a lack of understanding of the nature and function of urban open space. The Brackenridge Park system serves specific open space needs both as utility and as green open space. It is not only a major greenway leading into the central area of the city but, in the Olmos Basin, a major flood protection. It provides a range of open space needs for a great part of the urban population, not only for San Antonio itself but for its tourist and neighbor visitors in recreation and sports. It serves as a setting for institutional campus development and for cultural activities.

This system also serves as a great urban gathering place. On Easter it is the scene of a great spectacle of tens of thousands of people who come to this green space for observance and holiday—almost every square inch being taken up by family gatherings, picnicking, meeting, and play. Many come the day or evening before to claim a spot for the holiday. But all through the years—for many, many years—this has been the great play space for the military—from recruit to general of San Antonio's many famous military establishments.

An expressway route is a corridor space, not for stopping or gathering but for movement. It had been maintained that the expressway would give easier access to the park areas, but this is belied in the highway proposal itself. In fact, at least two key access streets would be closed off and the interchanges as proposed not only would give less easy access but more likely would create additional nonpark traffic loads. In one instance a proposed interchange at the doorstep of the college will create not only congestion and greater difficulty of access at this point but a major problem of safety.

The Brackenridge system is not a corridor open space. The route of the proposed expressway, twisting and turning and roller coasting over a high dam, reveals dramatically how it is imposed on land not appropriate for the purpose. It reveals how much distortion develops to convert one series of open space functions to another, basically not intended for the purpose and not suitable.

Why was this proposal made? It was assumed that all open space is "free" not only in cost—although the loss of trees alone is estimated in the millions—but even more in functions, that any open green space can and should be used for corridor space. There exists a corridor space long established and used as such to meet the problem of transportation—along the railroad from the north into the city, linking with the highway system.

The failure of the highway engineers, from the local district office to the Bureau of Public Roads, and of the interested promoters and planners locally to understand the nature of urban open space and the way to deal with it to meet all needs is dramatic in the case of the *North Expressway*. It highlights a basic issue in urban growth as well as raises questions of the highest order in relating the major transportation needs to the open space needs everywhere.

OPEN SPACE SYSTEM

The classic case of the *North Expressway* in San Antonio points up other problems of urban open space, particularly those of multiple functions. Open space can serve green space, utility, and corridor functions, if so planned and developed. Open spaces may change in function.

The separation of function is not so essential as the creation of a system of open spaces; that is, a related or planned arrangement which not only can provide the spaces to meet urban needs but a structural framework for urban development. At this point the planning of the urban area—community, metropolitan, or regional—must find a new approach, not by way of the areas for building but by areas not for building.

It is interesting to note that, where nature has provided a basic open space system, there is a universal response to it. San Francisco—beloved by dweller and visitor alike—in great part is defined by a magnificent open space system—the surrounding ocean and bay. Regardless of mistakes made in building, the city itself is a magnificent urban form.

The New York metropolitan area in its own way has another open space system—more than 30 percent of the regional area is taken up by river, sound, harbor, and ocean. These provide a framework for whatever building and rebuilding time, money, and men may produce. In many urban situations there are basic natural features on which to base open space systems—grand or small. The essential point is that an open space framework, once articulated, organized, developed, and kept, opens a great range of opportunities for urban design. Given such a framework, the urban builder can have a base from which to develop as his ingenuity and means permit. In the long perspective the test will not be whether man can build anywhere or whether the market controls or whether mistakes in building occur—for building is man-made and can be man-changed. But open space by nature cannot be replaced. In the design and planning sense, it is the "fixed" element, the building areas the "free." Up to now the general view was that the building areas were to be established as the fixed elements of urban growth; the open spaces—the leftover spaces—were free for building or not.

The change in view is taking place. Nationally we are in hot pursuit to hold or recapture such critical open spaces as the seashore and other waterfronts. The change comes out of our national history. About one hundred years ago, the great urban park reservation came into being with Central Park in New York, followed fifty years later by such other historic examples as the Cook County Forest Preserve, the Cleveland Park System, the Westchester Park System, the Ohio Conservancy District, and the Boston Metropolitan Park System. One great example is the system laid out for Boston by Frederick Law Olmsted in the plan which ties the Arnold Arboretum, Franklin Park, the Jamaica Way and Jamaica Pond, the Fenway, Commonwealth Avenue, and the Charles River. Whatever building changes have taken place in Boston, this glorious concept remains. Its lessons can be applied today, here.

San Antonio offers an example. Incorporating the Brackenridge Park system, now threatened, large metropolitan or regional reserves to the north could be linked with the Olmos Flood Basin, the Brackenridge Park complex, and along the river into and through the heart of the city and to the south along a proposed Mission Parkway following the river and including the historic missions—in themselves another form of open space—on to other major water and other open areas. The tributary creeks and the open spaces provided by encircling military bases and airfields, all forming a grand open space system together with the great north-south backbone of open space, in turn could link with the open spaces at the heart of the city.

The central area of San Antonio is characterized physically by the downtown river loop and a series of parks and plazas: Main Plaza, Military Plaza, Alamo Plaza, Travis Park, Milam Square, Romana Plaza, and Maverick, Columbus, and Madison parks. Together with streets and highways, this series of open spaces can be considered as a great structural framework of open space for San Antonio's growth, development, and renewal.

The downtown river loop—one of San Antonio's great physical features—is in itself an important lesson of the role of open space. In the 1920's, officials and others proposed to cover the river, converting it into a storm sewer. Among the chief arguments was that it would help traffic and parking and thus mean progress. Public opinion held otherwise, and, with the organization of the San Antonio Conservation Society to arouse the city, the river as open space was saved. Late in the 1930's, it was landscaped and developed as a river greenway. Today, the value of the river is being seen anew. A new surge of development is taking place along the river— old shops done over, new buildings designed. Whatever hope remains for rebuilding San Antonio's central area inevitably must relate to the river.

The Hierarchy of Open Spaces

The example of San Antonio illustrates not only the nature of an open space system but also the hierarchy of open spaces—from the large-scale metropolitan or regional space to the small, intimate place; from the great public park to the family yard or patio; from the great regional trunkline and express routes through major arteries, boulevards, parkways, and feeder streets to the residential street.

Within the hierarchy of scale is a hierarchy of use. Open areas do not mean sterilized land, although an open space system should provide for wilderness and untroubled area even at small-scale and close-in locations. The range includes multiple uses as well as campus areas and other man-made facilities. The essential point is that open space needs to be identified as *open* and not *building* space. When building use is involved, it is not as encroachment but as support of the primary open space. A recreational building does not, of itself, disaffect a recreational area; nor do properly handled park roads change the primary use of the park. The treatment of open space is not for the purpose of destroying it; but, as in the treatment of building area, it calls for judgment and intelligence and the skills and arts of those who understand landscape and the land.

POLICIES AND PROGRAMS

Open space in the past was, largely, a negative concept—the areas for non-building. It now is coming to be recognized as a positive element for urban growth. In the decades ahead open space as a system can become the means of control in development. If it is to achieve this role, a new text of planning policies and programs must be written—and followed into practice. The issues are not for planners alone. They will be fought in the political arena, and out of a public consensus may come the new tools and new means, both public and private.

And How

The existing legislative and regulatory tools are inadequate. The oldest tool is acquisition of lands for open space purposes. While the trend may be to public, governmental action, such as in the current federal open space program and such state programs as those in New York or New Jersey or in metropolitan or city programs throughout the country, a place remains open for private action for which there is much precedent in history.

Zoning seems to be a weak tool. William H. Whyte, Jr.,[9] cites the example of Santa Clara County, California, where to preserve rich farm and orchard land an exclusive agricultural zone was established, only to find that the state highway engineers were planning to lay a new highway right through the middle.

Special conservancy districts, open space dedication, open space easements, development rights compensation,[10] compensable regulations,[11] reservation in advance of acquisition, tax concessions, the guaranteed value scheme, and the official map principle[12]—all these in various terms have been suggested and are the subject of increasing attention and, in some cases, of legislative action.[13]

[9] "Urban Sprawl," in *The Exploding Metropolis* (Doubleday, 1958).
[10] Whyte, "Securing Open Space for Urban America: Conservation Easements," in Urban Land Institute Technical Bulletin No. 36 (1959).
[11] See Krasnowiecki and Strong, "Compensable Regulations for Open Space," in 20 *A.I.P.J.* (May, 1963).
[12] See Mandelker, "What Open Space Where? How?" in *Planning 1963* (Chicago: American Society of Planning Officials, 1963).
[13] California Government Code § 6950 (enacted 1959); Maryland Ann. Code, art. 66(c), § 357(A) (enacted 1960); New Jersey S.A.

Lawrence Levine[14] points out, "The very breadth and diversity of open space objectives pose difficult problems in developing a soundly conceived open space program"—and, it can be added, in finding the legal and political means to bring it into being. President Lyndon Johnson has said:

> "Open land is vanishing and old landmarks are violated. Worst of all, expansion is eroding the precious and time honored values of community with neighbors and communion with nature. . . . We have always prided ourselves on being not only America the strong and America the free but America the beautiful. Today that beauty is in danger. The water we drink, the food we eat, the very air we breathe are threatened with pollution. Our parks are overcrowded and our seashore overburdened. Green fields and dense forests are disappearing. A few years ago we were concerned about the Ugly American; today we must act to prevent the Ugly America. For once our natural splendor is destroyed, it can never be recaptured. Once man can no longer walk with beauty or wonder at nature, his spirit will wither and his sustenance be wasted."

If understanding of the role and function of open space in all its multiple uses and objectives can be reached—from the living space at home and street to the far reaches of the region—and if political skill can be brought to bear, we may be able to take a major step in fashioning a new urban environment that has both sense and sensitivity.

13:8A-1 (enacted 1961); New York Municipal Law § 247 (enacted 1961) and New York Conservation Law § 875 (enacted 1961); and West Virginia Code, ch. 20, § 2215 (enacted 1961). See also *Shirley Adelson Siegal* in *The Law of Open Space* (New York: Regional Plan Ass'n, 1960).

[14] "Land Conservation in Metropolitan Areas," in 30 *A.I.P.J.* 205 (Aug. 1964).

Chapter 8

METROPOLITAN FORM AND STRUCTURE

What is to be the spatial form and grain of the future metropolitan area or region? And how do we manage this inevitable spread city in an efficient and humanly rewarding fashion? Clearly the scale of mankind's city settlements has gone far beyond the old narrow political boundaries to sprawl over state lines in the United States and national frontiers in Western Europe—with rapidly burgeoning populations filling in the interstitial rural areas and rushing to the suburban fringes to be quasi-managed by amateur governments, as Robert Wood has named them. Overlapping, often chaotic, jurisdictions (1,400 plus in New York's metropolitan area) make rational decision-making and subsequent administration a chancy process at best.

Utopian dreams of optimal spatial form and governmental structure are intellectually satisfying, but generally have little results in the real world. The three articles which follow attempt to build on solid foundations of what is and what is possible in the reasonably immediate future. Alan Campbell and Seymour Sacks, "hard-nosed" empirical practitioners of the quantifiable fiscal arts, look hard at existing three-tiered American government fragmentation to discover what governmental level pays for what; in effect, who performs the services that get done today. They tentatively conclude that county government may conceivably be the best bet and growing force for above-the-political-city-management of the American urban scene with a higher level of and possibly more costly services.

Professor Thijsse, one of the Netherlands' most respected planners, discusses with characteristic Dutch thoroughness the extraordinary attempt made to control the megalopolitan area of central Holland, to preserve the amenities of scarce space despite a rapidly increasing and concentrating population, and to forward economic development at the same time. Even with the traditional Dutch reverence for the good earth, and despite, to us, quite extraordinary national powers, the cities of the horseshoe-shaped megalopolis continue to reach out to each other, and the small towns slowly spread at the edges. Thijsse recommends national plan-making above local plans with all of the Netherlands under consideration and flatly states that the co-operation of Germany, France, and Belgium are needed to manage the economic and spatial development of this urban place in Northwest Europe.

Arthur Row advocates strong governmental medicine (federal and state primarily) to manage the New York metropolitan area with four massive tissue grafts: (a) the development of twelve many-faceted regional urban centers, (b) a major transportation network of highways, (c) nodes of industrial concentration and (d) an open-space grid system. These steps, he feels, are financially possible and rewarding under present legislation, fit the mood of the times, and need no elaborate new governmental structures. By public sector leadership of this magnitude, economic gains of a high order are possible for the private sector and social gains for the often bewildered humans trapped by the urban octopus.

Administering the Spread City

ALAN K. CAMPBELL AND SEYMOUR SACKS*

Since the end of World War II increasing attention has been paid to the spatial redistribution of the American people. The urbanization and metropolitanization of the country have been widely discussed and its implications for the nature of American society vigorously debated. The full ramifications of this fundamental change defy summary since the change involves nearly all aspects of man's behavior. In fact, it has been argued that ". . . now, when the last rural threads of American society are being woven into the national urban fabric the idea of city is becoming indistinguishable from the idea of society.[1] Urban man has become 'every man.'"

While philosophers, statesmen, social critics and journalists debate the merits of this revolution with a colorful but imprecise language, day-to-day decision-makers must try to cope with the new reality. Among those most directly concerned are the local government administrators who daily make de-

* For a brief biography of Alan Campbell, see Chapter 1. Seymour Sacks, Professor of Economics at the Maxwell Graduate School, Syracuse University, has been on the faculties of Rensselaer Polytechnic Institute, Wayne State University and the University of Vermont; and has served New York State and a number of local government agencies in a professional capacity. He has contributed to a number of journals, mainly on tax and governmental tax problems, and is the author with William F. Hellmuth, Jr., of *Financing Government in a Metropolitan Area—The Cleveland Experience* (Glencoe, Ill.: The Free Press, 1962).

This article is reprinted from *Public Administration Review*, Vol. XXIV, No. 3, September 1964, by permission of the publisher.

[1] Melvin M. Webber, "Order in Diversity: Community Without Propinquity" in *Cities and Space: The Future Use of Urban Land* (Lowdon Wingo, Jr., ed.), The Johns Hopkins Press, 1963, p. 23.

cisions which reflect the revolution and, to some degree, influence its course.

Of the names this new environment is called, a few are flattering, most are damning, hardly any are value-free: urban sprawl, scatteration, cancerous growth, and slurbs are but a few of the value-loaded names which have been given to it. Perhaps the phrase "spread city" is as nearly a neutral one as is likely to be found although even it is likely to have a negative ring in the ears of most readers since a city is normally pictured as being compact rather than spread. The New York Regional Plan Association's definition of the term is, by implication at least, negative rather than positive: "It is not a true city because it lacks centers, nor a suburb because it is not a satellite of any city, nor is it truly rural because it is loosely covered with houses and urban facilities."[2] Others view the phenomenon in a more positive way, arguing that it provides a range of choices in living conditions and styles never before possible. They find ". . . in the dissolution of the urban settlement a liberation of human energies and a proliferation of opportunity for human interaction."[3]

Whether good or bad the urban future of this country is a "spread-city" future. It may be "less" rather than "more" spread if policies are geared to this end, but when compared to the compact city of the past it will be spread. For the local official the result is a new decision-making environment. Even under the simplifying assumption of a single governmental jurisdiction for the entire spread city area, the problems he faces will be new, if not in content at least in dimension. For a given level of services many of the infra-structure cost advantages possible through economies of scale in a compact city, for example, will not be realized in a spread city, whatever the jurisdictional pattern. Further, the spatial distribution of welfare, health and education needs would probably not be much altered by a one-jurisdictional governmental system.

Although the decision environment of the spread city, even with the assumption of a one-jurisdictional local system, will be vastly different from that of the compact cities, the reality is not one jurisdiction, but many. The fact of many jurisdictions operating in the same area has resulted in many defining

[2] Regional Plan Association, *Spread City: Projections of Development Trends and the Issues They Pose: The Tri-State New York Metropolitan Region 1960–85.* Bulletin 100, September 1962, p. 3.

[3] Melvin M. Webber, *op. cit.,* p. 18.

the metropolitan problem as governmental fragmentation.[4] Whether this is *the* metropolitan problem or if the situation is better described as problems in metropolitan areas is not the issue here. Rather it is the nature of the impact of spread city, plus governmental fragmentation, plus the state-local governmental system on the decision environment of administrators. The result is that no single set of officials within a spread city is responsible for the entire area or even a very large part of it.

The fact of fragmentation as a general feature of local government in the United States has led to the development of a variety of generalizations about its impact on policy-making at this level of government. These generalizations usually point to a lack of coordination, inequity in tax burdens, distortions in land-use patterns and unhealthy competition among local jurisdictions as the inevitable results of the fragmentation. It is normally assumed that these criticisms apply with equal or nearly equal validity to all spread cities in the country.

It is the lack of validity in this assumption of uniformity of impact which is the concern of this analysis. Governmental systems operative in spread cities across the country are not the same in every spread city area. Nor are these systems enough alike to assume that generalizations can be made about the impact of fragmented government on the nature and quality of public decisions.[5]

STATE-LOCAL GOVERNMENTAL SYSTEMS

The first step necessary, therefore, in an analysis of the significance of fragmentation for local decision-making in the spread city is to describe the kinds of governmental systems from which the decisions emerge. There are 50 state-local governmental systems and the District of Columbia system in the United States, each with its own unique characteristics;

[4] Council of State Governments (John C. Bollens, Director of Study): *The States and the Metropolitan Problem,* 1956. "The basis of the problem is the absence of general local government organizations broad enough to cope with metropolitan matters," p. 17.

[5] For a discussion of the implications of fragmentation which does not accept the easy assumption of a need for area-wide government see Vincent Ostrom, Charles M. Tiebout and Robert Warren, "The Organization of Government in Metropolitan Areas: A Theoretical Inquiry," *The American Political Science Review,* Vol. LV, No. 4 (December 1961), pp. 831–42.

and within each state-local system there are distinct local sub-systems, usually more than one within each state. Alongside these state-local systems and their sub-systems is the federal government with its state-local aid programs and, of particular relevance to spread city governmental systems, its recent efforts to encourage planning in urban areas.

Although there are various ways in which these systems can be described and classified, one of the most useful is to base the classification on fiscal characteristics. The relevant fiscal characteristics for describing state-local systems are: the allocation between state and local governments of general expenditure and general revenue responsibilities,[6] the extent and character of state aid, variation in local revenue sources, and the nature of the property tax. To illustrate the wide-spread variation in these factors the following table indicates the interstate differences within and between regions for each of the fiscal characteristics.

The allocation of expenditure responsibility to local government varies greatly from state to state although there are regional patterns. In 1962 local government expenditures ranged from 39.4 percent of total state-local expenditures in Vermont and 42.3 percent and 44.9 percent in Kentucky and West Virginia, respectively, to highs of 77.8 percent in New York, 74.8 percent in Wisconsin, and 74.4 percent in New Jersey. The state average expenditure allocation has remained remarkably constant over time: 59.1 percent in 1962 and 59.2 in 1957, with standard deviations of 9.1 and 9.2 for the same two years.

For tax allocation to local government, the range for individual states is from 71.1 percent in New Jersey to Delaware with 22.2 percent. The average state allocation for 1962 was 45.8 percent as compared to 44.9 percent in 1957, with standard deviations of 12.0 and 11.8 for the same two years.[7]

----

[6] General expenditure and revenue, rather than total, are used throughout this analysis in order to avoid comparing non-comparable packages of public services. Following the Census Bureau's definition, general expenditures include "all expenditures other than (a) benefit and refund payments of public-employee-retirement and other social-insurance systems and (b) spending for state and local liquor stores and for local water, electric, transit, and gas utilities." General revenue includes all revenue "except utility and liquor store revenue and insurance trust revenue."

[7] A comprehensive analysis of the impact of the allocation systems on fiscal behavior at the national and metropolitan levels will be provided in the forthcoming Brookings-sponsored study. As a part of this general

TABLE 1
STATE AND LOCAL FISCAL CHARACTERISTICS BY STATE FOR CONTINENTAL UNITED STATES: 1962

	General* State-Local Expenditures Per Capita $	Local General* Expenditures as Percent of State-Local Expenditures %	Local Taxes as Percent of State-Local Taxes %	State Aid as Percent of Local Taxes %	Local Property Taxes as Percent of Total Local General* Revenue %	Assessed Value of Commercial and Industrial as Percent of Assessed Value of All Property %
UNITED STATES						
NORTHEAST						
Maine	271.78	50.7	54.9	19.1	75.4	39.6
New Hampshire	302.33	52.6	62.5	8.5	78.5	N.A.
Vermont	372.66	39.4	44.6	30.0	70.8	N.A.
Massachusetts	343.25	72.0	60.8	37.6	63.3	32.3
Rhode Island	292.98	53.7	49.4	29.7	66.8	N.A.
Connecticut	367.37	59.4	53.4	23.0	70.1	N.A.
New York	398.26	77.8	56.9	49.7	44.4	N.A.
New Jersey	301.68	74.4	71.1	19.0	87.6	34.6
Pennsylvania	272.41	61.3	41.7	41.9	44.6	28.9
Delaware	335.37	49.3	22.2	159.8	31.2	31.6
Maryland	318.32	69.4	43.4	84.0	41.5	37.8

NORTH CENTRAL						
Michigan	343.25	65.7	47.0	68.4	51.3	N.A.
Ohio	290.52	72.0	55.3	45.1	49.7	51.9
Indiana	290.37	67.2	55.6	44.9	59.1	N.A.
Illinois	315.06	70.2	57.8	26.3	58.4	33.9
Wisconsin	350.78	74.8	53.1	63.4	50.4	36.5
Minnesota	362.81	70.5	53.5	56.8	53.1	35.2
Iowa	325.58	64.1	56.7	34.2	61.4	N.A.
Missouri	266.39	59.1	51.4	33.7	50.0	29.5
North Dakota	378.66	52.7	53.6	32.6	58.4	27.3
South Dakota	329.29	48.7	61.9	13.8	70.4	18.1
Nebraska	280.49	65.3	64.4	25.9	58.9	20.9
Kansas	321.35	66.6	55.8	40.7	58.4	N.A.
SOUTH						
Virginia	249.26	60.2	42.3	65.4	38.4	N.A.
West Virginia	250.95	44.9	30.6	77.8	40.6	N.A.
Kentucky	293.01	42.3	33.2	80.5	33.6	42.9
Tennessee	238.70	59.8	37.5	86.1	36.9	N.A.
North Carolina	229.38	62.1	37.1	121.8	30.4	39.9
South Carolina	202.11	50.8	26.4	125.4	32.3	53.9
Georgia	256.71	59.4	35.3	92.4	33.3	N.A.
Florida	282.67	67.8	48.6	46.9	42.6	N.A.
Alabama	244.81	52.4	30.3	122.9	18.3	N.A.
Mississippi	248.69	55.4	35.4	114.3	29.9	N.A.
Louisiana	332.78	47.8	25.8	152.4	26.6	34.9
Arkansas	221.10	49.1	31.1	95.2	37.0	N.A.
Oklahoma	290.52	48.2	32.5	81.4	40.5	N.A.
Texas	269.17	65.3	46.6	51.2	48.4	N.A.

	General* State-Local Expenditures Per Capita $	Local General* Expenditures as Percent of State-Local Expenditures %	Local Taxes as Percent of State-Local Taxes %	State Aid as Percent of Local Taxes %	Local Property Taxes as Percent of Total Local General* Revenue %	Assessed Value of Commercial and Industrial as Percent of Assessed Value of All Property %
United States						
WEST						
New Mexico	326.92	52.8	26.4	185.5	21.6	N.A.
Arizona	354.14	59.5	44.6	64.4	44.2	N.A.
Montana	350.93	52.4	55.6	24.9	62.4	N.A.
Idaho	310.82	54.4	46.3	52.3	51.4	46.6
Wyoming	497.60	53.0	46.2	64.6	44.3	N.A.
Colorado	362.19	67.8	51.5	58.2	48.1	43.7
Utah	332.71	55.2	53.5	53.3	45.2	55.5
Washington	385.15	57.8	31.2	110.5	29.8	N.A.
Oregon	382.63	55.0	48.8	48.6	51.5	41.0
Nevada	496.40	57.9	40.7	63.7	33.9	N.A.
California	429.34	71.8	54.2	58.8	47.0	N.A.

* See footnote 6.
SOURCES: U.S. Bureau of the Census, Governments Division, *Governmental Finances in 1962* and Census of Governments 1962, *Property Values.*
N.A.—not available.

In general, the major determinants of allocation are state and federal aid and the degree of urbanization. The most important determinant of this difference in allocation responsibility is the division of public welfare expenditures between state and local governments.[8] There are 31 states in which state governments take primary responsibility for this function and 17 in which local government is given such responsibility. Another determinant of allocation is the rather random year-to-year differences of federal grants for the interstate highway programs.

Another difference in state-local governmental systems revolves around state aid. The already discussed allocation of expenditures is greatly influenced by the amount of state aid. In 1962 this source of local revenue varied from $10.54 per capita in New Hampshire to $96.81 per capita in California, or a variation from 6.6 percent of local expenditures in New Hampshire to 52 percent of local expenditures in New Mexico with California's high per capita figure equivalent to 31.4 percent of local expenditures. These differences in state aid require the development of distinct local strategies by public officials if they are to maximize their benefits from this source of revenue. In Wisconsin, for example, the state aid system takes the form, in part, of shared taxes and this kind of system demands different local public finance decisions than the more usual pattern of having aid inversely related to fiscal resources.

It is a combination of the allocation of responsibility for state-local services, and the extent of state aid which determines, in part, the amounts of revenue which must be raised from local tax sources. As would be expected, the variations are very great. Per capita local taxes varied from $35.97 in South Carolina to $175.85 in New York, a substantially greater proportional variation than in the differences in local expenditures which varied from a low of $103 to a high of $310 per capita.

The chief source of local tax revenue is the property tax; this tax produced, in 1962, 88 percent of all local tax revenues. It is in spread cities, or portions thereof, where local

---

study a Ph.D. dissertation by Yong Hyo Cho is attempting to measure the determinants of the allocation systems.

[8] Selma J. Mushkin, "Intergovernmental Aspects of Local Expenditure Decisions" in *Public Expenditure Decisions in the Urban Community* (Howard G. Schaller, ed.), The Johns Hopkins Press, 1963.

non-property taxes have been most widely adopted. Although these taxes add a new dimension to the decision environment, the property tax usually remains the chief source of local taxes. In the case of New York City, even with its almost $600 million of non-property tax revenues, the property tax still contributed 69.6 percent of all local tax revenue in 1962.

The property tax varies greatly, too, in the content of its base. In all but four states both real and personal property are taxed, but even in these four the content of the base is by no means completely explained by the term "real." When both real and personal property are included in the base there is no way of knowing what property is taxed without examining the assessment rolls themselves.

Of particular significance is the proportion of the assessed base made up of different classes of property, for it is through these proportions that the contribution of different classes of property to total tax revenue is determined. In this instance assessed value is much more meaningful than "true" value. It is through specific assessment practices that it is possible to shift heavier fiscal responsibility from one class of property to another. There is, for example, great variation in the proportion which commercial and industrial property constitutes of total assessed value in different states. For the 22 states for which figures are available, commercial and industrial property constitute only 18.1 percent of the base in South Dakota, while the comparable percentage in South Carolina is 53.9.

These variations in fiscal characteristics, as between state and local governments and among local sub-systems, define a part of the differences among governmental systems. There are, however, at the local level, other significant differences which must be fitted to variations in fiscal characteristics before a complete classification is possible.

THE NON-FISCAL CHARACTERISTICS OF LOCAL SUB-SYSTEMS

Each state-local system has operating within it a number of local governmental sub-systems. These local sub-systems can be classified by a number of characteristics. The most useful, perhaps, are functional inclusiveness, size of jurisdiction, and the jurisdictional assignment of land-use controls.

Functional inclusiveness is a measure of the generalness of governments operating in spread cities. The empirical fact of overlapping governments in metropolitan areas is well known but the actual variations in the extent of this phenomenon is often overlooked.

One measure of functional inclusiveness is the proportion of total general governmental expenditures made in a particular jurisdiction by that jurisdiction itself. The central cities in metropolitan areas are among the most inclusive jurisdictions in the country but there is great variation even among these. The central cities in the 24 largest metropolitan areas vary in the proportion of general expenditures for which they are responsible within their own jurisdictional area from a low of 29.5 percent in Los Angeles to a high of 95.7 percent in Washington, D. C., with Baltimore, Boston, and New York all having proportions over 90 percent. Table 2 indicates the total per capita general expenditures in the central city areas and the proportion of these for which the central cities themselves are responsible for 1957.[9]

Functional inclusiveness also is related to local fiscal interdependence since the more governments operative in the same area the more taxing units there will be drawing on the same tax base. For any specific piece of property in a spread city the result may be the imposition of from one to a dozen tax rates on variable tax bases. Because of the multiplicity of special districts it is impossible in many areas to measure fiscal burden by any areal unit larger than individual parcels of property. Where there is greater functional inclusiveness or where the multiple units of government tend to be coterminous, it is possible to calculate burden by governmental unit rather than by individual pieces of property.

This characteristic is reflected through the substantial differences, even within the same spread city, in the division of taxes collected in a particular area by jurisdictions in that area. In the inclusive jurisdictions all taxes will go to the jurisdiction itself, while in other cases it will be divided among various jurisdictions operating in the same area. Table 3 shows the division of taxes collected within each municipality and urban township of over 50,000 population in the New York Metropolitan Region. In the case of the functional inclusive jurisdictions of Connecticut, all of it goes to the municipality; in New

---

[9] In a forthcoming Ph.D. dissertation done as a part of the Brookings study, Woo Sik Kee has analyzed the local fiscal patterns of all central cities in terms of their functional inclusiveness.

TABLE 2

GENERAL EXPENDITURES PER CAPITA IN CENTRAL CITY AREAS
MADE BY THE CENTRAL CITY GOVERNMENTS AND OTHER
OVERLYING GOVERNMENTS AND THEIR RELATIVE PROPORTIONS
IN THE 24 LARGEST METROPOLITAN AREAS—1957

City	Total General Expenditures Including Overlying Governments in Central City Area (Per Capita)	Central City Expenditures (Per Capita)	Central City Expenditures as a Percent of Total General Expenditure in Central City Area (Percent)
Atlanta	$158	$ 72	45.6%
Baltimore	199	189	95.0
Boston	273	258	94.5
Buffalo	193	142	73.6
Chicago	203	96	47.3
Cincinnati	246	138	56.1
Cleveland	180	88	48.9
Dallas	175	86	49.1
Detroit	202	111	55.0
Houston	155	61	39.4
Kansas City	157	86	54.8
Los Angeles	261	77	29.5
Long Beach	320	122	38.1
Milwaukee	229	101	44.1
Minneapolis	182	80	44.0
St. Paul	189	125	66.1
New York	257	237	92.2
Newark	243	181	74.5
Paterson	160	132	82.5
Clifton	141	113	80.1
Passaic	166	138	83.1
Philadelphia	165	109	66.1
Pittsburgh	188	88	46.8
St. Louis	147	91	61.9
San Diego	191	65	34.0
San Francisco	218	146	67.0
Oakland	231	89	38.5
Seattle	174	73	42.0
Washington, D. C.	234	224	95.7

SOURCE: Bureau of the Census: Local Government Finances in Standard Metropolitan Areas, Vol. III, No. 6, *1957 Census of Governments*, U.S. Government Printing Office (Washington, D. C.), 1959.

TABLE 3

THE ALLOCATION AMONG GOVERNMENTAL JURISDICTIONS OF TAXES
COLLECTED IN MUNICIPALITIES AND URBAN TOWNSHIPS OF OVER
50,000 POPULATION IN THE NEW YORK METROPOLITAN REGION—1962

| | Allocation of Taxes Collected in the Municipalities and Urban Townships to: | | | Per Capita |
Cities/Villages	The Municipality Itself	The County	The School District	Total Local Taxes
New York				
Mt. Vernon	44.1%	14.4%	41.5%	$163.42
New Rochelle	41.6	15.4	43.0	225.69
New York	100.0	—	—	219.87
White Plains	38.4	15.8	45.8	278.43
Yonkers	83.1	16.9	—	148.77
Connecticut				
Bridgeport	100.0	—	—	126.74
Norwalk	100.0	—	—	162.80
Stamford	100.0	—	—	192.55
New Jersey				
Bayonne	71.0	29.0	—	172.37
Clifton	77.3	22.8	—	139.08
East Orange	80.3	19.7	—	176.51
Elizabeth	89.1	10.9	—	144.15
Jersey City	82.4	17.6	—	191.47
Newark	85.2	14.8	—	194.89
Passaic	88.2	11.8	—	165.03
Paterson	88.5	11.5	—	130.95
Union	81.8	18.2	—	182.01
Urban Townships				
Connecticut				
Greenwich	100.0	—	—	221.76
New Jersey				
Bloomfield	74.9	25.0	—	167.34
Irvington	76.6	23.4	—	147.93
Union	23.7	19.9	56.5	155.50
Woodbridge	19.2	18.3	62.6	142.60

SOURCES: U.S. Bureau of the Census, *Compendium of City Government Finances in 1962.* Government Printing Office: Washington, D. C., 1963. New Jersey Taxpayers Association, *Financial Statistics of New Jersey Local Government,* September 1962. The Department of Audit and Control, State of New York. Unpublished data.

York it may all go to the municipality or may be shared by the municipality, the county and the school district.[10]

Jurisdictional geographic size is separate from but related to the characteristic of functional inclusiveness. Jurisdictions may be small but inclusive or large but fragmented. There are regional patterns, with exceptions, for this characteristic. New England (towns) and the South (counties) tend to have small but inclusive jurisdictions. The rest of the country combines large and small jurisdictions in the same area with a tendency to non-inclusiveness.

Finally, there are vast differences across the country in the jurisdictional assignment of land-use controls. In fact, in some instances these controls may be divided among different jurisdictions in the same area. For example, the zoning power may be assigned to municipalities or towns while the planning power is divided between these smaller jurisdictions and the county, with the addition recently of many regional planning agencies, usually advisory. The mix of these fiscal, structural and power characteristics will probably be different for every spread city in the country. Each particular mix carries with it implications for the public official who must seek the interest of his jurisdiction within the framework of the system within which he is operating.

One very clear example of the impact which differences in just the fiscal system may have can be shown through its impact on land-use zoning. A great deal has been written in recent years about fiscal zoning, i.e., the adoption of zoning practices which attempt to maximize the revenue gain from new land uses. The practice is usually deplored on the grounds that fiscal criteria for zoning are inferior to other criteria.[11]

Whatever the merits of fiscal zoning there are some situations where it is more attractive than in others. Where there is a high allocation of local expenditure responsibility and low state aid, the pressure on the local tax base will be very great. Fiscal zoning in this situation makes a great deal more sense than in the case where both state responsibility and state aid are high.

Other examples of the impact of the fiscal variables could be

[10] It should be noted that this comparison understates the complexity of the governmental pattern in New York State since it omits the unincorporated areas.

[11] Regional Plan Association, *op. cit.* "Tax considerations, in short, will play an expanding role in land development decisions, weakening the chance of planning for the best possible use of the land, unless the sources of local government revenues are modified," p. 3.

provided, but the addition of the governmental variables—functional inclusiveness, size of jurisdictions and land-use control—presents a more realistic picture of the decision environment. In one kind of situation these variables can reduce the complexity of the environment. Again using fiscal zoning as the policy area, the larger a local government jurisdiction is and the wider the range of governmental functions it performs, the simpler (although still difficult) is the calculation of possible financial gain from fiscal zoning. Further, the impact on other local governments drawing from the same tax base is eliminated when there are no other local governments operating in the same area.

The more common situation of small and overlapping jurisdictions presents a more complex picture. Assume the existence of several jurisdictions relying on the same tax base combined with high state aid for one type of jurisdiction. Another type jurisdiction in the same area, perhaps the county, may receive relatively little state aid while possessing high fiscal responsibility for those functions which it does perform, thereby placing a rather severe strain on its tax base. For the county, therefore, it may make good fiscal sense to zone heavily (if it possesses the zoning power) for land uses which are fiscally productive or, even if it does not have zoning power, to vigorously promote new industries for the area.

In the same area, however, the school districts may receive substantial state aid and this aid will normally be inversely related to property value per student. While the county, therefore, is increasing the tax base to improve its fiscal position, the school districts drawing on that same base will find that their property value per student is going up and, as a result, state aid will decline. The losses to the school district might well exceed the net gain which the county experiences through the improvement in its revenue base. Of particular interest is the lack of any governmental mechanism below the state able to even consider this kind of conflict situation, to say nothing of resolving it.

GOVERNMENTAL SYSTEMS IN THE NEW YORK METROPOLITAN REGION

The existence of quite different state-local governmental systems is well illustrated by the neighboring states of New York, New Jersey and Connecticut, all of which have within their boundaries a part of the spread city of New York. Rela-

TABLE 4

ASSIGNMENT OF FUNCTIONAL RESPONSIBILITIES AND PER CAPITA GENERAL EXPENDITURES OF MUNICIPALITIES AND URBAN TOWNSHIPS OVER 50,000 POPULATION IN THE NEW YORK METROPOLITAN REGION—FOR SELECTED FUNCTIONS—1962

Cities/Villages	Per Capita General Expenditures (own)	Education	Higher Education	Categorical Public Welfare	Non-Categorical Public Welfare	Sewerage and Sewerage Disposal	Hospital	Housing and Urban Renewal	Utilities Water	Utilities Other
New York State										
Mt. Vernon	$113.56	–	–	–	–	+	+	+	+	–
New Rochelle	170.31	+	–	–	–	+	+	+	–	–
New York	332.34	–	+	+	+	+	+	+	+	+
White Plains	139.90	+	–	–	–	+	–	+	+	–
Yonkers	200.89		–	–	–	+	–	+	+	–
Connecticut										
Bridgeport	158.55	+	–	–	+	+	+	+	–	–
Norwalk	251.89	+	–	–	+	+	–	+	–	–
Stamford	246.76		–	–	+	+	–	+	–	–
New Jersey										
Bayonne	150.05	+	–	–	+	+	+	–	+	–
Clifton	155.17	+	–	–	+	+	–	–	–	–
East Orange	161.45		–	–	+	+	+	–	+	–

	Value	1	2	3	4	5	6	7	8
Elizabeth	155.90	+	−	+	+	+	+	+	−
Jersey City	204.17	+	−	+	+	+	+	+	−
Newark	230.66	+	−	+	+	+	+	+	−
Passaic	166.13	+	−	+	+	+	−	−	−
Paterson	164.36	+	−	+	+	+	−	−	−
Union	156.88	+	−	+	+	−	−	−	−
Urban Township									
Connecticut									
Greenwich	294.57	+	−	+	+	+	−	−	−
New Jersey									
Bloomfield	162.13	+	−	−	+	−	−	+	−
Irvington	152.95	+	−	−	+	+	−	−	−
Union	76.30	−	−	−	+	−	−	−	−
Woodbridge	58.97	−	−	−	+	−	−	−	−

SOURCE: U.S. Bureau of the Census, *Compendium of City Government Finances in 1962.*

tive to the rest of the country, these states are all strong local-effort states as measured by per capita local taxes, but the similarity stops with this characteristic. In terms of local expenditures per capita, New York and New Jersey rank considerably ahead of Connecticut, while New York and Connecticut are considerably stronger state-aid states than New Jersey. Connecticut and New Jersey tend to have small general governmental jurisdictions; while the New York system is characterized by a fragmented governmental system with a great amount of overlapping.

Some of the differences in the assignment of functional responsibilities to municipalities and urban townships is shown in Table 4. All of the jurisdictions listed provide the normal municipal functions of fire, police, street maintenance and sanitation but here the similarity ends. Of the other functions included in the table only New York City provides them all, while some provide none beyond the basic municipal services. A great deal of the differences in per capita total expenditures are explained by these differences in functional assignment which, in turn, have an influence on the nature of the decision environment.

In a study of state aid in New York State,[12] six distinct sub-systems of local government were found to exist. These six systems are in stark contrast to the two which exist in Connecticut and the three in New Jersey. Since all of these systems are operative in the spread city of New York, it means that for this area there are three state-local systems and eleven subsystems.

Each of these systems carries its own imperatives for the local official administering it. The overlapping situation in New York, for example, might well cause jurisdictions to follow conflicting policies in relation to their common tax base. In contrast, the small functionally inclusive jurisdictions in New Jersey and Connecticut would be able to follow consistent intra-jurisdictional policies. Area-wide consistency in these states, however, would be unlikely while large area coordination is a possibility in New York because of its relatively strong counties. However, even here the lack of zoning power at the county level reduces the potential for such coordination.

The point is simply that it is not particularly useful to try to analyze the decision-making system in metropolitan areas on the assumption that the determinants of the environment are the same in all spread cities or even are alike in all parts of the same spread city. The need, as expressed by H. Douglas Price in discussing the politics of state-local government, is for comparative studies. He says, "The study of state and local politics is, of necessity, a problem in comparative government." He deplores the fact that "it has been treated as almost everything else: a problem in administrative organization, a matter of constitutional law, a question of 'power elites' or no 'power elites,' and so forth."[13] The need is no less urgent for comparative studies of state-local governmental systems and their local sub-systems, especially as they operate in urban areas.

GOVERNMENTAL SYSTEMS AND THE LOCAL OFFICIAL

For the local official, in contrast to the student of government, the need is not to understand all the governmental systems in the country but rather to understand his own jurisdiction and its relation to those of his neighbors. His role is to fit the policies for his jurisdiction to his own system in a way which will promote the interests of that jurisdiction. In one situation this might require him to push very hard for an increase in the industrial base of his community; in another his emphasis might better be placed on increasing state aid; in another his interest might be better served by trying to move a function to a higher level of government.

The only meaningful generalization possible is that he will try to serve the interest of his particular jurisdiction as he sees it. That interest is likely to be seen in terms of maximizing services and minimizing costs (however inconsistent these goals may be, both are sought), and maintaining an environment which fits the jurisdiction's image of itself.[14] To accomplish these ends will require very different decisions in different jurisdictions. For example, it is likely that the public finance differences already discussed may well cause the New Jersey portion of the New York spread city to emphasize fiscal zon-

[13] "Comparative Analysis in State and Local Politics: Potential and Problems." Paper prepared for delivery at 1963 Annual Meeting of American Political Science Association. (Mimeo)

[14] This image is a product of objective socio-economic characteristics as well as community aspirations. A comprehensive picture of the behavior of local officials would have to include both these classes of variables.

ing much more heavily than the New York portion. In Connecticut, with categorical welfare a state function, but with small functionally inclusive jurisdictions competing for revenue base, the pressure for fiscal zoning probably would rank between New Jersey and New York.

There are situations, of course, which lead to inter-local cooperation. Certain problems cannot be solved by an individual jurisdiction acting alone. In the areas of water supply, sewerage disposal, air pollution control, and transportation, the need for inter-local cooperation is most obvious. To the extent that local jurisdictions performing these functions in the same area can see a gain for themselves in inter-local cooperation, it is predictable that after a due amount of negotiation some form of inter-local cooperation will take place. The form of the cooperation can vary from an actual inter-local contract or agreement for the performance of the service to the movement of the service to a higher level of government or to the creation of a special jurisdiction specifically for that function.[15]

The possibility of gain relates, in part, to the governmental system operative in an area. For example, cooperation in sharing welfare costs is unlikely when the welfare function is assigned to municipalities rather than to a larger jurisdiction. Welfare needs tend to be concentrated in the core area of the spread city, although it can be argued that the financial responsibility for the function ought to be region-wide. As Harvey Brazer says, "To the extent that suburban communities, through zoning regulations and discriminatory practices in rentals and real estate transactions, contribute directly to the concentration in the central city of socio-economic groups which impose heavy demands upon local government services, they are in fact, exploiting the central city."[16]

It seems unlikely, however, that the central city could convince its suburban neighbors that they should assume a part of the fiscal responsibility for these costs. The city, of course, is left the political alternative of attempting to have the function performed at the state level and, as already pointed out, in a good number of states it has been moved to this level.

---

[15] For a comprehensive description of the cooperative techniques which are emerging in metropolitan areas see Roscoe Martin, *Metropolis in Transition,* Housing and Home Finance Agency, Washington, 1963.

[16] "Some Fiscal Implications of Metropolitanism," in *Metropolitan Issues: Social, Governmental, Fiscal,* Guthrie S. Birkhead, ed. (Syracuse University, Maxwell Graduate School, 1962), p. 77.

Another alternative is to retain the expenditure responsibility at the local level and yet reduce the direct costs to the local taxpayer by having the service more generously aided by the state.

Again, the significant calculation for the local official is the determination of the interest of his local jurisdiction. Because of the different governmental systems which surround each local official, it is not possible to predict the impact of the sum of the decisions made by all local officials in a particular urban area on the general well-being of the whole area. The only accurate generalization is that if the interests of the whole area are served it is a result of chance rather than design.

On the other hand, it should not be assumed, as it often is, that the general interest of a spread city is necessarily damaged by a fragmented decision environment. The outcome depends, of course, on how that interest is defined. For example, it is quite possible that the multiplicity of school districts in a spread city causes competition among these districts to provide high quality education. The result could well be a higher average quality of education for the area than would result from a one-jurisdiction education system. On the other hand expenditures might be lower in a one-jurisdiction system. For other functions the result could be the opposite. In the case of fire protection, for example, it would often be the case that quality of service over the whole area would be improved if there were a one-jurisdiction system, but expenditures probably would be higher. These results would follow from the professionalization of the service and the water supply requirements it would impose throughout the spread city area.

Jurisdictional Conflict and the County

These illustrations point up again one of the major characteristics of most spread-city governmental systems: the impact of decisions by one jurisdiction on the neighboring jurisdictions. The present system has no decision-making focus below the state to resolve conflict situations which emerge from this system. The potential for conflict has led many to advocate the adoption of some kind of metropolitan-wide government.

There is neither space nor the inclination to argue the merits or demerits of this proposal. It is enough to say that it is politically impossible, in most of our metropolitan areas, to accomplish this kind of fundamental change. Further, apart from the political issue surrounding metropolitan government, there are some positive virtues in attempting to adjust present local governmental systems in a way which will make it possible for them to resolve their conflicts of interest.

The unit most able, outside of New England, to assume a large role in performing this responsibility is the county. This unit is the most encompassing jurisdiction in many of America's spread cities. Leaving aside the special New England situation,[17] the county does include all the other types of local jurisdiction: towns, municipal corporations, school districts, special districts and authorities. There are, of course, metropolitan areas which include more than one county and emerging from this fact is the necessity for inter-county cooperation in multi-county spread cities. Within these larger areas the counties are sufficiently diverse within their own boundaries that the leaders are more likely to understand the interdependence of the area than is true with small urban town and village officials who, of necessity, see their jurisdiction's interests in provincial terms. Their social and economic homogeneity makes such provincialism inevitable.

Another advantage is that the county is a strong unit politically. The party system is normally based on the county committee. This relationship of the county to the political party system should enhance its ability to accomplish changes through the state legislature.

Despite the county's advantages in jurisdictional and political terms it has disadvantages relative to its power and structure. The county is weak, structurally, in a variety of ways. First, and perhaps most important, it often lacks an executive head. It is governed, in some parts of the country, by a board made up of representatives from the townships within the county and these representatives are likely to take their township responsibilities more seriously than their county obligations. In other sections of the country the county board, although representative of only county interests possesses some of the weaknesses of the city-commission form of government. Another structural weakness is caused by the election of many administrative officials. Such elections provide these officials with independent political bases and restrict the board's potential for county-wide administrative leadership. In terms of power the county's primary role to date, as agent of the state and its rural background, has tended to restrict the amount of general legislative power granted to it by the state.

If reform is needed a means should be found of capitalizing

[17] It is interesting to note that Connecticut, since abolishing its counties, has found it useful to establish regional planning units.

on the county's jurisdictional and political advantages while overcoming its power and structural weaknesses. The role of the federal government through its planning grants could help with this strengthening as could appropriate state policies.

SUMMARY

The spread city does impose a new environment on the local administrator. His task of finding the interest of his jurisdiction is made immensely complicated by this new form of human settlement. Further, the fragmentation of government within the spread city guarantees that policies for the area will be the sum of the individual policies of the jurisdictions which exist within it, plus whatever policy imposition is made by the state or encouraged by the federal government.

The federal government has an increasing role in these areas but thus far has developed no coherent policy orientation toward them. It is possible that there is beginning to emerge at the federal level some concern for such coherence —as expressed, for example, in the recently imposed planning requirements in many substantive programs,[18] plus the potential role of the Senate-passed bill requiring advisory metropolitan-wide planning agencies.[19]

As the federal government moves more and more into the provision of aid to local governments and develops planning requirements to qualify for such aid, its role in the state-local systems and local sub-systems will be enhanced. Its impact will obviously vary from system to system.

Over-all, the present systems of government in the United States lack uniformity. For the local administrator this characteristic requires the development of a strategy and a set of tactics which fit his own system. For the student of government the need is to develop a way of classifying governmental systems which aids in understanding the public policies that emerge from them. The variables which must be included in such a classification (there undoubtedly are others) are:

[18] See Advisory Commission on Intergovernmental Relations, *Impact of Federal Urban Development Programs on Local Government Organization and Planning,* 1964, Government Printing Office, Washington, D. C.

[19] For a discussion of the implications of this bill see *Metropolitan Planning:* Hearings Before the Sub-committee on Intergovernmental Relations of the Committee on Government Operations, U. S. Senate, Eighty-Eighth Congress, First Session, 1963.

(1) The allocation of expenditure and revenue responsibilities between state and local governments and between local governments
(2) The system of state aid
(3) The nature of the property tax
(4) The degree of functional inclusiveness
(5) Geographic size of local jurisdictions
(6) The jurisdictional assignment of land use and other controls

A realistic analysis of the behavior of local officials and the policies they pursue in the spread city must take into account the unique mix of these factors. It is this mix which constitutes the decision-making framework of state-local governmental systems.

Conurbation Holland

PROFESSOR JAC. P. THIJSSE*

1. LOCATION OF THE REGION IN THE NETHERLANDS

Conurbation[1] Holland consists of a cluster of towns in the western part of the Netherlands (See Figure 1). These towns are grouped in two lobes that together form a more or less urbanized area in the shape of a horseshoe. All these towns date from the middle ages—some are still older. For centuries they were quite independent of each other, except for competition. During the last ten years, as a consequence of their growth, they became interdependent and at present form *one* Conurbation.

* Chairman, Faculty of Comprehensive Planning, Institute of Social Studies, The Hague, Holland, 1958– ; formerly Head of the Central Physical Planning Office, Dutch East Indies, 1945–50; Professor of Physical Planning, Sanitary Engineering, Highway Engineering, etc., Technical Faculty, University of Bandung, 1950–54; General Advisor, Netherlands Government Physical Planning Service, 1954–58; and Deputy Rector, Institute of Social Studies, The Hague, 1959–65. He was graduated as a civil engineer from the University of Delft, and has contributed to various planning and geographic journals in Holland as well as to the Regional Science Association Papers and UN publications on housing and planning.

[1] Conurbation is a group of cities with strong interrelations within moderate distance of each other, but separated by rural areas.

FIGURE 1. Situation of Conurbation Holland in Western Europe

The northeastern lobe of the Conurbation covers an area which follows one of the waterways from the Rhine to the North Sea coast (See Figure 2). The sequence of towns includes Utrecht, Amersfoort, the Gooi area, Amsterdam, the Zaan area, the Ymond area and Haarlem. The waterway which forms the spine of this lobe is altogether artificial. The southwestern lobe follows another waterway from the Rhine to the North Sea; only its most westerly part is artificial. This is the most important waterway giving access to northwestern Europe. In this part of the Conurbation are Gorcum, Dordrecht, Rotterdam, Schiedam and Vlaardingen; in a northward branch we have Delft, The Hague and Leyden.

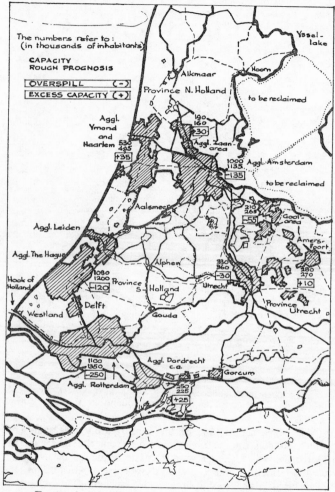

FIGURE 2. Possible Expansion of the Agglomerations

Being situated close to the world seas and having access to
the Rhine leading upstream to very important industrial and
mining areas in Germany and France have been two great
contributing factors in the development of the Conurbation.
The development of a cluster of important towns with strong

interrelations at this scale, is unique in its scale and unique in its shape. Activities in the field of commerce, industry, agriculture, transit and national government are most intensified in this part of the country. Consequently in the course of the ten years after World War II there has been a strong inland migration from the outer provinces to this centre of activities.

2. LOCATION OF THE REGION AS PART OF N.W. EUROPE

The greater part of the Netherlands is situated on a delta, which is formed by three rivers: the Rhine, the Maas, and the Scheldt. The Rhine, by far the most important, gives access to Germany, France and Switzerland, where the mining and industrial areas of the Saar and the Ruhr are of great international and economic importance. The river Maas, on the other hand, gives access to the mining and industrial areas of Belgium also accessible by the river Scheldt. A look at the population map of Europe shows that around Conurbation Holland the density is higher than in any other part of the continent. More than 170 million people live within a radius of 600 kilometers, with Conurbation Holland as the centre of the developed area. This is of the same degree of magnitude as the whole population of the USA.

Conurbation Holland is near conurbations in other countries. The distance between the centres of gravity of Conurbation Holland and the large Belgian cities (Antwerp, Brussels, Ghent) is only 115 kilometers; the distance between the centres of gravity of Conurbation Holland and the Ruhr area is 160 kilometers. It goes without saying that such close proximities cause strong interrelations. The areas in between are liable to be developed rapidly. Such development is spectacular in the province of North Brabant; but in the delta area between Conurbation Holland and the western part of the large Belgian cities, the development in the Netherlands has lagged behind.

After the big flood of February 1953 occurred in this delta, the central government decided to close the estuaries by a huge damming project. Upon completion of this work, which will take about twenty years, the opportunities for industrial and residential development in this area will show a much more satisfactory picture.

3. WHY THE CENTRAL GOVERNMENT TOOK PLANNING IN HAND

What was the justification for undertaking the comprehensive physical planning of the Conurbation? There were several reasons:

a. *Increase of population*

The annual increase in population in Conurbation Holland is about 1.35%. This means that within twenty-five years the population will have increased by 40%. In 1958 the urban areas of the Conurbation had a population of about four million. It was expected that by 1980 this population will have increased to five and a half or six million with resultant serious congestion and land will become even more scarce for every land use.

b. *Industrial development and its increase*

Although in the Conurbation the birth rate is lower than the average of the Netherlands, it is high in comparison with other European countries. Moreover the employment in the Conurbation offered by basic industries in the harbour areas and by other industries and activities which have strong relations with the basic industries, attracts many people from some of the outer provinces in the Netherlands. There has been a considerable inland migration up to 1960; the attraction of industries has been cumulative up to that date.

c. *Increase of transportation and traffic*

Increase of population and of industrial development causes increase of transportation and traffic.

d. *Increase of intensified agriculture*

As a consequence of the increase of population, the agricultural activities in the form of horticulture have been increasing as well. These are partly focussed on export through the great harbours or by aircraft to neighbouring countries.

e. *Unsuitable distribution of population over the country*

Industry, transportation and administration are for the greater part concentrated in the western part of the Netherlands. In many other provinces, industrial activities are developed but on a relatively much smaller scale. In the northeastern provinces livelihood is based for the major part on agriculture with a shortage of industries; unemployment appears first in these provinces and has caused many people to emigrate to the Conurbation. There is a definite threat that the towns of the Conurbation which at present are still separate will tend to grow together into one big muddled metropolis.

The Conurbation consists of many towns of moderate size; all these towns grow. As the distances between these towns are comparatively small, they are growing toward each other, and in many cases such towns have already met. They tend to form together a continuous ring of a *ciudad linear* with many centres. It is considered desirable to prevent this complete linkage in the future. The problems arising from the increase of activities in the Conurbation cannot be solved by measures of the local authorities. The Conurbation itself is situated in three provinces of the eleven provinces: North Holland and South Holland and Utrecht and is so powerful that it affects the whole country.

Thus, in 1951, the minister charged with physical planning in the Netherlands, created a committee consisting of representatives of various ministries, of the three provinces and the three large municipalities (Amsterdam, The Hague and Rotterdam) to study and report on the physical planning of the Conurbation as a unit. This method of planning is different from the usual manner decreed by Dutch law.

4. ORGANIZATION OF PHYSICAL PLANNING IN THE NETHERLANDS

a. *According to the legislation in force in the fifties*[2]

Municipal Plans. The municipalities have the obligation to draw up physical plans for their territory. These plans are submitted to the provincial government for approval. The provincial government is advised by the Provincial Physical Planning Service and by the provincial standing committee for physical planning. The composition of this committee warrants that interests of many facets, such as administration, housing, agriculture, transportation, forestry, water control and management, industry, etc. are fully taken into consideration. This prevents the municipal plans from being opposed to

[2] A new planning law was promulgated in August 1965, in which the organization has in principle been maintained.

the provincial and central government's interests. If the provincial government does not give its approval, the municipality has to modify the plan to meet the provincial requirements. The municipality, if unwilling to follow up the provincial suggestion, can appeal to the Crown.

Regional Plans. The provinces have the authority to draw up regional plans for specific parts of their domain. They do so when there are important and particular conditions requiring physical planning in an area covering more than one municipality. The regional plan is drawn up by the Provincial Physical Planning Service and submitted to the provincial government. If agreed to by the latter, it is then forwarded to the minister in charge of physical planning, who after having been advised by the Government Physical Planning Service and its standing committee, approves the plan or sends it back for modification.

By this arrangement the central government only judges regional plans and municipal plans. According to the legislation it does not plan itself.

b. *Special arrangements for Conurbation Holland*

This arrangement would not be satisfactory if the planning problems covered more than one province and were of importance to several of them. This is the reason why the aforementioned special arrangement was made for Conurbation Holland. The committee appointed by the minister established a technical working group consisting of the directors of the three provincial planning services and of the planning departments of Amsterdam, The Hague and Rotterdam, the highway and water-management services and railways, agriculture and the Zuyderzee Works. The Bureau of the Government Planning Service, which acts as a secretariat for the standing committee as well as for the Committee for the Conurbation, also joined the technical working group.

The committee's report, which contained a scheme and many suggestions, was approved by the national standing committee. It was submitted to the minister in February 1958, who in turn forwarded it to the Council of Ministers, where it has been discussed in the Physical Planning Council, which consists of seven ministers.

5. BASIC DATA OF THE PHYSICAL PLAN

a. *Population data of the Conurbation*

As has been mentioned the population of the Conurbation Holland is increasing at a rate of 1.35% and is concentrating. The density of population in the Netherlands is about 365 persons per square kilometer, which is one of the highest in the world. The density in the three western provinces (North Holland, South Holland and Utrecht) is more than 750 persons per square kilometer and in the municipalities, of which the Conurbation consists, more than 2,400 persons per square kilometer. The population in the area of the Conurbation grew from 600,000 in 1850 to more than four million in 1957. While in most other developed countries growth has slowed down and has even declined, the Netherlands people have maintained a high rate of increase throughout. Life expectancy is more than seventy years in the Netherlands. On the one hand, Holland has a relatively high birth rate (22%) and on the other, a low death rate (7.5%). Unless events prove different, a still further increase in the Dutch population can be expected. In practically all the neighbouring countries the population is showing a tendency to decrease.

In the Netherlands, the net reproduction factor is + 1.5. Even if the emigration of 30,000 persons per annum is taken into account, the period until 1980 will show an increase of about three million. It is expected that the population in the year 2000 may be twenty million or even more.

The population of Conurbation Holland will grow at about the same rate. If this rate and tendency continue during the period from 1956 until 1980, about half a million people would have immigrated into the Conurbation. Stopping internal migration and using the widest possibility of emigration on the international level, however, will not influence the development of industries and other activities in the Conurbation. If the Netherlands could not produce the people necessary for industrial development based on harbour activities and basic industries, imported labour would take the jobs. In view of the inevitability of European integration such a happening can be expected and this is what the development of the last five years clearly shows. The result of emigration has slowed down considerably and immigration from Italy, Spain, etc., has been constantly increasing. Consequently during the last three years the number of people entering the country has outnumbered the number of emigrants by 5,000 to 15,000. Recent prognoses based on economic development trends indicate a population of the Conurbation between five and six million in 1980 with the possibility of an even larger number thereafter.

b. *Prognosis of population based on economic tendencies for the individual agglomerations of the Conurbation*

The activities in the Conurbation are distributed over several urban agglomerations. Each of these agglomerations has still an independent life, and the functions of each may differ clearly from the other. For example, Amsterdam performs the function of commerce, Rotterdam of harbour activities and industries, while The Hague is the administrative city, seat of government and offices of private national and international companies. The increase of these different functions must be located next to or near the appropriate agglomeration. Based on the economic tendencies the probable increase of these agglomerations, being part of the Conurbation up to 1980 has been estimated, with the following result:

Utrecht with surroundings	¾ million
Amsterdam + Zaan area	1⅓ million
Haarlem + Ymond	½ million
Gooi area	¼ million
The Hague, Leyden and Delft	1¼ million
Rotterdam including Schiedam, Vlaardingen, etc.	1⅓ million
Dordrecht etc.	¼ million (See Figure 2)

6. TO WHAT WILL DEVELOPMENT LEAD WITHOUT THE APPLICATION OF PROPER PHYSICAL PLANNING AND THE IMPLEMENTATION OF PLANNING REGULATIONS

When no physical planning is done, the development follows natural tendencies.

Present tendencies are: (a) development of every agglomeration in all directions, (b) strongest development in the "magnetic" field between two agglomerations. Consequently the agglomerations Amsterdam and the Zaan area might well grow together with the agglomerations Haarlem and Ymond. Result: one city of more than two million people shaped in an approximately circular form. The agglomeration of The Hague, including that of Leyden and of Delft, might grow together with the agglomeration of Rotterdam; the open space between Rotterdam and Gouda would be filled up. Gouda, Alphen and Leyden would grow together and a new angular agglomeration would be the result. In a longer period the open space of the ring would be filled up. Ultimate result: one city of more than three million people. In the open space of the Conurbation, many still small villages would expand and result in the open area being completely filled in. Conclusion: one big amorphous, round-shaped agglomeration of dimensions similar to New York and with a population of more than ten million inhabitants. In the case of the Netherlands as a whole, the population distribution would become unharmonious.

Besides the formation of this enormous city, one could also expect that industry of all kinds would develop prolifically along the most important canals leading to the main harbours, especially near the coast. Areas which at present are still useful, or potentially fit, for recreation and agriculture would be taken up by industrial and residential uses. Essential and basically necessary activities near the coast would be hampered by such activities, which might as well be developed in other parts of the country.

7. TOWARDS WHAT ENDS SHOULD PLANNING ACTIVITIES AIM AS A CONSEQUENCE

a. In the Netherlands it is generally accepted, that agglomerations of very large sizes *are not desired*. One of the principles of planning in the Conurbation is that every inhabitant should live and work within a reasonable distance of an agricultural area or of large recreational areas. Consequently it was considered that the distance from any place in a residential or industrial agglomeration should be at the most four kilometers from open space (agricultural or recreational).

b. It is considered undesirable that agglomerations be of unlimited length without any articulation. Such articulations should divide the agglomerations in town units of not longer than ten to twelve kilometers and be formed by an agricultural or recreational strip of at least two kilometers wide. The space between the agglomerations should not be less than four kilometers. In this very flat, small-dimensioned country, this distance is psychologically felt as a wide-open space and a strong dividing element. Town enlargements violating these principles should be prohibited. Town-expansions directed toward the interior agricultural open area should only be allowed if the width of eight kilometers for the Conurbation at that place will not be exceeded. Stimulating activities and expansion of towns and villages in the interior area should not be encouraged. Another principle which is to be followed is that the expansion of residential and industrial development should be planned very economically in regard to use of land. The agricultural area on the one hand is losing to town, industrial and traffic development. On the other hand, since the thirteenth century the Netherlands have reclaimed land and this process is still going on; however after a few more decades this opportunity will be exhausted. Irrigation of the remaining wasteland may help for a short time, and agricultural intensification may increase the output to some extent, but in the end there will be only losses when no further reclamation is possible and residential and industrial expansion can only take place in former agricultural areas. The fact that very intensified and valuable agricultural land is not to be encroached on for economic reasons places some areas in the Conurbation out of the question for other development; for instance, the horticultural area, "The Westland," between The Hague and the Hook of Holland. This city of glass houses covers about the same area as The Hague itself, and a great part of its crop is exported. The agricultural "industry" is of strong economic importance to the Netherlands. The same is true of the flower industry especially in the district between Haarlem and Leyden, where the famous Dutch bulbs are grown and the flower area near Aalsmeer, from where flowers are constantly exported, via nearby Schiphol airport, to all countries in Europe and even outside Europe.

Along the coast of the North Sea is a strip of dunes which performs a triple function: (1) sea defense, (2) catchment area for water supply (retention), (3) recreation. The second function excludes building of residential or industrial premises.

There is another reason to put a brake on the increase of the Conurbation. The population should have areas for recreation not too far from where they are living so that unnecessary transport can be avoided. Consequently in and nearby the Conurbation extensive areas should be reserved for the recreation of the growing population. As a result of the expected rising economy and the increase of leisure time, the recreation area which will be required per head will have to be increased too. It will be difficult to meet this requirement even if the population of the Conurbation does not exceed five million.

If these limitations and principles are adhered to, it is quite clear that the Conurbation Holland cannot house any more than the number taken into account in the present municipal schemes. The total capacity of population planned for in these schemes is about five million people. Consequently if the population grows to five and a half to six million, a place must be found for the excess. If we exclude the interior area of the Conurbation, first, additional places might be found between successive agglomerations but keeping to our principle of four kilometers in between the agglomerations "on the ring." Second, there could also be made an effective outward expansion according to the British system of the New Towns and Expanding Towns. In the third place, the excessive population might be moved to the outer provinces, where density of population is considerably less. Employment in agriculture is getting scarcer with the adoption of modern methods and with the reallotment of land. Economic gains are increased by these measures, but fewer people are needed than before.

It would, therefore, be advisable to establish the overflow industries and business administrative headquarters preferably in the outer provinces where they should also find a satisfactory labour pool. Its effect would be to stop migration to the Conurbation of people who might be usefully employed in their own environments.

Decentralization of industries has already proved possible and successful. Many important industries have sprung up in the outer provinces, such as Philips at Eindhoven and in many other towns; textiles in Twente near the German border. The incentive for this kind of decentralization however has been the availability of plentiful and cheap labour. At present, however, labour in the outer provinces is not much cheaper than in the Conurbation. Thus new incentives had to be created to invite industries to establish themselves in the outer provinces. Therefore in the last few years the central government has developed an interministerial policy to promote the establishment of new industries in a limited number of centres in the outer provinces. The industrial climate in these centres has been greatly improved by better communication facilities, special facilities for new industries, and the extension of technical and vocational schools. Social and cultural conditions are being improved at the same time. As a result more than

50% of the newly established industries located in those areas in the course of the last six years. Consequently the migration flow to the Conurbation has stopped. In 1964 there was even an outward flow, although the natural increase of the population still caused a net increase at a much lesser rate.

The increase of the agglomerations based on present economic tendencies and compared with the capacity allowed for in the existing schemes shows the following overspill:

Agglomeration Amsterdam incl. Zaan and Gooi areas	160,000
Agglomeration Utrecht	30,000
Agglomeration The Hague (including Leyden and Delft)	120,000
Agglomeration Rotterdam etc.	250,000

(See Figure 2)

It is possible to expand Utrecht to the south to meet the overspill of 30,000. The agglomeration Rotterdam, as a consequence of the industrial and harbour development will have its extension along the New Waterway and to the west near to the coast of the North Sea.

For Amsterdam the possibilities are less favourable. It might be possible to expand the village Weesp between Amsterdam and the Gooi district, but this would only be for about 50,000 people. Particularly for the Gooi district, where there will be an overspill of about 55,000 people in 1980, it would be most welcome if use could be made of the new land reclaimed from the Ijsselmeer, but unfortunately these will not be ready to build on before 1980. From this reclaimed area, only the town of Lelystad can be used immediately to receive part of the overspill. For the first few years, use can be made of the expansion of some older towns in the province North Holland, 30 kilometers north of Amsterdam: Alkmaar and Hoorn.

Conditions are still less favourable in the agglomeration of The Hague. The Hague's growth is blocked in three directions: the North Sea to the west and parallel to the coast, the horticultural interests (Westland and bulb area) make growth impossible. As The Hague is the administrative centre of the Netherlands, the question arose whether it would be possible to establish a similar centre in the outer provinces which could take over part of the function of The Hague. The difficulties in developing such a town should not be underestimated.

Where efforts have been made to persuade the leaders of enterprises to establish their administrative headquarters in the outer provinces, the result has been mostly negative. Only a strong policy of the central government aiming at decentralization and setting the example itself could result in the realization of such an administrative centre.

Since The Hague area is practically filled by now, it has been necessary to develop a new urban area near The Hague. As the only possibility is inward toward the open central agricultural area, we will have to violate one of our principles. But there is no other choice possible. We should have started the idea of the second administrative centre more than fifteen years ago.

This new area should not be larger than necessary for its particular purpose. It should extend as little as possible into the open area. Communication with The Hague should be as easy and short as possible. Its locality and means of communications should not be placed in such a manner that it would attract inhabitants of other towns (Delft and Rotterdam). Its initial purpose should be to receive the overspill of The Hague caused by natural increase and slum clearance. A part of the ring around the old historical centre of The Hague, which was built during a poor period in architecture and town planning, needs clearance urgently. In this ring many small industries are mixed with residential houses. When these slums have been cleared the land will be destined for the expansion of the shopping and office centre as well as for green space and traffic (ringroad and parking areas). It will be impossible to rehouse the original industries and population in the rebuilt area. Most of them will have to move to another place.

As there was no agreement between the municipality, the central government and the province about the location of the new development, the discussions took a very long time. During that period one ambitious municipality near, but not near enough, to The Hague promoted its extension at such a rate that the authorities decided that it should perform the function of the intended development, although it did not meet completely the requirement which had been in view.

8. MAKING USE AND PROFITING BY NEW AREAS TO
   BE RECLAIMED: Zuiderzeepolders shortly, and the ex-
   ecution of other large technical projects (Delta Plan,
   Europoort).

a. *Zuiderzeepolders* (Reclamations)

It has been mentioned already that the work on the Zuiderzeepolders now under way or projected will be a help in receiving the overspill of Amsterdam. This help before 1980 will
be limited to Lelystad. After 1980 it was expected that the
work on all the proposed polders probably will be finished.
After their completion a great possibility for the development
of Amsterdam and the Gooi district will then have been created. This can be done without departing from our principles.
Along the canal between the two parts of the reclamations, industrial development can be developed. Along the south coast
of the new polder opposite the Gooi area, conditions will be
favourable for expansion by broadcasting and service industries.

b. *Delta Plan*

In 1953 there was an exceptionally high tide coinciding with
a strong hurricane (frequency ± 600 years). Some of the
dams in the southwestern provinces gave way, and large parts
of several polders were flooded. In order not to run such a
risk in the future, it was decided that the estuaries of the
delta should be closed by dams. Safety is the initial justification, but the consequences of dam building will extend much
further. The dams will provide excellent means of surface
transportation, so that the former islands in the delta will be
more easily accessible. The time at present needed to reach
Rotterdam from the islands will be decreased enormously. As
a result the potentiality for development of these areas will
increase accordingly. Up to now the activities in the islands
were mainly limited to fisheries and agriculture, although its
location between the Conurbation Holland and the centre of
Belgian activity (Antwerp, Brussels, Ghent) is most favourable for other more important purposes.

Further development depends mainly on better land transportation. The execution of this complete scheme will take a
long time; the last gap will not be closed until 1978. The advantage will—as in the case of the Zuiderzeepolders—come to

its full meaning in a later period. The isolation of the islands in the Delta area has already been minimized greatly by a new dam and two bridges by which all the islands have now been connected to the mainland, and by which support industrial development in the area will be speeded up. It will offer the possibility of a large new harbour area (Vlissingen Oost) in the Western Scheldt, which can take over part of the function of the port of Rotterdam where after a few decades no more land for extension will be available. In this way the development in the Delta area will help to avoid too much congestion in the southern part of the Conurbation.

Another important outcome of the damming of the estuaries will be the formation of a large freshwater basin, which is of great value to agriculture. As soon as some of the sea arms are dammed, new attractive possibilities for recreation will be available; there will be large areas for all kinds of water sport (yachting and sailing), and there will be many small islands and bathing beaches.

This will be very welcome because there is a considerable shortage of recreational areas in the Conurbation. The conditions in these new water sport areas will be so exceptionally favourable that they can be expected to become a considerable attraction to tourists from abroad.

Beautiful sailing possibilities and opportunities for shore recreation will also be created between the reclaimed Zuiderzeepolders and the existing countryside. To prevent the water level in the mainland being lowered as a result of the nearby low-lying polders, there will be canal lakes between polders and the mainland, which, besides their hydraulic function, will also serve as waterways for shipping and as recreation areas for water sports. In some of the polders, where the quality of the soil is not entirely suited to agriculture, a large area of new land will be used for recreational purposes. The Zuiderzee reclamation and the closing of the Delta will without doubt alleviate a great part of the congestion in later periods.

c. *New Subsidiary port of Rotterdam* (*Europoort*)

Another technical work of great importance, to further the development of the Conurbation and more particularly the harbour and industrial activities of the Rotterdam agglomeration, will be a new harbour entrance for deep draught vessels. There is a possibility that in connection with the new breakwaters a low part of the North Sea can be reclaimed and used for harbour and industrial development. This reclaimed land would be very expensive, but as it can be used for exceptionally deep draught vessels, its value will also be exceptional. This project is already in progress, although the exact area of the land to be reclaimed is still being studied.

9. DECENTRALISATION OF DOCK SPACE FOR DEEP SEA VESSELS

If the activities of the Conurbation become too intensified, decentralisation of port activities along deep water in other places where conditions are favourable must be carried out. This may be done at some future time in two places:

a. as mentioned above in the most southerly estuary of the Western Scheldt the technical works are already underway.
b. north of the present province North Holland on the Balgzand, which is planned to be reclaimed at a later period.

10. SUMMARY OF THE ORIGINAL SCHEME

The plan which as a result of the study of the Region was drawn up in 1958 is not statutory. It is advisory, and the planning committee suggested that provincial plans as well as municipal plans embody the essential principles of the over-all scheme.

A development scheme which is intended to give "a possible picture of the future development of the Conurbation" is given in a simplified version in Figure 3.

The land uses which are taken into account are:

a. residential and industrial zones
b. agricultural zone
c. horticultural zones of particular nature
d. zones for recreation
e. buffer zones between towns and agglomerations
f. lakes for water sports
g. nature reserves
h. airport
i. traffic connections

Here are some aspects of the general plan for land use:

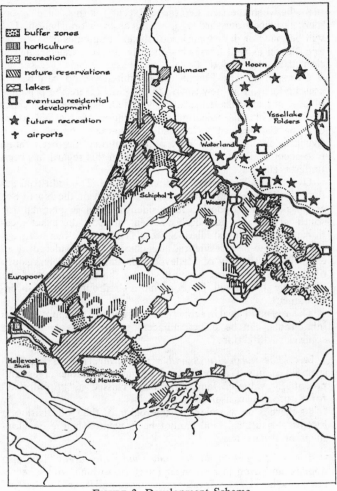

Legend:

- ▨ buffer zones
- ▥ horticulture
- ▦ recreation
- ▨ nature reservations
- ▱ lakes
- ▢ eventual residential development
- ★ future recreation
- ✦ airports

FIGURE 3. Development Scheme

a. *Residential and industrial zones*

The ultimate limit for 1980 has been set for the development of the present towns and agglomerations.

Plans for the overspill are:
For Amsterdam and the Gooi area: one limited develop-

ment between the two (Weesp). Except for this, all development is placed outward of the ring of the Conurbation. Use will be made of the expansion of the existing cities of Alkmaar and Hoorn as well as of new cities in the Ijsselmeer reclamation at a later period.

Overspill of The Hague for a limited period can be accommodated in a "new town" to the east. (Here the principle of outward expansion has to be violated, as there is no other choice.) With the indication and limitation of this new town, the establishment of a "second writing-desk" or administrative area in the eastern part of the country has been taken into account. But up till now no action in this regard has been undertaken.

Overspill of Rotterdam diverted outward. The industrial activities will be developed as near to the coast of the North Sea as possible (Europoort). Its residential area is planned for southward of this new harbour area. In 1958 the exact location was still being studied. Since a few years it has been decided that the new residential area should be considered as an extension of the city of Hellevoetsluis ± 10 kilometers south of the new Europoort harbour. Along the south bank of the Waterway there will be continuous harbour industrial development.

The overspill of Utrecht, which is limited to about 30,000 inhabitants, can be placed adjacent to the present city in a southward direction.

b. c. *The horticultural and agricultural area* has been respected as much as possible. The most valuable areas and potentially valuable land have been classed as "prohibited" for future urban use.

As there is no wasteland in the region of the Conurbation, a loss of agricultural land cannot be prevented in the development of urban areas.

d. e. f. *Recreation, buffer zones and water areas*. This also applies, and even in a stronger measure, to land with a recreational value. Urban development along and near the coast of the North Sea has been and will be detrimental to the existing recreation area. This is also the case in the development of the Gooi area and in Utrecht; the recreation area diminishes as the population increases. As a result the per capita availability of land for recreation diminishes very rapidly while actually the reverse is required. New recreational areas must be developed.

Good use can be made of new possibilities offered by reclamation in the Ijsselmeer and by the damming of the estuaries. Many other areas as well should be developed for this purpose, such as sites along the "Old Maas" south of Rotterdam and in "Waterland" north of Amsterdam. The buffer zones between towns and agglomerations will also fulfill an important function in this respect. Development of present recreational possibilities along the existing lakes in and near the region and a similar development along the borders of the new Ijsselmeer polders are also envisaged.

The agricultural inner area will also play an important role in this respect, along with the development of cycle paths and other amenities. One might also consider creating new recreation areas on submarginal rural farm land. In such cases conversion to recreational land use may be justified. Diminishing the area for agricultural land use might again necessitate intensive horticulture instead of ordinary (extensive) agriculture.

g. *Nature reserves* and recreation do not always go hand in hand. Nature reserves in many cases cannot be "for the enjoyment of the population." Their very nature prevents them from becoming an open playground. These special reserves must be considered of outstanding importance to nature investigation, natural science and history, zoology and botany.

h. i. *Traffic connections;* the development of the Conurbation and the diversion of population to other parts of the country will necessitate further development of traffic facilities: the railway system, highways and waterways. Some new railway connections will be necessary; e.g. a short cut from Amsterdam to The Hague via the area of Schiphol Airport, connections to the new harbour and industrial development west of Rotterdam and others. The railroad line which connects the towns forming the string on which the "pearls of the necklace" Conurbation have been threaded, performs a double function. Next to its use for long-distance traffic it will also be of outstanding importance for local traffic (commuting cannot be prevented). Consequently, as is already in process, the line has to be made four-tracked, and many small stops have to be added.

The highway system linking the agglomerations of the Conurbation and connecting it with the other parts of the country will need enlarging on an important scale in the near future. The number of motor vehicles keeps on growing at a high rate. It is estimated that the number of cars will probably be multiplied by five within a quarter of a century. For outward highway connections, effective use can be made of the new Ijsselmeer polders and the new dams in the estuaries. As for the waterways, the most important will be the doubling of the "New Waterway" and its connection with the hinterland. New canals near Amsterdam will avoid further congestion in the harbours near the heart of that city, while a new connection between the North Sea Canal and the North-Hollands Canal will facilitate the development of Alkmaar as a receiving town for population overspill.

The waterways between the Ijsselmeer polders and the existing land, as well as the canals which separate these polders, will also perform important functions; they will strongly aid in the development of the towns which will be established along their borders.

11. RESULTS OF THE ORIGINAL SCHEME

Since 1958 seven years have elapsed. It is interesting to review in how far the principles which were formulated in the report have been maintained.

The most important principles were: (a) to maintain the open inner area of the Conurbation and (b) to control the development of the various agglomerations in each other's direction.

The experience of the past seven years has shown that notwithstanding the strong Dutch planning legislation, it is very difficult to prevent semi-urban activities especially in areas between agglomerations.

Moreover, during the last decade intensive horticulture in the close environment of the agglomerations has shown a tremendous growth. Large areas of greenhouses have come into being, spoiling the former beautiful dairy-farming landscape. Consequently the area useful for future recreation is already diminishing rapidly.

There are also many open areas in the Conurbation—more than had been foreseen in 1958—which have to be converted to urban land use. The growth of the agglomerations of Amsterdam and Rotterdam will require more land than originally foreseen because of modern ideas of lesser population density in urban areas than prewar standards.

Moreover, there is a strong pressure by the municipality of Amsterdam to acquire land along the North Sea Canal for harbour industrial activities; much more than had been foreseen in 1958. It has also been proved difficult to control the growth of residential and industrial activities in small municipalities in close to the various urban agglomerations.

12. NEW ADMINISTRATIVE MEASURES ARE NEEDED

If full use is to be made of the suggestions contained in the study and by the planning committee, the central government must agree to the essential principles. It should also adopt a strong policy aiming at the realisation of these principles. Therefore the Council of Ministers (to which the report was presented) as a body and as individual ministers should devote their impartial interest to the carrying out of the proposed development.

Further it must be adopted as law and supported by the Dutch Parliament. And as mentioned above, provincial regional plans and municipal schemes should be undertaken in accordance with the principles of the planning committee. It is not expected that all this can be achieved without difficulties. Interests conflict often and the feelings of local autonomy and independence are very strong. Nevertheless, the tendency toward integration is becoming more manifest generally, so that municipalities are more willing to subordinate their individual characters to blend into the general well-being.

The fact that the agglomerations of the Conurbation have grown exceeding the municipal borders has clearly shown that our present local authorities are too small to cope with the present scale of development of urban growth. As in many other countries the small scale and the large number of such municipalities greatly hamper the planning process. Co-operation between two or more municipalities has not been successful in most cases where it has been applied. Although removing the old small-scale pattern and replacing it by a large-scale rational pattern seems politically not yet feasible.

As an effort to overcome those difficulties, in the Rotterdam area a new kind of local authority "the district" has been set up recently. It comprises a great number of municipalities (which will remain) and it has limited authority. It is governed by an elected district council with a high official in the chair who is appointed by the central government. The experience which will be gained by this new "metro" administrative setup, will certainly be useful for other parts of the country where similar conditions exist.

13. FURTHER CONSEQUENCES

The planning activities for the Region of the Conurbation Holland were not concluded with this report and scheme of 1958. Since implementation of the proposed scheme will affect other parts of the Netherlands, it will be necessary to study the impact on them as well. This study has already been started.

One of the points to be covered is the "second writing-desk."[3] Should it be established and where; how large should it be and would it be wise or advisable to add a university to it? *A second topic is* the more harmonious distribution of industry and population over the whole country; what would be the desirable form of distribution and by what means could it be achieved? Necessary improvements in the technical, economic, social and cultural fields ought to be studied in this regard. *A third subject* would be the possibility of distributing the harbour activities for deep-draught vessels.

Many of these subjects require the study and incorporation of interests of a larger area than the national territory. This will entail the liaison and co-operation of countries such as Germany, France and Belgium. It will be seen that European integration is not only essential in the field of economics but a dire necessity where physical planning is concerned and where the welfare of the population depends so much on each other.

[3] An administrative city.

Building Blocks for the New York Tri-State Metropolitan Region

ARTHUR T. ROW*

I. INTRODUCTION

In August 1961, the governors of the states of Connecticut, New Jersey and New York formed, by joint action, the Tri-State Transportation Committee. The committee was charged

* Professor of City Planning and formerly Department Chairman, Yale University. A graduate of Harvard, he holds an M.C.P. from that institution. Formerly Planning Director of the Portland, Maine, Plan-

both with developing long range solutions to transportation and development problems of the interstate New York Metropolitan Region, and with providing immediate recommendations for present and imminent problems.

Both long range and immediate action work programs were therefore set up by the committee staff. The work partially reproduced in this article was an early aspect of the long range program.

In the summer of 1963 I was asked, as a planning consultant, to undertake a quick reconnaissance appraisal of the Region and to submit some development ideas. In the fall I presented my conclusions to the Committee in oral form, supplemented by graphics, and in January 1964, I submitted the final written report.

City planning is a selective art expressed in developmental terms. All art is selective of course. But in the practice of planning we have been put off by an attempt to be comprehensive. Planners had been led into this for a variety of reasons. Exploration of the several roots and causes for this diversion would be a fascinating essay in itself. Let me simply say that the central theme of the following report is selectivity. I have attempted to concentrate on those elements of the metropolitan society which in my view will have the most significant influence in shaping the whole. Some are forcing and constricting, like a park system; others are growth centers for spawning secondary growths, like universities.

Over half of the full report is devoted to an analysis of the Region's present structure and dynamics, and quantitative estimates expressed spatially of the Region's future pressures in terms of population and employment. Important as these other chapters are in appraising the 1963 situation of the Region, and in providing a point of departure for the development plan ideas, the chapter on proposals stands reasonably well by itself. Therefore, with minor editing, and with the excision of

ning Board, he became subsequently Assistant Director of the Detroit Metropolitan Area Traffic Study (1953) and Assistant Executive Director of Philadelphia's City Planning Commission (1955) as well as lecturer at the University of Pennsylvania before coming to Yale in 1961; recently he has been on leave with the Ford Foundation team in Calcutta.

This article is an adaptation of certain concluding recommendations made as consultant to the New York-New Jersey-Connecticut Tri-State Transportation Committee, 1965, in *A Reconnaissance of the Tri-State Area*.

the last section on *re*development ideas, only the proposals for regional development are reproduced here.

II. SOME OBJECTIVES FOR A REGIONAL PLAN

Most of the goals of physical development planning are self-evident: to reduce pain in the environment; to improve the livability of the environment, and its workability; to reduce costs; to seek an environment that inspires and lifts the spirit.

Although planning is concerned with the total environment, choices must be made as to the situations in which the intervention of government will produce the greatest returns in terms of the goals set down above. In the Tri-State Region these situations are represented by two poles: the older built-up areas in varying stages of decay and obsolescence; the underdeveloped land on the periphery and in the interstices of the urbanized area. These are poles along the same scale, related to and influencing each other.

Since the Tri-State Transportation Committee is dealing with the problems of growth and change at the regional level, the objectives selected for pursuit should be demonstrably regional. The elements which the committee chooses to influence should be those components of the Region which are regional, as distinct from local, in character and influence.

Since we are by definition people of our time, we must deal with the artifacts of our time in the arena of the pressures of our time. There are no magic technological devices that will suddenly improve the livability of our urban regions; there are no simple political inventions that will suddenly ease the road to a more inspiring setting for our daily lives.

A few elements of regional structure have been selected as the critical components that will influence the total development pattern. They will be recognized from the first chapter in the full report: physiography; centers; industrial concentrations; transportation; and open space. Housing is not included for two reasons. First, it is assumed that, for the most part, housing is a derivative in location from these elements. Second, it is recognized that a variety of housing possibilities exists relative to the over-all structure, and these possibilities are best realized at a local scale of design.

Two objectives have been sought in the diagrammatic arrangement on the land of the selected regional components.

First, any plan for the Region must start with an objective

of taking advantage of the important features in the natural landscape.

Second, a plan for the Region built upon emphasis at the regional level of selected components of regional development must seek to arrange these in a manner which provides a basic framework or structure to which all the elements of the physical environment can be related, and, at the same time, an arrangement that permits variety and flexibility in the growth patterns of the more local units over a long period of time.

III. SOME PROPOSALS FOR REGIONAL DEVELOPMENT AND REDEVELOPMENT

The sequence of the discussion of the components of the plan has no significance. It simply represents the fact that everything cannot be said at once. All of the proposals are interdependent and should be thought of in terms of a single sketch.

Figure 1 is a distillation in sketch form of the significant topographic features of the Region. This is the natural setting for development. These dominant variations in the Region's natural landscape should be seen as opportunities for interest and drama in the Region's development. Maps such as this were once given such titles as "Barriers to Development" in planning reports. They are deterrents to the natural flow of developments as led by the real estate entrepreneur. But, in terms of public policy, such a point of view is grossly myopic. It simply does not make sense to permit the easy way in the first cycle of development and then to put tremendous effort into the resolution of problems that arise in succeeding cycles. There is no guarantee that a thoughtful utilization of natural landscape will reduce rates of obsolescence and decay. But there is every reason to believe that a sympathetic relation of new development to the land will, by virtue of providing a more interesting and in some cases inspiring setting for major regional activities, improve their first worth and reduce their rate of obsolescence. Any plan for the Region, therefore, must start with an objective of taking advantage in the public interest of the important features in the natural landscape. This is an objective to be sought in both renewal and in new development.

There are a number of ways by which order, amenity and common sense can be built into new suburban development. The most inclusive method would be the planning and con-

TRI-STATE REGION RECONNAISSANCE - SUMMER 1963

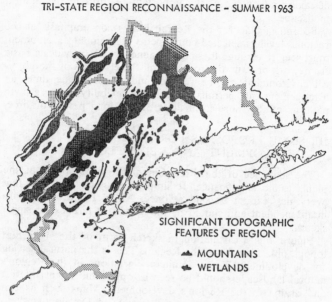

SIGNIFICANT TOPOGRAPHIC
FEATURES OF REGION

🔺 MOUNTAINS
🦐 WETLANDS

FIGURE 1

struction of complete new towns or cities on the periphery of the presently developed area. But if this approach is to be taken, then a great machinery must be developed for the necessary land acquisition and control, planning and design, and construction and early management. In Great Britain, the Western nation best known for this kind of development, only 130,000 dwelling units of some 3,500,000 built in the postwar period were actually located in new towns by 1963. Despite the tremendous effort made in this direction, one can question the extent to which this development has affected in any significant way the structure and development of greater London.

The new towns concept as represented by Western European policy is rejected here basically because it is believed to be an oversimplified solution to the needs of suburbia. Suburbia is both an extension of the urbanized area and a reorganization of the urbanized area. Viewed as a whole, the urban region is an intricate mixture of activities in space, and the regional planning task is to rationalize this arrangement without violating the basic internal relationships. In this mixture certain activities are arranged in a crude hierarchy of service area and area of influence. It is the argument here that identification of, and concentration upon, the planning of the primary elements in this hierarchy is a more effective route toward improving the urban region than concentrating effort upon the planning and design of discrete new towns.

There is another reason for choosing the method of selective activity concentration over a new towns program. In a structure of government in which several levels have identifiable responsibilities, it appears more reasonable to devise a planning and development process in which each extension of government can play its role responsive to the particular needs of its constituency, than by the creation of a machinery that cuts across the entire scale of planning and design.

The aim, then, is to identify those activities at the regional and subregional level in the hierarchy whose placement will influence if not produce an order in the Region, activities whose placement and development can be effected with modest changes in the present machinery of government in the Region. This means that the selected activities are clearly within the public realm insofar as location, site acquisition and planning, and capital investment are concerned.

These are: new centers; a major transportation system; major industrial concentrations; an open space system.

New Centers

Why new centers? What is their composition? In what way do they meet the criterion of public investment?

There are four reasons for making a proposal for new centers. These are:

a) A limited number will, in some form, be needed to perform a regional service for a variety of purposes;

b) They will tend to emerge anyway over time, but in the natural course of events many of the "natural" components will locate apart from one another,[1] and a long and costly period of readjustment will probably follow before the primary central places emerge;

c) They provide a base for the geographic arrangement of the new elements in the landscape to which other activities will tend to relate;

d) They represent a rather simple idea at the regional and

---

[1] Particularly if we look back at much of the incoherent pattern of postwar commercial development.

state scale that can be initiated by government exercising its present powers and responsibility.

These centers are conceived as central places for population service areas in the order of 500,000 people. Thus they would contain an array of activities suitable to the service of such a population. This array would include retail and consumer service activity, professional and business service activity, public and quasi-public services, certain kinds of industrial and industry-related activities. They are not simply regional shopping centers, although this function is included.

How can such an array be developed utilizing the initiative of government within our present system of powers?

It is proposed that the motivating force be the development of twelve new universities.[2] The university is rapidly becoming much more closely related to and involved in our society and our economy. The research parks at Stanford and at the Triangle Research Institute in North Carolina are examples. Sterling Forest represents an attempt in the New York Region. But these examples are quite simple ones. There is no question that continued growth in our economy requires an increase in the proportionate input of brain power . . . of which by definition, if not in fact, the university represents the seat.

Before spinning out this argument further, it is useful at this point to undertake some simple arithmetic to establish a quantitative base for the proposal.

It is forecast that the most rapidly growing segment of the population of the Region over the next twenty-five years will be the college and university age group. This group (18–24) is expected to double (91%). The next largest increase is expected in the next younger age group, those from 5–17 years of age. The college group is projected to increase by slightly over a million persons during this period.

Present enrollment in institutions of higher education in the Region is 350,000.[3] The Region is presently operating at a slight deficit, that is, more students are attending colleges and universities outside the Region than are entering the Region for such study. Enrollment rates in the United States appear to have increased at about 1 percentage point per year in the

[2] Twelve is not a magic number but the scale is probably at the order of 10–15. The number 12 is a derivative from the simple arithmetic shown.

[3] Material in this paragraph is taken from working papers prepared by Professor Netzer for the Regional Plan Association.

1950s. The Heald Committee investigating college and university needs for the State of New York estimated that enrollment would roughly triple between 1960 and 1985 in the state. The percentage of the population in the 18–24 age group enrolled in institutions of higher education in the Tri-State Region was 27%. If it is assumed that the rate of increase of enrollment between 1960 and 1985 is 50%, then 41% of the 18–24 age group would be enrolled in 1985. This would mean an enrollment figure of 970,000.

In summary, it is expected that the demand for higher education by 1985 will be in the order of 900,000 to one million students in the Region. If the mid-point of the range is taken, 950,000, then the Region must be prepared to support 600,000 additional students in college and graduate education. This is probably a conservative estimate. This demand will place a very heavy burden upon our economy, but it is a burden that must be borne if the economy is to continue to grow. It is critical that the impact be met by as effective and economic a use of facilities as possible.

Let us assume that one half of the new increment (300,000 students) can be educated in existing institutions. This assumption means that by some combination of new construction and changes in educational techniques, existing institutions can double their present load. This assumption still leaves 300,000 students to be absorbed by wholly new institutions.

We know from experience that a university can function with 25,000 students. This is the order of the magnitude of the University of California at Berkeley, certainly one of the top-ranking universities in the world. Columbia University is slightly smaller. New York University and the City College both exceed 25,000. Let us assume, therefore, that we shall invest in the Region in twelve new universities of approximately 25,000 students each to meet the demand of this remaining 300,000.

It is proposed that these new universities be largely day schools, that is that they be mainly non-residential universities. It is difficult to conceive how to meet this tremendous impact in residence universities because of the cost involved in providing such facilities and their services.

As largely day schools these universities must be accessible to daily commuters in the Region. Further, the number of full-time as distinct from part-time students is impossible to predict. These schools therefore, must be reasonably accessible to part-time job opportunities, and, conversely, as part-time educational opportunities. They must, in short, be urban universities. The rural setting sought out by new schools in the nineteenth century would not be suitable for the projected metropolitan needs.

It has been asserted above that the university is rapidly becoming heavily involved in the daily life of our society and its economy. Faculty are working in varying capacities in government and private industry. Professionals and executives in government and industry are increasingly entering universities as visiting lecturers and part-time teachers. Indeed, if one looks at the age distribution projected for the Region from which the university demand is drawn, one may properly ask where the teachers are going to come from. Whereas the college-age people are expected to increase by 90% by 1985, the working-age people are expected to increase by less than 20%. Considerable ingenuity will have to be exercised in staffing the teaching corps of the Region's institutions of higher education. It is reasonable to believe that two of the sources from which they will be drawn are the increasing number of educated women, and the persons working at professional tasks in government and industry. In each case, the need for proximity to other urban activities is self-evident.

It may be useful, before passing on to additional discussion of these new urban centers, to describe the kind of university center being proposed. These are not Princetons and Dartmouths . . . small private resident universities, dominating small towns. Rather they are big public universities woven into the fabric of the growing urban areas in the great metropolitan region surrounding New York. Perhaps the closest analogue is the state university program of California, where many state colleges and universities are organized and placed to meet state needs. In the case under discussion, however, three states are involved, each of which will undoubtedly develop its own program. The variety that would be so fostered is an attractive aspect of the proposal. The sites for these new institutions should be chosen with the end in view that these are major components of new cities in the Region, not simply university sites with their own limited criteria.

Other Central Elements

In the postwar shopping center construction boom, three levels of center have developed. They have been variously classified, but the terms "local," "intermediate" and "regional" are generally accepted as descriptive of their size and service function. The population market area of the last and largest of the three starts at 100,000 people and many run to 1,000,000. Assuming a population of 500,000 per center, twelve such centers could be developed.

Many of the suburban centers built solely as retail and consumer service operations are now attracting other activities, particularly offices, but including medical services and apartment houses. Besides retail stores and offices and apartments, the older and established business centers have included an array of public and quasi-public uses: churches, libraries, YMCAs, and the like. Postwar shopping centers (even the largest regional centers) have not included these other quasi-public activities, presumably because the centers have been built at one time as an integrated retail complex, by one entrepreneur. Provisions generally have not been made in the designs for the insertion of other activities over time. And indeed, from the point of view of the entrepreneur interested in return on investment, there is no reason to carry reserve unused land for ultimate use by these other activities. But if it is argued that a major component of metropolitan structure is the regional center, then it follows that there are more interests than simply those of the entrepreneur. It is so argued here, particularly in view of the longer-term pay-off of the community in contrast to the shorter-term turnover by a developer.

These proposed new business centers would not be simply regional shopping centers in the mode of the 1950s, but would be more inclusive developments, and more intricate, including a broad array of office and institutional activity, public and quasi-public services, parking, transit and residence. Even certain types of industrial development, an element that will be discussed separately below, could be related to these regional business centers.

The centers proposed are illustrated on Figure 2. The locations are diagrammatic, but they are not solely illustrative. The first step in their location was arithmetic: the geographic distribution that would provide reasonable service for the projected new population. The distribution of net new persons as estimated by the Regional Plan Association is summarized by sector of the Region in the accompanying Table 1.

In selecting locations for new centers a first question is whether to recognize the importance of older centers and build upon them or to seek out vacant land.

TRI-STATE REGION RECONNAISSANCE – SUMMER 1963

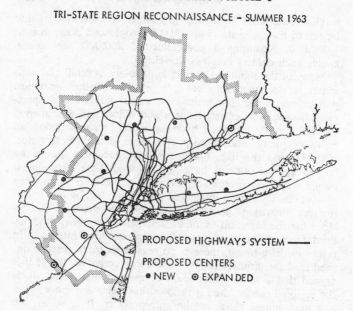

PROPOSED HIGHWAYS SYSTEM ——

PROPOSED CENTERS
● NEW   ◉ EXPANDED

FIGURE 2

TABLE 1

PROPOSED DISTRIBUTION OF NEW CENTERS BY SECTOR

Sector	1960–1985 Population Increment	No. of Universities[1]	No. of Regional Business Centers[2]
East	1,486,000	3	3
North	1,548,000	3	3
Jersey North	1,126,000	2	2
Jersey South	2,092,000	4	4
TOTAL	6,252,000	12	12

[1] @ 25,000 students each
[2] with a service area of approximately 500,000 persons each

There are certain advantages in selecting older centers. Some regional facilities already exist in varying stages of maturity. Existing transport facilities support these centers. Their market areas already exist and can be extended. A major regional investment would provide a strong input into the frequently thin re-use potential of these older centers. But there are significant disadvantages to this choice. Redevelopment is a slow and sometimes painful process, and the readjustments required of these older cities would be considerable. The existing supporting facilities would in most cases prove to be inadequate and would require major reconstruction, particularly in transportation. Design flexibility and alternatives would be limited; development patterns are set. Since few significant centers, and none of the composition under discussion here, have developed in the postwar period, the chief centers from which reasonable choices might be made are so surrounded by suburban development that their influence on new development would be limited.

The advantages of selecting vacant land locations are several. Planning and design flexibility is maximized. The potential for influencing the composition and form of new secondary development is considerable. New service and supporting facilities can be designed and built to the latest standards. Development could proceed more rapidly and probably at lower cost. But there are disadvantages too. Unless such new centers were well separated in space from older ones they would eat into the market and service areas of the older ones thus rendering more difficult an already tough task of renewal in these older cities. In the early years, the new center would develop its potential more slowly because it would not have an established market and service area. Their development would be particularly sensitive to the timing of supporting facilities . . . water, sewer, power, but most particularly transportation. Not least, a viable relationship with the existing local government would have to be worked out.

In the selection actually undertaken, diagrammatic as it is intended to be, the pros and cons, sector by sector, were tested as alternatives were considered. In this process one major criterion was brought to bear. The location chosen, whether vacant or developed, should be such that the new center could serve an existing market and service area but at the same time have sufficient vacant land in its immediate environs for expansion and for the new secondary development that would be influenced by the center. To this end the major new highways proposed were an important consideration.

It is clear from Figure 2 that the selected older centers are located in the historic and urbanized development corridor of the eastern seaboard. In the highly urbanized sectors southwest and northeast of New York City, vacant land choices are limited. Further, it is extremely difficult to find locations whose development would not detract actively from the older cities struggling to renew themselves. Therefore, in this corridor, the three locations chosen are old independent cities, each of which already plays a subregional role, and each of which is sufficiently distant from the urbanized area surrounding Manhattan to have vacant land in its own immediate environs. The three cities are Trenton and New Brunswick, New Jersey, and New Haven, Connecticut.

The "vacant" land choices comprise the majority of the new center locations. In their selection it was attempted to find locations near the periphery of the presently urbanized area, so that the center would be able to tap an existing market in its early years but would have a large generally undeveloped tributary area within which to build its clientele over the long future. Starting in Monmouth County, New Jersey, and reading clockwise to the northward, the locations are:

1) Monmouth County in the vicinity of Freehold.
2) Somerset County in the vicinity of Somerville.
3) Morris County (west) in the vicinity of Netcong.
4) Morris County (east) in the vicinity of Pequannock.
5) Orange County in the vicinity of Sterling Forest.
6) Putnam County in the vicinity of Camp Smith.
7) Fairfield County in the vicinity of Danbury-Ridgefield.
8) Suffolk County (east) in the vicinity of Huntington.
9) Suffolk County (west) in the vicinity of Brookhaven.

A word about site size may be in order so that the reader may place this proposal in scale. Where new centers are being proposed, sites in the order of five square miles should probably be acquired. These would constitute the central places of intensively developed urban subregions of a hundred or more square miles, and tributary areas of even greater size. In other words, this proposal is neither a proposal for new towns nor for new shopping centers, but for the centers of major new cities.

The conceptual basis is simple. These centers are new major structural elements of the Region. As such their location and planning is a matter of clear public interest at the level of the State governments acting in concert for the Region. Major public facilities at the level of regional service will have to be built in any case, particularly universities and medical centers. These should be located where they can perform economic and effective service. This means that they are inescapably related to the regional transportation system. They will in turn have considerable influence on the location and pattern of ancillary facilities . . . particularly housing which is the largest user of land. These centers are conceived also as the major new business centers of the Region. Again, although in this case most of the actual construction and operation of the units is a matter for the private sector of the economy, the location of these facilities is a matter of public concern. Moreover, since these are regional centers serving many municipalities, it is clear that a higher level of government such as the state must be responsible for the difficult location decision. The location and character of the secondary development that will be generated, of course, will largely be determined by private entrepreneurs and approved by local governments in the course of the exercise of local zoning and other powers. Further the public and private central place facilities at the level of regional service are . . . interdependent, and their locations should foster and facilitate this . . . interdependency. Therefore, it is argued that the governments should purchase land for the development of the necessary public facilities and build these facilities, and that the land purchase should include sufficient additional land for the development of the private facilities. The states,[4] or some agency thereof, should invest in the necessary utilities to service such a major development as is imagined here, and the state might then lease the land to entrepreneurs for the development of the privately owned and operated components of the center.

Critical to this concept of direct state involvement in these major central places is the idea that the remainder of the development pattern is not a concern of the state government, except in relatively general policy terms. The planning and development of tributary areas are the proper concerns of the county governments and the municipal governments, working out at their level the most effective partnership of government and the private sector of the economy.

Transportation

On Figure 2 a layout of a regional expressway net is drawn. It is intended to suggest the geographic scale of additions to the present regional system and to suggest a principle in system layout.

It is apparent that the present proposals for new highway construction in the Region are inadequate to provide the geographic spread of service required by the expected population

[4] An option to state action might be the establishment of a regional development agency.

expansion in the Region or by a system of centers such as those proposed above. The most obvious gaps in the present set of proposals are in non-radial or circumferential routes. The sketch suggests a system in which radial and non-radial (cross-region or distributor or bypass) service is more nearly balanced.

In a reconnaissance such as this, demand could not be estimated, and the proposals are diagrammatic. But the experience of other large urban regions can provide some reference points. The plan for the Chicago metropolitan region proposes an expressway for every 15,000 persons. In the Detroit plan the same relationship is on the order of 18,000. There are important variables of course that are different in the New York Region, residential density and car ownership for example, or the proportion of employment in the central business district, or the rail service. But in the new areas coming under the pressure of urbanization, the differences are much reduced. Thus one might reasonably expect a need for some four hundred miles of expressway simply to meet the incremental need of the additional six million people expected to inhabit the Region. Mileage to meet present deficiencies would be in addition to this. The image of Manhattan, served by railroad and subway, tends to obscure two facts that bear upon the need for automobile transportation service. The first is that the New York Region already has more expressway mileage than any other urban region. The second is that postwar suburban development in the Region has not been at a significantly higher residential density than other urban regions.

In short, the mileage of expressways suggested by the sketch is probably less than will be needed.

The other aspect of the sketch is the gridiron configuration of the proposed system. The present system in the Region is predominantly center-oriented. This center dominance probably reflects the demand in the historic corridors of movement. Such demand will continue. But demands already exist, and will increase for non-radial movements. This has been pointed out by other observers.[5]

The need for cross-region service will exist regardless of the density pattern. This would be true, although to a lesser degree, even in a rigorously controlled corridor development form such as that proposed for the Washington, D. C., urban

[5] See Chapter 21, *Metropolitan Transportation, 1980*, Comprehensive Planning Office, Port of New York Authority, N. Y., 1963.

region. (And, as Figure 2 suggests, such a highly controlled form is not the import of the ideas set forth in this reconnaissance.) The increasing interdependence of the diffuse parts of the Tri-State Region can be met only by a transport system with a more inclusive pattern of service than that provided by center-oriented radials. This is particularly true in a Region in which non-center-destined traffic demand must be met by reliance on the automotive vehicle.

But there is a more deep-seated reason for proposing the gridiron pattern than enhancing automotive transportation.

The fundamental question to be resolved in urban planning at the metropolitan scale in the United States is how to influence the development and redevelopment of the Region in the direction of economy and livability and at the same time to permit flexibility and variety at the level of local public decision making and private investment. Related to this question is how to choose objects of public investment that will stand up over time for the original purposes, even if new forms of urban development occur in the future. An expanding grid pattern of transportation would appear best suited to answer these questions.

The primary justification in human terms for the enormous urban regions of today is the variety of opportunity which they present to the individual. Since these opportunities have loci, a transportation system that makes these opportunities, wherever located, most accessible to the entire Region, is the grid. But these opportunities are not randomly distributed. Because certain activities are interdependent and serve either the Region as a whole, or definable sectors of it, centers develop. From the primary center a gradient in density toward the periphery is a natural response to the competing pressures for land. An evenly spaced rectangular grid would not be consistent with these aspects of a regional development pattern. Therefore, in principle, a polar grid, with cells expanding from center to periphery, would appear to be most suitable.

In the Tri-State Region, the chief center, Manhattan, cannot be served solely by automotive transportation; automotive transport should function as a necessary supplement to the rail system. All of the radial lines in a polar grid cannot be brought to the center. Therefore, the theoretical polar grid must be adapted to a shift in the relative importance of the two travel systems (highway and rail) in the environs of Manhattan. The eventual highway pattern would appear best described as a compromise between an expanding rectangular grid and a polar grid.

Three other aspects of the situation in the Tri-State Region act to modify this diagrammatic approach to highway system. The first of these is the present development pattern including transportation. The second is the physiography of the Region. The third is the location of this Region in the "megalopolitan corridor."

The first and second of these are related. The Hudson River was a deterrent to the integrated development of the Region in its formative years with the result that high proportions of land in residential use at high densities developed in the boroughs of the Bronx, Brooklyn and Queens to support the high level of employment in Manhattan. Subways were built to carry this home-to-work movement. These high-capacity carriers in turn justified further high intensity residential construction. On the New Jersey side of the river, separate work places developed, and much of the transportation development was oriented to their requirements. Although in the automobile era limited access facilities were first built, and in greater number, on the New York side of the river, much of the construction has been for parkway purposes, not designed for the workaday tasks of the urban expressway. In New Jersey, arterials were built for automobile service before the first limited access facilities were built. Although heavily congested today, they performed a service for automotive traffic and influenced the intensity of the land development pattern.

The result of this development history is a lopsided development and transportation pattern. Note the weighting of the high density areas to the north and east of Manhattan, or the undeveloped land in Middlesex and Monmouth Counties in New Jersey. The transportation problems of Long Island are aggravated by this historic pattern of density. The postwar building in Nassau and Suffolk Counties has been mostly composed of large-lot single-family detached housing, a development pattern requiring high dependence upon the automobile. Yet automobile entry to Manhattan is impeded by the barrier of high density development in Brooklyn and Queens. It is apparent that Long Island will have to depend heavily upon rail service for its entry to Manhattan for many years to come. The same is true in less degree for Westchester County and Connecticut. It is perhaps less severe for this northern sector because of the parkway system built into the Bronx so that the automobile can reach Manhattan without having to enter the local street system. But these routes are increasingly congested and as the Bronx and Queens intensify in development it will become increasingly difficult to construct new highway facilities. Thus the northern sector too will have to depend heavily upon rail service for entry to Manhattan. This increasingly difficult situation on the New York and Connecticut sides of the Hudson is not paralleled in the same degree in New Jersey. From this sector automobile and bus transport will continue to be an important and effective means of entry to Manhattan. It is difficult to foresee the growth of a density barrier on the New Jersey side of Manhattan comparable to that which has developed on the New York side.

This development pattern and its effect on present transport needs is a major factor in resolving today's problems. But, beyond overcoming the deficiencies of today, it represents real problems in future development strategy. The strategic problem has three components: development intensity and composition in land use terms; kinds of transportation facilities and investments; and timing of development and investment.

Another aspect of physiography influencing the layout of the transportation system is the ridges that traverse the Region on the west and north. The Watchung Mountains, the ridges to the west and the Ramapo Mountains suggest an obvious alignment for the circumferential routes in this part of the Region. The sketched routes have followed this natural bent.

The third aspect of the situation affecting the shape of a regional highway system is the location of this Region as an element of the urbanized eastern seaboard. This means two things: first that along this axis heavy radial demands will continue to exist and must be met; second that volumes of through traffic, though low in proportion to total traffic, are high enough to warrant bypass construction that will increase the requirements of bypass routes over what will be required for regional service per se.

The sketch plan of a regional highway system illustrated on Figure 2 is thus a compromise grid pattern reflecting the adjustment of diagrammatic objectives to other factors of the Region.

The maps in this report show no proposals for modifications to the rail system. There is no question that rail service will continue to be required for delivery of people to Manhattan. But it is believed that in the new areas of the Region no rail service is justified for other than Manhattan-oriented move-

ment. In this regard, the needs are more in the sphere of
program than of physical plan.

Industry

The third element of the proposals for new development
in the Region is industry. Once again, the first question to be
answered is: what properly constitute regional proposals as
distinct from local ones?

Although in the sketches undertaken and illustrated on Figure 3, no attempt has been made to quantify industrial pro-

TRI-STATE REGION RECONNAISSANCE – SUMMER 1963

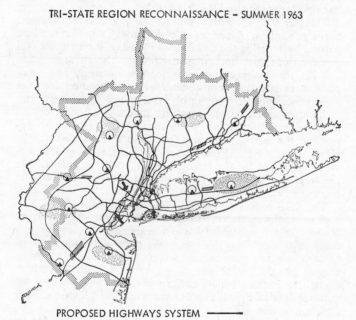

PROPOSED HIGHWAYS SYSTEM ———

PROPOSED INDUSTRY

    ⊚   IN CENTERS

    ▨   INDUSTRIAL PARK CONCENTRATION

    ⠿   DISPERSED AND CONTROLLED THROUGH
           PERFORMANCE STANDARDS

    ➡   INSERTED IN DEVELOPED AREAS

FIGURE 3

posals by location, the general weights of the Regional Plan Association's estimates have been kept in mind. It is useful to look at a summary of these projections set forth by sector. Industrial land requirements are primarily made up from manufacturing and wholesaling employment.

The Regional Plan Association in *The Spread City* estimates that the manufacturing and wholesaling employment increase will require ninety-five square miles of land. The amount of land that will be required for plant relocations from obsolete sites will increase the need considerably. Table 2 indicates the expected heavy growth of these kinds of activi-

TABLE 2
ESTIMATED EMPLOYMENT INCREMENT BY SECTOR*
TRI-STATE REGION, 1960–1985
(IN THOUSANDS)

Sector	Total Increase	Percent	Manufacturing and Wholesaling	Percent	Other	Percent
Manhattan	148	6	−71	−10	219	12
East	451	29	109	19	342	34
North	485	52	198	62	286	47
Jersey North	495	42	222	44	273	41
Jersey South	578	110	215	100	363	119
TOTAL	2,157	32	673	29	1,483	34

* Data from *The Spread City*, Regional Plan Association Bulletin 100, September, 1962.

ties in New Jersey, with Manhattan expected to show actual loss and the eastern sector (Long Island, including the boroughs of Queens and Brooklyn) expected to grow moderately.

Although the proportion of the regional economy devoted to manufacturing and wholesaling is expected to decline, the absolute numbers of people employed in these activities will be substantial, and in terms of the impact upon the landscape and on public services, particularly transportation, the effect will be of great importance.

Four separate development policies are suggested for dealing with this impact at the regional level.

The first suggested policy is the initiation of major industrial parks on vacant land along the major transportation axes of the Region. These parks would house the extensive and heavy industrial activities that require large tracts of land, have heavy goods movement and need high capacity transportation service, require industrial water and sewer service, and frequently attract smaller supporting industrial activities to their immediate vicinity. Major industrial centers of this type are of regional and subregional importance. They attract population and influence the location of residential construction and its supporting facilities; they influence the location of supporting industrial and commercial activities. Because they make particular demand upon regional utilities such as water and sewer, and have an obvious effect in imposing demands upon the transportation system, their location should not be a matter left entirely in the hands of the entrepreneur and the local zoning board. The location, public investment in utility service, and general use control is properly a matter of responsibility for a higher than local level of government . . . county and perhaps state government have both a responsibility for and a direct interest in such industrial development.

Diagrammatically, a suggested few major industrial concentrations of this type are shown on Figure 3. They are represented by the long rectangles aligned with the radial elements of the highway system.

The machinery for state intervention is less clear in this subject area than of the others discussed in this chapter. Yet it is clear that some intervention is required to guide these major regional activities to locations chosen with a long term view of the public interest. Perhaps a state development corporation is needed with powers of land assembly and utility investment.

The second of these industrial development policies relates to the major new centers suggested earlier in this chapter. All industry is not the heavy type requiring specialized services and large expanses of land. For a variety of reasons, certain industrial types continue to be appropriately urban, to be closely related to urban services, to depend upon a nearby labor force, to depend upon the resources of educational and research institutions. Research industry, printing and publishing, apparel, are samples of these. Therefore, provision should be made in the major new centers for industry of this type.

Since the first zoning ordinances were prepared in this country, industry has been looked upon as an activity that is incompatible with residential use. Yet there are many industrial activities that are housed today in plants that make perfectly suitable neighbors to residence, particularly in the low density suburb. Therefore, it is proposed that some thought be devoted at the regional level to drawing up criteria for those kinds of industrial activity which can be dealt with in local zoning ordinances with greater flexibility than most of these ordinances presently provide; the third proposal is therefore a simple graphic recognition of the need to meet some part of the Region's industrial land requirements in this policy manner.

The fourth policy is also one that must be met at the local level, but one that is properly a regional concern if one aspect of regional responsibility is to suggest modifications to present patterns in the directions of a more economic and livable Region. It is suggested that sites be sought out for the insertion of new employment in the fabric of the built-up areas of the Region. The development policy of New York City for example is very heavily housing-oriented. This is understandable in terms of the shortage of adequate housing accommodations for the large lower-income segment of the city's population. But this is questionable policy in the long run, even for the city itself. The counties of New York, with the exception of Manhattan, have the lowest ratio of employment to residence of all the counties of the Region. In order to balance better the demand for public service and to balance better the local tax base, and to strike at the economic problems of at least some of the city's population, it is proposed that new industry be inserted into the boroughs of Richmond, Queens and Brooklyn on land that is now vacant or in low intensity use.

Open Space

The fourth and last element of the proposals for new development in the Region is a suggested system of open space. Like other elements of structure dealt with in this reconnaissance, open space is not to be laid out merely for the sake of order or structure in the metropolitan landscape: it must serve useful purposes, both long and short run. The shape or form of the system must be rational on its own terms.

At the scale of the metropolitan region, two basic open-space schemes have been proposed in recent times. The first is the enclosure of urban development in open space. The second is the wedging of open space by sectors into urban development.

There are two variants to the enclosure idea. One is the "greenbelt" exemplified by the peripheral park system of Ottawa, the forest preserve on the fringe of Chicago, or the proposals by Sir Patrick Abercrombie for Greater London. The other is the idea of surrounding the metropolis by a series of new towns, each with its own surrounding greenbelt. This idea was conceived by Ebenezer Howard in the last century, and has been carried forward in the British new towns program.

In contrast to the surrounding belt system is the wedge system. This type of park and open space system was proposed in the Detroit Regional Plan and is most recently advocated in the *Plan for the Year 2000* for Washington, D. C. In this system, urban development is confined to corridors radiating from the primary center; these spokes, like fingers of development, are separated by wedges of rural and park open space.

Here a third system is proposed . . . a grid system of open space crisscrossing the entire Region. It should be evident from earlier discussion that neither of the two systems described above would be consistent with the general scheme of proposals made in this reconnaissance study, nor with the point of view of the Region as a highly complex and intricate system, the regional proposals for which should permit variety and flexibility in the development of its subsidiary parts.

There are several reasons for suggesting a grid such as that shown on Figure 4.

Open space is the opposite of developed urban space. A chief requirement for a high degree of urbanization is accessibility. Since open space is at the other end of the urban scale it is reasonable to conceive a system that is spatially offset from the transportation grid. But open space cannot be inaccessible or many of its purposes cannot be met. It is therefore reasonable that it should have direct contact with major traffic carriers. The open space grid meets both of these tests.

Open space is not unused space. One of its purposes is the preservation of natural features of the Region, both those which are rare or unique, and those which are simply of nature for the purpose of providing places for repair and refreshment. Open space may be cultivated. It may be the site for active recreation of urban people. It may be the right of way for urban services: water, sewer, power, pipeline. It may be the site of supporting urban activities whose site requirements are non-urban: special schools, defense activities, power generation, water resources. Although a grid system does not have inherent characteristics that meet all of these automatically, it does not create barriers to their attainment. And some of these needs can only be met in linear forms: the preservation of ridges and stream valleys, the rights of way for water and drainage. Others may be enhanced by linearity—the vista,

TRI-STATE REGION RECONNAISSANCE – SUMMER 1963

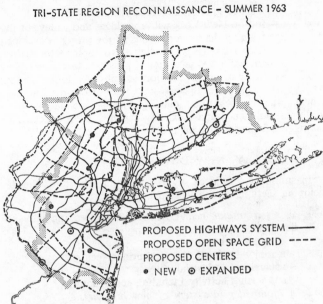

PROPOSED HIGHWAYS SYSTEM ———
PROPOSED OPEN SPACE GRID – – – –
PROPOSED CENTERS
● NEW   ⊙ EXPANDED

FIGURE 4

for example—or the kind of recreational activity that needs continuity, such as hiking.

The grid suggested has practically no limits as to width. It can be miles wide in some places, a few hundred feet perhaps in others. Thus it can permeate the developed fabric of the Region as well as help to shape the growing areas. And in this latter role, the grid provides reference in space without constricting development.

Finally, like most of the suggestions in this reconnaissance, it has the virtue of being a simple idea for execution at the regional level. It can be easily communicated and understood, no mean value in the field of public development.

Its accessibility should range from the immediate to the remote, insofar as the latter is achievable in an urban region.

Just as the highway grid cannot be as precisely reproduced on the landscape as on a paper diagram, neither can the grid of open space. A regional pattern of open space should take advantage of natural features of beauty or rarity that should be available to the public, tomorrow's as well as today's.

The open space grid on Figure 4 is aligned in New Jersey and trans-Hudson New York with the ridges and valleys of the mountains fringing the western limits of the present developed area. The lines running perpendicular to these natural lines follow stream valleys where that is possible. In eastern New York, and in Connecticut, the north-south lines follow stream valleys where possible; the east-west lines are somewhat arbitrarily placed across the ridges. Obviously such a proposed system should encompass existing regional open space. This is suggested graphically on the map.

IV. SUMMARY, NEW DEVELOPMENT

In summary, the ideas suggested in this report for the developing sections of the Region consist of:

1. *A set of major centers,* nine new, three radically redeveloped, and each comprising:
     a major university,
     a major business and institutional center,
     specialized industrial activity,
     supporting activity including some housing,
2. *A modified grid system of new highways,*
3. *Industrial development* consisting of:
     major industrial parks,
     industry in the proposed centers,
     industry mixed with residence under appropriate safeguards,
     industry inserted into older areas,
4. *A grid of open space.*

The chief arguments for these proposals are:

1. They constitute the primary structural elements of the developing areas;
2. thus they justify a particularly intense planning effort;
3. they are demonstrably regional in scope and nature;
4. they involve the use of, for the most part, existing public powers of the state governments;
5. they represent investments that the governments of the Region, in large degree, will have to make anyway.

Chapter 9

TRANSPORTATION AND COMMUNICATION

Human society is human interaction in patterned form; the optimum contact/movement of people, ideas and goods, with a minimum of friction, is thus basic to a high and rewarding urban civilization. Transportation is not only an instrumental and expensive must that enables a city to earn its living (as well as merely exist), but it is increasingly viewed as a powerful instrument for shaping metropolitan growth in a pattern of rational land use. Patently we are suffering everywhere today from a lopsided emphasis on the private sector (automobile), rather than decent public mass transport. It might even be wise to have "free" public people transportation in the city as a normal urban service; certainly heavy federal subsidies will be customary from now on. Colin Buchanan has outlined for Britain in his following article what he thinks can be done (and what it will cost) to cope successfully and humanistically with the traffic in towns. If transportation of goods and people be likened to a liquid piped through the city, the changes in mode at terminals are the most serious blockages in the whole system; Roger Gilman, chief planner for the Port of New York Authority, addresses himself to this problem with the enormous practical experience of that public corporation, indicating the multiplicity of considerations in terminal planning. On a more theoretical level, Ralph Gakenheimer from his vantage point as editor of the *Journal of the American Institute of Planners*, presents an overview of advanced metropolitan transportation planning as a form of system analysis and treads delicately into "Futurism" where "semisubstitutable" communications (videophone for example) may influence both transportation and life styles. Nor should we neglect, while heavily investing scarce resources in existent transportation technologies, the possible spread land-use patterns and radical emergent technologies of the future; the existence of huge unamortized capital investments in obsolescent systems might well block the utilization of advanced technology. We are probably already at this point with our urban road networks, which are already obsolete, but seemingly "unscrappable." Whether the Federal Department of Transportation centralizing functions now scattered among eleven different departments, agencies, administrations and bureaus is a "solution" to urban transactions in ideas, people and goods, from the CBD to suburbia is, at this juncture, by no means clear.

The Outlook for Traffic in Towns
COLIN BUCHANAN*

INTRODUCTION

I suppose that my colleagues and I can look at the reception of the report "Traffic in Towns"[1] with some satisfaction. The circulation has been extensive and world-wide, there has been a Penguin version, and there have been German and Japanese translations. I myself have had invitations from all over the world to expound the Report, beyond any possibility of coping with. There is evidence that it has influenced social thinking in ways which we never dreamed of.[2] Parts of it have crept into general examination papers and textbooks on English. I have heard, though I cannot confirm it, that someone has preached a sermon on it.

The Report moreover has run into very little criticism. There has been some adverse comment from certain groups in this country, but otherwise it has had a singularly good reception. This is not necessarily a good thing. It may be, and there is evidence to suggest it, that many people have done little more than skim through the Report. The severest critics have probably been the team who wrote it, and we have indeed spent much time going over the arguments again and again. On balance our conclusion is that the chain of reasoning has not as yet been seriously dented at any point.

Even so, there are misunderstandings about the Report which need to be put right; and there are some (as we think) valuable points in the Report which no one has yet picked up.

* Professor of Transportation at the Imperial College of Science and Technology, London; and formerly Principal Inspector, Ministry of Housing and Local Government, and Urban Planning Advisor, Ministry of Transport. Trained as an engineer, he is a Fellow of the Royal Institute of British Architects, Member of the Town Planning Institute, and Associate Member of the Institution of Civil Engineers. He is the author of *Mixed Blessing—The Motor in Britain* (1958), and the notable *Traffic in Towns* (H.M.S.O. 1963). This paper is based on a talk to the Society of Town Clerks at their Annual Conference in 1965, and published with their permission.

[1] "Traffic in Towns," Her Majesty's Stationery Office, London, 1963.
[2] See, for example, the "Art of Judgement," by Sir Geoffrey Vickers, Chapman and Hall, 1965.

In this paper I propose to try to correct the main misunderstanding that has arisen, and to pick out certain points hitherto overlooked which seem to have special relevance to current problems.

A SUMMARY OF "TRAFFIC IN TOWNS"

Before I proceed any further, I think I ought to recapitulate the main conclusions [as a series of propositions] of the Report in order to form a background to subsequent discussion:

1. The motor vehicle is a beneficial invention, outstandingly the most convenient form of mechanical transport yet invented for a wide variety of purposes, and unlikely to be generally supplanted within the foreseeable future by any other device for movement.

2. Assuming that no deliberately restrictive measures are imposed (the only possible justification for which would be the difficulty of accommodating the traffic) the number of vehicles in Britain (11½ million at present) is likely to double within ten years, to treble within twenty years, and possibly to increase to 40 million soon after the turn of the century. These figures take account of a likely national increase of population of 20 million by the end of the century.

3. Most of these vehicles will be used for one of two main purposes: first and very importantly for commercial business and industrial purposes, and secondly for a great variety of social uses. The second category, comprising in the main the use of cars, will form the major element in the increase of traffic in the future. It is plain that very substantial increases of traffic lie not so very far ahead.

4. The bulk of journeys begin and end in towns and cities, since it is here that the traffic generating activities are concentrated. The development of the road system *between* towns is comparatively simple in engineering terms, but the *planning* does need to take into account the future location of population; and vice versa, the planning of the location of population needs to take into account the possibilities for highway development.

5. *Inside* urban areas the problem of handling motor traffic is much more difficult for the simple reason that the advent of fast, heavy, dangerous vehicles in large numbers

has put our traditional urban layouts [both here and abroad] out of date at a stroke. If one designs an urban area deliberately for motor traffic, then something quite new emerges. However, the situation in existing areas has to be faced—even allowing for the new towns that must be built, it constitutes by far the greater part of the problem.

6. In existing urban areas there are two distinct aspects of the so-called traffic problem. First there is the *frustration of the door-to-door accessibility* which is the benefit the motor vehicle can provide. Secondly there is the *damage to the environment for living* which the motor vehicle is now causing and which is manifested in danger (especially for pedestrians), anxiety, noise, fumes and visual intrusion on an extensive scale. It can be shown that both these aspects together are costing the community very large sums of money annually—perhaps as much as 500 millions. The matter is complicated by the fact that these two aspects tend to be in conflict with each other: improve accessibility and you may worsen the environment, and vice versa.

7. There is only one principle whereby these problems of accessibility and environment can be sorted out. This is gradually to create, inside towns and cities, units or areas where considerations of environment are paramount and take precedence over the movement and parking of vehicles. These might be termed "environmental areas." The essential corollary is to have a highway network onto which longer movements of vehicles from locality to locality are concentrated, leaving the environmental areas to deal only with their own traffic. The principle may be crudely likened to the corridor-and-rooms system of a big building.

8. This principle opens the door to a quantitative approach. It can be seen, for example, that the *capacity* of the network to discharge traffic must be in balance with the ability of the environmental areas to generate or receive traffic. It can be seen again that the *pattern* of the network must depend largely on the location of the activities that cause traffic to flow, but conditioned by the requirements of the environmental areas. New techniques are now emerging which enable these aspects to be quantified in a manner not thought possible even a few years ago.

9. When the principle of networks and environmental areas is applied to existing urban areas in practice, it is found that environmental areas have strictly limited "capacities for traffic" according to the manner in which they are laid out. In other words if the anti-environmental effects of motor traffic are to be avoided, or at least kept under control, then the amount of traffic must be limited. But if an urban area can be reconstructed in a more advantageous form, then more traffic can be accommodated. Reconstruction costs money, however, so broadly it may be said that if certain environmental standards are desired then the amount of traffic an urban area can decently accommodate depends on what the community is prepared to invest in the necessary physical alterations.

10. However, in densely developed urban areas, there are absolute limits (dictated not by cost but by physical considerations) to the amount of traffic that can be accommodated. These limits are likely, in many instances, to be well below the future demands for the use of motor vehicles as numbers increase. Therefore, in such areas, future demands will have to be cut down to size. Broadly speaking the cut is bound to fall *not* on the use of motor vehicles for *essential* commercial and industrial purposes but on the use of cars for *optional purposes,* especially for the journey-to-work for which other means of transport either exists or can be devised. Herein lies an important range of implications for public transport.

11. Since the motor vehicle is in reality demanding new urban forms, much of our success in providing for it in urban areas will depend on our ability to secure the comprehensive redevelopment of sizeable areas. Obviously an enormous programme of redevelopment is coming to most urban areas, but we will fritter away all the opportunities if we simply allow each existing building to be redeveloped in isolation on its existing site. This will call for new co-operations amongst owners themselves and between owners and public authorities.

12. It will undoubtedly cost a great deal of money to accommodate traffic in towns. Society seems to be faced with the hard choice of either finding the money, or of deliberately curtailing the amount of traffic. What society cannot do very much longer is to go on [privately] investing at the present rate in the purchase and running of

motor vehicles and yet persistently refuse to put an equivalent [public] investment into accommodating the traffic that results. But even if some of the future "optional" traffic can be curtailed, there now seems to be a "rock bottom" level of essential traffic which is certain to demand road works and redevelopment on a scale and at a cost which few people have so far realised.

13. The broad conclusion was reached that virtually none of the statutory development plans really face up to future problems of traffic and transport. All of them needed radical review, with a determined effort to put them onto a more realistic and quantitative basis.

The above were the broad important conclusions of "Traffic in Towns." None of them were particularly "palatable" conclusions, and none of them tended to show that there were any easy, cheap "solutions" to the problems of traffic in towns to be had for the asking. The truth of the matter is that when a highly urbanised densely populated community decides to arm itself with motor vehicles on a big scale the results are most embarrassing.

A CRITICISM

A criticism which has been levelled against this chain of argument is that it failed to consider the possibilities of new urban forms in which the activities that create traffic would be arranged in ways that make for easier movement, and that it would be better to siphon off population from existing towns and cities (with their apparently insoluble problems) to newly developed areas where the scope was so much greater. One observation about this is that one of the important things that "Traffic in Towns" did was to demonstrate almost for the first time in this country the linkage that exists between activities involving the use of land and the movements that result. I find it a little hard to have this thrown back in our faces as something we neglected to exploit!

Of course, bearing in mind that another 20 million people will have to be accommodated in this country by the end of the century, and that there are still severe problems of accommodating people who must be displaced from overcrowded cities, there will be ample opportunities for experimenting with new urban forms. But two points are certain: first that the principles expounded in "Traffic in Towns" are applicable to every urban form that can be conceived of; and secondly that the problems of existing conurbations, cities and towns will not and cannot be expunged simply as a result of new development elsewhere. Existing urban areas and how to deal with their new traffic problems, will undoubtedly comprise the major part of future problems, and I feel quite confident that we were right in "Traffic in Towns" in concentrating on this aspect.

THE MAIN MISUNDERSTANDING

Although we did our best to write a report which was closely argued from paragraph to paragraph, and which would be understandable to the man in the street, it is obvious that we failed in one respect. This was in the impression we seem to have given that the Report contained positive recommendations for the early and very elaborate reconstruction of towns and cities at vast expense. I do not think anyone who reads the Report really carefully could receive this impression, but the fact is that many people have received it, which shows some deficiency in drafting, or possibly too much emphasis on pictorial illustrations showing urban areas as they might be.

The Three Variables

The fact of the matter is that the Report contains no such positive recommendations, nor does it postulate any particular level of investment. What the Report does do is to isolate three main variables that apply to all urban areas. The first is the *level of accessibility* that is required—that is to say the amount of usage of motor vehicles that is desired. This can obviously range from, say, the circulation of large numbers of private cars to permitting the entry of commercial vehicles only and in the small hours of the morning at that. The second variable is the *standard of environment* that is desired, which can range from complete separation of pedestrians and vehicles to allowing vehicles to park on the pavements, and accepting a high accident rate. The third variable is the *cost* one is prepared to incur upon altering the physical structure of the urban area in order to improve accessibility or environment or both.

Environment as a Variable

Having isolated these three variables we then applied our minds more closely to the second, i.e. the standard of environment,[3] and we concluded that if cities are to be reasonably civilised places, then there is not much scope for treating the standard of environment as a variable. Who, for example, could possibly opt for a highly dangerous urban area, or for one with high noise levels? This is not really a matter of asking people what they want or how much they are prepared to pay for better conditions, nor can environment be dismissed as a trivial frill which can easily be dispensed with. It is a matter of acting in the public interest and laying down standards in relation to certain extremely damaging side-effects of motor traffic. To demand a certain standard of safety in a residential street, for example, is to act in precisely the same reforming spirit that has secured all the social progress to date in matters of housing and public health. There is no basic difference. It just happens that the adverse effects of motor traffic, which have grown up slowly, are only now being recognised as presenting a social problem.

The "Law"

Accepting then that environment in the special sense that we used the term could not really be regarded as a variable, we were left with only two variables—the level of accessibility and the cost that can be incurred on physical alterations. This led us in the Report to formulate a rough and ready "law" in the following terms: "Within any urban area as it stands, the establishment of environmental standards automatically determines the accessibility, but the latter can be increased according to the amount of money that can be spent on physical alterations." This is really the key to the urban traffic problem and there is no escaping it. If a town wants the use of a great deal of traffic with civilised conditions, then it must be prepared to spend a great deal of money on physical alterations. If it does not desire to spend a lot of money then it need not do so as long as it reconciles itself to not having so much traffic. But what it cannot do is have a lot of traffic and not spend any money.

If one takes this "law" as the epitome of "Traffic in Towns" then it is correct to say, as I have done in public on many occasions, that the ideas in "Traffic in Towns" could in theory be implemented without spending any money at all. For if environmental standards are fixed and it is decided that no money can be spent, then application of the "law" shows that

[3] Editor's note: See Chapter 6 for an analysis of explicit and implicit planning values.

only a small amount of traffic can be accommodated. This is a perfectly fair application of "Traffic in Towns."

The Unavoidable Minimum

Although we made no firm recommendations in any of these cases [in "Traffic in Towns"], we did draw attention to one very important point. This is that in practice even the level of accessibility is not infinitely variable. For in all towns there appears to be a "rock bottom" amount of traffic which *must* be catered for if the towns are to survive. This traffic is the essential business and commercial traffic that keeps the place alive, it is not the use of cars for private convenience or pleasure. Our studies tended to show that even to accommodate this essential traffic in decent environmental conditions would require works at a cost and on a scale which few people have yet contemplated. From this situation there seems to be no escape. I wish people would be honest about this. You only have to look at the conditions in many streets, *outside the peak hours,* to appreciate the weight of essential traffic and the adverse effect it is having on the environment. Traffic does not consist, as many people seem to imagine solely of the frivolous use of cars.

Uncertainty about Investment

One very important reason why we did not make any positive recommendations was that we did not have any firm indications about the amount of money that any future government would make available for carrying out physical alterations. That is to say the third variable—cost—was completely indeterminate. As I have just explained we reached the pretty firm conclusion that if essential traffic alone was to be catered for in decent conditions it would cost a good deal more than most people had previously imagined. The only helpful way round this difficulty was to pick out certain examples to show what a certain level of accessibility would cost, not with the idea of recommending it but in order to provide some fixed point in an otherwise "uncharted sea." If, to draw a parallel, some person long resident overseas comes home with the idea of buying a house and settling down he may have no idea how much houses cost. So you suggest that he look at *Dalton's Weekly* or the back page of the *Times* just to get an idea of what he will have to pay for a house of a certain size and character. This was the spirit in which we costed our certain possibilities.

This question of the investment level is arising acutely in the case of certain studies of actual towns which I and my colleagues are now involved in. Whilst we are able to quantify many aspects of the traffic and transport problems, including the making of projections into the future, we are obliged in the absence of any government guidance, to work in the dark as far as the future level of investment is concerned. To get round this difficulty—as far as it is possible to get round it—we have evolved the following technique. We estimate the demands for movement (in terms of persons and goods) that are likely to arise at the time when motor vehicle ownership reaches saturation. This will happen round about the end of the century, and so we have to make predictions of population and land use to that date. Having obtained the detailed picture of movement demands we then interpret these in terms of a theoretical road system (i.e. primary network) on the assumption that there is unrestricted use of motor vehicles for all purposes. When we come to "bend on" this theoretical network to the town itself, making allowances for topography, environment, historic buildings, areas of recent development which cannot be changed, etc., we usually find that it is quite impossible of achievement. It is necessary to simplify it to something that appears reasonably practicable, but with the implication that *every act of simplification means that the level of accessibility is lower (i.e. less traffic can be accommodated)*. At each stage of simplification, since less traffic is being accommodated, there are different implications for public transport and parking policies.

All this we can work out with some accuracy, but the acute difficulty we run into is that we do not know how far to carry the process of simplification, because obviously it must be related to the investment resources that will be available. No one can tell us what this will be. So once again we are driven into the position of demonstrating what certain levels of investment will produce, but without making any recommendations. We have to leave it to our clients to take the policy decisions with such guidance as they can get from ministries.

THE INVESTMENT QUESTION

The position we have been in virtually ever since the motor vehicle arrived on the scene is that expenditure for the accommodation of traffic has had to take its place along with other claims on national funds, that is to say with defence, housing, schools, hospitals, etc. Against these other needs traffic has seldom established any priority. After the last war, for example, there was a shutdown on highway expenditure for many years in favour of spending on "welfare" projects. Many people thought this was right at the time, but looking back now I suspect that had we devoted our resources boldly to renewing the industrial sinews of the country, including the provision of an efficient road system, we would by now be in a greatly improved position vis-à-vis our competitors, and would have had more wealth available for welfare. As it is, as far as the road system is concerned, we are now burdened with the accumulated neglect of many years. The arrears are now so great that governments take fright and seek every imaginable excuse to avoid facing the situation. But it is difficult to see how this position can be maintained in the face of increasing pressures from a car-owning and car-desiring public, and the question arises whether we should not take a completely new look at the question of financing the accommodation of traffic.

This is not a field in which I claim any expertise, but I would like to discuss two ideas, neither of them new. The first is that, by transferring responsibility for the accommodation of traffic to some kind of national agency, a great deal of work could be financed out of loans. At present there is the strange anomaly that a local authority can finance housing estate roads, for example, out of loans, but the main national expenditure on motorways and trunk roads is dependent on what a reluctant Chancellor can squeeze out of his income budget in competition with other claims. It is difficult to think of anything that can be more surely relied upon to serve the needs of future generations than good communications, and it seems strange that the bulk of the expenditure should come from current revenue.

The second possibility (which could be exploited concurrently with the first) is to abandon all prejudices and to return to the idea of a road fund with resources allocated directly from vehicle and fuel taxation. American experience strongly suggests this as a workable principle. Even if it were only the future increment of revenue from this source arising from the increase of the national motor vehicle fleet that was taken into account, very considerable sums would accrue.

These are only suggestions. What I am really pleading for is for a new look to be taken at the situation. Is there no way of escaping from the dilemma which we seem to have drifted into? If not, I can see plainly what is going to happen: *one hundred years* after the introduction of the motor vehicle (1888) this country will find itself with no more than the shadow of a road system designed to exploit the most ingenious and versatile method of transport ever invented or likely to be invented. The motor vehicles will be there all right, in force, but operating in ever worsening conditions for industry and the community at large.

THE PROBLEM OF THE "GAP"

Even if progress could be made on the investment front, however, there remains the formidable problem of knowing what to do with traffic in the interim period until major works are completed. Even if funds unlimited could be allocated overnight it would still take years to catch up with the problem of traffic in towns. The problem will be intensified if, as seems to be present policy major works are postponed to some altogether distant future. This seems to be the central dilemma of our position: traffic is presenting an immediate problem whilst the creative measures to deal with it are slow and long term. How do we bridge this gap?

Now in "Traffic in Towns" we did not leave this question in mid-air and merely content ourselves with painting a picture of long-term ideas. We could see that this was the crucial issue. We said straight out (para. 467) that the full logic of the arguments we had put forward was that "ceilings" should be put on the amount of traffic in urban areas, and that these ceilings should be raised only as capital works were undertaken which would allow more traffic to be decently and efficiently accommodated. This is no different than saying that if it is desired to put more people in a house than it can properly accommodate then the increase should not be permitted until extra rooms have been built or the existing accommodation has been suitably rearranged.

We went on to say, however, that in practice this appeared to be a counsel of perfection that would be difficult to live up to. But we concluded that a practical approach to the same result could be achieved by means of a technique which we called "environmental management." This was probably the most important part of the whole report, but for some reason, perhaps because we did not spell it out with sufficient emphasis, it has largely escaped attention. It will perhaps be useful if I spell it out now.

Traffic Management

First, however, let me describe what appears to be the official policy, for this is a problem that has been recognised before. The official policy lies in the technique known loosely as "traffic management." This consists essentially of resorting to every possible inexpensive device to keep traffic on the move until capital works (whose prospects in terms of dates are usually extremely vague) can be executed. In slightly more detail the technique consists of "spreading the load" through as much of the existing street system as can be brought into use, improving signal installations, eliminating right-hand turns, instituting one-way systems, clearing the streets of parked cars, improving signs, and executing limited works (e.g. of "channelisation") to improve the flow of traffic.

Two objections attend this process in practice. The first is that by its very nature it tends to be carried out in disregard of environmental considerations. People living in some hitherto quiet street, for example, may suddenly find their amenities shattered by the introduction of heavy traffic flows, and it is by no means always the case that they have any chance to object. These invasions are the harder to bear when it is remembered that in many instances the pressure for "spreading the load" arises largely from the growth of commuter car traffic. As we said in "Traffic in Towns": "It seems to us a questionable ordering of social priorities that one group of people should find their established amenities ruined in order (in effect) to enable another group of people to use their cars for optional purposes" (para. 468). Nevertheless the present policy of the Ministry of Transport appears to be strongly aligned to the pursuance of traffic management measures designed primarily to facilitate the movement of vehicles. My forecast is that this policy will meet with increasing resistance from local communities, of which the opposition encountered by the previous Minister of Transport in the case of the Highgate Lorry Route was but a foretaste.

The second objection to traffic management as now pursued is that it often acts contrary to long-term planning objectives. Thus heavy traffic flows introduced into Gower Street and Russell Square appear to be entirely contrary to the long-cherished concept of a University of London central precinct. It is not much comfort to say that such measures are temporary only—if temporary means say twenty years, then twenty years of heavy traffic in a street can completely alter the character and the use, and possibly render the planning objective null and void.

An Alternative Approach

For these reasons we felt bound in "Traffic in Towns" to cast doubt on current traffic management policies. The proper approach, as we saw it, was to determine the network and environmental area plan, and then to work towards it by a carefully designed integration of constructional and traffic control measures. The principle, we suggested, was to get the network and environmental area system etched out on the ground in embryo form, as soon as possible. The network would in all probability consist largely of existing roads (out of which most networks are likely to be formed in any case, though eventually the roads will be reconstructed beyond recognition), but new links would be needed here and there to give continuity. Enclosed within the network would be the potential environmental areas. Once this embryo system had been established—and it should not take very long to do this—then a policy could be instituted of upgrading conditions in the potential environmental areas by the deliberate exclusion of cross-filtrating traffic, and by the reorganisation of internal circulations by means of a variety of comparatively simple engineering and control measures.

Such a policy would of course tend to throw additional loads of traffic on the embryo network, which might be overloaded as a result. Every conceivable device of traffic engineering would of course be applied to the embryo network to enable it to carry its load, but to the extent that congestion prevailed so this would be the most obvious means of applying the ceiling to the amount of traffic. But of course other means might be found, such as imposing road pricing techniques, to keep the amount of traffic on the network under control. Within each environmental area measures would be taken to relate, as far as possible, its traffic generating capacity to the capacity of the network. But as major improvements were carried out on the network, so could the traffic levels be increased.

I would emphasise, however, that we saw this technique as essentially a "gap bridging" operation. Every move would be a calculated move progressing consistently towards the long-term objectives. We called it "environmental management" partly because we could not think of a crisper term, but also as a counter to "traffic management" and because it conveyed the idea of a deliberate policy of checking and reversing the present widespread erosion of environment which the motor vehicle is causing. We were able to give only the outlines of the technique in "Traffic in Towns," and it has greatly disappointed us that no one has sought to develop it further. It is true that in the recent official report on Piccadilly Circus[4] there is a reference (para. 40) to the establishment of "at least the rudiments of an 'embryo' network . . . and to attract to these improved routes traffic which at present filters through the potential environmental areas," which at least indicates that the principle has been understood. But to seek to establish the rudiments of an embryo is not exactly to let oneself go in an act of creative planning.

I would like to emphasise once again that this question of bridging the gap between the current situation and the advent of the creative construction measures seems to be the crucial problem of the whole traffic situation. I hope I have shown that it is not one we neglected in "Traffic in Towns" in preference for very elaborate long-term constructional measures.

A New Concept for Development Plans

One important implication of this is that a development plan (in the statutory sense) begins to take on a new character or purpose. It becomes not merely a long-term plan for physical changes on the ground, but also provides a concise programme for achieving the desired objectives. This programme needs to be much more than a mere division (as at present) between development in the first five years and development after that period. It must postulate an investment programme, and, as far as traffic is concerned, a programme showing how traffic is to be handled at all the intermediate stages before completion of the major capital works.

WIDER OBJECTIVES

When we were writing "Traffic in Towns" we were very conscious of the fact that we were dealing with a problem which was really an integral part of a much larger problem, namely the form and organisation of urban areas. We ventured the view that this was now coming into perspective as probably the outstanding social problem for the rest of this century. It seemed to us terribly important that people should understand what was at stake. By the end of the century this

[4] Piccadilly Circus, *Report of the Working Party*, H.M.S.O. 1965.

small country is likely to have 66 million people living in towns, and it really does not require much imagination to see how important the quality of the physical surroundings of these towns will be to the lives of the people who live in them. Such quality as we may achieve in these physical surroundings will be, I suspect, as accurate an indication as any other measure of the quality of our civilisation and our standard of culture. The world will judge us by what it sees of our physical surroundings, especially our towns.

We were anxious however not to let the matter rest simply at the problem of towns. Consideration of the form of urban areas implies "by subtraction" consideration of the rest of the country. In this respect we could only record our great anxiety, so formidable are the pressures now developing, that it would be well within our capacity as a society to ruin the environment of this island by the end of the century. For myself I do not go back on this statement at all—I think this terrible result could be achieved by a combination of public indifference and the effect of thousands of individual decisions on land use and development taken in isolation without regard to the cumulative effect. The process can be seen at work at this very moment.

In the spring of 1965 I had the honour to accept an invitation from the President of the United States to attend his White House Conference on Natural Beauty. I doubt whether even the President himself would deny that there was a political background to the conference. I know that it took place in a country where wealth, even if it be unequally distributed, is growing beyond the dreams of avarice. I know that the title of the conference sounded a little strange to my English ears on account of the undertones I associate with the words "natural beauty." But even allowing for these points the total effect of the conference was overwhelming.

Fifteen different themes were discussed covering the main environmental problems of town and countryside, highway design, and education in the art of appreciating physical surroundings. All this at the highest level. One session comprised an open sitting of the Recreation Advisory Council consisting of the Secretaries (equivalent to our Ministers) of Defense, Interior, Agriculture, Commerce and Health, Education and Welfare, the Administrator of the Housing and Home Finance Agency, and the Chairman of the Tennessee Valley Authority. All spoke seriously and movingly about the need to conserve and where necessary to re-create the American environment.

It was suggested that this council should be reconstituted as the National Council on Natural Beauty and Recreation with a full-time staff. Compared with this proposition, the idea which I broached last year at the Town Planning Institute's London Conference that this country now urgently needs a Central Council for the Physical Environment seems comparatively modest.

A parallel demonstration in this country to the White House Conference would be for the Prime Minister and all his senior ministers to meet in special public session in the full glare of press and television, and to pledge themselves to the cause of the physical environment of the island as a major permanent item of government policy. How far we seem to be from achieving any such thing. With very few exceptions—Lord Silkin, I would say, when he was Minister of Town and Country Planning, and Mr. Duncan Sandys to whom we owe the Civic Trust—no politician with power seems either to have grasped the importance of the physical environment nor to have been able to see the political capital that could be made from harnessing the imagination of the people of this country to the idea of making something extraordinary and marvellous out of the surface of the island.

Terminal Planning

ROGER H. GILMAN[*]

In our highly complex and inter-related economy and society, passenger or freight terminals must be built with careful thought about their relationship to the total transportation demand and over-all planning of the region. The location, layout and design of terminals for all modes of transportation have a significant effect on land use and business activity and, as such, have a major influence on the area's over-all development. Indeed, the area's welfare and prosperity receive a major boost from a well planned terminal. This development is becoming even more significant in the light of the high-speed transportation and technological developments which are so basic to current and future terminal demands.

* Director of Planning and Development, The Port of New York Authority. A graduate in engineering sciences from Harvard, he is the author of a number of articles on transportation and port planning in various technical and professional publications.

TERMINALS AND THE TOTAL TRANSPORTATION TASK

If the terminal planning is to be effective, it must take into account the total movement of passengers and goods which are involved. Terminal planning cannot be done effectively if it is isolated from these broad considerations.

It is, for example, becoming commonplace for a businessman to make a one-day air round trip—in effect, a commuting trip—for distances of five hundred and more miles. Of obvious importance to such a commuter, therefore, is the time, convenience and comfort he experiences in getting to and from and through the two airports he uses. He has come to expect that he will have a one- or two-hour flight time in the air without any more likelihood of delay than on his normal commuter train to work. The related aspects of the ground trip to and from both terminals are, therefore, apt to concern him the most.

Another example is in freight handling, where a revolution is taking place in ocean shipping, with the advent of containers and their use on trade routes all over the world. The ability to pack a container at the plant, ship it by truck or rail to the port and then transfer it to a container ship is attractive only if the land and port facilities at the near and far ends of the ocean trip are equipped to discharge and handle the van efficiently. In this case, both land and port terminals are of crucial importance to the total transportation task and must be planned within this context.

THE TERMINAL'S THREE BASIC FUNCTIONS

1. *A Transfer Point*

Obviously, a basic function of a transportation terminal is to provide for an interchange of people and freight between modes of transportation or between two carriers of the same mode.

A bus, transit or rail terminal accommodates an arriving passenger and his interchange with subway, local bus, taxicab or private automobile, or simply provides access to the sidewalk for the continuation of his trip to his ultimate destination. At an air terminal, the traveler transfers to or from a taxicab or limousine, a city-chartered bus or other mass transit, a helicopter or air taxi or a private automobile. He may also transfer to a connecting flight or another airline. Similarly, at a marine terminal, the steamship passenger seeks a taxicab, private automobile or bus to take him to his next destination— his home, a hotel, railroad, bus or air terminal. The important point in all of these cases is that the terminal is a transfer station within a trip; it rarely marks the termination of a trip.

This same transfer function takes place in the handling of freight shipments. When a cargo ship arrives at a marine terminal, its freight is unloaded and transferred to land carriers, local cartage companies, over-the-road motor truck carriers, or to railroad cars. Rail freight arriving at a freight yard or terminal is transferred to motor trucks for delivery to its final destination. In some cases, the freight train is broken up into shorter trains or individual cars for delivery to local industrial sidings. Likewise, air cargo coming into an airport is shifted to trucks for quick movement to its destination. In some instances, over-the-road truck freight may be shifted at a metropolitan area terminal from a tractor-trailer to smaller trucks for local pickup or delivery.

2. *The Terminal as a Temporary Holding Area*

Transit storage is also an important consideration in planning for the movement of freight through a terminal. At a marine terminal, for example, outgoing shipments are delivered to the terminal days before the sailing date; incoming freight may remain at the terminal for as long as a week or more before it is picked up by its consignee or by the domestic highway or rail carrier responsible for its further movement. The freight houses of the railroads fulfill a comparable function, as do cargo sheds at airports.

Tie-up berths for cargo ships waiting for sailing schedules and the parking and storage areas at truck terminals also illustrate this phase of a terminal's operation. This is a terminal function which requires extensive space, and often it is uneconomical to provide for it on the same site as the other terminal functions. However, this part of a terminal's operation cannot be separated from its other functions by too great a travel-time distance.

3. *The Rhythm of Demand and Transit Storage*

The natural rhythm of the pattern of demand for transport service plays a dominant part in the over-all planning of a terminal and in its transit storage requirements. On a metropolitan scale, the peaks and valleys of demand reflect the basic rhythms of urban living.

Their effects are sharply apparent in passenger travel. Most people travel from home to work in the morning and from work to home in the evening. In the middle of the day there is much less need for transport, at least in the journey-to-work category. The buses, subway cars and commuter railroad cars must be stored during the off-peak period, in parking lots, garages, or storage yards, ready to be called upon for the next peak-demand time. This holding function is thus an integral part of the basic task of a terminal.

At a minimum, therefore, the operation of the terminal during the peak-departure hours must be precise and wide variations in the time of deliveries of empties from storage yards or lots can impair smooth outward flow of both passengers and goods. Planning for a transportation terminal thus requires the provision of a sufficient amount of space so that all of these functions can be carried on smoothly and efficiently. In particular, space must be adequate during the normal periods of high demand.

PLANNING TERMINAL CAPACITY

Some caution must be exercised in planning for "normal periods of high demand." There are occasional periods of highest demand for which it would be uneconomical to provide quick and easy accommodation of every passenger or piece of freight. An illustration in the passenger field is the extremely high demands placed on a rail, bus and air terminal on Christmas Eve. To accommodate this demand without any crowding would require a vast amount of terminal space, most of which would be unused during the rest of the year. In other words, terminal planning requires the assumption that occasional and infrequent periods of some overload will occur and will be tolerated.

In planning the capacity of a terminal, the demand during departure times is of controlling importance. Most passengers arrive at the terminal some time before the scheduled departure time, and their accumulation must be provided for. The number of peak-hour departure schedules and the duration of the vehicle's departure platform occupancy determine the needed number of such platforms. Here the mode of transportation controls the duration. In contrast to minutes for a bus, rail or air terminal, it can amount to hours at a marine passenger terminal and days at a marine or rail cargo terminal.

Thus, the goal in planning and developing terminals is to provide adequate capacity to meet most demand. On the other hand, a capacity should not be such that a substantial portion goes unused for so much of the time that the facility becomes uneconomic. One solution to this dilemma may be the incorporation in the design of the ability to expand without rebuilding the entire terminal, so that growth can be accommodated if and when needed.

TERMINALS IN THE NEW YORK-NEW JERSEY AREA

Three major terminal complexes in the New York-New Jersey area illustrate the wide variety and scope of approaches to planning which are needed to provide adequately for the handling of passengers and freight. In each case they were developed and are operated by The Port of New York Authority, the joint public agency of the States of New York and New Jersey. They are part of the Authority's self-supporting transportation and terminal program, carried on without the power of taxation or pledge of the states' credit.

1. Union Bus Terminals

In the New York-New Jersey area, the interstate bus has assumed a major role in the handling of commuter traffic. It basically serves persons living in northern New Jersey who work in Manhattan. Following the opening of the Lincoln Tunnel in 1937 and the expansion of the state arterial highway system in northern Jersey, the bus became a favored means of commuting for thousands of new residents whose homes were built in a widely scattered and extensive suburban region, inadequately served by the few rail branch lines which were oriented toward lower Manhattan. Rapid expansion of bus movements led to a public recognition of the need for a union bus terminal in midtown Manhattan which would take the buses entirely off the city streets.

As a result, The Port of New York Authority studied the problem and analyzed the needs of the bus lines, their equipment and passengers. Following extensive discussions with the two states, the city of New York, the bus industry and many civic and trade groups, and the enactment of bi-state legislation, the Authority proceeded with the development and opened the Port Authority Bus Terminal in 1950. The increasing bus travel demand led to a substantial expansion of the terminal in 1963 by adding several levels to the existing facility. Even more capacity will be needed in the future.

A major concern in locating and designing this terminal was the need to move the buses quickly from the Lincoln Tunnel to the loading and unloading platforms. It was designed to give passengers a convenient and comfortable terminal facility, making it possible for easy transfer, where necessary, to other local transportation (subway, intercity bus, taxi or walking) in the city.

Traffic and engineering studies led to the planning and construction of direct ramps between the tunnel and the terminal, removing all short haul and much of the long haul buses entirely from city streets. Platforms were designed to permit quick unloading of arriving buses, as well as for loading of departing buses operated by thirty-seven different bus companies. Internal access among various levels of the terminal was provided for the comfort and convenience of over 200,000 daily terminal users.

A similar but smaller bus facility is the George Washington Bridge Bus Station, built as a part of the project for adding a second deck to the bridge. This station was located at the Manhattan plaza, utilizing air rights over the expressway approach to the bridge. Direct ramps to and from the bridge have now removed most interstate buses from the streets of upper Manhattan. The bus station also provides a direct passenger transfer connection to the north-south subway line carrying traffic to midtown and downtown Manhattan.

These two terminals are a major element in the journey-to-work travel of the New Jersey-New York metropolitan area, serving 83,000 daily commuters crossing the Hudson River.

2. Modern Marine Cargo Terminals

Public port agencies in the United States have become the major instruments for planning, constructing and marketing of marine terminals used by steamship lines, private terminal operators and stevedoring companies. They are providing both general cargo and bulk cargo facilities.

Planners, designers and builders of steamship piers must take into account the framework of economics imposed by large ocean carriers, the need for fast in-port ship turnaround time, the increasing importance of the motor carrier for land haul, and the high cost of longshore operations per unit of cargo handled.

As a result, the modern pier for conventional general cargo is usually a wide one-story structure, capable of handling truck freight at tailgate-high platforms, with aisles in the transit shed for inside delivery or receipt of motor freight. The modern terminal must also provide for the handling of railroad freight either by lighter or by direct land access of railroad cars. Abundant transit shed space, supplemented by spacious paved, fenced and well-lighted open upland areas, are vital in the over-all function of loading and unloading ships, trucks, lighters, barges and railroad cars which converge on today's modern pier.

The Brooklyn Marine Terminal illustrates the trend toward developing such facilities through public agencies. The terminal was formerly owned by a private dock company which had neither the funds nor inclination to rebuild this prime cargo-handling waterfront. The Port Authority purchased the company's two-mile stretch of property and has provided twelve modern and spacious piers to replace twenty-six narrow and cramped piers, some dating back to the nineteenth century. Extensive upland areas for the parking and maneuvering of tractor-trailers were made available by tearing down old dilapidated warehouses back of the piers. Efficiency and productivity at the marine terminal were vastly increased and the total capacity for handling oceanborne cargoes greatly expanded.

The development of Port Newark is another illustration of the trend toward public development of marine facilities. Municipally owned Port Newark on the New Jersey side of the harbor was leased to the Port Authority after World War II, when the city of Newark was faced with capital demands for other public needs which did not permit the rebuilding of its waterfront. Starting in 1948, the Port Authority redeveloped this area into a completely new, greatly expanded and extremely busy marine terminal. Tonnage using the marginal wharves of Port Newark has increased from 800,000 tons in 1948 to more than 4 million tons in 1965.

Essential to the seaport's growth has been the development of supporting facilities on the upland areas in back of the wharves and cargo sheds. These include cargo distribution buildings for waterborne freight, a cold-storage warehouse, a cargo fumigation plant, specialized terminals for handling a wide variety of cargoes and many other installations for processing and distributing ocean freight.

Future marine terminals in the modern harbor will change

even more as a result of the accelerated introduction of containerization in ocean shipping. In its most ideal form, containerization involves the loading of a container or detachable van at an inland point and moving it as a unit by land and sea to an inland destination overseas without rehandling of its contents en route.

Containerization of ocean cargoes has tremendous implications in the planning of marine terminals. More spacious container and land vehicle marshaling areas will have to be provided adjacent to the vessel berthing area. They will have to be served by networks of excellent highways and provided with railroad trackage for direct rail delivery and receipt of containers. Fewer vessel berths will be needed, inasmuch as port turnaround time for a container ship is exceedingly brief due to the highly mechanized handling of containers—only one day compared to four or five days on the average breakbulk ships. In addition, the anticipated increase in size of future container ships will undoubtedly require longer berths than many now in use.

Containerization of oceanborne commerce is growing at a constantly faster pace. Its needs are being met at the Port of New York by the development of the Elizabeth-Port Authority Marine Terminal on the Newark Bay waterfront. This entirely new seaport facility will, when completed in 1975, have twenty-four deep-water berths, all designed to handle container ships if the demand justifies such use. Combined with thirty-seven deep-water berths at Port Newark, five of which are being designed for container ships, this vast marine terminal development is planned with an eye to the future of ocean shipping.

3. *Aviation Terminals*

The third illustration of terminal planning by The Port of New York Authority is its regional commercial airport program. This includes John F. Kennedy International and La-Guardia in New York, Newark and Teterboro Airports in New Jersey and two commercial heliports in Manhattan.

The largest and busiest of these is Kennedy Airport. Air passengers moving on eighteen domestic and twenty-three foreign flag lines are handled in the 655-acre Terminal City. Here are located eight individual terminals for the major airlines handling domestic flights and departing overseas trips. Two more are expected in the near future. Most arriving international passengers are handled in the International Arrival

Building where the various federal inspection agencies have their facilities and personnel for clearance.

The magnitude of the problem of passenger handling is evidenced by Kennedy Airport's volume of over 16 million domestic and overseas air passengers in 1965, expected to rise to over 30 million in 1975.

With this tremendous flow of air passengers, airport visitors and employees, the planning of the internal circulation of Terminal City became a major consideration. A comprehensive network of roadways provides access to individual terminals and easy movement to, from and within the airport itself. An intramural bus service accommodates movements between terminals. Space was set aside for expansion of terminals, hangars and maintenance areas. Air cargo centers have had to be continually enlarged to take care of this increasingly vital service. All of these, of course, had to be planned within the framework of the extensive runway system which serves the increasing air traffic demand.

JOHN F. KENNEDY INTERNATIONAL AIRPORT
TERMINAL CITY

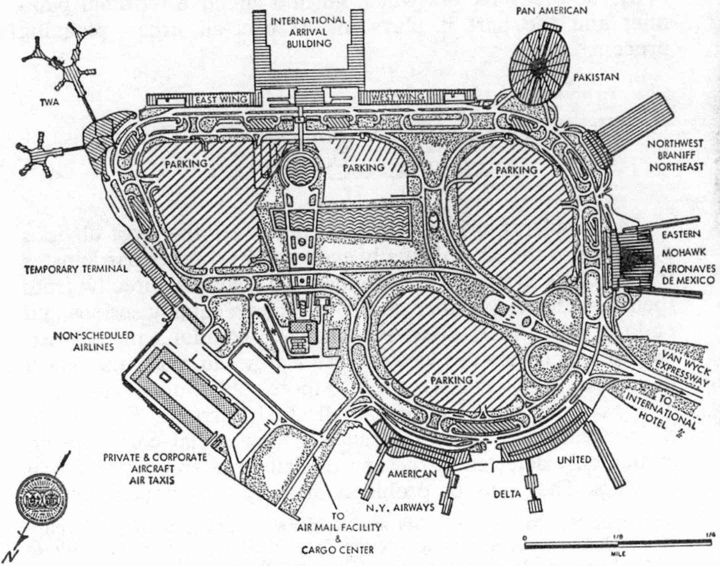

FIGURE 1.

The spectacular growth of air travel has made necessary the rebuilding of the old terminals at LaGuardia and Newark Airports. The LaGuardia redevelopment is completed while the new terminal area at Newark is under construction, to be opened in stages beginning in 1969.

The consistent increase in air traffic demand will require a fourth major commercial airport in the region by the 1970s. Vitally important to these airports is the provision of ground access which will meet the needs of the travelers, visitors and employees, and will take advantage of technological advances and transportation developments in the years to come.

SUMMARY

In all of the cases, the relationships of these terminal facilities to the total transportation system and urban planning were carefully considered. The need for interchange of various travel modes had a strong bearing on the plans for terminal layout, parking facilities, internal roadways, highway access, public transportation to the facilities, passenger and cargo service and many other elements. These terminals thus embody the many factors which go into effective terminal planning and the part it plays in the over-all urban planning process.

Urban Transportation Planning: An Overview
RALPH A. GAKENHEIMER*

The problems of urban transportation are the most obvious problems of the city. Virtually every urban dweller participates in the city's systems of movement and suffers directly from their inefficiencies. Other problems may be equally serious and enduring, but their discovery, their explanation, and the extent to which they are viewed with alarm and made the object of corrective policy are subject to more subtle influences. They may be uncovered by new intellectual currents, brought to wide attention by the appearance of new social commitment, or suddenly detected in the unarticulated preferences of urban dwellers. They may be problems of a minority which become

* Associate Professor of City and Regional Planning at the University of North Carolina, and editor of the *Journal of the American Institute of Planners*. He holds a Master of Regional Planning from Cornell and a planning Ph.D. from the University of Pennsylvania.

general concerns only when the majority is educated to a responsibility toward them or to the indirect benefits realized by solution. Through these changing patterns of concern for problems like housing, automation, poverty, economic growth, integrity of the natural environment and revitalization of downtowns, the transportation problem continues as one of the longest recognized of the "serious urban problems." Its most visible dimension, loss of time and money through inefficiencies imposed on the normal movements of people and goods, is modified and yields to more advanced interpretations when related to current perspectives on the other problems to which it is linked.

Thus the gravity of the transportation problem depends on relative concern for the others. During periods of relative slack in social commitment, such as the 1950s, transportation is regarded as the prominent urban problem. During times of greater commitment and new fears, like the late sixties, it assumes a more modest place. Because there are at present other significant social concerns, it has become current to think of transportation as a luxury problem which can be given priority only by an affluent society that has solved its more fundamental ones, but in view of the linkages between transportation systems and other troubled urban activities this position must be accepted with great qualification.

The question of whether the problem is getting worse at the present time, and if so in what sense, bears some attention. Taking the simplistic concept that the transportation problem is the one that gets worse as movements in the city are slowed down by congestion and other impairments, there is no firm evidence that the situation is currently getting worse. The major traffic problems have been associated with central business districts, where in most major cities the number of entering and leaving trips has been slightly reducing,[1] reflecting losses in employment and resident population in them. Thus while rapid urban growth in the outer rings of the metropolis would reduce travel speeds if destination preferences remained the same, it seems that this growth has taken a sufficient number of the downtown functions with it to adjust the movement systems away from the central focus and largely avoid this consequence.

Perhaps the problem takes its most extreme form when we consider the speeds of urban movement in contrast to the

[1] J. R. Meyer, J. F. Kain and M. Wohl, *The Urban Transportation Problem* (Cambridge: Harvard University Press, 1965), p. 35.

maximum speeds offered by available transportation technology. This form of the problem may be more intuitive to the urban dweller, and it exposes great limitations in the movement networks. We have a far greater capacity to build machines that move fast than to remove the external constraints on their speed in practical use. The automobile has a much higher ratio of maximum speed to speed in urban use than any previous mode. Horse-drawn urban vehicles probably had only a slightly lower average real in-town speed at less than a quarter of the maximum speed. It is necessary to emphasize this point because of the cultural inclination of Americans to assume that our transportation problems are rapidly getting worse and that their only salvation lies in our rapidly improving technology. In fact, the technology itself is in large measure defining the problem.

Given the limitations to reducing these constraints on automotive travel, only partly mitigated by increasing the capacities of facilities and limiting access to them, the obvious answer seems to lie with vehicles on independent rights of way, where they are isolated from most of these external effects. Thus the transportation problem becomes easily interpreted as one of how to make rapid transit work. With trends toward the loss of transit ridership in some cities and little gain in any of the others, maintaining present levels of service is often regarded as the more feasible problem.

There has been much discussion and research on the matter of consumer choice between modes of travel, based on relative costs, length of trip, time of travel, waiting time, psychic responses to the modes, and so forth. But the various interests which affect this choice are underlain by the evolving pattern of the city. Though there are undoubtedly social, economic, and psychological attractions to independent vehicles, the choice is primarily for a living environment which requires the use of automobiles to be accessible. The values that have motivated people to move to the urban periphery have been largely independent of consideration of transportation costs or conveniences. On the level of public policy also, therefore, the balance between modes of transportation is in good measure a residual of the primary choice, that of the structure of the city which best provides for the preferences and maximum opportunities of the people as created by policy and the independent locational decisions of urban dwellers. It is at that point, land use and activities patterns, that transportation planning must begin.

RESPONSIBILITIES OF URBAN TRANSPORTATION PLANNING

As reflected by the various perceptions of the problem, urban transportation is a superficially simple activity whose planning is subject to a multitude of interpretations, owing to its linkages with other urban problems. The nature of this series of linkages with other urban problems is clarified by considering the participation of transport in the most basic purpose of the city, that of creating proximity. Many advanced forms of human accomplishment are complex in the sense that they require close interrelations among large numbers of people in order to be achieved. Since long-distance communication is not a satisfactory form presently for many of these interrelations, people resort to locations of dense habitation in order to facilitate them. In the city an individual has access from his bases of operation to the maximum number of participants in other activities, thus maximizing potential interaction. Without the need or desire for this access there would be no cohesion within densely populated areas, and, our sentimentalities notwithstanding, we would resume the dispersed pattern of living which has been the overwhelmingly dominant style of living throughout human history.

The primary function of urban transportation, then, is to provide the characteristic of accessibility to locations in the city, and the objective of transportation planning is to increase it. This accessibility is unevenly spread because some locations are necessarily closer to the rest than others are, because it depends on the use of a network of facilities which cannot provide completely uniform coverage, and because of externalities which impede movement unevenly on the network. For similar reasons public policy cannot be effectuated to increase accessibility uniformly. In any case there is no reason why it should. The value of an increment in accessibility varies widely among the various users of urban locations; some benefit from it much more than others. Consequently, we can define transportation planning as the selective distribution of access in urban space.[2]

The more familiar objective, expediting projected movement flow where it is expected most seriously to overload the

[2] Lowdon Wingo, Jr., and Harvey S. Perloff, "The Washington Transportation Plan: Technics or Politics?" *Papers of the Regional Science Association,* Vol. 7, 1961, pp. 249–62.

existing network (or reducing congestion), can be regarded as derivative from the access concept. But this requires the implicit assumption that future expressed desire for movement will conform in pattern to the relative levels of benefit from access derived by the involved locations. It is nonetheless useful in approaching much of the problem and is tempting to policy action because it makes the problem subject to direct measurement. It also requires fewer normative judgments, since solution becomes a matter of correcting visible malignancy rather than weighing the relative merits of increased access at various locations. But this is dangerous for a variety of reasons. A person's concept of his opportunities, for example, may be very much controlled by his current reach. Further, it is not a completely politically acceptable interpretation because pressures for public action reflect the need for greater access by particular urban establishments, their forcefulness in demanding it, or their increasing loss of it because of growing externalities. In the case of the transportation industries, pressures arise from the desire of each to provide for a greater share of the movement.

As a result, the operational objectives of transportation planning reflect the relative strengths of these access-seekers and public sympathies toward them, as well as the need to facilitate movement where the network is found or expected to be overloaded. The loudest voice among the access-seekers in most cities is that of the central business district interests, who are becoming less accessible to the urban populations spreading over larger areas, and who are affected by the externalities that work upon the extended radial routes to the center. These effects are, of course, also subject to direct observation, so solution to this problem may also stem from an effort to treat network overload. But given the current decrease in trips to most CBDs, the strongest influence is usually the voices of access-seekers or a public determination that the core be saved. The voices of other, less unified, access-seekers are added to these, such as those of industries desiring to expand their access to labor or those of the electorate in general, who are usually concerned with facilitating the trip to work, which is their most troublesome one. The spatially ununified nature of these latter interests normally requires that they be solved by analysis of network overloading. Similarly, the objective of gaining a larger share of the trips for transit (or providing a greater choice between modes) reflects the industry's concern for its survival or an effort to relax network overload by a mode that uses urban space more efficiently in moving people.

Combinations of these objectives, together with others less closely related to transportation, can be represented by comprehensive decisions as to the way the form of the city should develop. This level of solution is preferable because in its comprehensiveness it establishes a balance among the immediate objectives and represents related interests outside this framework which are likely to be equally important, if not more so.

No matter how the objectives are approached, effort is made to provide specific levels of network service at least cost.

Though transportation planning has not yet been accomplished on a systematic basis for a mix of all the goals implied above, it has, in a qualified sense, been more systematic and internally logical than other aspects of planning.[3] This is true in the sense that minimum cost solutions (although within rigid limitations of benefit-cost measurement) have been sought and attained within stated criteria, lending more logical consistency to this aspect of the planning field than to many others. This accomplishment has been possible largely because of the nature of transportation—traffic on the streets—which can be easily and directly measured. This gives rise to an exact calculus for the field that also enables some measurement of the effects of policy and tends to define future change as tractable. That is, the unpredictability of human behavior patterns notwithstanding, direct dealings with the uncertainties that complicate other aspects of planning have to some extent been avoided, partly because the field has a fairly elaborate and standard analytical approach which permits the systematic entry of change estimates into the process. Moreover, the fact that most causes of urban movement are fundamental, and to some extent irreducible, makes these systems less liable to unpredictable change than others which depend more on popular tastes or more changeable commitment. Finally, the facilities which constitute the physical recommendations of the plan are provided by reliable sources (mostly the federal government) and are mainly within the public domain. This provides opportunity for direct cost measurement, which is not the case for planning in the private sector where effectuation is limited to indirect encouragement and controls.

[3] Britton Harris, Roger L. Creighton and Edward F. R. Hearle, "Have We Learned Anything from Transportation Studies," *Planning 1963*, American Society of Planning Officials, 1963, pp. 175–91.

This is not to say that transportation planning is without great uncertainties. Its confidence comes in good measure from a misleading specificity in its analytical methods; the ability to project systematically does not insure accuracy. Indeed, its uncertainties ultimately represent those of all the other urban systems to which transportation is related. Perhaps the greatest unreliability lies in our poor understanding of change in transportation and communication technology, where elemental changes have telling impacts on urban movement and location patterns.

THE PLANNING OF TRANSPORTATION

Regular professional attention to urban transportation problems began in the early years of the twentieth century. Streetcars had played major roles in the large cities for a sufficient length of time to create active concern for their standards of service, management effectiveness and effects on the urban physical structure. At this time contentions between the viabilities of private and public ownership began. Within the first fifteen years of the century methods were worked out for the measurement of origin-destination patterns, time of travel, and traffic volumes and changes in these with alteration of the route patterns and standards of service. The effects of transit routing on land value also received considerable attention, but only hortatory remarks were made about the capabilities of the transit systems for building or structuring cities. The orientation was toward providing service to meet demand.

By virtue of this development, concern for problems of automobile traffic, beginning in the late 1920s, could call upon sources of diagnostic method. The adjustment of these methods to the relative flexibility of automobile movement and the less centralized pattern of origins and destinations was eventually accomplished. More developed means of measurement and prediction appeared, but the prevailing understanding through the 1930s, that the populations of U.S. cities would cease to grow within the following twenty-five years, kept the problem from being dealt with as a crucial one.[4] Partly for this reason, the rapid increases in population and car ownership after World War II caused the transportation

---

[4] This understanding was expressed in many reports of the 1920s and '30s. See, for example, Ernest P. Goodrich, "Transit Facilities and Urban Development," unpublished ms. at the Library of the University of Pennsylvania, 1936, p. 54.

problem to reach professional as well as public recognition with explosive force. Aided by automatic data processing equipment, traffic flow characteristics and origin-destination studies were accomplished at increasing levels of detail. This greater capacity for detail made it possible to break down trip-making recorded in the origin-destination surveys by purposes of trips and characteristics of the trip-makers to understand the systems more clearly, thus introducing the possibility of the quantitative behavioral study of transportation.

In 1954 the analytical basis for studying interdependencies between land use and transportation was presented by Robert B. Mitchell and Chester Rapkin.[5] The concept was not entirely new that use of transportation facilities is determined by activities on proximate land and that the use of land is partially determined by its level of accessibility. But systematic means for the analysis of these relationships was a powerful tool that reset the approach of transportation planning. It provided a means for relating movement systems with other systems of activity in the city, represented as generators of person trips from fixed locations. This brought transportation analysis into the potentiality of full contact with planning concerns for land development and complex sets of activities of urban dwellers.

An operational form for this relationship was soon determined in a basic four-step procedure for the analysis and projection of transportation systems. The generation of trips from specific subareas is explained by its correlations to the values of variables representing the trip-making inclinations of the subareas' occupants; their purposes for making trips, income, car ownership, family size, distance from the CBD, and other measures. The variables are chosen as suitable for predicting the generation of trips at a future date when the occupation of the zones and other trip generation characteristics have changed. These trips are then distributed; their origins or destinations in other subareas are considered and interchanges between pairs of zones are simulated by equations. Trips which form the interchange between each pair of subareas are then divided between available modes of transportation. Finally, the interchange by modes is assigned to existing traffic facilities and thereby represented as traffic on the streets. This whole set of procedures is done once to

[5] Robert B. Mitchell and Chester Rapkin, *Urban Traffic: A Function of Land Use* (New York: Columbia University Press, 1954).

reliably simulate the existing pattern of movement by use of equations which can take future changes in trip-making characteristics as input variables to predict future systems of travel based on a new pattern of land use and new trip-making characteristics.

The procedure for analyzing transportation systems, even in this very simplistic form, suggests the principal problems met in an effort to establish future needs for transportation facilities. The predictive reliability of the process depends upon (1) the usefulness of the variables involved (or of any available) to properly register change in trip-making, (2) the extent to which principles of movement, reflected by the mathematics of the analysis, sufficiently approximate forces in the real world, and (3) the extent to which each variable can be usefully predicted. Considerable attention has been given to these topics. Comparisons of the fit of variables to generation equations, for example, have been made.[6] Controversy has continued for several years on the usefulness of alternative equations for predicting trip distribution, which assume different responses of generated trips to the availability of new origins and destinations. Limited verifications have been developed,[7] but since the equations are applied on the basis of assumptions which cannot be directly verified, only extensive review of their success in prediction can suggest their value. The predictability of variables is even more difficult to examine, but efforts have been made to understand the stability and change characteristics of some of the better behaved ones.[8] All of these assurances are, of course, circumscribed by the relatively unknown shape of matters such as future life styles, technology, and changes in other elements of public policy, which forbear against the view that any projection of travel can be regarded as accurate. Still, an understanding of knowable trends provides a stronger base to underlie consideration of the open questions, and leads to an answer useful in the absence of major impingements by unknowns on the present course of events.

A second set of problems emerges from the need to recog-

[6] See Walter Y. Oi and Paul W. Shuldiner, *An Analysis of Urban Travel Demands* (Evanston, Northwestern University Press, 1964).

[7] Donald M. Hill and Norman Dodd, "Studies of Trends of Travel Between 1954 and 1964 in a Large Metropolitan Area," *Record of the Highway Research Board,* forthcoming.

[8] J. F. Kain and M. E. Beesley, "Forecasting Car Ownership and Use," *Urban Studies,* Vol. 2, No. 2, November 1965, pp. 163–85.

nize the interdependency between changes in movement systems and changes in activities taking place at fixed urban locations. A concomitant to the basic analytic procedures of the field is the interpretation that a transportation facility network cannot be designed merely to serve a previously devised or predicted land-use pattern because the network itself will stimulate trip-making that will change the future of that pattern. Correspondingly, a land-use pattern cannot be projected after a transportation plan, because the existence of these new activities will alter the requirements for the transportation network. This situation requires that the planning of the two areas be somehow simultaneous in order that the effects of each on the other be properly accounted for. The obvious means for doing this by current methodology is to pass several times through the planning of each in turn in order to absorb the effects upon each of the planning of the previous one. That is to say, land development can be planned or projected; then the transportation system can be designed for it; then the land-use plan is revised for transportation impacts upon it; in turn the transportation plan is revised to meet the new demands upon it, and so forth. This procedure would presumably achieve a reasonably stable relationship between the two components within a short number of iterations. This process has actually never been accomplished for a transportation study, but the impediments have been lack of time and money. It contains few fundamental technical problems.

Another problem, symptomatic of the relationship between transportation planning and other aspects of urban planning, stems from the hesitancy of transportation planners to accommodate planned change in other urban systems when they establish future facility networks. Transportation planning is based primarily on projections rather than plans. One of the reasons for this is that the specificity of transportation planning analysis requires more detailed statements of the policy objectives of other system plans than is normally provided, or can be provided by those aspects of the process. Even projections of land use provided by municipal agencies have generally been found unsatisfactory, so that the transportation agencies have made their own. But more significant than this is the orientation of transportation planning to directly purchased facilities in the public domain, which are less frequently obstructed politically than other planning recommendations. The relatively high assurance of effectuation offered by these conditions, when compared to the indirect means by which other urban systems must be planned, leaves transportation planners in the position of needing to cover rather long shot bets by other components of planning. They are not generally disposed to do this. Problems arise on account of this which are related to the interdependency argument above. Transportation planning based on a projection tends to "implement" the projection as though it were policy statement. Correspondingly, if based on a plan, the projected network would tend to validate that statement. Still, in view of the poor record of comprehensive planning, the risks are considered too high.

A final basic problem is the difficulty in measuring consequences of investment.[9] By virtue of the links between movement systems and other systems of urban activities, transportation investments cause a wide array of benefits and disbenefits in the city which are impossible to evaluate fully by the present state of knowledge on this subject. Further, facilities of this type have long lives, remaining parts of the urban plant through considerable changes in the conditions which determine their usefulness. Moreover, these facilities represent series of large single investments with considerable economies of scale, so that the level of effect from different series of such expenditures becomes a matter of difficult balance. The absence of a conventional market for these facilities also confuses the analysis. Most importantly, the widely different approaches to the accomplishment of objectives and broad choice among mixes of objectives themselves make it very difficult to identify an optimum investment mix among one set of investments, to which optima of others can be compared. There is, nonetheless, a substantial amount of work being done on this topic to describe workable boundaries for the effects of network changes,[10] to estimate network costs,[11] to clarify network planning principles implied by cost-benefit

[9] Britton Harris, comment on Tillo E. Kuhn, "The Economics of Transportation Planning in Urban Areas," *Transportation Economics* (New York: Columbia University Press, 1965) pp. 321–22.

[10] A. R. Prest and R. Turvey, "Cost-Benefit Analysis: A Survey," *Economic Journal*, December 1965, see pp. 711–14. Also, Herbert Monring and Mitchell Harwitz, *Highway Benefits; an Analytical Framework* (Evanston: Northwestern University Press, 1962).

[11] Abe Gottlieb, "The Economic Context of 1985: Transportation Costs in the PJ Region," Penn-Jersey Paper No. 23, 1965.

relationships,[12] to better understand movement system costs,[13] and to explore broader series of network effects.[14]

FORCES AND RESPONSES CONDITIONING THE FUTURE OF URBAN TRANSPORTATION PLANNING

The surest thing about the future shape of transportation planning is its growth as an active process in metropolitan areas. The present trend of federal legislation in this field bears similarities to the development of urban renewal legislation during the last two decades, which has been a decisive force in the expansion of planning work in that area. Since 1961 the Department of Commerce and the former HHFA have encouraged the use of the 1½ percent highway survey planning funds for metropolitan transportation planning, thus joining the interests of urban transportation with urban renewal and paving the way for financial participation by the Department of Housing and Urban Development in the major transportation studies. The Federal Aid Highway Act of 1962 formally joined the transportation and urban planning efforts by requiring that highway projects since mid-1965 be based on continuing comprehensive planning. The trend represented by these and other federal acts will increase the amount of transportation planning activity and, hopefully, the store of useful experience in solving its difficult problems.

Current development of models for the allocation of new land uses promises to provide for transportation planning based on less limited policy assumptions, and to provide more understanding of the effects of relations between transportation and other urban systems. Past models for this purpose have normally predicted change in terms of aggregate behavioral data with changes in the land-use system stated in the same aggregate structural terms. A new generation of models is now being operationalized which focuses instead on the action of the individual decision unit—for example, the household, or single industrial plant—and adds these elemental de-

[12] R. L. Creighton, I. Hock and N. Schneider, "Estimating Efficient Spacing for Arterials and Expressways," Highway Research Board *Bulletin 253.*

[13] J. R. Meyer, J. F. Kain and M. Wohl, *op. cit.,* Part II, "Comparative Costs," pp. 171–308.

[14] Morris Hill, "Evaluation of Plans in One Sector," doctoral dissertation, University of Pennsylvania, Department of City and Regional Planning, 1966.

cisions into a net effect.[15] In view of the close contact of these concepts with the real course of policy impact, response to policy by individual actors in the city, they should facilitate predictions which are better conditioned to changes which are expected to occur or are considered as policy alternatives. This would provide for removal of some of the unfortunate rigidities in transportation planning which are characteristic of the process to the present time.

Considerable work is also being done in the development and qualification of methods for the projection of zonal interchanges. Though the work in this area has tended to be more incremental than in that of land-use projection, some additional concepts in the systematic study of trip-making have appeared.[16]

More generally, improvements of this type offer an increased capacity to simulate entire series of urban systems. The model-building has been done in each of these subareas of the problem with the assumption that the various analyses can be linked together to provide a full picture of interactions between the subsystems. This development is countercyclical to the previous tendency to aggregate knowledge of the interactions from a more and more detailed knowledge of intuitively related parts. At this level, of course, the development is not fundamentally one of transportation planning, since its involvements are comprehensive within the field of urbanism. Nevertheless, most of the development has come from efforts in transportation planning because of the particular needs and analytical style of the field.

Problems may soon beset trip-making analysis on account of changes of balance among trip types. At the present time work trips dominate planning considerations because they are the most numerous single type, are highly convergent in pattern, and occur during very limited periods of the day. They therefore tend to fix the minimum capacity of transport networks. But with workplaces dispersing as the city grows, and with increased affluence and leisure time, work trips will become a less significant network determinant. Unfortunately, the trip purposes which are rising in significance, especially

---

[15] J. Herbert and B. Stevens, "A Model for the Distribution of Residential Activity in Urban Areas," *Journal of Regional Science*, Vol. 2, No. 2, 1960, pp. 21–36.

[16] Anthony R. Tomazinis, "A New Method of Trip Distribution in an Urban Area," (mimeo) Penn-Jersey Transportation Study Research Paper, 1963.

recreational, have different and less tractable characteristics. They are closely related in quantity and pattern to current fashions; they are flexible for time of travel and so can be made during off-peak hours (within serious limitations); they can be discouraged or diverted by congestion. In short, their patterns are far less reliable than those of work trips, and their projection requires dangerous assumptions about very changeable motivations. Though studies on these movements to the present time mostly emphasize travel at the supraurban scale,[17] where changes in volume will probably be greatest, the concern for their planning in urban areas is bound to increase.

Technology

The technologies of transportation and of other urban activities present perhaps the most difficult problems in estimating future facility needs and urban structure. A considerable amount of research is going on toward the improvement of intra-urban transportation vehicles and networks, but the inconclusive likelihoods of particular innovations have made it impossible for planning to be based on assumptions of changed future technology. No public urban transportation plan to the present time has been based on technology other than that now existing and in common use.

Work in transportation technology is emphasizing the objectives of increased speed and acceleration, more economical power, abatement of noise and other nuisances, more comfort, more efficient use of urban space, lowering operating costs through automation, and increasing the efficiency of movement through systems design of networks and control of networks. Although most of this work is not likely to affect the dimensions of urban trip-making to the extent that it would invalidate projections of trip-making and locational choices, some of it seems to offer potentialities for this. Discounting possibilities of intracity air travel as leading to insurmountable traffic control problems, the research on very high speed ground transit systems could have considerable impact.[18]

[17] Outdoor Recreation Resources Review Commission, *Projections to the Years 1976 and 2000: Economic Growth, Population, Labor Force and Leisure, and Transportation* (Washington, D.C.: Government Printing Office, 1962), Part III, pp. 73–119.

[18] Project Transport, M.I.T., *Survey of Technology for High Speed Ground Transport* (Washington, D.C.: U. S. Department of Commerce, 1965).

Though it is being considered primarily for intercity movement, the limitations of single-point destinations in major cities
are likely to encourage two-scale networks with intra-urban
distribution systems. Operational designs for acceleration and
deceleration ramps would reinforce this impact enormously.[19]
These ramps, off the main trunk of a transit system, would
store small cars which would be boarded by a few passengers
headed for the same destination. The car would accelerate
to full cruising speed before entering the trunk line, and maintain that speed until it reached the deceleration ramp at its
destination. By eliminating the intermediate stops, which seriously limit the speed of any current urban transit mode, high
speed vehicles could be used to great effect.

Resistance against this type of innovation is offered by a
number of factors, including the vested interests in other
modes, need for large-scale initial network construction, and
especially the increasingly dispersed location patterns of residences in American cities. In any case, current construction
of the Bay Area Rapid Transit System in the San Francisco
area and the recent Toronto subway construction serve to
remind us that local introduction of a different technology is
not impossible, even without the unique advantages of some
of the developing forms.

With respect to transportation planning, the greatest question about future transport technology seems not the details
of speed, economy and external effects upon transportation
vehicles, but innovations which sharply affect preference between individual and mass movement. The important difference between these two is that individual movement encourages dispersed residential location patterns, while an
overwhelmingly superior transit system could conceivably re-
structure the city into a series of density peaks at the transit
stops, or into a larger-scale version of the star-shaped streetcar-
dominated city of the late nineteenth and early twentieth centuries.

This conflict between the two basic modes is fundamentally
between automotive life style and transit technology. Three
decades of increasing use of individual vehicles has induced
location and trip-making patterns that are increasingly resistant to service by transit which requires heavy patronage
along a single line. The locational dispersion will undoubtedly increase. On the other hand, individual vehicles are not

---

[19] This feature is not presently operational, but has been suggested
by the Industrial Systems Group at Westinghouse.

susceptible to much technological improvement. Their usefulness can be measurably increased only by greater dispersion
of the population. Thus technological impacts are sure to be
on the side of transit. It seems quite possible that restructuring
of Eastern U.S. urban areas might occur through the local
distribution systems of very rapid transit designed primarily
as an inter-city mode.

At the present time, most professionals in urban transportation planning do not consider major change in technology
likely during the next twenty to thirty years, and adherence
to this position seems to become more definite as time goes
on. This is understandable as a working assumption since no
specific alternative to it would be really viable at present. And
it is surely to some extent reinforced by increasing vested professional interests in a detailed series of analytical methods
whose value would be seriously limited by expectations of
change in this magnitude. But as feasibilities of innovation become clearer, new demands for major policy decisions in the
planning process will occur.

Communications—the movement of ideas rather than people or goods—is another aspect of technology that is gradually
altering the shape of urban activity. It is clear that transportation and communication are to some extent substitutable as
means of completing transactions. In parts of the world
where telephones are uncommon there is much street traffic
incurred for purposes that would elsewhere be met by phone
calls. Since transactions which can be accommodated by communications media are almost always less costly by that
means, increasing adjustment of activity to the media usually
follows their introduction. Extensive reliance on communications media partly releases the participant from the need
for proximity to locations at which he interacts since the cost
of communication, within broad bounds, does not increase
with distance. Thus increasing reliance on mass media
for information and recreation and on personal electronic
media for individual transactions has in some measure made
possible the dispersed pattern of suburban residences at the
present time.[20] This effect is sure to continue in the future,

[20] Melvin M. Webber, "The Urban Place and the Nonplace Urban
Realm," in Melvin M. Webber, *Explorations into Urban Structure*,
(Philadelphia: University of Pennsylvania Press, 1964). For comments
on the details of substitutability see Frederick W. Memmott, III, "The
Substitutability of Communications for Transportation," *Traffic Engi-
neering*, Vol. 33, No. 5, February 1963, pp. 20–24.

reinforced by increasing social and physical mobility. Increased availability of closed-circuit television, telephone conference call arrangements, expansion of coverage by the mass media and so forth will be significant.

The trend for dispersing location patterns, however, is based not so much on additional innovation as on continued adaption to presently available media. Many transactions are now accomplished by the physical presence of people only because social propriety seems to demand it, because a feeling of trust is conveyed by personal contact, or in order to control the actions of a participant (to make sure he works a full eight hours a day, for instance). Yet the increasing complexity of bureaucratic and administrative networks served by improving communications networks tends to overcome these barriers. Central control of management functions is expedited, and systems of activity lap over each other such that collateral checks on facts and obligations become increasingly available. The effect is to regularize activity and "keep people honest," such that personalized control and intuitive assurances become less necessary. As a result more transactions can be accomplished by the more efficient means of communication. (Comparisons of business methods between underdeveloped and developed countries show differences partly explained by this.) To the extent that we cling to personal means of transaction because they are more pleasant and sociable, the transition can be slowed; but since some participants in every relevant activity will seek to maximize their efficiency through communication, the others will be forced to follow in order to remain competitive.

It is not clear how far trends in this direction will go, particularly since they imply gross changes in social style. Since they involve change of well-ingrained patterns of activity, their advance, as in the past, is apt to be slow. Nonetheless, they present difficult problems to transportation planning, in which it would be useful to consider transportation and communications systems together and develop a better understanding of the partial substitutability between them. Unfortunately, this is very difficult because of the measurement problems in communications. Though there is theoretical basis for these measurements, meaningful empirical survey of transmission is not possible at the present time.

As a joint result of increased mobility and reliance on communications, it is clear that many people will take the option of greater physical isolation to gain a larger living space at less expense. Thus the city will continue to regionalize; to spread over larger areas with looser ties to its central locations and require a more even pattern of access to its various parts. Friedmann and Miller[21] have suggested a pattern of this type, in which the metropolitan area is circumscribed by a radius of two hours' driving time from the core (about a hundred miles by today's technology), urban facilities are widely dispersed, and a much broader series of interaction possibilities available, whether in the central metropolis or in the non-metropolitan periphery now fused to the city. A trend in this direction is presently in motion. Its advanced stages will present transportation network requirements of a different type from those of the core-dominated city. Required networks will convey more even access, rather than the unified converging radial network of the traditional city. With the access-seekers more widely distributed, problems of multiple point access and relative location will rise in significance; and current problems of congestion, minimization of the use of scarce central city land for transportation facilities, and damage by proximity of incompatible activities should decline.

Spread of the Boundaries of Concern

Aside from developments within the field, transportation planning is subject to change because of altered approaches to other urban problems. The existence of a much greater and more detailed quantity of diagnostic data than in many other areas is encouraging the study of many urban activities through their access and movement characteristics. This has included studies in commercial location, urban land values,[22] the locational consequences of racial segregation,[23] alternatives in urban physical structure[24] and a number of other

[21] John Friedmann and John Miller, "The Urban Field," *Journal of the American Institute of Planners,* Vol. 31, No. 4, November 1965, pp. 312–20.

[22] Stanislaw Czamanski, "Effects of Public Investment on Urban Land Values," *Journal of the American Institute of Planners,* Vol. 32, No. 4, July 1966.

[23] John F. Kain, "The Effect of the Ghetto on the Distribution and Level of Nonwhite Employment in Urban Areas," paper presented to the annual meeting of the American Statistical Association, Chicago, December 1964.

[24] Work on this topic is being pursued at the Department of City and Regional Planning at M.I.T. under the leadership of Professor Aaron Fleisher. See George C. Hemmens, "An Analysis of Urban Travel and the Spatial Structure of Urban Activities," doctoral dissertation, Department of City and Regional Planning, M.I.T., 1966.

topics. Some of this work is filtering back into the planning of transportation in the form of new methods for analysis and qualification of objectives. The work in urban structural alternatives is particularly promising for transportation planning, since it approaches more closely the basic alternatives in life style and economic character which are the most fundamental impacts of transportation networks. Beginnings in this direction have been made.[25]

Along with this continual broadening and detailing of the analytical net, there are reactions against the increasing complexity and cost of comprehensive studies which are likely to increase. These take the form of militant conservatism, narrowly circumscribed simplistic solutions, or ad hoc solutions. Desire for the simplistic solution seems symptomized by the popularity of the recent Buchanan Report[26] on urban traffic planning in Great Britain. Ad hoc solutions to localized problems or to specific viewpoints on broader problems will, of course, always be necessary, at least as detailed solutions within larger policy frameworks. It seems likely, however, that efforts will arise to devise specific detailed solutions and then link them together, in the manner of social action trends, in order to avoid the complexities of the over-all job.

In the end, these rapidly expanding bounds of the applicability of transportation analysis and planning threaten on one hand to engulf a good part of the planning field, and on the other to disappear by assimilation. Broadening efforts in the projection and planning of urban activities by the major transportation studies (as necessary background to fulfill their responsibility of recommending facilities networks) and the unusual formative strength of the networks, have caused some observers to believe that soon little may be left to the rest of planning but residual tasks outside these interests. It seems more likely, however, that as the methods are diffused into other urban policy professions the broad urban structure analyses and decisions may become the responsibility of other fields, leaving to transportation planning only its more fundamental concern for network development. Their use in the

---

[25] The New York Regional Plan Association has developed such structural alternatives and related them to the particular transportation networks they imply.

[26] Great Britain, Ministry of Transport, *Traffic in Towns: A Study of the Long Term Problems of Traffic in Urban Areas* (London: H. M. Stationery Office, 1963). See also remarks on the book by John W. Dyckman, "Transportation in Cities," *Scientific American*, Vol. 213, No. 3, September 1965, p. 169.

recent Community Renewal Plans of San Francisco, Philadelphia, New York, and other cities is symptomatic. Should this happen, urban transportation planning in its present sense will have disappeared. This is no reason for concern, since it is only part of a larger current trend toward the redefinition of professionalized activity by problem areas, rather than skill areas. The contributions and skills of transportation planning would continue developing in the decision sectors where maximum use could be made of them.

Chapter 10

THE ECONOMIC FUNCTION

A city must earn its living; unless outputs of goods and services exceed inputs *nekropolis* will be the result. But how to define "a city"? Is a political city even remotely a *closed* economic system? Is a functional metropolitan area a system, or must the scale of the physical area be expanded to the region, to the nation and even beyond? In the introduction to Chapter 4, it was pointed out that the economist has had considerable difficulty—specifically in an advanced interconnected expanding economy—in carrying out economic analysis within a valid urban spatial framework. And yet there is evidence, both historical and contemporary, that cities and/or city sectors wither on the vine. There must be local and non-local economic reasons for such decline, or intracity and intercity factors as Wilbur R. Thompson names them in his treatment of urban economics.[1] Further, planning bodies, as well as private and public community goals, are pretty generally atomistic in scope. In the narrowly centered public jurisdictions of the political city and of the suburbs, there is little or no sense of metropolitan "togetherness" and of common economic goals for the entire area.

Despite the unclarity of the system's physical limits, serious studies of the urban economic base[2] have been in progress for well over a decade with attempts made to measure the export or basic industrial components of a city economy. An interesting short cut is "the minimum requirements approach,"[3] which attempts to simplify the job of analysis and subsequent development by reducing the economic base to key components of crucial or determining importance. The regional Science Association, based at the University of Pennsylvania, has investigated an accounting system, similar to a cost/benefit analysis, for urban areas. But it has been obliged to deal with larger than political city systems up through the metropolis to include the regional hinterland in order to carry out meaningful studies and make valid planning recommendations of an economic order. As a sophisticated planning device, Arthur Row's scheme (Chapter 8),

---

[1] See Chapter 4.

[2] See Charles M. Tiebout, *The Community Economic Base Study*, Supplementary Paper No. 16, Committee for Economic Development, 1962 for a useful summary and instructions for practical application of this device.

[3] Edward Ullman and Michael Dacey, "The Minimum Requirements Approach to Urban Economic Base," *Papers and Proceedings, Regional Science Association*, Vol. VI (1960), pp. 175–94.

places industrial development strategically throughout the entire New York Metropolitan Area, as well as siting twelve new or expanded general purpose centers or nodes of varied activities to increase the well-being of and structure the entire area. This economic overview of an entire metro is not general.

It would appear to be a relatively safe assertion to say that a weak or decaying central city can hardly—at this stage of Western urbanization and despite the California autopolis of Los Angeles—lead to a virile metropolitan area. Even L.A. itself, is commencing to "center" with new public transportation planned and the higher culture laid on in the core with a trowel! Thus city planners tend, probably rightly, to concentrate initially on saving downtown as does almost the entire federal urban redevelopment effort. Uncle Sam is betting billions on the CBD (Central Business District) thus luring many more billions of private capital investment in a multiplier effect. Jean Gottmann, geographical student of megalopolis, believes in central city with its patent external economies of financial gain and good living; he makes a plea below for the functional rightness of high density expressed by the skyscraper to meet the high level of *transactions* (interaction more or less in sociological terms) of modern urbanized society—a paper society of white collar workers! Some question might well be raised as to how long such a functional necessity for extreme centrality will continue in the face of the electronic communications revolution in business and human relations practices. William L. Baldwin takes a "conservative" economist's position in arguing cogently that in a "free market" such as we admire, governmental operations should be minimized and private operations maximized to create external economies which will encourage renewal in and development of urban places. This is a thoroughly realistic exploration of possible urban economic planning within the parameters of our present society; most urban plans are private plans—public plans are neither comprehensive nor compelling enough and their rationality cannot be guaranteed either. Baldwin suggests minimal ordinances to nudge the "free market" in land and accepts a level of controlled "congestion" as conducive to a healthy central city with an expanding local economy. In the feasibility study for Philadelphia's proposed Chestnut Street Mall, Arthur C. Kaufmann and Associates, Inc., carried out a thorough canvass of existent pedestrian precincts. In a bold fashion these economic consultants have "proven" the economic viability of a two-mile pedestrian mall for the CBD of that grand old city, which has experienced such a remarkable renaissance in recent years under an active coterie of citizens often leading the government as John Bodine's article indicates.[4] Thus "the city fights back against suburban sprawl" with the lessons learned from shopping centers molded into the central area with its heavy valuable freight of culture, finance, learning, life, political action and a wide spectrum of trade. And the revivified

[4] See Chapter 20 in Volume II.

center with a balanced relationship to the fringe can make a most important contribution to the economic and human viability of the entire metropolis. Eventually, of course, these metropolitan areas must be linked, but that will be beyond "urban planning" to the regional and national levels.

Economic Aspects of Business Blight and Traffic Congestion

WILLIAM L. BALDWIN*

I. INTRODUCTION

If any two symbols can conjure up a vision of the troubles of our cities today, they are physical blight and traffic congestion. Blight and congestion are symptoms, not causes. The point is well recognized, virtually a truism, and need not be belabored here. Yet if a medical analogy is to be used, blight and congestion must be viewed as scars rather than measles spots. They may or may not go away by themselves when the underlying causes are recognized and corrected. Thus, planning for the future of the city is inevitably coupled with urban renewal, area redevelopment, highway, street, parking and mass-transit projects which in substantial part are designed to erase the visible results of the past. The analogy must, however, be carried one step further before being dropped. A competent physician would hesitate to recommend plastic surgery when less drastic treatment would aid the natural recuperative powers of the body, or when the scar tissue served useful functions and the disfigurement was minor.

The present essay focuses on blight and congestion as they are caused by and in turn affect industrial and commercial activities in the city. There is certainly no intention of slighting the importance of problems of residential slums. I recognize their primacy in any analysis of the city's ills. However, an-

* Associate Professor, Department of Economics, Dartmouth College. He received his doctorate in economics from Princeton University where he also served as Visiting Assistant Professor in 1961–62; in 1963–64 he was at the Brookings Institute as Research Professor. The author of a number of professional articles, this contribution draws heavily on an unpublished study prepared several years ago for Arthur D. Little, Inc., Cambridge, Massachusetts. Professor Baldwin wishes to express his gratitude to them for permission to make use of portions of the earlier study in both original and revised form here.

other commonplace observation is that the *raison d'être* for most American cities is the performance of economic functions rather than religious, military or political. It therefore follows that it is essential for the city planner to understand the strengths and weaknesses of the city as an environment for business activity. A significant part of the planner's efforts must be aimed at bolstering the economic advantages of his city and countering its economic shortcomings.

Perhaps the single most important concept that economic theory has to contribute to city planning is that of "externalities," or social costs and benefits accruing to others than the initiators of a decision. Given the fundamental locational, topographic and historical features which have shaped an urban area, externalities account for most of the unique advantages and disadvantages of the city as a place for business enterprise. In this paper, externalities as a basic source of urban economic strength will first be noted; and the concept will then be applied to an analysis of the causes of and appropriate remedies for business blight and congestion.

II. INTERDEPENDENCE AND EXTERNAL ECONOMIES IN THE CITY

The city's business vitality is largely based on interactions among the various functions performed there. A major stock exchange, for example, requires the proximity of brokers' and dealers' offices, banks, other financial establishments and law firms. The existence of many nearby firms, either of the same type or dependent upon each other for sales, supplies and services, leads to the creation of certain "external economies." These may be defined as advantages which a firm derives from the independently determined activities of other firms or as benefits which the firm receives without the need for any changes in its internal structure, organization or output.

Raymond Vernon has shown that the central cities in the United States today have far more than their proportionate share of industrial firms which are of small size and which produce non-standard products.[1] These two features of small size and versatility are interrelated. A firm which expands in order to achieve economies of large-scale production generally reduces unit costs by acquiring and installing specialized machinery and gearing its manufacturing operations to rapid pro-

[1] *The Changing Economic Function of the Central City* (New York: Committee for Economic Development, 1959), esp. pp. 28–37.

duction of a large volume of relatively standardized goods. But the complex interactions among city firms will not permit any such standardization. A major segment of the printing industry of New York, for example, is designed to meet day-to-day variations in the requirements of law firms, the advertising agencies and the financial community. Legal briefs, advertising material and securities prospectuses are printed on a job-order basis, with each job having its own unique characteristics. We may note in passing that the locational advantages of advertising, legal and financial institutions are as much based on the existence of a convenient printing industry as *vice versa*.

A similar case is posed by job-order shops meeting the ever-fluctuating design, material and processing demands of New York's clothing industry. Another, more frequently mentioned feature of the garment district is the advantage that accrues to each firm as a result of having many show rooms in the same area, giving department store buyers the opportunity to visit a large number of displays conveniently.

These small, flexible and non-standardized firms derive genuine external economies from a central city location. They enjoy numerous services which could be obtained only by large expenditures on the parts of individual firms in less concentrated locations. A firm in the central city can make use of freight forwarders for less than carload or less than truckload shipments, take advantage of other specialized distribution services in transportation such as the terminal facilities of the Port of New York Authority, purchase skilled labor time by the hour as needed, rent heavy equipment for part-time use, and benefit from the existence of municipal power, water, sewage, and fire and police protection.

Still another advantage, which serves as an excellent example of an external economy, is the reduction in uncertainty which results from the flexibility inherent in the fact that a small firm meeting special job orders is not dependent on one or a few customers, nor must the customer rely upon a single supplier or a small number of potential suppliers.

A central business district containing office buildings, hotels and entertainment facilities attracts large numbers of people. Theater, concert or sporting event crowds, office workers on their lunch hours and transients simply looking over the city or spending time between engagements are all potential customers for downtown restaurants and other retail stores, particularly if these shops have an appeal to the "impulse" buyer who is in the city primarily for other reasons. The use of downtown land for retail and other business uses may be mutually beneficial. An attractive group of retail stores may encourage theatergoing, for example, or ease the problem of recruiting clerical help for downtown offices.

Although wire connections can handle routine communications, a great part of top-level business activity seems to require face-to-face contact and the rather delicate interplay of exchanges of opinion, information and even emotion in direct discussion. At least the present generation of business executives appears to regard the telephone conference and the use of closed-circuit television as poor substitutes for personal meetings, especially over a good expense-account dinner with two martinis thrown in. Not only may a firm wish to have many of its executives and specialists located in the same building, but it may desire to have these key employees in close proximity to customers' and suppliers' representatives, lawyers, financiers, outside directors, and even competitors. The advantages of luncheon meetings at first-rate restaurants, shop talk, and frequent business and social contacts among those concerned with similar business problems may be elusive, but they are considered to be important. Further, the central offices require assistants, secretaries, clerks and stenographers of a high caliber who can be readily recruited in large enough quantities only in and around major centers of population possessing all of the real or putative advantages of the urban scene.

The business structure of a city, then, is similar to that of a house of cards. Almost every industry and branch of trade which finds an urban location particularly hospitable both supports and is supported by others. It is impossible to assess the future of any one aspect of a city's business in isolation, and to ignore the interdependencies and external economies of a city location is to grossly underestimate the vitality and future prospects of any city.

III. CAUSES OF BLIGHT AND CONGESTION

Blight of business areas may be a rational reaction to other failings of the city, or it may be an independent cause of over-all deterioration. The immediate indication of blight is a decline in the quality of the physical facilities of an area. For one reason or another, natural wear and tear of buildings and their eventual declines into dilapidated states are not checked by repairs and maintenance, improvements and new construction. Blight does not consist alone, however, of decay of buildings. Another aspect of a blighted area is that its facilities are devoted to progressively "lower" business uses.

A distinction between "higher" and "lower" business uses often implies some sort of value judgment, such as the "class" of customer being served, rather than measurement by some objective standard. Yet if, throughout an area, book stores were being replaced by magazine stands with racks full of comic books, girlie magazines and cheap candy, if restaurants with table service were giving way to hamburger stalls and hotdog stands, and if the number of bars and poolrooms were growing relative to other business facilities, very few would deny that these shifts indicated "lower" retail uses of the area. Some rather general indications of "lower" uses and the onset of blight may be suggested. A relative growth of industry and trade paying lower wages, an increase in the number of workers per unit of floor space and decline in both pleasantness and safety of working conditions, shoddier products and less reliable services, an increase in nuisances such as noise, odor, vibrations and obnoxious wastes, and a decline in the stability of individual firms as evidenced by higher turnover of real estate and more frequent bankruptcies would all seem to indicate "lower" business uses and at least incipient blight. Paradoxically, rents and land values in blighted areas may remain high because the "lower use" firms are excluded by zoning, building codes or public health ordinances from other parts of the city; and their collective demand for land and buildings may be strong enough to sustain or even push up real estate prices.

Blight may well be the result of perfectly rational behavior on the parts of the business firms involved. A firm which finds its markets declining or its transportation costs rising or the difficulties of recruiting and retaining satisfactory employees increasing, and which believes that its difficulties grow out of its present location, will have no incentive to maintain or improve its facilities. Its best course of action might well be to convert its investment in the property into liquid assets as rapidly as possible. This objective could be achieved by selling or renting the building, or by retaining the funds which otherwise would be devoted to upkeep of the premises. While a firm may "liquidate" a building by selling it or letting it deteriorate, the building itself is not liquidated from the viewpoint of the community until it is physically destroyed.

Firms acquiring such premises from defunct or relocated predecessors will often have no incentive to improve or maintain the building. In most cases, the operations of these second-generation tenants do not require modern, well-equipped buildings, for if their situations were otherwise they would never have located in the rundown sites in the first place. Some of these firms may require little more than a roof and space off of the street; others may be fly-by-night types of business interested in the profit possibilities of temporary and short-lived ventures. Blight of this sort is not a cause of urban decay, but an effect. If, for other reasons, an area becomes an unsatisfactory place for "higher" types of business, the normal and sound functioning of the economy will encourage out-migration unless the weaknesses can be and are corrected. When such migration is occurring, "lower" business uses of the abandoned areas may represent the best possible uses. The costs of purchase and demolition of the existing building must be added to the costs of the site and construction in a decision as to whether putting up a new building is a reasonable investment. The market allocation of city land and present buildings to the highest bidders may well be functioning to prevent vacancy, even worse deterioration and more rapid blight.

However, blight may be just as much a contributing cause to a city's decay as an effect of other evils. In the first place, business blight is not always the result of rational and economically beneficial behavior. In the second place, the most insidious feature of urban blight is that, like the biological phenomenon from which it draws its name, it is contagious.

Deterioration of a firm's buildings and equipment is occasionally the result of a misguided and shortsighted management which has not provided sufficient funds to allow for maintenance and modernization, only to regret this policy at a later date. Such unplanned obsolescence is probably most prevalent among small firms. Cases of inept management may be relatively rare in comparison with the number of intelligently run firms, but in a close-packed city with numerous small firms their importance far exceeds their number.[2] Simply because of the contagious nature of blight their errors or sins may be

[2] "Over-optimistic" and "unrealistic" views were found to be fairly widespread among a group of small firms displaced by urban renewal and highway projects in B. G. Zimmer, *Rebuilding Cities: The Effects of Displacement and Relocation on Small Business* (Chicago: Quadrangle Books, 1964), p. 275.

magnified and aggravated to the point where the original causes of blight are unrecognizable.

Any urban firm which, as a result of rational decision or error, permits its facilities to decay or which turns its building over to "lower" uses, makes the environment that much less suitable to its neighbors. Thus, the beginnings of blight encourage planned deterioration among rationally managed firms in the area, and the process feeds upon itself and tends to accelerate in scope and speed. The decline, deterioration and even ruin of a suburban or rural firm may be a severe blow to the firm's employees and to a small community; but the effects are less likely to be cumulative than in the city. The problem is particularly severe when blight takes the forms of increased fire hazards and greater nuisances such as noise and smoke; but the impact of lower quality in surrounding stores or even a worsening of the neighborhood's reputation can be serious or fatal to a retail establishment.

The contagious character of urban blight offers a virtually perfect example of the concept of an "external diseconomy." External diseconomies may be defined as the reverse of external economies, as damages done to the community or to a firm by the independently determined activities of other firms, or as costs which are imposed without the recipient having made any change in its internal structure, organization or output. Blight spreads simply because the activities of some firms have adverse effects on other firms. The firms which suffer from the erosion in quality of their environment may neither have initiated the deteriorating actions nor be able to exercise any sort of control over the firms whose policies and behavior are imposing increasing costs, declining revenues or both on all nearby businesses. Once the process of blight is under way, it makes little difference whether it began as a rational policy by a few businesses to adjust to changing conditions within the city or whether it resulted from error and shortsighted business policies. Its spread, in either case, will be the same, as firms which otherwise would have maintained the quality of their facilities and processes react to the initial stimulus.

Externalities are also at the core of the problem of traffic congestion. There are perfectly good reasons for many commuters and shoppers to use private automobiles in preference to mass-transit systems and for business firms increasingly to rely on truck transport. But neither the commuter nor the truck user can be expected to take into account the impact of his decision on other users of the streets and highways. A potential road user presumably considers existing or predicted degrees of congestion in comparing the costs to him (private costs) of various means of transportation, but no one driver has any reason to estimate the costs he imposes on other drivers or the community as a whole (social costs) by adding to the congestion. Following a similar line of reasoning, it has been argued that subsidization of mass transit is justified, since the benefit accrues not only to those who use the transportation service provided, but also to those who continue to drive on streets made less congested by those who have switched to the bus or train.

Other drivers are not the only victims of vehicular externalities. An increase in the number of employees and customers traveling to a business establishment by automobile, or a rise in the numbers traveling to a firm's neighbors in this fashion, increases the need for the employer to provide off-street parking places. Frequent physical inability of individual firms or groups of neighboring firms to do so in city locations has been recognized as one reason for the rapid relative growth of business establishments in the suburbs.

Two or more trucks being loaded or unloaded at the same time may block a street even though any one truck could be parked without obstructing traffic. In such a situation, no firm may feel that it is the one which should provide off-street loading and unloading facilities. Even if a firm does not increase its own volume of truck shipments, it will suffer delays and additional costs in transport if other firms in its area are generating a greater volume of truck traffic and if the local streets and private facilities are inadequate to handle the increase. Or, if a number of neighboring firms plan, independently of each other, to increase their production levels and as a result increase shipments of raw materials into and finished goods out of their plants, each one may find that its costs have risen far more than it had anticipated or than would have been the case if it had been the only one in the area to expand.

Traffic congestion, abstracting for the moment from increased use of the motor vehicle as a substitute for other means of transportation, illustrates an external diseconomy which results from an expansion of business activity. Blight, on the other hand, can inflict a host of external diseconomies on a firm as a result of a decline in the amount of business carried on in the vicinity. Yet congestion and blight are not unrelated when the rise of the motor vehicle at the expense of the railroads is considered. It is quite possible, for example, that if enough firms substituted motor vehicle transportation for rail, many more firms would be forced to follow as rail service was curtailed, that increased street congestion would result without any connection to increased production, that some firms would find the increased congestion serious enough to justify a move or planned deterioration of their buildings, and that blight would then begin to spread.

Thus, the interdependence of firms in a city—the house-of-cards aspect of an urban economy—is hardly an unmixed blessing. Not only may geographical areas of the city become blighted, but entire industries may become "sick" when their suppliers or customers run into trouble. This is a problem which is certainly not confined to the city. But to the extent that a city's business population is composed of small firms finding an urban location desirable because of the proximity of other businesses, the city may be particularly vulnerable to a decline in the fortunes of any one of its basic industries and services.

IV. COMBATING BLIGHT AND CONGESTION

If we can assume both rational profit-seeking behavior and an absence of emotional prejudice and discrimination against certain forms of enterprise within the business community, economic reasoning should be able to contribute meaningful and valuable insights into the problems and requirements of city-based industry and commerce. Assumptions of rationality and tolerance seem appropriate as working hypotheses.

To a very large extent, the impersonal operations of the market for land and buildings in a free-enterprise economy operate to assure fairly good allocation of urban land for business uses. Without any zoning ordinances or conscious city-wide planning, manufacturing, wholesale and retail activities do in fact tend to establish themselves and develop as the city grows in relatively rational land-use groupings, at least from the point of view of private interest. Thus, industry seeks sites along major rail routes, and both retailers and housing developers regard the proximity of a rail line as a nuisance. A warehousing firm would not pay a premium for a corner location at a busy pedestrian intersection and would undoubtedly be outbid for such a lot by a department store. Even in cases where land sites are suitable to a number of business uses and competition is keen, the prices offered should be based on relative profit potentialities; and the highest bidder, who gets the site in a properly functioning land market, is normally the businessman who can make the best use of it provided that he, in turn, sells his product in a competitive market.

Nevertheless, land for business use will be misallocated and blight and congestion will be heightened if a free market in real estate rentals and sales is permitted to operate unhampered in a city which has already had intensive development of available land. Although we can assume that land for business purposes is bought and sold rationally, in terms of maximizing the profit potentialities of each plot, we cannot assume that the businessman is omniscient. The public benefit will not be assured by a free market in which the participants are constructing facilities which will last for fifty years and in which reasonably accurate projections and estimates cannot be made for more than ten years ahead. The problem is likely to be particularly acute for smaller firms with uncertain markets and inability to establish and maintain planning staffs. But the effect on the environment is obviously in part a function of size, and the errors of a large firm may have a devastating impact.

Further, the economy of an urban area is certainly a "mixed" one, with many essential functions performed by public enterprise. Today, market allocation of land is not expected to determine the space available for parks, playgrounds, schools, fire and police stations, libraries, nor, often, for cultural facilities such as concert halls. While private enterprise could provide for such needs, as has been the case many times in the past, there have been widely accepted social judgments that private demand calls forth insufficient private resources for recreation, education, public safety and culture and also that there is a fundamental lack of equity in permitting distribution of these services according to ability to pay.

We have already seen that still another and most crucial reason why a free real estate market will not assure optimum use of a city's space and facilities is the widespread existence of external economies and diseconomies. These aspects of a firm's environment become more important as businesses crowd together and as less and less space is available relative to the demand for it. If a firm would benefit other firms by locating on a particular site, the social value of devoting that site to the firm in question is higher than the purely private value of the land to the firm. Conceivably, firms which would benefit from the external economies might pay part of the purchase price of the land, or they might make direct contributions to the firm considering the location. Although such payments and partial subsidies are not unknown in the development of shopping centers, they are of interest mainly as theoretical measures of external economies. Such transfers on the part of independent urban businessmen are most unlikely because each firm would benefit if the others subsidized the newcomer while it stood pat, and because the extent of the benefits accruing to each firm would be extremely difficult to assess. In most instances, the firm which would benefit the others will not bid as much for the site as it would if it could appropriate the full social value; and the site may very well be bought by another purchaser whose private interest is stronger. Conversely, and probably of greater significance to the city planner, firms which bring external diseconomies to an area will be able and willing to bid more for sites than the sites would be worth to them if they had to pay the costs inflicted on others. Thus, because a bidder will take into account only his own costs and benefits in planning his operations and in estimating the value of a plot of land and its facilities, a free market excludes firms from plots they could most efficiently occupy and places other firms on sites which, from the larger point of view of the city as a whole, represent uneconomic use of scarce land and buildings.

Nevertheless, any business renewal or redevelopment project should proceed with a profound respect for the existing results of the operation of the market. In the absence of important external diseconomies or overriding public needs, the first assumption ought to be that the present structures are being used as efficiently as possible. Undoubtedly, many business buildings are obsolete, no longer suited to their original functions; and if the original owners did not take account of obsolescence as the prime cause of depreciation they may well have suffered a loss on their investment. However, the market prices and rentals of such buildings ought to reflect their current value for various business uses other than those originally intended. Whenever urban land values become high enough and buildings decrepit enough to justify razing, private investment searching for profitable opportunities could be expected to do the job.

If the sources of contagious blight in business districts can be identified, preventive measures may not only check the spread of the infection, but may stimulate private redevelopment of the area. Thus, traffic congestion may require passage of ordinances prohibiting loading and unloading in the streets or all-day parking of automobiles. Nuisance features can be attacked by similar laws dealing with smoke control, abatement of noise, treatment and disposal of offensive wastes and safety, public health and fire prevention standards. If the occupant of a building finds that he cannot continue profitable operation under strict enforcement of these measures, he will simply have to vacate the premises. Presumably the next tenant would be someone who could use the building to advantage. If no one can use the building appropriately at any positive rental, and if there is in fact demand for urban space, its demolition by private investors will be hastened by rigorous enforcement of anti-nuisance standards. If off-street parking and loading facilities are required, and if the curtailment of nuisance features substantially reduces external diseconomies in the area, the value of land sites should rise at the same time that the values of some buildings are declining. In this fashion, via the automatic workings of the market, razing of substandard buildings by private interests in order to provide land for parking and for new businesses which can meet adequate antinuisance standards would be encouraged with only infrequent need for public authorities to perform the leveling themselves. Firms which survived would have less reason for permitting their facilities to decay and greater incentive to stay in the area.

Such an approach to a city's business area would be brutal, even though effective. One compelling argument in favor of condemnation and compensation is that the use of regulations and prohibitions, designed to compel property owners to check blight, destroys property values derived from existing use. *Indeed, in encouraging private redevelopment, our proposed program relies heavily upon lowering the values of properties which have adverse effects upon neighbors.* If arbitrary and unjust confiscation through uncompensated destruction of private property values is to be avoided, the authorities should draft and make public a long-range, scheduled conservation program and should put various features into enforcement gradually, with substantial advance notice, thus easing the impact upon individual businessmen to the greatest extent consistent with the needs of the area being conserved.

Conservation of business areas will, occasionally, have to be supplemented with some public renewal and redevelopment. No matter how much advance notice is given and no matter how considerate of existing interests the planners may be, there will be a few cases in which businessmen cannot be expected in equity and fairness to make the necessary adjustments or sales without compensation. In such situations, condemnation or negotiated purchases are justifiable. If blight has reached emergency proportions and business emigration threatens to become a headlong stampede, immediate renewal can be defended on the grounds that the private market works too slowly. Although the economic theory used here assumes rationality behind private investment decisions, one or two well-conceived public renewal projects may be necessary catalysts, demonstrating the potentialities for private profit in similar ventures. In the mixed economy of the city, there are needs for parks, fire and police stations, libraries and other public facilities even in business districts. The present contention is that public renewal and redevelopment projects in business areas should be held to a minimum, not that they should never be undertaken.

Both the need for and the availability of engineering solutions to the most pressing urban traffic woes are widely recognized. There is a common and rather caustic comment made about our cities, that the only direction in which to expand is upward. The significance of this quip for the fight against traffic congestion has only belatedly been recognized in the replacement of open parking lots by multi-story parking garages. Similarly, newly designed warehouses are using interior ramps so that trucks can be loaded and unloaded on each of the upper stories, and Macy's new store on Long Island has parking ramps at all levels. Multi-level highways, pedestrian podiums, causeways and arcades, and the suspended monorail have long been envisaged as permitting a vertical expansion of a city's traffic facilities. Underground garages indicate the possibility of downward expansion. On the ground level, belt highways and limited-access throughways can relieve other streets of all but local traffic. Intelligent use of one-way streets, synchronized lights under direction of a computer, parking regulations and special lanes can do a great deal to speed traffic flow. Most important, new and improved mass-transit facilities, aided by public subsidy where necessary and advisable, can remove many private automobiles from the streets.

Commonly, a lack of co-ordination among governments in metropolitan areas is given as the major impediment to effective action against congestion. The problem is said to be political, not technical. Proposals for equating social and private costs through increased tolls, parking charges, and highway taxes (with the proceeds perhaps going to subsidization of mass-transit systems) and through required installation of exhaust control devices, have run into strong political opposition. The objections of one suburb either to excessive through traffic or to being completely bypassed, the financial problems involved in sharing the burdens of condemnation and construction costs among political subdivisions for the indivisible benefit of the entire area, and the sacrifices that some must make for the convenience of others all militate against a rational, area-wide motor vehicle network. Similar problems of rights-of-way, franchises and subsidies, particularly who should pay how much of the subsidy, may plague efforts to establish area-wide and heavily patronized mass-transit systems. Yet it would appear that widespread concern over such political problems and efforts to resolve inter-governmental issues have obscured an even more fundamental economic problem. Succinctly, economic use of valuable urban land implies extremely intensive use of this land and a resulting heavy use of streets by both vehicles and pedestrians—or, in harsher language, *planned and deliberate congestion.*

It is difficult to prescribe an optimum degree of congestion. If the demand for urban land could be assumed to be constant, and if there were no opportunities to shift from or to land outside of the metropolitan complex, then a simple economic rule for optimum street and sidewalk development could be formulated. As long as additional investment in streets and pedestrian facilities lowered metropolitan land rents per unit of land and the total reduction exceeded the costs of construction, the investment should be made. With demand given, a reduction in rent charges would indicate that street construction and improvement were increasing the supply of available land and permitting more intensive use. A rise in rents coupled with constant demand would indicate that streets had been overbuilt, cutting into the supply of land available for productive use. In the real world, in which our assumptions must be relaxed, improved access may increase rent values as the land becomes still more preferable to outside alternatives, and demand in a dynamic economy is certainly not constant. The practical working goal should be to make, as far as possible, the sheer unavailability of physical space the limiting factor on expanded use of urban land, rather than either wasteful use of this space for excessive roadways or blockages to intensive development resulting from lack of adequate access and unnecessary congestion.

Streets, admittedly, serve important functions other than transportation. Below the surface are mazes of pipes, sewers, electrical conduits and other tunnels of various sorts, requiring occasional access from the street level. Above the surface, streets bring light and air to close-packed buildings. Yet there may be external economies if these essential functions of open spaces can be performed by playgrounds, parks, and other unencumbered uses of land which would be more pleasant to the urban residents than streets. The final concern must be with the health and safety of the city's residents. In arguing for an optimum degree of congestion and intensive use of streets as well as the rest of the urban land, with the optimum measured in terms of efficient performance of the city's economic function, we must not neglect the noise, noxious exhaust fumes and dangers to pedestrians posed by the motor vehicle. Any measure of the most efficient economic use of land for streets must take into account human resources and the desire for pleasant, safe, and healthy living conditions.

V. CONCLUSION

Restraint has been the essential theme of this essay. Several years ago I heard an urban renewal official argue that even if city authorities were not quite sure of what they were doing to their city or what the long-run consequences of their actions would be, they should nevertheless act, because the consequences of inaction were obvious and dire. I suspect that at that time, in the late 1950s, many city planners would have been sympathetic to the sentiment. The bulldozer driver, in this view, is the modern equivalent of the mounted knight, thrown into a desperate struggle to drive back the looming forces of chaos. Since the consequences of inaction are in fact neither obvious nor dire, a reaction has set in which envisages the bulldozer as a dragon running amuck in and literally through the city.[3]

[3] See, especially, Martin Anderson, *The Federal Bulldozer: A Critical Analysis of Urban Renewal, 1949–1962* (Cambridge: The M.I.T. Press, 1964). There is a thoughtful and critical review of this book by Harvey S. Perloff, *American Economic Review,* LV (June 1965), pp. 628–30.

In regard to residential problems of the city, Raymond Vernon views developing patterns throughout the metropolitan area as seriously detrimental to the living conditions of only the very rich and the intellec-

Insofar as its economic life is concerned, I see no evidence that the American city faces a crisis so severe and urgent that only a crash program can save it. If left alone, it would continue to function tolerably, as it does at present. On the other hand, there are challenging opportunities for significant improvement. A degree of economic sophistication is needed for effective realization of these opportunities. The full potential of external economies must be appreciated. The market allocation of urban land and facilities should be treated as an aid to efficient business use, rather than as a hindrance, once the market has been purged of avoidable external diseconomies. Traffic congestion should be controlled to optimize use of limited space, not be eliminated. Inaction, in the face of the urbanization of our society, is indeed unacceptable. But so is action without understanding and deep reflection on need and consequences.

Why the Skyscraper?

JEAN GOTTMANN*

It may seem superfluous in these days to explain what a skyscraper is; nevertheless, its present definition is relatively recent. In the multivolume edition of 1933 the Oxford English Dictionary lists six definitions for "skyscraper." The first, a

tuals. *The Myth and Reality of Our Urban Problems* (Cambridge: Harvard University Press, 1962).

* Professor of Human and Economic Geography of the United States at the *École des Hautes Études, Université de Paris.* Since 1943 he has specialized in the economic and political geography of Western Europe, the Mediterranean world and North America. Professor Gottmann has been a Rockefeller Fellow as well as a member of the Institute for Advanced Study at Princeton a number of times from 1943–65; he has lectured widely in European and North American Universities and served as Visiting Professor at Columbia, Newcastle-on-Tyne (England), Laval (Quebec), University of Pittsburgh, Hebrew University (Jerusalem), University of California (Berkeley), and Southern Illinois. He is the author of over one hundred articles in collective volumes or scholarly periodicals, and eleven books; the best known here being *Megalopolis* (New York, 1961), a study of the great northeastern seaboard urban belt in the United States. From 1945 to 1963, he was a consultant to the French National Planning Office and has done professional work for both public authorities and private organizations in the United States, Canada, France, and the Netherlands in recent years. This article is reprinted with the permission of the *Geographical Review*, April 1966, and the author.

nautical meaning, is a triangular sky-sail. Then follow several colloquial meanings: a high-standing horse; a bicycle with a very high wheel in the back; an exceptionally tall man; and an exaggerated tale, or "tall story." Finally comes "a high building of many stories, especially one of those characteristic of American cities." Here we get into geography: in 1933 skyscrapers were apparently to be found more extensively in American cities than in cities in other parts of the world. However, the single-volume Oxford Illustrated Dictionary, published in 1962, gives only the last meaning, the many-storied building, and location in American cities is not mentioned, which indicates an evolution not only in the term but in the areal distribution of the structure.

This was a significant change. Indeed, the skyscraper has over the last twenty years come to be an important geographical phenomenon, for several reasons. First, it stands for a specific formula in land use. Second, it reflects a certain type of economic activity, with economic and social connotations rooted in some locations and not in others. Third, it is found mainly in large cities, and especially in American cities. Fourth, it is a distinctive landmark, stamping an original imprint on the urban landscape. We speak of a group of skyscrapers as forming a "skyline," a term commonly accepted to describe certain landscape characteristics of downtown districts in large cities. And finally, it is a phenomenon that is spreading all over the world, to the point where it has become typical not just of American cities but of the architecture of our time. As the skyscraper has spread to other continents, one may even wonder whether it still has the same meaning and function it had in the beginning. These trends may be better understood if we ask, and try to answer, the questions, Why have skyscrapers been built? And when and where?

HISTORICAL BACKGROUND

Since the most impressive skyline in the world—in extent, density, and height—is definitely in Manhattan, many people think that the birthplace of the skyscraper was on that crowded island, and perhaps for the simple reason of lack of space. But this is not so. The skyscraper was born at the end of the nineteenth century in Chicago, a city much less hemmed in by nature but with a strong tradition in daring architecture. The first such building was the Home Insurance Building, ten stories high, designed by William Le Baron Jenney and completed in 1885. The fact that it was built for an insurance company is noteworthy for our understanding of the entire phenomenon, as we shall shortly see.

The multistoried building of considerable height was made possible by a remarkable contraption, the passenger elevator —an American invention now just about a hundred years old. Lifting devices had been operated for specific purposes for a long time. The use of a pulley to move things vertically, particularly in wells, is ancient, and animal-powered devices to lift heavy weights have been known for centuries around the Mediterranean world. But a passenger elevator, merely to transport people up and down within a building to save them the trouble of walking up and down stairs or ramps—that was something new, and the idea probably came out of the coal mine.

The first passenger elevator officially recorded, and definitely an ancestor of the present ones, was installed in 1857 by the Otis Elevator Company in a not very high building in New York City. It was soon followed by others. Indeed, European visitors to the city in the 1860's were impressed by the elevators in the hotels.

The first elevators were hydraulic, and their rise was limited by the physical laws of the pressure of the water column. An elevator could be lifted by hydraulic force to a height of eighteen or twenty stories, but not much more than that, especially in the nineteenth century. To be liberated from this ceiling, architecture needed the electric elevator, which made its appearance about 1887. From then on, the height to which people could be lifted mechanically was no longer restricted by physical laws, and the sky became the limit.

Still, there were other restrictions, in the weight the structure could carry. Walls of masonry were heavy and if very high would crush the foundation of the building. In the 1870's and 1880's the idea developed of using a cast-iron skeleton frame and covering it with whatever masonry was necessary to mask it. Later the cast iron was either complemented or replaced by steel. The first very high structure of cast iron and steel was completed in Paris in 1889—the Eiffel Tower. This shaft rises almost one thousand feet above the ground, nearly as high as the Empire State Building constructed in Manhattan half a century later, but the tower had only four stories. It was, said the architectural profession, not a tower but a huge bridge that Eiffel had made to stand up! However, the elements were there. The metal skeleton and the passenger elevator were the two technological innovations that made the skyscraper feasible.

Little by little, especially during the 1890's, it became feasible to build the steel skeleton stronger and higher; around it only thin curtain walls were needed, to serve merely as an enclosing screen or wrapping. Such walls could be made of the kinds of materials that were at hand if they had the necessary strength and malleability. In short, the principles of construction that led to today's glass towers were already available in the late nineteenth century.

Chicago, of course, was not the only city to build skyscrapers. New York City soon began to catch up, first with a few rows of high buildings. In 1892 the New York City Building Law made provisions for skeleton construction that gave some assurance of control and strength for the building of high towers. The first of the buildings now standing in Manhattan that was a true skyscraper is the curiously shaped Flatiron Building, completed in 1902. In 1908 the Metropolitan Life Insurance Tower was opened, and in the next few years New York kept producing buildings of increasing size. In 1913 a height of sixty stories was reached with Cass Gilbert's Woolworth Building, a much more daring structure than any previously built.

In 1916 the City of New York adopted a "Building Zone Resolution," which established legal control over the height and arrangement of buildings and imposed a progressive setback of exterior walls above a height determined according to the rule of the "sky angle." That was the beginning of the lean towers rising above a much wider base; the grouping of these towers took on the form that evokes the image of "skyscraping," or the indented skyline.

Thus several technological and legal factors contributed to the skyscraper's shape. And to them must be added also a certain taste for building in height.

THE SPREAD OF THE SKYSCRAPER

In foreign encyclopedias and dictionaries one finds different characterizations and definitions of skyscrapers. The strongest anti-skyscraper stand I have found is in the Soviet Encyclopedia, in the edition dated 1954.[1] *Neboskrëb,* the word that means "skyscraper" in Russian, is defined as a multistoried,

[1] Bol'shaya sovetskaya entsiklopediya (2nd edit.; Moscow, 1954), Vol. 29, p. 332.

high building, again characteristic of American cities, and its existence is explained by the excessive greed of the capitalists who want to make the most they can out of a piece of real estate. The entry also indicates that as a result of skyline building some American cities, and especially downtown New York, are built up in such a disorderly mass of overpowering structures that community values and architectural quality are destroyed in the city. The skyscraper is condemned both as an architectural style and as a social or economic phenomenon.

But in the last dozen years Moscow has built at least eight skyscrapers—which they call "tall buildings"—that dominate any panoramic view of the Soviet capital.[2] Photographs of these buildings, especially the Moscow State University and the Hotel Ukraine, reveal that they are reminiscent of the skyscrapers of Chicago or New York in the early part of this century. They recall such structures as the Wrigley Building in Chicago or the Waldorf-Astoria Hotel in New York. Such resemblances show that even the Soviets, despite their virtuous condemnation of skyscrapers, could not withstand the modern urge—a strong one—to build them. Moreover, it was the Soviet authorities who directed the erection in the middle of Warsaw of the Palace of Culture, which dominates the Polish capital.

In 1962 officials in charge of housing programs in Sweden told me how annoyed they were that small towns, with perhaps ten to twenty thousand inhabitants, each wanted a high tower. They were asking for a skyscraper, whether for apartments or some other use, as a matter of self-respect. Every city now has to have a high-rise building, since without it the city lacks status. Travelers in both South America and Africa know how impressive a skyline many of the cities have, and these cities are not running out of space!

Some areas, however, have resisted the skyscraper much more stubbornly than others. Among those that have held out against it for some time are not only the Communist countries but places where the greed of the capitalists may be just as great as it is in New York or Chicago and where the same economic factors and trends in real-estate values could be expected to operate. London, for example, until recently had only one skyscraper; now it has half a dozen. In Paris one skyscraper has recently been completed, and a second, which will be a tall tower above a vast lower project over the Mont-

[2] Arthur Ling: "Skyscrapers and Their Siting in Cities," *Journ. Royal Soc. of Arts*, Vol. 111, 1962–1963, pp. 368–383; reference on p. 377.

parnasse Railroad Station, is just beginning to rise. Several earlier plans for high towers in these congested cities were defeated. In Paris especially, where the Eiffel Tower has become a beloved monument, such opposition to the skyscraper may seem surprising.

THE SKYSCRAPER AND THE CATHEDRAL

The skyscraper as a structural form poses two basic questions. First, is it essentially the result of a technology that is imposed, or is there an economic necessity for it? Second, does it herald some new kind of art or taste that impels architects to build in this form? Recently an article by Aldous Huxley about beauty in modern art was called to my attention, one of the last articles the novelist wrote.[8] Huxley begins with architecture and paraphrases Henry Adams about the great achievements of the Middle Ages in construction and in art, comparing them to those of our time and symbolizing the essential difference between the men of the Middle Ages and ourselves: "With their kind of power our ancestors built cathedrals; with ours we broadcast Westerns, make ice cubes, run computers. . . . We are primarily technologists; they were primarily metaphysicians. That is why they built Chartres and we build the New York Hilton."

This is not quite a fair comparison, but as he develops his views in the article Huxley recognizes that man does not live by bread alone and that he does not live by faith alone, either. Faith is not enough to build vast and magnificent cathedrals such as those constructed during the twelfth to the fifteenth century in so many European cities. Technological knowledge was also needed, and confidence in the technological ability of the people to build. For it was not easy at that time to embark on such huge enterprises; relatively, it was much more difficult than to build a modern skyscraper.

Still, there is some kind of symbolism that architecture applies to the materials with which it works, and that symbolism expresses not only a psychological, intellectual state of mind but also a social system. Cathedrals were built because at that time a great church was the symbol of the community in the hands of God. The huge nave was supposedly capable of enclosing the entire population of the city, and even more, for on holidays people came from the countryside around. Essen-

[8] Aldous Huxley: "The New Frontiers in Beauty," *Show Magazine*, Vol. 3, No. 12, 1963, pp. 92–94 and 152.

tially, the cathedral was a kind of meetinghouse. And it had to express in many ways all the lore and the emotions of the community, and to be, as such art historians as Émile Mâle[4] and Henri Focillon have shown, an "encyclopedia," put together piece by piece, of stone and glass. We must think of what the sculptured figures described, of what the stained-glass windows represented, recounting the stories of the Bible, of the Crusades, of the famous heroes of the time, of the best and most beloved things or important notables of the city. As the rays of light streamed into the cathedral through the stained-glass windows, animating their images, coloring the interior, the vast structure would come alive.

By contrast, there is a certain impersonality, something abstract, about the skyscraper. Some may say that this impersonality fits our times, because as a people we are so mathematically or materialistically minded, or perhaps we just like to take one pattern and put it in another perspective. It has been suggested that the skyscraper is merely a three-dimensional variant of the gridiron street plan made to stand up vertically instead of lying horizontally, an interesting view in a century of abstract art. However, the matter is not quite so simple as that. The modern skyscraper was not so impersonal to start with; it once had decorations and embellishments. But admittedly it is growing more and more impersonal, and perhaps this trend better reflects the modern social philosophy of the common man. There may also be something else that pushed all those towers up toward the sky, that fostered the use of such designs to express modern thrusts—something other than just the need to house the crowds of workers.

THE CASE OF MANHATTAN

In the December, 1963, issue of *Show,* the distinguished architect Wolf Von Eckardt reviewed the major projects of urban renewal in sixteen large American cities.[5] His interesting article, full of information and wisdom, begins by commenting on New York City's "spectacular comeback." Indeed it is striking as one remembers how everybody was "selling down the river the future of New York City" in the years 1945 to 1949. It was commonly agreed that New York would

[4] The basic study of the cathedral as a "book of stones" is by Émile Mâle: *L'art religieux au xiii⁰ siècle en France* (Paris, 1925).

[5] Wolf Von Eckardt: "Metropolis USA: A Judgment on 16 Cities," *Show Magazine,* Vol. 3, No. 12, 1963, pp. 78–81 and 142–152.

decline in importance in the future. The city was not advantageously located for the era of airplane travel, and the time seemed past when transport by sea made it essential to have the country's main economic center a seaport.

It was also agreed that Manhattan Island was far too crowded, that the rest of New York was too blighted, and that the costs of improving the situation would be prohibitive. Every major corporation that did not have particularly local roots—and even some that did—was planning new headquarters elsewhere, in Chicago, Denver, Los Angeles, and so on. In a few lines Von Eckardt sums it up: "I rejoice in the city's spectacular comeback—a boom of new apartment buildings, and some one hundred and fifty new office towers built since the end of World War II, when the Cassandras pronounced Manhattan doomed to the fate of a congested poorhouse."[6] In the last dozen years more than a hundred apartment buildings or hotels have been built on the island, each with more than twenty stories and therefore in the old skyscraper category. But the office-building towers alone would form quite a skyline anywhere. Practically all of them are located below 60th Street, and the crowding of the sky in the hub of New York is becoming unpleasant unless seen in a far perspective.

In January, 1964, plans were announced for the building of a World Trade Center on the lower West Side of Manhattan, along the Hudson River. This will consist of twin towers above an open plaza surrounded by much lower buildings on a sixteen-acre site. The towers will have 110 stories each and will rise to 1350 feet, higher than the Empire State Building. The entire project will contain about ten million square feet of floor space to rent (that is, besides the corridors, foyers, and so on). Some people feel that with 150 or more postwar office towers Manhattan has already overbuilt, but apparently there is room for more skyscraping. The World Trade Center is being developed by the Port of New York Authority, an agency of New York State and New Jersey, and there is every reason to expect that it will rise as planned. Legislation for its construction was supported by New York City and was passed by the legislatures of both states by 1963.

THE OFFICE INDUSTRY AND THE SKYSCRAPER

There must be good reason behind New York's unquenchable thirst for skyscrapers and the spread of this structural

[6] Von Eckardt, *op. cit.*, p. 79.

form throughout the world, despite the severe esthetic criticism the existing structures have aroused. The reason may be that the skyscraper is not only a landmark and an art form; it is also the expression of a social and intellectual revolution characteristic of our era. Skyscrapers are, in fact, highly functional buildings. It is noteworthy that the first skyscraper in Chicago and some of the early ones in New York were built by insurance companies—that is, by companies whose business is entirely bureaucratic. Their work is all on paper and in transactions. The expression "office industry" is a debatable one, but so far as it is in use let us stress its significance: to perform its function, an office industry does not need anything but space for executive offices, filing and clerical work, meetings, discussions, and the like. The insurance companies are not the only ones characteristic of the office industry, and not the only ones to locate in skyscrapers, of course.

Some of the high towers are hotels, a use of space rather obviously associated with the kinds of transactions that go on in offices—a large agglomeration of offices would naturally attract a great many visitors to the city for short periods. Some are built for apartment houses or for parking facilities or for both, as is illustrated by Chicago's Marina City. But basically the skyscraper expresses the need to accumulate floor space for offices and related activities.

Until recently, there seemed little demand to provide so many offices in the centers of the smaller cities, but now, with the rapidly growing urban populations, this demand appears there also. Thus in 1959 Houston, Texas, had only four tall buildings rising above the general level of the spread-out city; today it has many more. One of the four, a rather fat building, was a hotel, another was a Veterans Hospital, and the remaining two were private medical buildings in which offices and other facilities—for consultation, for treatment, for laboratory analysis, for radiology and similar technical specialties—had piled up on top of one another. This raises another point. Medicine today is becoming highly specialized; a really sick person seldom accepts just the judgment of a general practitioner, and he in turn often wants his patient to be examined by specialists, and these specialists may need a corps of technical assistants. Medical practice is much better integrated if the whole complex is housed in a massive building in which one can move from one facility to another simply by crossing a corridor and taking an elevator. Hence large hospitals all around the world are increasingly being built in high-rise fashion.

A modern skyscraper provides concentration for many interconnected activities. Most of them do not have the ten million square feet of floor space that the projected New York World Trade Center will have, but many easily contain a million square feet or more. If such an area were distributed horizontally it would require a great deal of land. It would also greatly increase the distance, and therefore the time, needed to go from one office to another and would be more costly to service adequately. In the skyscraper the same amount of floor space does not require the same cost and traffic time, because of that excellent means of rapid mass transit, the elevator.

Some years ago I had the opportunity of witnessing the change made by a large organization from an enormous one-story office building, with only a small part on a second floor, to a tall, compact tower. That happened in 1951, when the United Nations Secretariat moved from the Sperry plant at Lake Success, Long Island, where it had been since 1946, to the now-familiar great shaft on 42nd Street on the East River. In the Lake Success building people spent much time walking around the corridors. I recall often taking a visitor through that maze when I worked there in 1946–1947; if you did not want him to get lost you had to see him to the outside gate, where he would emerge saying, "Oh, now we have come out of the underground." The building was not underground at all, but since it had originally been a large wartime industrial plant, with windows on the periphery only, sunlight entered few of the offices. The structure was air-conditioned and well lighted, but in it one felt as if one were in a cave.

In the new glass tower overlooking the East River, there are some parts in the center of every floor where not much outside light penetrates, but most of the floor space is fairly well in touch with the outside. At least nobody has much doubt about the altitude at which he is situated! However, people on the United Nations staff soon began to protest. They no longer spent much time in transit between offices, but they missed meeting one another and the nice chats they had had in the corridors. In the new building, even if they met someone in the automatic elevator, there was no time to talk. Thus the established system of community communication, the exchange of news and views, had been disrupted as rapid vertical transit replaced the more leisurely horizontal variety. Habits and schedules had to be rearranged, and the transition took years. For the very special system of communication needed inside the Secretariat, and for some particular purposes, it is hard to say which is preferable, the corridor or the coffee break. But in efficiency of work and in time spent in door-to-door inner traffic, the vertical system brought about a tremendous saving.

THE EVOLUTION OF THE LABOR FORCE

The basic question of why we need the skyscraper mode of life brings us to another of the skyscraper's functions. The main reason for its development is not the intensive use of real estate, though the real-estate market has done very well with the high towers, nor is it the efficiency of office organization. The skyscraper is an expression of the social evolution of employment, of the labor force today.

It is a long-accepted truth that the labor force is leaving the farms and going to the cities. Therefore the cities are expanding. But why do they have to expand in height? They used not to; they grew sideways. Urban sprawl is still with us, but it is not necessarily in opposition to building in height. The real point is that employment is no longer going into manufacturing pursuits or the manipulation of goods as it once did. Besides the exodus of people from farms to cities, two other migrations are displacing labor. First, the exodus of the manufacturing plants out of the densely built-up urban centers, and particularly out of the cores of the cities, is an important trend; the warehouses follow the factories, and consequently the storage and processing of goods in bulk are both going out of the cities. Second, these two capital sectors of economic activity are replaced in the heart of the modern metropolis by the influx of white-collar labor of a special kind.

A significant trend, denoting rapid change, has developed in nonagricultural employment in the United States in the last twenty-five years.[7] Employment in nonagricultural establishments—which covers most of the labor force—totaled 32.4 million jobs in 1940, rose to 45.2 million in 1950, and reached 58.2 million in 1964. Thus from 1950 to 1964 there was an increase of about 13 million jobs, or some 28 percent. This increase was unequal in the various categories of employment.

[7] Employment data cited in this section are from the *Statistical Abstract of the United States 1965*, 86th edit., U. S. Bureau of the Census, Washington, D. C. 1965, pp. 220–223.

Mining, as is well known, declined rapidly: from about 900,-000 workers in 1940 and in 1950 to 635,000 in 1964. Contract construction, on the other hand, has been one of the boom activities in recent times. As a result of all the building, of urban sprawl and skyline rise, employment in contract construction increased from 1.3 million in 1940 to 2.3 million in 1950 and 3.1 million in 1964. In the manufacturing industries employment rose from 11 million in 1940 to 15.2 million in 1950 and 17.3 million in 1964; this means an increase in the last decade and a half of only about two million jobs. Transportation and public utilities increased from 3 million in 1940 to 4 million in 1950 and remained at about the same level from 1950 to 1964. This is important; in the growth of the labor force now taking place in the service industries, transportation and the utilities—the traditional services par excellence—are not instrumental.

It is in the other service industries that the most rapid growth of employment has taken place recently. Wholesale and retail trade employed 6.75 million people in 1940, 9.4 million in 1950, and 12.2 million in 1964. The rapid rise in the 1950–1964 period was due mainly to retail trade. However, this rate of growth was slow as compared with the expansion of employment in the "financial community"; that is, in financial, insurance, and real-estate operations. This sector of the labor force grew from 1.5 million in 1940 to 1.9 million in 1950 and 3 million in 1964, a rise of more than 50 percent. This rate of increase is matched by the so-called "miscellaneous services" (medical services, radio and television, news agencies, the hotel industry, and so on), which employed 3.7 million people in 1940, 5.4 million in 1950, and 8.5 million in 1964. Finally, another fast-growing sector of employment is government, which increased from 4.2 million in 1940 to 6 million in 1950 and 9.5 million in 1964. The increase in the last fifteen years was largely due, not to federal employment, but to employment by state and local governments, which alone accounted for more than three-quarters of the total increase in all government employment.

To understand better what is actually happening, it is necessary to analyze the statistics of employment in manufacturing, which still is by far the largest category of nonagricultural employment, with about 30 percent of the total. Within the manufacturing sector the Bureau of Labor Statistics distinguishes two major categories: production workers and nonproduction workers. Nonproduction workers are those who work in management, research, financial operations, sales, marketing, economic analysis, and legal departments. They are on the company's payroll but are considered nonproduction workers. From 1950 to 1964 employment in manufacturing establishments increased by only 13 percent, from 15.2 million to 17.3 million, but these 2.1 million additional jobs were not for production workers. The number of production workers in manufacturing has since 1950 remained almost constant, at about 12.5 million (12.8 in 1964), while production itself has been rapidly increasing. From 1950 to 1964 the total manufacturing production of this country increased by at least 60 percent in volume, the population increased by 40 million, and the rise of the per capita consumption rate of the population kept pace.

The same situation has been recognized in agriculture for a long time. To produce more on the farms, and to produce it better and more cheaply, a great many people must come off the farms. In the industrialized countries at least, the fewer farmers left on the land, the more efficiently they usually produce. This trend, for similar reasons of mechanization, automation, and rationalization, is reaching into manufacturing production, and it is affecting the processes of manipulating and transporting manufactured goods. A few years ago in New York there was a joke that if one projected into the future the rise of employment in finance, banking, and insurance in the United States over the past twenty years as a percentage of the total labor force the curve would reach 100 percent about 2056; that is, by the middle of the next century everybody would be employed in banking! The same kind of projection could be done for government employment or for education, where the curve is rising even more steeply—so steeply, in fact, that everyone would be a professor before everyone would be a bank teller.

But the real point here is that those sectors of employment which were, and still are, regarded by the classical economists as *external* activities because they did not seem to be important elements in the economic process (production through processing and distribution to consumption)—those external activities are now becoming major sectors of employment. They were, of course, peripheral to the economic process of old. It was useful to have people to do the research, take care of management, look after speculation and investment, gather and spread information, but though qualitatively important, quantitatively the group was negligible. Now their number is increasing fast:

nonproduction workers employed by manufacturing establishments numbered 2.7 million in 1950 and 4.5 million in 1964, by which time they constituted more than one-quarter of all manufacturing employment. To understand what this means, think of the skyscrapers in Manhattan, many of which bear the names of manufacturing corporations. The older ones may display the names of insurance companies, but there are also the Chrysler Building, the General Motors Building, the RCA Building, and Lever House. Still newer ones have been built by Seagram, Union Carbide, Sperry Rand, and Corning Glass. Now we see why the total employment in manufacturing establishments in Manhattan may be high, but the figure does not simply represent people who work at producing manufactured goods; it largely represents people who work in the offices, the brain and nerve centers of the corporations.[8]

A TRANSACTIONAL CIVILIZATION

Technological progress is aimed at liberating us from the hard, compelling work of production so that we can indulge in something else—administration, communication, art, research, and also leisure. To run our plants and factories, what we depend on most is not the supervision of the machines or the transfer of the goods, but the effectiveness of communication. How well do the persons in the offices and the professions understand what they say to one another? How well informed are they when they enter into the transactions among themselves that decide the fate of the rest of the economy—in agriculture, manufacturing, transportation, public utilities, and the like? There is an "abstract transaction factor" here, which encompasses not only management but also the entire financial community associated with management. The exchange of information—whether it is scientific or political or economic—is a part of this as well. It is not enough to have data recorded on paper; they must be correctly understood and competently

[8] For an elaboration of this theory, though without specific reference to the architectural consequences, see Jean Gottmann: *Megalopolis: The Urbanized Northeastern Seaboard of the United States* (New York, 1961), Chapter 11 (pp. 565–630), "The White-Collar Revolution." It should also be noted that in 1958 the manufacturing industries in Manhattan employed 471,208 persons, with a payroll of $2.17 million, of whom 132,000 were nonproduction workers earning $881,000. Thus 28 percent of the jobs, and 40 percent of the pay, in manufacturing were nonproduction.

weighed, otherwise their worth and efficiency will be diminished. Proximity and direct communication promote better understanding. In skyscrapers grouped in the city a million white-collar workers can be close to one another. They can meet easily to exchange opinions, transact business, acquire information, and obtain whatever expert interpretation, legal counsel, or technological advice they may need.

One of the large buildings of Chicago that can be classified as a skyscraper, though not one of the highest, is the Merchandise Mart. It exemplifies an essential urban function for which the city since ancient times has been the center: a meeting place for the market. The city was also the place for the administration of justice, for the management of politics, and for the observance of rites on religious holidays since the dawn of history. These functions brought the cities into being, and no other helped more in their development than the market function. The Merchandise Mart offers basically the same thing as is achieved in every market. It was Chicago's good idea to gather some of the exhibits of merchandise under one roof, to receive the wholesaler customers, and to give them a choice among a great variety of goods and prices; space is leased to anyone who wishes to offer his goods. The project contributed to Chicago's role as a great trading center. More and more cities are finding it desirable to have adequate buildings for national or international conventions. Material goods are no longer the only important objects of transaction; "marts" are needed for such matters as scientific, political, economic, and technological information. Why all the professional meetings and conferences that take up so much of our time today? Because that is how we give and receive ideas, data, results of work in office, field, and laboratory. In meetings we can test these things, we can choose among them, and we can make as certain as possible of adequate interpretation.

The daily work of decision making requires consultations with many specialists; the specialists cannot be expected to gather where there are only one or two customers, but rather where there are several thousand.[9] Also, the specialists prefer to be near one another. This proximity is what the proposed World Trade Center in New York intends to provide in its own field—"a one-stop service and information center for

[9] For a discussion of the development of headquarters offices see William Goodwin: "The Management Center in the United States," *Geogr. Rev.*, Vol. 55, 1965, pp. 1–16.

world trade."[10] At least several million square feet of floor space is needed for such a purpose. Obviously these requirements mean high structures; in no other way could a comparable area be made available in the immediate vicinity of the large banks, insurance companies, trading houses, corporation-law firms, and other technological specialists. This is what makes the skyscraper and creates the skyline: the need for agglomeration. Now we begin to see in the skyline an expression of the intricate web and huge volume of communication generated by, and indispensable to, the modern transactional way of life.

CONSEQUENCES OF SKYLINES

There have been precedents for today's skylines, particularly in the curious narrow towers—in which, however, many workers would *not* fit—of the medieval cities of central Italy. At the time that Florence was one of the leading centers in the then all-important world of the Mediterranean, hundreds and hundreds of towers pointed up to the sky in Florence, and in Bologna, in Siena, and in the smaller towns of Tuscany. In the small town of San Gimignano, now a famous tourist attraction, thirteen of the fourteenth-century towers are still standing and are well preserved. These miniature skyscrapers were usually put up by the notable local families, the merchants or bankers of that age. They were built partly for prestige, partly because they were the fashion, and partly because they provided a good defense device for the palazzos above which they rose. When there was a time of trouble in Florence, the winning party would commonly require the towers of the losing party to be razed. At least one case is on record when more than three hundred towers were knocked down in Florence alone by political decree.

When the Medici family asserted control over the management of Florence and concentrated all matters of government and most of the city's banking in their hands, only two towers were left standing. One, useful for scanning the horizon around the city, still rises above the then government headquarters, the Palazzo Vecchio; a smaller tower above the police headquarters, the Bargello. The medieval skyline of Italy may be related to the competitive and transactional mode of life of that time, and also to its intellectual and esthetic ideas.

[10] The quotation is from a promotional brochure on the World Trade Center issued by the Port of New York Authority.

The skyline expresses the need of concentration in a competitive civilization. If the American economy had come to be directed by a small number of persons who made all the essential decisions, the concentration of so many people and so many facilities for transacting business would not, perhaps, have been necessary. A free economy devours more space, more time, and more endeavor on the part of a much larger number of people. But crowding seems a price well worth paying for the freedom, the opportunity, and the many other benefits that derive from a free society.

The compulsion to gather in a central core so much space organized and equipped for white-collar work does not necessarily mean a compulsion toward dense grouping of residences nearby. In fact, the skyscraper contributes to the increasing sprawl, urban and suburban, of housing and of the economic activities, such as retail trade, that follow the customers. It is impossible for all the many thousands of workers gathered in tall structures within a small area during office hours to live nearby. Moreover, the high price of land and services in the crowded downtown area adds prohibitively to the cost of living. The residences of the labor force must therefore spread out, and as a result the skyscrapers must be provided with rapid mass-transit facilities for passenger traffic, preferably at underground and elevated levels. In most of the European cities where skyscrapers are now rising the towers are on top of or near railroad stations that handle much suburban commuter traffic. In Chicago the Loop is still defined by the elevated rails that encircle it, and more high buildings are rising along or above the Illinois Central rail lines. In New York, the Pan American World Airways building has been built over Grand Central Terminal, and a massive new Madison Square Garden is being constructed over Pennsylvania Station. The World Trade Center was first proposed and planned in 1958–1960 with a different design from that which has now been adopted. It was to rise on Manhattan's East Side, along the East River. In 1961 that proposal was approved by the New York State Legislature but was rejected by the New Jersey State Legislature. Since both states must agree to such an undertaking, the Port of New York Authority had to re-do the plan, to fit it to a site on the Hudson River. The new design is composed of differently shaped buildings and higher towers. In 1963 the New Jersey State Legislature accepted the revised plan.

One important factor in this decision was that on the Hudson side the new center is going to be on top of the Port Authority tubes that connect lower Manhattan with New Jersey under the river. The people who will work in the World Trade Center towers, many thousands of them, will be able to go down into the basement and take a rapid tube connection to the New Jersey side of the Hudson; this would not be the case were the center to be built on the other side of Manhattan, with better connections to Long Island. There is now a fair chance that Jersey City—which could benefit from some renewal—and other New Jersey areas will profit from the new center. This is a clear example of how the skyscraper affects urban sprawl, pushing it out in a given direction as a result of political decisions and existing transportation facilities.

As the skyscraper increases the sprawl, more is heard about subterranean transport—tubes and subways—and about suburban railroads. Does the commuting pattern ruin both the central city and community life in the region as a whole? Such an effect is doubtful. It is well known that the headquarters of some corporations in the center of New York had planned to move out of Manhattan, perhaps only to the Jersey side of the Hudson, or to the Bronx or Long Island. They explored how their personnel would like this, for they need good personnel, the more so since their work depends heavily on the effectiveness of communication among their staffs. They need people who not only are competent but also have certain attributes. They found great difficulty in recruiting the same quality of personnel to work in outlying locations. Many still preferred to work in the city, where they had the choice of sophisticated stores, services, theaters, restaurants, and other places of entertainment.

SKYSCRAPERS AND THE ART OF LIVING

The curtain walls of the skyscraper office building are increasingly being drawn open. The steel and cement skeletons are now sheathed largely or partly with glass. The new fifty-story Pan Am Building in New York, for example, is enclosed by 240,000 square feet of tinted glass. Thus one who walks along the avenues in the relatively narrow canyons between glass walls or who works in one of those buildings sees more and more of what goes on inside the hundreds of windows up and down the street.

Let us return briefly to the concept of the medieval Gothic cathedral as an encyclopedia. Its high walls of rather narrow stone pillars let the light stream in from the outside through the wide windows of stained glass, and that stained glass provided a good part of the "book" that the cathedral was supposed to offer—the pictures of famous knights, of great heroes, of Biblical prophets, and so on. Today it is the common man's world that one views behind the tinted glass of the skyscraper's walls; from the streets the life inside the buildings can be followed. The inner life of the city, or at least of its downtown section, is projected toward the outside, toward the rest of the community. In the past it was the person inside a building who looked out to the street and who was the observer. Now it is the person outside the building who can "read," so to speak, an enormous window of "animated stained glass."[11]

This kind of spectacle creates social and esthetic feeling; it is a certain expression of the art of living.[12] Luxury offices or apartments provide interesting tableaus in these buildings, though the pictures may be less artistic for more ordinary occupants. Still another aspect of urban art is beginning to take shape owing to modern skyscrapers: the color of the light within the building can be coordinated or contrasted with the color and texture of the material framing the glass of the walls. This trend is visible along Park Avenue in New York, with the golden light of the Seagram Building framed in dark bronze, or the clear silvery light of the Union Carbide Building framed in glinting stainless steel. All this opens up a new avenue for art; it creates a unique atmosphere in the big-city canyons and stimulates the senses in this huge man-made milieu. The new City Hall of Toronto, with its "opening oyster" design, symbolizes this modern trend toward an inward-looking but more open society and a freer architecture.

If people of certain occupations prefer to work in this environment it is because the skyscraper system, even when crowded, offers to the urban community a social life which is new, which is being arranged and elaborated, but which has not yet reached its ultimate kind of renovated Gothic expression. For it is a new Gothic in architectural style. It has excitement and beauty. All this, together with the economic functions that congregate here, causes the skyscraper to ex-

[11] See Jean Gottmann: "L'urbanisation en Amérique du Nord et en Europe Occidentale: Notes comparatives," *Social Science Information*, UNESCO, Vol. 2, No. 3, Paris, 1963, pp. 33–52.

[12] For interesting views and information concerning the new skyscraper architecture see Ada Louise Huxtable: *Four Walking Tours of Modern Architecture in New York City* (Garden City, N. Y., 1961).

hibit something fundamentally geographical that has to do with density of population and with kinds of economic activity that are growing ever more important. It has also to do with a landscape that has always expressed—not determined, but expressed—the social, economic, and intellectual evolution of a society.

The Economic Feasibility of the Chestnut Street Mall, Philadelphia

ARTHUR C. KAUFMANN AND ASSOCIATES, INC.*

I. THE PROBLEM IN ITS SETTING

There is little doubt that among the major cities in this country, Philadelphia has been in the vanguard in revitalization of its physical properties, with resultant benefit to its national and international reputation. To quote *Time* (November 6, 1964):

> Of all the cities under the planner's knife, none has been deeply and continuously committed to renewing itself as the city where the Declaration of Independence was signed: Philadelphia. For twelve years, the nation's fourth largest city has been tearing down and digging up, burrowing, building, restoring, condemning, relocating and spending what will amount to more than $2 billion in private, city, state and federal funds to carry out the most thoughtfully planned, thoroughly rounded, skillfully coordinated of all the big-city programs in the U.S.

Penn Center and the Independence Hall-Society Hill area developments are but two of the larger examples of the imaginative thinking and progressive action that has taken place —and, indeed, more is yet to come. At Penn Center, a highly unusual set of circumstances culminated in the unique oppor-

* Management Consultants, Philadelphia, Pennsylvania. This is an adapted summary of a report, contracted for in August 1965 by the Philadelphia City Planning Commission, on the economic feasibility of the Chestnut Street Mall as presented in *The Plan for Center City Philadelphia, 1963*, and is reprinted here with the permission of Arthur C. Kaufmann and Associates, Inc., and the Philadelphia City Planning Commission.

tunity for redevelopment of eighteen acres in the Central Business District. Certainly, through intelligent planning, the most has been made of this opportunity. The Society Hill-Independence Hall sector is on its way to becoming an even more comprehensive national shrine. Add to these the number of other fine residential, commercial, and recreational developments that have taken place, or are under way, in the city. In between the two major CBD development areas mentioned above, however, stretches the main business thoroughfares of the city. Precious little had been done to tie these two areas together, or to help the businessmen located on the connecting thoroughfares to combat the economic and physical deterioration that have occurred. Chestnut Street—long considered Philadelphia's "quality thoroughfare"—has shared in this deterioration. Total retail sales in the Philadelphia CBD have declined in the period 1948 to 1963 for which Chestnut Street must bear at least partial responsibility. This decline has taken place in a period of unprecedented prosperity in our country—a time during which the city as a whole and the entire Metropolitan Area have recorded impressive gains. Similarly, real estate assessments have declined along Chestnut Street, while those for the CBD and the city as a whole have moved forward.

But even these statistics do not tell the whole story. The aesthetics, the quality of many of the stores and the very atmosphere of the street are further evidence of the deterioration that has set in. It is only fair, however, to point out that this problem is not confined to Philadelphia—it is one that confronts nearly all of our large cities. Indeed, it confronts countless cities, large and small, throughout the world.

Philadelphia has tackled the problem imaginatively and, as evidenced by the Market Street East plan and the proposed two-mile long Chestnut Street Mall, gives every intention of continuing to do so. An arterial highway system which will provide easier access to downtown—and, at the same time, divert unproductive through-traffic from the core area—is under way. Add to this the overall improvements planned for mass transit. *Conditions will exist, then, which will facilitate access to center city.* The Mall, as visualized, will integrate and at the same time lengthen the CBD. It is designed to tie historical Philadelphia to the business-paced Philadelphia of the twentieth century, and add excitement to the very life of the city.

II. OBJECTIVES OF THE STUDY

The Philadelphia Planning Commission has chosen to approach this important matter from two standpoints: 1. Economic Feasibility; 2. Traffic and Engineering. Our study covers solely the *economic feasibility*.

In carrying out the *basic purpose* of this study of a proposed pedestrian Mall on Chestnut Street—and in so doing to lend guidance to the City Planning Commission in its final determinations in this matter—we view this work as having *three major objectives:*

1. To determine the anticipated economic effects on business and property values along that portion of Chestnut Street under consideration;

2. To determine, in part, the anticipated economic effects on business and property values in the CBD, and the city itself;

3. To determine the anticipated intangible effects on not only those areas aforementioned, but the effect on the character and reputation of the city itself, together with the pride of its citizens in their city.

In order to arrive at the most intelligent conclusions possible, this study has encompassed:

1. The current and projected shopping and travel characteristics of pedestrians along that area of Chestnut Street under consideration.

2. The current and projected shopping and travel characteristics of pedestrians in the major shopping centers and areas in the Philadelphia Standard Metropolitan Statistical Area.

3. The current and projected shopping and travel characteristics of visitors to Independence Hall National Historical Shrine.

4. The experiences of Chestnut Street businessmen and property owners under existing conditions, the anticipated effects of the proposed Chestnut Street Mall on their businesses and property values, as well as their reactions to the proposed plan.

5. The past and current experiences of representative cities, both domestic and foreign, which now have, or have tried and discontinued, or are currently considering pedestrian malls for the CBD.

III. TREND IN PHILADELPHIA REAL ESTATE ASSESSMENTS AND SALES

In our *Proposal for a Market and Feasibility Study* we said, in part, "as we view the matter, the decision as to whether to proceed with the conversion of Chestnut Street into a Mall should be based primarily on the practical benefits that will accrue to business on Chestnut Street and adjacent thoroughfares." Consequently, it was necessary to determine what the trends in real estate assessments and in retail sales have been.

a. *Assessments*

Assessments for 1950, 1955, 1960, and 1965 were reviewed —for the city as a whole, for the Central Business District, and for the thirteen-block center portion of Chestnut Street. Chestnut Street assessments peaked in 1955, and have declined at an accelerating rate since. CBD assessments peaked in 1960, and have declined since, due entirely to the decline of assessments for Chestnut Street; in fact, other than for the Chestnut Street segments, the CBD assessments increased during each of the three five-year intervals, as did those for the city as a whole. The new buildings in and around Penn Center, Independence Hall and Society Hill have more than accounted for the increase in CBD assessments during the last fifteen years —they have more than offset the Chestnut Street decreases. Here, it should be noted that the area that was the Pennsylvania Railroad right-of-way, was completely tax-exempt. Even to the eye, it is noticeable that fewer improvements have been made on Chestnut Street than in the balance of CBD. Apparently, lack of confidence in the future had caused Chestnut Street property owners to postpone improvement expenditures. Over the past ten years, Chestnut Street assessments declined 13.1%; CBD assessments increased 2.8%; while total assessments for the city increased 17.7%. During this period, Chestnut Street assessments, expressed as a percentage of total city assessments, declined from 3.32% to 2.45% (−26%). CBD assessments including those for Chestnut Street, similarly expressed, declined from 13.59% to 11.88% (−12.6%).

b. *Retail Sales*

During the fifteen years ending with 1963, CBD[1] retail

[1] Central Business District is the area between the Delaware and Schuylkill Rivers, Vine and South Streets.

sales declined $81 million (−12.6%), while total city sales (including the CBD loss,) increased $435 million (22.6%) and The Philadelphia Standard Metropolitan Statistical Area[2] sales (including the CBD loss,) increased $2,428 million (78.1%). The rate of CBD loss accelerated during the past ten years.

CBD sales, in percent of total city and SMSA sales, declined steadily over these fifteen years, as revealed in the following tabulation:

CBD SALES IN PERCENT OF

	1948	1954	1958	1963
City Sales	33.4%	26.8%	26.3%	23.9%
SMSA Sales	20.7%	14.9%	13.0%	10.2%

The number of retail stores decreased during the fifteen years ending with 1963 for all four categories (CBD, City, SMSA and U.S.), as shown below. This trend to fewer stores bears no direct relationship to sales—for example, city sales increased 22.6%, while number of stores declined 27%. It is simply indicative of the nationwide trend to fewer but larger stores—particularly in outskirts and suburbs with roominess and lower land values.

NUMBER OF STORES

	1948	1954	1958	1963	% of 15-year decline
CBD	3,060	2,767	2,621	2,293	−25
City	26,103	23,819	22,934	18,980	−27
SMSA	42,410	41,667	41,667	37,321	−12

IV. OTHER CITIES HAVING MALL EXPERIENCE

Obviously, in this feasibility determination, the actual experience of cities in this country and in Europe, which either have or have had a pedestrian mall in service or under consideration, has great value. Our organization decided to contact *every* city that has been reported to have had experience of some sort with a mall in its downtown core area. The first

[2] Standard Metropolitan Statistical Area, the eight-county area (Philadelphia, surrounded by Bucks, Montgomery, Delaware, Chester, Gloucester, Camden, and Burlington).

step in accomplishing this was to compile a master list of those cities from various sources. This resulted in a master list of 104 cities, 70 domestic and 34 foreign. Information concerning these cities was gathered by any one, or combination of three basic methods: personal staff visits, a questionnaire to the cities themselves, and through correspondence, published material and/or other miscellaneous material.

To summarize our findings on malls in this country: a definite pattern of prerequisite steps emerged—prerequisites which are generally accepted as being conducive to the successful application of the mall concept. Of course, latitude in this regard exists; the highly individualistic conditions in each particular city precludes adherence to any hard and fast rules.

In domestic mall cities, these prerequisites have been provided in varying degrees, with varying success. Nevertheless, those individuals most intimately concerned with pedestrian malls agree that, where applicable, when the following prerequisites are satisfied, the chances for success are materially enhanced:

1. The mall should be but one part of a comprehensive master plan for the entire CBD.

2. Temporary or expedient planning has no part in an undertaking of this nature.

3. From the very beginning, all sectors of the community should be fully informed, and their cooperation and support actively solicited.

4. The street on which the mall is to be installed should be a sensible choice—one that is, and will continue to be, the natural center of business and social activity. Further, it should be a street on which there are no physical features that would deter pedestrian circulation.

5. Access to the CBD should be made convenient. Expressways, etc.,—with ample capacity—and full utilization of mass transit should be provided to make the trip downtown as easy as possible.

6. Peripheral roads, by any name, should be provided to divert through and other unnecessary traffic from the CBD.

7. Provision should be made so that traffic removed from the mall street is rerouted in a manner that does not create congestion in other areas.

8. Plentiful, conveniently located and inexpensive parking should be provided.

9. The mall should be aggressively promoted by all concerned.

10. Every effort should be expended for the convenience and attraction of the pedestrian.

V. GENERAL CONCLUSIONS AND RECOMMENDATIONS

All of the foregoing research and study was undertaken for *one basic purpose*—to bring as much objective and substantiating information as possible to the final determination of whether or not the proposed Chestnut Street Mall is economically feasible. It is our opinion that if time and money permitted—and there were twice as many malls available for study—little more could be gained which would have any direct bearing on our mission.

During five months' concentrated work on such a study, thoughts gradually mature, and the pattern slowly takes form; hence, reaching a conclusion takes on added significance by reason of its maturity, as differentiated from firsthand impressions.

In arriving at our recommendations, full weight has been given to *all* opinions that have been expressed in the many collective and individual discussions which were held with: public officials, architects and city planners, businessmen in widely diversified fields, shoppers, pedestrians, motorists, public transportation operators, and civic organizations. There is one common underlying fact. Of all the businessmen interviewed—both "pros and cons"—never were their worst fears realized—except in Toledo, Ohio—which was ill-conceived and ill-executed. We conclude:

1. That the traffic and engineering study clearly indicates it *is* possible to solve the traffic problem through sensible rerouting off Chestnut Street, and that the vehicles utilizing north-south streets crossing Chestnut would move smoothly and swiftly across the Mall;

2. That ample additional parking *surrounding* the Mall can be provided, as well as that contemplated at both the east and west terminals;

3. That this parking be made available at modest, controlled prices, possibly through use of the City Parking Authority; and that rates be scaled to produce a minimum of three to four times daily turnover;

4. That agreement be reached on a satisfactory vehicle to move two ways on Chestnut Street, and that this service be provided at a fare not to exceed ten cents per passenger. It

also seems advisable to offer a no-cost transfer system to this vehicle from all public transportation contiguous to Chestnut Street. "The man on the street" phase of our study clearly points up the necessity for such transportation, which will certainly require something of a more substantial nature than that presently being used on Lincoln Road or Pomona Mall. It will have to accommodate more passengers, and be adaptable to Philadelphia's variable weather conditions, for an average ride of longer duration.

5. That pickups and deliveries be permitted at those businesses which do not have rear loading facilities—until 11 A.M. daily—and that these, and all regulations governing the use of the Mall, be strictly enforced. *Every effort must be made to give the pedestrian the right-of-way.* The only permanent exception to this should be for emergency vehicles—police, fire, ambulances, etc.

Our research makes it abundantly clear that it is, and will be, economically feasible to convert Chestnut Street into a pedestrian mall—that in so doing, business and property values *will* increase. To that end, we recommend that this project commence at the earliest possible date, consistent with the satisfactory solution of the foregoing five qualifying conditions.

We heartily concur in the thinking that the Chestnut Street Mall must be considered in context with whatever is ultimately decided for the Market Street East area, but should not be delayed until this more complex and costly project is begun.

We now set forth thirteen practical reasons for our recommendation of the Chestnut Street Mall:

1. The sheer necessity of separating vehicular and pedestrian traffic, which problem, in some form, is recognized by architects and city planners in every progressive city in the civilized world. Automobiles are slowly but surely "strangulating" business in CBDs, a trend that will only accelerate in the years to come.

2. While, as Victor Gruen says, "A mall isn't all"—it has proven successful as an integral part of over-all downtown redevelopment, such as has been planned for Philadelphia's CBD.

3. Our evaluation of what has actually transpired on Chestnut Street, with reference to the quality deterioration of the thoroughfare and the consistent decline of property values, points up the need for action of such a drastic nature.

4. We completely share the philosophy of the many non-Philadelphia businessmen and groups who said to us—"We

have only two alternatives: (a) *To do nothing,* and permit the situation to worsen; (b) *To take positive action* towards *successfully* coping with the rapidly growing trend in all business to locate or relocate in the suburbs." We are convinced the latter is the sensible and enlightened approach; and, hence, should be taken notwithstanding the opposition of local businessmen and property owners, whose negative views of this project certainly predominate. In making this recommendation, we do not wish to appear disrespectful of their opinions, but firmly believe—as has been true in many other cities—that these very "conscientious objectors" will eventually become the Mall's most enthusiastic supporters.

5. Our study convinces us that the Mall, when completed and beautified, will prove to be such an attraction that it will help *all* downtown business—on the Mall, as well as on the thoroughfares adjacent to it. To achieve this goal, it has to be well done, thoroughly planned, carefully maintained and co-operatively promoted.

Malls have proven to be an excellent device for unifying the merchants—and lend themselves admirably to joint, all-year-round promotion. Experience has proven that all citizens eventually share in the pride of such an endeavor.

One objection to construction of the Mall will surely be based on the amount of money to be expended. Businessmen, property owners and citizens from other parts of the city may well object to money being spent seemingly for benefit of one group. It must be made abundantly clear to these individuals that if the CBD is allowed to decline, it is they who will have to make up the difference in paying for the ever-increasing costs of running a modern city. It should also be recognized that anything which helps one area in the CBD, helps every business in the entire downtown core.

To others who are directly concerned with just who is going to pay for the Mall, it should be pointed out that the increased valuations, which have resulted from well-planned and successful malls in other cities, will, over the succeeding years, gradually defray the costs.

6. The three consumer surveys which are a part of this study clearly point out that the idea of a pedestrian mall is well received by present and potential customers. The responses from each group surveyed indicated, in varying degrees, an anticipated increase in purchases and purchase days, were the Mall in existence.

7. It is also factual that the merchants on a mall who run

their businesses well, do better in both sales and profits—even when they are required to pay more rent. Their prosperity is, of course, in direct ratio to the sound management of the individual business and the extent of the mall co-operation —which, in turn, is dependent on strong leadership and the enthusiasm of the tenants and owners.

8. We have ascertained that businesses catering to people in all walks of life and all categories of trade benefit, once again, dependent on their own skill in "cashing in" on the superior opportunities which a mall presents.

9. While it is true that no metropolitan city the size of Philadelphia has yet had mall experience, there is no reason we can discern (once those five qualifications are complied with) why it should not succeed. Since the plan is fundamentally sound, we can see no barrier simply in the size of the city. It just takes a little more courage to do it—and, by the same token, should add even more to Philadelphia's reputation as a progressive city. In addition, it will induce thousands of people from all over the world to see it. We start with a great advantage—the location of Independence Hall on Chestnut Street, and, consequently, the Mall as a tourist attraction is more readily assured. This, too, is part of our philosophy, that—exactly like a store—a city can't sell people anything if it doesn't at least bring them downtown to look—and this includes our own citizens, as well as countless visitors from near and far!

10. We submit that the most successful suburban shopping centers are built around malls—so much so that the old "strip developments" have already been made obsolete. It is also a well-known fact that suburban malls are now being built with, or converted to, the "all-weather," covered variety—but this is not presently recommended for Chestnut Street. It is conceivable that the success the Chestnut Street Mall will achieve, may ultimately merit the expense of a covered mall as one additional device to meet and beat suburban competition. One thing sure, all of the benefits of leisurely shopping and relaxed atmosphere cannot be brought from the suburbs to the cities—but a mall can bring many of them.

11. On this latter subject, we mention the social significance which these malls have assumed. They *do* become the focal point of a city and, eventually, the meeting place for both residents and visitors to these communities. This does not alone hold true during regular business hours, but after hours, on holidays and weekends as well. Some opponents of a mall call

attention to the fact that it may become the headquarters for beatniks and bums, but these characters presently gather from the Spanish Steps in Rome to Rittenhouse Square in Philadelphia—consequently, this is not a valid reason for failing to do the necessary to pull Chestnut Street up by its bootstraps.

12. For what is commonly known as Philadelphia's "Quality Thoroughfare," few new buildings have been built, few new businesses of character have located on the Street, and few renovations have taken place, hence, the sheer necessity for such positive action.

13. There persists in the minds of many businessmen—not only in Philadelphia, but elsewhere, as well—that automobile traffic passing their doors represents business. This is the philosophy that accepts congestion, and even confusion, as beneficial. Countless studies, including our own, have shown the reverse to be true. This fact will undoubtedly be substantiated by the current Traffic and Engineering Study, authorized by the City Planning Commission. While it is hazardous to generalize, we feel safe in stating that no more than three out of ten cars on Chestnut Street have a Chestnut Street destination.

Further, the two-way transportation recommended will provide equal viewer exposure to stores and show-windows on *both* sides of Chestnut Street; and, it will do so under conditions most conducive to full attention—freedom from all the necessary and diverting factors that are part of operating a car on a busy downtown thoroughfare.

The Plan For Center City Philadelphia, 1963 proposes a Chestnut Street Mall, which would run from the Delaware River to the Schuylkill River, with two-way transportation along its length, and possibly, to important points beyond. However, inasmuch as this plan calls for a mall of approximately two miles—more than twice as long as any presently existing—it is our suggestion that consideration be given to accomplishing the objectives in two stages, rather than in its entirety. In no way is this suggestion to be interpreted as an espousal of the "temporary" or "experimental" school of thought—in many instances, such planning has only proven detrimental—but, rather, that such an approach would effect the minimum disturbance in accustomed procedures.

We believe that a more conservative approach would be to proceed with the removal of vehicular traffic and the installation of the proposed two-way transportation along the street for the length envisioned, but limiting the construction of actual Mall amenities, etc., to one portion thereof. This program would then involve the expenditure of only that money necessary for resurfacing and beautification in that part of the street selected. It is our opinion that, in so doing, valuable lessons may be learned, and that the over-all objectives may be achieved with less "wear and tear" on everyone concerned.

We are not making any hard-and-fast recommendations as to what portion of the street should constitute the first stage, for the Planning Commission must rely on its own expert judgment, as well as on all information available to it.

We conclude—by repeating—that, from every standpoint of our evaluation, constructing a mall on Chestnut Street will, if given ample opportunity, prove economically feasible. Sooner or later, Philadelphia, like every other metropolitan city, will be forced to recognize the necessity for the separation of vehicular and pedestrian traffic. We firmly feel that a Chestnut Street Mall, as contemplated, is the first important step in coping with the situation which confronts our city. Consequently, we recommend that it be done *sooner,* rather than later—and the sooner the better, as still another progressive step in Philadelphia's renaissance.

Chapter 11

HOUSING AND COMMUNITY

Housing provides the frame for living; in some as yet not completely clear way the character of the family dwelling molds and is molded by its inhabitants. Further, as a family goes through its life cycle of childless early years, young children, crowded peak years to childless later years, the function and form of this frame must change. Housing is more than the mere physical dwelling; it is interior space, equipment and furnishings; the immediate exterior space; and importantly its relationship to the surrounding neighborhood or community—even in our mobile society. Prodded by our mores and the powerful consortium of businesses profiting from the housing industry, Americans try hard to "own" houses—even if ownership is merely the token percentage of a heavy mortgage; by 1961 an estimated 62% of American families "owned" their homes. The federal government has aided and abetted this ownership through the FHA mortgage system which has been such a heavy factor in the typical free-standing single dwelling sprawl around central city in suburbia.

The need for *good* housing everywhere exceeds the supply; effective demand in free market economies or the ability to purchase or rent reasonable quarters is far below need. In socialist countries, there simply is not enough housing. In the United States our present total supply is (1961) approximately 58.3 million units for an estimated 52.6 million families—the overage accounted for by second or vacation homes. Theoretically the quantity of dwellings is adequate but it is not distributed into the "right" hands, and the quality is distressing. Some 27% of the U.S. housing stock is unsound or lacks minimal plumbing. There has been, however, a consistent overall gain in the elimination of substandard dwellings especially in owner-occupied units, but the rapidly increasing population (showing itself in new family formation at an estimated yearly rate of 1,200,000), the wearing out of the existent supply and the destruction of dwellings by the curiously self-defeating massive urban renewal and urban transportation operations run ahead of good housing stock. It has been estimated that we need a minimum of 2,000,000 housing starts yearly to cope with the above factors and to clean up the physical slums; we get about only 1,500,000 starts yearly on the average.

In central city, the supply is deteriorating and most especially in the non-community of the jungle slums into which the poor nonwhites of our society are herded along with the remnants of earlier immigrant or migrant waves. Thus the "long hot summers" of contemporary America with death and violence in a miasma of heat, dirt and fear become normal throughout this land from Harlem to Watts.[1] Our city slums are poverty holes of despair—not as Lisa Peattie has pointed out "the slums of hope" to be found in the *bidonvilles*, *favelas*, and *ranchos*—the squatter camps of underdeveloped lands. What is needed is not better housing but a better chance as the Model Cities Program hopes to accomplish and the OEO is stumbling toward with Neighborhood Job Corps, Summer Work Training Programs, VISTA, Community Action Programs, etc. Social planning is now slowly joining physical planning as it must; Chapter 19 explores this.

In Scandinavian countries, housing has become a quasi-public utility or a service beyond profit linked to a total community planning approach. Not only must it be recognized that poverty is the root of slums, but that every conceivable device must be harnessed, as the consultants' report to New York's mayor recommends, to upgrade the quality, to increase the housing supply, and to civilize the inhabitants themselves, brutalized by lives with no foreseeable "out," locked in ghettos within a wall of "lily-white" suburbs.

Beyond the dismal slums of our central cities are the unrewarding gray areas of the outer city and the banal suburbs in characterless tens of square miles. The "best" housing of America is often "bad" both by design and human standards. William H. Whyte, sensitive both to the good land and the good life, has taken up the cudgel for cluster housing, and his article makes clear that there is both profit and satisfaction in this advanced way to group town houses and country houses. With massive populations of the future seemingly inevitable, Michael Hugo-Brunt's lauding of fantastic housing densities (3,900 to the acre) in Hong Kong shows that what would be considered slums here can be rewarding communities in that crowded land; these appear to be dwellings of hope with all the excitement of lively human interaction and convenient in-town living. Is this a partial rebuttal of "garden city" and suburban sprawl? Finally, a truly magnificent idea fountain was assembled by Mayor Lindsay to give him leads as to what might be done about the appalling housing/slum tangle in New York; fifty suggestions quite possibly applicable throughout the United States were reported out by his Advisory Committee. They are worth pondering, since they deal with nine common facets of the massive housing problem facing every American city: administrative organization; discrimination; segregation and integration; public housing; limited profit housing; rehabilitation and inspection; rent subsidies; the federal relationship; design, materials and open space; and land policy.

And yet the city is where the action has been historically, and

[1] 34 dead, 1,032 wounded, 3,952 arrested, $40 million damage in this one city during the 1965 riots.

still is despite auto-designed America. In a 1964 replication[2] of a 1960 housing and community preference study[3] made by sampling techniques at an Ivy League college, 38% of the 1964 seniors were willing to locate initially and 17%, with an established family, to remain in central city; as compared with 18% and 3% for 1960 seniors. Seniors today tended further to accept multiple family dwellings slightly more readily than a college generation ago: for initial housing, 76% compared to 61%, and for an established family, 17% to 4%. While the opinions of these possible "future opinion molders" may be no more than straws in the wind, they may well indicate a trend toward re-accepting central city, slowly upgrading as it is today through urban renewal, as *the* truly rewarding civilized place to live—despite the patent clear and present dangers.

Bernard J. Frieden, socially oriented planner, in a bridging article between this chapter and the one on social planning, shows how traditional planners have taken a very limited view of "planning"—neglecting in urban development policies "the improvement of living conditions and opportunities for currently disadvantaged groups." Actually many urban development and planning efforts hurt certain groups considerably, although returning measurable economic gains. Fragmented suburban and central city governments often seem to be used as devices to protect the affluent and corral the disadvantaged. Frieden proposes four major policies in the realm of 1) intergovernment relations, 2) land use controls, 3) the administration of laws against discrimination and 4) direct assistance to people damaged by development. He recommends advocacy planning, discussed by Paul Davidoff in Chapter 13 of Volume II, "Advocacy and Pluralism in Planning," and his insistence on socially oriented policies (that is, complex administrative tools) is increasingly characteristic of modern planning orientation.

[2] H. Wentworth Eldredge, Paul S. Feinberg and Derek L. Phillips, "Changing Housing Preferences in the U.S.A.: An Empirical Examination" (unpublished manuscript).

[3] H. Wentworth Eldredge, "Housing Preferences in the U.S.A.," *Town and Country Planning*, Vol. XXX (September 1961), pp. 369–73.

Cluster Development

WILLIAM H. WHYTE*

Cluster is on the verge of becoming the dominant pattern of new residential development, and probably for many years to come.

* Author and formerly assistant managing editor of *Fortune* magazine. He is the author of *Is Anybody Listening?* (1955) and *The Organization Man* (1957). He became involved with practical action for

It is a counter revolutionary movement that is taking place. The cluster idea is ancient; what it calls for, simply, is grouping the houses more tightly together and using the land thus saved for common greens and squares. It is the principle of the early New England town; it is the principle of the medieval village, it is, in fact, the basic principle of community design since we first started building several millennia ago.

The revolution took place here, and quite recently. Fifty years ago we clustered housing without thinking much about it. For all the nostalgic image of the American homestead, most Americans lived quite close to each other, in towns and cities, and many of the best people lived in row houses. But then in the twenties the expansion of suburbia began gathering force, and what is known as the American's historic yearning for a home in the country was soon to be established.

By the fifties it was official. A growing urban population had now turned the move to suburbia into a great surge. This had the effect of under-cutting the reason for the move, for the countryside was always vanishing over the next hill, but the momentum was unstoppable. The detached house on a lot of one's own seemed to have become the norm of middle class aspiration.

There was no alternative, or so it seemed. With few exceptions the new subdivisions homogenized the land with lots strung out as far apart as income or pride could enforce. The design was embedded in countless local ordinances, in the lending requirements of the FHA and mortgage institutions, and perhaps more important, in the widespread conviction that Americans would accept no other design.

"Garden city" advocates had tried to prove otherwise, and through the efforts of Clarence Stein and others several model communities had been built on the cluster principle. There was Radburn in the late twenties, the Greenbelt towns of the early

open space while editing the *Fortune* series later published as *The Exploding Metropolis* (Doubleday Anchor, 1958). He did a study for the Urban Land Institute on conservation easement and in 1961 *Open Space Action* for the *Outdoor Recreation Resources Review Committee*. Appointed in the summer of 1964 by President Johnson as a member of the Task Force on Natural Beauty, he drafted the Task Force's final report, and aided Laurance S. Rockefeller to organize the White House Conference on Natural Beauty in May 1965 at which he chaired the landscape Panel. This article has been adapted and reprinted with permission from his study: *Cluster Development* (New York: American Conservation Association, 30 Rockefeller Plaza, 1964) highly recommended as an excellent summary of modern siting practice both in town and in the suburbs. It includes important visual material.

New Deal and in the late thirties Baldwin Hills in Los Angeles. Some of the Utopian expectations with which these experiments were freighted were never borne out, but as individual communities they were, and still are, quite successful. But they remained outside the mainstream. Some of their features were copied, such as the super block and the cul-de-sac, but the basic cluster principle was not. Few developers even bothered to go look.

By the late fifties, however, the conventional pattern had been pushed close to the breaking point. No matter how far out developers pushed, land prices kept soaring ahead of them. Thus, as they moved further away from the center of their market, they found the cost of the land and of improving it was taking up a sharply increasing portion of the final housing costs. If developers were not to price themselves out of the mass market something had to give.

One solution would be to squeeze more houses onto the tract. But communities wouldn't allow this; indeed, they were more zealous than ever in using large lot zoning to keep down the number of newcomers they would have to school and service. For the developer the only practical solution would be to concentrate the allowable number of houses on the most buildable part of the tract and leave the rest open. The Urban Land Institute, the National Association of Home Builders, and the leading housing journals commenced an impressive educational campaign on this concept.

Sprawl had been hurting the public most of all, and the fact was at last becoming quite visible. Large lot zoning was not keeping the subdivisions in check; it was making them chew up more and more of the landscape. This not only looked like hell, it was proving costly for the community to service. And what would happen when the next wave hit?

The Regional Plan Association has made such an estimate for the New York metropolitan region. By 1985 there should be an additional six and a half million people to house; on the remaining vacant land, however, the average lot size is now up to $\frac{2}{3}$ of an acre, and if the pattern persists there could only be one result. The Association, which fervently hopes it never comes to pass, calls it "spread city"—"not a true city because it lacks centers, nor a suburb because it is not a satellite of any city, nor is it truly rural because it is loosely covered with houses and urban facilities."

In every metropolitan area the warning has been sounded. The mathematics has become inexorable; with just so much land and many more people we simply cannot continue to waste land the way we have been. If there is to be any environment worth living in, there must be a much more efficient use of the land. This calls for many approaches but the essence is the cluster idea, on the regional as well as the community scale, and with increasing urgency this point has been expounded in hundreds of local meetings.

Citizens have been interested, but cautious. Why be the guinea pigs? If we approved cluster wouldn't the jerry-builders come swarming in? How do you solve the problem of who takes care of the open space? That's a fine plan but did it ever get built? If this is such a hot idea, why haven't more communities tried it? Citizens want to be shown.

Now they can be. Many of the projects which were initiated three or four years ago have finally broken through the last crust of resistance. A few have been up for some time, a fair number have been completed and are shaking down, and an impressive number are now getting the final approval and are ready for the land grading phase. There has been a pick-up in the number of communities which have adopted ordinances to permit cluster development, and the increase could soon be geometric.

What are the chief denominators? We must first define terms—but not too finely. Cluster goes under many different names—density zoning, planned unit development, environmental planning—but it is the basic approach that concerns us. Rather than attempt a highly specific definition, let us think of a range. At one end we have the conventional subdivision in which there is no common open space. At the other end we have the cluster development of high density, siting towers, or town houses around small common greens.

What is significant is not the exact degree of clustering. Lot sizes, after all, are relative, and what in one area would constitute high density clusters—one-half acre plots around a green, for example, in a four acre zone—would in a more urban area seem anything but cluster. What is significant is the direction. There is a definite shift towards the cluster end of the scale, and this shift may presage a later move to higher net densities for all kinds of developments.

This does not mean that paradise is imminent. Nor does it mean that large lots and detached houses are on their way out, or that they should be. There is a place for each, and for the maligned rancher too. What we are really talking about is a more effective land use, and it is the new range of choice cluster provides that opens up the great opportunities.

They could be well seized, or they could be abused; at this stage the cluster movement is still highly malleable. That is the reason for this report. It is an effort to bring together what has been learned so far; to see which approaches are working out well, and which are not. The initial chapters concentrate on the major legal and economic factors. The middle chapters take up the specific cluster developments. In the concluding chapters we set down what we believe are the major lessons. In the Appendix is a tabulation of data for a cross section of 46 developments, and as a help to civic officials and citizen groups a selection of model ordinances, articles of incorporation for homeowners associations and deed forms are provided.

Here is a five point summary of the basic findings.

1. *The verdict of the market place is yes.* The sales data we have gathered have to be interpreted with care; every development is something of a special case and in any event sales figures have to be judged in relation to the local market. Nevertheless, one fact is becoming evident; in most cases cluster developments have been outselling conventional developments of the same price range.

It doesn't follow from this that people buy because of the cluster principle; other factors, most notably the house itself, may be more compelling. But one reason it is difficult to sort out cause and effect is that these factors tend to have an underlying unity in most cluster developments.

Those developers who have the imagination to try a new approach are most likely to be the developers with the best eye for house design. Cluster developments, as a consequence, tend to be better developments than the competition in a host of details as well as in overall concept. What weighting do buyers give the common green? The walkways? The swim club? Even they don't know. But they are buying and this is the key fact.

2. *People like to live in cluster developments.* Talks with homeowners indicate that while they may be quite unaware that there's anything particularly unusual about their subdivision, they show a high degree of satisfaction with it. Similarly, while the cluster element may not have been the motivating factor, it is one that they come to appreciate. When they were shopping their questions were primarily about the house itself, schools, nearby transportation and such. Once they be-

come owners, however, the usefulness and amenity of the open space layout becomes more important and in talking to other people about the community they are likely to give it some emphasis.

Interestingly, there is often something of a time lag problem. People have to know how to use open space to appreciate it. Where the people have come from the central city, the kind of open spaces—such as stream, valleys and woods, for example—so familiar to country people can seem a downright menace, and mothers forbid their children to go near them. It will be interesting to see how the new generations respond.

3. *The "town house" development is catching on fast.* In most cases the town house is a row house that is not in town at all and is often extremely expensive. One could deduce that it's all wrong for the market, suburbia most of all. Add a Williamsburg facade, such touches as old fashioned gas street lamps, group them around common greens, and the result is a sales package that may turn out to be the "revolutionary" new concept of the next decade.

Some of the most successful of such developments have been in the upper brackets; Dudley Square in Shreveport, Louisiana, with its $40,000 houses, is a notable example. While town house developments do seem to have a certain taste-maker appeal the market success has been equally strong at the other end of the range, and it is in this bracket that developers are now sensing a bandwagon. In the Los Angeles area, the success of one town house development has been so great that developers all over the area have been junking conventional plans and have virtually swamped the local FHA office with applications for town house units.

4. *There is a growing emphasis on recreation as a core element.* Recreation facilities have worked well for many conventional developments and golf course subdivisions date back to the twenties. Such facilities are virtually called for, however, by a cluster layout. Some of the new cluster developments include golf courses, bridle trails, tennis courts and such, and several of the largest make recreation so integral a feature that they could be called "recreational communities." These feature a series of villages, each centered around a special recreational activity—swimming in one, for example; riding in another.

While facilities are much less elaborate in the smaller developments, as a minimum almost all include swim clubs and children's playgrounds. The day is close at hand, indeed, when a developer will have to provide them if he is to compete.

5. *The basic procedures for common open space ownership and maintenance are working well*. There are three basic methods. One, favored in New Jersey, is to deed the space to the local government. This seems the simplest course but for reasons which this report will detail later, it may prove the least effective. The second method is to set up a special governmental district, the boundaries of which coincide with that of the development, and deed the land to the district. Such districts are empowered to levy assessments on the residents for maintenance and development of the open space. The third is basically the same except that the vehicle is a nonprofit corporation consisting of the homeowners.

There has been considerable experience with such associations, and as a study of them by the Urban Land Institute indicates, they have worked quite well. Key requirements: they should be set up at the very beginning; membership should be mandatory for all homeowners; there should be provision for assessments to cover costs, and for adjusting the assessments to meet new conditions.

It may seem premature to worry about the disadvantages of success, but several warnings are in order. Because the developers who are pioneering cluster tend to be among the best, the overall standards tend to be well above average. But this is likely to be temporary; and the defects that are already apparent could well be magnified as the idea is taken up by more and more developers. Here are six potential problems:

1. *Cluster could be frozen into a format as stereotyped as the conventional layout it is replacing*. The enthusiasm with which Los Angeles builders are hopping on the town house bandwagon may be a foretaste of what is yet to come: the externals of the best selling developments are likely to be repeated time and time again, whatever the site, the latitude, or the character of the area. If one had to guess the specifications of the all-American development five years from now, they would probably run something like this: two-story row houses, Georgetown facade spiced up with West Coast Cinderella; the first floor featuring an open kitchen leading to living room, in turn opening out through sliding glass doors onto a patio twenty feet square, with a fence eight feet high, the gate opening out onto a common area roughly 100 feet across to the next row of houses, a play yard at one end with

swings and abstract forms—the whole garlanded with gas street lamps.

There is nothing inherently wrong with this layout, save for those gas lamps, and some cluster developments that come close to these specifications are excellent ones. But what about the copies? Imitation has a way of missing the quality of the prototype, and as the copies go up the uniformity could be appalling.

2. *Cluster development calls for a fresh approach to house design.* In the outlying areas there can be clustering with relatively large lots and here the conventional detached house can work well. As lot sizes get smaller, however, there comes a point where the conventional design doesn't quite work. Windows on the side, for example, tend to lose their function. There's nothing to see except the neighbor's windows, and the vestigial strip of yard becomes a positive disadvantage.

More important, the relationship of one house's design to another becomes much more critical. In a conventional large lot subdivision with, say, five basic models, there may be enough space that a split level, barn red colonial can be sited next to a rancher without visual clash, and even a few Hansel and Gretels won't foul things up too badly. Bring the disparate elements close together, however, and what strikes the eye is chaos.

3. *There is too much hack site planning.* Cluster offers unparalleled advantages for imaginative use of topography—the use of trees as focal points, the use of rock formations, and overburden from grading operations. But there is far too little exploitation of these advantages.

In researching developments for this report one of the most disconcerting tasks was finding out who did the basic site plan. In some cases, evidently, no one did; in others, it started on the back of an envelope and then was handed over to a civil engineer to fill in. For the best developments trained site planners were used but in too many of these cases they were brought in only after the first plans proved unworkable. Developers would save money if they started with them in the first place.

There should be more experimentation with uses of open space—in particular, the relationship between private and common spaces. There is a lot of dogma about how people should use open spaces, but remarkably little attention paid as to how people actually do use them. Formal play areas are an example: children seem to play almost anywhere else.

4. *Cluster should not be used as a device to achieve unreasonable densities.* Standardization would be bad enough; worse yet would be both standardization and compression. What appeals most to many developers, let us remember, is the cluster, not the open space: the doughnut and not the hole. Clustering can achieve higher densities and a more pleasant environment at the same time. But somewhere along the line the two part company.

There is a fine line between a comfortable sense of enclosure and being cramped, and some developments have pushed compression to the point of claustrophobia. In recognizing the effectiveness of a small open space it is easy to forget that the effectiveness is possible because the development has borrowed space from surrounding areas. Take away the larger areas and the smaller open spaces have a far different feeling.

5. *Communities should not use cluster as a cut-rate substitute for buying park land.* Just as developers should not make too much of a good thing of cluster, neither should communities. A number have been trying very hard, most notably in New Jersey. As part of the bargain for approving cluster developments, they are requiring that common open spaces be deeded outright to the town. It seems to be working well enough. The courts have indicated approval, the developers have not raised a fuss, and the towns have been getting a great deal of land without having to pay a cent.

But it is a bad precedent. To make municipal ownership an invariable condition is to undercut the basic rationale of cluster. It is the homeowners who are really paying for the common land, and they should be able to enjoy it.

This does not mean that dedication to the community is necessarily against their interests; in many cases, it is the best way for all concerned to handle the common area, in full or in part. But in many other cases it is not, and dedication to a homeowners association would be preferable. The community should demand guarantees that the open space remain open; it should decide the precise form of ownership, however, on the basis of the particular case.

Thus to our final point: the great promise of cluster is in the exciting opportunities there are for linking spaces together. For the community it is the connective quality of cluster open space that is most important and a relatively small part of the open space may be the link that ties many more acres together. The key is to anticipate cluster development and to lay down in advance the skeleton of an open space network that would unite the open spaces of one cluster development with the open spaces of others—and with the school and park sites of the community. It can be done; Philadelphia has demonstrated this.

The potential of cluster is great and that is what makes this particular point in time so tantalizing. The concept is not frozen yet. Eventually, the cluster concept may become codified and imbedded in various legislative and administrative regulations, much as the once new "super-block" pattern became virtually dictated by law. But not quite yet.

Cluster is still in the formative period. The very fact that cluster can mean so many different things may make definition difficult, but it does provide a rich field of experimentation. We have a chance to see which approaches are not proving fruitful, and what new ones ought to be tried. The time ahead is the critical one. Several years from now decisions will have been made that will probably set the pattern of American residential development for a long time to come. But the decisions are still ours to make.

THE ECONOMICS OF CLUSTER

Good aesthetics, it is said, make good economics. Cluster development, as this chapter will outline, is one instance where the thought is demonstrably true. Whether considered from the community's interest or the developer's or the homeowner's, the factors that make cluster developments look better are the same factors that make them more economical.

Until recently, the economic case had to be somewhat hypothetical. Most presentations would be based on a detailed comparison of the cost of putting up a conventional subdivision on a given tract of land and the cost of the cluster alternative. Since rules of thumb for costs are fairly standard—so many dollars per lineal foot of curbing, and the like—the comparisons could be realistic. Invariably, they favored cluster.

On aesthetics the comparisons favored cluster even more. Here imagination would be displayed, often very enthusiastically, and what with sketches of children gamboling on greenswards, outdoor cafes with striped umbrellas, and such, the vision held up approached idyllic proportions.

But the basic case is a strong one and it has been well presented. The National Association of Home Builders put together a travelling road show which has been shown to builders across the U.S. The FHA has been energetic in missionary work; it has been revising its regulations to encourage the new approach and as an invitation to builders recently published "Planned Unit Development With a Homes Association" (available at 50¢ a copy from the U.S. Government Printing Office, Washington, D.C.).

City and county planning agencies have also been assiduous, and over the past few years they have been putting out some notable why-don't-we-try-this presentations of the cluster idea. One of the best, shown below is that prepared by Karl Belser and his associates on the planning commission of Santa Clara County, California. It was used to good effect by planners

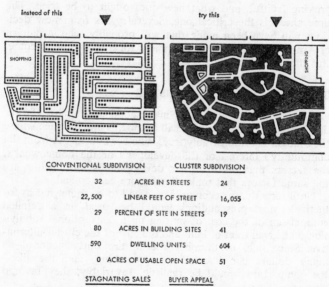

Instead of this ▼   try this ▼

	CONVENTIONAL SUBDIVISION	CLUSTER SUBDIVISION
	32	ACRES IN STREETS	24
	22,500	LINEAR FEET OF STREET	16,055
	29	PERCENT OF SITE IN STREETS	19
	80	ACRES IN BUILDING SITES	41
	590	DWELLING UNITS	604
	0	ACRES OF USABLE OPEN SPACE	51

STAGNATING SALES

The typical tract house has been overproduced. Buyers are tired of:
Peas-in-a-pod uniformity
Gimmicks in place of real values
A forest of overhead wires
Weed growing, trash collecting, useless side yards.

BUYER APPEAL

The dwelling oriented to the Common Green is a fresh concept with a great potential. Buyers are looking for:
Variety in housing
Nearby open space
Sky views uncluttered with overhead wires
Minimum yard maintenance.

FIGURE 1. Excerpts from "The Common Green" Brochure, Fomented by Santa Clara County Planners in 1961

and builders all over the country (eventually, Belser is happy to note, in Santa Clara County too).

Now the case need no longer be hypothetical; enough cluster developments are actually on the ground to afford first hand tests. One of the most significant is Village Green in Hillsborough, New Jersey. It is significant because there is nothing particularly unusual about it. Some of the very large developments may make a more striking case economically, but they tend to be complicated by a number of special factors. Village Green is characteristic of the kind of problems faced by the great bulk of builders.

Hillsborough is a semi-rural community whose 8,000 people want it to stay semi-rural. In 1958 the town had decided to raise the bars. With New York forty miles away and new highways going up, a mass invasion by developers seemed imminent, and to forestall this the town changed its zoning from a half acre to one acre lots. For a while this seemed to work.

In 1960 real estate man Sidney Halpern acquired a 79 acre tract and proceeded to plot it for one acre lots. Fortuitously the county planner, William Roach, was a member of the Hillsborough planning board, and he was keen on cluster. One afternoon he sat down with Halpern and sketched out on a piece of paper how a cluster plan would be a better proposition for Halpern than his conventional one. Roach's idea was to group the houses in three clusters on 35 acres and leave the remaining 40 acres open.

Halpern and his associate, Seymour Tuschak, liked the idea. So did the town planning board. It retained planner Robert Catlin to make zoning and designing recommendations. In 1961 the board unanimously approved a cluster zoning ordinance and subsequently approved the Village Green plan.

Builder Melvin Konwiser, who bought the package from Halpern, started off with a good edge on the competition. He could not only put up more houses, he could concentrate them on the prime sites. Under the conventional plan, he would have been forced by the topography to put up only 69 houses, and many of them would have to have been placed on less desirable portions of the periphery—land abutting the railroad tracks, a highway, an industrial zone, and low cost homes of a neighboring township. Under the cluster plan, he was able to gain three more house sites. All of the houses, furthermore, were placed on the choicest part of the tract and the outermost of them, instead of being out the peripheral land, were bordered by the common open space.

Another saving was in water and sewerage. In the conventional plan Konwiser would have had to put in septic tanks and dig wells; because the tighter grouping of the cluster plan allowed shorter pipe runs, he would be able to tie them in with the water and sewerage facilities of adjoining Manville borough. Land development costs, estimated at $6,500 per lot for the conventional plan, were shaved to $5,500. There was less roadway and less grading. The trees, including a fine stand of hardwood, didn't have to be sawn away.

As he began to build the development, Konwiser discovered there were additional savings. He built the development a cluster at a time, and in doing so found he was able to concentrate all his materials and equipment in one place with a considerable savings in man hours and convenience. As soon as one cluster was finished he moved everything to the next cluster site.

The first cluster was ready for occupancy in the middle of October 1962; a month later it was fully occupied. The second cluster was opened up in December, the third in March. While there is no precise way of measuring the time savings, the speed of construction cut down Konwiser's overhead by a considerable margin and got him off to an earlier start on sales.

The inevitable extras cut somewhat into the savings of cluster: Konwiser installed a drinking fountain, water lines, a baseball diamond, two bus stop shelters. He could well afford to. The houses outsold the competition—indeed, they knocked the bottom out of the market in the area for some time. . . .

In establishing the economic case for cluster, it is the community aspect that is the crux of the matter. If anything, the benefits of cluster are even stronger for the community than for the developer but though this may seem self-evident to planners and developers it is by no means evident to local officials and the general citizenry. Nor is it self-evident to municipal engineers. They are a conservative group, and are naturally suspicious of innovations, especially those that seem to call for watering down accepted civic standards for construction.

Technical objections to cluster, we must note, are often more a rationalization for resisting cluster than the reason. The amenity appeal is what will sell cluster and as time goes on and there are more such developments to see, the technical objections will dwindle. It is important, however, to compress that time. Over the next year or so there are going to be bruising debates in hundreds of communities over cluster and the more fully the economic case is presented the less wear and tear for all concerned.

[There are clear economic gains for all concerned by well-designed sanitary sewers, natural storm drainage systems, and site planning in cluster development.]

* * *

As communities get more experience with cluster development, many of the troublesome questions will be cleared up. But a more positive approach is needed: the processing should be expedited as a carrot for developers. Whatever the defects of conventional subdivisions for developers, it is the easy way as far as the civic machinery is concerned, and this has a great bearing on developers' costs. Each month that capital is tied up means higher costs—and a declining interest in projects that depart from the conventional.

Developers could do a lot to help if they would spend a little more money on their initial site planning. Platting a conventional FHA subdivision is such a cut and dried matter that many developers have been in the habit of having a civil engineer do all the work on the site plans, landscaping and all. Applied to cluster development, however, this penny-pinching can produce some pretty bad plans, and civic officials have been quite right to insist on changes and redrafts. Some of the most encouraging data encountered in this study, we should add, were the plans that *didn't* get built.

Less encouraging was the number of times that professional site planners were not brought in until it was obvious the initial cut rate plan wouldn't work very well. (Several of the best plans shown in this report began as rescue jobs.) A good site plan almost invariably produces savings far beyond whatever extra fee is involved; it would provide even more savings if such a plan had been drawn up in the first place. Good aesthetics, to repeat, make good economics.

TWO EXAMPLES: TOWN HOUSES IN THE CITY AND TOWN HOUSES IN SUBURBIA

River Park (*Washington, D.C.*)

In the southwest redevelopment area is River Park. It combines town houses and towers, but with quite a different approach. The word here is "striking." For the Reynolds Metals Company, sponsor of the project, architect Charles Goodman designed a large tower with a foreground of town houses. The town houses are something of a composition; with their mixture of flat roofs and barrel vault roofs set off with different primary colors, they provide from a number of angles views with the fascination of a puzzle. Visually, River Park is a knockout.

Here the emphasis is on privacy. There is very little green; the common areas are paved and they function primarily as walkways. Between these and the patios there is no ambiguity whatsoever. The walls surrounding the individual patios are seven feet high, and it is impossible for the passerby to see what's going on inside. The people in the towers can, of course, but the possibility doesn't seem to have been inhibiting.

It certainly didn't dampen the interest of purchasers. River Park's units are cooperatives and their price ranges from $22,000 for a two-story town house to $31,550 for a three-story one. All were sold out before construction was completed and no model house ever had to be operated. The tower units went more slowly, but by fall 1963 virtually all units were sold.

Georgetown South (A Virginia Suburb of Washington, D.C.)

Town houses may go well in town, many people argue, but could they ever really catch on in suburbia? And would they go over with the middle income group? Thirty miles south of River Park an important market test has been taking place. For some time Merit Developers, Inc. wanted to try a town house and village green project in the suburbs of Washington. Under the zoning of most adjacent Virginia counties, town houses could be constructed only if they were rental units, so the developers pushed on to Prince William County. This was stretching the limit of commutation pretty far, but the local authorities eventually proved willing to revise their ordinances to allow the building of a town house cluster development.

The result is a clean, economic layout. Architect Marion Bagley has laid out the houses in straight rows, with the rows grouped to make a series of blocks, each with its own common green in the center. The developers did not provide the customary swimming pools, only sites, but they have dressed up the greens with barbecue pits, swings, and play equipment, and they merchandise the package very effectively. Common areas will be deeded to a homeowners association; pending its formation each home is assessed $3 a month for maintenance.

There is a nod to the suburban front yard (though setbacks were reduced to fifteen feet from the previously required thirty-five), but in other respects the design salutes the city as its inspiration, especially Georgetown, Alexandria, and Williamsburg. The street scenes have been carefully composed for this effect, with some thirty-five basic exteriors used to give variation.

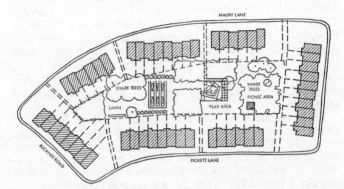

FIGURE 2. Typical Georgetown South Block

It may not be Georgetown, but at $11,490 to $14,990 a house, it is quite a sales package. Construction began in January 1963. By June, 170 houses had been sold; by December, 205. Most of the buyers have been people who work in Washington, with government workers the biggest single group. It's a big market to tap, and the chances of selling out the total 900 units planned seem rather good.

Hong Kong Housing

MICHAEL HUGO-BRUNT*

This British colony today covers 398 square miles. The capital, Victoria, on Hong Kong Island and the industrial city of Kowloon on the mainland, are the largest urban areas. To-

* Associate Professor, Department of City and Regional Planning, School of Architecture, Cornell University. Holder of a Bachelor of Architecture from Cape Town University, South Africa, and a master's

gether they cover 12 square miles and overlook each other from the opposing coast lines of the large natural harbour. There are several market towns, Tsun Wan, Taipo, Shatin and Yuen Long in the New Territories as well as several smaller centres on the island at Aberdeen, Stanley, Repulse Bay and Shekko. These are either resort areas or fishing villages.

Hong Kong is an industrial, tourist, administrative and educational centre. It is also a free port, a military base and transportation terminal; it is an exchange mart between China and the West and might be described as a "Western listening post" on the China coast. The trading centre also functioned as the Far Eastern base for the Royal Navy prior to 1941. Since 1945 refugees, industries, American fleets, shipping lines and airways have stimulated such growth that the British have had to struggle to sustain the growing population.

The population, now numbering almost 4 million, is continuously increased by an influx of refugees from Communist China. In 1971 it will rise to be 4.8 million and, if present growth rates continue will be 7.4 million in 1981. The majority of the inhabitants are Kwangtung Chinese; the British number a mere 15,000, but there are 5,000 other Europeans. Gross densities are high: Hong Kong Island, with an area of 2 square miles, has 3,900 persons per acre, while Kowloon, covering 3 square miles, has 2,250 persons per acre. Over 93.6 percent of the population live in urban areas; most of the 1,579,825 inhabitants of the New Territories reside in small market towns.

THE ABERCROMBIE REPORT

In 1947–48 it seemed as if there might be a "New Jerusalem" in the colony's muddled planning history when the Hong Kong Government requested Sir Patrick Abercrombie,

degree in Civic Design from the University of Liverpool, he was a Senior Lecturer in Architecture at the University of Hong Kong, carrying out university-sponsored research in China, Thailand, Malaya, Cambodia, Macao and Japan over a period of years. Prior to coming to Cornell, he served as Assistant Professor and Research Associate of the Division of Town and Regional Planning at the University of Toronto, as well as planning consultant to the University. Professor Hugo-Brunt has received a Fulbright Scholarship from the United States, a Canadian Central Mortgage and Housing Corporation Senior Fellowship and a Canada Council Research Grant.

who had done the trailbreaking greater London Plan of 1943, to prepare a preliminary Town Planning Report, which was "to provide a land use pattern for future development." His recommendations, which included a Master Plan, were not implemented because the government maintained that it was committed to the immediate problems of housing and industry —presumably this precluded planning! Abercrombie suggested that a series of immediate projects be undertaken of ten years duration in conjunction with a long range policy involving a fifty-year phase. He also discerned the need for urban space and the implications of population increase.

The detailed proposals concentrated upon 1. The improvement of maritime facilities, 2. The determination of a maximum population limit, 3. Housing density and distribution standards, 4. New shopping and industrial areas, 5. Road improvement, 6. A Victoria-Kowloon tunnel, 7. The removal of Defence Establishments from the central area, 8. Open spaces, 9. The tourist industry, 10. The administrative, business and commercial functions of the cities, 11. The appointment of a Town Planning Officer and Planning Office.

The recommendations were rejected. A Planning Officer was later appointed who produced a zoning ordinance, but his efforts were hampered by a lack of statistical data and departmental policies. Abercrombie's analysis has proved sound; maritime installations have been improved, tourism has blossomed while the population increase has spurred extensive industrial expansion. The urgent demands for housing between 1947–57 finally spawned a Housing Authority.

Between 1947–65 it was government practice to engage consultants for particular developments, but although the need for planning specialists was apparent—and many were available—none were ever used. Hong Kong has thrived and prospered without systematic planning for two decades, although crucial decisions have been made and extensive developments completed. Finally the government decided recently to implement the Abercrombie recommendations—now eighteen years old.

HOUSING

Sixty-four percent of the present housing stock was erected before World War II and over 62 percent of it is subject to rental controls. Only 16.6 percent accommodates the owners, but their buildings have often been renovated. Over 1,000 new buildings are constructed each year; most of these are multi-storied apartments ranging from eight to twenty floors in height.

Private houses and apartments are frequently speculative buildings, the rents of which vary—depending upon the degree of luxury—from HK $400[1] to HK $3,500 per month. The speculator leases and erects a multi-storied apartment. His prospective tenants pay him "key" money to be able to get an apartment and this may be in the region of from HK $500 to HK $3,000. Thus, the entrepreneur before he has completed the building has already received some return on his principal which he expects to be repaid with interest in five to seven years. He frequently borrows most of the money using the building as collateral.

A line of hills, known as "The Peak," form a backdrop to Victoria and there is also an escarpment behind Kowloon. Luxury apartments and housing of a "suburban" character concentrate in these areas which accommodate middle and upper income groups. Most buildings are subject to the 1955 Buildings Ordinance and Regulations, which restricts any structure exceeding five stories, but since accommodation is at a premium this has not been stringently observed. Since 1956 zoning schedules permit more intensive development and encourage the erection of multi-storied buildings. A suburban coverage scale reduces ground coverage when buildings are higher: the plot ratio varies from 1.65 for three floors to 5 for twenty floors, i.e. the maximum building height. The maximum plot ratio is 6 and building lines must be observed in most cases.

The 1963 Regulations permitted maximum plot ratios of 10 for domestic constructions and 15 for non-domestic constructions—as well as 100 percent ground coverage up to five stories in non-domestic buildings. Sixty-six percent coverage was permitted for domestic buildings. Open space controls apply for buildings on a street lot, a corner lot and on an island lot. If, however, a developer sets his building back at ground level and preserves frontage for public use, he may increase his maximum floor area by five times the designated area, nor does he need to conform to building lines.

New Territories' properties are classified as either agricultural or building lands. There is no restriction on the erection of a house of less than 700 square feet in area and 25 feet in

[1] There are about 5 HK $ in 1 U.S. $.

height on private property. The owners of the new town development areas surrender their land to the government in return for leases which terminate at the cessation of the British lease. A developer pays the difference between the agricultural and new use value. In all development areas 3 square feet of public land are allocated for services, schools, roads and open space to every 2 square feet of private land.

Most recent speculative buildings have been built in Victoria or Kowloon, but a new phase of speculation may be anticipated in new development areas. Co-operative or condominium ownership, the selling of individual apartments has also been introduced. Thus, there can be between three hundred to four hundred separate owners in a single building.

THE TENEMENTS

Notwithstanding extensive housing building activity and demolition, the better buildings are civic, industrial or commercial. There is perpetual housing shortage due to a natural increase of 75,000 births annually and the continuing influx of refugees. Numerous residents live in overcrowded and unhealthy tenements which are devoid of services, but do provide needed shelter. Many, despite a Rents Restriction Act, cannot compete in the open market for better accommodation. The authorities believe that over 600,000 persons remain to be rehoused. It is policy, therefore, to utilize every available dwelling.

The typical brick tenements are adaptations of those used in England during the 1880s. They copied the 1875 Bylaw tunnel-back row plans having two or three rooms per floor. Party walls support a staircase unless there is a special well between the ground floor shops. An arcade covers the sidewalk and leads to open-fronted shops with sliding, folding doors or removable screens. The upper residential floors are lit and ventilated on the street and rear façades. Walled backyards are standard. The ground floor and the basement are built of local granite, while upper stories are made of rendered brick and are whitewashed or painted. The flat Canton tile roofs are used for recreation, small animal housing or washing. Timber or cast iron verandahs overlook the streets. Over the years most have been enclosed with "Portuguese" shutters, casements or bamboo sun blinds. Bamboo drying poles are also suspended from windows or verandahs, which contrast with vertical shop signs set against the façades.

The first tenements were built by local contractors and craftsmen under the direction of English surveyors. They had unified façades and sheltered the pedestrian from both rain and sun. The wide cast-iron or terra cotta gutters were characteristic features as were the thick walls, high ceilings and large windows which provided cross ventilation and kept rooms cool. As buildings they were virtually noncombustible, but their sanitary facilities and water supply were hopelessly inadequate despite the communal taps, pumps or washhouses which were provided by some speculators.

Corporations or individuals commissioned "designer-builders" to erect the tenements and occasionally approved of stylistic revival embellishment such as column capitals, bases, pediments, string courses, cornices and window surrounds. Even today they still retain many excellent features when compared to some of the new air-conditioned apartments.

Victorian architecture and civic design preserved contiguity, height, tone, colour and texture control along streets, unconsciously directing the visitor towards the civic or administrative monuments or the open spaces and markets. The tenement, when associated with the gridiron plan, made the most economic use of land. It was only after the wars that the pedestrian street was endangered by the automobile. Such tenements were erected as late as 1927—probably because they afforded high returns on investment.

The surviving tenements contribute much to the indigenous character of Hong Kong although most should be classified as overcrowded "slums." They provide much needed low rental commercial and residential accommodation and are extensively used by gold- and silversmiths, jewellers, rattan workers, coffin, furniture and chest makers or antique dealers. Others accommodate Chinese food and tea shops and yet others are leased to business corporations, professional specialists or merchants. Those blocks in primary locations have been modified and adapted for these purposes, but the majority remain residential.

In 1956–57 two residential surveys of 1912 tenements were carried out by architectural students of the University of Hong Kong.[2] Typical four-floor tenements were selected in Kowloon between Kansu Street, Temple Street and Shanghai Street. The results were revealing and were later confirmed,

---

[2] Under the direction of the author, then a Senior Lecturer in Architecture (1952–59) at the university.

to some extent, by the Maunder-Szczepanik Survey of 1957.

It was discovered that 3,200 persons lived in a 19-unit tenement covering 49,400 square feet. The average household consisted of 4.7 persons. There was an average of 11.8 persons on each floor of a unit. However, some units had as many as 81 persons. Over 79 percent of the households shared their premises, while 50 percent of the remainder had one room and 29 percent three rooms. About a quarter of the shared premises had four or more households, but most averaged between two to three families. There was acute overcrowding: only one water closet was available per unit, and there were no washing facilities.

Sub-tenants erected partitions on each floor, but though deprived of light these provided families with a unified space for living. Five percent of the families inhabited verandahs and yet another 5 percent cocklofts. Only 8 percent possessed areas not used for sleeping. The cooking area was communal and contained the ubiquitous Chinese stoves.

The landlord of this tenement received a gross rent of HK $1,120 per month. His tenants paid him HK $210 per month for a floor. These were then partitioned and rented by the tenant for HK $13 to HK $18 per cubicle. Some premises rented as low as HK $10 while others were as high as HK $36. The ground floor shops were rented by carpenters, hairdressers, Chinese herbalists, eating houses, haberdashers, rattan workers, jewellers, furniture makers and goldsmiths for between HK $150 to HK $600—an average of HK $233. These rents were set by the landlord, who based the rental upon a percentage of the estimated turnover; individual variations were considerable.

Bed space was frequently rented by sub-tenants on night shift to outside persons or friends for between HK $5 to HK $50. The rental was higher for a landing or a verandah and lower for space under stairs, on roofs, in passages or circulating areas.

There were 5 adult males, 6 adult females, 5.5 male and 4 female children on each floor and these included four married couples. One hundred and twenty-five children attended government or government-aided schools within a mile of each block. Private schools absorbed another 12. In the area at least 290 more children were either infants or those who could not attend school because their parents could not afford the fees. The average monthly income of the household was

HK $175 with two or three wage-earners but a small minority had incomes which ranged between HK $600 and HK $6,000.

GOVERNMENT HOUSING

Governmental and institutional housing is erected for expatriate civil service officers. The rents are low, since an apartment is deemed a fringe benefit, and the accommodation standards vary according to status, income and race. The government also assists other organizations by granting beneficial leases or even waiving some holding restrictions if this will encourage them to resolve accommodation problems for their personnel. The administration erects its own staff apartments, which may be used in emergencies as communication centres or hospitals. Both point or rectangular blocks (emulating those of the English new towns) have been built. The materials, while not luxurious, are excellent. The space standards, including servant accommodation, are extravagant and would otherwise be economically unjustifiable.

PHILANTHROPIC HOUSING

Church and philanthropic institutions such as the Hong Kong Housing Society assisted in various ways by the government despite limited funds, have been active promoters of better housing. Many of their projects are on the outskirts of the harbour cities where small dwellings or apartments have been built. The rents have been made as small as possible and standards have been reduced to a basic minimum, although sanitary and cooking facilities are provided. None are outstanding examples of architecture, but they do reflect sincere attempts to improve conditions.

THE SQUATTER AND RESETTLEMENT

Between 1947–57 HK $100,000,000 has been invested in rehousing, but this was incapable of accommodating the majority of those living in substandard accommodation. Slum clearance was contemplated but social surveys indicated that all existing housing stock must be conserved. The problem has been compounded by between 260,000–300,000 squatters who are a source of embarrassment to the authorities. Most of them are refugees; without employment or shelter they constitute a serious drain upon the welfare resources, a health hazard and a potential danger to security. Their shanty dwellings surround the built-up areas, constituting squatter suburbs which are periodically devastated by fire, flood and typhoon. While most fires are accidental, arson also occurs, since it has stimulated the erection of new housing—or returned property to landowners for redevelopment. Such disasters drive the squatters into the streets and force the government to devise further resettlement programmes and restrict legal immigration. Seventy-five thousand destitutes still bed down in streets, on rooftops or under any available cover. One hundred and thirty thousand "floating" squatters live on junks and sampans which were once the homes and workshops of fisherfolk. As squatter areas are difficult to supervise they become sanctuaries for criminals, prostitutes and other derelicts.

The resettlement policy of the Hong Kong Government was to evoke unusual interest. New housing was fraught with insurmountable difficulties, since non-combustible shelter which would be cheap, speedy in erection and adaptable was urgently needed. Minimum acceptable standards for housing and space, inspired by British practice, proved uneconomic and beyond the means of the squatter.

The government made a shrewd reappraisal of the available resources, the building industry and the number of units needed. Standards were pared to an unbelievable minimum so that a single room could shelter a household. The buildings were of prefabricated concrete and used standardized communal facilities wherever possible. These new "slums," as they have been described, replaced some of the squatter housing and were erected quickly. In 1955 a series of experimental units were built. These were three stories high and consisted of rooms having access from open balconies and staircases. They were the prototype designs for the multi-storied apartment blocks later used in Kowloon.

These early Ship Kip Mei blocks have been extensively publicized in recent years. They were fireproof, accommodated large numbers of people and were cheap. The plans were H-shaped having two blocks of back-to-back rooms sharing a service-cooking link. The roof was available for use as drying, recreation or school area. Each room had a wooden door, a shuttered window and electric lighting. If the housing demand ever eased it was hoped that an enlarged apartment could be made by opening up a door between each unit of back-to-back rooms.

Site layout was the worst aspect of the complex. A gridiron

plan was adopted which did afford fire engines, ambulances, police and service vehicles access to every unit. Unfortunately, open space was severely restricted and the renting of ground floor shops turned each street into a pedestrian market play area. The monotony of the many identical blocks with their long façades facing west was unforgivable, nor did the application of pastel colours redeem their brutalism. Unexpectedly, resettlement aggravated the water shortage, since in Ship Kip Mei alone the tenants consumed over three million gallons a month.

THE HOUSING AUTHORITY

The largest residential programmes are undertaken today by the Hong Kong Housing Authority, a public corporation created in April 1954. The Executive consists of members of the Urban Council and three government nominated appointees. A Commissioner of Housing is the senior executive officer of the Authority, which also has sections dealing with administration, accounts, estate management, statistics and architectural planning.

Housing Authority rents are kept low and must cover all expenditures. The new tenants are chosen from overpopulated areas where households share accommodation. Family inconvenience, war service, Hong Kong residence and service in the auxiliary Defence Forces are taken into account when determining an applicant's status. He must also have a total monthly income of between HK $300 and HK $900 a month before being placed on the Register. Rents are then adjusted to the individual's means. Although the government grants no subsidies, it does sell Crown Land to the Authority at a third of the estimated market value as well as providing low interest loans from a Development Fund. The Housing Authority is an obvious descendant of the Singapore and the Malaya Improvement Trusts. It exercises restricted jurisdiction and cannot be held responsible for poor planning as its developments have never been integrated into a comprehensive city plan.

The analytical operations are European in concept; that is they are determined and interpreted by architect-planners and tend to be empirical and utilitarian.

Housing estates of considerable size but possessing a "conventional municipal character" have been built on vacant sites. Although the accommodation standards are utilitarian the buildings are architectural assets but, as white collar workers predominate as tenants, the Authority has been subjected to criticism. The architects have little choice: they could reduce standards to an absolute minimum, or they could determine an acceptable living standard or a basic Western standard, but in Hong Kong this means that those who need the housing most are excluded.

As sites are limited, multi-storied development became essential. The Housing Authority plans to provide 5,000 dwelling units a year at densities of 1,500 persons per acre. The first housing estates, all designed by consultants, were 6½ acres off North Point, 3.7 acres at Kennedy Town, 18.79 acres in Kowloon (the So Uk Estate), 21 acres at Clearwater Bay and another 10 acres in Kowloon (the Ma Tau Chung Estate). Nearly all had irregular terrain and boundaries.

The apartment blocks now have eleven floors or more and use reinforced concrete frame, brick panelling as well as standard steel windows, doors and partitions. The foundations are supported upon piles driven into the reclaimed land; many are over 105 feet in depth. The apartments have kitchens, sanitary facilities, utility balconies and simple electrical installations. All estates are self-contained with primary schools, clinics, post offices, halls, shops, pharmacies and electrical substations. Flushing water is provided by wells or from the sea.

The So Uk Estate, which is one of the largest housing developments in the Orient, will have 4,600 apartments for 30,-000 persons in twelve- to sixteen-story blocks. It will be provided with primary schools, an assembly hall, thirty shops, an estate office, a clinic and a post office.

Perhaps it is inevitable that there is a superhuman scale in most of these housing estates and it is unfortunate that repetition of similar elements leads to overpowering monotony. The high densities require formal spatial treatment, but the intense use of site, and the need to reduce maintenance costs leaves the landscape architect with a restricted vocabulary. Yet, the architecture is generally sound and Housing Authority projects have more imaginative layouts than previous mass housing.

The population increase and the shortage of industrial sites has forced the administration to underwrite three new industrial towns in the New Territories. Each satellite will accommodate a million persons: eventually 5,000,000 will reside in them. Together these will cover 1,220 acres at the ratio of 350 workers per acre on Hong Kong Island, Kowloon and Kowloom, including Kwun Tong.

THE CITIZEN AND THE ENVIRONMENT[3]

Despite the administrative failures, Hong Kong has indigenous lessons for the planner. With fantastic densities up to 3,900 persons per acre, with the subsequent strain upon traffic facilities and services, with inadequate housing standards and with the inequities of casual laissez faire, the citizens (and particularly those with low incomes) have triumphed over their environment.

The resident Chinese are seemingly by nature, adaptable, gregarious and capable of utilizing the most meagre resources to enrich their environment. Their needs are few and simple: food, shelter and a livelihood. The new industries, being dependant upon imported resources, has utilized their industriousness, considerable skills and their cheap labour. Short of open space, provided with the simplest shelter and enjoying but the barest of necessities, the endurance, humour and sensitivity of the inhabitants has produced an environment which is mobile, exhilarating and rich in experience.

The Chinese are city dwellers, not from choice but through circumstance, yet they have turned the street, the shop, the eating house and the tenement into theatre, market and community. All have blended together in an intricate and unusual social pattern. The open-fronted shops and occasional markets with their odors of dry fish, joss and scented materials, together with the bustling pedestrian movement, the haggling in purchase and sale, create an unforgettable atmosphere. The noise of musical instruments, the Ma Jong players, the perpetual honk-honk of vehicles, the yells of greeting or outrage, the siren of police, fire brigade or ambulance, the rumble of the streetcar, radio and the jukebox are an essential ingredient of the perpetual hum in the built up areas by day and night. The colour of the traditional advertisements, the neon signs, the shop displays, the sensitivity or vulgarity of decorative materials provide unusual visual stimuli. All activity is intensified by the birthday or the marriage celebrations, the funeral processions, the business contracts; by New Year, political or national celebration, any of which may focus upon the restaurant, the temple or the church, or the club, and these all have their own peculiarities of sound and colour. At night, after the intense heat of the day, the effects are intensified. The stores

---

[3] The author lived for five months in a Chinese tenement in order to observe the nature of high density residence.

and restaurants operate into the early hours of the morning, and the ugliness, the shoddiness, the poverty as well as the opulence are all hidden by a variety of electrical demonstrations which put Coney Island to second place.

The population diversity is reflected in dress and custom, by the industrial worker, white-collar worker, scholar, student, merchant, coolie, amah, Cantonese, Shanghaiese, Pekinese, agriculturist, landowner, peasant, fisherman, lighterman, taxi-driver, hawker, Pakistani and Hakka; all of whom have their own image of their city. Social groups emerge which are associated with a common pattern of movement, with a common patronage of establishment or a tendency to group together through diet, area of origin, language, occupation and relationship.

Perhaps it is significant that the visitor bypasses the European commercial establishments in the central area and gravitates to the Chinese streets where he searches the curio, jewelry and ceramics shops, watches the craftsmen tailoring, designing, polishing and shaping, or observes others gourmandizing in the restaurants.

There is life and vitality in these high-density areas swarming with people which, contrary to various laboratory rat experiments, do produce interest, liveliness, sense of community and well-being amongst the inhabitants. Vice, crime and prostitution are also present, but rarely to the extent that the news media would indicate. Many of the inhabitants have fled from the puritanism of the communist-organized and drilled society in which basic food, shelter and clothing are perhaps more adequately provided than in the "free society." The Hong Kong resident can exercise his abilities and enjoy his leisure. Western academic planning tends to overlook the simple fact that the human being is adaptable, resilient and invariably triumphs over his environment as has apparently happened here.

THE IMPLICATIONS OF HIGH DENSITIES

The Hong Kong lessons are obvious; there are many advantages to high density:

1. Most residents are between two to fifteen minutes distant from their place of employment.

2. Within a five-minute radius, they enjoy a variety of shops, markets, commercial institutions, restaurants, cinemas and other recreational facilities. They can compare prices,

hunt for bargains and enjoy a range of choice from department store to standing. There is extraordinary commercial flexibility. A neighbourhood will include light industries, craft operations, offices and a diversity of other occupations—since mixed uses are permitted. These are accompanied with variety, contrast, interest and convenience—a situation which rarely emerges under Western zoning.

3. Pedestrian circulation predominates since the inhabitants have "taken over" all smaller streets or lanes. These have become malls in effect and are lined with open standings throughout their length. Thus, pedestrian concentration has forced a desirable pattern of development. Service circulations occur during the early morning or the late evening since overcrowding renders day loading inconvenient. Both wholesaler and retailer have adopted a service technique in smaller streets similar to the closed streets of Holland. It may be inferred, therefore, that the inhabitants of areas with high densities can capture space for exclusive pedestrian use and so fulfill desirable planning ends.

4. Variety, smell, tone, colour, texture, contrast, discord and harmony are all characteristics of high-density living. These stimulate activities of all types and provide efficient service to all citizens. Shops remain open as long as possible to obtain customers. Their late closing and early opening changes the character of a community. It affects the life of every inhabitant and forcibly introduces him to those of different races, areas of origin, languages, customs and creeds. It destroys social isolation and forces all into close association with one another—thus enriching the individual's life and experience.

5. Higher densities are conducive to the maximum usage of facilities and one is not left with idle and uneconomic urban elements. Furthermore, the street in the absence of facilities becomes a viable recreation space—a lesson which has been adapted in several European cities.

6. High-density living and intensive land use are compatible in mutual association with each other. Both benefit from the convenience. The "image" of the city for most inhabitants is that of a street or a block which is virtually self-contained. A natural selectivity is displayed by larger industries such as machine shops, textile mills, etc. which, because of servicing inconvenience, group in industrial areas as close to the available labour pools as possible. There is a strong case for in-

corporating light and heavy industrial elements into the fringes
of new neighbourhoods.

7. The neighbourhood emerges naturally in areas of high
density. It occupies much smaller acreage as most facilities
concentrate in a street, a block or a small open space. The
inhabitant identifies himself in the points of maximum activity,
with the restaurant, the club, the clinic, the temple or the
church, which are invariably in close proximity to each other.

8. These communities manifest many of the advantages
that Le Corbusier has postulated for his Ville Radieuse, although he attempted to blend green space with building and
thus create an urban-rural balance. The Hong Kong gridiron
is a distinctively urban métier, but the geographical advantages of mountain enclosure, shore line and bay have provided
the townsman with environmental beauty. These, in relation
to the character, symbols and forms in his district, make him
unusually conscious of physical elements and change—even in
the smallest detail.

9. The lineal gridiron has divided the town into easily identifiable sectors. Within fifteen minutes any citizen can reach
the hillside or the waterfront. This is an inherent effect of lineal
sprawl, which, as it grows, eventually consolidates into a comprehensive urban area. Lineal growth is accompanied by desirable dispersion. Hong Kong certainly substantiates the
theories of Sorio Y Mata and Le Corbusier. A lineal city combined with Le Corbusier's high-density residential concepts is
an operative thesis for developing a realistic master plan where
population densities are greater than 145 persons per acre.

10. As the vehicle does not operate effectively in such concentrations, it will adapt and restrict itself. Public transport
is the only effective communication between various areas.
Consequently the revitalization of the streetcar or some vehicle which affords the passenger observation of the shifting
urban scene is most desirable. Severe restrictions should be
imposed on other vehicles or they should be banned from
congested areas.

Today the emergency service of police, fire, medical and
security personnel, encounter severe problems, but the lack
of space at ground level for sidewalk, square and street could
have been overcome with intelligent planning. It must be admitted that high densities are conducive to crime and disaster,
particularly where inadequate residential accommodation has
been associated with overused meagre service and facilities.
Metropolitan areas must install service systems far exceeding

anticipated demands despite the heavy initial cost; the water and sewage systems of Hong Kong have proved totally inadequate for the present population simply because no one ever foresaw the present expansion.

Despite all the criticisms levelled at the Hong Kong Colonial Government, the postwar achievements have been noteworthy; the authorities are at last analysing their resources and initiating planning. They have developed a viable economy and created a new industrial base for the community. They have pioneered in the mass production of housing and, despite a lack of aesthetic sensitivity have, in large measure, made sincere attempts to meet their obligations. They are developing satellite industrial communities. Their ability to utilise the resources of contemporary planning will become apparent within the next decade and perhaps it is only then that the critic may give an impartial assessment of their achievements.

BIBLIOGRAPHY

The author acknowledges the assistance he received in the direction of the Kowloon and Aberdeen Surveys from the Town Planning Office of the Public Works Department of Hong Kong and the fourth-year students of the former Faculty of Architecture, Hong Kong University, 1954–55.

Abrams, Charles, *Man's Struggle for Shelter in the Urbanizing World*, M.I.T., Cambridge, Mass., 1964.

Abercrombie, Sir Patrick, *Hong Kong—Preliminary Planning Report*, London and Hong Kong, 1948.

Dark, J. W. (A.M.T.P.I.), Letter, *Journal of the Town Planning Institute*, London, November 1965, Vol. 51, No. 9, p. 381.

David, M. C., *The Resettlement Survey*, Hong Kong Council of Social Service, Social Welfare Office, June–September 1957.

Davis, S. G., *Hong Kong in Its Geographical Setting*, Wm. Collins Sons and Co. Ltd., 1949, London.

Department of Economics and Political Science, *A Cost of Living Survey*, University of Hong Kong, Hong Kong University Press, December 1955.

Endacott, G. B., *A History of Hong Kong*, Oxford University Press, London, 1958.

Far Eastern Economic Review, *Resettlement Areas*, Vol. 23, p. 694.

Fraser, J. M., *Housing and Planning in Singapore,* Town Planning Review, Vol. 23, No. 1, April 1952.

Hambro, Dr. E., *Survey: The United Nations Refugee Survey,* Hong Kong, 1954.

Hong Kong Government, *Historical and Statistical Abstract of the Colony of Hong Kong,* Noronha and Co., Hong Kong, 1907.

Hong Kong Government, *Report of the District Commissioners of the New Territories,* 1957, Hong Kong Government Printer.

Hong Kong Government, *Squatters: 1955 Survey Resettlement Department,* Hong Kong Government Printer.

Hong Kong Housing Authority, *Report for April 1957 to March 1958,* Hong Kong Government Printer.

Hurlimann, Martin, *Hong Kong,* Viking Press, New York, 1962.

Maunder, W. F., and Szczepanik, E. F., *The Hong Kong Housing Survey,* Vols. I, II and III, University of Hong Kong, May 1957.

Orange, James, *The Chater Collection,* Thornton Butterworth, London, 1924.

Peplow, S. H., and Barker, M., *Hongkong, Around and About,* Ye Olde Printerie, Inc., Hong Kong, 1931.

Sayer, Geoffrey Robley, *Hong Kong, Birth, Adolescence and Coming of Age,* Oxford University Press, London, 1937.

Scott, Francis, *Statements and Suggestions Regarding Hong Kong,* Blades and East, London, 1850.

Szczepanik, E. F., *The Hong Kong Population Puzzle:* Far East Economic Review, Vol. 19, 1955.

Tregear, Thomas R., *A Survey of Land Use in Hong Kong and the New Territories,* Hong Kong University Press, Hong Kong, 1958.

Tregear, Thomas R., and Berry, L., *The Developments in Hong Kong and Kowloon as Told in Maps,* Hong Kong University Press, Hong Kong, 1958.

Trelawney, Saunders, *Further Statements and Suggestions Regarding Hong Kong,* London, 1851.

Weiss, K., *Hong Kong Guide,* Graphic Press Ltd., 1953.

Wigglesworth, J. M., "Planning in Hong Kong," *Journal of the Town Planning Institute* (G.B.), Vol. 51, No. 7, 1955.

Wood, Winifred A., *A Brief History of Hong Kong,* South China Morning Post Ltd., 1940.

Report of the Housing and Urban Renewal Task Force to Mayor John V. Lindsay*

Respectfully submitted:

CHARLES ABRAMS (CHAIRMAN)

DR. PAGET ALVES

MR. DAVID CRANE

MR. VICTOR DE GRAZIA

DR. WILLIAM G. GRIGSBY

MR. JUSTIN HERMAN

MR. WILLIAM HUDGINS

MRS. R. H. JACOBS, JR.

MR. EDWARD J. LOGUE

MR. I. M. PEI

MR. WILLIAM L. RAFSKY

MR. I. D. ROBBINS

MR. ALAN G. RUDOLPH

DR. WILLIAM L. C. WHEATON

The year in which the incoming administration takes over responsibility for the city's housing operations also marks the passage of a generation since the city was given the power to clear slums and build decent housing. Although hundreds of millions have been spent and lent in the effort and although the city now has a fund of more laws, devices and agencies for housing improvement than any city in the nation, its slums stubbornly persist; crowded and rundown housing continues to frustrate decent family life; racial segregation solidifies; the housing shortage continues to penalize poor and middle-income families seeking decent shelter within their means.

During the past five years, in fact, slum housing has increased more swiftly than it has been eliminated. Unsound units (exclusive of rooming houses) have increased from 420,000 in 1960 to 525,000 in 1965. The median rent-to-income ratio in the same period has gone up from 18.4 percent to 20.4 percent. Taken as a whole, the people of New York are paying a higher proportion of their incomes for a less satisfactory inventory of housing than they were five years ago.

The very amplitude of devices and agencies moreover, has brought cross purposes and stalemate to the city's housing efforts. Federal public housing funds are now suffering a steady curtailment. State appropriations are approaching their end owing to repeated rejection of additional appropriations at the polls.

We dare not accept this bleak situation as a forecast of the

* The report was dated January 10, 1966.

future. Cities are history's record of a civilization's progress, and what a particular generation contributes to its own physical environment will survive as the ineradicable account of its performance or its failure. No level of government can therefore afford to shun responsibility for improving the shelter in which its people live or for elevating the environment which conditions the lives of their children. The commitment by Congress to "a decent home and a suitable environment for every American family" still remains to be translated from rhetoric to reality in the nation's greatest city. Nor can any society become a great society while its cities are allowed to deteriorate.

Although the nation is now overwhelmingly urbanized and more than $7 billion of the federal budget still goes to subsidize agriculture, less than one per cent of the federal budget is devoted to housing and to the development of its urban communities. If our central cities are to be salvaged for the great society, effective pressures must be mobilized by the nation's central cities to impress a higher responsibility upon the Congress, and the new mayor of the nation's largest city must be in the vanguard of the effort "to make the American city a better and more stimulating place to live."[1]

If we are to keep faith with the present and the future, new goals must be written, a new central strategy devised, major adjustments of policy made. The city must have new housing but not at the expense of losing sound housing, businesses and industries. It must eliminate slums, not shift slums. It must conserve what can be repaired and must radically rehabilitate what can be salvaged. It must keep what is sound from degenerating. It must fortify racial and income diversity wherever it already exists, and encourage and provide for it where it does not. It must recognize that good design is not a luxury but a necessity and that solving the housing problem means not only more and better housing but also functioning communities. It must experiment. It must employ not only government funds in these efforts, but must encourage the use of private and foundation funds. It must work with, not against, the people to overcome their housing and neighborhood problems and must listen to their constructive ideas and act upon them.

[1] The quotation is from President Johnson's State of the Union Message, January 4, 1965.

The recommendations that follow* represent the general consensus of the fourteen-member Task Force on Housing appointed by Mayor-elect John V. Lindsay on November 26, 1965. No consensus can be expected to resolve all the complicated problems involved with the building industry, the public health aspects of housing, the involutions of rent control practices or the difficulties of relocating tenants during a housing shortage. A consensus, moreover, can only be a statement of guidelines and general recommendations that depend for their fulfillment not merely upon laws and appropriations or the form of the agency that administers them. The past record of changes, abolitions, consolidations and reorganizations of the city's housing and building agencies underscores the endless quest for a foolproof administrative mechanism. There is none, for whether the administrator be individual, board or commission, no substitute has ever been found for competence, integrity and imagination.

ORGANIZATION

1. New York City's housing and neighborhood development programs require unified direction under a single administrator. The most prominent defect in the city's present program is that its various components lack a direction and a sense of relationship to any over-all conception of goals and planning. Conflicts of jurisdiction and competition for sites on the one hand, and areas neglected or overlooked on the other hand, add to the present confusion of planning—for industries, schools, libraries, parks and other services. If the city's housing program is to contribute to the more orderly planning of the neighborhoods of which it is a part, more order must be brought into its own fragmented administration.

2. The functions of the Housing and Redevelopment Board, the Housing Authority, the Department of Relocation, the rehabilitation and conservation functions of the Rent and Rehabilitation Administration, the receivership and emergency repair functions of the Department of Real Estate, and the residential code inspection and enforcement functions of the Department of Buildings, Health, Fire and Water Supply, Gas and Electricity, should be combined in one agency under the new Administrator of Housing. The administrator should have jurisdiction over all capital expenditures involving housing and

_____

* Only those recommendations of more general application are included here. The Editor.

urban renewal programs and be equipped to deal directly with the new federal Secretary of Housing and Urban Development on all federal matters affecting such programs.

3. The new Housing Administrator should review the Community Renewal Program of the City Planning Commission and provide policy direction in its future preparation. He should immediately review the city's current roster of housing, rehabilitation and renewal plans and make a realistic determination of those which can be carried out in the immediate future and set target dates for each of them. Those which are unrealistic should be eliminated from the roster and the action made known so that the people living in the areas can be relieved of uncertainty and hardship, and so that mortgagees, owners and businessmen can again be poised to invest in these areas and improve them. . . .

DISCRIMINATION, SEGREGATION AND INTEGRATION

Although New York City is subject to the most comprehensive anti-bias laws in the nation, segregation on account of race and color continues in its housing and neighborhoods as well as in the city's environs.

5. Segregation and discrimination in housing cannot be abolished solely by the resolution of individual housing complaints in adversary proceedings. The city and state must be prepared to move directly into areas of housing discrimination without depending upon the resolution of individual complaints.

6. It has become as essential to prevent segregation as to ban it and when an existing housing project in a neighborhood is threatened with segregation, it becomes the duty of a public agency to prevent it by positive policy, even where the public agency concerned must become conscious of color to do so. . . .

7. The city must strive to stabilize neighborhoods that are integrated, by rehabilitation of housing, by new housing for present residents, and by improvement of educational services and the addition of needed public facilities.

8. Discrimination can no longer be identified solely by an individual's or official's exclusionary actions and devices. Discrimination and segregation can exist also by implication or omission, as in the case of a deliberate failure by the federal or state governments to provide freedom of access to shelter

in areas surrounding the city; failure to encourage programs or enact laws which make it possible for a minority family of low income to compete for housing; by zoning so restrictively that none but the wealthy can afford to build or rent; by failing to appropriate funds or subsidies for programs benefiting minorities. It is elimination of these subtle forms of discrimination and segregation which needs new emphasis if equality of housing opportunity is to be established in the city and its suburbs.

PUBLIC HOUSING

9. The public housing "project" should no longer be the norm for public housing endeavors. New York City's share of the 35,000 units of new public housing construction authorized annually under the Housing Act of 1965 (about 3,500 per year for the city) should be primarily devoted to providing buildings, not "self-contained" projects. The buildings should be inserted as part of existing neighborhoods, not massively superimposed upon them. They should encourage and reinforce integration where it already exists; they should help house the "overflow" families from older buildings which are being radically rehabilitated and uncrowded; they should add to the net supply of housing by taking advantage of potential building sites now idle or grossly under-used as well as replace abandoned or unsalvageable buildings that mar a neighborhood. The Housing Authority should experiment with differing types and sizes of buildings. Operational policy should (as in Philadelphia) allow for the management of groups of scattered buildings; similarly, contracts should be let for the simultaneous construction or rehabilitation of groups of scattered buildings. . . .

10. While pressing for more state and federal appropriations for public housing, immediate plans should be made to take advantage of New York's share of the 15,000 public housing rehabilitation units provided annually under the Housing Act of 1965, and the city's share of the 10,000 units to be leased from private enterprise annually. . . .

11. The Housing Authority should develop programs for leasing some of its existing housing projects to non-profit corporations as a pilot effort. . . .

12. The Authority should simultaneously experiment with cooperative arrangements for its operations. Tenants in state and city projects who increase their incomes could be sold

their apartments under a condominium plan. As rents of some tenants rise, the excess above the maximum rent could be deposited in escrow to be used as future down payments for the dwelling units. This would help stabilize the tenancy and reduce the way-station aspect of housing projects. . . .

13. There is considerable research to be undertaken that would help improve public housing operations. This includes: study of operational policies here and abroad for the housing of problem families (funds should be sought for this study from the Office of Economic Opportunity); research into more efficient building materials, kitchen designs and equipment (as one of the world's largest builders of multiple dwellings, the New York City Housing Authority should also be the authoritative laboratory for the study of materials, methods and design); a study of reactions to public housing by a cross-section sample of the more than 139,000 families living in public housing projects. It should seek to determine their needs, wants and desires and weigh their suggestions for change and improvement of policy, facilities, design and equipment. . . .

15. The write-down of land cost for public housing sites should be authorized, whether or not they are in renewal areas. Simultaneously, state legislation should be introduced to provide $5 million for site subsidies for public housing. Annual appropriations for the purpose can be made by the state legislature without formal approval by the people.

16. Provision for public housing should be made on residential urban renewal sites. This would help achieve a sound balance in schools and community facilities. The emphasis should be on preserving, enhancing and, where necessary, creating better neighborhoods and a functioning community life.

17. Special authorizations should be sought in future state and federal legislation to provide more dwelling units for large families. Some of the city's older public housing projects require rehabilitation; where they are rehabilitated, some of the smaller apartments should be combined for use by larger families where possible. . . .

LIMITED PROFIT HOUSING

20. State and city Mitchell-Lama funds [for middle class housing] should be augmented by a substantial commitment of 221(d)(3) low-interest funds from the federal government. Such low-interest loans coupled with partial tax exemption

should continue available until the housing shortage is eased. Mitchell-Lama buildings should accommodate some subsidized lower-income families. . . .

22. The emphasis should be upon vacant sites, sites that contain abandoned buildings, and grossly under-used industrial or commercial sites; sites should be promptly rezoned where necessary. Not only should the single site qualify for state and city aid; scattered sites as part of a single contract should qualify also.

23. Limited-profit construction should be undertaken not only by limited-profit corporations. It should also be undertaken under suitable financial controls by general contractors, and the completed buildings should then be sold to limited-profit corporations to be operated either as co-operatives or rental properties; some could also be leased in whole or in part to the Housing Authority.

24. Land should be purchased both by the city for resale and directly by limited-profit sponsors. Land write-downs should be authorized where necessary, without the requirement that the buildings be in a renewal area. Powers of condemnation should be invoked where necessary to obtain idle and grossly under-used sites.

25. The city should encourage the establishment of organizations with foundation assistance for aiding and advising religious, community and other non-profit groups to sponsor limited- and non-profit housing.

REHABILITATION AND INSPECTION

26. The city should embark upon a major program of rehabilitation of all salvageable structures, and of conservation of all good and repairable structures. This program should embrace (a) radical rehabilitation (providing new and modern dwelling units within old but sound walls), (b) strict enforcement of maintenance to meet codes, and (c) as and when the housing shortage is overcome, strict enforcement of the laws against overcrowding. . . .

28. Since radical rehabilitation for families living in squalor nearly always entails uncrowding, new construction of public housing buildings and limited-profit buildings must be dovetailed with rehabilitation and made available to overflow families.

29. The city's stock of 1,150,000 existing dwelling units in old masonry structures should be surveyed and reassessed in

the light of the new possibilities opened up by technological advances in materials, ventilating equipment and lighting (e.g., installing prefabricated kitchen equipment in tenements, providing duplexes on the third and fourth and the fifth and sixth stories for large families, etc.).

30. The Housing Authority should be prepared to acquire salvageable structures for sale to non-profit or limited-profit corporations for radical rehabilitation. Funds could be obtained either by its own bond issues or through other available city, state or federal sources. . . .

33. In prior years, owners of old-law tenements made major investments in providing central heating, toilets for each family, fire retardation of cellars and stairways and provision of roof scuttles and angular fire escapes, without a penny of public investment. More recently the type of owners has changed for the worse, and responsible institutions that once made mortgage loans have withdrawn from the field. The result has been a dearth of capital for improvements coupled with an inability or unwillingness of owners to invest their own funds for major improvements. The consequence has been the rapid and continued deterioration of buildings in which major investments by previous owners had once been made. Not the least of the reasons for deterioration has been the public cavil heaped upon ownership in slum areas (a slum owner is automatically a slumlord) and the fear of criminal penalties to which responsible owners willing to invest and institutional mortgage lenders willing to lend might become subject. Slums are now contraband, and fear of investment and deterioration will grow unless public policy and official attitudes take a more realistic view. Criminal liability should be suspended (as in 1936) for a reasonable period when new owners or purchasers file plans in good faith to rehabilitate or when mortgage-lenders come into possession through foreclosure and file such plans.

34. Many low-income families currently experience hardship because of rent increases resulting from improvements made by owners. To hold down rent increases that may prove a hardship to such families, low interest loans and rent supplements as well as tax abatement should be made available. . . .

37. Inspection and code enforcement should be taken seriously for every building, including those scheduled for eventual clearance. . . .

SUBSIDIES

38. Employment of family rent subsidies is essential as a tool for solving the housing problem. Obviously rent subsidies will not meet the specific problems of all low-income families and their administration requires careful policy determinations to avoid the appearance of their being just another form of welfare payments. Its use should be considered in combination with low interest loans, limited-profit sponsorship, tax abatement, federal public housing construction, rehabilitation and leasing arrangements. But although Congress has authorized rent supplements, it has not yet provided funds for them.* . . .

39. All too often, the indiscriminate payment of rents for welfare families tends to perpetuate slums and disrepair when it might provide an opportunity to promote rehabilitation and better housing. Pilot undertakings should test the possibilities of financing rehabilitation through leasing of dwellings or dwelling units and making special arrangements with non-profit corporations through combined low interest loans, rent subsidies and welfare advances made to supplement capital requirements.

THE FEDERAL RELATIONSHIP

40. New York City, as the nation's largest city and as its main port of immigration, has always been viewed as one of the principal focal points of the housing problem and it used to be a main source of the pressures for remedial and pioneering legislation; it supplied much of the impetus and ideas for the first federal housing legislation after 1934. In recent years, however, legislation has originated in Washington and after its submission to Congress, the city has been poised only to approve, disapprove or ask for modifications after the fact; that the state has given substantial aid supplemental to federal assistance never received any special consideration or acknowledgment. There has in fact been a frequent subordination of the city's special needs and a premium placed upon its higher land and building costs. This has been the case even when the city has given substantial tax subsidies. Where maximum cost or income limitations on public housing

---

* Funds now available. The Editor.

are unrealistic for the city, the mayor should make that fact known to federal officials and to Congress in advance of its final determination. Comparisons of costs with those of other cities are useful and necessary, insofar as they may expose fundamentally uneconomic methods or policies, but this should not be confused with costs which are inescapably higher than those elsewhere because of the differences in wage levels, densities, more rigid code requirements than exist in less populated areas, or higher land values.

41. Similarly, federal administrative rulings and regulations, particularly those with respect to urban renewal programs, should be vigorously opposed, and timely substitutions submitted when such regulations, rulings and procedures are detrimental to the city's people or irrelevant to their situation. . . . Where federal bills or aids are irrelevant or penalize the city, all city departments should be prepared well in advance to make it known to the mayor in time to press for changes.

42. Federal legislation should be sought to make landmarks eligible for federal write-downs, whether or not they are in renewal areas. The city should also seek a larger federal contribution for community facilities; it should be privileged to locate the facilities outside, as well as in, renewal areas.

43. The federal poverty program offers vast opportunities for demonstrating new types of programs in housing, neighborhood and social improvement which can vitally influence future federal policy. The city should explore these opportunities and pioneer in new types of OEO grants to improve neighborhood life in the less privileged areas. . . .

DESIGN, MATERIALS AND OPEN SPACE

44. Design of private buildings will usually resist improvement if the economics of investment are against it. But too often public regulations unnecessarily compound the problem. The zoning law needs re-examination for its impact on the use and design of smaller plots. The Building Code not only needs reassessment in line with a current study but there should be continuing restudy both of the code and the zoning law by a standing commission or committee that takes continuing notice of new materials and methods, of standards suggested by the Federal Housing Administration, by other states and cities and by foreign experience. . . .

45. Since design of speculative architecture frequently fol-

lows a prototype (witness the old- and new-law tenements, the four- and five-story walk-up, and the six-story automatic elevator building), the City Planning Commission and the Department of Buildings should, whenever codes and zoning laws are proposed, prepare model design types on varying plots and under given land costs and rental ranges so as to anticipate the economic as well as the structural problems and potentials.

46. Public architecture should set the example of design excellence; mediocrity in this sector invites a general decline in the design contributions by the private sector as well. Public building and in fact all public contributions of any kind (street lights, street furniture, etc.) bear the public imprimatur and should therefore be built to equally high standards and with variety wherever possible. The limitation of costs on public housing is poor economy, for the product will survive and condition the city's horizons long after the bonds have been amortized. . . .

47. The proper use and development of open space is as vital to good design as the development of the enclosed spaces. Any master plan of the city should therefore include a master plan of the city's visual environment. Small vest-pocket parks should be created, particularly in those neighborhoods inhabited by the poorer families. Where public densities must be high, space requirements should be based on the concept of useable open space for outdoor enjoyment and recreation rather than on rigid formulas governing courts, setbacks or parking spaces. Design of public areas should include contiguous open space that can be used in common by residents of adjacent buildings. In new subdivisions, the effort should be made to avoid routine lot-by-lot developments that are unrelieved by open areas for common use.

48. Since urban renewal and limited-profit undertakings are also publicly assisted, they similarly call for higher and more imaginative design and open space standards. Provision of stores should not be restricted and can often add not only to the attractiveness of the buildings but help reduce the rents of dwelling units. The Housing Administrator should have the authority to convene all relevant city departments for the purpose of expediting an undertaking or speeding provision of the essential services and facilities.

49. In the tendency to think primarily in terms of larger projects, the smaller improvements and amenities that can make the city more interesting and more tolerable are too

often overlooked by the professionals. Yet these smaller improvements and amenities can do much to upgrade neighborhoods and even generate investment in housing, rehabilitation and in the humanization of neighborhoods. They can be particularly useful when made part of an area services or neighborhood conservation program. The ideas for them often originate in the people themselves or in their local planning boards. They are frequently sound ideas but there is no forum to which they can be exposed and no laboratory in which they can be tested. They might involve such matters as the improvement in the design of particular street furniture or play equipment, a special use of streets or walks for recreation, improvement of public lighting or other public equipment, the organization of a neighborhood improvement or tree planting campaign, the better use of open or unused spaces for recreational forms of various sorts, and similar proposals that normally escape the attention of the public official. A "clinic" should be available—perhaps at one of the architectural and city planning departments of a university—which could serve as the testing ground at which the ideas can be assessed; if found valid they can be taken up with the appropriate departments for implementation.

LAND POLICY

50. In a city with a land inventory that is rapidly being consumed, a sound land policy is indispensable to its rational development and the strengthening of its economic base. The city lacks such a policy. City-owned land has been sold that might be needed in the future for public use or other essential needs. Sites have been acquired for schools which had buildings that were ripe for rehabilitation. No plan exists for earmarking land needed for public housing, recreation, schools, or for a combination of public or public-private uses. A land bank should be set up for land reserves for future use and development by the city. Where city land is sold, the terms of sale should, wherever possible, require development within a reasonable time in accordance with the best interests of the area and the city. Where public improvements are contemplated, the city should consider acquiring more land than is needed for the improvements and after completing them, reselling the excess subject to requirements as to what may be built. What is prescribed should blend with the public contribution.

CONCLUSION

If one spans the three decades that separate First Houses—the half-block of rehabilitated old tenements on East Third Street that was the city's first public housing venture—to its most recent pilot scheme on West 114th Street, it would seem that we have simply completed a cycle and are still groping for solutions. So with Harlem River Houses, the vest-pocket project built thirty years ago, when the term vest-pocket housing had not even been coined.

The answer, however, is that we have learned much and that there is still much to be learned. Not the least important of the lessons is that there is no single formula that will apply to all people at all times. Nor should there be one. For if one of our main objectives is to enlarge the choices available to the individual, there must also be a variety of housing formulas—Authority-owned housing; rehabilitated, limited-profit and non-profit housing; rent supplements; home ownership, rental and hire-purchase housing; co-operatives and condominiums; planned neighborhoods and unplanned ones and above all a large supply of private housing with a multiplicity of landlords and a diversity of dwelling types from which to make a selection.

The major obstacle is that these choices do not actually exist in New York City and as long as housing shortage continues, they will never come into being. The housing situation will continue to require a rent-controlled instead of a normally free market to govern the relationships between landlord and tenant; it will continue to be a main cause of the discontents that are now part of city life and that are partly responsible for the flight of middle-class families.

If, therefore, there is one overriding objective that should guide official policy, it is that a vacancy ratio must again be created at all rent levels and for all income groups that will restore to the city's families the privilege of bargaining without duress. It means that we must strive to increase the housing supply; it means that we must use all the help, federal, state and city, that we can get; it means that we must hold down all but essential demolitions until our objective is attained; it means that the emphasis of all publicly assisted housing should be on vacant and underdeveloped land until there is again a normal market and a variety of dwellings from which to choose.

Mayor John V. Lindsay has said: "I want to capture the vision and grandeur of the people of this city and reflect them in their physical environment. I believe *cities* are for *people,* and I want to make *this* city—its housing, its parks, its community facilities—for *its* people—and a joy for generations to come." To many who have lived with the frustrations of New York City life, this may seem a distant hope—but if we know our objectives, the distance will be shortened and the hope become a reality in the years that lie ahead.

Toward Equality of Urban Opportunity

BERNARD J. FRIEDEN*

It is no accident that social reform movements in the United States have been preoccupied with the quality of life in the cities. Many of our national problems are not only highly visible in urban areas, but are even reinforced and made more difficult to solve by the way we build and organize our cities. Now the United States has dedicated itself to the achievement of important objectives in civil rights, education, housing, and the war on poverty. These national purposes imply parallel goals in the planning of our urban areas. Extending equal opportunities to minority groups means, among other things, making it possible for minorities to find decent housing throughout metropolitan areas. And the attack on poverty means, in part, giving disadvantaged groups access to better education and other health and welfare programs. President Johnson placed these goals in an urban context in his 1965 Message to Congress on the Cities: "We must extend the range of choices available to all our people so that all, not just the fortunate, can have access to decent homes and schools, to recreation and to culture."

* Associate Professor of City Planning at M.I.T. and formerly editor of the *Journal of the American Institute of Planners* (1962–1965). His teaching and research interests include specialized work in the area of urban planning and social policy. He is the author of *The Future of Old Neighborhoods* (M.I.T. Press, 1964) and has written on metropolitan planning and development. Earlier versions of this article appeared in the *U.C.L.A. Law Review,* Vol. XII (March 1965), pp. 856–79, and in the *Journal of the American Institute of Planners,* Vol. XXXI, No. 4, (November 1965) and is reprinted with the permission of both publications. The author wishes to acknowledge his indebtedness to Charles Haar, Norman Williams, Jr., and Norman Beckman for their helpful comments and suggestions on the first draft of this article.

The achievement of these national objectives poses a special challenge to urban planners. The purposes of urban planning are sometimes obscured in day-to-day efforts to sort out incompatible land uses, maintain reasonable environmental standards, and program public facilities. More broadly, the job of urban planning is to allocate land and living space in accord with social goals. As a first step, it is important to translate national purposes into goals that can be made operational in the planning of urban areas. This is a twofold assignment, involving not only identifying relevant goals for urban development, but also finding ways to orient public policies in support of these goals.

The social goals of urban planning have been debated ever since planning emerged as a profession. In an important recent paper on the social responsibilities of urban planners, which was received enthusiastically at a national planning conference,[1] Melvin Webber summarized three major objectives: to extend access to opportunity, to integrate urban development planning with other public and private planning for facilities and services, and to enlarge the range of choices available to individuals. Webber urged a joining of professions concerned with urban life and welfare, and looked to this new partnership to produce "imaginative social inventions that will increase the city's riches, while distributing them to all the city's people."

These rather broad and abstract objectives can be applied to a number of specific issues of urban policy, centering mainly around questions of where the poor and minority groups are to live and what levels of public service they are to receive. These are not the only issues relevant for urban development today, but they are among the most important. Few planning programs make adequate provision for the disadvantaged. In many cases, the tools of planning are being employed in ways that restrict residential choices for the poor and deny them access to reasonable housing and services. To reverse this situation will require more than the good will and dedication of city planners: it will require legal and governmental innovation to curb specific abuses of land use controls,

---

[1] Melvin M. Webber, "Comprehensive Planning and Social Responsibility: Toward an AIP Consensus on the Profession's Role and Purpose," *Journal of the American Institute of Planners,* XXIX (November 1963), pp. 232–41. This paper was originally prepared for the 1963 American Institute of Planners Government Relations and Planning Policy Conference.

moderate the incentives that lead local governments to adopt socially detrimental policies, and to redirect urban development policies toward an improvement of living conditions and of opportunities for currently disadvantaged groups.

URBAN DEVELOPMENT POLICIES

1. *Residence and Mobility*

Where people live is significant in many ways. Different cities and towns in metropolitan areas have varying tax resources and provide vastly different quantities and qualities of public service. The resources available depend to a large extent upon the assessed value of taxable property, which in turn depends upon the income level of the residents and the amount and value of industrial and commercial property. The variation in expenditures can be considerable. As James B. Conant has pointed out, wealthy suburban schools may spend one thousand dollars per pupil in a year and provide a staff of seventy professionals per thousand students; while slum schools, where the job of education is more difficult, often spend less than half as much and provide forty or fewer professionals per thousand students.[2] Even within a single community, public services often differ from one neighborhood to another, with favored areas receiving preferential treatment in school programs, recreation, sanitation, street maintenance, and so on. Residential location is a base for the provision of services; when the poor are restricted to certain locations, they are likely to receive inferior services.

The significance of residential location can be seen most clearly in the case of the group in American society that has been most sharply restricted in its choice of where to live: the Negroes. Within our metropolitan areas, the nonwhite population grew from some six million in 1940 to approximately thirteen million in 1960. Most of this growth took place in the central cities, and within these cities the Negro population remained segregated in well-defined areas. One result has been de facto school segregation, arising from the fact that residential location is the usual basis for assigning children to school districts. Another result has been that Negroes made only limited gains in improving their housing conditions, at a time when conditions improved markedly for

[2] James B. Conant, *Slums and Suburbs* (New York: McGraw-Hill, 1961), p. 3.

the urban population at large. Freedom of movement is a prerequisite for acquiring better housing: families must be able to enter new neighborhoods or move to other communities in order to take advantage of vacancies that they can afford. Negroes are limited in their ability to move to new locations, and hence in their ability to find good housing. Instead, they compete for housing in a restricted market where good housing is scarce and where prices are high for whatever is available.[3]

Residential location also implies certain social consequences. Many working-class people find it desirable and beneficial to live in distinct ethnic communities, among friends and relatives, with special clubs, churches, and other neighborhood institutions nearby. For many, these areas provide support in time of need and a bulwark against the different values of a middle-class world outside. Historically, such neighborhoods have served as way stations for migrant groups as they adjusted to urban life, improved their status, and moved on to new surroundings. For the family not yet ready to move, the availability of such a community can be extremely important. Many people who have been forced to leave because of urban renewal or highway construction have found it a shattering experience, with profound psychological and social after-effects comparable to the grief that one experiences with the loss of a family member.[4]

For those who aspire to a higher status but are forced to remain where they are because of barriers outside, the consequences can also be severe. Many Negroes, particularly, have been compelled to remain in social circumstances that they find incompatible with their personal aspirations. They do not approve of their neighbors' ways of life; they feel their children threatened by constant exposure to rougher patterns of behavior; they feel victimized by a society that allows them no escape from the working-class world. This enforced resi-

[3] For a general summary and analysis of research on segregation in housing and the characteristics of the nonwhite housing market, see Davis McEntire, *Residence and Race* (Berkeley: University of California Press, 1960). The extent of recent improvement in housing conditions for whites and nonwhites is discussed in Bernard J. Frieden, *The Future of Old Neighborhoods* (Cambridge, Mass.: M.I.T. Press, 1964), pp. 12–30.

[4] See Marc Fried, "Grieving for a Lost Home," *The Urban Condition*, ed. Leonard J. Duhl (New York: Basic Books, 1963), pp. 151–71; and Peter Marris, "A Report on Urban Renewal in the United States," *The Urban Condition, op. cit.,* pp. 113–34.

dence in objectionable surroundings can in turn destroy incentives for personal advancement and replace ambition with apathy. A lack of residential mobility may thus lead to a lack of social mobility. Robert C. Weaver has contrasted the situation confronting urban Negroes today with that confronting earlier migrant groups in the cities. Previous minority groups, he notes,

> moved out of the slums of yesterday into the suburbs and middle-class neighborhoods of today. This Nation offered them middle-class status when and if they evidenced adherence to the dominant culture. For them, there were and are real, tangible, and demonstrable rewards for industry, conformity, and ambition.
>
> Similar rewards are far less general for non-whites. Thus, the degree of social and economic mobility among this group is less.
>
> . . . It is both unrealistic and an evidence of the projection of one's own middle-class values to expect most of those who are denied middle-class rewards to strive for what experience has demonstrated to be unobtainable to them.[5]

The social import of residential location is thus complex and far-reaching. Other illustrations could be cited, but these few examples are sufficient to indicate that neighborhoods and communities satisfy or frustrate a great variety of human needs. Urban planning and policymaking cannot cope directly with these differing needs, except by attempting to ensure a wide variety of choices—including, wherever possible, the choice *not* to move from a community—and by removing barriers that prevent people from moving freely throughout our cities and suburbs. The additional significance of residential choices in enabling people to enter areas where they may receive improved public services, and where they may find better housing, also argues strongly for policies that will maximize freedom of movement for all, and particularly for disadvantaged groups.

2. *Migration and Intergovernmental Conflict*

In the 1930's, when agricultural upheavals sent migrants streaming across state borders in the movement chronicled in

---

[5] Robert C. Weaver, *The Urban Complex: Human Values in Urban Life* (Garden City, N.Y.: Doubleday & Company, 1964), pp. 264, 267.

The Grapes of Wrath, national issues were posed that have not yet been adequately resolved. California and other states that poor migrants sought to enter attempted to exclude them by means of settlement laws, residence requirements for public assistance payments, and a number of extra-legal methods including border patrols. The Supreme Court in 1941 invalidated a California statute which made it a misdemeanor for a person to assist any non-resident indigent in entering the state. Justice Douglas, in a concurring opinion, reaffirmed the right of free movement and noted its significance in the light of state efforts to curtail this right:

> The conclusion that the right of free movement is a right of *national* citizenship stands on firm historical ground. . . . A state statute which obstructs or in substance prevents that movement must fall. That result necessarily follows unless perchance a State can curtail the right of free movement of those who are poor or destitute. But to allow such an exception to be engrafted on the rights of *national* citizenship would be to contravene every conception of national unity. It would also introduce a caste system utterly incompatible with the spirit of our system of government. It would permit those who were stigmatized by a State as indigents, paupers, or vagabonds to be relegated to an inferior class of citizenship. It would prevent a citizen because he was poor from seeking new horizons in other States. It might thus withhold from large segments of our people that mobility which is basic to any guarantee of freedom of opportunity. The result would be a substantial dilution of the rights of *national* citizenship, a serious impairment of the principles of equality.[6]

At the same time, one of the country's foremost students of urbanism, Louis Wirth, saw the long-range implications of this migration and the hostile governmental responses that it engendered. His interpretation is still relevant for today's problems:

> Freedom to move is perhaps the most basic of human liberties. It is the very antithesis of bondage or slavery. For the perpetuation of our institutions, therefore, it is essential that this freedom be preserved. Without it, our national union could not long survive. If the States and

[6] Edwards *vs.* California, 314 U.S. 160, 181 (1940).

localities should be allowed to undermine this freedom by the erection of barriers, the unhappy prospect of the crystallization of separate civic bodies hostile to and jealous of one another is not an unlikely one in this country.[7]

The intergovernmental warfare that Wirth foresaw is at the root of many of our current problems in urban areas. The sphere of conflict is no longer primarily at the state level. Now the cities and towns of metropolitan areas are engaged in mutually hostile policies that restrict opportunities for the poor. The planning tools that should be applied to translating national social goals into effective local action are instead deployed for the protection of provincial interests. Within many of our large urban areas, the poor, the elderly, and minority groups are concentrated mainly in central cities and a handful of older outlying towns; within these communities, they are often concentrated further in specific neighborhoods. The more affluent suburban towns are eager to preserve their social status and to keep their tax rates low: for these purposes, many are attempting to use land development controls to keep out the poor, who would contribute little to tax resources and would require considerable public outlays for education and welfare programs. At the same time, many central cities are trying to reverse the population movements that have left them with concentrations of the poor, high service demands, and a stagnant tax base. Their efforts to retain or win back middle-income families often lead to development programs that eliminate areas of low-cost housing without providing reasonable alternatives that the occupants can afford. Together, these policies threaten to victimize those who are already disadvantaged by displacing them from their homes in central cities and making it difficult for them to find places to live in the suburbs.

This emerging conflict between local governments is a matter of first importance for city planners and for all professions concerned with urban development. It arises from a context of intergovernmental relations in which considerations of municipal finance join with social prejudices in creating incentives for public officials to prevent the poor from living within their jurisdictions, or at least to hold their number to a minimum. A fundamental objective for all groups concerned

[7] Statement by Louis Wirth in U. S. Congress, House, Select Committee to Investigate the Interstate Migration of Destitute Citizens, *Hearings, Interstate Migration,* 76th Cong., 3rd Sess., 1940, p. 888.

with human welfare in urban America must be to change the intergovernmental setting in ways that will provide greater incentives for socially responsible policies. Until the legal and political context of local government is changed in this direction, city planners alone will be able to accomplish little in enlarging the choices available to the poor or opening the gates for a freer movement of all people throughout urban areas.

3. Suburban Policies

Before a path can be found for governmental reform, it is important to understand the pressures that shape local development policies and the forms that these policies take. Since World War II, the suburbs of our metropolitan areas have struggled with the costs of rapid growth. By 1960, nearly half the people living in metropolitan areas lived outside the central cities. Today, we are not only an urban nation but a suburban one as well. The pace of this suburban growth necessitated vastly increased outlays for schools, roads, utility systems, and the operating expenses of local government. The spending of all local governments in the United States rose from $9 billion in 1946 to almost $45 billion in 1962.[8]

Rising local expenditures have been financed largely out of local property taxes. Increasing tax outlays have prompted suburban governments to take a closer look at their planning programs and land use controls—and in many cases to institute these controls for the first time. Methods of economic analysis have been developed so that the local costs and revenues resulting from each type of land use may be estimated in advance and projected for the future. The accurate application of these techniques requires a detailed study of the local community, and consideration of marginal rather than average service costs.[9] Nevertheless, certain generalizations can be made about the impact of different kinds of new development. In general, inexpensive new housing tends to necessitate greater costs (for schools and public services) than the income that it yields via property taxes, resulting in an increase in the

[8] U. S. Bureau of the Census, *Historical Statistics of the United States, Colonial Times to 1957* (Washington: Government Printing Office, 1960), p. 730; U. S. Bureau of the Census, *Statistical Abstract of the United States: 1964* (Washington: Government Printing Office, 1964), p. 417.

[9] See Walter Isard and Robert E. Coughlin, *Municipal Costs and Revenues Resulting from Community Growth* (Wellesley, Mass.: Chandler-Davis, 1957); and William L. C. Wheaton and Morton J. Schussheim, *The Cost of Municipal Services in Residential Areas* (Washington: Government Printing Office, 1957).

over-all local property tax rate for the community. Clean suburban industry, shopping centers, and high-value housing generally have the opposite effect and tend to show a net gain in property tax terms over the service costs that they bring. Forewarned by this type of analysis, many sophisticated suburbs have responded by adopting land use controls that limit or exclude inexpensive housing and encourage the development of varying combinations of costly housing, "desirable" industry, and retailing.

Screening Out the Undesirables

Robert C. Wood has documented this response in a part of the New York metropolitan region where it has dominated local planning:

> At least since World War I, Westchester has been stereotyped as a refuge of upper-income families from the City who settle in "quality" neighborhoods and consequently enjoy high-quality public services with relatively low "tax effort." During the same period, the county's political leadership has devoted most of its energies to public policies which support the pattern of low densities which topography originally encouraged. Though exceptions exist among its municipalities, Westchester remains, as someone has quipped, dedicated to "zoning against 'Bronxification.'" The stand against "Bronxification" consists fundamentally of policies designed to maintain reasonably low levels of density; to exclude developments of a character likely to result in more public expenditures than they return in revenue. . . . More recently, the expansion of "Westchester-type" industry has been encouraged; outsiders have been excluded from the county's well-developed park system; and considerable attention has been paid to keeping out what has been termed "the undesirable element."[10]

The New York *Times* has made the same point editorially about local zoning in New Jersey, which it claims is "too often . . . intended to discourage the growth of a community, in order to spare its present residents the cost of new schools and other public works for newcomers."[11] Similar approaches

[10] Robert C. Wood, *1400 Governments* (Cambridge, Mass.: Harvard University Press, 1961), pp. 93–94.
[11] "New Jersey's Future Growth" (editorial), New York *Times*, December 21, 1964, p. 28.

in other metropolitan areas have been noted by many observers, including the U. S. Commission on Civil Rights, the Advisory Commission on Intergovernmental Relations, the Commission on Race and Housing, and the National Housing Policy Committee of the American Institute of Planners.[12]

As Wood's account of Westchester makes clear, tax and fiscal considerations are often accompanied by an unmistakable undertone of determination to keep socially "undesirable" people out of the community. The strategy is essentially one of economic exclusion, however, and has come to be known as fiscal zoning. This approach usually takes the form of requiring large minimum lot sizes for new single-family houses, and making little or no zoning provision for single-family houses on lots of less than one-half acre or for multifamily construction. (In New Jersey and a few other states, some local zoning controls even specify minimum house sizes.) In desirable suburban locations where land prices are high, restricting new home building to lots of one or two acres or more can add a few thousand dollars to the minimum cost of a new house and can effectively discourage builders of inexpensive houses from operating in the community. Large-lot zoning may thus slow the rate of population growth in a community as well as raise the sales price of whatever new housing is built.

[12] See U. S. Commission on Civil Rights 1959 Report, *Housing* (Washington: Government Printing Office, 1959), p. 338; U. S. Advisory Commission on Intergovernmental Relations, *Metropolitan Social and Economic Disparities: Implications for Intergovernmental Relations in Central Cities and Suburbs* (Washington: Advisory Commission on Intergovernmental Relations, January 1965), p. 95; Davis McEntire, *op. cit.;* and American Institute of Planners, Report of the Planning-Policy Committee on National Housing Policy (January 1964). The AIP committee report states: "Present patterns of residential development in most outlying areas, under the influence of local zoning and subdivision practices and financing policies, meet the housing needs of a limited and privileged sector of the population and effectively exclude minority groups. Extension of typical suburban patterns of land use, density and housing types, with the consequent effects on the political, social, economic and physical patterns of metropolitan areas should not be supported by the planning profession. Rather, the profession should work to create diversified developments necessary to permit an expanded housing choice for all Americans," p. 6. See also William F. Doebele, "Key Issues in Land Development Controls," *Planning 1963*, Selected Papers from the ASPO National Planning Conference (Chicago: American Society of Planning Officials, 1963), pp. 5–14; and Norman Williams, Jr., "Planning Law and Democratic Living," *Law and Contemporary Problems*, XX (Spring 1955), pp. 317–50.

Building codes and subdivision regulations are often used for the same effect. Building codes typically vary a great deal in different jurisdictions of a metropolitan area; stringent codes can raise the price of new housing by requiring expensive construction methods. Similarly, subdivision regulations can raise the cost of new houses by requiring the developer to invest heavily in wide streets and sidewalks built to demanding specifications even when the density of population does not call for such elaborate installations. It should be noted that these local policies are directly opposed to long-standing federal policies of promoting a high volume of new homebuilding and increasing the supply of good low-cost housing.

Suburban governments can reinforce policies of this kind by acts of omission as well as by regulation. Abuses of zoning, building code, and subdivision controls serve to price housing beyond the reach of lower middle-income families. Even if these regulations were to be relaxed, low-income families would not be able to afford new private housing. A number of federal and state subsidy programs have been devised to enable local housing authorities to build for low-income families. These programs are optional: no locality is required to provide decent housing for the poor. The housing problems of the poor, however, are truly regional in nature. Low-income wage-earners are part of the metropolitan economy and in fact are needed for certain industries that help support the region at large. Nevertheless, the suburbs can easily avoid making a contribution to the solution of low-income housing problems by failing to utilize subsidy programs in their own communities. Most suburbs build little if any subsidized housing, and leave this responsibility to the cities where the poor are more numerous.

Policies of exclusion can be reinforced further by the practices of private businesses concerned with the development and sale of housing. Real estate brokers have their own policies for deciding which listings of houses for sale will be shown to which potential clients. Negroes and members of other minority groups may be shown listings for certain locations only, or may be shown none at all. Banks and financial institutions can exclude minority families from selected areas by declining to issue mortgages to them. Practices of this kind are not actually matters of local public policy, but they are subject to public regulation, and many states have brought them within the sphere of public action by means of laws against discrimination in housing.

The main impact of suburban exclusion policies falls upon low-income groups and lower middle-income groups at large rather than upon specific ethnic or racial minorities. Nevertheless these effects cannot be separated from today's concern for integrating Negroes more fully into our urban society. The vast majority of Negro families are part of the low-income housing market, and policies that exclude the poor will automatically exclude most Negroes. Thus, while economic exclusion may or may not be accompanied by practices designed to keep Negroes out of a community, land use controls that limit new housing to upper middle-income groups and to the wealthy will permit no more than token integration of Negroes into the community. Fiscal zoning and related policies are therefore also significant in the light of current attempts to eliminate racial segregation.

4. *Central City Policies*

Public officials in the central cities and in the older suburban towns are well aware of the effects of suburban exclusion policies. Former Mayor Frank P. Zeidler of Milwaukee once indicated how suburban development policies appear from the vantage point of City Hall downtown:

> The housing problem is in the central core of the cities. Here the people are packed in densities upwards of 10,000 persons per square mile and in many cities with densities many times that. As the houses deteriorate there is no method to move the people around and clear the sites.
>
> The cities are surrounded by suburbs with zoning restrictions that restrict residence to the upper income groups or that restrict the number of families per acre. Consequently, the pressure between the masses of people in the city seeking to go outward and the suburb exclusiveness creates a continual area of conflict.[13]

While the suburbs have been coping with their problems of growth, the central cities have had to deal with equally pressing problems of decline. In most large metropolitan areas, the movement of middle-income and more affluent families from central cities to suburbs has left striking concentrations of the elderly, racial minorities, and the poor in the central cities.

[13] Quoted in Edward C. Banfield and Morton Grodzins, *Government and Housing in Metropolitan Areas* (New York: McGraw-Hill, 1958), p. 85.

The service needs of this population are great—for welfare, education, police and fire protection, and public health. At the same time, the tax resources of these central cities have failed to grow correspondingly with rising service costs: not only have the more prosperous residential taxpayers been leaving, but industries and retail businesses have also been moving to the suburbs.

The conflict that Mayor Zeidler had in mind is now very clear. The wealth of the central cities is passing to the suburbs, while service needs of these cities continue to grow. Most of the large central cities have responded with development programs designed to make them more attractive to middle-income citizens and to industry. Two major components of these programs are urban renewal—aimed at clearing or renovating old structures and attracting new taxable real estate investment—and highway construction to provide better access from in-town locations to the rest of the metropolitan area. These programs to revitalize the old cities have unfortunate implications for the poor, however.

Both urban renewal and highway building destroy a good deal of low-cost housing and displace many families. In 99 cities over one hundred thousand in population surveyed in the summer of 1964, these two programs had displaced twenty-four thousand families in the past year and were expected to displace an additional seventy-six thousand families in the next two years.[14] It has been estimated independently that as the pace of operations grows, urban renewal and the federally aided highway program together will displace more than a million families by 1972.[15] Highway construction clears housing without replacing any of it; and routes through residential areas destroy mainly low-cost housing, since highway planners try to keep land acquisition costs low. Urban renewal programs build housing as well as destroying it, but they build much less than they destroy and most of the new housing is far too expensive for the people who are displaced. The ef-

[14] U. S. Advisory Commission on Intergovernmental Relations, *Relocation: Unequal Treatment of People and Businesses Displaced by Governments* (Washington: Advisory Commission on Intergovernmental Relations, January 1965), p. 12.

[15] Cited in address by Representative Clifford Davis, Chairman, House Select Subcommittee on Real Property Acquisition, reprinted in *Congressional Record*, 88th Cong., 2nd Sess., 1964, Vol. 110, No. 111, p. A2998. See also Alvin L. Schorr, *Slums and Social Insecurity* (Washington: Government Printing Office, 1963), p. 61.

fects of these programs in destroying low-cost housing may be offset by other housing market trends that place additional vacancies at the disposal of lower-income groups. A large volume of clearance, however, always creates immediate hardship, and may slow the rate of improvement of housing conditions for the poor or may even reverse market trends and cause housing conditions to deteriorate further.

EXCHANGING THE POOR FOR THE PROSPEROUS

Unless these programs are accompanied by positive measures to provide good alternative housing for those who are displaced, the revitalization of central cities will increasingly restrict the housing choices available to the poor. They will have to leave areas where they now live, and the total supply of low-cost housing in the city will be reduced. For a number of reasons, central city policies appear to be working in this direction. Although relocation assistance is now available under the federally aided highway program as well as under urban renewal, relocation is clearly an incidental function in the case of highways, and there is no strong motivation to extend more than a minimum of aid. Urban renewal, according to the Housing Act of 1949, had as one of its original purposes "the realization as soon as feasible of the goal of a decent home and a suitable living environment for every American family," but the goals of the program now appear to be somewhat different. Commissioner William L. Slayton of the Urban Renewal Administration, in testimony before Congress in 1963, gave assurances that relocation planning would receive careful attention, but his presentation suggested that it is seen locally mainly as a byproduct of renewal—an obstacle to be overcome—rather than a central objective. Mr. Slayton interpreted the original legislation in 1949 as an indication "that the clearance and redevelopment of blighted areas was a national objective"[16]—more so, apparently, than the improvement of living conditions for families in the blighted areas. Elsewhere in the same statement, Mr. Slayton observes that "Because one of the objectives of urban renewal has always been to sustain and increase the capacity of cities to meet rising needs for essential public facilities and services, the

[16] Statement of William L. Slayton, Commissioner, Urban Renewal Administration, in U. S. Congress, House, Subcommittee on Housing of the Committee on Banking and Currency, *Hearings, Urban Renewal,* 88th Cong., 1st Sess., 1963, pp. 391–92.

impact of urban renewal upon taxable values is particularly important."[17]

Urban renewal is an exceedingly complex program and raises many issues that cannot be examined adequately in a short article.[18] I suggest, however, that central-city renewal programs can generally be best understood as part of the conflict between central cities and suburbs, and this of intergovernmental competition lie a number of ominous implications. Highway building in the central cities is caught up in the same effort to refurbish the core areas to make them more desirable locations for taxpaying businesses and residents, but the major new highways are usually part of metropolitan and statewide road building plans, so that they reflect other influences in addition to central-city policies. Thus the pressure to build new highways in the central cities may originate with suburbanites who want convenient auto access to their downtown offices, as well as with downtown businessmen trying to attract suburban shoppers. Highway building is less clearly a weapon of intergovernmental warfare than urban renewal, but it is often an integral part of plans to make the cities able to compete more effectively with the suburbs, and it tends to create displacement effects similar to those of renewal.

The current program of the Boston Redevelopment Authority, one of the most active and sophisticated renewal agencies in the country, illustrates with unusual candor the intention to build a development policy around the goal of attracting a more prosperous population to the central city. After reviewing recent population changes, including an increase in "population groups most dependent on public services—racial minorities, the elderly, and low-income groups generally," the General Plan states clearly:

> The Policy of the Development Program and this Plan is . . . to promote stability in the size of Boston's population while increasing the diversity of its composition, so that it more nearly reflects the composition of the Region's population as a whole. This would, of course, entail a reversal of present trends toward increasing pro-

[17] *Ibid.*, p. 425.

[18] For an informed critique and discussion of urban renewal, see Herbert J. Gans, "The Failure of Urban Renewal: A Critique and Some Proposals," *Commentary*, XXXIX (April 1965), pp. 29–37; and a subsequent exchange of views on this article, "Urban Renewal," *Commentary*, XL (July 1965), pp. 72–80.

portions of low-income groups and non-whites in the core City.[19]

To achieve this goal, an exchange of population is indicated, in which some of Boston's poor are to be relocated outside the city and some present or potential middle-income suburbanites would live in new housing in the central city. The General Plan contemplates eliminating twenty-nine thousand units of presumably low-cost housing, and building thirteen thousand to fourteen thousand luxury units (for small families with incomes of nine thousand dollars or more); fifteen thousand units of moderate-income housing; and five thousand new units of low-cost public housing. The statement of relocation policy further underlines the exchange of population that is implied:

> Boston can provide a substantial amount of new housing for low and middle income families, but it cannot meet the entire need. Unless suburban cities and towns change their zoning policies to make presently vacant land outside the City available for low and middle income housing, the time required for eliminating sub-standard housing in the metropolitan area will be needlessly extended.[20]

RELOCATION: FEDERAL INNOVATION AND LOCAL NEGLECT

Central-city policies conceived in this spirit are understandable, but they do not augur well for people who will be caught in the squeeze between central-city displacement and suburban exclusion. Core cities are tempted to wage war on poverty by eliminating some of the poor from their jurisdiction—with federal aid. If the intent is to encourage the poor to leave the city, the city will have no motivation to provide them with new low-cost housing to replace what they had before. Relocation aid, for both renewal and highway programs, will consist mainly of assistance in finding vacancies in private housing and reimbursement for moving expenses, plus such innovations as the newly authorized payment of a short-term subsidy under renewal to help eligible families meet increased housing costs. Yet the Advisory Commission on Intergovernmental Relations, in its recent report on national relocation experience, concludes unequivocally: "The worst problem in

[19] Boston Redevelopment Authority, "1965–1975 General Plan for the City of Boston and the Regional Core" (November 1964), p. VI–3.
[20] Ibid., p. VI–5.

relocating families and individuals is the shortage of standard housing for low income groups."[21] What is needed most is not counseling but an expansion of the supply of low-cost housing, which would have to involve either the construction of new subsidized housing or direct rent subsidies on a long-term basis to enable poor families to afford adequate private housing.

Far from assisting low-income families and enlarging their opportunities to find decent housing and satisfactory neighborhoods in which to live, the rebuilding of central cities is a threat to their welfare. Further, the incidence of hardship is not random but quite selective. The majority of families displaced by urban renewal have been nonwhite, and many of the white displacees are members of other minority groups that also suffer from special disabilities in the housing market: Puerto Ricans, people of Mexican background, large families, the very poor. A recent survey of sixty-eight renewal areas conducted by the Urban Renewal Administration indicated that almost 29 percent of the families had monthly incomes below two hundred dollars.[22] According to usual budget allowances, a family earning two hundred dollars a month can afford to pay no more than forty dollars to fifty dollars for rent. Most urban areas have little private housing in sound condition available at this rent level. Even rehabilitated housing in renewal areas assisted under the federal moderate-income ["221 (d)(3)"] program involves monthly charges greater than fifty dollars.

The literature on relocation experience to date is extensive, and it is clear from many studies that the results have been a good deal less than satisfactory. It is now conceded that relocation in the 1950's often failed to improve housing conditions for the families affected and typically resulted in higher rents. Reliable evaluators of relocation experience have found good reason to question the rosy statistics compiled by local renewal agencies in their own accounts of relocation.[23]

[21] U. S. Advisory Commission on Intergovernmental Relations, *Relocation, op. cit.,* p. 104.

[22] William L. Slayton, *op. cit.,* p. 414.

[23] For a review and analysis of relocation experience to date, see Chester Hartman, "The Housing of Relocated Families," *Journal of the American Institute of Planners,* XXX (November 1964), pp. 266–86. A national survey sponsored by the Housing and Home Finance Agency in 1964–65 reports greatly improved performance in relocation resulting from urban renewal. See Housing and Home Finance Agency, *The Housing of Relocated Families* (Washington: Office of the Administra-

Robert C. Weaver, Administrator of the Housing and Home Finance Agency, grants that through the mid-1950's "relocation often created additional slums and brought blight into new areas" and that "relocation was often poorly done and human suffering frequently occasioned."[24] Further, he notes that the clearance of racially mixed areas was usually followed by the construction of new housing that few Negroes could afford, and that "urban renewal too often seemed to be an instrument for wiping out racially integrated living in one area at the same time that it failed to provide for an equal degree of racial integration on the site or in another section of the city."[25]

Under Dr. Weaver's leadership, federal policy has changed in the past few years and new legislation passed during the administrations of Presidents Kennedy and Johnson has made more liberal relocation assistance available. The federal response to problems of relocation has indeed been a positive one, and nowhere more so than in the case of urban renewal and public housing. Since 1962, relocation advisory assistance and payment for moving costs have also been authorized for people displaced by federally aided highways. Legislation now before Congress would equalize relocation aid under all federal programs to match the standards set by urban renewal and public housing. In addition, federal housing programs included in the Housing Act of 1965—particularly the rent subsidies for low-income families—should make it possible for larger numbers of displaced families to find decent places to live at prices they can afford.

But federal action alone does not solve the problem of re-

tor, Housing and Home Finance Agency, March 1965). The finding that 94 per cent of displaced families were relocated in standard housing is subject to several important qualifications, however. Among the major limitations of this study are the following: the survey covered only displaced families and not separated individuals; of the original sample of 2,842 families, 542 were "lost" and no information was secured on their rehousing; no information is given on the number of families relocated into other areas slated for clearance in the near future; data are not reported by city but on a national basis which includes many small cities outside of metropolitan areas.

[24] Robert C. Weaver, *op. cit.*, pp. 53, 54.

[25] *Ibid.*, p. 54. Additional discussion of the implications of urban renewal for class segregation appears in Peter H. Rossi and Robert A. Dentler, *The Politics of Urban Renewal* (New York: Free Press of Glencoe, 1961); and James Q. Wilson, "Planning and Politics: Citizen Participation in Urban Renewal," *Journal of the American Institute of Planners*, XXIX (November 1963), pp. 242–49.

location. Urban development programs are essentially local in nature and execution. Enlightened federal politics will not produce better results in practice if local governments continue to use urban programs to attract middle-income families rather than to give fresh opportunities to the poor. Additional and current evidence of poor local performance came to light recently when the New York State Commissioner of Housing and Community Renewal disclosed that his office had rejected twenty-eight of thirty-eight urban renewal relocation plans submitted by New York communities in the past three years. He noted that "too many renewal agencies overlooked their social responsibility and would create new ghettos in their haste to get funds and clear slums for new housing and stores." "Everyone wants to get rid of slums," he observed, "but no one wants to have the former slum dweller live down the block."[26]

An effective reshaping of local policies will call for changes closer to the local scene and for innovations that planners and their allies can help to bring about.

STRATEGIES FOR URBAN REFORM

This review of urban development policies in central cities and suburbs has emphasized certain trends that have an adverse impact on disadvantaged groups and that result in part from the present pattern of local competition in urban areas. A number of approaches are worth exploring as ways to reorient development policies toward the goals of extending equal opportunities to all, enlarging the range of residential choices for the poor, and giving them access to high levels of public service. These approaches are: (1) changing the context of intergovernmental relations in which local decisions are made; (2) reforming present abuses of land use controls; (3) improving the administration of laws against discrimination in housing; and (4) providing direct planning assistance to people adversely affected by urban development policies.

1. *Intergovernmental Relations*

Policies of suburban exclusion and central-city displacement do not necessarily result from ill-feeling toward the poor: they result in large part from a situation in which local governments find that they can operate at lower cost by excluding

[26] "State Housing Chief Denounces 'Soft Heads' Who Snag Renewal," New York *Times*, June 15, 1965, p. 35.

the poor. If the presence of low-income families made no difference to the public treasury, it is likely that far fewer communities would use their development programs to control the kind of people who will live in the community. Social snobbery will no doubt have some effect in any case, but the removal of economic incentives would be an important step forward.

The cost of providing public services is now divided among local governments, the states, and the federal government. Most states provide significant grants-in-aid to localities for such services as welfare assistance, education, highways, and public health. The federal government also makes important contributions for public works, welfare programs, hospitals, and other facilities. The impact of this outside aid differs considerably from one place to another, depending to a great extent upon differences in the amount of aid that the state makes available to localities and, within any state, upon the aid distribution formulas that it uses. Where grants-in-aid cover a substantial part of local service costs, local governments will be able to cope with the needs of low-income residents without major increases in local taxes. State and federal grants for certain categories of public welfare assistance now go a long way toward meeting local needs, but localities must still rely heavily upon their own tax resources—primarily the property tax—to pay for school expenses and many other local services.

Increased aid from the states and federal government would of course moderate existing incentives to exclude the poor from local jurisdictions. A revision of present aid distribution practices could have a similar effect. Allocation formulas that give increased assistance to communities that have a larger number of poor families, such as the proposals in President Johnson's education program, could create new incentives counter to the present ones. More generally, a desirable distribution system would be sensitive to community needs as well as resources, and would work to equalize the burden of providing services for the poor. If the basic principle is that no community shall suffer financial penalties because it has low-income occupants, then a redistribution of tax revenue is clearly necessary, and the more affluent taxpayers will no longer be able to insulate themselves from regional problems by living in favored communities. More effective equalization of tax burdens would thus eliminate part of the motivation for suburban exclusion as well as central-city displacement.

The case for increasing state and federal grants and gearing aid distribution to measures of local needs and resources does not rest solely on the desirability of redirecting local development policies. Where a problem is regional or national in nature, state or federal assistance is appropriate to avoid penalizing particular localities and to ensure that necessary measures are taken at the local level. The federal anti-poverty program recognizes national responsibility to help local government provide certain types of education for the poor. To a considerable extent, the central cities of our large metropolitan areas are attempting to cope with problems resulting from large migrations of people from other parts of the country— particularly from southern states and Puerto Rico. Here, too, substantial federal assistance would appear to be warranted to share the costs more broadly and to provide newcomers with a high level of public services for education, health, and welfare.

Changes in the structure of intergovernmental grants-in-aid will obviously depend upon political and legislative solutions. Planners can prepare the way for such changes by analyzing local needs and resources, studying the present methods of distribution, and devising new standards for assigning financial responsibilities and allocating grants-in-aid. The needs of disadvantaged groups should receive special attention in the planning of public programs. The Advisory Commission on Intergovernmental Relations has made an impressive start in this direction,[27] but much work remains to be done at the state and local level.

2. Reviewing Development Controls

The use of suburban development controls to exclude lower income groups has attracted increasing attention, and several eminent lawyers have suggested that the courts may now be prepared to give more weight to the discriminatory nature of

[27] See Advisory Commission on Intergovernmental Relations, *Metropolitan Social and Economic Disparities, op. cit.* The first recommendation of the Advisory Commission in this report is of special significance to urban planning: "The Commission recommends that each local governmental unit and agency within metropolitan areas, whether central city or suburban, ascertain, analyze, and give recognition to economic and social disparities affecting its programs. Federal planning aids for urban development, including 'Section 701' urban planning assistance and comprehensive transportation planning, should specifically authorize and encourage economic and social policy planning for the community as a basic justification for physical planning," p. 91.

these controls in judicial review. Charles Haar has observed that "the relationship between planning controls and discrimination, since the Supreme Court's decision in the School Cases, has been subjected to increasing judicial scrutiny."[28] Norman Williams, noting that "zoning regulations directed against people have been increasingly important in recent years," finds an important breakaway from past approval of such zoning in a strong dissent by two judges in Vickers *vs.* Gloucester Township (New Jersey) in 1962.[29]

Two paths warrant exploration in such cases. One is for planners and legal counsel to present the discrimination issues more clearly when exclusionary development controls are considered by local governments or are challenged in court. The other, as the Advisory Commission on Intergovernmental Relations has suggested, is to propose changes in enabling legislation that would require zoning authority to be exercised in a manner to permit a wide range of housing prices within each jurisdiction. A separate but related proposal of the Advisory Commission on Intergovernmental Relations would change enabling legislation to give zoning authority in metropolitan areas only to large municipalities and to counties.

Still another approach to the problem would be to introduce metropolitan housing and planning considerations more explicitly in judicial review of local development controls. Questions of the misuse of these controls to exclude unwanted people are difficult for the courts to decide. The effects of local controls on the metropolitan housing market are usually complex and indirect, and can best be evaluated with the help of a technical planning staff. An independent review of local controls by a technically competent agency would clearly be helpful to the courts, and the growth of metropolitan planning opens up important possibilities for such review. The majority of our urban areas have metropolitan planning agencies. When these agencies have conducted metropolitan housing market studies that delineate over-all housing needs, or when metropolitan plans have been prepared indicating land use allocations consistent with over-all needs, this information

[28] Charles M. Haar, "The Social Control of Urban Space," *Cities and Space: The Future Use of Urban Land,* ed. Lowdon Wingo, Jr. (Baltimore: Johns Hopkins Press for Resources for the Future, 1963), p. 219.

[29] Norman Williams, Jr., "Annual Judicial Review, Recent Decisions on Planning Law: 1962," *Journal of the American Institute of Planners,* XXIX (May 1963), p. 130.

should be brought to the attention of the courts as background for reviewing local ordinances.[30] A further step in this direction would be to develop a system of administrative review in which the metropolitan planning body itself would comment on the metropolitan impact of local controls.

Large-lot zoning is sometimes justified when topographic considerations make high densities undesirable, as in flood plains. Metropolitan studies and review could be useful in these cases as well, since local large-lot zoning for topographic reasons should be in accord with regional studies of drainage basins or soil quality. Further, changes in enabling legislation could limit the use of large-lot zoning to instances when it is part of a regional plan based upon these or similar considerations.

In curbing local exclusionary policies, a metropolitan approach is also important to ensure that no single community bears the full brunt of development pressures by letting down the barriers while other localities still maintain them. Judicial challenges to local controls should therefore be handled so as to apply as quickly as possible to all communities practicing policies of exclusion. If local controls permit inexpensive housing in a great number of jurisdictions, it is unlikely that one or two will be overcome by sudden increases in service demands.

3. Anti-discrimination Laws

By the end of 1963, twelve states had laws prohibiting discrimination in various categories of private housing; a number of others had laws applying to public and publicly assisted housing.[31] The President's Committee on Equal Opportunity in Housing is now coordinating the work of various federal agencies concerned with carrying out President Kennedy's executive order prohibiting discrimination in federally aided housing. In addition, many private fair-housing groups are helping members of minority groups to enter previously segregated areas.

Although the number of public and private agencies in this field is growing rapidly, much remains to be done. Procedures

[30] For a fuller discussion of metropolitan planning and its relevance for housing and urban development problems, see Joint Center for Urban Studies of M.I.T. and Harvard University, *The Effectiveness of Metropolitan Planning* (Washington: Government Printing Office, 1964), pp. 3–24, 147–48.

[31] American Jewish Congress, "Summary of 1962 and 1963 State Anti-Discrimination Laws" (New York: 1964).

need to be developed for coordinating the enforcement of fair housing laws by all government agencies concerned with housing, and for rapid disposition of cases of alleged discrimination. Private groups in particular need the advice of informed planners on ways of directing their efforts most effectively toward the elimination of discriminatory practices. Observers have noted a tendency among both public and private agencies to become enmeshed in individual cases rather than focusing on institutional practices that exclude minority groups from entire sections of our metropolitan areas.[32]

A continuing evaluation of experience under the various state laws and agencies is also important, so that appropriate changes can be proposed. Close observation will be necessary to probe relationships between economic exclusion and racial segregation—both in suburban development controls and central-city renewal programs—and to challenge discriminatory practices in the light of state laws.

4. Direct Assistance and "Advocacy Planning"

It is clear that disadvantaged groups often suffer considerable hardship as a result of development programs that affect the neighborhoods where they live. These groups generally lack the political power to modify local programs so that their detrimental effects may be reduced. Programs of urban renewal and highway construction are extremely complicated, and considerable expertise is needed to register effective protests, propose reasonable alternatives, and obtain a fair hearing for the views of those who are affected.

Professionals in several different fields are currently attempting a new approach for assisting groups of people, usually on a neighborhood basis, in their dealings with local officials. A handful of urban planners, social workers, and lawyers have been working directly for neighborhood groups rather than for city-wide agencies. In Chicago, a neighborhood group hired Saul Alinsky to head a program of community organization that led to the creation of The Woodlawn Organization. Alinsky's work focused on increasing the political effectiveness of people in this neighborhood and their capacity to cope with their social and economic problems. When the community was threatened by a proposed urban renewal

---

[32] For an analysis of comparable experience in the area of fair employment practices, see Herbert Hill, "Twenty Years of State F.E.P.C.: A Critical Analysis with Recommendations," *Buffalo Law Review*, XIV (Fall 1964), pp. 22–69.

program, the Organization hired its own planning consultants to evaluate the city's proposals and present more acceptable alternatives. As a result, the city's original plan was modified to include the construction of low-cost housing on vacant land in the area before any existing housing is cleared.[33] A few neighborhood associations in the New York area have also hired planning consultants to prepare renewal plans in their behalf. Mobilization for Youth, an independent community agency supported primarily by federal funds, has taken a similar approach in its community organization activities for the residents of New York's Lower East Side.

These efforts have placed professional staff in a new relationship to the people of the communities for which they work. Staff members are not responsible to city governments and do not assume the function of weighing neighborhood needs against citywide considerations. Their purpose is rather that of articulating the felt needs of people in the neighborhood and serving as professional advocates for local groups. They may advise local people on rent strikes, represent them in their dealings with local officials, propose educational and housing programs and give aid at administrative hearings and in court. An important aspect of the philosophy underlying this advocacy function is to end the feelings of dependence and passivity that usually characterize relationships between the poor and the public agencies that provide them with various kinds of service. Efforts are made to assert the rights of the poor to receive public service; the service is not regarded as a favor.

The advocacy approach has already attracted considerable attention in legal circles. Former Attorney General Robert F. Kennedy, in an address at the University of Chicago Law

[33] See Charles E. Silberman, "Up from Apathy—The Woodlawn Experiment," *Commentary*, XXXVII (May 1964), pp. 51–58. The philosophy and experience of Mobilization for Youth in carrying out comparable legal programs in New York are described in Charles Grosser, "Neighborhood Legal Service: A Strategy to Meet Human Need," paper presented at the Conference on the Extension of Legal Services to the Poor, Washington, D.C. November 12, 1964; Charles F. Grosser and Edward V. Sparer, "Social Welfare and Social Justice," *Social Work*, forthcoming; and Edward V. Sparer, "The Role of the Welfare Client's Lawyer," *U.C.L.A. Law Review*, XII (January 1965), pp. 361–80. The role of urban planners as advocates for disadvantaged community groups is discussed in Paul Davidoff, "The Role of the City Planner in Social Planning," American Institute of Planners, *Proceedings of the 1964 Annual Conference* (Washington: American Institute of Planners, 1964), pp. 125–31.

School, thought in these terms when he delineated the contribution that lawyers can make to the attack on poverty:

> . . . We have to begin asserting rights which the poor have always had in theory—but which they have never been able to assert on their own behalf. Unasserted, unknown, unavailable rights are no rights at all.

> Helplessness does not stem from the absence of theoretical rights. It can stem from an inability to assert real rights. The tenants of slums, and public housing projects, the purchasers from disreputable finance companies, the minority group member who is discriminated against —all these may have legal rights which—if we are candid —remain in the limbo of the law.

> . . . We need to begin to develop new kinds of legal rights in situations that are not now perceived as involving legal issues. We live in a society that has a vast bureaucracy charged with many responsibilities. When those responsibilities are not properly discharged, it is the poor and the helpless who are most likely to be hurt and to have no remedy whatsoever.

> We need to define those responsibilities and convert them into legal obligations. We need to create new remedies to deal with the multitude of daily injuries that persons suffer in this complex society simply because it is complex.

> I am not talking about persons who injure others out of selfish or evil motives. I am talking about the injuries which result simply from administrative convenience, injuries which may be done inadvertently by those endeavoring to help—teachers and social workers and urban planners.[34]

Professional help in this spirit is needed for urban development programs as well as for other purposes. Edgar S. and Jean C. Cahn have recently presented a most significant proposal for a "neighborhood law firm" that would represent people in the community in a great variety of circumstances involving public officials, private service agencies, and busi-

---

[34] Attorney General Robert F. Kennedy, Address on Law Day, May 1, 1964, at the University of Chicago Law School, cited in Edgar S. and Jean C. Cahn, "The War on Poverty: A Civilian Perspective," *Yale Law Journal,* LXXIII (July 1964), p. 1337.

nessmen.[35] It should be clear by now, however, that the regulations and programs associated with urban development —urban renewal, highway construction, housing code enforcement, public housing—can have a critical impact upon the lives of the poor, and can either frustrate or promote the goals of equal opportunity and freedom of residential choice. Neighborhood planning advisers would thus have a special role in influencing these programs by making public officials more aware of local needs, advising local citizens on presentations at public hearings, making citizens aware of their rights and opportunities under the various programs, and, where necessary, by challenging administrative findings such as those upon which federal renewal aid depends—that the area is blighted, that adequate relocation housing is available.

Finally, planners in these areas could help prepare positive plans and programs incorporating the neighborhood's own assessment of its problems and needs. Before agreeing to such plans, the city would of course evaluate them in a wider perspective and no doubt they would be modified. Nevertheless, the programs that emerge from this interplay of ideas will almost certainly reflect greater sensitivity to local needs than programs for the neighborhood formulated by city officials. Further, it is likely that growing interprofessional concern for the problems of people who now suffer from urban development policies will lead to many proposals for totally new approaches to urban problems. For example, metropolitan approaches to relocation might be investigated: perhaps a state agency with the power to subsidize rents on a long-term basis, build low-cost housing in any jurisdiction, and assist localities in providing services for low-income displacees, could operate effectively in meeting the varied housing needs of displaced people throughout the metropolitan area.

The major obstacle blocking more widespread use of the advocacy approach to planning is the difficulty of paying for professional staffs. Neighborhoods of disadvantaged people are unlikely to have funds available for this purpose. Foundations, churches, and labor unions, as well as neighborhood associations, have participated in some of the current experiments. Federal funds administered by the President's Committee on Juvenile Delinquency and Youth Crime have also supported community agencies using the advocacy approach. Additional funds may well become available under the fed-

[35] *Op. cit., Yale Law Journal,* LXXIII (July 1964), pp. 1317–52.

eral poverty program. The Cahns' proposal for a neighborhood law firm would have it affiliated with a university. University sponsorship may be particularly appropriate when the neighborhood agency also services teaching and research functions or when it is part of a university-sponsored "urban extension" program.[36] In short, financing may be available from a number of sources, and the prospects at this point are by no means discouraging.

URBAN DEVELOPMENT AND SOCIAL CONFLICT

Within the space limitations of this article it has been possible to sketch only briefly some of the problems posed by current urban development policies and some ways in which planners can contribute to their solution. Urban planning and land development controls are both concerned with the allocation of urban space among competing interests. Intergovernmental competition in our metropolitan areas has tended to sharpen certain conflicts for space: public programs in the older communities have laid claim to living space occupied by the poor and by minority groups, while development controls in many of the newer suburbs tend to exclude these groups from space available there. Conflict over living space can shade easily into social and class antagonism. Consider the following accounts of interviews with people in Washington, D.C. who were living in the path of a proposed highway:

A white homeowner who had purchased his property a few years ago and was proud to live in an integrated neighborhood, said that he felt strongly that "changes effected thus far and those contemplated . . . have been made or considered without due regard for the interests of citizens in general, the underprivileged especially, Negroes in particular." He believes that major changes are generally made in the interests of large property owners and builders who profit from these developments.

A well-informed elderly lady commented that "It just isn't just for those people out in Maryland and Virginia with such beautiful homes to expect us to give up the little we have just so they can get into the city more con-

[36] See Kirk R. Petshek, "A New Role for City Universities—Urban Extension Programs," *Journal of the American Institute of Planners,* XXX (November 1964), pp. 304–16.

veniently." She said that she hoped that she will be dead before they begin displacing people . . .

A dental student with a young family who had grown up in the area said: "You can tell whoever you are working for that I want to be relocated in Silver Spring or Takoma Park. I want to live where I want to, not where somebody says I got to. I want to live in one of those apartment buildings that's got a swimming pool and be able to get out with my white neighbors. Sure I know why they want to get that freeway through here. It's so the white folks will have a better way to get to the suburbs."[37]

The bitterness and antagonism reflected in these interviews is likely to become much more widespread as our urban areas grow and rebuild, unless we take corrective action. Urban planning can serve to ameliorate social conflict, if it is properly oriented. Planners can help establish favorable conditions for socially oriented development policies, and can give content to these policies by using their special skills to advance the interests of people who do not yet enjoy the full benefits of our urban society.

[37] Barbara Kemp, "The Social Impact of a Highway on an Urban Community," paper presented at 43rd Annual Meeting, Highway Research Board, January 1964, pp. 5, 8–9.

Chapter 12

RECREATION, LEISURE AND THE HIGHER CULTURE

Man is most certainly a playful as well as a social animal. Non-purposive elaboration of physical and intellectual pursuits has been part of human culture since its beginning. The plastic, performing and literary arts have been useful tools for man's search for understanding of himself and his environment, only lately rivaled by science with its empirical methodology. The re-creation of human energy and spirit through relaxing and "ennobling" play may quite likely be an end value for life on earth. Even when and where it was "root hog or die" men found time to decorate visually, tonally and verbally the humdrum; the vigorous quality of primitive art entrances us still. Today with our powerful automated productivity galloping ahead—after the grindingly grim start of the industrial revolution—we now have time. Time during the day, time during the week, time during the year and time during a lifetime; "free time" to kill or to build into leisure as the thoughtful pursuit of enriching experience that makes life worth its troubles. This is especially so as earning one's living turns dull. Sebastian De Grazia has explored[1] in a most sensitive fashion both *time*, concluding that we do not have as much daily and yearly time as we imagine, since moonlighting to buy gadgets to be cared for is so common; and *leisure*, concluding, as indicated above, that sophisticated leisure is "work" requiring the investment of time, energy and someone's capital. In fact, for large numbers of its citizens the world of affluent society is tending to be turned upside down: "work" is a cinch and leisure is "work"—at least in foot-pounds of energy. Western mass society seems as ill-prepared for massive inputs of free time as developing areas are ready for democracy. De Grazia undoubtedly has a point in putting his finger on the quasi-illusion of heavy recent net dollops of free time. However, if the burgeoning U.S. recreation industry is any clue, with a guess-estimated $40 billion gross yearly take "for fun," then at least we are equipping ourselves well and spending ourselves into an active non-working nirvana. Finally, the long debate is by no means settled as to whether mass society can only produce mass culture as offshoot of its huge expanding populations and mass production, although there is already some evidence that a slightly higher average culture rather than "excellence" may be our fate.

[1] *Of Time, Work, and Leisure* (New York, 1962).

Where does the planner, urban and beyond, fit into all this? It should be obvious that extended space and extensive furniture (both organizational and physical) are needed to cope with the enormous publicly and privately manufactured wishes of the free time/leisure-seeking hordes. Ample private individual dollars can buy a great deal, but hardly much city greenery, a playing baseball diamond or an opera house—much less natural wilderness or much seaside frontage in the late 1960s. Unfortunately too few have ample dollars. *Spectatorship* is expensive enough, but *participation* by large numbers must come out of the public till—aided and abetted in a mixed economy by private and community capital infusions. Further, if planners have the high goal values which they claim, they should be aware that the measure of the style and quality of American life in the twentieth century will not be based on the production of clothespins and bombs but on the creation, display/performance, and consumption of the intellectualized and aesthetically developed arts, as well as a sensitive and loving respect for Mother Earth.

Some indication of the complexity of the free-time problem is indicated by the wide spectrum of needs or functions that must be met by a recreational program of physical and socio-economic-political structures. Although the following categories are not mutually exclusive, the following examples can serve as an indication of the way the cake must be cut. The recreational spectrum must meet difference of:

1) *age*
   a) infant
   b) child
   c) youth
   d) adult
   e) old people
2) *sex*
   a) male
   b) female
3) *time/distance*
   a) the daily lunch or evening hour
   b) the weekend trip
   c) the yearly two weeks to one month holiday
   d) "senior citizens" fifteen-year "vacations"
   e) the unemployable in an automating economy
4) *physical/intellectual*
   a) football field
          to
   b) concert hall

"Doing," most seem to agree, is better than "watching"; participation is more valuable than spectatorship—although some alteration may be immensely rewarding even to the most dedicated participant. The private sector of the economy has profitably exploited spectatorship all the way from "the great wasteland" of TV to the millions of classical recordings sold yearly; however, to provide the higher reaches of aesthetics and intellectual leisure—as well as participation of both a physical and mental variety—demands organizational and capital resources far beyond the private person's pocket or profit-making recreation industry. In the latter case of the higher culture, it would appear that there can be no pecuniary profit, only profit in non-quantifiable human returns. Thus the leisure pattern of a mixed economy seems to be to let private industry profit, by answering (often created) wants whenever it can; filling in the interstitial areas and going beyond by some combination of public and community, plus private non-profit making whenever available. The *creation*, moreover, of higher culture demands special educational facilities and rare, expensive teaching skills; *performance/display* may bring small pecuniary returns but requires essentially expensive public investment; while *consumption* is only the result of the society's entire youth and adult educational process. In short, the cultivation and production of leisure becomes increasingly a government utility or *service* must—joining education, health, and housing in modern advanced society and, symbolically at least, in developing ones too.

Unquestionably the United States (following belatedly English, French and other models) is experiencing a terrific cultural explosion with the public sector thrusting into a leading role by the establishment of a National Council on the Arts in 1964 and a National Arts Foundation as August Heckscher's ground-breaking report to President Kennedy recommended in 1963. President Johnson's enthusiastic crusade for "Natural Beauty" reaches deeply into the redevelopment, rehabilitation and conservation of our entire urban and rural environment both national *and* man-made. One must not delude oneself by these exciting beginnings with all their promise, and measure culture by the numbers; here is the record for the USA in 1963:[2]

- 1,401 symphony orchestras (twice the number of 1939)
- 754 groups presenting opera
- 40,000 theatrical enterprises
- 200 dance companies

BUT

Broadway, the creative center of the American theater, has reduced its annual production from 142 to 60 plays and its playhouses from 54 to 36 within the past thirty years.

There are only 200 commercial theaters in the USA compared to 590 in 1927.

Only 54 of the 1,401 symphony orchestras are composed predominately of professionals.

There are only 5 or 6 dance companies in the USA that meet professional standards.

[2] Rockefeller Panel Report, *The Performing Arts: Problems and Prospects* (New York: McGraw-Hill Book Co., 1965).

Of the 754 opera-producing groups, only 35 or 40 are fully professional and not more than 10 of them provide performers more than 15 days in the year.

There are some eighty "cultural centers" built, building or planned in urban America today. But what goes on inside? One singled out by *Life* several years ago as worthy of note opened with a local community orchestra to be followed the next day by Captain Kangaroo in the afternoon and Bob Hope in the evening — live!

There is much yet to be done at both the social and physical planning level, if we would match our peers. The city of Munich spends approximately what Britain does through her arts council on the higher culture, and Britain, if population size and GNP be taken into account, spends at least four or five times nationally what we are presently prepared to do.

Ian McHarg, landscape architect and regional planner, below has given a wonderful poem of praise for nature and a savage indictment of modern America's rape of this lovely thing. Christopher Tunnard makes a plea for reguilding the water frame of urban life and suggests ways to enhance its impact. Jane Jacobs puts the spotlight on precious city greenery and makes abundantly clear that with almost automatic over-use by starved urban dwellers we must budget heavily far beyond present practice—neglecting the further dimension of savage vandalism—if the provision of civilizing areas to our urban desert is to survive the citizens. Perhaps a new flexibility for urban play space at the simple aesthetic or recreational level must be attained beyond present practice as now prefigured by ingenious experiments with vest pocket parks, mobile parks, and "instant" parks.

With August Heckscher's report to President Kennedy, we move into the multiplier effects of the federal dollar, which could draw five to ten matching private and local government dollars. Whether some Americans like it or not, respect for a discriminating civilized culture can be forwarded mightily by the national government's symbolic and financial concern as André Malraux's Ministry of Culture in Gaullist France illustrates. No one wants to limit and badger the creative artist, but he cannot exist without costly training, display/performing and consumer facilities. In a society of increasing scale and interrelationship, the leading sector for the provision of such cultural infrastructure is the national government, which is almost automatically bound to increase its role.

*The Place of Man in Nature and the Place of
Nature in the Environment of Man*

IAN MC HARG*

Nature has been erased from the city of man which spreads
inexorably into the countryside—its image the bulldozer, hot
dog stand, gas station, diner, billboard, sagging wire, split-
level, rancher, asphalt and concrete. Contemplate the prospect of New York adding 1,500 square miles of sterilizing
smear in the next 20 years, consider the 55 million acres of
presently rural land in the United States which will be transformed during the same period to urban anarchy and despoliation.

Yet the paradox and tragedy of urbanization and growth is
that, while based upon a profound and pervasive desire for
more natural environments, it destroys its own objectives. The
American dream recedes with each annular ring of suburbanization to a more distant area and a future generation. For
this is the sad pattern by which those who escape to the country are encased with their disillusions in the enveloping suburb.
It is a Utopia only for those who make it and profit thereby—
insensitive beings, despoilers, acute only to money.

We cannot indulge the despoiler any longer. He must be
identified for what he is, as one who destroys the inheritance
of living and unborn Americans, an uglifier who is unworthy
of the right to look his fellows in the eye—be he who he is—
industrialist, merchant, developer, Christian, Jew or agnostic.

Yet growth is inevitable and must be accommodated. What
rules should guide the nature and location of development,

* Professor and Chairman of the Department of Landscape Architecture and Regional Planning, University of Pennsylvania. He holds a
B.L.A. and a M.C.P. from Harvard and has practiced as a private consultant extensively in both city planning and landscape architecture with
the Philadelphia City Planning Commission, the United States Geological Survey and the Committee of Environmental Variables and Mental
Health as clients, among others. Lecturer in Landscape Architecture,
Royal College of Art, Edinburgh, and Royal Technical College, Glas-
gow, Scotland, he has published professionally on both sides of the Atlantic on environmental problems connected with urban planning. The
brief excerpt that follows was a very well received and forcefully delivered contribution as member of the Landscape Action Panel at the
White House Conference on Natural Beauty, May 1965.

the preservation of natural processes and beauty? Certainly not the prevailing process which, observed dispassionately, would seem to suggest that water is made to be befouled, air to be polluted, marshes to be filled, streams to be culverted, rivers to be dammed, farms subdivided, forests felled, flood plains occupied and wildlife eradicated.

If one examined the face of man-made America as a product of conscious choice it would appear that we preferred a dilute soup of dead bacteria in a chlorine solution to clean water, an admixture of lead, hydrocarbons and carcinogens in our air, selected beautiful rivers for dumps, junkyards and sewage disposal, and had formulated a national policy for the eradication of natural beauty and integrated this into policies for highways, housing, industry, transportation and agriculture. It would further appear as if anarchy and ugliness were the criteria of excellence for cities. The automobile was preeminent over man. Open space in cities was a positive evil to be eradicated. God's Own Junkyard—the chosen symbol of our time and society.

Clearly this is not the conscious choice of the American people, not the physical image of democracy, not the face of The Great Society. What simple rules can lead to a fairer image? Some guide lines are necessary so that men of good will and intelligence in both private and public domains can contribute to preservation and creation of noble and ennobling environments. Land use regulations have a high priority. They cannot ensure art but they can avert folly, avarice and mindless destruction. They can provide the basis and the context for excellence. These should devolve in the first case from an understanding of nature and natural processes, the values of land, its air, water and biotic resources, their roles, their tolerance and intolerance to man and his artifacts.

A research project which I have conducted for the Urban Renewal Administration on the development of criteria for selecting metropolitan open space for the Philadelphia Metropolitan area can illustrate this approach. Given abundant land and choice, given an understanding of the major physiographic regions, their ecological communities, their permissiveness and prohibition to development, then certain restraints, upon land use, based upon natural processes, seem both inevitable and desirable. These are the eight simple rules for the New Conservation.

1. Surface water and riparian lands should be utilized only for functions inseparable from waterfront locations—ports,

harbors, marinas, water-related and water-using industries. In the Philadelphia region where there are 5,000 miles of rivers, such uses as would be permitted might consume 50 miles of waterfront location. For the remainder agriculture, forestry, recreation, open space for housing, and also institutions would be appropriate.

2. Water quality would be regulated by the natural capacity of rivers and streams to reduce pollutants and sewer outfalls would be located in response to this capacity to ensure continuous high quality water for both consumption and recreation. Water quality standards would be defined—not by dead bacteria or chlorine but by the number and distribution of living aquatic organisms as advocated by Dr. Ruth Patrick.

3. Marshes would be preserved as flood storage areas and wildlife habitats. Filling or development would be prohibited.

4. Fifty-year-flood-plains would be prohibited to all development save those inseparable from waterfront locations plus agriculture, forestry, recreation and open space uses. Flood plains are not for people.

5. Ground water or aquifers are an invaluable resource. In New Jersey the water below is the valuable constituent of the land above. The factors of percolation, storage, water quality, recharge and withdrawals, flood and drought control should be managed. These require restraints upon land use. Injection wells, toxic wastes, atomic reactors, sewage treatment plants, and similar hazards to water resources should be explicitly prohibited and other land uses permitted in relation to their effect upon the water regimen.

6. Soils are living systems, the most productive soils are products of geological time and are irreplaceable. Given land abundance and choice, it is recommended that prime agricultural land be prohibited to development.

7. Steep slopes and the ridges and mountains they constitute are a major source of erosion and sediment, disequilibrium in water systems, increased turbidity, diminished biotic habitats, natural water purification, threat to flood control structures and reservoirs. Such erosion presents enormous problems and costs for flood control, water treatment, navigation, and channel maintenance. Regulation on steep slopes of 12 degrees or more would forbid cultivation or development where unforested and limit development on forested slopes to not more than one house per three acres.

8. Forests and woodlands are the major regulators of equilibrium in the water system and diminish oscillation between

flood and drought. They are important to water quality. They exercise a profound effect upon climate and microclimate and represent a prime scenic and recreational resource. In principle, forests and woodlands are recommended for forestry, water catchment areas, airsheds, recreation and, under certain conditions, for housing but in clusters at a density not exceeding one home per acre.

These restraints, if imposed upon the 3,500 square miles of the Philadelphia Metropolitan area, would not, according to Dr. William Grigsby, incur any total economic costs. They would canalize development and structure growth but they would not consequentially affect time-distance from city to suburb or the aggregate of value added by development. They would protect natural beauty and natural processes, provide structure for growth, ensure a functional interfusion of open space and development.

I therefore recommend to this Conference the formulation of a National Land Use Policy based upon ecology, with explicit regulations. From this may emerge the image of the place of nature in the metropolis of man, the place of man in nature.

Recapturing the Waterfront
CHRISTOPHER TUNNARD*

Think of an urban waterfront—river, lake, or ocean—and be reminded of its blighted condition. It is a refuse dump, perhaps, the garbage filling in the space between rotting piers, where once proud clipper ships or river steamers rode the ways. Or, lately, some huge new installation like a power-plant or a nest of oil storage tanks may have been erected on new fill, blocking off the view of the water. Or, equally bulky and also noisy, a giant freeway may interrupt the prospect, with its thousands of shiny automobiles and trailer trucks. Access will also be blocked; and in many American cities, the residents are scarcely aware that their city is water-based. They are conditioned to traveling many miles for a glimpse of open water. The two-year battle that was recently fought and

* For a biography, see Chapter 1. The following was adapted from *Beauty for America: Proceedings of the White House Conference on Natural Beauty* (Washington, D.C., 1965), pp. 154–58.

won for Breezy Point Park in New York City, the last stretch of beach available to subway riders, is an example of the energy that must be put into claiming waterfronts for the public.

Paradoxically, the very existence of decay on the waterfront gives Americans a second chance to improve its appearance and amenities. Although there is still competition for land on the water's edge, the existence of decay is evidence that certain older uses are no longer necessary there and that we should be thinking seriously of the kind of uses which should replace them. Some older harbor cities no longer consider the harbor as part of their economy—long-range truck transportation has been a major factor here—and the result is that refuse and objectionable land uses like wrecking yards find their way to the shoreline.

There is already in existence a trend to reclaim those areas for community use. The new Liberty State Park (part of the Statue of Liberty National Monument in New York Harbor) will be designed on the site of old wharves and ancient industries in Jersey City. It will be the only waterfront park on that stretch of upper New York Bay.

Why should not the new land uses at the waterfront provide an amenity rather than a hazard to health or an eyesore? If the economy no longer requires so much industry or commerce on the waterfront, why cannot we consider it for more pleasurable uses? The answer is: we can. Our urban waterfronts can be treated as a new resource for the economy of leisure. But there must be safeguards, or they will be despoiled all over again in the very name of the public. Of this, more anon.

The San Francisco waterfront provides an illustration of the possibilities of reclamation. There are piers all the way around from Fisherman's Wharf to the China Basin. They were built in a generation when visions of expanding world trade coupled with an already obsolete docking technology led shipping and port authorities to "cover the waterfront" with these facilities.

Today, one marginal berthing facility of sufficient width could accommodate all the ocean-going ships ever to be found at one time in San Francisco Bay.

San Francisco's Marine Museum at the Embarcadero, with its six vessels giving a realistic picture of life aboard ship in former times, shows what can be done by private enterprise in an educational way. New York City has as yet nothing like this. The idea of recreational piers put forward by Jane Jacobs for the latter city deserves implementation. Here recreational programs could join hands with historic preservation, saving for posterity the Chelsea Piers built for Mayor McClellan by the noted architect Whitney Warren.

A combination of technical know-how and local-to-state government strategy is necessary to renovate our waterfronts. The inertia of years and of obsolete institutions must be overcome. Further, the existence of rotting piers and abandoned ferry slips has encouraged inappropriate commercial enterprise to fill land and even to make new islands in historic harbors. On these reclaimed areas (some of them provided by federal dredging operations) motel-marina developments are promoted, with free public access banned. Some of them are even braving existing conditions of pollution in order to stake their claim.

Not only new commercial facilities, but new industrial and public utilities projects are under way on waterfront land. Many of these are only there because public regulations have not been devised to keep them away. For example, although oil is still brought in by ship on much of our coastline, the new pipelines have made it unnecessary for oil storage tanks to be located exclusively on the waterfront. Where it must be carried by ship, oil can be pumped inland to more suitable locations in many areas.

Similarly, long-term land contract agreements could insure the removal of scrap-metal yards on waterfront land (a common present-day use), with a view to future inland location or to coming advance in technology demanding less space. We should not be thinking of renovating our coasts in short-term measures. They are worth considerable negotiation and trouble.

Meanwhile, new highways are usurping the best waterfront sites, much as the railroads did in the nineteenth century. A spectacular example is the area of Harlem west of Broadway between 125th and 135th Streets, which is losing its view of the river with the addition of three highway viaducts.

Recommendations for various types of action appear below:

1. To insure the urban waterfront becoming a cultural resource, establish urban waterfront districts along the lines of the soil conservation districts, set up by the states and counties. These to be staffed and funded from Washington, and to include in a planning staff an architectural historian, a biologist, city planner, park planner, etc. The districts would not replace port authorities, which are not concerned with scenic charac-

ter, but supplement their activities. It is possible that they might have a task-force character and eventually turn over their functions to existing county or state planning bodies.

2. The urban waterfront districts should establish scenic zones on the lines of Item 16 in UNESCO's "Recommendation concerning the Safeguarding of the Beauty and Character of Landscapes and Sites," December 11, 1962. In these zones permission would have to be obtained for new installations, including highways.

3. Historic district legislation should be applied to waterfront land wherever appropriate. For example, when Brooklyn Navy Yard is given over to a new use, the Admiral's house, the Martin Thompson Hospital and a surrounding historic area should be preserved for the public, since for a long time, beginning with the assembling of the Monitor, the history of this area has been the history of the U. S. Navy.

In some waterfront situations, linear historic districts can be established. In all cases the planning district, as regional planner Harold Wise, has suggested, should be at least six blocks deep, to allow for consolidation of existing railroad uses, etc.

4. County boards of supervisors should refuse permits for shoreline development unless sewerage is taken care of by the developers. Example: The current activities of the gambling and subdivision promotion dynasty on the south shore of Lake Tahoe, which are turning the lake into a sewer.

5. New installations of public utilities and water-needing industries, not to mention the high-rise apartments and hotels which threaten historic scenic areas like the Annapolis waterfront, require co-ordinated planning on the part of regional authorities. In many cases, they do not belong on the urban waterfront at all. Think what this means when it is admitted that the urban shore of Connecticut now extends from the New York State line to New Haven. The historic district, which can save eighteenth-century harbors like Greenwich, and pleasant nineteenth-century fishing villages like Stonington, cannot be expected to do the whole job in these cases.

The real significance of the conflict between scenic preservationists and Consolidated Edison in the New York region is that this public utility serves 10 million now, and that the population of this area will probably increase by 80 percent by the year 2000. Regional planning boards which do not replace but are superimposed upon existing levels of administration are badly needed in these areas. They can be formed of associations of local governments, with democratic representation. In some matters they should be empowered to deal directly with Washington.

This is not the occasion on which to describe a regional authority. I would merely add that private corporations might assist in the location process by hiring environmental designers and wildlife experts on their own staffs.

To end with a slogan: Access to urban waterfront, both physically and visually, will give our citizens that sense of enlarged freedom, which, exactly one hundred years ago, Frederick Law Olmsted claimed for the U. S. public park movement.

Maintenance in Urban Parks and Open Spaces

JANE JACOBS*

Let us suppose, perhaps wistfully, that this crusade for beauty will aim at bringing pleasure and delight to all city people.

In that case, as far as parks and open spaces are concerned, the first order of business must be to reform park maintenance and operation. When we speak of beauty, character, or even usability and cleanliness, we are talking of quality. Park quality, unlike quantity, cannot be bought with capital grants. Park quality requires, forever and forever, good, healthy operating budgets.

I assume you are aware of today's typical deteriorations; neglected plantings, broken equipment, pockets of litter, disintegrated pavements. I assume you are aware of the dreary and humdrum designs that anticipate perfunctory maintenance. More parks has a nice sound, but what does it mean? Today it means that manpower and money already spread much too thin will have to spread thinner.

This does not mean we need be defeatist about affording

* Author and formerly Associate Editor of *Architectural Forum* (1952–62). She is best known for her shattering critique, from a "people-oriented" position, of current city planning and redevelopment practices, *The Death and Life of Great American Cities* (1961). The brief section here is drawn from *Beauty for America: Proceedings of the White House Conference on Natural Beauty,* May 1965, U. S. Government Printing Office, pp. 119–21, and published with the author's permission.

more city parks and outdoor recreation. But it does mean that it is irresponsible to wish more parks upon cities that lack funds to maintain those they have.

I am proposing three interlocked programs: Employment, training and experimentation, all three to be financed—and generously financed too—by the federal government. Nobody else can afford to be generous.

Under the employment part of the program, a co-operating city would receive annual grants for park operation. In return, the city would agree to maintain at least its current park budgets, and also to hire workers from the training program. The more trained workers hired, the larger the grant.

The training program would supply workers equipped with many kinds of skills and many degrees of skill. Trainees whose interest and capacity merited it, would have received advanced training and specialized experience.

This program would not work if it were only to supply menial labor. It would not work if it were cynically meant to placate angry unemployed youth during the summers. It would not work if it were motivated by fear of the people, rather than confidence in the people. It would not work unless there were jobs open and waiting at the end of training. It must be a way of opening up permanent, genuine and responsible park careers—including careers that do not now exist. We need new blood, and new blood always comes from below.

The training program would use city parks leased by the federal government. These classroom parks would also serve simultaneously as experimental parks. While each classroom park were under lease, it would be done over in part or in whole without reference to existing practices and standards. Training would combine with the work of creating these experimental parks and learning to operate them. This would be training not for things as they are now done, necessarily; but as they can be done.

Experiment must be at the heart of our search for quality. And by experiment, I do not mean drawing up new sets of specifications. It ought to be a sin, if not a crime, to standardize the design, material or equipment of parks.

Today many park departments, imprisoned as they are in their low budgets and fine print, seem to have lost the capacity to want parks intended for more than minimal maintenance. Does the cheapest fence to maintain happen also to be the ugliest? Is one monster skating rink or pool cheaper to operate than five smaller, scattered rinks or pools? And no rink at all still cheaper? Is asphalt cheaper to maintain than sand or stabilized earth? Is grass a cheaper green than a garden? Is a concrete wall less troublesome than a slope? Is a Keep Off sign cheaper than building a good turf? The thing is decided. All kinds of possibilities are ruled out in advance. A recent English visitor, Lady Allen, noting the effects of such prudence and the mentalities of the people who are good at it, has observed with scorn that American playgrounds are designed for administrators, not for children.

If beauty is only this year's bandwagon, let us have a good and virtuous time discussing it and then forget it. If beauty is to be next year's justification for renewal developers and highway builders, let us forget it even faster. But if we are serious, let us concentrate generously and urgently upon the operation of city parks, in the full understanding that this is expensive but worth it—worth it not only for the obvious advantages of good maintenance and loving management, but because this is the only way we can tap new reservoirs of talent and enthusiasm for city park and recreation work, and because this is also the only foundation for creating parks worthy of being maintained.

The Arts and the National Government: A Report to the President
AUGUST HECKSCHER*

INTRODUCTION

Growth of the Arts

Recent years have witnessed in the United States a rapidly developing interest in the arts. Attendance at museums and concerts has increased dramatically. Symphony orchestras,

* Journalist, author and Director of the Twentieth Century Fund, Parks Commissioner of New York, formerly President of the Woodrow Wilson Foundation, and chief editorial writer of the New York *Herald Tribune*. He has been associated with a very considerable number of civic and educational organizations as director, trustee, and member: including Chairman of the Board of the Museum of Modern Art (New York), trustee of St. Paul's School, International House, and the New School for Social Research. His publications include: *A Pattern of Politics* (1947); *Diversity of Worlds* (1957) with Raymond Aron; and *The Public Happiness* (1962). He was briefly an Instructor of Government

community theaters, opera groups and other cultural institutions exist in numbers that would have been thought impossible a generation ago. The artist, the writer and the performer hold new positions of respect in our society. Good books are bought in large quantities, as are recordings of good music and reproductions of the great art of all ages. The crafts are developing new standards of creativity.

The causes of this widespread popular interest lie, it appears, deep within the nature of our society. What might be taken at first glance as a fad, a passing enthusiasm, is actually related to some of the basic currents of the sixties in America. An increasing amount of free time, not only in the working week but in the life cycle as a whole; a new sense of the importance of cities; a recognition that life is more than the acquisition of material goods—these have contributed to the search for a new dimension of experience and enjoyment.

At the same time there has been a growing awareness that the United States will be judged—and its place in history ultimately assessed—not alone by its military or economic power, but by the quality of its civilization. The evident desirability of sending the best examples of America's artistic achievements abroad has led to our looking within, to asking whether we have in fact cultivated deeply enough the fields of creativity. We have come to feel as a people not only that we should be stronger but that we should have a higher degree of national well-being in proportion as the arts come into their own.

Despite this new enthusiasm, despite favorable social and political tendencies, the condition of the professional arts in the United States is not in all regards satisfactory. The very demands which changing public tastes have made upon established artistic institutions have strained the financial resources available to them. Older forms of patronage have not in all cases been adequately replaced. A long-standing weakness in what might be called the cultural infrastructure has led to institutions inadequately supported and managed and, as in the theater, to a lack of the stability and continuity which provide the grounds where talent can develop and mature. Often inadvertently, government has imposed obstacles to the growth of the arts and to the well-being of the individual artist.

at Yale (1939–41), and is now a Fellow of Jonathan Edwards College at that university. This report to President Kennedy was submitted on May 28, 1963, as Special Consultant on the Arts and is reprinted in abridged form with the author's permission.

The Role of Government

Government in the United States has not in the past showed consistent concern for the state of the arts. There have been moments, particularly the formative period of the Republic, when statesmen possessed the clear realization that the forms of art reflected the inner ideals of the social order. The planning of cities and the construction of public buildings were expected to match the concepts of order and human dignity inherent in the country's laws and institutions. This awareness was dimmed during most of the period of westward expansion and industrial progress. But in the twentieth century American Presidents again began to sense a relationship between government and the health of the cultural life. Before Franklin Roosevelt inaugurated immensely fertile experiments in this field, Theodore Roosevelt had brought to the White House artists, scholars and poets; William Howard Taft had established the Commission of Fine Arts.

Since the Second World War the role of government in the arts has been repeatedly stressed. In 1958 Congress passed legislation establishing the National Cultural Center.[1] A report on "Art and Government" requested of the Fine Arts Commission by President Harry S Truman surveyed the field methodically and formed a starting point for much of the work done by the Special Consultant in recent months. Significantly, too, when President Eisenhower established a Commission on National Goals, the cultural life of the United States was one of the areas subjected to inquiry.

A New Phase

These two trends—mounting popular enthusiasm for the arts and a growing concern on the part of the government—came together at the start of the present Administration. Attendance at the Inaugural ceremonies of outstanding artists, writers and scholars was understandably hailed as signaling a new partnership in the national life. Reconstitution of the White House as a dramatic symbol of America's cultural heritage, and the hospitality provided to outstanding representatives of the intellectual and artistic community, carried further the idea that government and art have a basic relationship.

Against this background the first Special Consultant on the

---

[1] Renamed "The John F. Kennedy Center for the Performing Arts." The Editor.

Arts was named. It was understood that he would be concerned with the progress of the arts primarily as they affect, not our international posture, but the well-being, the happiness and the personal fulfillment of the citizens of our democracy. In this sense the appointment, modest in scope and tentative in form though it was, marked the beginning of a new phase in the history of art and government.

I. OFFICE OF THE SPECIAL CONSULTANT

Named in March 1962, with the understanding that he would serve part time, approximately two days a week, and for approximately six months,[2] the Special Consultant has had a small White House office with one full-time assistant.

During this period work has been carried forward in the following major areas.

1. *Collecting Information on the Arts,* 2. *Legislative Activities,* 3. *Survey of Federal Programs,* 4. *Advisory Activities.*

II. THE ARTS AND THE EXECUTIVE AGENCIES

The federal government touches the arts at many points. By its programs and activities it can affect the cultural life of the country in important ways. If all is done well, much will have been accomplished, not only in making the government a setter of standards but in giving support to creative talent.

In this section existing government programs and policies are reviewed and broad objectives stated. Governmental activities have been grouped not according to departmental and agency lines but in terms of broad functions. Thus, government acquires art; it creates objects which are marked by quality and good design; it shapes the cultural environment, etc. It has seemed most useful in dealing with this wide variety of material to concentrate on general policies and objectives and avoid administrative or operating detail.

1. THE ACQUISITION OF ART

Government in the normal course of its operations acquires by purchase or commission a considerable number of works of art. In this way, government is a patron of the arts. It creates a market for the work of artists; it sets an example to others,

[2] Report actually made to President Kennedy, May 28, 1963. The Editor.

including public and private bodies, which may have an important effect on the general cultural climate. Memorials, statues, murals, fountains, historic and decorative paintings—as well as works of art for public museums—are among the objects which government in some degree or other makes its own.

The role of government as a patron of the arts in this sense could well be increased. . . . Art is now acquired in a variety of ways and through a variety of agencies. Three areas offer particular possibilities.

Government Collections of Art

The federal institutions chiefly concerned with the acquisition of art do a splendid job within their resources and their authority of preservation, display and research. But the National Gallery, the Smithsonian Institution and the Library of Congress have virtually no funds, except more or less accidental private bequests, for adding to their collections. As a result, these collections cannot be truly representative either of our artistic heritage or of contemporary American art. . . .

Public Buildings

A current list of works of art commissioned in the last two years in connection with public buildings suggests that the harvest has been meager, though the General Services Administration is now attempting to practice a policy of using for fine arts one half of one percent of the cost of buildings over $250,000. . . .

American Embassies

American embassies are important cultural outposts. The purchase by the government of American art, supplemented by private gifts, could lead to a collection administered by the National Gallery or some other Bureau of the Smithsonian Institution and displayed, perhaps on a revolving basis, in United States embassies. . . .

In addition, in a number of often unrecognized ways the government is constantly "acquiring" art—by purchase, commission, or creation by its own designers and producers. . . .

Too often, unfortunately, the criteria observed are solely documentary or functional. . . . In the selection of artists for public portraits or historic events we should as a matter of course wish to be represented by the best American talent, as we do in all other fields of endeavor, whether it be weapons, scientific developments or public buildings. Clear recognition of this principle is hardly less important than the provision of adequate funds.

2. RAISING DESIGN STANDARDS

Many of government's activities are related to the arts indirectly in that they consist of a normal part of its operations which may be done with a sense of beauty and fitness, or may be done tastelessly. Government is a printer and coiner; it strikes medals and makes stamps. It is also a builder on a grand scale. Should it not consistently promote—as Pericles said in his funeral oration to the Athenians—a "beauty in our public buildings to cheer the heart and to delight the eye day by day"?

The task throughout this area is to inject into the process of planning and execution a concern for aesthetic standards, for the quality of good design and good workmanship. . . .

Government Posters—An Example

Government posters may be cited as an example of the way in which a seemingly utilitarian process—in this case the communication of simple facts or ideas—can be raised to the level of art. A group of government posters collected for this survey by the Prints and Photographs Division of the Library of Congress shows how frequently inferior American work is to European in this field; it also reveals the difference of quality which exists between different initiating agencies. . . .

Administrators Alert to the Importance of Good Design

The first requisite for improving design is that men in responsible positions be encouraged to concern themselves with more than practical utility in their respective fields. They may not themselves be knowledgeable in art and design, but they must have an awareness of the need for the highest quality in all that the Federal Government produces or sponsors. They must be ready to take advantage of expert advice wherever it is available. . . .

Recruiting and Encouraging Talent

The recruiting and encouragement of talented individuals in those areas where design is carried out has not been sufficiently recognized as a policy objective. There are small incentives at present for men of ability in the arts to think of the Federal Government as a place where they can do good work. Rewards tend to go to the conventional and the mediocre. At the same time there is slight disposition among government agencies to make use of outside talent. . . .

The Use of Advisory Committees on the Arts

In a number of departments special committees have been created to advise on matters of art and design. Such committees can play a highly useful role, depending upon their composition, their quality, and the weight attached to their recommendations. Outstanding representatives from the world of fine arts and architecture have shown themselves ready to give generously of their time when called on for these purposes.

The most notable example of such a committee has been that which advises the State Department on the design of its embassies and consulates. Composed of a small rotating group of gifted architects, ready to take advantage of talented young men as well as famous names, this committee has been responsible in the postwar years for buildings abroad in every way worthy of America's role in the world. In the last several years, the value of this achievement has not been fully recognized. The foreign building program of the State Department has received inadequate support and has been cut back. . . .

Public Buildings—A Major Area of Concern

In areas where design factors are involved, the advisory committee should be adapted to special needs; thus graphic artists should advise on postage stamps, sculptors on medals, etc. These committees, perhaps under some system of loose co-ordination, should continue to work within separate departments and agencies. In the case of public buildings, however, a more centralized structure might well be explored.

The most striking and most enduring objects created by government are buildings. Construction is carried on through many agencies—principally by the General Services Administration, but also by the Army Corps of Engineers, the Space Administration, the Post Office Department, etc. Here the possibility arises of an over-all panel which would oversee, from the point of view of design, all government building. It could determine occasions where competitions are appropriate and keep open ways to the use of fresh talent and novel concepts. . . .

The implementation of the President's directive of May 23, 1962, on Guiding Principles for Federal Architecture is of first importance. This directive recommended a three-point architectural policy for the Federal Government. It restated in affirmative and contemporary terms the conviction held by Washington, Jefferson and other early American statesmen that public buildings should set an example for public taste and in the words of the directive "provide visual testimony to the dignity, enterprise, vigor and stability of the American Government." It recommended: (1) the selection of distinguished designs that embody the finest contemporary American architectural thought (2) the avoidance of an official style and the encouragement of professional creativity through competitions and other means and (3) the special importance of landscaping and site development in relation to the surrounding area. . . .

3. Impact on the Cultural Environment

We have been speaking of government's responsibility in the design of specific objects—from postage stamps to buildings. But government's responsibility does not stop there. Not always is it recognized how large a role government plays in preserving cultural assets and creating an environment within which cultural values can be realized. Public buildings, if they are to be genuinely significant, must not only be well designed but must be part of a setting in which life can be lived with some sense of spaciousness, dignity and aesthetic delight. Again, roads are not only per se susceptible of being improved in appearance and in the aesthetic experience they provide; what is even more important, they must be so conceived and carried out as not to dehumanize the landscape or run roughshod over the living community.

The scale upon which modern government acts makes it vital that this responsibility to the total environment be acknowledged. The constant tendency is to think only of the immediate task, forgetting the wider implications of governmental action.

Preservation of the Cultural Heritage

The Historic Sites Act, passed nearly thirty years ago, established the government's concern with the preservation of historic sites and buildings. Under this act a program of identifying, recording and promoting preservation, by acquisition where appropriate, has been carried out.

The problem is broader, however, than can be met by such an approach. Government policies and programs directed toward legitimate and accepted ends have had the secondary results of destroying sites and buildings which ought to be preserved. It is important that in all federal policy governing construction, highways and community development the interest of the nation in historic preservation be given weight. This is an area where the vigilance of a Consultant on the Arts can make sure that such an interest is heard and adequately represented. . . .

Preservation in this sense requires prudence and sensitivity in administering federal projects. It requires a willingness to give weight to views in the community which may not always be very loudly expressed but which speak for the long-range national interest. . . .

Shaping the Environment

To shape an environment which meets the needs of men and women for a civilized existence is a long-range federal interest going beyond mere preservation. The National Parks should be seen in this light: they are important for recreation, but also, more broadly, as a means to fulfilling the characteristic American concept of the good life. . . .

Within the urban context, as well, government policies to enhance the environment and to assist in the achievement of this objective by the private as well as the public sector should be encouraged. . . .

The government's responsibility for good housing was clearly stated in the Housing Act of 1949 which established a national housing objective. This act declared that the goal of a national housing policy was "a decent home and a *suitable living environment* for every American."

In the fourteen years since that act was passed, the government has continued and initiated many programs to carry out this aim. With this experience has come increasing recognition of the importance of environmental factors, especially the use of space. Thus the Housing Act of 1961 authorized a program of grants to help states and metropolitan areas create and preserve open space.

Urban renewal has shown itself in many instances to be the only effective and practical means of saving and redeveloping urban areas. The recognition by the Urban Renewal Administration that plans should be concerned with historic preservation, with the provision of such public services and amenities as theaters, libraries and cultural centers, and with standards of good architectural design, is important. A recent URA policy statement makes the point that "urban renewal provides an unprecedented opportunity to rebuild major parts of our cities. Well designed, these can become great assets—functionally and aesthetically. But if these areas are poorly designed, rebuilt in uninteresting and unproductive patterns, a basic purpose for the expenditure of public funds and public effort will be lost."

Public housing is an area in which the Federal Government has even greater and more direct responsibility and opportunity.

Unfortunately public housing has too often been the victim of indifference, suspicion, and even hostility on the part of officials and politicians, private builders, the general public and even the architectural profession. There is a widely held view that public housing should by its very nature be drab, standardized and functional and that materials and "appurtenances" should be held to the minimum type and quality necessary to build what the law describes as a "decent, safe and sanitary dwelling."

The law further prescribes that such housing be developed and administered to promote "serviceability, efficiency, economy and stability," that no "elaborate or extravagant design or materials" be used, and that economy of construction and administration be promoted. These criteria have often been unnecessarily interpreted to mean that public housing units under the law cannot be well and imaginatively designed and that essential amenities and services cannot be provided.

The Public Housing Administration should be encouraged and supported in its new efforts to improve the design of public housing and to make its projects more responsive to the needs of its tenants. It is actively working with the American Institute of Architects on improving architects' fees (which have generally been too low) and revising standard contracts. It has asked the AIA also for recommendations on ways to improve design, development and review procedures, the desirability of competitions, design award programs, exhibitions and methods of increasing public and professional appreciation of design and environmental factors.

A consultant program has been established to aid local housing authorities and their technicians on design problems. The program includes architects, landscape architects and planners, and their function will be to consult with and advise on specific plans and designs, land use, site development and assist in the conduct of seminars. A National Panel of Design and Planning Consultants, composed of thirty or more leading architects and planners, has been set up. . . .

4. PRESENTATION AND DISPLAY OF ART

Government responsibility is not discharged in acquiring and conserving works of art and other objects of historic and artistic merit. To be enjoyed and appreciated by the people and to make the contribution they should to our cultural life they must be made available and accessible in a much more extensive and varied manner than they have been to date.

The Visual Arts

A large number of federal agencies are involved in one way or another with the display and presentation of the visual and graphic arts. Chief of these, of course, are the great galleries in Washington and the Congressional Library. Some individual departments and agencies operate specialized museums and exhibit programs, for example, activities of the Armed Services, historic sites and buildings administered by the National Park Service, national memorials of various kinds, etc.

The quality of existing activities and the competence and dedication of the staff responsible for them was found in the cases which this office was able to study to be unusually good. On the other hand, the casual and unimportant role accorded such programs as far as policy and financial support was concerned has meant that as a practical matter they are generally inadequate and haphazard. Lack of funds, limited exhibit space, duplication and ineffective co-ordination and liaison between the different government agencies involved, and above all the absence of any positive policy and program to make our national collections more available to the public have all contributed to this state of neglect. . . .

Finally, it should be pointed out that the lack of any central system of exercising over-all co-ordinating, recording and policy functions has probably contributed to the greatly varying character of professional care, preservation, accessibility and even knowledge of the art treasures belonging to the government. This should be a matter of some concern. . . .

The National Collections

A positive program should be adopted to expand the educational and presentation activities of the national collections.

The many excellent recommendations in this regard of the Report to the President submitted by the Fine Arts Commission in 1953 should be carried out. In this report, the commission urged that in addition to providing authority and funds to the National Collection to make this a truly representative museum of American art, a greatly expanded program of traveling exhibitions, catalogues and publications and reproductions should be initiated. . . .

Presentation of the Performing Arts

The Federal Government should fulfill its responsibility for the performing as well as the visual arts. Government auditoriums have generally been built with little or no concern for this important function. The sponsorship of concerts and theatrical performances has been very limited, primarily restricted to the city of Washington, and in most instances entirely dependent on private gifts to the government.

The programs of chamber music, literary readings and dramatic performances taking place in the Library of Congress, the National Gallery Symphony Orchestra concerts, and the few programs, including experiments with *Son et Lumière*, sponsored by the National Park Service, are the main examples. Tours and performances sponsored by the Armed Services provide an opportunity for presenting the performing arts to an audience which is in a position greatly to influence the future cultural life of American communities.

The National Cultural Center

Creation of the National Cultural Center will enhance the Federal Government's role in presenting American cultural achievements and in stimulating and supporting the performing arts throughout the country. To fulfill its aim, the Center must be more than a group of splendid stages for the benefit of Washington audiences.

The general policy of the Cultural Center is outside the scope of this report; but it may be stressed here that if it is to fulfill its role of presenting the performing arts to a broad national audience it must from the start conceive a program keyed to diverse and wide-ranging interests. Not only must it be expected to present the best of orchestras, repertory theater, opera, choral and dance groups from this country and overseas; it must also reach out through competitions, festivals, youth programs and commissioned works into the heart of the nation's cultural life. The motion picture, that most characteristic and indigenous of American art forms, should have an important place in the program. The organization of the motion picture industry tends to emphasize the expensive commercial feature picture. The Center can provide a means to encourage both the production and the opportunity for public viewing as well as a way of recognizing the best of our documentary and shorter fine arts films.

The Cultural Center must use all means to make its presentations extend beyond the area of its halls. A program of education and dissemination activities must be central in its planning. Plans must be made for bringing the programs to the country at large through full use of television.

Promoting New Facilities

A major obstacle hindering the development of the performing arts throughout the country is the lack of proper facilities. There are a number of ways in which the government can contribute with little or no increased expenditure of federal funds. In many of the construction programs in which the government exercises a financial or advisory role, auditoriums are built or could be built—and at little relative additional cost—with adequate facilities for the performing arts. It is strongly urged that the government not overlook this opportunity.

Specifically it is suggested that the provision of facilities for the performing arts be considered in: (1) plans for new federal centers and buildings throughout the country as well as Washington (2) urban renewal and community development programs (3) public works programs (4) the National Park Service (5) business and building financial and service assistance and (6) the school construction program and advisory service on school facilities administered by the Office of Education.

The Urban Renewal Administration has already taken steps to suggest that the provision of auditoriums and civic and cultural centers be considered eligible and desirable objectives in renewal plans. This policy should be encouraged and extended to other appropriate programs. . . .

Presentation in the International Sphere

Cultural exchange is one of the most important means by which government fulfills its role of presenting and displaying American arts. The foreign policy aspects of this program are not considered here. It must be stressed, however, that the cultural life at home is stimulated and benefited by the effectiveness with which this responsibility is carried out. The recognition American artists receive through the exhibition of their works abroad is an important element in their development. Those who have the experience of working abroad and coming to know the artists of other countries bring back fresh skills and new sources of inspiration. . . . For these reasons it is urged that an active exchange program be furthered by all government agencies directly or indirectly involved. . . .

International Fairs and Conferences

The Commerce Department, responsible for trade fairs and exhibitions, can also play a role in presenting before foreign publics the best work of American architects, graphic artists and designers. . . .

The Department of Justice should make every effort to put into effect simpler and more realistic entry requirements, thus encouraging the holding in this country of international conferences, competitions and festivals. It must be hoped that ways will be found for providing the funds which other countries authorize for hospitality to foreign visitiors at such gatherings. At present, due largely to legislative obstacles and stringencies, international groups rarely meet within the United States. . . .

5. EDUCATION, TRAINING, AND RESEARCH

The Federal Government affects the arts through what it does, or fails to do, in the related fields of education, training, and research. In developing these potentialities there is opportunity for much positive and useful support. Programs in these areas are well-established and recognized as a natural governmental operation. But at present, the arts are given a low priority, or are even excluded in most educational and training programs; and basic research information in this field is scarcely pursued at all. . . .

The National Defense Education Act

The major program of federal assistance (aside from aid to special construction, vocational and minority groups) is that authorized by the National Defense Education Act. Assistance is limited to those fields of education which contribute to the national defense—specifically science, mathematics and modern languages. Initially the act was interpreted to permit a limited program of fellowship awards in the arts, but this was later terminated as being contrary to congressional intent.[3]

The Office of Education

The Office of Education, the chief agency of the government concerned with education, has until recently given little attention to the arts. Recommendations for increasing the art programs of the Office of Education have been submitted after a study by a consultant who reviewed for HEW its activities in this area. A new division has been established to deal with educational needs beyond formal school programs. This division will be responsible for the Library Services and Adult Education programs and through a new Cultural Affairs Branch will give increased attention to the arts.

It is recommended that further consideration be given to increasing the share of the Federal Government's support to education which is concerned with the arts and the humanities. This should include the same type of across-the-board assistance now given to modern languages, mathematics and science: for example, facilities and equipment, teacher training, teaching techniques and materials, scholarship and fellowship programs. The predominant emphasis given to science and engineering implies a distortion of resources and values which is disturbing the academic profession throughout the country.

Other Federal Institutions

The activities of the Library of Congress and the several museums comprising the Smithsonian Institution are often classified as educational in nature. Those agencies do carry on a variety of educational services, but they are to a large extent dependent on private funds and volunteer staff, necessarily limited in nature and primarily restricted to Washington. A major recommendation of the Fine Arts Commission Report of 1953 was the allocation of funds to make color reproductions, photographs, slides and motion pictures available to schools and colleges on a national basis. This recommendation should be put into effect.

Research in Art Education

Encouraged by its success in stimulating the preparation of new teaching materials in science and mathematics, the Panel on Educational Research and Development (a committee

---

[3] Now liberalized. The Editor.

sponsored by the Office of Education, the National Science Foundation and the President's Science Advisory Committee) has initiated a project on the teaching of art and music in elementary and secondary schools. . . . Generally speaking, however, no more attention has been given to research on and in the arts than to training and education in the arts. . . .

Gathering Statistical Information

A major obstacle to the assessment of the problems and needs of the arts and the formulation of sound and realistic public policies is the lack of adequate up-to-date factual and statistical information. Professional organizations or associations of the arts have not had the resources to collect such information as is commonly collected by business, labor or other professions. None of the fact-collecting agencies of the Federal Government collect comprehensive or consistent data on any detailed or meaningful basis. The problem is not easy, as much of the data relating to the arts is not available through standard methods of collecting information on economic and social activities. At the same time, the growing social and economic role played by the arts makes the collection of such information increasingly necessary. For example, Department of Commerce figures on recreation and entertainment show that in 1961 expenditures on admissions to legitimate theater, opera and entertainments of non-profit institutions amounted to $400 million dollars, which is substantially more than total admissions to spectator sports. The importance of the performing arts in the employment picture has been recognized by the Department of Labor in including data in the annual Occupational Outlook Handbook of 1961 for the first time. But there is little reliable information on such elementary facts as numbers of performing groups, character of facilities, types of services, sources of financial support including state and municipal subsidies, etc. To be of value this information must be collected on a continuing, systematic and detailed basis.

6. Government Recognition of the Artist

Most of the great countries of the world have traditionally given national recognition not only to outstanding military and government service but also to individuals for distinguished accomplishment in science, the arts and the humanities. Britain has an Honors List; France the Legion of Honor and the Academy; the Soviet Union a variety of awards.

Japan gives recognition by designating her artists as "living cultural assets."

In recent years there has been growing support in the United States for a system of national recognition of achievement in the arts and the humanities. Presidential recognition has been given in several different ways through special dinners, individual invitations to the White House, and occasional performances by leading professional artists or youth groups. This method, however, is necessarily irregular and personal and can scarcely answer the requirements of a formal and continuing system, though a more official system does not, of course, exclude the continuation of the various forms of personal presidential recognition, noted above, which have important values of their own.

A number of bills to establish a system of medals or awards in various fields of civilian endeavor have been introduced in Congress in recent years but have never been passed. An occasional individual, such as Robert Frost, has been honored by a medal authorized by special legislation. Until very recently, however, there has been no system of regularly honoring accomplishment or contribution in all fields of human endeavor. As a result of legislation passed in 1959, a National Medal of Science was established and the first award made in February 1963. Also in the scientific field are the Fermi and Lawrence Awards, which include cash prizes, and are granted by the Atomic Energy Commission, as authorized in its basic legislation, for meritorious contributions to the development of atomic energy.

The highest civil honor of the United States has been the Medal of Freedom originally established by President Truman as an award for meritorious service in connection with the war. Its scope and purpose have recently been broadened, and from now on it will be awarded on a systematic annual basis to a limited but unspecified number of persons who have made especially meritorious contributions to the security or national interests of the United States, world peace, cultural or other significant public or private endeavors. . . .

III. THE NATIONAL CAPITAL

The city of Washington has an importance far outweighing its relatively small population of less than 800,000 people. As the national capital of the country, it is the center of a metropolitan population of two million (over half of whom live not only beyond its municipal borders but in other states), it plays host to more than fifteen million tourists a year (estimated to rise to twenty-four million in the next decade), and as a political and diplomatic capital is visited by hundreds of thousands of business and professional men, public officials and foreigners.

It should be an example to the rest of the country, a symbol of the finest in our architecture, city planning and cultural amenities and achievements—a symbol in fact of what the environment of democracy ought to be.

A New Era for Washington

For more than a hundred and fifty years Washington's chief problem has been growing up to the dimensions of the L'Enfant Plan. The original conception of the city was in every sense magnificent; but for long periods Washington was allowed to grow without order, design or a true appreciation of its aesthetic potentialities. Federal architecture has been largely second-rate, with the new State Department Building standing as a particular monument to false functionalism and false grandeur.

In the past decade Washington has suddenly outgrown not only the original plan but also the political and administrative system which has been relied on to date to guide its development and maintain its distinction.

In any discussion of Washington, or of the relationship of government and the arts, the responsibility of the Federal Government for Washington should be stressed. It is the Federal Government—through the executive branch and the Congress—which makes the ultimate decisions and authorizes the funds which determine the quality and character of the city.

Much of the problem is due to overlapping, conflicting or inadequate policies, agencies and interests. In the aesthetic field, we have the General Services Administration, the Fine Arts Commission, the National Park Service, the Office of the Architect of the Capitol (Congress has complete authority over buildings and grounds in the 135 acres comprising the Capitol area), the National Capital Planning Commission and, if we include the metropolitan area and the Potomac River, the National Capital Regional Planning Council and the States of Virginia and Maryland.

What is needed is an imaginative new approach which will realize the concept of a capital city fully expressing the standards and values of the nation. A beginning has been made in the new policy on federal architecture contained in the President's Memorandum of May 23, 1962, in the establishment of the Pennsylvania Avenue Advisory Council charged with drawing up plans for the redevelopment of Pennsylvania Avenue as the "great thoroughfare" it was originally intended to be, and in the President's Memorandum of November 27, 1962, establishing "guidelines" for the development of the National Capital Region. These policies and projects should be vigorously pursued and implemented. . . .

Federal policies applicable to cities should be applied with special care and imagination to Washington itself. Thus it is fortunate and fitting that what is potentially the country's best urban renewal project in terms of planning and design is situated within a stone's throw of the Capitol. . . .

The Fine Arts Commission

It is vitally important that the Fine Arts Commission be made capable of carrying out its mission of helping to ensure that the architecture and environment of federal buildings in the capital be worthy of the best of our times. It should take a positive attitude toward achieving good design in the capital. . . .

Planning the Capital Region

A more difficult but equally urgent task is to create some means to eliminate the present piece-meal approach to the planning and development of the national capital region. A plan worthy of L'Enfant, for example, would provide for the preservation and enhancement of the Potomac River as a natural resource offering amenities to our citizens as well as assuring the capital the beautiful setting it deserves.

Cultural Opportunities

The capital should, however, be more than a collection of buildings, monuments, museums and parks. It should also offer both opportunity and recognition to the best dramatic and musical talent, both from here and abroad, as expressed in performances of composers, playwrights and choreographers new and old.

It has never had a stage appropriate to this role, and this is what in essence the National Cultural Center will be. It is, therefore, of utmost importance that the efforts now under way to bring to reality the Center with its several halls and stages should be given every possible encouragement.

In addition, Washington should be an example to other cities in seeing that the artistic institutions and programs needed to provide the city with a broad range of cultural opportunities are flourishing and responsive to new needs as they develop. . . . Washington could well be a laboratory for the working out of effective relationships between public agencies and private institutions.

IV. GENERAL POLICIES AFFECTING THE ARTS

There is a broad range of general government policies which are designed to accomplish objectives not primarily or specifically related to the arts, but which do affect and concern the state of the arts and the position of the individual artist, often adversely and mainly through inadvertence. These are in such fields as taxation, copyright laws, postal rates, disposition of surplus government property, public works and general assistance programs.

1. TAXATION

Of these, the impact of the tax laws is undoubtedly the most important, mainly because the earning and income pattern of the writer and artist differs strikingly from that of most other professions and occupations.

Our tax laws have traditionally been more concerned with providing relief and incentive to the "inventor" than to the "artist." The argument has been that tax relief to the inventor is necessary to encourage the inventive genius essential to economic growth. . . .

Income Tax

It has been widely recognized that the progressive tax rate principle affects individuals whose incomes fluctuate from one year to the next much more harshly than it does those with steady annual earnings. This result violates a basic principle of equity providing that equal incomes should bear equal tax liabilities. Existing tax laws make some provision for averaging income over a period of years but for narrowly prescribed and limited situations. For example, although the writer can qualify for a three-year spread of income (even if his book takes ten years to write), it appears that the preforming artist cannot. Frequently the writer's earning pattern does not permit any real relief because it does not fit the specific requirements of the law. Existing law is quite restrictive and limits the benefits of averaging to a particular invention or artistic work the completion of which took two years or more, and requires that 80 percent of the income from the work be received in a single taxable year. The economics of book publishing and selling are such that few writers can qualify under the law.

Revision of the tax laws to create a fair income-averaging provision which will provide realistic and equitable tax relief to the artist is of first importance to the growth of the arts.

Tax Deductibility for Contributions to the Arts

The President's new tax proposals contain a number of recommendations which affect the tax deductibility of contributions. This report welcomes the proposed extension of the 30 percent ceiling to such non-profit organizations as symphony orchestras, museums, libraries and other cultural institutions. Under existing law contributions to these types of organizations are limited to 20 percent. It is strongly urged that the higher limit be applicable to all recognized cultural institutions. The proposed revision should embody this principle very clearly in its final wording.

The Tax Message also urges the repeal of the unlimited charitable deduction provision on the grounds that no group of taxpayers, no matter how small nor how beneficial their contributions, should be permitted to escape income tax entirely. Under present law some taxpayers need give little more than the otherwise allowable 30 percent in order to escape from the payment of any tax. Although the $10 million involved is small, relative to total philanthropic giving, repeal could seriously affect specific institutions and organizations, especially in the cultural field.

The major proposal which may adversely affect the level of private support of non-profit cultural institutions and programs is the recommendation for a 5 percent floor on itemized deductions. . . .

In any case the tax benefit is considered of crucial importance by those responsible for the managing and financing of our cultural institutions. They state with virtual unanimity that a 5 percent floor would seriously affect contributions. To the argument of Treasury officials and other tax experts that over the years the level of voluntary giving has been unaffected by tax changes, they answer that the psychological effect of such a change introduced at this point would be severe, and that individual contributors would definitely decrease their giving.

This report strongly urges that contributions to non-profit organizations and institutions be considered a quite separate category of personal expenditure entirely different in nature and purpose from other deductible items of personal expenditure, such as taxes, interest, employment and investment expenses. Complete tax deductibility for contributions is a method, deeply imbedded in American tradition, of support for philanthropic and non-profit enterprise. In many ways it is a substitute for the direct public subsidy these organizations would need in the absence of private contributions. The eligible organizations and institutions are providing important services, are not run for profit, and can by their nature never be self-supporting. Government policy should be to provide the maximum positive encouragement and contributions should be wholly and not partially exempt from taxation as a matter of principle.

Admissions Tax

Other countries give positive support to their theaters; the United States by contrast "penalizes" the theater by imposing a 10 percent admissions tax.[4] . . .

Professional Tax Deductions

Artists and writers often find themselves penalized by not being permitted to deduct what they consider legitimate professional expenses under existing tax laws. The issues are basically technical and frequently a matter of regulation and administrative interpretation. They relate generally to the fact that the practicing artist must often earn his living through other employment, notably teaching, and is often unable to earn any money from his creative output for years at a time. . . .

Tax Treatment of Copyrights

The creator of a work of art is denied the rights available to holders of patents and other property under the capital assets tax provisions.

2. OTHER POLICIES

Postal Rates

Existing special rates for organizations and educational and library materials are important to the maintenance of com-

---

[4] Repealed January, 1966. The Editor.

munications within the cultural community. It is important that rates for all legitimate cultural materials be kept as low as possible as a matter of principle.

Copyright Laws

The Register of Copyrights is preparing legislative proposals for the first general revision of the U.S. Copyright Laws since 1909. This step is long overdue. Technological developments entirely unknown in 1909 have rendered the existing laws in many respects uncertain, inconsistent, inequitable and inadequate. . . .

A more radical proposal, the merit and feasibility of which should be seriously studied, is the suggestion that royalties on works in the public domain should be paid to the government to be used to support and advance the arts.

Government Surplus Property

Many millions of dollars worth of surplus real and personal federal property becomes available annually for free disposal or sale. Under present law such non-federal and non-profit use as schools, libraries, health, recreation, and wildlife conservation programs, etc., are eligible to acquire this property on a free or low-cost basis. . . .

Public Works and Community Development

Although such cultural facilities and institutions as auditoriums, museums, theaters and cultural centers are not specifically excluded from federal public works and community development programs, very few projects of this type have been aided.

In a few instances assistance has been given to libraries, civic auditoriums and zoos. In general, however, such projects are given low priority as not meeting essential public needs or contributing to either economic growth or the reduction of unemployment.

It is suggested here that the existence of adequate cultural facilities in a community is often an important factor in plant location and therefore economic development. In any case, the concept of the public interest should be interpreted to include cultural opportunities as well as basic material needs.

Special Assistance and Service Programs

Federal programs of service and assistance have not usually taken into account environmental factors or considerations of good design. The Small Business Administration and the Community Facilities Administration could well include these considerations in their advisory services and in their planning and research assistance. Better design is not only to be desired on aesthetic grounds but, as manufacturers are increasingly aware, can be important to efficiency, public relations and sales, particularly exports. Similarly, plant location could be subjected more effectively to considerations of environmental planning, including cultural factors.

Media of Mass Communication

Government has long been recognized as having responsibility to ensure that radio and television are operated in the public interest. Within the scope of this authority, through exhortation and encouragement, the Federal Communications Commission has recently been able to raise in some degree the level of programing, with the result that the arts and cultural activities in general have received a better hearing. But this indirect method has definite limits. The Federal Communications Commission is a quasi-judicial body, not a watchdog on behalf of the great community of listeners. The commercial broadcasters, though not infrequently surprised at the broad appeal which programs of a high cultural level achieve, can scarcely be convinced that this appeal is *numerically greater* than that of popular entertainment.

The Federal Communications Commission cannot be expected to carry the burden of determining the cultural level of programs. But through other machinery it should be possible to report periodically upon the advance or decline of current programing insofar as it relates to the specific field of the arts and cultural activities. It is recommended that a panel of the President's Advisory Council regularly issue such reports based upon a review of actual developments. In this way a series of benchmarks might at least be provided, in place of the scattered and unsystematic impressions on which judgment is now formed.

A second area of general government policy related to the quality and the cultural content of programing is through the ability to increase the number and effectiveness of educational television stations. Here, as in other fields, government's long established concern with education can be properly used as a means of stimulating the arts. Educational television as it has developed in the United States is only partially geared in with the educational system narrowly defined; it is also—and not least importantly—a means of bringing to the broad public a high level of programing, with stress upon literature and the other arts. Educational television may become the kind of yardstick—testing new ideas and audience response—which many have urged be established by one means or another.

For this reason the encouragement of educational television becomes a major means by which the government through its regular activities can affect the arts. Particularly to be noticed is the precedent of recent legislation authorizing federal assistance on a matching basis to facilitate the creation of educational television facilities. . . .

Tariff Policy

It is most important that the necessary legislation be passed to implement the Florence Agreement to establish duty-free status for educational scientific and cultural materials. This agreement is one of several international conventions drawn up under the auspices of UNESCO to promote the free flow of cultural materials. It was adopted in 1950 and has since been ratified by approximately forty countries, including the United States.

V. ADMINISTRATIVE MACHINERY RELATING TO THE ARTS

Experience during recent months suggests the need for setting up continuing administrative means for dealing with issues of the arts. The public has come to anticipate that the expressed concern of the government will be formalized in some way. It is important that nothing pretentious or heavy-handed be created, and equally important that recent initiatives not be allowed to expire. The following suggestions build upon what has already been done, and look ahead to what seems a natural development in the light of increased and deep-lying national interest in the arts.

These three suggested steps presuppose a constant concern with the enhancing and development of the arts through normal activities of the federal government. They also look forward to a more direct involvement of government through a new institutional body with operating funds. They do not envisage any effort to direct or influence the work of artists; their purpose is to keep the arts free, not to organize or regiment them.

1. SPECIAL ADVISOR[5]

A major recommendation of this report is that the post of Special Consultant on the Arts be continued after the present trial period. Consideration should be given to its being full-time and having the status of Special Advisor. Detailed day-by-day attention is necessary if governmental operations, often seemingly unrelated to the arts, are to be brought to the standards advocated by this report.

Principal areas of work for which the Special Advisor would be responsible have been described in the first chapter of this report. Besides the policy-planning and review functions which formed the major part of the original assignment, he should be available for advice on all matters pertaining to the arts which arise in the course of the Administration's work. He should be the President's liaison with the National Cultural Center, should sit in on panels and meetings where matters of federal architecture, design, graphics, etc., are being discussed.

In addition, the Special Advisor should have, as described below, a close relationship with the President's Advisory Council on the Arts.

2. THE ADVISORY COUNCIL[6]

Detailed recommendations relating to the establishment and functions of an Advisory Council within the Executive Office of the President have been separately submitted. This Council provides an essential part in an orderly and representative structure dealing with the arts. Its basic function is to continue and fill out the work of study and gathering information begun with the limited resources of the Special Consultant; to review federal policies and make recommendations for improving design; to recommend long-range programs; and to assure the active participation of the artistic community in the government effort.

The Special Advisor can call upon the council and its specialized committees for assistance. The Advisory Council will thus become part of the machinery through which advice is provided to the various agencies of government as they en-

[5] "Special Assistant to the President on the Arts," 1966 title. The Editor.

[6] National Council on the Arts, established by law in 1963. The Editor.

deavor to set up art committees of their own, to organize competitions, or otherwise to raise the level of design.

The President will appoint the chairman of the council, who presumably will be the Special Advisor. Following experience in the science field, the Advisory Council should achieve effectiveness and stature through being related to the President's advisor and having its recommendations go through him directly to the President.

3. A NATIONAL ARTS FOUNDATION[7]

An arts foundation, on the model of the existing foundations in science and health and as already proposed in legislation before the Congress, would appear to be the logical crowning step in a national cultural policy. Such a foundation would be a means of administering grants-in-aid, generally on a matching basis, to states and institutions of the arts. It might thus administer matching grants to states setting up arts councils. It might make available grants for demonstration projects proposed by particular cultural institutions. Thus it could consider helping support experiments designed to increase attendance, to foster creativity and introduce contemporary works to new audiences, or to offer services on an experimental basis. The foundation would not provide subsidies to carry the deficits of such institutions, but would aim at promoting cultural diversity, innovation and excellence.

Such an arts foundation should be thought of as supplementing the goals of the National Cultural Center, for it would help develop and stimulate the cultural activities and institutions of the country. And these, in turn, would have for their ultimate showcase the stages of the National Cultural Center in Washington.

What is sketched here represents the beginning of what could become a permanent policy giving form to the relationship between government and the arts. It is a limited policy; for government's role in this area must always be marginal. It is a policy not copied after European models, but keyed to the particular conditions of diversity and decentralization prevailing in the United States.

There will always remain those who feel that art and government should exist in different spheres, having nothing to do with each other. But in fact the government of the United States comes up constantly against choices and decisions

[7] National Endowment for the Arts, established by law in 1964. The Editor.

where aesthetic considerations are involved. In today's world, moreover, artistic talent and creativity are resources vitally important to the nation, and the well-being of the people is related to progress in the arts as surely as to progress in fields such as recreation and education where government's responsibility is fully recognized. Although government's role in the arts must always remain peripheral, with individual creativity and private support being central, that is no reason why the things which the government can properly do in this field should not be done confidently and expertly.

AUTHOR'S NOTE

In the writing of this report, as in all the work of the office of the Special Consultant on the Arts, I am immensely indebted to my assistant, Miss Barbara Donald. Without her constant and effective help it would have been impossible to fulfill even a part of the assignment. Mrs. Nancy Newhouse also deserves my thanks for her valuable assistance.

INDEX